PROGRESS IN
SEXOLOGY

PERSPECTIVES IN SEXUALITY
Behavior, Research, and Therapy

Series Editor: RICHARD GREEN
State University of New York at Stony Brook

A Continuation Order Plan is available for this series. A continuation order will bring delivery of each new volume immediately upon publication. Volumes are billed only upon actual shipment. For further information please contact the publisher.

PROGRESS IN SEXOLOGY

Selected papers from the Proceedings of the 1976 International Congress
of Sexology

Edited by

Robert Gemme
Department of Sexology
Université du Québec à Montréal, Canada

and

Connie Christine Wheeler
The Society for the
Scientific Study of Sex, United States

PLENUM PRESS · NEW YORK AND LONDON

Library of Congress Cataloging in Publication Data

International Congress of Sexology, Montréal, Québec, 1976.
    Progress in sexology.

    Includes index.
    1. Sex-Congresses. I. Gemme, Robert. II. Wheeler, Connie Christine. III. Title.
[DNLM: 1. Sex disorders—Etiology—Congresses. 2. Sex disorders—Therapy—Congresses. 3. Sex education—Congresses. 4. Sex—Congresses. 5. Sex Behavior—Congresses. WM610 163s 1976]
    ISBN 0-306-31104-6   301.41   77-13011

Selected papers from the Proceedings of the 1976 International Congress of Sexology
held in Montreal, October 28-31, 1976

© 1977 Plenum Press, New York
A Division of Plenum Publishing Corporation
227 West 17th Street, New York, N.Y. 10011

Printed in the United States of America

1976 INTERNATIONAL CONGRESS OF SEXOLOGY

MONTREAL, OCTOBER 28-31, 1976

PATRONS

Canada
The Department of Sexology of Université du Québec à Montréal
The Quebec Federation for Planned Parenthood

France
The French Society for Clinical Sexology

United States
The Society for the Scientific Study of Sex
The American Association of Sex Educators, Counselors and Therapists

SPONSORS

Canada
Sex Information and Education Council of Canada
Canadian Sex Research Forum

German Federal Republic
Deutsche Gesellschaft für Sexualforschung

Italy
Il Centro Italiano de Sessuologia

Japan
The Japanese Association for Sex Education

United States
Erikson Educational Foundation
Sex Information and Education Council of United States
The American Humanist Association

Acknowledgments

We wish to express our thanks to Dr. Marc Bélanger, Vice-Rector Academic of the Université du Québec à Montréal and Honorary President of the 1976 International Congress of Sexology, and to the Department of Sexology, Université du Québec à Montréal, for their continued support in the publication of these proceedings.

We also thank Michèle Pépin, whose skillful attention to the typing and indefatigable devotion toward our tasks completion, most assuredly made its publication possible.

Foreword

As editor of the series "Perspectives in Sexuality: Behavior, Research, and Therapy," I consider it a major scholarly achievement to publish selected proceedings of the Second International Congress of Sexology. Never before have so many professional organizations supported such a conference or so many scholars, from so many countries, participated in such a conference. Eighteen countries were represented; over one hundred papers were presented.

The Congress and these proceedings mark an historical milestone for sexology in international scientific cooperation. The collaboration of so many researchers from diverse disciplines further illuminates the interdisciplinary approach. The papers presented reflect the challenge accepted by scientists to compare varieties of techniques and programs, to develop new theories and creative approaches in their investigations, and to initiate scientific study of heretofore taboo areas of inquiry.

Clearly, sexology has come of age. It takes its place among the respected scientific disciplines. This monumental achievement, the Second International Congress of Sexology, signals the emergence at the international level of Sexology as Science.

Richard Green

Preface

The Second International Congress of Sexology was held in Montreal, Canada on October 28-31, 1976. Researchers of international acclaim from eighteen countries presented progress reports in specialities as endocrinology, neurophysiology, infertility, contraception, sexual dysfunction, ethics in sex research and sex education. The Congress, whose theme was "international progress in sexology," had as its scientific objective a wide range of subjects concerning the interdisciplinary study of sexology from many areas of the world.

This volume constitutes the published record of selected proceedings of the scientific papers and presentations made at that Congress.

Selection from 113 papers to adequately represent an overview of the Congress theme was made exceptionally difficult by the general high quality of presentations made, the limiting parameters set by the publisher for the number of papers to be published, the diversification of research areas reported on, the necessity to have the proceedings reflect the representation of most countries participating in the Congress, and the desire for a balance of reports on research, theory, description of techniques, etc. Emphasis for selection was placed on new and innovative original presentations, research oriented work, current relevance for a balance of topic areas, and geographical representation.

Papers presented by speakers from fourteen countries reported findings in topic areas as sexual dimorphism and sexual differentiation, sexual dysfunction, sexual response and erotic fantasy, fertility-infertility-contraception, sex education, and sexology in foreign countries. We have approached our task of editing with a genuine concern to maintain as much cultural flavor from translated manuscripts as prudence will allow, without sacrificing comprehension and without altering individual writing styles.

The Congress meetings were unique. They provided a single, topically oriented forum for an interdisciplinary group of research workers concerned with the scientific study of sex. Challenging ideas were presented. It is our conviction that this Congress has proven its worth and that it establishes a pattern for future meetings.

This compilation of much of the latest findings, hypotheses, ideas and suggestions of a dedicated group of investigators emerges as a mosaic of the united effort being made toward the understanding of sexology worldwide. It is our hope that this volume will be a useful tool for our colleagues now and in the future.

Robert Gemme
Connie Christine Wheeler

Contents

SECTION 5:   ANTHROPOLOGICAL AND SOCIOLOGICAL STUDIES

SECTION 6:   SEX EDUCATION

SECTION 7:   SEXOLOGY IN THREE COUNTRIES - AN OVERVIEW

SECTION 8:   CONCLUSION

SEXUAL DIFFERENTIATION IN THE HUMAN MALE AND FEMALE: SCIENCE,

STRATEGIES AND POLITICS

Richard Green

United States

We are all male or female. To varying degrees we have feelings, attitudes, and behaviors which carry connotations of masculinity and femininity. Our sexual fantasies and overt activities
engage males, females, or both. How much more fundamental to the
core of one's personality can a subject be for scientific study?
Current research into sexual differentiation has engaged greater
numbers of scientists, of both sexes, and has harnessed more sophisticated research designs. Regrettably, the topic has concurrently become politicized such that dispassionate inquiry is frequently replaced by passionate rhetoric.

Sexual differentiation in the male and female continues to
puzzle representatives of the several scientific disciplines, and
to infuriate those of varied political persuasions. The war against
ignorance is being pursued by, among others, warriors from the
disciplines of neuroendocrinology, clinical psychology, psychiatry,
anthropology, developmental psychology, and sociology. A discordant note in this effort, however, is that allies frequently have
difficulty recognizing allies (often seeing them as enemies), there
is no integrated battle strategy, and a Fifth Column has insinuated
itself into the objective findings of serious research. Battles
are being fought where there should be no battleground. There is
no sign of a truce and no Henry Kissinger to shuttle between the
disciplines and positions seeking to reconcile diversity.

1

THE ARMIES

What are the battle strategies of these various warriors? Consider first the neuroendocrinologists. The seas in which their battles are fought are the amniotic fluid or the fetal plasma. They measure levels of sex steroid, pollute the waters with more hormones, and then await the long range effects of what they have done. Occasionally they are aided by their ally, nature, who does the manipulation for them.

The classic warriors have been Young, Goy and Phoenix (1964). Their strategy included exposing pregnant female rhesus monkeys to large amounts of testosterone proprionate (male hormone) and study- ing the effect on postnatal behaviors of a female fetus. The ef- fect was that juvenile females exposed before birth to high levels of androgen behaved more like young males. They were more involved in rough-and-tumble, chasing, and aggressive behavior and have been commonly termed "tomboy" monkeys. This finding demonstrated the potential for a prenatal influence on the central nervous system which has an enduring postnatal effect on male/female behaviors.

The human parallel to this research is well known. Here we have nature's experiment: the virilizing adrenogenital syndrome in the female. Females with this syndrome, beginning in fetal life, are exposed to elevated levels of androgen which derive from the adrenal cortex. This is due to an inborn error of metabolism. These girls show behavioral changes during their juvenile years like those in the monkey research. When compared to their sisters, they are more rough-and-tumble and athletically oriented, and are less interested in doll play. They are called "tomboys" (Ehrhardt and Baker, 1974). Thus, there is evidence that prenatal levels of androgen affect the developing central nervous system for some be- haviors which have sex typed connotations. The influences are subtle, however. There is no increased incidence of more dramatic cross- sexed behavior such as transsexualism or homosexuality (Ehrhardt, Evers, and Money, 1968).

What of the male? Research is underway on the effect of ex- posing the male fetus to elevated levels of female hormones, nota- bly diethylstilbestrol and progestational drugs. An earlier study found that 6 and 16 year-old males whose diabetic mothers had re- ceived diethylstilbestrol and progesterone during pregnancy were less rough-and-tumble and less athletic and aggressive than a con- trast group of males not given hormones. However, the contrast group mothers were not diabetic and so it is not possible to rule out the effects of the mothers' illness on the boys' development (Yalom, Green and Fisk, 1973). More recently, we have conducted a study of 141 adult males whose mothers, during pregnancy, received diethyl- stilbestrol (DES), DES plus progesterone, progesterone, or no

hormone. These data are currently being analyzed and will be available shortly. Other findings of a similar project with younger subjects will be reported later at this Congress by Meyer-Bahlburg.

The next column of warriors are the neonatalogists. These
baby and mother watchers observe newborn males and females and
their patterns of interaction with parents. They excitedly report
that female children are talked to more by their mother and male
children more often have their limbs stretched (Moss, 1967). Males
are more able to raise their head from the prone position when
placed on their abdomen. This finding is interpreted as due to
greater muscle development at birth, a consequence of higher levels of prenatal androgen (Bell and Darling, 1965). At five months
of age, males appear to spend less time in physical contact with
their mother and at twelve months when placed beside their mother,
are more likely to crawl away (Goldberg and Lewis, 1969). These
findings parallel those in the non-human primate where our close
relative, the squirrel monkey, is more likely to move away from
his mother in spite of her efforts to retrieve him (Rosenblum,
1974).

At twelve months of age, male and female children may respond
differently to a barrier placed between themselves and toys. Their
play style with these toys may also differ. In one study male children tended to crawl toward the end of the barrier, in an apparent
effort to get at the toys, while females tended to sit where placed
and cry. Males were more likely to fling the toys about, while females tended to gather them together   (Golberg and Lewis, 1969).
Two other soldiers failed to replicate this finding, however
(Maccoby and Jackling, 1974).

Two provocative, but as yet unreplicated findings, suggest
that at twelve months of age human beings are able to discriminate
infants of the same and other sex. When photographs of twelve
month old children revealing only facial features are shown to
adults, the adults are unable to identify the sex of the child.
However, when the same photographs are shown to twelve month old
infants, they tend to look at pictures of their sex longer (Lewis
and Weinraub, 1974). When two male and two female children are
placed in the corners of a rectangular enclosure and one child
at a time is permitted to crawl toward the other children, they
tend to crawl to the child of the same sex. The odds against their
doing so are 2:1 (Lewis, 1976).

What might this mean in terms of sexual differentiation in the
male and female? If children at one year are able to discriminate
their own sex from the other, this may have a significant influence
on establishing an appropriate core-morphologic sexual identity.
Core-morphologic identity is here defined as the earliest self-
concept of being male or female (Stoller, 1968; Green, 1974).

Thus, there may be a cognitive capacity for self versus other sex discrimination which is the first cue which children use as they correctly label their sex. This could be construed as having evolutionary value in that when persons establish a core-morphologic identity contrary to their anatomy, this will likely lead to trans-sexualism (Benjamin, 1966). Transsexuals typically are well below the norm in producing children and therefore contribute little to continuation of the species. Thus, it can be argued that at twelve months of age, species survival is served by the establishment of appropriate core-morphologic identity giving this cognitive capacity evolutionary merit during this phase of the life cycle. The discriminative capacity for labeling the photographs would be less important for an adult when core-morphologic identity has long since been established.

The next set of warriors are the officers of the Society for the Scientific Study of Sex. The process of differentiation of male and female has been extensively studied by the President and President-Elect of the SSSS via two complementary strategies. John Money and co-workers have focussed on anatomically intersexed children who develop a sexual identity consistent with their sex of assignment. Richard Green and co-workers, notably Robert Stoller, have focussed on children who develop a sexual identity contradictory to sex of assignment. Money's work demonstrated that postnatal socialization factors, primarily the parents' conviction that the newborn belongs to one or the other sex and the resultant signals the child receives, firmly establishes identity. The pattern is established even when the input contradicts other criteria of sex including gonadal sex, chromosomal sex, internal reproductive structures, etc. (Money and Ehrhardt, 1972). More recently, Lev-Ran (1974) has shown that even when the appearance of the external genitalia dramatically contradict sex of assignment, persons will establish an identity consistent with that sex of assignment. Lev-Ran describes a person with the female adrenogenital syndrome, who was raised as a female, has a female identity, behaves in a feminine way, and is heterosexual, in spite of a 9cm. (when erect) phallus. Similarly a 5 year old is described who was considered male, has a male identity, and behaves in a masculine way, in spite of a phallus of 1.5 cm.

The matched pairs of hermaphrodites studied by Money offer dramatic evidence that two persons with the same physiological status (female virilizing adrenogenital syndrome) can be assigned to opposite sex roles and develop a psychology consistent with sex of assignment. Thus the one considered female at birth will receive cortisone and genital reconstruction, be raised as female and behave in a feminine manner (the above "tomboy" data, notwithstanding). She will usually be sexually attracted to males. While this is not all that surprising, consider that the infant born with the same degree of genital ambiguity assigned to male status will

develop a male identity, show masculine behavior, and will usually
be sexually attracted to females.

There are skeptics who question the validity of studying the
anatomically intersexed as a model of psychosexual differentiation
in the typical person. They point out that intersexed persons are
exposed to unusual hormonal and genetic influences, beginning prenatally, and thus may be more "plastic" postnatally (Diamond, 1965).
As a counter case, Money and Ehrhardt have reported a pair of monozygotic male twins, one of whom is being raised as a female. At
six months of age, the penis of one co-twin sloughed after circumcision trauma. At eighteen months of age the twin was reassigned
to female status. Now, some nine years later, they appear as a
typical brother and sister. Here, we have better control over
prenatal hormonal and genetic composition, with sex of assignment
and rearing being the major independent variables.

Two other pairs of monozygotic twins discordant for sexual
identity have been studied by myself and Stoller (1971). One is
a set of ten year old boys, one of whom fantasies being a female,
and behaves in a feminine way. His brother is unremarkably masculine. The other set is a pair of twenty-five year old females,
one of whom wants sex reassignment to live as a male, and a sister
who is unremarkably feminine. In both sets of twins it was possible
to identify socialization experiences, divergent for the co-twins,
which appear consistent with their diverse patterns of sexual
identity.

My primary research strategy has been to identify a sample of
anatomically normal children whose sexual identity is atypical
(Green, 1974, 1976). Their behavior is similar to that retrospec-
tively reported by adults with an atypical identity. Nearly all
transsexuals, about half of transvestites, and perhaps the majority
of homosexuals report varying degrees of cross-gender behavior
since childhood. The transsexuals typically report "as far back
as I can remember," having felt like someone of the other sex and
preferring the activities and clothes of the other sex. The male
transvestites, (there are no female transvestites), report, in
about half the cases, commencing their fetishistic cross-dressing
prior to puberty (Prince and Bentler, 1972). For adult male homosexuals, in two studies, about two-thirds reported a "girl-like
syndrome" during grade school years. For one female homosexual
sample, significantly more reported having been tomboyish during
pre-adolescence and remaining tomboyish into teenage (Saghir and
Robins, 1973). Studying adults is frought with obvious methodologic
pitfalls. Retrospective falsification occurs, important events are
forgotten, and significant others present during the early life of
the individuals are not available. Thus, our strategy has been to
draw a composite picture of children who are now behaving in the
way many atypical adults recall their childhood.

We have generated a sample of 60 boys, age 4 to 10 when initially seen, who prefer the toys, dress, activities and companion-
ship of girls, typically role-play as female, and state their wish
to be girls. Also, we have generated a sample of 50 females, in
the same age range, who strongly prefer boys' clothes, show no interest in doll-play, typically role play as male, are actively engaged in rough-and-tumble play and sports, and state their wish to
be boys. These children and their parents have been studied by a
variety of psychological tests, clinical interviews, and direct
observation. The children and their families have been matched
with a family in which a same age, same sex child is showing typical sex-typed behavior. Matching has also been accomplished on
sibling sequence of the child, plus family marital status, ethnic
background and educational level.

The male children are quite diverse in their activities. Cross-
dressing begins early in the feminine boy group, with three-fourths
commencing by the fourth birthday. When genuine articles of feminine
clothing are not available for dressup, there is improvisation from
other materials. Doll play begins early, again by the fourth birthday,
"Barbie" doll is the favorite toy. Roles typically portrayed in
family or house games are female. The peer group is female. The
boys strongly prefer their mothers. Forty percent were separated
from their biological father before the fourth birthday. However,
half of those separated had a father substitute living in the home.
Thus one must look more closely at the 60 to 80 percent in which
the father is living in the home so as not to simply indict "father
absence" as etiologic for feminine development in the male. Marital role division in the families of feminine and masculine boys
is not significantly different. There is also no difference in
the amount of time spent by the parents with the masculine and
feminine boys in the first two years of life. The contrast group
for the tomboy sample is being generated and thus no comparative
data are available.

The research strategy is to follow the four samples of children
into adolescence and young adulthood and to correlate later patterns
of sexuality with earlier behavioral patterns and parental attributes. We will also assess intervening events as the children
mature into adolescence and adulthood. The males are approaching
adolescence and during the next two and a half years an extensive
effort will be made to conduct follow-up evaluations. For the
females, we will study in detail the early adolescent experience
to understand why most tomboys abandon tomboyism with teenage
while a smaller minority maintain this behavioral pattern.

Another strategy being waged by this warrior for studying
psychosexual differentiation is the converse of that just outlined.
Rather than studying children with an atypical identity but whose
parents are typical, we have initiated a study of the children of

the sexually atypical. To date we have evaluated over two dozen
children being raised by transsexual or homosexual parents. Whether
it be from a psychoanalytic or a social-learning viewpoint, having
a parent with a dramatically atypical sexual identity, such as seen
in the transsexual, or with a variant pattern of sexual orientation
as seen in the homosexual, should have an effect on the child.
Whether one posits resolution of the Oedipal phase, penis envy, and
castration fear as pivotal points for the development of typical
sexual identity, or whether one relies on role modeling of parents,
divergent outcomes should be expected in these children.

Consider the atypicality of the following experience: in one
family four female children between 5 and 10 watched their mother,
over a period of five years, undergo metamorphosis through male
hormone injections and surgery to emerge as their "father." These
children, now in their early to late teens, all have a female core-
morphologic identity, are behaviorally feminine, and are hetero-
sexually oriented. Consider another family in which two teenage
males, fifteen and sixteen, have lived in the home in which their
"step-father" was a preoperative female-to-male transsexual since
the boys were one and two years. Extreme household modesty pre-
cluded the boys' opportunities of discovering that their father had,
until 2 years ago, female-appearing breasts, and still has a female perineum. These two males have a male core-morphologic identity, are masculine, and are heterosexual. Similarly, a 10 year
old male who watched his father metamorphose to become his mother
over the past three years, is male identified, masculine, and
heterosexually-oriented. All of the children (still pre-teen)
being raised by their now lesbian mothers who have been evaluated
to date, show a core-morphologic identity consistent with anatomy,
gender-role behavior which is culturally typical, and look forward
to heterosexual dating and marriage.

The next wave of warriors are the androgynists. Unquestionable, male and female children are treated differentially in our
culture, as well as in most. Argument persists as to whether the
sex differences shown by children are a coincidental accident of
many cultures reinforcing the same behaviors, or whether these differences are biologically programmed, with culture following the
tail of genetics.

Considerable energy is being expended by some segments of our
culture in raising children in a more androgynous manner. Research
is underway assessing the degree to which breaking some stereotyp-
ically male-female type patterns of early childrearing effects
early personality and later sexuality. The methodologic difficulty
here is that the experience of a given set of parents or in a given
pre-school is only a part of the total life experience of the growing child. Children are exposed to mass media and the influence
of the peer group. Thus, it is difficult to systematically manip-

ulate all the sex-typed input to a child, making experiments of
"nurture" difficult to control.

There has been considerable blurring of clinical, social, and
scientific responsibility. There is no question that biased attitudes have been rampant in this culture, discriminating on the basis of sex. However, a clear distinction must be made between the
real differences between the sexes, overlap between the sexes, and
the manners by which the sexes are discriminantly treated. Whether
there exist innate sex differences with respect to styles or levels
of aggressive behavior, physical strength, or scores on the embed-
ded figures test, this can in no way justify prejudicial employment,
salary, voting rights, or credit ratings. While no one looking at
the Olympic records would deny that biological sex differences
exist, this fact must remain distinct from social prejudice. However, it is scientifically unjustified to deny the existence of sex
differences, if they can be demonstrated with sound methodology,
merely because that knowledge might be misused by those who would
like to reinforce sexism. It is the responsibility of those who
conduct research to both report their findings in an objective manner and to safeguard against the misuse and misapplication of such
findings.

Reverse discrimination must also not be tolerated. There are
those who wage war against girls dressing in frilly dresses and
playing all day with "Barbie" dolls, while defending to the last,
the right of a male child to do the same. Children must not be
made the prisoners of war in an honestly motivated campaign against
sexual injustice and individual psychic pain.

                              CONCLUSION

This war is being waged on several fronts. One enemy is ignorance; ignorance of how a most basic personality feature which
permeates our entire existence comes to be. Another enemy, ironi-
cally, in keeping with the metaphor, might be considered the pa-
cifists. They do not feel this war should be waged at all. They
would put a halt to research on typical and atypical patterns of
psychosexual differentiation in the belief that study of the process
reinforces sexism. Others consider the subject of human sexuality
frivolous, without serious scientific or social significance, or
else so riddled with sin and shame as to be rightfully buried
beneath bedrock.

It has never been fashionable to be a sex researcher. The
term "sexology" has fallen into considerable disrepute. Governmental funding agencies and private foundations are not jostling
for position to provide monetary resource to pursue these studies.

A recent U.S. Health, Education and Welfare Appropriation bill set
a unique precedent, of horrifying implication. Tacked onto it was
a rider prohibiting the conduct of one research project which had
been previously approved by the appropriate University and Federal
Agencies. This project fell victim to political pressure because
it dealt with two controversial areas, human sexuality and mari-
juana.

Scientific research into psychosexual development must proceed
on all fronts. This war against ignorance will be won. Scientific
facts will not be discarded by those with placards or those who
disrupt scientific meetings. Nor, will they be bankrupted by prigs
who want this fundamental aspect of the human condition to go away.

This conference is a symbol of the continuing success in our
quest for knowledge in understanding human sexuality. By the end
of four days' time, reports from the various fronts, by the many
warriors seated here before me, will expand the base of our wisdom.
On behalf on this Congress' sponsoring agencies, I welcome you all
from the battlefields to the Conference Table.

REFERENCES

Bell, R. and Darling, N. (1965). The prone head reaction in the
human newborn. Child Develop. 36: 943-949.

Benjamin, H. (1966). The Transsexual Phenomenon, Julian Press,
New York.

Diamond, M. (1965). A critical evaluation of the ontogeny of
human sexual behavior. Quart. Rev. Biol. 40: 147-175.

Ehrhardt, A., Evers, A. and Money, J. (1968). Influence of androgen on some aspects of sexually dimorphic behavior in women
with the late-treated adrenogenital syndrome. Johns Hopkins
Med. J. 123: 115-122.

Ehrhardt, A. and Baker, S. (1974). Fetal androgens, human central
nervous system differentiation, and behavior sex differences.
In Friedman, R., Richart, R., and Van de Wiele, R. (eds.),
Sex Differences in Behavior, Wiley, New York.

Goldberg, S. and Lewis, M. (1969). Play behavior in the year-old
infant: early sex differences. Child Develop. 40: 21-31.

Green, R. and Stoller, R. (1971). Two monozygotic (identical) twin
pairs discordant for gender identity. Arch. Sex. Behav. 1:
321-327.

Green, R. (1974). Sexual Identity Conflict in Children and Adults,
  Basic Books, New York.

Green, R. (1976). One-hundred ten feminine and masculine boys:
  behavioral contrasts and demographic similarities. Arch.
  Sex. Behav. 5: 425-446.

Lev-Ran, A. (1974). Gender role differentiation in hermaphrodites.
  Arch. Sex. Beahv. 3: 339-424.

Lewis, M. and Weinraub, M. (1974). Sex of parent and sex of child:
  socioemotional development. In Friedman, R. Richard, R.,
  and R. Van de Wiele, R. (eds.), Sex Difference in Behavior,
  Wiley, New York.

Lewis, M. (1976). Early sex differences in the human: studies of
  socioemotional development. In Rubinstein, E., Green, R.
  and Brecher, E. (eds.), New Directions in Sex Research,
  Plenum, New York.

Maccoby, E. and Jacklin, C. (1974). The Psychology of Sex Differences, Stanford Press, Stanford.

Money, J. and Ehrhardt, A. (1972). Man and Woman; Boy and Girl,
  Johns Hopkins Press, Baltimore.

Moss, H. (1967). Sex, age, and state as determinants of mother-
  infant interaction. Merrill - Palmer Quart. 13: 19-36.

Prince, C. and Bentler, P. (1972). Survey of 504 cases of transvestism. Psychol. Rep. 31: 903-917.

Rosenblum, L. (1974). Sex differences, environmental complexity
  and mother-infant relations. Arch. Sex. Beahv. 3: 117-128.

Saghir, M. and Robins, E. (1973). Male and Female Homosexuality,
  Williams and Wilkins, Baltimore.

Stoller, R. (1968). Sex and Gender, Science House, New York.

Yalom, I., Green, R. and Fisk, N. (1973). Prenatal exposure to
  female hormones: effect on psychosexual development in boys.
  Arch. Gen. Psychiat. 28: 554-561.

Young, W., Goy, R. and Phoenix, C. (1964). Hormones and sexual
  behavior. Science 143: 212-218.

SEXUAL DIMORPHISM IN EROTIC FUNCTION: A PSYCHOSOCIAL APPROACH

John H. Gagnon

United States

The choice of any particular theoretical or explanatory perspective and its application in a systematic and coherent fashion
is a significant decision in all areas of scientific inquiry. As
we all know, our theoretical preferences have consequences in that
they determine what we decide are the "facts," what significance
the "facts" might have, as well as the relationships between the
"facts." Our theories guide our scientific conduct, they are a
set of instructions about what to notice and what to ignore, what
is important and what is trivial. The tension between theory and
data, hypothesis and test, explanation and example is the chronic
condition of scientific activity.

The importance of a thoughtful choice of a theoretical perspective is nowhere more profound than in the study of sexuality.
In part this is the result of the peculiar importance that sexuality has both collectively and individually in western cultures.
In the long process of the secularization of social life, sexuality
has still managed to retain its status as our major exemplar of
the margin between the sacred and the profane.[1] Only in the last
ten years has sexuality been accessible to research and many researchers themselves have been overwhelmed by a need to defend
their interest in the morally taboo. As a result sexual theory
has more often than not been sexual ideology, often representing
either an impulse to conform or oppose established values, both

---

[1]See the Vatican statement on masturbation quoted in Gagnon, 1977,
p. 148.

sexual and non-sexual.[2]

Even though there has been a major surge in cultural interest
in sexuality as expressed by the flood of mass media materials
since 1960, there has been only a modest relaxation of the taboos
against sex research. Consequently our accumulated body of knowledge about sexuality remains scanty and much of what has been
done lacks methodological precision. As a result of this absence
of a strong body of data, our choice of theories takes on an even
greater significance. It is primarily through our theories that
we have attempted to sketch in the landscape of sexuality, often
by making large and speculative leaps from one isolated study to
another.

These problems of the relation between sexual theory and sexual ideology, and sexual theory and data are crucial in the study
of gender dimorphism in erotic function.[3] The existence of differences in patterns of sexual conduct between men and women has
been one of the most common findings in the history of sex research.
The sexual revolutionaries of the turn of the century (whom Paul
Robinson has recently and accurately labelled sexual enthusiasts)
confirmed what the sexual folklore of the times recorded: that
women and men seemed to differ in erotic function (Robinson, 1976).
From the clinical impressions of the psychoanalytic movement to
the survey researches that occurred in the United States during
the 1920s to the work of Kinsey and even after, it was the differences between men and women that caught the researchers' attention.
While different differences were thought to be important by various
researchers, it was the differences that were systematically noted.
Even the work of Masters and Johnson which focuses on the common-
alities between female and male sexual response at the physiological level leaves substantial room for variation at the psychological and social level (Masters and Johnson, 1966).

The issue, however, is not whether or not differences in
erotic function between women and men were observed (differences

---

[2]D.H. Lawrence uses the power of sexual rule breaking in his novel
Lady Chatterly's Lover to criticize the existing class structure;
a similar use of a different sexual theory was used for a similar
end, though more Marxist in character, by Wilhelm Reich. Conservative sexual theorists still abound; for them obeying the sexual
rules affirms other cultural values (cf. footnote 1).

[3]Erotic function is conceived most broadly in this paper; it is
coterminous with the phrase sexual conduct as William Simon and I
have used it (cf. Gagnon and Simon, 1973).

in incidences, rates, preferences, feelings, stimuli have all been
adequately recorded). The issue is our explanations or theories
about how these differences have come about, how stable they are
in terms of either societal or individual histories and how such
differences are maintained.

In general, theories or explanations of the erotic dimorphism
in women and men suffer from a developmental and/or a biological
prejudice. We can find the beginning of this prejudice in "scientific sexology" with Freud's choice to continue to use the anatomic
differences between men and women as the ground out of which both
what we call gender identity, roles and performances and sexual
conduct emerges. The goal of psychosexual development was the
gender and erotic dimorphism that appeared to be or was thought
to be common in the middle class of middle Europe in the 19th
Century. Heterosexuality and biological reproduction remained
the basis for the judging of psychosexual normality. This search
for the biological roots for the sources of the differences between women and men and as the basis for judging what is sexually
normal has recently moved further in two new biological directions,
first into the chemical sublevels of the organism and second into
evolutionary theory. Hormones and the hunting and gathering origins of human groups are the current biological justifications of
contemporary cultural conduct (Lunde, 1975; Tiger and Fox, 1971).
Even Kinsey with his emphasis on the variability of sexual conduct
as a species characteristic still treated males and females as
relatively unvariable creatures. While he viewed heterosexuals
and homosexuals as linked to each other on a continuum of acts,
males and females appeared to be members of different species
(Kinsey, 1948, pp. 610-666; Kinsey, 1953, pp. 642-689).

GENDER DIMORPHISM AND EROTIC DIMORPHISM

At the present time the most common developmental model for
the acquisition of erotic dimorphism rests upon the preexistence
of gender dimorphism. It is generally argued that early in life
male and female children acquire gender identities and then cumulate
roles and performances congruent with those identities (Money and
Ehrhardt, 1972). Thus in contemporary western cultures, most young
people learn to be girls and boys and in some cases young men and
young women long before they learn or practice sexuality. Most
western societies do not overtly encourage sexual conduct among
young people until their late teens, but do emphasize from an
early point in life relatively sharp differences in gender identities and roles. When sexual conduct (both as scripts for conduct
and concrete sexual acts) begins to be practiced, young people
commonly proceed using the previously acquired self-labels and
cognitive materials associated with the boy/girl-man/woman distinctions. Since the acquisition of sexual conduct is structured

by the dimorphic adolescent learning environments in which sexual
conduct is coded in terms of gender roles it is at this point that
the erotic stage of psychosexual dimorphism begins in this society
(Gagnon, 1971).

What is important to recognize, however, is that regardless
of the strength of the gender self-label at age 3 or 4 (tested by
such statements as "I am a boy" - "I am a girl") this label has
very little substantive content. It is only because the later
learning environments are themselves coded in terms of girl/boy
in specific kinds of ways that the child acquires further senses
of difference. It is not that the child has passed through a
unitary transition point after which all future gender choices
are programmed, but rather that the child has acquired a volitional
self-label that makes for the easier acquisition and assimilation
of the next learnings in contexts that are labelled boy or girl.
If the occupational structure and the world of sexuality were not
coded in terms of male-female then the original self-label as boy
or girl would be irrelevant to those domains of conduct.

The issue is that gender identity, roles and performances are
not developmental constants but are in fact variable. The conventional model of development as the sequential unfolding of fixed
attributes, stage following stage, tends to obscure the range of
conduct variation around the stereotypical average. The interaction of intra-gender differences with patterns of acquisition
and performance of sexual conduct are rarely examined and understood.
Most developmental theory is linear in emphasis, that which comes
earlier is exclusively causative of that which comes after. Such
theory depends on the belief in the constant taking into the individual programs or dispositions to act which are relatively irreversible. The aging of the organism is seen as involving increasing response fixity and decreasing adaptive flexibility. Thus
male-female differences in erotic function are viewed as both necessary outgrowths of prior gender experience and as nearly irreversible characterological or personality components. Such versions
of development view the difficulties involved in behavior change as
the result of individual rigidities rather than examining the set
of continuing environmental contingencies which reinforce a wide
range of dimorphic conduct.

SOCIAL LEARNING AND EROTIC DIMORPHISM

In contrast to this perspective, there are two examples of
erotic dimorphism that may well be better interpreted by explanations which depend on an environmentally disposed social learning
model. This latter model emphasizes the role of continuous environmental contingencies in the maintenance of behavior (in contrast to internalized predispositions) and the relative ease with

which sexual conduct varies or changes under naturalistic circumstances. The first of the examples, the acquisition of masturbation and its role in accelerating divergent gender role learning in adolescence, suggests the nonlinearity of development. The second, the reports of a convergence of female-male response to common erotic stimuli, suggests the ability of men and women to relatively easily change their sexual conduct under given environmental conditions.

Young persons come into puberty with some differences between boys and girls on a number of psychological and social dimensions but with considerable variability and overlap in performances. The rapid and dramatic differences in the acquisition of masturbation in young men and women and the different patterns between the sexes among those who masturbate is only in a limited way a function of the gender role history of these young people. What appears critical is that learning environments for masturbation during adolescence are very different for boys and girls and the sexual conduct acquired in these environments changes or affirms gender roles and performances. As we all know, masturbation remains in the United States predominantly a male activity with substantial incidences and frequencies (Kinsey et al., 1948, 1953; Gagnon, Simon, Berger, 1970; Clifford, 1975). On the other hand a substantial number of young women do masturbate and some do so at high rates – what we do not possess is an adequate body of information about how differences from what appears to be the norm (the males who do not masturbate, the females who do at high rates) derive from prior or effect future gender role development.

The fact that masturbation is environmentally-coded male means that it is acquired more easily by males, but its acquisition creates a new context for gender dimorphic conduct. If masturbation of this type (performed by a majority of a group at moderate to high rates accompanied by fantasy) had been coded female then we would have seen a quite different set of interactions between gender predispositions and sexual conduct. Indeed we (as sex researchers) might then assert that there was in female gender development a particular set of factors that made women more likely to masturbate. Perhaps the "female" traits of passivity, dependency and submission would have been used to explain the passive, solitary, unsocial practice of self-masturbation. The problem is that what is is not what has to be. Because environments are sequentially coded does not mean that persons who perform correctly in them have been previously internally programmed.

The flexibility of erotic dimorphism is suggested by the recent research findings that previously observed differences in men and women in their responsiveness to erotic materials have not been replicated in more recent survey and experimental studies. Kinsey

in his researches in the late 1940s and early 1950s found (as did
other survey researchers) that fewer women than men reported being
aroused by erotic materials (Kinsey et al., 1953: 642-689).
Recall it was not that women were not aroused as intensely by such
materials as were men, but that fewer women than men were so aroused.
We did not have a measure of differential intensity, we had a measure of differential frequency. Kinsey chose as his most plausible
explanation of these reports of differences in arousal a difference
in conditionability of men and women based on inferred gender differences in the central nervous system. Alternative environmental
explanations of this gender dimorphism of response to visual erotica
could be: 1) that most women in the 1940s did not see much of these
kinds of materials, 2) the materials were largely prepared for men
(that is they did not connect with women's sexual scripts, though
romantic movies did) and finally 3) women had learned to talk about
these materials in a negative manner. The observed differences between men and women then could partly rest on: 1) some women who
saw the materials did not define them as sexually arousing (and
there is no reason why they should have) and 2) some women did
find them arousing, but did not want to say so.

    More recent studies of visual arousal, conducted in the 1960s
and 1970s suggest that the differences between men and women are
less than in earlier studies (for a sociological summary of these
studies, see Victor, 1977). More men were aroused by seeing pictures of naked women than women aroused by pictures of naked men,
including men with erections. However when offered pictures of
sexual activity (petting or coitus) or a film showing extended
sexual activity (petting through coitus) both men and women registered quite similar responses (erections in men, vaginal lubrication in women). Blood flow changes in the genitalia of a significant sort were found in both men and women when they were exposed to erotic materials either on film or auditorily - and about
the same proportions report a similar degree of arousal on verbal
scales.

    A similar gender dimorphism in erotic arousal noted between
men and women is that many men seem relatively unresponsive to
generalized body touching in sexual activity and have a greater
genital focus for sexual pleasure while many women are more erotically (that is, interpret stimuli as erotic) responsive over their
entire body, have orgasm more easily from non-genital contacts and
are less dependent on the genitalia for arousal and orgasm. Much
of the reporting of these differences are anecdotal and come from
therapeutic and clinical sources, but do seem to be expressive of
an erotic dimorphism between women and men. In the past the lack
of genital focus on the part of women was seen as one possible
source of lack of orgasm and many clinicians looked for ways to
increase women's focus on their genitals, at one time the vagina
(now the clitoris). More recently however the male focus on the

genitals has become defined as a sexual lack as well - a lack that might be producing both premature ejaculation and, in some cases, erectile dysfunction when the capacity for erection becomes part of a demanded performance. The sensate focus exercises are techniques to increase the range of male sexual response - to increase the sensitivity to general tactile stimuli (Masters and Johnson, 1970). Indeed at the present time there is considerable interest in the male nipple and breast as a newly defined erogenous zone.

What these two examples of changing dimorphisms suggest is that there existed at one time in the United States relatively separate learning systems in which men and women acquired certain aspects of eroticism. Thus women and men differed in their rates of exposure to sexual materials, in their ways of talking about sexuality and in the sexual script elements that seemed to be particularly arousing to them. As men and women have developed more common histories of exposure to sexual materials, have been offered materials and experiences that contain elements of both male and female sexual scripts they have converged in preferences and practices.

The same convergences may be observed in learning about the body as a source of erotic pleasure. Masturbation among men created a genital focus in sexual response, women, in contrast, often had a less focused genital committment. As masturbation grows more common among women a greater genital focus will develop and as men are trained by women (and sex counselors, therapists and advice manuals) to respond to sex over more of their bodies their non-genital sexual responses will increase (Heiman, LoPiccolo and LoPiccolo, 1976).

SEXUAL LEARNING AND SEXUAL THEORY

Such observations require a movement away from the view that current sexual patterns are a property of the individual organism either in a biological or developmental sense. For instance, there is no evidence that a high rate of masturbation must be associated with "masculinity" or low rates with "femininity", the fit between these two categories is a function of specific learning environments which code both classes of conduct with the same labels. Further, the erotic dimorphism in the case of masturbation may be powerfully influential in increasing gender dimorphism - the experiences of the later stage dramatically extending the more modest differences of the earlier. Our dilemma is that we have taken the processes of a single set of historical examples and have assumed that they have universal validity. In this sense most of sex research is anti-historical and also anti-cultural. We often insist that men and women and sexual conduct are not only the same in similar places, but that all combinations of gender and sexual activity also have common trans-historical origins and meanings. The patterns of gender role and erotic development that we observe in Western European societies are only one of the potential designs available for humans.

In contrast to models emphasizing developmental fixity and the singular priority of early experience there is evidence that even after having experienced the conventional gender divergent processes of psychosexual development there can be a remarkable convergence in female-male patterns of erotic conduct later in life. What appeared to a researcher of less than three decades ago as an inviolable difference in neurology turns out to be merely a difference in environmental contingencies. The convergence of patterns between men and women in various areas and the use of learning programs in sex therapy suggest the importance of not only viewing sexuality through a social learning perspective, but also one that gives particular weight to the continuing environmental factors for either the maintenance of conduct or its change.

As has been said, the theories that one uses provide the meanings for the evidence one examines. An environmental social learning model not only affects specific interpretations of specific information but has a more significant set of consequences. Sexuality can be viewed not as a special domain of conduct with special theories, special researchers, special curricula, but rather more mundanely, as part of conventional social life.

REFERENCES

Clifford, R. (1975). Female Masturbation in Developmental and Clinical Application, Unpublished PhD Dissertation, Department of Psychology, State University of New York, Stony Brook.

Gagnon, J.H., Simon, W. and Berger, A.J. (1970). Some Aspects of Adjustment in Early and Later Adolescence. In Zubin, J. and Freedman, A.M. (eds.), The Psychopathology of Adolescence, Grune and Stratton, New York.

Gagnon, J.H. (1971). The Creation of the Sexual in Early Adolescence. In Kagan, J. and Coles R. (eds.), Twelve to Sixteen: Early Adolescence, Norton, New York.

Gagnon, J.H. and Simon, W. (1973). Sexual Conduct: The Social Sources of Human Sexuality, Aldine, Chicago.

Gagnon, J.H. (1977). Human Sexualities, Scott Foresman, Glenview.

Heiman, J., LoPiccolo, L. and LoPiccolo, J. (1976). Becoming
    Orgasmic: A Sexual Growth Program for Women, Prentice
    Hall, Englewood Cliffs.

Kinsey, A.C., et al. (1948). Sexual Behavior in the Human Male,
    Saunders, Philadelphia.

Kinsey, A.C., et al. (1953). Sexual Behavior in the Human Female,
    Saunders, Philadelphia.

Lunde, D.T. (1975). Sex Hormones, Mood and Behavior. In Adelson,
    E.T. (ed.), Sexuality and Psychoanalysis, Brunner/Mazel, New
    York.

Maccoby, E. and Jacklin, C. (1974). The Psychology of Sex Dif-
    ferences, Stanford University Press, Palo Alto.

Masters, W. and Johnson, V. (1966). Human Sexual Response, Little,
    Brown and Co., Boston.

Masters, W. and Johnson, V. (1970). Human Sexual Inadequacy, Little,
    Brown and Co., Boston.

Money, J. and Ehrhardt, A. (1972). Man Woman; Boy Girl. Johns
    Hopkins Press, Baltimore.

Robinson, P. (1976). The Modernization of Sex, Harper and Row,
    New York.

Tiger, L. and Fox, R. (1971). The Imperial Animal, Holt, Rinehart,
    and Winston, New York.

Victor, J.L. (forthcoming, 1977). The Social Psychology of Sexual
    Arousal. In Denzin, N. (ed.), Studies in Symbolic Inter-
    action, J.A.L. Press, New York.

Means of investigation of sexual differentiation:
Inducible distinctive LH surge following oestrogen administration in homosexual ♂ compared with heterosexual ♂'s.

HORMONE DEPENDENT DIFFERENTIATION, MATURATION AND FUNCTION OF THE BRAIN AND SEXUAL BEHAVIOR

Günter Dörner

German Democratic Republic

Neuroendocrine Control of the
Gonads and Sexual Behavior

The first outstanding experiment in sexual endocrinology was done by Berthold (1849). Castration of roosters resulted in atrophy of the genital organs and decrease of sexual activity, which could be prevented by reimplantation of the testes. It was therefore suggested that a substance was produced by the testes responsible for the development and function of the sex organs and also for the appearance and maintenance of sexual behavior.

The gonadotropic function of the pituitary gland was first demonstrated by Aschner (1912) who observed gonadal atrophy in dogs following hypophysectomy. Subsequently, the gonadotropins were discovered by Aschheim and Zondek (1927) in our laboratories and simultaneously by Smith and Engle (1927) in America.

In 1932, Hohlweg and Junkmann envisaged the central nervous system as controller of the hypophyseal gonadotropic functions, and later Barraclough and Gorski (1961) distinguished a rostral sex center located in the preoptic hypothalamic region and regulating cyclic gonadotropin secretion in females and a caudal center located in the hypothalamic ventromedial arcuate region responsible for tonic gonadotropin secretion in both sexes. Recent data suggest, that structures of the limbic system, especially of the amygdala, are also responsible for cyclic gonadotropin release in females (Kawakami and Terasawa, 1974; Döcke et al., 1975).

Present day knowledge regarding the hypothalamo-hypophyseal-gonadal system may be summarized in the following manner (Figure 1): in the medial basal hypothalamus a gonadotropin releasing hormone (Schally et al., 1971) is secreted under the influence of neuro-transmitters (Kamberi, 1974; Sawyer et al., 1974). It is transported by the hypothalamo-hypophyseal portal vessels to the anterior pituitary stimulating there the secretion of gonadotropins. In females, an additional so-called cyclic sex center is responsible for a cyclically increased liberation of this gonadotropin-releaser. In consequence, a periodic over-release of hypophyseal gonadotropins occurs, promoting the induction of ovulation.

The hypophyseal gonadotropic hormones control the generative functions as well as the secretion of the gonadal hormones. The sex hormones, in turn, exert either only an inhibitory (negative) or also a stimulatory (positive) feedback effect on gonadotropin secretion depending on sex hormone concentrations during a critical hypothalamic differention period and the postpubertal functional period as well (Dörner, 1976).

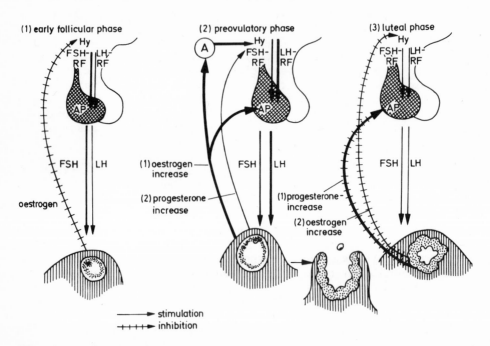

Fig. 1. Schematic drawing of the neuroendocrine regulation of the ovarian cycle. CHO: optic chiasm; A: amygdalar-preoptic-anterior hypothalamic continuum; HY: basomedial hypothalamus; AP: anterior pituitary.

Finally, sex hormones can sensitize hypothalamic mating centers to sensory stimulations which reach the diencephalon by pathways from the cerebral cortex and/or subcortex mediated by neurotransmitters (Dörner, 1972 and 1976). In 1941, Brookhart and Dey
demonstrated by means of intrahypothalamic lesions in guinea pigs
a central nervous mating center responsible for sexual behavior.
In 1968-1969, we distinguished a male mating center located in the
preoptic anterior hypothalamic area and a female center located in
the hypothalamic ventromedial nuclear region (Dörner et al., 1968;
Dorner et al., 1969). In rats of either sex, predominantly male
or female sexual behavior could be selectively stimulated or abolished either by intrahypothalamic sex hormone implants or by hypothalamic electrolytic lesions in these regions. Similar findings
were meanwhile described by other authors (Nadler, 1972; Powers,
1972; Carrer et al., 1973, 1974).

Moreover, we have found that the decrease of female sexual
behavior following bilateral or even unilateral hypothalamic
lesions of the ventromedial nuclear region, i.e. of the female
center, was associated with a simultaneous increase of male behavior in rats (Dorner et al., 1968 and 1969). Similar findings
were obtained in homosexual men (Roeder and Müller, 1969; Müller
et al., 1974; Dieckmann and Hassler, 1975). On the other hand,
lesions of the medial preoptic area, i.e. of the male center,
resulted in decreased male and increased female behavior in rats
(Powers and Valenstein, 1972).

Therefore, the following conclusion may be drawn: different
neuronal reflex circuits are responsible for male and female sexual behavior. In the medial preoptic anterior hypothalamic area
a sex hormone sensitive control center is located belonging to a
neuronal reflex circuit responsible for male behavior, whereas in
the ventromedial nucelar region a sex hormone sensitive control
center is located belonging to a neuronal reflex circuit regulating female behavior. Some antagonistic interrelationships appear
to exist between these male and female mating centers (Dörner, 1976).

Sex Hormone Dependent Differentiation of
Gonadotropin Secretion and Sexual Behavior

As early as in 1936, Pfeiffer observed that in rats, independent of the genetic sex, the lack of testes during a critical neonatal differentiation phase resulted in cyclic hypophyseal gonadotropin release, whereas the presence of testes during this critical phase gave rise to tonic hypophyseal gonadotropin secretion
in later life. Thus, ovarian cycles could be induced in male rats
castrated immediately after birth and implanted with ovaries after
becoming adults. On the other hand, ovulations could not be induced

in female rats neonatally implanted with testes. Consequently,
male and female rats are born with the latent capacity of cyclic
gonadotropin secretion. In the presence of testicular tissue and/or
a high testosterone level during the first days of life a male-
type brain differentiation takes place resulting in tonic gonadotropin secretion throughout the life. In case of lacking testes
and a low testosterone level during this critical period, on the
other hand, a female-type brain differentiation occurs. When
becoming adult, these animals show the capability of cyclic gonadotropin secretion.

Regarding sex hormone dependent brain differentiation and sexual behavior a remarkable observation was reported by Vera Dantchakoff in 1938, which was later confirmed by Phoenix and coworkers
(Phoenix et al., 1959). Female guinea pigs, androgenized prenatally, exhibited increased male and decreased female behavior
in adulthood. On the basis of these results, Phoenix and his coworkers distinguished an early organization period and a postpubertal activation period.

Adult females of other species, e.g. rats (Barraclough and
Gorski, 1961; Dörner, 1972), golden hamsters (Carter et al., 1972;
Swanson et al., 1974) or rhesus monkeys (Eaton et al., 1973) were
then also found to exhibit predominantly masculine behavioral patterns in adulthood after androgen administration during critical
organization periods.

On the other hand, Grady and Phoenix (1963) and Harris (1964)
reported that male rats orchidectomized shortly after birth showed
especially strong female sexual behavior when treated with estrogen
in adulthood. Similar findings were obtained in adult male rats
which had been treated with anti-androgen during perinatal life
(Neumann et al., 1967). All these observations pointed to the
significance of the sex hormone level during a critical differentiation phase for the development of sexual behavior.

                        Investigations on Sex Hormone
                        Dependent Brain Differentiation

During the last decade, the following findings were obtained
in our laboratories on sex hormone dependent brain differentiation
and sexual behavior (Dörner, 1976):

1. Male rats castrated on the first day of life showed predominantly heterotypical behavior, following androgen substitution
in adulthood (Dörner, 1967, 1969, 1970, 1972). In other words,
genetic males exposed to a temporary androgen deficiency during
the hypothalamic organization period, but normal or approximately

normal androgen levels in adulthood were sexually excited prefer-
entially by partners of the same sex.

2.   This neuroendocrine conditioned male homosexuality could
be prevented by androgens administered during the critical hypothalamic differentiation period (Dörner and Hinz, 1971).

3.   The higher the androgen level during the hypothalamic
differentiation phase, the stronger was the male and the weaker
the female sexual behavior during the postpubertal functional
phase, irrespective of the genetic sex. Even a complete inver-
sion of sexual behavior was observed in male and female rats following androgen deficiency in males and androgen overdosage in
females during the hypothalamic differentiation period. According to these findings a neuroendocrine predisposition for primary
hypo-, bi- and homosexuality may be based on different degrees of
androgen deficiency in males and androgen (or even estrogen) over-
doses in females during sex-specific brain differentiation (Dörner,
1969, 1970).

4.   The higher the androgen level during the critical hypothalamic differentiation period, the smaller were the nuclear
volumes of neurons in specific hypothalamic regions regulating
sexual behavior and/or gonadotropin secretion as well as in the
medial amygdala throughout the life (Dörner and Staudt, 1968 and
1969; Staudt et al., 1976).

5.   In male rats castrated on the first day of life, a strong
positive estrogen feedback effect (Hohlweg effect) could be induced in a similar way as in normal females, but not in males
castrated on the 14th day of life or in neonatally androgenized
(or estrogenized) females (Dörner and Döcke, 1964; Döcke and Dörner,
1966). In view of these findings a strong positive estrogen feedback effect appears to be only evocable in adulthood if there existed a low androgen level during brain differentiation.

6.   Recently, the following correlations between sex hormone
levels during the hypothalamic differentiation and/or functional
periods, on the one hand, and the evocability of a positive estrogen feedback effect on LH secretion were observed in rats (Figure 2): following a single estrogen injection in postpubertally
castrated and estrogen-primed female rats a distinct surge of LH
secretion was evoked, while castrated and androgen-primed females
displayed a diminished and delayed surge of LH secretion. On the
other hand, postpubertally castrated and estrogen-primed male rats
exhibited only a slight, but significant surge of LH secretion,
whereas castrated and androgen-primed males did not display any
surge of LH secretion following estrogen injection. In view of
these findings the evocability of a positive estrogen feedback
action on LH secretion is dependent on the sex hormone level during

the critical hypothalamic differentiation phase and the postpubertal
priming phase as well.

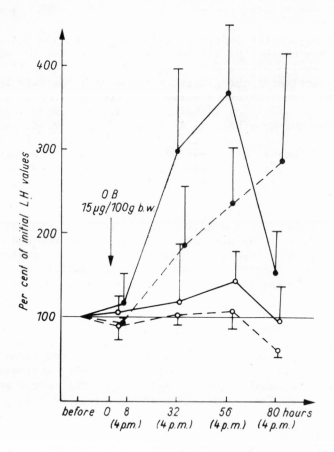

Fig. 2.   Serum LH response to a subcutaneous injection of estradiol
benzoate (15 ug/100 g b.w.) expressed as per cent of the mean initial
LH values in postpubertally castrated and oestrogen- or androgen-
primed female and male rats (Means ± SEM).

●———●   castrated and oestrogen-primed female rats (n = 8)

●— — —●   castrated and androgen-primed female rats (n = 5)

0———0   castrated and oestrogen-primed male rats (n = 4)

0 — — —0   castrated and andorgen-primed male rats (n = 5)

7. A positive estrogen feedback effect could also be elicited in intact homosexual men in contrast to intact heterosexual and bisexual men (Figure 3). Thus, in homosexual men, an intravenous injection of estrogen (20 mg Presomen[R], which is comparable to Premarin[R]) produced primarily a decrease of the LH serum level followed secondarily by a significant increase above the initial LH values. In intact heterosexual men, on the other hand, the estrogen administration also produced a decrease of the LH serum level which was not followed, however, by an increase above the initial LH values (Dörner, Rohde, Krell, 1972; Dörner, Rohde et al., 1975). This finding suggests that homosexual men possess – at least in part – a predominantly female-differentiated brain.

8. The apparently free, i.e. the biologically active plasma testosterone level (Table 1) was slightly, but significantly decreased in homosexual men (Stahl et al., 1976), whereas the plasma FSH level was significantly increased (Dörner et al., in preparation) in effeminized homosexual or transsexual men as compared to heterosexual men (Table 2).

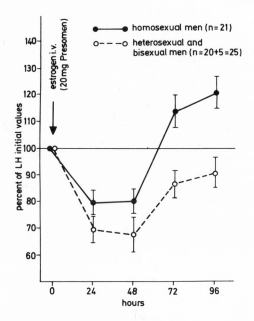

Fig. 3. Serum LH response to an intravenous estrogen injection expressed as per cent of the mean initial LH values in homosexual and hetero- or bisexual men (Means ± SEM).

TABLE 1

TOTAL AND FREE PLASMA TESTOSTERONE (T) AND TESTOSTERONE
BINDING GLOBULIN (TeBG) CAPACITY IN MALE HETEROSEXUALS
AND HOMOSEXUALS (MEANS ± SD)

Subjects	Number	Age (years)	Total T (ng/100 ml)	Free T (ng/100 ml)	TeBG (x 10^{-8} M)
Male Hetero- sexuals	38	20 - 40	562 ± 126	13.3 ± 4.5	4.8 ± 2.7
Male Homo- sexuals	35	19 - 40	590 ± 148	10.7 ± 3.3*	6.5 ± 2.6*

* $P < 0.01$ as compared to the heterosexuals

TABLE 2

SERUM FSH LEVELS (MEANS ± SD) IN HETEROSEXUAL MALES,
NONEFFEMINIZED HOMOSEXUAL MALES, EFFEMINIZED HOMOSEX-
UAL MALES AND TRANSSEXUAL MALES

Subjects		N	Serum FSH level (mIU/ml)
I	Heterosexual males	20	4.36 ± 2.57
II	Noneffeminized homosexual males	24	5.58 ± 3.32
III	Effeminized homosexual males	20	8.55 ± 6.40*
IV	Transsexual males	4	10.60 ± 5.05
V (= III + IV) Effeminized homosexual or trans- sexual males		24	8.89 ± 5.57**

* $P < 0.02$ and $P < 0.01$ vs. heterosexual males

9.   In female rats, unphysiologically high androgen and/or
estrogen levels during the hypothalamic differentiation period
caused anovulatory sterility and/or a neuroendocrine predisposition for female hypo-, bi- or homosexuality (Dörner, Döcke and
Hinz, 1971; Dörner and Hinz, 1972).   In this context, it may be
mentioned that androgens are converted to estrogens, at least in
part, by neural tissues from fetal and neonatal rats (Reddy, Naf-
tolin and Ryan, 1974).   A complete masculinization of sexual behavior in female animals was observed following a combined pre-
and postnatal androgen treatment (Dörner et al., 1968; Ward, 1969;
Sachs and Pollak, 1973).

10.   In adult homosexual women, a significant increase of the
plasma testosterone level was found as compared to heterosexual
women (Griffith et al., 1974; Dörner et al., still unpublished
data).

In summary, the following correlations were found between
changes of the androgen and/or estrogen levels during the hypothalamic differentiation phase and permanent sexual disorders during the postpubertal hypothalamic functional phase:

1.   In genetic males, androgen deficiency during the hypothalamic differentiation phase can result in a more or less female
differentiation of the brain; i.e. a neuroendocrine predisposition
of the brain; i.e. a neuroendocrine predisposition for male hypo-,
bi- or even homosexuality.

2.   In genetic females, androgen (or estrogen) overdosage
during the hypothalamic differentiation phase can lead to more
or less male differentiation of the brain, i.e. anovulatory sterility and/or neuroendocrine predisposition for female hypo-, bi-
or homosexuality.

In view of these findings, important disturbances of sexual
functions may be based on discrepancies between the genetic sex
and the sex hormone level during the hypothalamic differentiation
phase.   A causal prophylaxis may become possible in the future by
preventing such discrepancies during the time of sex specific brain
organization.

Three preconditions towards this aim have been achieved in
our laboratories:

1.   Comparative studies of hypothalamic biomorphosis in human
fetuses and rats have led to the conclusion that the critical hypothalamic differentiation period may be timed in the human between
the 4th and 7th month of fetal life (Dörner and Staudt, 1972;
Dörner, 1976).

2. A simple and reliable method for the prenatal diagnosis of genetic sex was developed using fluorescence microscopy of amniotic fluid cells (Dörner, Rohde et al., 1973).

3. Significantly higher testosterone concentrations were found in amniotic fluids of male fetuses than in those of female fetuses (Dörner, Stahl et al., 1973; Giles et al., 1974).

Sex Hormone Dependent Brain
Maturation and Sexual Behavior

The influence of sex hormones on brain maturation was also investigated. For this reason, male rats were castrated on the 14th day of life, i.e. at the beginning of the prepubertal maturation phase and substituted with androgens during adulthood. In these animals, permanently reduced male sexual behavior (Figure 4) was found, despite long-term androgen replacement in adulthood (Götz and Dörner, 1976).

These findings suggest that in genetic males a sex-specific androgen level is necessary, not only during brain differentiation but also during brain maturation in order to obtain normal male sexual behavior. In view of these data primary male hyposexuality can also be based on androgen deficiency during the prepubertal maturation phase of the brain.

Organization Rules for the
Ontogeny of Neuroendocrine Systems

The following organization (differentiation) rules were deduced from our experimental and clinical studies on sex hormone dependent brain differentiation (Figure 5).

1. Transformation rule. During a critical hypothalamic differentiation phase, an open-loop regulatory system (e.g. placenta and/or hypophysis - fetal gonad - fetal hypothalamus) is converted into a feedback control system (hypothalamic-hypophyseal-gonadal system). The regulating variable and the regulated element of the primary open-loop regulatory system (e.g. sex hormone and hypothalamus) are then transformed into the controlled condition (homeostatic variable) and the central nervous controller of the secondary feedback control system.

2. Determination rule. The quantity of the primarily regulating and secondarily homeostatic variable (e.g. sex hormone) determines during brain differentiation the quality (responsiveness) of the central nervous controller, and hence the functional and tolerance ranges of the feedback control system throughout the life.

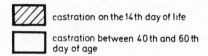

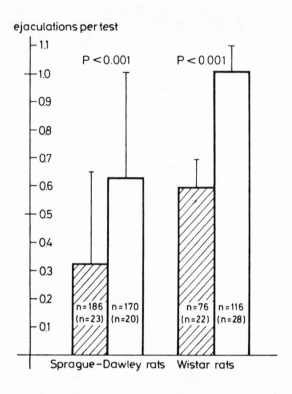

Fig. 4. The influence of the endogenous androgen level during the prepubertal maturation phase on the ejaculatory behaviour during the postpubertal functional phase in male rats. All rats were equally substituted with androgens in adult life; n = number of tests and SEM; (n) = number of rats.

These organization rules deduced from animal experiments and clinical studies for the hypothalamic-hypophyseal-gonadal system regulating reproduction appears to hold also true for other neuro-endocrine systems controlling metabolism and information processing (Dörner, 1974 and 1976).

Thus, the following ontogenetic basic rule may be valid for fundamental processes of life, such as reproduction, metabolism and information processing: during critical differentiation

I. Prenatal open-loop regulatory system

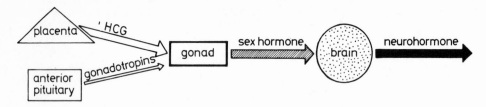

II. Postnatal feedback control system (closed-loop regulatory system)

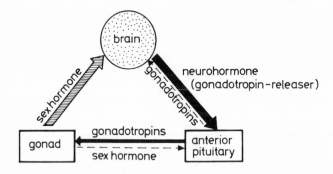

Fig. 5.   Ontogenesis of the feedback control system for reproduction.

periods of the brain, the quantity of local or blood-borne systemic hormones can predetermine the quality, i.e. the reactivity and adaptability of their own central nervous controllers, and hence the functional and tolerance ranges of their own feedback control system throughtout the life.

Neurotransmitters as Local
Hormones of the Brain

In my opinion, hormones may be defined as intercellularly active chemical messengers that are produced in specifically differentiated cells and exert biological effects on other cells of the same organism by acting either locally, i.e. as local hormones, or at distant target cells, i.e. as blood-borne or systemic hormones. They affect reversibly (during functional periods) or even more or less irreversibly (during differentiation and maturation periods) cell activities, especially enzyme activities, by intracellular receptors or by cell membrane receptors, cyclases and

intracellular messengers. Thus, hormones can be classified according to their chemical structure, their site of production, their
site of action, their biological action and/or their mechanism of
action.

   In view of this definition, central nervous neurotransmitters
may be regarded as local hormones of the brain, and a strict differentiation between neurohumors or neurotransmitters and blood-
borne neurohormones appears to be no longer justified.

Neurotransmitters and Sexual Behavior

   In recent years, it was demonstrated that neurotransmitters
are also responsible for the control of sexual behavior. Male
behavior was found to be stimulated by acetylcholine and β-adrener-
gic activators, but inhibited by serotonin and χ-adrenergic activators (Gessa and Tagliamonte, 1975; Soulairac and Soulairac, 1975).
On the other hand, female behavior was reported to be stimulated
by noradrenaline, but inhibited by serotonin, dopamine and adre-
naline (Everitt et al., 1975; Crowley et al., 1976).

   Fascinating enough, such neurotransmitters appear to represent
not only temporary activators or inhibitors, but also organizers
of the brain. Most recently, we have obtained some experimental
data suggesting that the quantity of neurotransmitter concentrations and/or turnover rates during brain differentiation is also
able to predetermine the quality, i.e. the reactivity of central
nervous controllers for sexual behavior.

   Rats were treated with pargyline, reserpine or pyridostigmine
during the first two weeks of life. These animals showed significant permanent changes not only of sexual behavior, but also of
conditioned learning behavior and emotional reactivity in juvenile
and/or adult life (Dörner, Hecht and Hinz, 1976; Dörner, 1976).
Male sexual activity was permanently decreased in neonatally par-
gyline- or reserpine-treated animals, but permanently increased
in neonatally pyridostigmine-treated rats (Figure 6). In addition,
learning and/or memory capacity also appeared to be permanently
decreased in neonatally pargyline- or reserpine-treated animals,
but permanently increased in neonatally pyridostigmine-treated
rats. Thus, it was demonstrated that nonphysiological concentrations and/or turnover rates of neurotransmitters during brain differentiation can act as teratogens leading to permanent behavioral
changes.

   Furthermore, these findings indicate that external environment
dependent brain differentiation may be mediated by neurotransmitters, since changes of the external environment during brain differentiation can permanently affect the responsiveness of the

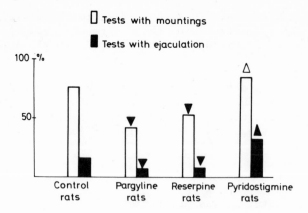

Fig. 6. Male sexual behavior in juvenile and adult male rats following the treatment with pargyline, reserpine or pyridostigmine
during the first two weeks of life. Male sexuality was expressed
in per cent of positive tests with mounting and ejaculation when
exposed to castrated and estrogen-treated female rats; ▼ significantly decreased and ▲ significantly increased as compared to the
controls (▼ and ▲ P 0.001; ▲ P 0.05).

central nervous system in a similar imprinting way (Denenberg,
1964; Rosenzweig, 1971).

In view of all these findings, numerous relevant disturbances
of reproduction, metabolism and information processing called "idiopathic, primary, endogenous, genuine or essential" so far can be
based on hormone dependent differentiation disturbances of the
brain and hence appear to be accessible, at least in part, to a
preventive therapy.

CONCLUSIONS

Critical Differentiation Period

Four critical differentiation periods may be distinguished
for sex-specific development in mammals:

1. Determination of the gonosomal sex. Fertilization of an
ovum by an androsperme (with a Y gonosome) results in a genetic
male, whereas fertilization of an ovum by a gynosperme (with a X
gonosome) results in a genetic female.

2. <u>Organization of the gonads</u>. If the somatic cells of the gonadal blastema contain a Y gonosome, testes will be organized, whereas in the absence of a Y gonosome and in the presence of 2 X gonosomes ovaries will be differentiated.

3. <u>Sex hormone dependent differentiation of the genital organs and the brain</u>. The organization of the gonads is followed by (a) the differentiation of male or female gonaducts (month 2 to 3 of fetal life in the human), (b) of male or female external genitalia (month 3 to 4), and finally (c) of a male or female hypothalamus (apparently between month 4 and 7 of fetal life). In the presence of testes and a high androgen level there is a male differentiation, whereas in the absence of testes there is a female differentiation, irrespective of the presence or absence of ovaries. The sex-specific differentiation of sexual behavior may be mediated not only by sex hormones but also by neurotransmitters.

4. <u>Development of the gender role</u>. The gender role appears to be affected (a) by sex hormone dependent differentiation processes, especially of the brain, and (b) by educational and sociocultural factors, in particular during a critical period of early postnatal life. This environment dependent determination of sexual self-identity may also be mediated by neurotransmitters.

Disorders of Sex Differentiation

Consequently, the following disorders of sex differentiation may be distinguished:

1. <u>Gonosomal disorders</u>: XO (gonadal dysgenesis), XXY (sex chromatin positive Klinefelter's syndrome), XYY (supermale) and gonosomal mosaics.

2. <u>Gonadal organization disturbances</u>: pure gonadal dysgenesis, sex chromatin negative Klinefelter's syndrome or hermaphroditism with XY or XX.

3. <u>Differentiation disturbances of the genital organs and/or of the central nervous system</u>: internal and/or external and/or central nervous pseudohermàphroditism in males and females.

4. <u>Disorders of the gender role</u>: transvestitism and transsexualism.

Thus, relevant disorders of sex differentiation can be based on gonosomal disturbances (genetic defects) or on discrepancies between the gonosomal sex, i.e. the genetic material, and a sex-specific hormonal environment during critical differentiation periods of the internal and/or external genital organs and/or, in particular, of the brain.

In genetic males, androgen deficiency during a critical differentiation period may lead to a more or less female differentiation of the brain, i.e. a neuroendocrine predisposition for male
hypo-, bi- or even homosexuality. In favor of this theory,
primarily deduced from extensive animal experiments, we have found
in homosexual men (a) the evocability of a positive estrogen feedback effect (b) a slight, but significant decrease of the apparently
free, i.e. biologically active plasma testosterone level (Table 1)
and (c) a significant increase of the plasma FSH level in effeminized homosexual and transsexual men (Table 2).

In genetic females, on the other hand, an unphysiological increase of the androgen and/or estrogen level during the differentiation phase may result in a more or less male differentiation of the
brain, i.e. a neuroendocrine predisposition for female hypo-, bi-
or homosexuality and/or acyclic hypophyseal gonadotropin secretion.
In this context, it may be mentioned that an increased plasma
testosterone level was observed in masculinized homosexual women
(Griffith et al., 1974; Dörner et al., still unpublished data).

Up to the present all treatment of genetic defects is purely
symptomatic. Since important sexual disorders can be based, however, on discrepancies between the genetic sex and sex-specific
hormone concentrations during critical differentiation periods, a
causal prophylaxis may become possible in future by preventing
such discrepancies in early development.

This aim has been approached by 3 preconditions (Dörner, 1976):

1. Timing of hormone dependent differentiation periods;

2. Development of reliable methods for prenatal diagnosis of
   genetic sex;

3. Demonstration of sex-specific concentrations of hormones
   in fetal blood and in amniotic fluids.

REFERENCES

Aschheim, S. and Zondek, B. (1927). Hypophysenvorderlappenhormon
    und Schwangerenhormon im Harn von Schwangeren. Klin. Wschr.
    6: 1322.

Aschner, B. (1912). Uber die Beziehungen zwischen Hypophysis und
    Genitale. Arch. Gynak. 97: 200-228.

Barraclough, C.A. and Gorski, R.A. (1961). Evidence that the hypothalamus is responsible for androgen-induced sterility in the female rat. Endocrinology 68: 68-70.

Berthold, A.A. (1849). Transplantation der Hoden. Arch. Anat. Physiol. 42-46.

Brookhart, J.M. and Dey, F.L. (1941). Reduction of sexual behavior in male guinea pigs by hypothalamic lesions. Amer. J. Physiol. 133: 551-554.

Carrer, H., Asch, G. and Aron, C. (1973, 1974). New facts concerning the role played by the ventromedial nucleus in the control of estrous cycle duration and sexual receptivity in the rat. Neuroendocrinology, 13: 129-138.

Carter, C.S., Clemens, L.G. and Hoekema, D.J. (1972). Neonatal androgen and adult sexual behavior in the golden hamster. Physiol. and Behav. 9: 89-95.

Crowley, W.R., Feder, H.H. and Morin, L.P. (1976). Role of monoamines in sexual behavior of the female guinea pig. Pharmacol. Biochem. Behav. 4: 67-71.

Dantchakoff, V. (1938). Role des hormones dans la manifestation des instincts sexuels. Acad. Sci. 206: 945-947.

Denenberg, V.H. (1964). Critical periods, stimulus input, and emotional reactivity: a theory of infantile stimulation. Psychological Review, 71: 335-351.

Dieckmann, G. and Hassler, R. (1975). Unilateral hypothalamotomy in sexual delinquents. Report on six cases. Confinia Neurologica, 37: 177-186.

Döcke, F. and Dörner, G. (1966). Tierexperimentelle Untersuchungen zur Ovulationsauslösung mit Gonadotropinen and Östrogenen. 4. Mittl., Zur neurohormonalen Regulation der Ovulation. Zbl. Gynäk. 88: 273-282.

Döcke, F., Smollich, A., Rohde, W., Okrasa, R. and Dörner, G. (1975). Studies on extrahypophyseal sites of estrogen action in the induction of ovulation in rats. Endokrinologie, 65: 274-287.

Dörner, G. (1967). Tierexperimentelle untersuchungen zur Frage einer hormonalen Pathogenese der Homosexualität. Acta Biol. Med. Germ. 19: 569:584.

Dörner, G. (1969). Zur Frage einer neuroendokrinen Pathogenese,
     Prophylaxe und Therapie angeborener Sexualdeviationen.
     Dtsch. Med. Wschr. 94: 390-396.

Dörner, G. (1970). The influence of sex hormones during the
     hypothalamic differentiation and maturation phases on
     gonadal function and sexual behavior during the hypothalamic
     functional phase. Endokrinologie, 56: 280-291.

Dörner, G. (1972). Sexualhormonabhängige Gehirndifferenzierung und
     Sexualität, Jena, Gustav Fischer und Springer, Wien.

Dörner, G. (1974). Environment-dependent brain differentiation
     and fundamental processes of life. Acta Biol. Med. Germ.
     33: 129-148.

Dörner, G. (1976). Hormones and Brain Differentiation, Elsevier,
     Amsterdam.

Dörner, G. (1976). Further evidence of permanent behavioral changes
     in rats treated neonatally with neurodrugs. Endokrinologie,
     in press.

Dörner, G. and Döcke, F. (1964). Sex-specific reaction of the
     hypothalamo-hypophysial system of rats. J. Endocr. 30:
     265-266.

Dörner, G. Döcke, F. and Hinz, G. (1968). Entwicklung und Rück-
     bildung neuroendokrin bedingter männlicher Homosexualität.
     Acta Biol. Med. Germ. 21: 577-580.

Dörner, G., Döcke, F. and Hinz, G. (1969). Homo- and hypersexuality
     in rats with hypothalamic lesions. Neuroendocrinology, 4:
     20-24.

Dörner, G., Döcke, F. and Hinz, G. (1971). Paradoxical effects of
     estrogen on brain differentiation. Neuroendocrinology, 7:
     146-155.

Dörner, G., Döcke, F. and Moustafa, S. (1968). Differential lo-
     calization of a male and a female hypothalamic mating centre.
     J. Reprod. Fert. 17: 583-586.

Dörner, G., Götz, F. and Rohde, W. (1975). On the evocability of
     a positive oestrogen feedback action on LH secretion in
     male and female rats. Endokrinologie, 66: 369-372.

Dörner, G. and Hinz, G. (1971). Männlicher Hypogonadismus mit sekundärer Hyposexualität nach hochdosierten Gaben von Östrogenen während der hypothalamischen Differenzierungsphase. Endokrinologie, 58: 227-233.

Dörner, G. and Hinz, G. (1972). Neuroendokrin bedingte Prädisposition für weibliche Homosexualität bei erhaltener zyklischer Ovarialfunktion. Endokrinologie, 59: 48-52.

Dörner, G., Rohde, W., Baumgarten, G., Herter, U., Halle, H., Gruber, G., Rössner, P., Bergmann, K.H., Götz, F. and Zillman, R. (1973). Zur pränatalen Geschlechtsbestimmung im Fruchtwasser und peripheren mütterlichen Blut durch fluoreszenzmikroskopischen Nachweis des Y-Chromosoms. Zbl. Gynäk. 95: 625-634.

Dörner, G., Rohde, W. and Krell, L. (1972). Auslösung eines positiven Östrogenfeedback-Effekt bei homosexuellen Männern. Endokrinologie, 60: 297-301.

Dörner, G., Rohde, W., Stahl, F., Krell, L. and Masius, W. (1975). Neuroendocrine conditioned predisposition for homosexuality in men. Arch. Sex. Behav. 4: 1-8.

Dörner, G., Stahl, F., Rohde, W., Halle, H., Rössner, P., Gruber, D. and Herter, U. (1973). Radioimmunologische Bestimmung des Testosterongehalts in fruchtwasser männlicher und weiblicher Feten. Endokrinologie, 61: 317-320.

Dörner, G. and Staudt, J. (1968). Structural changes in the preoptic anterior hypothalamic area of the male rat, following neonatal castration and androgen substitution. Neuroendocrinology, 3: 136-140.

Dörner, G. and Staudt, J. (1969). Structural changes in the hypothalamic ventromedial nucleus of the male rat, following neonatal castration and androgen treatment. Neuroendocrinology, 4: 278-281.

Dörner, G. and Staudt, J. (1972). Vergleichende morphologische Untersuchungen der Hypothalamusdifferenzierung bei Ratte und Mensch. Endokrinologie, 59: 151-155.

Eaton, G.G., Goy, R.W. and Phoenix, C.H. (1973). Effects of testosterone treatment in adulthood on sexual behavior of female pseudohermaphrodite Rhesus monkeys. Nature, 242: 119-120.

Everitt, B.J., Fuxe, K., Hökfelt, T. and Jonsson, G. (1975). Role of monoamines in the control by hormones of sexual receptivity in the female rat. J. Comp. Physiol. Psychol. 89: 556–572.

Gessa, G.L. and Tagliamonte, A. (1975). Role of brain serotonin and dopamine in male sexual behavior. In Sandler, M. and Gesse, G.L. (eds.), Sexual Behavior: Pharmacology and Biochemistry, Raven Press, New York.

Giles, H.R., Lox, Ch.D., Heine, M.W. and Christian, C.D. (1974). Intrauterine fetal sex determination by radioimmunoassay of amniotic fluid testosterone. Gynaec. Investigation 5: 317–323.

Götz, F. and Dörner, G. (1976). Sex hormone-dependent brain maturation and sexual behavior in rats. Endokrinologie, in press.

Grady, K.L. and Phoenix, C.H. (1963). Hormonal determinants of mating behavior; the display of feminine behavior by adult male rats castrated neonatally. Amer. Zool. 3: 482–483.

Griffith, P.D., Merry, J., Browning, M.C.K., Eisinger, A.H., Huntsman, R.G., Lord, E., Polani, P.E., Tanner, J.M. and Whitehouse, R.H. (1974). Homosexual women: an endocrine and psychological study. J. Endocr. 63: 549–556.

Harris, G.W. (1964). Sex hormones, brain development and brain function. Endocrinology, 75: 627–648.

Hohlweg, W. and Junkmann, K. (1932). Die hormonal-nervöse Regulierung der Funktion des Hypophysenvorderlappens. Klin. Wschr. 11: 321–323.

Kamberi, I. (1974). Catecholaminergic, indolaminergic and cholinergic pathways and the hypothalamic hypophysiotropic neurohormones involved in control of gonadotropin secretion. In Dörner, G. (ed.), Endocrinology of Sex, Leipzig, Barth.

Kawakami, M. and Terasawa, E. (1974). Role of limbic forebrain structures on reproductive cycles. In Kawakami, M. (ed.), Biological Rhythms in Neuroendocrine Activity, Igaku Shoin Ltd, Tokyo.

Müller, D., Orthner, H., Roeder, F., König, A., Bosse, K. and Kloos, G. (1974). The effect of hypothalamic lesions on sex behavior and gonadotropic functions in the human. In Dorner, G. (ed.), Endocrinology of Sex, Barth, Leipzig.

Nadler, R.D. (1972). Intrahypothalamic exploration of androgen-
     sensitive brain loci in neonatal female rats. Transactions
     New York Academy of Sciences Series II, 34: 572-581.

Napoli, A., Powers, J.B. and Valenstein, E.S. (1972). Hormonal
     induction of behavioral estrus modified by electrical stim-
     ulation of hypothalamus. Physiol. Behav. 9: 115-117.

Neumann, F., Elger, W. and von Berswordt-Wallrabe, R. (1967).
     Intersexualität männlicher Feten und Hemmung androgenab-
     hängiger Funktionen bei erwachsenen Tieren durch Testos-
     teronblocker. Dtsch. Med. Wschr. 92: 360-366.

Pfeiffer, C.A. (1936). Sexual differences of the hypophyses and
     their determination by the gonads. Amer. J. Anat. 58:
     195-225.

Phoenix, C.H., Goy, R.W., Gerall, A.A. and Young, W.C. (1959).
     Organizing action of prenatally administered testosterone
     propionate on the tissues mediating mating behavior in the
     female guinea pig. Endocrinology, 65: 369-382.

Powers, J.B. (1972). Facilitation of lordosis in ovariectomized
     rats by intracerebral progesterone implants. Brain Res.
     48: 311-325.

Powers, J.B. and Valenstein, E.S. (1972). Sexual receptivity
     facilitation by medial preoptic lesions in female rats.
     Science, 175: 1003-1005.

Roeder, F. and Müller, D. (1969). Zur stereotaktischen Heilung
     der pädophilen Homosexualität. Dtsch. Med. Wschr. 94:

Rosenzweig, M.R. (1971). Effects of environment on development
     of brain and behavior. In Tobach, E., Aronson, L. and Shaw,
     E. (eds.), The Biopsychology of Development, Academic Press,
     New York.

Schally, A.V., Kastin, A.J. and Arimura, A. (1971). Hypothalamic
     follicle stimulating hormone (FSH) and luteinizing hormone
     (LH)-regulating hormone: structure, physiology and clinical
     studies. Fertil. and Steril. 22: 703-721.

Soulairac, M.L. and Soulairac, A. (1975). A Monoaminergic and
     cholinergic control of sexual behavior in the male rat.
     In Sandler, M., and Gessa, G.L. (eds.), Sexual Behavior:
     Pharmacology and Biochemistry, Raven Press, New York.

Stahl, F., Dörner, G., Ahrens, L. and Graudenz, W. (1976). Sig-
    nificantly decreased apparently free testosterone levels
    in plasma of male homosexuals. Endokrinologie, in press.

Staudt, J. and Dörner, G. (1976). Structural changes in the medial
    and central amygdala of the male rat, following neonatal
    castration and androgen treatment. Endokrinologie, 67:
    296-300.

Swanson, H., Brayshow, J.S. and Payne, A.P. (1974). Effects of
    neonatal androgenization on sexual and aggressive behavior
    in the golden hamster. In Dörner, G. (ed.), Endocrinology
    of Sex, Barth, Leipzig.

Ward, I.L. (1969). Differential effect of pre- and postnatal
    androgen on the sexual behavior of intact and spayed female
    rats. Hormones and Behav. 1: 25-36.

SEXUAL IDENTITY AND EROTICISM

Jules Bureau

Canada

A phenomenon which has apparently paralleled the recent development in sexology is on one hand the increasing breakdown and
parcelling out in the studies on human sexuality. Attention is
focused on the various types of orgasm, hormonal levels, karyo-
types, average and abnormal erotic behaviors, and sexual subcul-
tures, etc. However, on the other hand such dissection of human
sexuality has encouraged the emergence of an even greater morcel-
lement in the labelling which isolates and separates a fundamen-
tally human and integrated dimension; to wit, the differentiation
between sexuality and gender identity, sexuality and genitality,
and especially between eroticism and sexuality.

In separating eroticism from sexuality, a differentiation
which suggests two distinct realities to many, there has been a
growing tendency among researchers and public alike to explain all
human sexuality in terms of eroticism, i.e., a desire to experience
a specific or vague pleasure, be it enriching or degrading. This
tendency, jeopardizes the entire significance of sexuality and
its meaning in human life. To reduce sexuality to eroticism de-
prives it of its essential human dimension; in truth, to be or not
to be sexual, to be a man or else a woman, surpasses the mere erotic
being: it transforms this being and gives it meaning. It is sexuality which should explain eroticism rather than the contrary, and
to do so, sexuality must recover its human, that is, its global
and integrated specificity without, however, becoming enmeshed in
vague and incoherent philosophism or in unyielding psychologism.
Indeed, if all present research in sexology allow for a better
understanding and development of human sexuality, we must endeavor
to centralize the observations and results obtained in an integrating principle which will bridge the chasm between the sexed and the

sexual body, the sexual parts and the sexual whole.

In truth, just as the understanding of human sexuality is not the prerogative of the intellect alone, but is also the fruit of the intimate union of all human functions (emotive, intellectual and instinctive) whose interaction leads to the highest levels of knowledge, the same holds true for the full meaning of the reality of human sexuality which does not belong exclusively to the sociologist, or the biologist, or to the physician or the psychologist, but should be attained in all its dimensions by a conjugated effort of interdisciplinary, interprofessionalization and even interpersonalization approach. In order to protect this notion of sexual reality from a loss in meaning and a "de-substantiation" of its strength, sexology should be on guard against the following dogmatic tenets: to refuse the acceptance of the sexual phenomenon in itself by considering it to be a mere indication of internal dynamics (Freud, 1905); or to limit oneself to a simple examination of the external manifestations as though they were the only real aspect of the phenomenon.

In my opinion, the sexual identity of the human being is the integrating principle which gives the sexuality of a man or a woman, its human specificity. We shall attempt to illustrate this principle in spite of the difficulties involved in tackling the problem in operational terms.

THE NECESSITY FOR SEXUAL IDENTITY

The human identity of a person is the magnetic pole of all his actions, emotions and experiences, and it is by experiencing this identity that a person appropriates his behaviors which will become part of his life and for which he feels awareness and responsibility. More than a structure or a substance, it is a process which allows man bypass the shallow conformism, the "dasman," i.e. the anonymous mediocre and dull man, a constant threat in this day and age. This is indeed the threat which contemporary man faces, wherein he is emptied of his own being to conform with the crowd (Fromm, 1945), where he loses the experience of belonging to himself, deprived of doing his own thing, he finds himself condemned to be a number among others. It is by an attempt to single out and understand the intrapersonality of each human being that it becomes possible to set up barriers before this all invading conformism. To this task humanistic psychology has devoted its resources. Allport (1967), Jourard (1974), Bugental (1964) and many others are trying to reach this dimension of man's humanity. The "who and I?", "I am myself" - which, when stripped of all trappings, rests on "I am... and therefore..." with all the consequences at the level of awareness and responsibility, "I have the right to be and it is not the conformity to others that justifies my existence."

In like manner, the same dangers surround man's sexual identity and we must refer to the same sources if man is to retain the meaning of his sexual identity and not be submerged in the sum total of sexual behavior averages like a robot with computerized reflexes. Only a sharp awareness of his sexual identity will allow a human being to direct, individualize, and fully live his sexuality, using it as an ownership which gives form to his fantasies, caresses, sexual interests, or garments.

Human Identity and Sexual Identity

A person's sexual identity is the most pregnant identity with consequences affecting the individual's life and its development. Among the various aspects of his identity (Figure 1), sexual identity has an inherent strength or weakness which invades the entire individual.

Human identity:

"I am myself"

(Bugental, 1964; Allport, 1967; Jourard, 1974)

Identity of species:
"I am human" (Kohlberg, 1966)

Identity of sex:
"I am a boy - a girl"
(Money, 1972; Stoller, 1968)

Identity of age:
"I am a child" (Kohlberg, 1966; Lécuyer, 1975)

Identity of race:
"I am White" (Lécuyer, 1975)

Identity of culture:
"I am a Quebecer"

Identity of social status:
"I am poor" (Rainwater, 1960)

Identity of religion:
"I am a Catholic"

ETC.

Fig. 1. The various aspects of human identity.

This trail leads to the question: "What am I, sexually-speaking?" and not "What should I do, sexually-speaking?", a question unfortunately too often asked. The individual has no choice but to attribute himself a value whatsoever to this personal dimension (Kagan, 1969) and without outlining the entire genesis (Bureau, 1976[a]), we observe that a child acquires a sexual identity before acquiring any other single identity (Kohlberg, 1966; Lécuyer, 1975; Rainwater, 1960) except for the identity of species. The sexual identity is co-occurrent with that of age (Kohlberg, 1966) and its irreversibility is several months prior to the child's grasp of the principle of material conservation (Kohlberg, 1966; Piaget, 1956). From the "I am a sexed, sexual and erotic being arises "I act sexually and erotically." The strength, conciseness, and precision with which the individual lives himself and tells himself ("I am sexed, sexual, and erotic") vitalize the whole of his psychic sexual and erotic existence (sentiments, interests, emotions, conscience, ideas, and responsibilities). It will also influence his outward sexual and erotic behaviors. Such is the impact of sexual identity on the human being.

The Content of Sexual Identity and Means of Attainment

Since we have elsewhere elaborated upon the various contents of sexual identity and the different means of attainment (Bureau, 1976) we will here, only summarize our position. Greenson (1965) states that sexual identity is acquired in three stages and is experienced in three categories of content: 1) "I am myself, John;" 2) "I am myself, John, a male;" 3) "I am myself, John, a male who desires females." Montgrain et al. (1974) would rewrite this classification as follows: 1) "I am myself, different from my mother;" 2) "I am myself, John, a male;" 3) "I am myself, John, a male with my masculine sexual attribute, a penis, the characteristic which differentiates the sexes." Such explanations, in our opinion, rely too much on the primacy of eroticism or of genitality concept over sexuality. We are inclined to believe that the stages of acquisition and the categories of sexual identity content are much more subtle and organized in sexuality in general than confined merely to eroticism and the genital concept.

Following the inevitable separation from the maternal body which leads, on the one hand, to the concept, "I am myself" resulting from "I am my own stomach, my own hunger, my own body" (Allport, 1967), and on the other hand, to the identity of the species, "I am a human being, different from cats, birds, etc." we find entwined within these aspects the first category of content and the first phase of sexual identity, "I am sexed and sexual" as in a sexual monad, minus sexual distinction and differentiation (Figure 2).

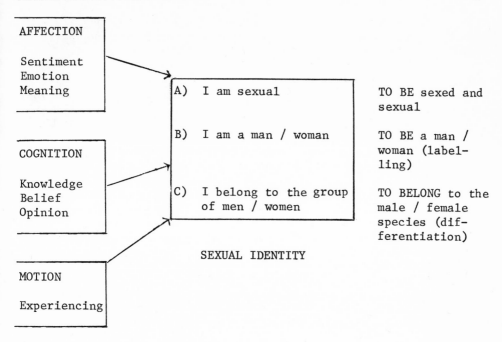

Fig. 2. The means of attaining sexual identity and the categories of sexual identity content.

THE REQUEST FOR SEXUAL CONVERSION: THE PRIVILEGE SCENE FOR THE STUDY OF SEXUAL IDENTITY

Since 1973, more than ninety requests for sexual conversion have been evaluated at the Université du Québec à Montréal (UQAM). The incidences and ratio of male/female requests for sexual conversion are illustrated in Table 1. Without going into detailed reports about this incidence (Bureau et al., 1975) we must note the following: our own male/female ratio is close to 1:1 which, with reference to Pauly's most recent statistics (1975) differs from the figures set down in the literature; this can probably be explained by the type of work we are engaged in. As we are not part of a surgical or hormonal - dispensing center and since we are interested in consultative dimensions, we have been able to recruit candidates who would not have presented themselves at hospital centers. Because such subjects are uncertain of their decision to resort to sexual conversion and are more in need of help in their search for identity, they feel more at ease when they present themselves for consultation than they would if hormonal or surgical intervention were offered. Thus, our case incidence is

TABLE 1

INCIDENCE AND MALE/FEMALE RATIO
IN REQUEST FOR SEXUAL CONVERSION

Source	Male	Female	Ratio M/F
1) Pauly (1975)	1148	286	4.0:1[1]
2) Quebec hospitals[2]	25	8	3.1:1
3) U.Q.A.M.	55	35	1.5:1

[1]In the literature, true problems of transsexuality are not always identified in requests for sexual conversion. Some authors only report true cases; others report all requests for sexual correction.

[2]Following an investigation conducted by U.Q.A.M. in 1975, it is possible that some non-identified candidates were also included in the U.Q.A.M. sampling.

near equal in the number of male/female candidates, a condition which has allowed us to come into contact with both masculine and feminine sexual identity conflicts. As a consequence, we are less impressed by the masculine aspect of such conflicts, thanks to the illuminating contribution of our female subjects, which has prevented us from falling into the prejudicial trap of considering the almighty role of the penis in the process of sexual identity confusion.

Accidents in the Sexual Identification Process
at Various Biopsychosociographic Stages of
our Candidates for Sexual Conversion

Sexual identity conflict may be approached through its origin and considered as an accident occurring in the course of one of its stages in the aforementioned process. Such a perspective allows us if we do limit ourselves to his view, to observe the idiosyncrasy of human sexual identity and its conflicts. Figure 3 (adapted from Money and Ehrhardt, 1972 by Bureau et al., 1975) clearly illustrates the individualization of possible accidents during the various stages of the process in twenty-five candidates for sexual conversion. Such accidents may occur in various sites, physiologic, intrapsychic and interpersonal. For instance, sexual differentiation in the

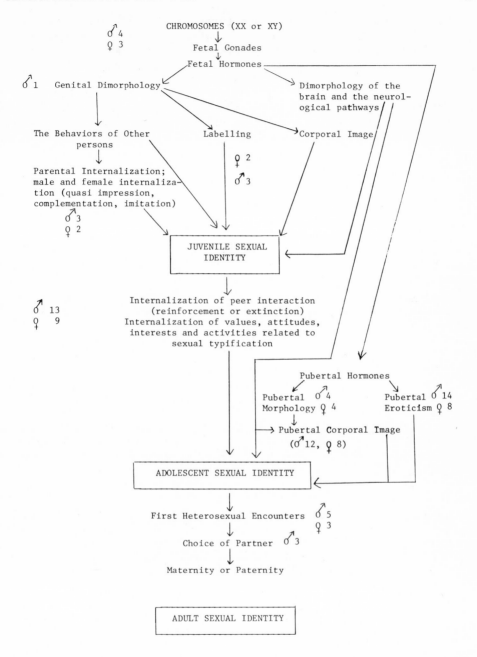

Fig. 3. Accidents occurring in sexual identification process in 25 cases of transsexual subjects evaluated at U.Q.A.M. (16 male to female transsexuals, 9 female to male transsexuals). Adapted from the sexual identification figure, of Money and Ehrhardt, 1972.

embryonic period of four male and three female candidates was affected by hormones absorbed by the gestating mother in order to
avoid spontaneous termination of pregnancy, or by genital infan-
tilism in the mother. Two female and three male subjects were
victims of parental ambivalence as regards sexual labelling (a
given name of one sex and a nick name of another) all of which
illustrate the necessary interaction between the somatic and the
psychic and between the inter and intrapersonal aspects. It is
difficult to consider only certain factors as crucial (e.g., the
physical contact between mother and child during its first two
years), putting aside the numerous variables and factors paving
the way toward mishaps and accidents which may become the elements
of sexual identity. Nor should the understanding and explanation
of this phenomenon be limited to a single school of thought, however illustrious it may appear.

Another consideration parallels the idiosyncrasy of sexual
identification and of the accidents which may occur during its
development; it is the extremely lengthy presence of this sexual
identification in the individual's life. It is more of a process
than a particular genetic trait and is initiated when the ovum
first comes into contact with the spermatozoon. Its "content"
ends with paternity or maternity. During his entire existence,
the individual will identify himself during this inexorable unfolding of self-knowledge.

Apart from its evolution sites (Figure 3), the conflict may
be observed on a certain point of the continuum, from the well
established intrapsychic into erotic behavior itself. The con-
centric zones illustrated in Figure 4 represent the various levels
between sexual identity and erotic behavior, alternating with the
different sites of conflict or dissatisfaction. Certain sexual
conversion candidates have truly set up a sexual identity which
is in contradiction with their biological sex and the conflict
will disappear when their body finds an equation to their identity; others will develop an identity corresponding to their
biological sex but are always dissatisfied with this identity,
such as a woman who is not satisfied with being a woman. As we
draw away from the first zones, the conflict, in a way, becomes
more superficial. At this point in our knowledge, it is not possible to alter a fixed, irreversible sexual identity; however, it
is possible to find a solution to such a conflict by means of
psychotherapeutic methods, should the conflict appear in other
zones, even though the candidate would insist at first on a
solution involving physical transformation.

Many subjects seek a "new identity" through sexual conversion,
and some again continue to live the discomfort of an erotic interest
at war with their sexual identity, whereas others, who are dissatisfied with their general sexual role, will attempt reconciliation

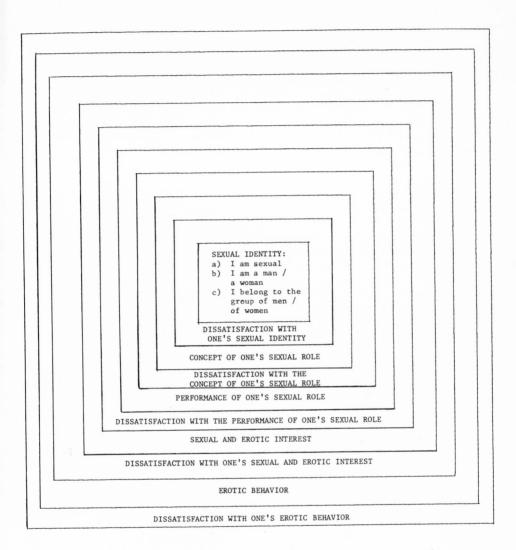

Fig. 4. The various levels in the sexual identity continuum, sexual role and erotic behavior and the various sites of conflict in candidates for sexual conversion.

by means of physical transformation. Figure 4 illustrates with
more subtlety a certain typology of sexual conversion candidate
in a context where erotism is non-permeating, but well in place.

The "Defects" in the Attainment
Of Sexual Identity or in its Content

In an attempt to understand the explanation of this individualization of the origin and the phenomenon of experience in sexual
identity conflict, it is necessary to penetrate the field of implication leading to this identity. In Table 2 we refer to the
enumeration of the accidents affecting sexual conversion candidates
in attaining their sexual identity, i.e., the difficulty in the
cognition of one's sexed and sexual personality, its acceptance,
feeling, experience, the agreement between the sexual role and
sexual identity, and finally, the different categories of content
surrounding this most complex identity. We shall not analyze
Table 2 which has already been reviewed elsewhere (Bureau 1976[c]),
but we will point out as an example that the refusal to recognize
one's own sexual self through fear of overwhelming rejection would
result in the subject living out conflict in the sexual role and
the acceptance by others of this role. The request for sexual
conversion will stem more from a desire to be accepted by peers
rather than finding the equation between one's sexed and sexual
body and sexual identity, e.g., an individual living with an
identity unrelated to a given sex and seeking to adapt the body
to this unrelated state (i.e., the desire to have breasts and yet
retain his penis). Each request for sexual conversion may thus
be explained by a given difficulty (Bureau, 1976[c]).

The preceding paragraphs have served to illustrate the density
and fullness of sexual identity and the idiosyncrasy peculiar to
this conflict as well as the scope of its definition which overreaches
simple eroticism. The presence of a sexual identity conflict is not
confined to persons seeking sexual conversion - it may be found in
all human beings. To illustrate this theory, we will now treat the
impact of sexual identity in erotic dysfunctions.

THE SEXUAL IDENTITY OF PERSONS
SUFFERING FROM EROTIC DYSFUNCTIONS

Among the variables studied for their relation to eroticism
such as social status (Kinsey, 1948, 1953), personality traits
(Cooper, 1968), types of interpersonal relationships (Kirkendall,
1966), sexual identity is too easily neglected, but this too is a
variable, because there are various types of sexual identity and
different ways of experiencing this identity, all of which may have
a differential impact on erotic behavior. This is known as the

TABLE 2

LIST OF ACCIDENTS IN THE PHENOMENON OF EXPERIENCING SEXUAL IDENTITY IN CANDIDATES FOR SEXUAL CONVERSION

1- Defects and difficulties in acquisition of self-knowledge as a sexed, sexual and erotic being:
   A) biased self-knowledge,
   B) limited self-knowledge,
   C) absence (or altered) self-knowledge,
   D) refusal of self-knowledge,
   E) paralogic thoughts: equation between a part and the whole.

2- Defects and difficulties in self acceptance as a sexed, sexual and erotic being:
   A) rejection of one's true self,
   B) indifference toward one's true self,
   C) partial acceptance of oneself,
   D) denial of an important part of oneself,
   E) fear and refusal of one's homosexuality.

3- Defects and difficulties in feeling as a sexed, sexual and erotic being:
   A) sentiment of dissociation with either sex,
   B) masculine or feminine ambivalence,
   C) refutation of association with a given sex,
   D) fear of awakening to life,
   E) fear of surpassing oneself.

4- Defects and difficulties in self-experiencing as a sexed, sexual and erotic being:
   A) self rigidness,
   B) denial of self mobility,
   C) rigidity in self-expression,
   D) refusal to accomplish oneself in personal identity,
   E) fear of making decisions.

5- Defects and difficulties in one's sexual and erotic role:
   A) expression contrary to one's sexual identity,
   B) hesitation and anxiety in the expression of one's sexual identity,
   C) rigidity in one's sexual and erotic role,
   D) stereotyped dependence in the exercise of one's sexual and erotic role.

6- Defects and difficulties in the various categories of sexual identity:
   A) experiencing one's identity as a sexual monad,
   B) experiencing one's identity as a search to belong to a sex,
   C) experiencing one's identity as belonging to either one of the sexes,
   D) experiencing one's identity merely as an affective interiorization,
   E) experiencing one's identity merely as a rational interiorization.

intrapersonal mode in the sexual life of an individual who experiences such a dysfunction.

Erotic dysfunction is experienced in one's body, the non-
ejaculating penis or the contracting vulva, and this living dysfunction cannot be seen merely as confined to the epidermal layers
or to hormonal balance, nor as an instrument inherent to man or
the object of his intervention; a sexed, sexual and erotic body
is endowed with an animal, vegetative, hormonal apparatus, the
domain which "belongs immediately to human existence" (Boss, 1954;
33). An erotic body is a route through which the interiority of
man, the identified individual, reaches out toward the exterior
world. The hand, the penis, the vulva, the breast, may accomplish
their mission because they represent the whole human being. To
be there presumes an identity, male or female, and all the degrees
and variables of this sexual identity will influence the functioning of a sexual and erotic body.

In our research on the psychosocial characteristics of the
clients of a sexological clinic, involving the types of intervention used (deconditioning, Wolpe, 1961; love-making communication, Masters and Johnson, 1970; rationalization of emotions,
Ellis, 1968; client centered approach, Rogers, 1966) and on their
effectiveness of one hundred and forty-eight cases of erotic maladjustment, eighty-seven were of female origin and sixty-one of
masculine origin (Table 3). Our findings are detailed and analyzed
elsewhere (Bureau, 1976c) but we would like to highlight a particular category which is not frequently mentioned in the literature,
i.e., insufficient sexual interest.

If we would uncover the deficiencies or defects in sexual
identity underlying such erotic manifestations, we must first
explain that several of these dysfunctions may stem from peripheral
factors (lack of sex information, physiological traumatism) or else
from interpersonal factors (refusal of regular erotic exercise on
the part of one's sexual partner). Even if the sexual intrapersonal factor may always at least refer indirectly to the erotic
dysfunction, sexual identity should not be considered the "be-all
and end-all" of erotic functioning.

DEFECTS IN SEXUAL IDENTITY IN EROTIC MALADJUSTMENT

In several cases of erotic dysfunction among male and female
subjects however, many sexual identity defects have been detected
and a certain number of these are listed in Table 4. This explanation of dysfunction due to identity insufficiency is not a simple
mental exercise but a means of setting up a more appropriate form
of individual treatment suited to the identity of the afflicted
subject.

TABLE 3

THE DISTRIBUTION OF MASCULINE AND
FEMININE EROTIC MALADJUSTMENTS IN OUR SAMPLING

Erotic difficulties	Number of cases	Relative fre-quency (%)
In women		
Secondary anorgasm	44	50.0
Insufficient sexual interest	21	23.9
Primary anorgasm	13	14.8
Non consummation	3	3.4
Erotic ambivalence	2	2.3
The integration of communicative and procreative sexuality	2	2.3
Vaginismus	1	1.1
Greater sexual needs	1	1.1
TOTAL	87	100.0
In men		
Secondary impotence	17	27.9
Insufficient sexual interest	17	27.9
Premature ejaculation	11	18.0
Erotic ambivalence	6	9.8
Retarded ejaculation	3	4.9
Integration of communicative and procreative sexuality	2	3.3
Primary impotence	2	3.3
Exhibitionism	1	1.6
Greater sexual needs	1	1.6
Transvestism	1	1.6
TOTAL	61	100.0

TABLE 4

SOME DEFECTS IN SEXUAL IDENTITY
PERTAINING TO PARTICULAR EROTIC MALADJUSTMENTS

Erotic difficulties	Defects in sexual identity
In women	
Secondary anorgasm (50%)	- refusal or difficulty experiencing dimorphism in erotic behavior - absence or difficulty in acknowledging and accepting one's receptivity - rigid sexual passivity related to one's concept of the female erotic role
Insufficient sexual interest (23.9%)	- decorporalization of one's sexuality - refusal or difficulty mastering one's sexuality - over expectation of male performance in awakening one's eroticism - peripheralism of corporality
Primary anorgasm (14.8%)	- difficulty in accepting or refusing to be a woman - spiritual and incorporal female experience - fusion of sexual concept with total subjection through loss of control
Non consummation (3.4%) and Vaginismus (1.1%)	- fear of annihilation through male invasion - lack of sexual assurance and fear of personal loss through coitus with male partner - refusal to accept inevitable pain leading to pleasurable experience
In Men	
Secondary impotence (27.9%)	- selectivity in the concept of women (the "right" woman ; the "dirty" woman) - extinction of erotic interiority due to the extinction of one's interior limits of reference
Insufficient sexual interest (27.9%)	- overdependence on an external point of reference in one's sexual interest - lack of erotic interest in women - refusal to resort to erotic activity once interest is aroused
Premature ejaculation (18%)	- experiencing male behavior as a function of woman's requirements - loss of contact with personal sexuality due to overanxiety about female responsivity - interior erotic emptiness - complete dependence on female responsivity for pleasurable experience
Delayed ejaculation (4.9%)	- fear of annihilation through loss of control - refusal to complete pleasurable experience - fear of partner's refusal to acknowledge ejaculation and pleasure
Primary impotence (3.3%)	- refusal to assume positive and agressive masculinity - refusal to accept, or lack of contact with one's sexual and genital corporality

In women suffering from secondary anorgasm, especially of the coital type (which constitutes fifty percent of our cases), we may observe a difficulty or a refusal to experience sexual dimorphism in erotic behavior as if there were not two forms of behavior to be experienced. Other subjects experience difficulties resulting from a lack of contact with the forms of acknowledgment and acceptance of their physical femininity. Finally, the rigid sexual passivity associated with one's concept of the female erotic role incites some women to consider the vagina as an inert instrument to be used as a corridor rather than a means of global, living experience.

Secondary impotence in men (twenty-seven percent) includes such defects as selectivity in their concept of "good" and "bad" women, wherein the latter alone may be erotic or else, be capable of becoming so. The "good" woman, his loved partner, thus becomes a disembodied, anonymous, sexless symbol. Other men exhibit a certain limitation of their erotic interior, following the extinction of their interior source of reference, because their partners have become their source of reference. Living experience is therefore peripheral to and dependent upon the reactions of another person. Some men lose their claim to erotic existence due to a loss of their zest for life. They feel they have no right to living, and this attitude affects their erotic existence, their right to pleasure and physical enjoyment.

CONCLUSION

We have try in this paper to show some of the relations between sexual identity, eroticism and human experience. Human sexual identity is not just a set of biological, psychological and cultural contents. It is the experential process in which biological, psychological and cultural contents are carried forward and given a meaning. Man may loose the simple unity between his eroticism and his humanity if he does not find and live the integrating dimension of his sexual identity.

REFERENCES

Allport, G.W. (1967). Pattern and Growth in Personality, Holt, Rinehart & Winston, New York.

Boss, M. (1954). Introduction à la Médecine Psychosomatique, Presses Universitaires de France, Paris.

Bugental, J.F.T. (1964). Investigations into the self-concept: III. Instructions for the W - A - Y experiment. Psychological Reports, 13: 643-650.

Bureau, J., Trempe, J.P., and Jodoin, L. (1975). Transexualité:
Catégorie Diagnostique ou Expérience d'un Individu, Miméo,
Department of Sexology, U.Q.A.M., Montréal.

Bureau, J. (1976a). L'ontogénèse sexuelle, tout l'humain y par-
ticipe. Etudes de sexologie: Théorie et Recherches.

Bureau, J. (1976b). Conflits d'idendité sexuelle chez l'enfant
et l'adulte. Colloque International sur Psychologie et
Sexualité, Privat, Toulouse.

Bureau, J. (1976c). La congruence entre l'identité sexuelle et
le rôle sexuel. Cahiers de Sexologie Clinique, Les Nou-
velles Editions Médicales, Paris (in press).

Bureau, J. (1976d). Identité sexuelle et transexualité: essai de
typologie des demandes de conversion sexuelle. Unpublished
Ph.D. dissertation, Department of Psychology, Université de
Montréal.

Bureau, J. (1976e). Les caractéristiques psycho-sociales de la
clientèle d'une clinique de sexologie. In Press.

Bureau, J. (1977). Mésadaptations Erotiques et Failles de l'Identité Sexuelle, In Press.

Cooper, A.J. (1968). A Factual Study of Male Potency Disorders.
Brit. Journal of Psychiat., 114: 719-731.

Ellis, A. (1960). The Art and Science of Love, Lyle-Stuart, New
York.

Freud, S. (1905). Trois Essais sur la Théorie de la Sexualité,
Standard Edition, 7: 135-243.

Fromm, E. (1945). Escape From Freedom. Norton, New York.

Greenson, R.R. (1965). Homosexualité et identité sexuelle, Revue
Française de Psychanalyse, 39: 343-348.

Jourard, S. (1974). La Transparence de Soi, St-Yves, Québec.

Kagan, J. (1969). Acquisition and Significance of Sex Typing and
Sex Role, in Hoffman, M.L. (ed.), Child Development Research,
Russel Sage Foundation, New York.

Kando, T. (1973). Sex Change, C.C. Thomas, Springfield.

Kinsey, A.C., Pomeroy, W.C. and Martin, C.E. (1948). Sexual Behavior in the Human Male, Saunders, Philadelphia.

Kinsey, A.C., Pomeroy, W.C., Martin, C.E. and Gebhard, P.H. (1953). Sexual Beahvior in the Human Female, Saunders, Philadelphia.

Kirkendall, L. (1966). Interpersonal Relationship and Sexual Relation. C.C. Thomas, Boston.

Kohlberg, L. (1966). A Cognitive-development Analysis of Children: Sex-role concepts and attitudes, In Macoby, E. (ed.), The Development of Sex Differences, Stanford University Press, Stanford.

L'Ecuyer, R. (1975). La Génèse du Concept de Soi: Théorie et Recherches, Editions Naaman, Sherbrooke.

Masters, W.H., Johnson, V. (1970). Les Mésententes Sexuelles, Laffont, Paris.

Money, J., Ehrhardt, A. (1972). Boy and Girl, Man and Woman, John Hopkins Press, Baltimore.

Montgrain, N.H., Bury, J.A., Bernachez, J.P. and Painchaud, G. (1974). Le Transexualisme: réflexions psychanalytiques. La Vie Médicale au Canada-Français, 3: 1160-1170.

Pauly, I. (1974). Female Transexualism. Archives of Sexual Behavior, 3: 487-526.

Piaget, J. (1956). La Psychologie de l'Intelligence, Armand Colin, Paris.

Rainwater, L. (1960). And the Poor Get Children, Wiley, New York.

Rogers, C. and Kinget, M. (1966). Psychothérapie et Relations Humaines, Institut de Recherches Psychologiques, Montréal.

Stoller, R.J. (1968). Sex and Gender, Science House, New York.

Wolpe, C. (1961). The systematic densensitization treatment of neurose. Journ. of New Mental Disease, 132: 189-203.

Genetic makeup (XY) did not affect
subsequent sexual development + orientation
—all female (1 homo)

ANDROGEN INSENSITIVITY SYNDROME: EROTIC COMPONENT OF GENDER

IDENTITY IN NINE WOMEN

Viola G. Lewis

United States

The androgen insensitivity syndrome is genetically transmitted
as an X-linked recessive trait, or male-limited dominant trait; the
karyotype is 46,XY. The primary pathognomonic feature of the syndrome is that the tissues of the body are insensitive to androgen.
This insensitivity may be attributed to a reduced affinity of the
cellular nuclear receptors for androgen. The plasma level of testosterone is normal for males as is the level of estrogen. The
external genitalia of a baby born with the complete form of this
syndrome are entirely feminine in appearance. The internal genitalia are defective. The shortened vagina ends blindly and does
not communicate with a cervix, a defect generally not discovered
until later in the patient's life. In congruence with the external genital appearance, affected babies are assigned and reared
female. Puberty is feminizing, as the effects of estrogen are
virtually unopposed. Breast development and contours are feminine.
Without a uterus, there is no menstruation.

I have studied longitudinal data on the psychosexual status
of nine androgen-insensitive women, now aged 17 to 38 years. Their
sex of rearing was concordant with external morphology and discordant with chromosomal and hormonal status. One might expect the
genetic and/or gonadal status to produce a masculinizing effect on
psychosexual differentiation, but the findings were otherwise.
Gender identity differentiated congruently with the cultural/social
training of an individual reared as female. In this context, I
have examined particularly the occurrence of erotic heterosexuality,
bisexuality and homosexuality in the gender identities of the nine
patients.

The findings strongly support the propositions that: 1) the chromosomal status had no masculinizing effect on psychosexual status; 2) the increased postpubertal level of androgen had no masculinizing effect on either bodily or psychosexual status; 3) the female level of estrogen produced by the testes or taken post-surgically as substitution therapy may have had a feminizing effect on psychosexual status as it did on the body; and 4) each patient's sex of assignment and rearing as female contributed to the differentiation of a feminine psychosexuality and eroticism in adult gender identity.

Seven of the nine women were exclusively heterosexual in practice and preference. None of these seven reported imagery of, or an interest in homosexual relations. The other two patients were primarily heterosexual, but reported a trivial history of homosexual relations. In one case the homosexual encounter involved only a brief period of pubertal kissing and fondling with one partner. In the second case, there were two late adolescent incidents of homosexual kissing and fondling and a third experience of bisexual troilism. This patient had a severe episode of psychiatric breakdown. In therapy, it appeared that self-doubt as to her sexual identity was secondary to the refusal of others to discuss with her, the facts of her diagnosis which she had secretly discovered. In the course of psychotherapy, she came to believe that she would not have any further homosexual encounters.

Statistically these findings are within the limits that one might encounter in any group of nine female patients. They correspond with the findings of a matched group of nine women (chromosomally and gonadally female) with Rokitansky's syndrome of atresia of the vagina. The similarity of the two groups permits the conclusion that sex chromosomal status per se does not directly influence the erotic component of gender identity.

PAIR-BONDING EXPERIENCE OF 26 EARLY TREATED ADRENOGENITAL FEMALES

AGED 17-27

Mark F. Schwartz

United States

The adrenogenital syndrome is a genetically transmitted defect which expresses itself as a hormonal malfunction of the adrenal cortices, from fetal life onward. The adrenal cortices fail to synthesize cortisol and instead release into the bloodstream a precursor hormone that is androgenic. Females with the syndrome are born hermaphroditic.

The patients of this report constitute the first generation of young adults treated from infancy onward with cortisone, which in 1950 was discovered to be the effective therapeutic agent. Complete treatment includes also surgical correction of the genitalia as needed.

The purpose of this report is to document impairment of pair-bonding as manifested in dating (social and erotic) in teenage and young adulthood. Social dating refers to accompanying a male to any social event like a football game, movie or party. Table 1 shows that by age 17 only three of the 26 patients had had her first date. Of the 26 patients who were at least between the ages of 17 and 20 at the time of the study, only 11 had a first date. Four of the 14 patients older than 20 had not yet dated. Table 2, in which the criterion is more than three dates with the same person, parallels the finding of Table 1.

The delay in dating and romantic pair-bonding was not related to unattractiveness of appearance. In fact, as a group, these young women were more than usually attractive in physique and appearance in terms of today's cosmetic standards.

TABLE 1

ADRENOGENITAL FEMALES:
AGE AT FIRST DATE

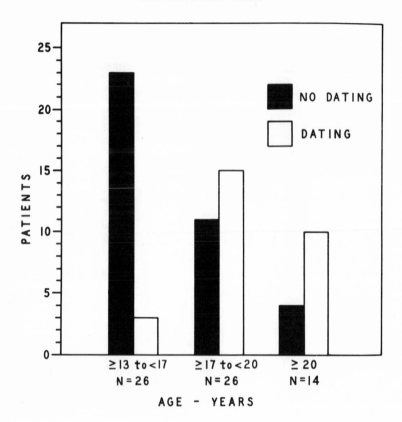

     The delay in establishing a romantic and erotic pair-bond
might be related to a more general disability in interacting with
peers. Eight of the group judged themselves as social outcasts
in high school and 17 claimed that they had difficulty making
friends.

     Also related to difficulty in establishing a pair-bond might
be reluctance or inhibition in expressing bisexuality or homosexuality. Pilot data indicate that incidence of bisexuality either
in imagery or experience is higher for adrenogenital women than
would be expected by chance.

TABLE 2

ADRENOGENITAL FEMALES WHO DATED
ONE PARTNER MORE THAN THREE TIMES

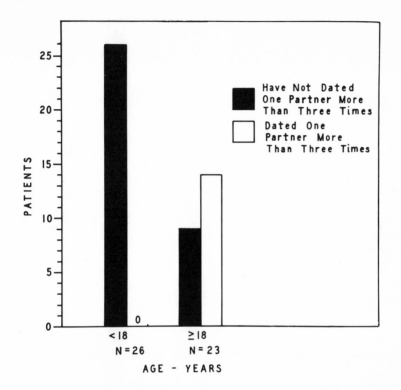

It is not yet possible to formulate a definitive explanation
for these results. They probably are not a secondary effect of
having a chronic condition requiring pharmacologic treatment, for
in other syndromes requiring long-term therapy the same effects
do not necessarily appear. They could be an unknown side effect
of long-term cortisone therapy. The most likely hypothesis, however, is that they represent a delayed action effect of prenatal
androgenization (defeminization) of as yet unknown pathways in the
limbic system of the brain.

EROTIC IMAGERY AND MALE/FEMALE DISCORDANCE IN HERMAPHRODITIC SIBLINGS

Florence C. Clarke

United States

This report is about erotic imagery relative to gender identity in two sisters who were diagnosed as virilizing male hermaphrodites. Both had 46, XY chromosomes and testes (lacking spermatogenesis). In accordance with the Eve principle, namely that in the absence of androgenization the external genitals differentiate as female, these girls appeared phenotypically female at birth. The unusual feature of these patients is that they masculinized hormonally at puberty, even though they appeared likely candidates for a diagnosis of the androgen insensitivity syndrome, in which puberty is feminizing.

The anomaly of the older sister was first observed by the mother when the child was about two. At that time she noted the patient had clitoral enlargement. The girl had three hospital admissions which included a laparotomy at 8 years of age. The surgery revealed absence of an uterus and fallopian tubes. At the age of 14, she was referred to The Johns Hopkins Hospital for another opinion, after a conflict in case management, in which a surgeon imposed an edict to reassign her sex as a boy. With coordination of endocrine, surgical and psychological opinions, which is the routine approach at Johns Hopkins for the treatment of hermaphroditic patients, it was determined unequivocally she continue living as a female. At that time she underwent gonadectomy and surgical feminization of the external genitalia and was put on estrogenic hormonal replacement therapy (1.25 mg Premarin twice a day). Vaginoplasty was performed two years later.

In taped interviews, the patient willingly described her erotic imagery. She denied any arousal from looking at sexually explicit

pictures. However, she was aroused by erotic stories and books.
Before feminization from surgery and hormonal replacement she
stated that these books aroused her and she masturbated. After
feminization, the stories no longer induced the desire to masturbate.

The younger sibling was not suspected of being a male herma-
phrodite until she was 13. At this time the mother noted hair on
her upper lip. There was minimal clitoral enlargement. The patient came to The Johns Hopkins Hospital and had the same feminizing surgery and hormonal therapy as her sister. The special gender
significance of her report on her sexual arousal, was that during
the period she was masculinized she taped a report of a positive
erotic feeling from looking at pictures of cute boys in the clothing
section of the Sears-Roebuck catalogue. Two years after feminizing
she did not recall this statement, and stated she was aroused only
by thinking about dating and marriage.

Neither patient ever verbalized to us or to the mother any
doubt as to their female gender identity. Both expressed their
positive reaction to breast development and feminizing. In a follow-up telephone conversation (August, 1976) the younger sister
stated her satisfaction with her gender role. The older girl was
likewise contented with her role.

The girls enjoyed when growing up what would be considered
tomboy activities such as riding horseback, fishing and hiking.
This tendency was more pronounced in the case of the older sister.
She never enjoyed dolls or playing house, whereas the younger one
was more inclined to home-making play.

The significance of these two cases is that both girls had
what may be interpreted as a masculine threshold for arousal in
response to visual-narrative erotic material, whereas the content
of their erotic imagery was feminine.

POSTPUBERTAL PSYCHOSEXUAL FUNCTION IN MALES WITH HYPOPITUITARISM

Richard R. Clopper

United States

Hypopituitarism signifies deficient release into the blood stream of one or more of the pituitary hormones. Individuals with this endocrine anomaly are of particular interest to sexology because they provide an opportunity to study the effect of pituitary mediated sex hormone deficiency on psychosexual behavior. The purpose of this paper is to summarize recent findings on the postpubertal psychosexual function of male hypopituitary patients (Money and Clopper, 1975; Clopper, Adelson and Money, 1976; Clopper et al., 1976).

Nine patients were selected according to the criterion that their missing hormones did not include pituitary gonadotropins. Therefore, they were able to maintain their own puberty in adolescence and did not require sex hormone therapy. They did, however, require growth hormone therapy as a result of which they achieved a minimum adult height of 5 feet (152cm). The age at last follow-up ranged from $17\frac{1}{2}$ to 25 years.

Self report data from structured interviews with the patients and available relatives yielded data on psychosocial and psychosexual behavior.

All nine patients experienced some degree of social isolation from peers and other age groups. Data on friendships and group memberships indicated that socializing was primarily by way of membership in a club or work group and required little or no personal initiative. Only one patient reported any self-initiated social contacts which he described as "a test" to see if he could pick up a woman in a single's bar.

Current dating frequencies for the group were low. One patient had not begun to date and four others were not dating at last follow-up even though they had had some prior dating experience. Two others were dating sporadically. Only one patient was dating once per week or more. One other had quit dating because he was married.

The criteria of erotic function were frequency of masturbation or sexual participation with a partner, the frequency of episodes of erotic imagery or fantasy and the history of reported active erotic interest. By these criteria there were only three patients who barely qualified as not being hypoerotic. The other six were given ratings of hypoerotic. They had a history of being able to get erections and ejaculations but very infrequently did so.

The findings on this group of nine patients are paralleled by the findings on another group of male patients with a history of hypopituitarism since puberty secondary to surgery for removal of a benign pituitary tumor. All were maintained at a normal level of sex hormone functioning. Nonetheless, they manifested the same hypoeroticism as the idiopathic group.

The pooled evidence of both groups indicates that hypoeroticism could not be attributed to a postpubertal deficiency of sex hormone per se, nor to a simple deficiency of gonadotropins. It is possible that hypoeroticism is mediated through an as yet unknown neurohormonal mechanism in the hypothalamus. It is also possible that the pathways which mediate sexual imagery and behavior in the hypothalamus are independent of the pathways that regulate sex hormonal function via the pituitary and that the former are impaired independently of the latter in hypopituitarism of both the idiopathic and postsurgical type. Secondary to this inferred deficit there may be overlay from the social environment, for all short statured people are infantalized by others due to underestimations of chronologic age and ability based on physique alone. Comparison with other short stature groups, however, suggests that the discrepancy between statural age and chronologic age with social age somewhere in between may not be sufficient to account for the hypoeroticism seen in hypopituitary patients.

REFERENCES

Clopper, R.R., Adelson, J.M., and Money, J. (1976). Postpubertal psychosexual function in male hypopituitarism without hypogonadotropinism after growth hormone therapy. J. of Sex Res., 12: 14-32.

Clopper, R.R., Meyer, W.J., Udvarhelyi, G.B., Money, J., Mulvihill,
    J.J., and Piasio, M. (1976). Postsurgical IQ and behavioral
    data on twenty patients with a history of childhood cranio-
    pharyngioma. Psychoneuroendocrinology, in Press.

Money, J., and Clopper, R.R. (1975). Postpubertal psychosexual
    function in post-surgical male hypopituitarism. J. of Sex
    Res., 11: 25-38.

THE TRANSVESTITE/TRANSSEXUAL: GENDER-IDENTITY CONTINUUM AND TRANSPOSITION

Eileen Higham

United States

Patients with an error in gender-identity differentiation occasionally present vexing problems of diagnosis and case management. The transvestite/transsexual patient illustrates this problem. Neither transvestite nor transsexual, the patient shares characteristics of each diagnosis, with the process of change from transvestism to transsexualism a prominent feature of the condition.

The idealized male transsexual presents a history of gender incongruity dating from a very early age. With hormonal puberty, virilization of the body is despised, especially the genitals and the erotic sensations they produce. The condition, once established, is experienced as a continuous and persistent urge to live and be accepted as a female in public and private life.

The idealized transvestite also reports a history of gender transposition from an early age, manifested mainly in cross-dressing, partially or completely, in female clothing. With hormonal puberty, virilization of the body is accepted, along with the erotic sensations obtained from the genitals during masturbation with the imagery or the percept of the self in female clothing. The choice of partner for sexual pair-bonding is female, as in heterosexualism, except for the inclusion of female clothing as a fetish for erotic response and orgasm. Unlike transsexualism, the gender transposition is episodic, alternating male and female gender roles. The dissociation of gender identity/role is not limited to the private, erotic life, but includes also dissociation of the male and female personality, with two personalities, two wardrobes and even two names, respectively.

DISSOCIATION

In a sample of six consecutive cases of transvestite/transsexual patients collected in the past four years, the dissociation of masculine and feminine gender identity/role emerged gradually between childhood and young adulthood. Reports of being dressed in girl's clothing, for punishment, or to portray the female child the mother wanted, were given by four of six patients. In one of these patients, a feminine personality, complete with name, began at age 7, subsequent to the initiation of "petticoat punishment." All, however, required themselves to try adapting to the role of husband and father, and all of them undertook highly skilled, "macho" work, for which they were well-equipped intellectually, and at which they were unusually successful.

While retrospective accounts yield too little to trace the etiology of dissociative development in one's own biography, contemporaneous accounts are clear and unequivocal. Neither personality is whole; both are stereotypic and rigid, frequently a travesty of femininity and masculinity, respectively. In one patient, a whimpering, frightened, lonely girl is paired with an exaggerated male bragadoccio, cruel and pitiless. In another, a flirtatious, vibrant woman is paired with an angry, hot-tempered, heavy drinker; in still another, a genteel society matron is coupled with a sailor's vocabulary and biceps. In all of the patients, feminine clothing released a sense of calm, contentment and satisfaction, somewhat akin to the post-ejaculatory phase of copulation.

METAMORPHOSIS

The threshold for the emergence of femininity as a fixed, persistent gender identity/role is altered by a critical event in adulthood; alternating periods of masculinity became increasingly difficult to sustain, especially as the passage of years produced the feeling that time was running out.

Economic and career pressures, disruption of the family group through illness or death, a wife's increasing dissatisfaction with a transvestitic partner, and growing abhorrence of the psychosocial and psychosexual aspects of the masculine personality, were the critical contingencies which preceded the request for consultation. Depression, anxiety, suicidal thoughts and body-image pathology accompanied the request for sex reassignment.

To settle the various family and financial commitments which accompany middle age, and to avoid an impulsive decision for sex reassignment, the two-year, real-life test was in each case recommended prior to irreversible surgical rehabilitation.

In a transitional disorder, described in this paper, life circumstances and aging, interact to alter the threshold for the emergence of a feminine gender identity/role. In some instances, a new, whole personality differentiates after sex reassignment.

Reasonable elevation of voice pitch in ♀ transsexual — chewing exercises

VOICE THERAPY WITH A TRANSSEXUAL

Meryle A. Kalra

Canada

This paper was designed to present and evaluate a therapeutic approach to the vocal rehabilitation of a transsexual. The objective was to raise the habitual pitch of a 27 year old morphological male, who became a female.

Procedures included a therapy log of the clinician's observations, laryngological examinations during and after therapy; spectographic analysis of selected speech tasks served to provide objective data on fundamental frequency changes throughout therapy.

Review and discussion of the literature demonstrate that the male voice is about one octave lower than that of the female. The average normal range of the male voice lies between 100 and 132 hz while the habitual pitch levels in normal females reported from study samples range between 142-256 hz.

No specific data on the incidence of transsexualism have been compiled in Canada or the U.S.A. However, the Erickson Foundation of New York estimates that 2000 transsexuals in the U.S. have had sexual conversion up until 1975.

Gender alteration male to female is four times more frequent than female to male. Hoenig and Kenna (1973), found the incidence in England and Wales to be 1.51 transsexuals per 100,000 population. Approximately 1 male per 40,000 population and 1 female per 154,000 population, the male to female ratio being 3.41:1.

MATERIALS AND METHODS

The subject, B.L., was a normally developed physiological male whose sexual identity at age 32 was altered to become that of a female. B.L., the second son of eleven children, described herself as being close to her mother, and having a strict, controlling father; she remembers feeling sensitive and expressing continuously the wish and desire to become a girl. After successive experiences as a homosexual, a female impersonator and transvestite, B.L. decided at 29 years to seek sexual identity change and become a female. In 1969 hormone therapy was commenced while several months later sexual reassignment surgery was performed. At the time of her referral for voice therapy B.L. appeared feminine; however, the distinct male quality to the voice was the most likely characteristic to betray her masculinity. B.L. complained of being mistaken for a male over the telephone. At the time of her referral her vocal characteristics were judged subjectively to be: 1) male vocal quality; 2) poorly controlled pitch levels; 3) clavicular and shallow breathing patterns; 4) laryngeal tension; 5) absence of vocal resonance; 6) poorly controlled loudness which was associated with irregular pitch use.

Without professional guidance the client had obvious difficulty in adjusting the male larynx to the functioning requirements of a female larynx.

At present no precise histological data describes the effects of oestrogen on the intrinsic muscle mass of the human larynx.

THERAPEUTIC PROCEDURES

Voice Therapy was administered over a three month period, once a week for approximately 45 minutes each session. Optimum pitch at this time was in the area of D sharp well below middle C at approximately 150 hz. Treatment was directed toward controlling intercostal and diaphragmatic muscle activity to reduce clavicular breathing patterns and lessen pharyngeal tension.

Elevation of the optimum pitch to more appropriate and desirable pitch levels was achieved through exercises which reinforced resonance and maintained a balance between the vocal generator and supraglottal resonators. As new pitch levels were acquired, Foreschel's chewing method was used to increase anterior oral resonance.

The first pitch level above optimum pitch was F below middle C at approximately 170 hz. Gradually the fundamental

frequency of the voice was moved up the musical scale to G below
middle C or approximately 220 hz and the therapeutic procedures
were repeated.

DATA ANALYSIS

Analysis of data collected throughout the therapeutic process consisted of both subjective and objective measures.

RESULTS

Subjective data contained a condensed therapy log as well
as laryngological examinations during and after therapy to determine whether any structural changes had occurred to the client's
vocal mechanism as a result of therapeutic procedures.

Laryngological examination during the course of therapy
described the normal configuration of the male larynx in size and
appearance and indicated improved function of the crico-thyroid
muscle two years post-therapy. No vocal strain or pathology had
been induced by raising the client's original male pitch level to
within a low average female pitch range. Optimum pitch had been
obtained with maximum comfort for the client's laryngeal mechanism
and integrated into the client's spontaneous speech patterns.

Objective data was demonstrated using a Kay sonograph to determine the fundamental frequency through spectographic printouts
of voice samples using narrow band widths (45 hz) and wide band
widths analysis (300 hz).

Procedures for Extraction of Fundamental Frequencies

Narrow band analysis permits the investigator to select non
fluctuating periods from within the intonational patterns of the
voice. These represent an average or habitual pitch level.

In Figure 1 the dark horizontal lines represent the harmonics of the voice. If a rising or falling pitch pattern is encountered in contextual speech the horizontal lines are shifted
in a corresponding manner. Section A of this figure displays an
upward shift in the pitch of the voice. Section B illustrates a
stable, habitual pitch level. The harmonics are parallel to the
base line, and the chosen criterion for selecting sample points
on the speech tasks in this analysis.

A wide band width analysis was made to determine the fundamental frequency once a stable pitch level was isolated. An

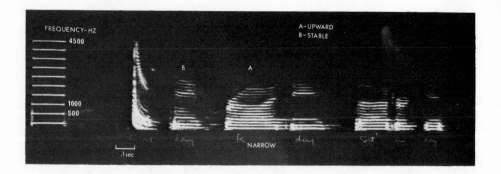

Fig. 1.   Narrow Band Analysis of Voice Print.

increase in the band width of the spectographic filters produces
a temporal compression within the frequency spectrum which consequently displays discrete vertical striations on the spectographic
printout.   Thus each opening and closing of the vocal folds is represented as a vertical striation on the wide band spectographic
analysis.

In figure 2 the vertical striations in a period of one
second equals the fundamental frequency of the voice at a given
point.   To gain a close approximation of this value without count-
ing all striations in a one second period, a one tenth second sample
was taken and the number multiplied by ten to determine the fundamental frequency of the voice.   The duration of one tenth of a second represented on the sonograph expressed a distance of 1.325 cm.
This value was determined by measuring the rotation of the spectographic drum which proved to be 2.4 seconds per rotation.   The
scale used to measure the calibration is shown in figure 1 and 2.
The mean speech sample values were calculated by averaging three
measures from each imitative and spontaneous speech task.   The
same procedure was used for establishing the fundamental frequency
on subsequent recorded samples.

On examination of the spectographic data the fundamental
frequency for all speech tasks showed a consistent increase.
Table 1 illustrates the fundamental frequency level of B.L.'s
speech on imitative and spontaneous speech tasks.

Fig. 2.   Wide Band Analysis of Voice Print.

TABLE 1

FUNDAMENTAL FREQUENCY LEVELS OF B.L.'S SPEECH
ON IMITATIVE AND SPONTANEOUS SPEECH TASKS

Habitual Fundamental Frequency Levels

| Recorded Therapy Session | Imitative Tasks | | | Spontaneous Speech | |
	Chewing	Days of week*	Months of year*		Mean
1	180	180	160	153	168
2	180	185	173	168	176
3	200	185	187	200	193
4	200	196	190	198	196
Mean	190	186	177	180	

* The patient was asked to chew and talk simultaneously while
repeating the days of the week and the months of the year.

In the first recording for both imitative and spontaneous speech tasks B.L. produced an average fundamental frequency of 168 hz. In the second recording the same measurements showed a mean increase of 8 hz, raising the fundamental frequency to 176 hz. Further upward shifts at the fundamental frequency were found in the third recording (193 hz) and the fourth recording (196 hz). On comparison of the first and fourth recording a total gain of 28 hz in the fundamental frequency was realized. This constant increasing trend was found across all speech levels measured.

Table 2 demonstrates the comparison of the fundamental frequency between the clinician and the client on imitative and spontaneous speech tasks.

TABLE 2

A COMPARISON OF FUNDAMENTAL FREQUENCY
BETWEEN THE CLINICIAN'S MODEL AND
CLIENT'S RESPONSE ON IMITATIVE
AND SPONTANEOUS SPEECH TASKS

	Clinician's Model	Imitative	Difference	B.L. Spontaneous	Difference
Average of Recording 1	150 hz	173 hz	+ 23 hz	153 hz	+ 3 hz
Average of Recording 2	193	179	− 14	168	− 25
Average of Recording 3	193	190	− 3	200	+ 7
Average of Recording 4	220	195	− 25	198	− 22

X = 184   x = 179

Reevaluation two years after the termination of regular therapy resulted in a stabilization of spontaneous speech at 200 hz. On imitative speech tasks the client slightly fell below the given model of 200 hz (Table 3).

CONCLUSION

The object of this study was a) to prescribe a therapeutic model for altering the vocal pitch of a male-to-female transsexual, thereby creating a vocal quality more appropriate for a female, and b) to assess the efficacy of this model.

Results indicate that in the initial period of therapy the subject exceeded the provided model on imitative speech tasks. At this time excessive laryngeal tension was evident and repeatedly the clinician had to reestablish correct breathing patterns and improve supraglottal resonance through chewing practice.

In the second recording, although laryngeal tension had been reduced, the client was unable to achieve a model of 193 hz introduced on imitative speech tasks. Although an increase in the habitual pitch between the first two recordings could be demonstrated, spontaneous speech deviated from the model by a minus 25 hz. Carry over into imitative tasks or transfer to spontaneous speech was not occurring.

TABLE 3

A REEVALUATION OF THE CLIENT'S VOICE
ON IDENTICAL SPEECH TASKS
TWO YEARS POST-THERAPY

Imitative Tasks			Spontaneous Speech
Chewing	Days of Week*	Months of the Year*	
190-	185	185-	200

*The patient was asked to chew and talk simultaneously while repeating the days of the week and the months of the year.

For a period of four weeks therapy concentrated on improving carry over from imitative speech work at 193 hz to spontaneous speech. Spectographic measures for spontaneous speech in the third recording showed the client had increased her habitual pitch to a level close to the stated mode. Her speech had become more functional and stabilized in every day use. Laryngeal tension was less apparent during spontaneous speech, demonstrating an overall increase in the complementary use of the vocal generator and oral resonator. Improvement in vocal resonance appeared to be directly connected to accentuated anterior oral resonance which best accommodated this higher vocal pitch.

In a later recording a relatively stable pitch level of 200 hz had been established in the subject's spontaneous speech. Further efforts to elevate this pitch level were unsuccessful. Laryngeal tension reappeared when a vocal model of 220 hz was provided and the subject was unable to reach this pitch level on either imitative or spontaneous speech tasks. Upon return to a pitch level of 200 hz vocal stabilization was achieved again. Therapy was terminated at this point since any further increase in the fundamental frequency appeared to induce both laryngeal strain and vocal discomfort.

In summarizing the findings of this case study it was found:

1. That a modified Froeschel's chewing approach to vocal therapy with a male transsexual resulted in an upward shift in the fundamental frequency of the voice.

2. That the influence of hormonal agents on the human larynx are still unassessed at present.

3. That elevation of vocal pitch occurred in the first four months of therapy. Stabilization continued for a further period of five months, despite an intervening period of three months when therapy was discontinued.

4. The therapeutic success in this case appeared to be an important and significant factor contributing greatly to the improvement of the self-image of the client who now perceives herself more completely as a woman; she is also perceived by others as a woman. This serves to enhance her self-image and reinforce her new gender identity.

REFERENCES

Hoenig, J. and Kenna, J. (1973). Epideminological aspects of transsexuals. Psychiatria Clinica, 6: 65-80.

No effect of administration of medroxy-progesterone acetate during pregnancy - on IQ of children Good controls. Differs from Katharina Dalton's findings

EFFECTS OF PRENATAL HORMONE TREATMENT ON MENTAL ABILITIES[1]

Heino F.L. Meyer-Bahlburg and Anke A. Ehrhardt

United States

The research on the influence of sex hormones on the developing brain focuses on two aspects: one is the influence on the whole brain, learning ability, and intelligence; the other is the influence on specific brain systems, especially those that relate to sex-dimorphic behavior. We are currently conducting a study on the effects of various hormones on both aspects but will limit this report to the effects of a synthetic steroid hormone, medroxy-progesterone acetate (MPA), on general mental abilities.

The highest rate of brain development in the young human extends from midgestation to about three to four years after birth (Dobbing and Sands, 1973). It is well documented that the presence of thyroid hormone in certain amounts during this sensitive phase is necessary for normal brain growth. Also other hormones have been suspected of playing a role in early brain development, particularly progestogens, i.e. naturally occurring or synthetic pregnancy hormones. Many different progestogens have been used as therapeutics in difficult pregnancies and some have been investigated as to their effects on developmental milestones and mental abilities.

The earliest and often-cited report is by Reifenstein (1958). He studied offspring from mothers who took hydroxyprogesterone caproate (delalutin) during pregnancy and found some increase of

---

[1]This work was supported by a grant from the Spencer Foundation.

birth weight above published norms which he took as evidence for
promotion of early maturation by the hormone. Unfortunately, he
did not use a control group, and those differences in his data
which can be analyzed statistically are far from significant.
Ehrhardt and Money (1967) presented data on ten girls who had
been exposed prenatally to various progestins which had caused
masculinization of the genitalia in nine of them. As a group,
these girls had unusually high IQs but it is not clear to what
extent this was a reflection of the elevated status of their
parents, since no control group had been used.

A series of progesterone studies was reported by Dalton (1968)
in England. She had available children whose mothers were treated
with high dosages of progesterone for pre-eclamptic toxemia of
pregnancy, a condition which may lead to intellectual impairment,
especially under unfavorable rearing conditions (Bailey, 1963). A
pilot study of 32 children aged 6 to 13 years showed that the offspring of these mothers received intelligence ratings of "above
average" by their head teachers slightly more frequently than the
children of a matched normal control group. Dalton then investigated the offspring of mothers with toxemic pregnancies who had
been random-assigned to the progesterone-treatment or to a non-
progesterone control condition. At age one year, the 29 progesterone-exposed children appeared somewhat more advanced in standing
and possibly in walking, but not with regard to other milestones.
Dalton also compared a sample of twenty-nine 9-10 year old progesterone-exposed children to normal controls and to untreated toxemic
controls, and teacher ratings suggested elevated school performance
significantly more frequently for the hormone-exposed subjects than
for the controls. In a very recent follow-up study of 34 progesterone-exposed children from toxemic pregnancies, Dalton (1976)
noted that a higher proportion of exposed children left school
with advanced grades and entered a university than of the normal
controls or untreated toxemic controls.

It appears that the four studies by Dalton are not independent
but involve largely overlapping samples of progesterone-exposed
children and controls. Unfortunately, the reports lack detail in
data presentation, statistical analysis, and background information so that it is difficult to judge to what degree possible
confounding variables have been controlled. Dalton's samples have
been restudied with psychological tests by Zussman et al. (1975).
These authors noted elevations in subtests of the Differential
Aptitude Test - statistically significant only for Numerical Ability - although their preliminary report does not yet allow conclusive interpretations. As in the earlier studies by Dalton, the
major problem is the control-group selection.

Our research team in Buffalo had an opportunity to study the
effects of another progestogen, medroxyprogesterone acetate (MPA),

in a sample of children from a study population which also served as a source of pair-matched controls. This study is part of a larger project on the effects of prenatal exogenous hormones on mental abilities and behavior.

METHOD

Subjects

The experimental subjects of the larger project had been drawn from the Buffalo sample of the Collaborative Perinatal Study of the National Institute of Neurological Diseases and Stroke (1972) in which approximately 50,000 white and negro children were enrolled to be followed from prenatal life to 8 years of age. The Buffalo sample is a private-practice population, comprised of approximately 2,400 predominantly white children. From this sample, subjects who were exposed to exogenous progestogens, estrogens, and/or thyroid hormone in utero were selected by computer analysis (provided by Dr. Dennis Slone in Boston). We selected all subjects with exogenous hormone exposure for more than one week during the second to 8th month after the last menstrual period. 15 girls and 13 boys had been exposed only to exogenous MPA.

Matched control subjects with documented lack of hormonal exposure were selected from the same study population by a computer program (made available by Dr. Dennis Slone) which selected 4 controls per experimental subject. Match criteria were sex, race, birth date (±6 months), and socioeconomic status (±10 points on a SES scale from 0-95, as developed by the Collaborative Perinatal Study on the basis of national census data - U.S. Bureau of the Census, 1963). Subsequently, the study records of the subjects were screened in an effort to match for vaginal bleeding in pregnancy. A number of subjects had to be excluded because of death, incomplete charts, moving out of the area, and so on. Finally, by random selection from equivalent controls, one control subject was chosen for each experimental subject.

Table 1 compares the sample characteristics of the MPA-exposed (experimental) subjects with the pair-matched controls. (All earlier data on these subjects were extracted from the research records of the Collaborative Perinatal Study.) All subjects were white. The socioeconomic status (SES) rating was based on education, occupation, and income of the parents at the time of the pregnancy and placed the subjects in the middle and higher strata of the population. Mother's IQ had been assessed by Form AH of the SRA Non-Verbal Form (1947) at the children's 4-year examination and varied approximately ± 2 standard deviations around the population mean.

TABLE 1

SAMPLE CHARACTERISTICS

Variables	Exp. Subjects	Control Subjects	N(pairs)	t_{dep}	p(2-tailed)
Race	Caucasian	Caucasian	28		
Socioeconomic Status:					
Mean	76.4	77.4	28	-1.55	>.10
Range	40-93	40-93			
Mother's IQ:					
Mean	105.0	97.8	25	1.71	>.05
Range	73-129	68-129			
Length of Gestation (weeks; days post-LMP):					
Mean	38;3	39;3	28	-1.42	>.10
Range	30;5-42;3	33;6-34;1			
Birth Weight (lbs.; oz.):					
Mean	6;12	7;0	28	-1.00	>.10
Range	3;10-9;4	4;14-8;10			
Age at testing (years;months)					
Mean	10;11	11;7	28	-10.40	<.001
Range	8;7-12;8	9;3-14;0			

Mean age of the children at the current testing was approximately 11 years with a range from 8-14 years; this was the only variable in which the two samples differed significantly, the control group being about 8 months older on average. For the experimental sample, average duration of the MPA administration during pregnancy was 17.7 weeks, ranging from 2 to 34 weeks. Average total MPA dosage was 1268 mg with a range of 140-3900 mg.

Procedure

The subjects were recalled for a double-blind comprehensive psychological follow-up examination involving the Wechsler Intelligence Scale for Children-Revised (Wechsler, 1974) and other psychometric tests, questionnaires, and interviews with mother and child (Meyer-Bahlburg et al., in press; Ehrhardt et al., in press).

RESULTS

Both the experimental and control groups showed an elevated IQ distribution (Figure 1) as is to be expected on the basis of the socioeconomic data. Mean Full-IQ was 111.6 for the MPA-exposed

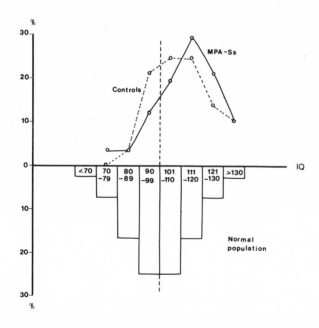

Fig. 1.   Prenatal MPA Study: IQ Distribution (WISC-R)

group and 111.1 for the controls; the difference was not significant (t_{dep}= 0.16, p >.10, 2-tailed).   The correlation between Full-IQ and MPA dosage was negligible and not statistically significant (r = -0.12, p >.10, 2-tailed).

Table 2 compares the experimental and control samples with regard to the correlation of IQ with background variables. SES and IQ were positively correlated as usual. Mother's IQ correlated significantly positive, as expected in normal samples, with the control children's IQ but the correlation was zero with the experimental children's IQ. Length of gestation and birth weight did not correlate significantly with IQ. Age at testing did also not correlate with IQ; consequently, the small age difference between the experimental and control samples is not relevant for the interpretation of the results.

As to test patterns, there were no remarkable differences between Verbal and Performance IQ, or between Cohen's (1957, 1959) Verbal, Number and Perceptual factors, within or between the experimental and control group. There were also no treatment effects on individual WISC-R subtests.

DISCUSSION

The results show no significant influence of prenatal MPA on later cognitive functioning since all control group comparisons with regard to the WISC-R are statistically insignificant. The only exception is the correlation between children's and mother's IQ, which is positive and significant, for the control subjects, but zero for the experimental group. This finding is in need of further analysis.

With regard to IQ mean differences, our results do not corroborate earlier reports of significant elevation of mental abilities by progestogens. The earlier Dalton studies used teachers' ratings rather than intelligence testing, and teachers' ratings tend to take into consideration both mental abilities and behavior. Thus, teachers' ratings of mental abilities might be positively affected if MPA would slightly influence behavior, for instance, would render the children more docile and adjusted; in fact, similar behavior changes have been found in these children (Ehrhardt and Meyer-Bahlburg, 1977). Another important difference between our and Dalton's studies is that Dalton used a higher total progesterone dose than our MPA mothers had taken during pregnancy.

However, in comparison to all previous studies in which the comparability of subjects and controls leaves much to be desired, our close pair-matching of experimental and control subjects

TABLE 2

CORRELATES OF WISC-R FULL-IQ

Variables	Experimentals			Controls		
	r	N	p(2-tailed)	r	N	p(2-tailed)
SES	.30	28	>.10	.50	28	<.01
Mother's IQ	-.01	25	>.10	.47	28	<.05
Length of Gestation	.19	28	>.10	.17	28	>.10
Birth Weight	-.30	28	>.10	-.10	28	>.10
Age at Testing	-.24	28	>.10	.05	28	>.10

eliminated differences in socioeconomic level and other background variables. Therefore, we can conclude that the synthetic progestogen MPA in dosages as it has commonly been used in mild forms of pregnancy disturbance does not elevate mental abilities in offspring as measured here. This does not rule out possible effects of higher MPA dosages on brain development and intelligence.

REFERENCES

Bailey, M.A. (1963). Toxemia of pregnancy: cognitive and emotional effects in children from consistent and non-consistent environments. Ph.D. thesis. Xerox University Microfilms, Ann Arbor, Michigan.

Cohen, J. (1957). A factor-analytically based rationale for the Wechsler Adult Intelligence Scale. J. Consult. Psychol. 21: 451-457.

Cohen, J. (1959). The factorial structure of the WISC at ages 7-6, 10-6, 13-6. J. Consult. Psychol. 23: 285-299.

The Collaborative Perinatal Study of the National Institute of
     Neurological Diseases and Stroke. (1972). The Women and
     Their Pregnancies, W.B. Saunders, Philadelphia.

Dalton, K. (1968). Ante-natal progesterone and intelligence.
     Brit. J. Psychiat. 114: 1377-1382.

Dalton, K. (1976). Prenatal progesterone and educational attain-
     ments. Brit. J. Psychiat. 129: 438-442.

Dobbing, J., and Sands, J. (1973). Quantitative growth and de-
     velopment of human brain. Arch. Dis. Child., 48: 757-767.

Ehrhardt, A.A., Grisanti, G.C., and Meyer-Bahlburg, H.F.L. (In
     press). Prenatal exposure to medroxyprogesterone acetate
     (MPA) in girls. Psychoneuroendocrinology.

Ehrhardt, A.A., and Meyer-Bahlburg, H.F.L. (1977). Prenatal pro-
     gestogen and gender-role behavior in childhood. Paper
     presented at the 34th Annual Meeting of the American
     Psychosomatic Society, Atlanta, Georgia, March 25-27, 1977.

Ehrhardt, A.A., and Money, J. (1967). Progestin-induced herma-
     phroditism, IQ and psychosexual identity in a study of 10
     girls. J. Sex Res. 3:83-100.

Meyer-Bahlburg, H.F.L., Grisanti, G.C., and Ehrhardt, A.A. (In
     press). Prenatal exposure to medroxyprogesterone acetate
     (MPA): behavioral effects in boys. Psychoneuroendocrinol-
     ogy.

Reifenstein, E.C., Jr. (1958). Clinical use of 17 α-hydroxyproges-
     terone 17-η-caproate in habitual abortion. Annals New York
     Acad. Sci. 71: 762-786.

SRA Non-Verbal Form. (1947). Science Research Associates, Inc.,
     Chicago, Illinois.

U.S. Bureau of the Census. (1963). Methodology and scores of
     socioeconomic status. Working paper no. 15. Washington,
     D.C.

Wechsler, D. (1974). Wechsler Intelligence Scale for Children-
     Revised. Psychological Corporation, New York.

Zussman, J.U., Zussman, P.P., and Dalton, K. (1975). Post-pubertal
     effects of prenatal administration of progesterone. Paper
     presented at the meeting of the Society for Research in
     Child Development, Denver, Colorado, April 1975.

SEXUAL FUNCTIONING RECONSIDERED

Bernard Apfelbaum

United States

Despite its obvious significance there is little in the literature of sexology and sex therapy on the relation between sexual
arousal and sexual performance. There are systematic and historical reasons for this which must be recognized before they can be
transcended.

In the pre-Masters and Johnson period there had been no concern with performance criteria. "Impotence" included both erectile
and ejaculatory dysfunction, and "frigidity," a term that seemed
more like a complaint than a diagnosis, had no clear referents.
This ambiguity on the performance level reflected the single-minded
preoccupation with finding ways to heighten erotic arousal that
dominated pre-Masters and Johnson sex therapy. Masters and Johnson
recognized the heavy demand pressure this created, and the effect of
their work was to make obsolete the preoccupation with techniques
of extended "foreplay."

Sexual Arousal Subordinated

Masters and Johnson's innovation was, of course, a total reversal of emphasis. Rather than concentrating on techniques of
erotic arousal, they focussed on solving sexual performance problems on the principle that sexual arousal is most likely to appear
when it is ignored. It is less clear why they also ignored degree
of arousal diagnostically, though presumably it was their hope that
by defining all sexual problems in performance terms, we could be
spared having to cope with all the complexities of sexuality.
Although this solution has saved us from the ambiguities of the

previous era, another source of ambiguity is created by leaving
degree of arousal unspecified, as Kaplan (1974b) has pointed out.
Taking the case of "orgasmic dysfunction," Masters and Johnson's
reformulation of "frigidity," Kaplan argues that:

> "orgastic dysfunction" has no real conceptual advantage over
> the old "frigidity" because it also fails to distinguish be-
> tween the sexually unresponsive woman and the responsive
> woman who has difficulty reaching orgasm.

She contends that female "responsiveness," that is degree of arousal, cannot be measured by frequency of orgasm. In a bold diver-
gence from the Masters and Johnson diagnostic scheme, Kaplan as-
serts that women with orgasmic dysfunction, rather than being sexually unresponsive in general, are _typically_ aroused: "As a general
rule, women who suffer from orgastic dysfunction are responsive
sexually. They may fall in love, experience erotic feelings, lubricate copiously, and also show genital swelling (1974b: 343)."

Kaplan's association of dysfunction with a high degree of
arousal has no counterpart in Human Sexual Inadequacy. There,
dysfunction and lack of arousal are treated as essentially equivalent. For example, in describing women who are infrequently orgasmic, Masters and Johnson say that "these women are rarely orgasmic
and usually are aware of little or no physical need for sexual expression (1970: 240)." The implication is that infrequent orgasms and lack of sexual interest go together. Further, there is
no other mention of lack of erotic arousal in Human Sexual Inadequacy.

Masters and Johnson do not include a diagnosis of lack of sexual interest or desire. The women just described who lack desire
and are rarely orgasmic are given the diagnosis of "random orgasmic
inadequacy." This diagnosis is based on the infrequent orgasms
such patients experience _despite_ their lack of sexual interest.
This follows Masters and Johnson's practice of defining sexual disorders as disorders of function, hence, their term sexual dysfunction. This practice implies that there are no separate disorders
of arousal.

Sexual Aversion

I have mentioned Kaplan's challenge to the position that arousal and functioning can be treated as equivalent. A second challenge
comes from Masters and Johnson's (1976) own later work. In keeping
with their naturalistic, atheoretical bias, they do not acknowledge
the conceptual shift indicated by the inclusion of an arousal disorder in their diagnostic system. In as yet unpublished data covering the period 1972-1975, they present outcome data for the treatment

of <u>sexual aversion</u>. It is the only diagnostic category they have
added to those reported on in <u>Human Sexual Inadequacy</u>, and it represents an interesting departure from that work since it does not
refer to a dysfunction. They state that of the 98 patients so
diagnosed, 75 women and 23 men, "the great majority in either sex is
not dysfunctional." These patients are sexually functional despite
what Masters and Johnson describe as an aversion to sex that is not
merely a dislike but an aversion of "phobic proportions."

     The term "sexual dysfunction," introduced in <u>Human Sexual</u>
<u>Inadequacy</u>, has become so much a part of our language that it can
indeed seem strange to be presented with a symptom that is not a
dysfunction. Perhaps this makes it easier to notice that the term
"sexual dysfunction" carries the assumption that sexual problems
are to be defined in terms of behavioral outcomes, erections and
orgasms, and that the achievement of these outcomes signifies sexual fulfillment. We have come to associate unimpaired sexual functioning with sexual well-being. Yet consider the way arousal disorders can be masked by nonsymptomatic sexual functioning in people
whose sexual alienation is less severe than that found in Masters
and Johnson's sexual aversives. In fact, in this Masters and Johnson sample sexual alienation may well have been masked until it
reached phobic proportions and then could no longer be ignored.

Autonomous Excitement-Phase Functioning

     If functioning can mask lack of arousal then the equivalence
between performance and arousal that Masters and Johnson have assumed clearly does not hold. This means that the whole question
of the relation between arousal and performance must be reopened
To make it clear that the lack of equivalence between performance
and arousal found in Masters and Johnson's sexual aversives is also
found in other kinds of patients and in non-patients, I would like
to give you some of my own observations of sexual functioning autonomous from arousal. Although Masters and Johnson's sexual aversives
presumably can function autonomously in all phases of the response
cycle, the population I will be drawing from next is made up of
men with orgasmic and ejaculatory disorders who display autonomous
excitement-phase functioning. The opportunity to study such patients is provided by our method of individual body-work sex therapy. This method makes it possible to control and monitor the
patient's responses to behavioral assignments in review sessions
that painstakingly examine the events of each body-work session,
providing a fund of data not available in couple therapy (Apfelbaum,
1977b; Greene, 1977; Williams, 1977a).

     In our work we have come to see erection alone as a limited
indication of arousal, at best. We have seen cases of men who
invariably develop rapid and sustained erections, but who insist

that they experience no subjective sense of arousal. Some of them resent the presence of erection because they then feel called upon to have intercourse knowing that they will either have a premature orgasm or none at all.

When they become impotent, men who have learned to expect autonomous erections can be especially difficult to treat because they have no conception of any way their erectile response is vulnerable to their level of arousal. Thus in one such case a man had been accustomed for many years to accommodating his wife's demand that before she would allow intromission, he had to take a shower and to emerge from the shower with a complete erection. He claims to have accomplished this without difficulty until his wife told him that she had a lover and was considering a separation. Despite this severe and unexpected trauma, and despite his background as an OB-GYN specialist, he was unable to comprehend his subsequent inability to meet his wife's expectations.

We have also had the opportunity to recognize that many men who suffer from premature ejaculation also exhibit rapid and sustained autonomous erections. Even when showing signs of their chronic characterological tension as well as experiencing heavy emotional stress in the therapeutic situation, their erections may be unaffected. Thus I can see them as suffering from premature erection as well as premature ejaculation.

Retarded ejaculators provide another such example. When seen in couple sex therapy they may report lack of coital orgasm despite feeling aroused, making them Kaplan's (1974b) male analogue to female orgasmic dysfunction. When seen in individual body-work sex therapy they report a low degree of arousal, but still exhibit the sustained erection characteristic of the retarded ejaculator.

One such patient was given the task of relaxing the pubococcygeus muscle, an assignment more suitable for the premature ejaculator. However, he had exhibited the involuntary penile throbbing that is often found in the severe premature ejaculator, suggesting that relaxation of the PC muscle might be of some value. He became so proficient at this task that he claimed to be able to pass some urine through his erect penis. This was not observed clinically, but we can at least guess that being preoccupied with this task signified a low level of arousal. Yet his erection remained unaffected.

On the basis of these observations, our therapeutic approach often differs from the standard approaches. Clearly, whether or not the retarded ejaculator is seen as aroused will be a central determinant of one's treatment strategy. Masters and Johnson abandon their non demand strategy with retarded ejaculators, presumbly because they consider these patients to be already capable

of sexual arousal (Williams, 1977b). In contrast, we see retarded
ejaculation as an arousal disorder masked by the autonomous erection
that convinces the patient and others that he must be aroused. Our
first move, then, is to help the patient lose this erectile autonomy to facilitate his getting in touch with the ways he is not
aroused when with a partner (as contrasted with his much higher
level of arousal in masturbation).

If we now direct our attention to women we can find parallel
examples of sexual functioning autonomous from arousal. It is not
at all unusual for a woman to lubricate in response to purely
physical stimulation without experiencing any subjective sense of
arousal. For many women this is their typical way of experiencing
sex; for others this is at least the way sex is initiated. Kaplan
(1974a) mentions the woman who can "experience orgasm rather easily" despite being "severely inhibited in the arousal component
of the sexual response." This description would, of course, also
apply to Masters and Johnson's sexual aversives.

                            Bypassing

What is it that makes autonomous sexual functioning possible
and how are we to think about it?

Kaplan's (1974b) concept of bypassing is useful here. Although
she uses it to describe the therapist's overlooking tensions and
conflict in a relationship in the service of restoring sexual functioning, the term can also be applied to the same maneuver when
done deliberately or instinctively by the patient. When seen as
a form of sexual response, bypassing can refer both to the ability
to overlook tensions in order to become aroused (for an example of
this, see Apfelbaum, 1977a) and to the ability to overlook lack of
arousal in order to function, as by focussing on sensation. Here
is an illustrative vignette of this latter form of bypassing, the
kind more pertinent to my present discussion:

> This woman was brought into therapy by her partner because he
> had lost all sexual feeling for her after the initial phase
> of the relationship. She reported that she never fails to
> reach orgasm whenever there is the opportunity for manual
> stimulation by any partner. During an assignment her partner
> became aroused when she was stroking him, but reported that
> he was responding to a fantasy of another, sexier, woman.
> She felt hurt and angry, but suppressed it. Then when it was
> time for him to stroke her, he acted reluctant and asked to
> postpone it on some pretext. She again suppressed her feel-
> ings and also managed to conceal a strong urge to put on her
> clothes and leave. Instead she refused to give up her turn,
> and in due time reached orgasm. On being questioned, she

said that she saw nothing remarkable in this, adding that she saw no reason why her feelings should interfere.

As I see it, bypassing is one of the two opposing (ultimately synergistic) functions of sexuality, either one of which may be elaborated into a disorder. Although I must reserve further discussion of this point for a later time, I can here reduce my analysis to a quip by saying that the two opposing functions of sex are to gain relief from 1) loneliness, and 2) relationships.

Our Reference Population

I think it likely that the reason bypassing has not yet been studied is that it is built into our reference model. If, as I have suggested, sexual arousal was implied in Human Sexual Inadequacy, we could say it was assumed in Human Sexual Response (1966). Masters and Johnson thought of this work as a textbook of sexual physiology and were concerned with the detection and differentiation of physiological changes. They were not concerned with subjectively experienced sexual arousal, and did not get self-ratings on this from their subjects (the closest they came to it was to get subjective descriptions of the experience of orgasm). In other words, they were not concerned with what initiated the physiological patterns they observed. Their book could have been called Human Sexual Performance.

Further, there is reason to believe that the majority of the subjects in Masters and Johnson's study sample were adept sexual bypassers. Thus, of the "7500 complete cycles of sexual response" recorded for the female subjects, there were only 10 failures to reach orgasm in masturbation and only 108 failures to reach coital orgasm (Masters and Johnson, 1966: 313). These are striking statistics in view of the base rates in the general population, and even more striking when we note that these coital orgasms were frequently reached not with established partners but with "anonymous" partners and with the artificial phallus.

These are the people who have given us our model of the sexual response systems, or "phases," as they are presently called. It is a highly appropriate sample for a textbook of sexual physiology, but a highly skewed sample for a study of the relation between sexual arousal and sexual performance. Even Masters and Johnson's clinical sample does not sufficiently correct for this bias because in this carefully selected group sexual rapport and, consequently, the potential for a high level of arousal could be taken for granted. It may take data from patients ordinarily screened out of sex therapy as well as those not motivated for it to correct for this bias. In other words, we may now need to investigate the sexuality of those who exhibit more complex relations among the sexual response systems (phases).

Dysfunction or Disorder?

We may also need to reconsider the now widespread use of "sex-ual dysfunction" to refer to all sexual disorders. My own view is that although Masters and Johnson's exclusive focus on dysfunction has saved us from the impressionistic ambiguities of the previous era, it has created an obstacle to thinking about the relation be-tween performance and subjective arousal. A safeguard against further ambiguity would be to use the term dysfunction to refer only to performance impairments. This has apparently been Masters and Johnson's own view since they can say that most of the sexual aversives in their sample are not dysfunctional.

However, Kaplan (1976) has argued in favor of keeping dysfunc-tion as the generic term. Her reasoning is that arousal is as much a "function" as is vasocongestion and orgasm. She sees "desire" as a phase of the response cycle, and hence sees lack of desire as a "true psychophysiologic" reaction. (I will propose in a subsequent paper that the desire "phase" is not a phase of the response cycle and is best considered the expression of a separate response system).

Kaplan's position is shared by the Subcommittee on Sexual Dis-orders in the unpublished draft of their provisional nomenclature for DSM III, the Third Edition of the American Psychiatric Associa-tion's Diagnostic and Statistical Manual. Their inclusion of a "desire phase," at the suggestion of Harold Lief, is "a major theoretical and clinical advance," as Kaplan (1976) put it. Even in Kaplan's The New Sex Therapy (1974) lack of sexual interest or desire is not present as a diagnostic entity and lack of subjective arousal is discussed only when it results in dysfunction, though the fact that it is discussed is itself an advance over Masters and Johnson's work.

One might say that in recognizing the diagnostic significance of subjective arousal, or "desire," the Subcommittee has taken the next step in the rediscovery of sexual arousal. However, "desire" is defined as a sexual function, just as Kaplan has recommended, presumably resulting in the diagnosis of a "desire dysfunction." The concept of a dysfunction of desire, and with it the possibility of feeling sexually dysfunctional, would seem to reflect the con-ceptual strain created by the introduction of subjective arousal into what has been an exlcusively performance-oriented system.

REFERENCES

Apfelbaum, B. (1977a). On the etiology of sexual dysfunction. J. Sex Marital Ther. 3 (1): 50-62.

Apfelbaum, B. (1977b). The myth of the surrogate. J. Sex Res. 13: in press.

Greene, S.E. (1977). Resisting the pressure to become a surrogate: a case study. J. Sex Marital Ther. 3 (1): 40-49.

Kaplan, H.S. (1974a). A new classification of the female sexual dysfunctions. J. Sex Marital Ther. 1: 124-138.

Kaplan, H.S. (1974b). The New Sex Therapy. Brunner/Mazel, New York.

Kaplan, H.S. (1976). Toward a rational classification of the sexual dysfunctions. J. Sex Marital Ther. 2: 83-84.

Masters, W.H. and Johnson, V.E. (1966). Human Sexual Response, Little, Brown and Co., Boston.

Masters, W.H. and Johnson, V.E. (1970). Human Sexual Inadequacy. Little, Brown and Co., Boston.

Masters, W.H. and Johnson, V.E. (1976). Seminar, New York.

Williams, M.H. (1977a). Individual sex therapy. In LoPiccolo, J., and LoPiccolo, L. (eds.), Handbood of Sex Therapy, Plenum, New York, in press.

Williams, M.H. (1977b). An unnoted inconsistency in Masters and Johnson's use of nondemand techniques: retarded ejaculation. Presented at Calif. State Psychol. Assoc. Conv., San Francisco.

MALE ERECTILE IMPOTENCE

Gilbert Tordjman

France

In sex therapy difficulties begin the very moment the patient starts describing his problem. These difficulties have two main causes: a) the embarrassment felt by the physician vis-à-vis the symptom, impotence or frigidity, and b) the lack of clarity in the client's descriptions and the not meaningless ambiguity of medical terms.

This ambiguity can be traced back to the different sexual roles which society assigns to men and women: a man is only defined by his ability to have an erection, and a woman by her receptivity and her good expression of erotic warmth. Hence the use of the terms "impotence" and "frigidity" to which we prefer that of sexual dysfunction.

The lack of clarity in the patient's descriptions is due to the fact that these problems touch upon the very core of his personality and conjure up in him an aura of anxiety and other emotions. More than any other patient's the questions the impotent man asks of the physician are questions he has long tried to answer himself. His symptom points to a lack and loss of an identity he must be helped to recover. All he is saying boils down to: "I am not a man. Do you think something can be done about it?" Therefore his verbal description never fully accounts for what he is experiencing. He tries, not always successfully, to go beyond the physiological facts: lack of desire, inability to control the ejaculatory reflex, etc. Every confidence is marked by a very personal coefficient of dissatisfaction, incompleteness, humiliation, even despair, which the therapist has to evaluate. In this respect, the infra-verbal message, contained in the patient's attitude, tone of voice, hesitations, silences, proves to be more revealing than what he actually says. And in this first interview, what is essential is more often what is left unsaid than the words actually spoken.

Male erectile dysfunctions, at any rate, usually referred to as impotence, must be clearly distinguished from libidinal deficiency and ejaculatory disorders, which, until about the 60's, were often confused with each other and therefore treated in the same way. Almost always co-existing with anxiety, the erectile dysfunction may occur at the very beginning of foreplay, often dissociating psychical desire from its objective realization, at the moment of penetration, or after a more or less prolonged period of intercourse.

In some cases, intercourse has never been possible; the term of primary impotence used to describe this condition disregards the actual frequency of erections and the man may well know "triumphant mornings" and masturbate successfully. In other cases, penile ballistics, which had long proved satisfactory, meets with failure in some trivial circumstances. The term of secondary impotence can only be used if the percentage of coital failures reaches 25%. This is the definition given by Masters and Johnson, and this definition states only the obvious, for every man will eventually have some momentary sexual difficulties and to classify them as impotence would be wrong, and even dangerous.

THE CLINICAL FORMS OF
ERECTILE IMPOTENCE

The erection may be incomplete (the penis semi flaccid or semi erected according to whether one opts for the pessimistic or optimistic point of view). It may fail with any one given partner, the man's wife or possibly his mistress. Impotence may occur when coitus is attempted and disappear when the man is stimulated manually or orally. We have even known patients whose sexual functioning could only be satisfactory if they remained fully dressed.

Secondary Erectile Impotence
Leading to Premature Ejaculation

This clinical form is particularly interesting in so far as it brings to light, in an almost experimental manner, a man's reactions to his sexual dysfunction. Humiliated, frustrated, sometimes desperate, he may prefer to abstain from sex altogether rather than meet with another failure; in the majority of cases, a marital conflict will eventually break out and it cannot always be ascertained whether impotence was its cause or a consequence.

Finally, the impotent man may be forced into homosexual, voyeuristic or pedophillic behaviors, when he does not seek refuge in alcohol, which, to quote Shakespeare, "provokes the desire but ... takes away the performance."

CAUSES OF ERECTILE IMPOTENCE

The Relationship between Psychogenic and Physiogenic Causes

The study of erection shows that it is both an autonomous and interpersonal function and it usually allows a distinction between psychogenic and physiogenic erectile impotence. When the erectile impotence is psychogenic, erection remains possible as long as the man is not in a relational situation or when coitus is not intended. Thus, one of our patients always regained potency during his partner's menses. Others can only retain their erection if they remain fully dressed.

But the fact that the etiology of erectile impotence is as a rule overdetermined makes the matter much more complex: a long period of psychogenic sexual abstinence will eventually affect the amount of plasma testosterone secreted. Conversely, a patent neurological or metabolic vascular lesion is in the long run, bound to bring about an anxiety which will precipitate failure or cause a degeneration of the marital relationship.

Some cases are even more difficult: for some patients, who suffer from manifest organic disorders, erectile impotence is but a psychogenic epiphenomena resulting from the anxiety provoked by the disease itself. Thus, erectile impotence can be observed in the context of diabetes or medullary sclerosis, but is not a direct consequence of diabetes or of the neurological disorder itself, and that is confirmed by the favorable progress brought about by psychotherapy. The physician's role may primarily consist in distinguishing the psychogenic from the physiogenic, and this is not always easy.

Organic Causes

Diabetes. A very large number of impotent men show abnormal results when submitted to the glucose tolerance test, and it is still not known whether they are in a prediabetic condition or reacting to the stress of impotence itself. When the sexual dysfunction is provoked by a diabetic neuropathy, it is most likely to be associated with other neurovegetative phenomena like nocturnal

diarrhoea, sudation disorder, orthostatic hypotension, atonic bladder and partial anaesthesia when the testis is strongly pressed
between thumb and forefinger and retarded ejaculation or lack of
ejaculation where the patient may lose his ability to have an
ejaculation several months before losing his erectile potency.

Arterial causes. Selective arteriographic exploration of
the hypogastric and internal pudental arteries has recently brought
to light a specific vascular pathology in the genital sphere.

We take two shots of the penis, at an interval of 5 minutes,
the first before cooling and the second after cooling. In subjects
whose inhibitions are psychogenic, the drop in penile temperature,
once stabilization by the usual regulation mechanisms has taken
place, does not exceed 3°C. When the distal gradient of the penis
reaches or goes beyond 4°C., there are usually arterial vascular
disorders which are confirmed by the arteriography.

In these cases, selective arteriography of the left and right
hypogastric arteries reveals an amputation of one of the internal
pudendal arteries at any point of its course (a substitution anas-
tomatic network of thin aterioles can then be observed in the
symphisis pubic area) or a series of stenoses along the length of
the arteries, a lack of vascular irrigation of the whole of the
penis, and an amputation of the dorsal artery of the penis, and
especially, of the deep artery of the penis itself, which plays
such a major role in the erection process.

However this arteriography is only to be carried out in cases
when the clinical and biological factors both point to this particular etiology and when the thermography of the penis reveals
an arterial cause.

Venous causes of impotence. We are currently studying patients
whose dysfunctions lie in the field of this new pathology heretofore undescribed. In these cases the patient has an erection, but
is unable to maintain it for more than a minute or two. But what
is most significant is that he reports that he can more easily
maintain his erection when standing or in a dorsal or lateral
decubitus than in the classical missionary position.

The clinical, and particularly the thermographic examinations
show a venous stasis at one of the 3 following levels: at the root
of the penis and in the abdominal area where superficial varices
are sometimes directly palpable, in the area covered by the internal
saphena and in the spermatic plexuses where a varicocele is to be
found. Indeed, the deep dorsal vein which drains off most of the
venous blood from the penis anastomoses to these three networks.

Most of the time, this venous pathogeny is due to a valvular incontinence of the deep dorsal vein of the penis. This incontinence, phlebographically demonstrated, provokes a hypertension in the deep dorsal vein of the penis. The situation could be pictured in the following way: the penis, threatened with priapism by this venous hypertension, hurriedly reduces the flow of arterial blood and drains off the venous blood.

Medicamentous Impotence. Under no circumstances should the practitioner fail to ask his patients what medicines they are currently taking. Many of them may alter the vascular process or the neuroendocrinal mechanisms which control erection and ejaculation.

Thus alcohol, absorbed in large quantities, provokes a depression of the central and parasympathetic system and influences sexuality. Anticholinergics, such as atropine and other antispasmodics, have a parasymptholytic action which may also imperil erection. Experimentation with animals, which has often been confirmed with human beings, shows that dopamine stimulates sexual and aggressive behaviors, while serotonin or 5-hydroxytryptamin excerts an inhibiting and calming influence. Dopamine would particularly speed up the secretion of LH-RH and inhibit that of LTH.

Thus all the drugs which shut off the dopamine receptors at the level of the central nervous system are shown to inhibit sexuality, and most of the time hasten prolactinemia. This is the case with chlopromazine, haloperidol, reserpine, methydopa, sulpiride and certainly with a great number of tranquilizers which we are now investigating. On the contrary, all drugs which slow down the secretion or synthesis of serotonin strongly stimulate sexuality and aggressivity; this is particularly true with PCPA, LSD and testosterone.

This opposition between dopamine and prolactine hormone has led us to experiment in certain cases of sexual inhibitions provoked by antidopaminergic drug, the CB 154 (2 Bromo α ergocryptine) in fact, CB 154 not only inhibits prolactine secretion by a direct action on the pituitary gland but also stimulates the dopaminergic neurones of the central nervous system and particularly in the hypothalamus. Thus a new chemotherapeutic era is dawning and it could lead to a discovery of the perfect chemical aphrodisiac.

CONCLUSION

It nevertheless remains true that in all forms of erectile impotence a common denominator is always present: vulnerability to those emotions which condition 3 forms of negative affect: 1) fear of failure, anticipation of failure, anxiety; 2) inability to concentrate on erotic feelings; and 3) excessive vulnerability to the partner's reactions.

The frustrated woman's aggressiveness mainly emerges during
intercourse and/or during the sensate focus exercises prescribed
by the therapist.   What every woman ought to know is that all
pressures brought to bear on sexual desire or performance hinder
the achievement of the chosen goal.

We feel we have demonstrated that erectile impotence is in
most cases a psychosomatic disorder, and that equal amounts of
attention should be paid to both its somatic and psychiatric components.

THE EFFECTS OF DEPRESSION ON SEXUAL BEHAVIOR: PRELIMINARY RESULTS OF RESEARCH

Antonino Tamburello and Marisa Feliciotti Seppecher

Italy

In an examination of the literature on sexology the small amount of data available on the relationship between human sexual behavior and depression becomes obvious. This is not just our personal point of view but one shared by other writers who have attempted a synthesis on the area in question (Renshaw et al., in press).

This is extremely surprising in light of the high frequency with which the clinician, working in the field of the treatment of sexual dysfunctions, finds depression sometimes, and unfortunately, playing a leading role.

In such publications as do exist a hierarchy of varying view points can be traced, the most prevalent being that depression is an inhibiting and limiting factor in human sexuality. The most fervent exponents of this view are Bailey (1973) and Horn (1971) who respectively and almost categorically state: 1) "Frigidity is in every case associated with depression," and that "one of the most important inhibiting factors in depression," and 2) "sexual behavior is the most precise index of the remissive state of endogenous depression." Going down the hierarchical ladder from the level of rigid perspective and interdependence of the factors of depression and sexual behavior (the latter ingenuously considered as a single variable), we come to the more balanced positions of those who assert that there is a loss of interest and that while there is still a complete physiological sexual response, it is separated from the emotive and cognitive response, or, as a patient has expressed it most clearly, "I don't laugh any more after I climax."

Even further down the ladder we find those who assert that only the frequency of activity is altered (Brown, 1973) and even those who suggest that it is the sexual dysfunction itself which causes depression (Bagadia, 1972).

There is even a minority group who claim to note an increased frequency in sexual activity in depression (Michaelis, 1971; Ming, 1975). This last viewpoint has not had much influence because it is more than balanced by the high correlation discovered between maniacal excitement and personality (Winokur, 1969; Knoff, 1975) and by the discovered role of biogenic amines in depression and of their potential role in the hypothalamic-hypophyseal connections and hence in the gonadotrophin secretion which have stimulated the organicistic attitudes.

Moreover, the relationship between remission in the psycho-pathological picture and sexual behavior has been neglected, but the only two statements on this aspects admit to a parallel re-versibility of the induced changes (on mania, Winokur, 1969; on depression, Renshaw, in press).

Coming back to a global evaluation of the contributions so far available, we can only confirm the insufficiency of the data and the methodological inadequacy of the evaluation of the data which has led, in some cases, to statements being put in the form of general impressions, and, in others, in the form of authoritarian expressions.

However, as there is a lack of precise observation and sys-tematic evaluation, we feel that nothing more could have been done. The fact is that the clinician working in the field of sexual dys-functions is deprived of data which could serve to orient him in his work. Let us take as an example the decision as to whether to accept or not in an intensive therapy programme a sexually dys-functioning couple, one of whom is clearly depressed. In such a case one's uncertainty, as to whether to precede the intervention with psycho-pharmacological therapy or some kind of psycho-therapy, is understandable. Even with a more specific evaluation of the phenomenon, for example, taking into consideration its duration, stability, and whether it preceded or followed the sexual inade-quacy, the lack of reference data annuls every significance.

Put into different terms the basic question could be formulated thus: is the organism of the patient in this dynamic moment (that is, in the depressive state) in its potential to exhibit a phys-iological model of sexual response? (Here we do not take into ac-count the stimulus condition as this comes into the area which can be more directly attacked by the therapeutic strategy).

The clinician who asks this question would still be in doubt, and a series of nonverbal and involuntary signals could be interpolated in the communication between therapists and the couple, thus raising the anxiety level of the latter. We at least have found this to be true. Certainly it could be avoided by waiving the selection of patients and thus treating 200 couples in which one member is consistently depressed and see what happens. But there is no need to point out the debateable professional correctness of such behavior. There is no comfort either in the observation that in certain cases the cognitive and perceptive modifications prevent the depressive from defining personal goals and individual needs which cannot be communicated, and leave the couple (and also the therapists) up in the air concerning the interpersonal and environmental reinforcements which alone are capable of positive mood controls.

The path chosen was to explore the sexual behavior of a large number of depressives in order to verify a series of hypotheses formulated through clinical impressions.

HYPOTHESES FOR WORK (OR RESEARCH)

The first hypothesis is to determine the existence or non-existence of a correlation between the intensity of the depressive state and the extent and significance of the changes in the single behavioral units considered and of the sexual repertoire taken as a whole.

The second hypothesis is to determine the existence or non-existence of a correlation between the level of development and the adequacy of the sexual repertoire before the onset of the depression and the extent and significance of the changes in the single behavioral units or in the repertoire taken as a whole.

The third hypothesis is to determine the existence or non-existence of a correlation between the level of deterioration in the marital relationship and the extent and significance of the changes in depression in the single behavioral units or the repertoire taken as a whole.

The fourth hypothesis is to determine the existence or non-existence of the restoration, to the original level of the sexual repertoire, of depression corrected by psycho-pharmaceutical means.

METHODOLOGY

Evaluation Methods and Instruments

Verification of the hypotheses listed before, necessitated the measurement of two fundamental dimensions: the intensity of the depressive state (let me stress here the fact that we intentionally referred only to the "status," avoiding the thorny question of the definition of the diagnostic subgroupings of depression) and the state of the marital relationship in correspondence to 2 or 3 clinical moments, that is 1) in the last phase free from the depression (M1), 2) in the acute depressive phase (M2), 3) in the phase of partial or total remission (M3).

The instruments used are respectively the "Hamilton Psychiatric Rating Scale for Depression" and the "Locke Wallace Marriage Inventory," and the data was obtained through interviews carried out by the same interviewer (in order to reduce the possibility of uncontrollable variables linked to the behavior of the interviewer).

The information on the basic units of the sexual behavior repertoire, relative principally, but not exclusively, to aspects that involve interactions between the two members of the couple, (in fact data which concern fantasy, dreams, masturbation, and other sources extraneous to the diadic life have been taken into consideration) was obtained through guided interviews based on a form elaborated by the Institute and composed of 41 items.

The items were arranged on the form in such an order so as to ensure a constant control, during the interview, of the data being collected.

Besides the three groups of data mentioned up to now, which have allowed us to organize the numerous subgroups which appear in Table 1, for each of which have been calculated the changes relative to each single behavioral component, a considerable amount of other information was gathered on every patient: of a social nature, on their alimentary habits with particular attention to the assumption of toxic substances, on the psychiatric history of the depressive disturbance, on psycho-pharmaceutics and relative dosages taken in the period of treatment and in particular on the verbal expressions used by the patient to explain clearly and with more efficacy some concepts relative to the items under consideration. We did not wish to lose the potential information which the rigidity of the methodology could have sacrified, even if it is not used in the verification of formulated hypotheses.

TABLE 1

COMPOSITION OF THE SAMPLE'S SUBGROUPS

Complete group: including all the subjects, divided only by sex.

Group H1: including all the subjects with Hamilton value up to 50.

Group H2: including all the subjects with Hamilton value between 50 and 70.

Group H3: including all the subjects with Hamilton value over 70.

Group L&W1: including all the subjects with Locke and Wallace value up to 80.

Group L&W2: including all the subjects with Locke and Wallace value between 80 and 100.

Group L&W3: including all the subjects with Locke and Wallace value over 100.

Group R1: including all the subjects with a so called "good previous sexual repertoire," rated on our scale (which is composed of seven behavioral items) between 19 and 28.

Group R2: including all the subjects with a so called "average previous sexual repertoire," rated on our scale between 13 and 19.

Group R3: including all the subjects with a so called "poor previous sexual repertoire" rated on our scale between 0 and 13.

Group L̄&W̄1: including all the subjects with a diminution in depression of L W value less than −5.

Group L̄&W̄2: including all the subjects with a diminution in depression of L W value between −5 and −15.

Group L̄&W̄3: including all the subjects with a diminution in depression of L W value more than −15.

Sample Group

Research was carried out on 107 depressed patients of differing gravity, ranging from the moderate form between 30 and 50 on the Hamilton Scale to the serious form > 70. The patients were 69 females and 38 males, 71 under ambulatory treatment and 36 undergoing in-patient therapy. The average age of the selection was 43 (42 for women, 47.5 for men) with a range of 17 to 73.

The patients chosen had to be married or living with a fixed partner over a period of time sufficient to include the measurement moments that could be two or three.

Other necessary conditions were the exclusion of local pathologies of the genitals: peripheric neuro-pathies, diabetes, other syndromes which could affect the sexual life. This exclusion was made with the collaboration of the medical examiner or other specialists.

The sample group was composed of subjects belonging to the lower middle-class living in central Italy, Latium and Tuscany.

Depressed patients who had requested treatment at the Sex Clinic section of our Institute were excluded from our study as they were clearly not representative of the population of depressives but formed a selective group. Also patients in psychotherapy were excluded, in order to evaluate more correctly the spontaneous recovery of the sexual repertoire, when the correction of the depression was obtained through pharmaceutics.

The patients were found through the collaboration of many psychiatrists from the Center for Mental Health, from the Psychiatric Hospital of Rome, the Center for the Study of Depression of the University of Pisa, and from some private clinics.

Statistical Test

The significance of differences $\overline{M1M2}$, $\overline{M2M3}$, $\overline{M1M3}$, relative to the three measurements of each behavioral unit, was calculated through the Wilcoxon Test.

RESULTS

The results must be considered preliminary and insufficient to verify all the above formulated hypotheses. Research is still being continued, in fact, on some subgroups of the sample, especially those of males whose number among patients was insufficient. These groups will not however be considered in this paper.

Frequency of Sexual Intercourse

Examining the frequency of sexual intercourse (Tables 2, 3), the first point to note is that in the complete group of male patients the tapering of depression (for both p<0.01) is more marked (from 4.3 to 6) than in the female group (from 4.3 to 5.4).

The second point concerns the extent of the tapering in relation to the intensity of the depressive state.

For the males the difference in the extent of tapering between the three groups (H1, H2, H3) is very marked. The more serious the depression the more marked is the tapering of frequency (for Hamilton 3, from 4.2 to 7.2; for Hamilton 1, from 4.1 to 4.8). For the females there is almost no difference in the extent of the drop in frequency (H1, 0.6; H2, 0.6; H3, 0.8).

Most likely these first two differences between the male and female can be attributed to the cultural and environmental conditioning on initiating sexual intercourse where even today it is more often the male who is active and the female passive.

Of definite interest is the extent of frequency tapering in the three groups distinguished by the quality of the marital relationship (L&W1, L&W2, L&W3), especially in the female where it is much more evident (L&W1, 1.71; L&W2 and L&W3 respectively 0.5 and 1.1). That is there is a greater drop in frequency of sexual intercourse in those subjects where the quality of the marital relationship was already poor before the onset of depression.

A consideration of another variable, the extent of damage to the marital relationship (evaluated by a drop in the Locke & Wallace point system between M1 and M2) which occurs at the time of the depressive episode, bears perhaps the most interesting point: group $\overline{L\&W3}$ with the greater damage (which makes us suspect a dynamic relationship between the factor "damage of the relationship" and the factor "depression," and hence an etiologic role of the latter), and males in $\overline{L\&W2}$ (the number of patients in $\overline{L\&W3}$ being too few) show clearly a greater tapering in frequency.

Unfortunately, we do not have enough time to explore in depth a cognitive aspect such as the desired frequency, but we can say that here the "double standard" effect can be found: the males would have desired a greater frequency (5) than that actually achieved in depression (5.7) while the females would have desired a lesser frequency (6.8 instead of 5.4).[1]

------

[1] It should be remembered that in our system of valuing, a higher point corresponds to a lower frequency.

TABLE 2

FREQUENCY OF SEXUAL ACTIVITY BY SAMPLE'S
SUBGROUPS AND BY CLINICAL MOMENTS (MALES)

Sample's Subgroups	Clinical Moment					
	Last phase free from depression		Acute depressive phase		Phase of partial or total remission	
Complete group:	M1	154	M2	227	M3	52
	mv [1]	4.36	mv	5.97	mv	5.7
	M1M2	p<0.01	M2M3	p<0.01	M1M3	p<0.01
H1:	M1	58	M2	68	M3	8
	mv	4.142	mv	4.85	mv	4
	M1M2	p<0.01	M2M3	p=0	M1M3	p<0.01
H2:	M1	58	M2	93	M3	31
	mv	3.866	mv	6.2	mv	6.2
	M1M2	p<0.01	M2M3	p<0.05	M1M3	p<0.01
H3:	M1	38	M2	65	M3	20
	mv	4.222	mv	7.222	mv	6.666
	M1M2	p<0.01	M2M3	p<0.01	M1M3	p<0.01
L&W1:	M1	48	M2	69	M3	9
	mv	4.363	mv	6.272	mv	9
	M1M2	p<0.01	M2M3	p<0.01	M1M3	p<0.01
D&W2:	M1	28	M2	49	M3	23
	mv	3.5	mv	6.125	mv	2.87
	M1M2	p<0.01	M2M3	p<0.05	M1M3	p<0.01
L&W3:	M1	78	M2	110	M3	8
	mv	4.105	mv	5.78	mv	4
	M1M2	p<0.01	M2M3	p = 0	M1M3	p<0.01
R1:	M1	101	M2	163	M3	30
	mv	3.607	mv	5.821	mv	1.71
	M1M2	p<0.01	M2M3	p<0.05	M1M3	p<0.01
R2:	M1	50	M2	54	M3	0
	mv	5.55	mv	6	mv	0
	M1M2	p<0.01	M2M3	p -	M1M3	p -
R3:	M1	6	M2	9	M3	9
	mv	6	mv	9	mv	9
	M1M2	p<0.01	M2M3	p<0.01	M1M3	p<0.01
L̄&W̄1̄:	M1	119	M2	172	M3	50
	mv	4.103	mv	5.931	mv	1.724
	M1M2	p<0.01	M2M3	p<0.02	M1M3	p<0.01
L̄&W̄2̄:	M1	18	M2	39	M3	0
	mv	3	mv	6.5	mv	0
	M1M2	p<0.05	M2M3	p -	M1M3	p -
L̄&W̄3̄:	M1	13	M2	15	M3	0
	mv	4.33	mv	5	mv	0
	M1M2	p<0.01	M2M3	p -	M1M3	p -

[1]mv = medium value for subject

TABLE 3

FREQUENCY OF SEXUAL ACTIVITY BY SAMPLE'S
SUBGROUPS AND BY CLINICAL MOMENTS (FEMALES)

Sample's Subgroups	Clinical Moment							
	Last phase free from depression			Acute depressive phase			Phase of partial or total remission	
Complete group:	M1	296		M2	371		M3	129
	mv [1]	4.289		mv	5.376		mv	4.961
	M1M2	p<0.01		M2M3	p<0.01		M1M3	p<0.01
H1:	M1	130		M2	145		M3	27
	mv	4.81		mv	5.37		mv	4.5
	M1M2	p<0.01		M2M3	p<0.01		M1M3	p>0.05
H2:	M1	126		M2	143		M3	53
	mv	4.66		mv	5.29		mv	4.81
	M1M2	p<0.01		M2M3	p<0.01		M1M3	p<0.01
H3:	M1	62		M2	74		M3	38
	mv	4.13		mv	4.93		mv	4.75
	M1M2	p<0.01		M2M3	p<0.05		M1M3	p<0.01
L&W1:	M1	88		M2	124		M3	68
	mv	4.19		mv	5.9		mv	5.66
	M1M2	p<0.01		M2M3	p=0		M1M3	p<0.01
L&W2:	M1	129		M2	138		M3	28
	mv	4.59		mv	5.11		mv	4
	M1M2	p<0.01		M2M3	p<0.01		M1M3	p<0.05
L&W3:	M1	89		M2	112		M3	24
	mv	4.23		mv	5.33		mv	4
	M1M2	p<0.01		M2M3	p<0.01		M1M3	p>0.05
R1:	M1	121		M2	154		M3	40
	mv	3.55		mv	4.529		mv	4.44
	M1M2	p<0.01		M2M3	p<0.01		M1M3	p<0.01
R2:	M1	126		M2	152		M3	76
	mv	4.846		mv	5.84		mv	5.06
	M1M2	p<0.01		M2M3	p=0		M1M3	p< 0.01
R3:	M1	54		M2	68		M3	9
	mv	6		mv	7.55		mv	4.5
	M1M2	p<0.01		M2M3	p<0.01		M1M3	p<0.01
L̄&W̄1:	M1	223		M2	275		M3	68
	mv	4.55		mv	5.61		mv	4.53
	M1M2	p<0.01		M2M3	p<0.01		M1M3	p<0.01
L̄&W̄2:	M1	49		M2	60		M3	23
	mv	3.76		mv	4.61		mv	4.6
	M1M2	p<0.01		M2M3	p<0.05		M1M3	p<0.05
L̄&W̄3	M1	26		M2	41		M3	25
	mv	3.71		mv	5.85		mv	6.25
	M1M2	p<0.01		M2M3	p=0		M1M3	p<0.01

[1]mv = medium value for subject

It seems that for the first group, the males, there is an effort to adjust to a good level of performance and for the second group, the females, there is a renewal of the original sexual guilt association.

Initiative in Sexual Intercourse

If we examine the behavioral component of the taking of initiative in sexual intercourse (Tables 4, 5), we note that this is much less subject to influence compared with other variables in the repertoire; the tendency however of the whole sample is significant ($p < 0.01$).

The average shift for both sexes (for males from 2.6 to 3.04; for females from 4.3 to 4.5) is expressed in only fractions of units in our scale of measurement in which the higher points correspond to a lower percentage of initiative.

An interesting point is that in this case the greater change appears in the group H3 both for the males (for H3, 0.7; for H2, 0; for H1, 0.2) and for the females (for H3, 0.4; for H2, 0.2; for H1, 0.2); that is, only high levels of depression are able to influence this exceptionally stable behavioral pattern. The only other element worthy of consideration is that the greatest value shift can be observed in that group of patients in which a greater damage to the relationship concomitant to the depression is noticeable, that is, L&W2 and L&W3; and also in this case both in the males (for L&W2, 0.9; for L&W1, 0.05) and in the females (for L&W3, 0.7; for L&W2, 1.4) and expresses nothing less than a reduction of the stimulus value of the partner or, anyway, a way to refuse.

Activity in Sexual Intercourse

Keeping in mind that for "activity" we mean the capacity to orient the sexual experience through one's own or one's partner's behavior towards the satisfaction of personal needs, we would point out that, in the sample population considered as a whole, (Tables 6, 7), there is, in depression, a slide towards the reduction of activity, statistically significant, although results were 0.5 and 0.4 units respectively for males and females in our scale.[2]

Therefore, there is a reduction in the "activity" in depression, whatever the preexisting level which, as can easily be imagined,

---

[2] In which also this time the increasing values refer to diminishing values in the degree of "activity."

TABLE 4

INITIATIVE IN SEXUAL INTERCOURSE BY SAMPLE'S
SUBGROUPS AND BY CLINICAL MOMENTS (MALES)

Sample's Subgroups	Clinical Moment		
	Last phase free from depression	Acute depressive phase	Phase of partial or total remission
Complete group:	M1 77	M2 70	M3 18
	mv [1] 2.96	mv 3.04	mv 2
	M1M2 p<0.01	M2M3 p<0.01	M1M3 p<0.01
H1:	M1 33	M2 36	M3 5
	mv 2.3	mv 2.57	mv 2.5
	M1M2 p<0.01	M2M3 p<0.01	M1M3 p<0.01
H2:	M1 29	M2 28	M3 17
	mv 1.93	mv 1.86	mv 3.4
	M1M2 p = 0	M2M3 p<0.01	M1M3 p<0.01
H3:	M1 17	M2 23	M3 2
	mv 1.88	mv 2.55	mv 1
	M1M2 p<0.01	M2M3 p<0.01	M1M3 p<0.01
L&W1:	M1 22	M2 27	M3 1
	mv 2	mv 2.45	mv 1
	M1M2 p<0.01	M2M3 p<0.01	M1M3 p<0.01
L&W2:	M1 18	M2 19	M3 12
	mv 2.25	mv 2.37	mv 2.4
	M1M2 p<0.01	M2M3 p<0.01	M1M3 p<0.01
L&W3:	M1 40	M2 42	M3 9
	mv 2.105	mv 2.21	mv 3
	M1M2 p<0.01	M2M3 p<0.01	M1M3 p<0.01
R1:	M1 60	M2 66	M3 15
	mv 2.142	mv 2.357	mv 1.87
	M1M2 p<0.01	M2M3 p<0.01	M1M3 p<0.01
R2:	M1 13	M2 14	M3 0
	mv 1.44	mv 1.55	mv 0
	M1M2 p<0.01	M2M3 p -	M1M3 p -
R3:	M1 1	M2 1	M3 1
	mv 1	mv 1	mv 1
	M1M2 p<0.01	M2M3 p<0.01	M1M3 p<0.01
$\overline{L\&W1}$:	M1 52	M2 54	M3 16
	mv 1.79	mv 1.86	mv 1.77
	M1M2 p<0.01	M2M3 p<0.01	M1M3 p<0.01
$\overline{L\&W2}$:	M1 15	M2 20	M3 0
	mv 2.5	mv 3.33	mv 0
	M1M2 p>0.05	M2M3 p -	M1M3 p -
$\overline{L\&W3}$:	M1 5	M2 6	M3 0
	mv 1.66	mv 2	mv 0
	M1M2 p<0.01	M2M3 p -	M1M3 p -

[1]mv = medium value for subject

TABLE 5

INITIATIVE IN SEXUAL INTERCOURSE BY SAMPLE'S
SUBGROUPS AND BY CLINICAL MOMENTS (FEMALES)

Sample's Subgroups	Clinical Moment		
	Last phase free from depression	Acute depressive phase	Phase of partial or total remission
Complete group:	M1 297	M2 307	M3 111
	mv^1 4.3	mv 4.5	mv 4.3
	M1M2 p<0.01	M2M3 p<0.01	M1M3 p = 0
H1:	M1 114	M2 123	M3 20
	mv 4.22	mv 4.55	mv 4
	M1M2 p<0.01	M2M3 p = 0	M1M3 p = 0
H2:	M1 118	M2 123	M3 50
	mv 4.37	mv 4.55	mv 4.54
	M1M2 p<0.01	M2M3 p = 0	M1M3 p<0.01
H3:	M1 65	M2 72	M3 34
	mv 4.33	mv 4.8	mv 4.25
	M1M2 p<0.01	M2M3 p<0.01	M1M3 p<0.01
L&W1:	M1 93	M2 102	M3 50
	mv 4.42	mv 4.85	mv 4.54
	M1M2 p<0.01	M2M3 p = 0	M1M3 p<0.01
L&W2:	M1 119	M2 121	M3 33
	mv 4.407	mv 4.48	mv 4.71
	M1M2 p<0.01	M2M3 p<0.01	M1M3 p<0.01
L&W3:	M1 86	M2 95	M3 25
	mv 4.09	mv 4.52	mv 4.16
	M1M2 p<0.01	M2M3 p<0.01	M1M3 p<0.01
R1:	M1 137	M2 152	M3 39
	mv 4.02	mv 4.47	mv 4.33
	M1M2 p<0.01	M2M3 p<0.01	M1M3 p = 0
R2:	M1 117	M2 122	M3 67
	mv 4.5	mv 4.69	mv 4.78
	M1M2 p<0.01	M2M3 p = 0	M1M3 p<0.01
R3:	M1 44	M2 44	M3 3
	mv 4.8	mv 4.8	mv 3
	M1M2 p<0.01	M2M3 p<0.01	M1M3 p<0.01
L&W1:	M1 213	M2 223	M3 56
	mv 4.34	mv 4.55	mv 4.3
	M1M2 p<0.01	M2M3 p<0.01	M1M3 p<0.01
L&W2:	M1 41	M2 61	M3 29
	mv 3.15	mv 4.6	mv 2.23
	M1M2 p<0.01	M2M3 p<0.01	M1M3 p<0.01
L&W3:	M1 27	M2 32	M3 15
	mv 3.85	mv 4.57	mv 5
	M1M2 p<0.01	M2M3 p<0.01	M1M3 p<0.01

[1] mv = medium value for subject

TABLE 6

ACTIVITY IN SEXUAL INTERCOURSE BY SAMPLE'S
SUBGROUPS AND BY CLINICAL MOMENTS (MALES)

Sample's Subgroups	Clinical Moment					
	Last phase free from depression		Acute depressive phase		Phase of partial or total remission	
Complete group:	M1	87	M2	106	M3	24
	mv [1]	2.28	mv	2.78	mv	2.66
	M1M2	p <0.01	M2M3	p = 0	M1M3	p <0.01
H1:	M1	32	M2	36	M3	7
	mv	2.28	mv	2.57	mv	2.33
	M1M2	p <0.01	M2M3	p <0.01	M1M3	p <0.01
H2:	M1	38	M2	44	M3	8
	mv	2.53	mv	2.93	mv	2
	M1M2	p <0.01	M2M3	p <0.01	M1M3	p <0.01
H3:	M1	20	M2	26	M3	3
	mv	2.22	mv	2.88	mv	1.5
	M1M2	p <0.01	M2M3	p <0.01	M1M3	p <0.01
L&W1:	M1	23	M2	29	M3	1
	mv	2.09	mv	2.63	mv	1
	M1M2	p <0.01	M2M3	p <0.01	M1M3	p <0.01
L&W2:	M1	18	M2	20	M3	11
	mv	2.25	mv	2.5	mv	2.2
	M1M2	p = 0	M2M3	p <0.01	M1M3	p <0.01
L&W3:	M1	47	M2	54	M3	8
	mv	2.47	mv	2.84	mv	2.66
	M1M2	p <0.01	M2M3	p <0.01	M1M3	p <0.01
R1:	M1	69	M2	81	M3	20
	mv	2.46	mv	2.89	mv	2.5
	M1M2	p <0.01	M2M3	p <0.01	M1M3	p <0.01
R2:	M1	17	M2	21	M3	0
	mv	1.88	mv	2.33	mv	0
	M1M2	p <0.01	M2M3	p -	M1M3	p -
R3:	M1	1	M2	5	M3	5
	mv	1	mv	5	mv	5
	M1M2	p <0.01	M2M3	p <0.01	M1M3	p <0.01
L̄&W̄1̄:	M1	66	M2	74	M3	20
	mv	2.27	mv	2.55	mv	2.22
	M1M2	p <0.01	M2M3	p <0.01	M1M3	p <0.01
L̄&W̄2̄:	M1	13	M2	21	M3	0
	mv	2.16	mv	3.5	mv	0
	M1M2	p <0.01	M2M3	p -	M1M3	p -
L&W3:	M1	8	M2	8	M3	0
	mv	2.66	mv	2.66	mv	0
	M1M2	p <0.01	M2M3	p -	M1M3	p -

[1] mv = medium value for subject

TABLE 7

ACTIVITY IN SEXUAL INTERCOURSE BY SAMPLE'S SUBGROUPS AND BY CLINICAL MOMENTS (FEMALES)

Sample's Subgroups	Clinical Moment		
	Last phase free from depression	Acute depressive phase	Phase of partial or total remission
Complete group:	M1 262 mv[1] 3.79 M1M2 p<0.01	M2 288 mv 4.17 M2M3 p<0.01	M3 103 mv 4.29 M1M3 p<0.01
H1:	M1 101 mv 3.74 M1M2 p<0.01	M2 109 mv 4.03 M2M3 p = 0	M3 21 mv 4.2 M1M3 p = 0
H2:	M1 104 mv 3.85 M1M2 p<0.01	M2 110 mv 4.07 M2M3 p<0.01	M3 48 mv 4.36 M1M3 p<0.01
H3:	M1 57 mv 3.8 M1M2 p<0.01	M2 68 mv 4.53 M2M3 p<0.01	M3 33 mv 4.125 M1M3 p = 0
L&W1:	M1 86 mv 4.09 M1M2 p<0.01	M2 97 mv 4.61 M2M3 p<0.01	M3 48 mv 4.36 M1M3 p = 0
L&W2:	M1 97 mv 3.59 M1M2 p<0.01	M2 105 mv 3.88 M2M3 p<0.01	M3 31 mv 4.42 M1M3 p<0.01
L&W3:	M1 77 mv 3.66 M1M2 p<0.01	M2 82 mv 3.904 M2M3 p<0.01	M3 25 mv 1.19 M1M3 p<0.01
R1:	M1 113 mv 3.32 M1M2 p<0.01	M2 129 mv 3.79 M2M3 p = 0	M3 35 mv 3.5 M1M3 p<0.01
R2:	M1 107 mv 4.11 M1M2 p<0.01	M2 116 mv 4.46 M2M3 p<0.01	M3 66 mv 2.53 M1M3 p<0.01
R3:	M1 43 mv 4.77 M1M2 p<0.01	M2 43 mv 4.77 M2M3 p<0.01	M3 8 mv 2 M1M3 p<0.01
L&W1 (overline):	M1 189 mv 3.857 M1M2 p<0.01	M2 203 mv 4.142 M2M3 p = 0	M3 64 mv 4.26 M1M3 p<0.01
L&W2 (overline):	M1 47 mv 3.61 M1M2 p<0.01	M2 54 mv 4.153 M2M3 p<0.01	M3 21 mv 4.2 M1M3 p<0.01
L&W3 (overline):	M1 27 mv 3.85 M1M2 p<0.01	M2 32 mv 4.57 M2M3 p<0.01	M3 19 mv 4.75 M1M3 p<0.01

[1]mv = medium value for subject

distinguishes clearly the male group (2.28) from the female group (3.79).

Moreover, as was valid for the previously examined concepts of "frequency" and "initiative" the most obvious changes are correlated with the intensity of the depression, and the concomitant damage to the quality of the relationship between the marital partners.

Capacity of Orgasmic Response

Two different stimulus situations were considered for orgasmic reactivity: touching of the external genitalia (Table 8) and coitus (Table 9).

If we consider the whole sample population we can observe that in depression a tendency in the reduction of orgasmic response capacity is verified for both situations examined,[3] which is less than one unit of measure (respectively 0.7 and 0.9, which corresponds to a change of 25% in the percentage of response), and is statistically significant, with complete correction on remission of the depression for the first (touching) and only slightly noticeable for the second (coitus). Also in this case the correlation between the extent of the percentage diminution of the orgasmic responses and the depression (Table 8: H3, 1.6, H2, 0.5, H1, 0.3; Table 9: H3, 1.6, H2, 1, H1, 0.5) is very clear in both the stimulus evaluated.

For the second time the correlation between the extent of the reduction of capacity of orgasmic response and the quality of the relationship with the partner pre-depression is strikingly clear. In those depressives with a more deteriorated marital relationship we can observe a more extensive reduction of the orgasmic potential, both in touching and in coitus, (L&W1 1.3, L&W2 0.5-0.9, L&W3 0.7).

Also to this factor can be added the by now familiar correlation between the extent of the damage to the marital relationship concomitant to depression (Table 9: $\overline{L\&W3}$, 1.3, $\overline{L\&W2}$, 1.15, $\overline{L\&W1}$, 0.5).

Erectile Response Capacity

Two different stimulus situations were considered for erectile response: foreplay (Table 10) and coitus (Table 11). In both cases

---

[3]This proved by increases in value on our scale in which the higher values indicate a lower percentage of orgasmic response.

TABLE 8

CAPACITY OF ORGASMIC RESPONSE IN TOUCHING OF THE EXTERNAL
GENITALIA BY SAMPLE'S SUBGROUPS AND CLINICAL MOMENTS (FEMALES)

Sample's Subgroups	Clinical Moment		
	Last phase free from depression	Acute depressive phase	Phase of partial or total remission
Complete group:	M1 212 mv[1] 3.07 M1M2 p<0.01	M2 259 mv 3.75 M2M3 p<0.01	M3 77 mv 2.96 M1M3 p<0.01
H1:	M1 84 mv 3.11 M1M2 p<0.01	M2 92 mv 3.407 M2M3 p = 0	M3 16 mv 3.2 M1M3 p>0.05
H2:	M1 93 mv 3.44 M1M2 p<0.01	M2 108 mv 4 M2M3 p<0.01	M3 41 mv 3.72 M1M3 p<0.01
H3:	M1 32 mv 2.13 M1M2 p<0.01	M2 58 mv 3.86 M2M3 p<0.02	M3 20 mv 2.5 M1M3 p<0.01
L&W1:	M1 66 mv 3.142 M1M2 p<0.01	M2 93 mv 4.42 M2M3 p<0.01	M3 40 mv 3.63 M1M3 p<0.01
L&W2:	M1 82 mv 3.03 M1M2 p<0.01	M2 97 mv 3.59 M2M3 p<0.01	M3 23 mv 3.28 M1M3 p<0.01
L&W3:	M1 54 mv 2.57 M1M2 p<0.01	M2 69 mv 3.28 M2M3 p<0.01	M3 14 mv 2.33 M1M3 p = 0
R1:	M1 58 mv 1.705 M1M2 p<0.01	M2 90 mv 2.64 M2M3 p = 0.01	M3 23 mv 2.55 M1M3 p = 0.02
R2:	M1 102 mv 3.92 M1M2 p<0.01	M2 117 mv 4.5 M2M3 p<0.01	M3 48 mv 3.69 M1M3 p<0.01
R3:	M1 50 mv 5.55 M1M2 p<0.01	M2 52 mv 5.77 M2M3 p<0.01	M3 6 mv 3 M1M3 p<0.01
L&W1 (overline):	M1 154 mv 3.142 M1M2 p<0.01	M2 182 mv 3.71 M2M3 p<0.01	M3 44 mv 2.93 M1M3 p<0.01
L&W2 (overline):	M1 35 mv 2.69 M1M2 p<0.01	M2 50 mv 3.84 M2M3 p<0.01	M3 14 mv 2.8 M1M3 p<0.01
L&W3 (overline):	M1 22 mv 3.142 M1M2 p<0.01	M2 30 mv 4.28 M2M3 p<0.01	M3 19 mv 4.75 M1M3 p<0.01

[1]mv = medium value for subject

TABLE 9

CAPACTIY OF ORGASMIC RESPONSE IN COITUS
SAMPLE'S SUBGROUPS AND BY CLINICAL MOMENTS (FEMALES)

Sample's Subgroups	Clinical Moment		
	Last phase free from depression	Acute depressive phase	Phase of partial or total remission
Complete group:	M1 191 mv[1] 2.76 M1M2 p<0.01	M2 251 mv 3.63 M2M3 p<0.01	M3 82 mv 3.41 M1M3 p<0.01
H1:	M1 74 mv 2.74 M1M2 p<0.01	M2 89 mv 3.29 M2M3 p = 0	M3 15 mv 3 M1M3 p>0.05
H2:	M1 74 mv 2.74 M1M2 p<0.01	M2 102 mv 3.77 M2M3 p<0.01	M3 38 mv 3.45 M1M3 p<0.01
H3:	M1 42 mv 2.8 M1M2 p<0.01	M2 65 mv 4.33 M2M3 p>0.05	M3 31 mv 3.87 M1M3 p<0.01
L&W1:	M1 62 mv 2.95 M1M2 p<0.01	M2 90 mv 4.28 M2M3 p<0.01	M3 42 mv 3.81 M1M3 p<0.01
L&W2:	M1 60 mv 2.22 M1M2 p<0.01	M2 84 mv 3.11 M2M3 p<0.01	M3 22 mv 3.14 M1M3 p<0.01
L&W3:	M1 52 mv 2.47 M1M2 p<0.01	M2 67 mv 3.19 M2M3 p<0.01	M3 20 mv 3.33 M1M3 p = 0
R1:	M1 76 mv 2.23 M1M2 p<0.01	M2 107 mv 3.14 M2M3 p<0.01	M3 30 mv 3.33 M1M3 p<0.01
R2:	M1 77 mv 2.96 M1M2 p<0.01	M2 100 mv 3.84 M2M3 p<0.01	M3 48 mv 3.69 M1M3 p<0.01
R3:	M1 43 mv 4.77 M1M2 p<0.01	M2 49 mv 5.44 M2M3 p<0.01	M3 6 mv 3 M1M3 p<0.01
$\overline{L\&W1}$:	M1 136 mv 2.77 M1M2 p<0.01	M2 171 mv 3.48 M2M3 p<0.01	M3 51 mv 3.4 M1M3 p = 0
$\overline{L\&W2}$:	M1 35 mv 2.69 M1M2 p<0.01	M2 58 mv 4.46 M2M3 p<0.01	M3 16 mv 3.2 M1M3 p<0.01
$\overline{L\&W3}$:	M1 19 mv 2.71 M1M2 p<0.01	M2 30 mv 4.28 M2M3 p<0.01	M3 17 mv 4.25 M1M3 p<0.01

[1]mv = medium value for subject

A. TAMBURELLO AND M. FELICIOTTI SEPPECHER

TABLE 10

ERECTILE RESPONSE CAPACITY IN FOREPLAY BY
SAMPLE'S SUBGROUPS AND BY CLINICAL MOMENTS (MALES)

Sample's Subgroups		Clinical Moment				
	Last phase free from depression		Acute depressive phase		Phase of partial or total remission	
Complete group:	M1	50	M2	97	M3	17
	mv [1]	1.315	mv	2.55	mv	1.888
	M1M2	p<0.01	M2M3	p = 0.02	M1M3	p<0.01
H1:	M1	15	M2	23	M3	2
	mv	1.071	mv	1.64	mv	1
	M1M2	p<0.01	M2M3	p<0.01	M1M3	p<0.01
H2:	M1	25	M2	50	M3	15
	mv	1.66	mv	3.33	mv	3
	M1M2	p<0.01	M2M3	p>0.05	M1M3	p<0.01
H3:	M1	9	M2	25	M3	3
	mv	1	mv	2.77	mv	1.5
	M1M2	p<0.01	M2M3	p = 0	M1M3	p<0.01
L&W1:	M1	21	M2	29	M3	6
	mv	1.909	mv	2.636	mv	6
	M1M2	p<0.01	M2M3	p<0.01	M1M3	p<0.01
L&W2:	M1	8	M2	18	M3	6
	mv	1	mv	2.25	mv	1.2
	M1M2	p<0.01	M2M3	p>0.05	M1M3	p<0.01
L&W3:	M1	22	M2	51	M3	8
	mv	1.15	mv	2.68	mv	2.66
	M1M2	p<0.01	M2M3	p = 0	M1M3	p<0.01
R1:	M1	28	M2	73	M3	14
	mv	1	mv	2.607	mv	1.75
	M1M2	p<0.01	M2M3	p<0.05	M1M3	p<0.01
R2:	M1	17	M2	21	M3	0
	mv	1.88	mv	2.33	mv	0
	M1M2	p = 0.01	M2M3	p -	M1M3	p -
R3:	M1	4	M2	6	M3	6
	mv	4	mv	6	mv	6
	M1M2	p<0.01	M2M3	p<0.01	M1M3	p<0.01
L&W1:	M1	34	M2	75	M3	20
	mv	1.172	mv	2.58	mv	2.22
	M1M2	p<0.01	M2M3	p = 0.02	M1M3	p<0.01
L&W2:	M1	11	M2	17	M3	0
	mv	1.83	mv	2.83	mv	0
	M1M2	p>0.05	M2M3	p -	M1M3	p -
L&W3:	M1	4	M2	6	M3	0
	mv	1.33	mv	2	mv	0
	M1M2	p<0.01	M2M3	p -	M1M3	p -

[1] mv = medium value for subject

TABLE 11

ERECTILE RESPONSE CAPACITY IN COITUS BY
SAMPLE'S SUBGROUPS AND BY CLINICAL MOMENTS (MALES)

Sample's Subgroups	Clinical Moment					
	Last phase free from depression		Acute depressive phase		Phase of partial or total remission	
Complete group:	M1	43	M2	83	M3	21
	mv [1]	1.131	mv	2.18	mv	2.33
	M1M2	p<0.01	M2M3	p = 0.02	M1M3	p<0.01
H1:	M1	14	M2	19	M3	2
	mv	1	mv	1.35	mv	1
	M1M2	p<0.01	M2M3	p<0.01	M1M3	p<0.01
H2:	M1	20	M2	42	M3	16
	mv	1.33	mv	2.8	mv	3.2
	M1M2	p<0.01	M2M3	p>0.05	M1M3	p<0.01
H3:	M1	9	M2	22	M3	3
	mv	1	mv	2.44	mv	1.5
	M1M2	p<0.01	M2M3	p = 0	M1M3	p<0.01
L&W1:	M1	16	M2	21	M3	6
	mv	1.45	mv	1.909	mv	6
	M1M2	p<0.01	M2M3	p<0.01	M1M3	p<0.01
L&W2:	M1	8	M2	18	M3	6
	mv	1	mv	2.25	mv	1.2
	M1M2	p<0.01	M2M3	p<0.01	M1M3	p<0.01
L&W3:	M1	24	M2	52	M3	8
	mv	1.26	mv	2.73	mv	2.66
	M1M2	p<0.01	M2M3	p<0.01	M1M3	p<0.01
R1:	M1	28	M2	62	M3	14
	mv	1	mv	2.21	mv	1.75
	M1M2	p<0.01	M2M3	p>0.05	M1M3	p<0.01
R2:	M1	14	M2	18	M3	0
	mv	1.55	mv	2	mv	0
	M1M2	p = 0.01	M2M3	p -	M1M3	p -
R3:	M1	2	M2	6	M3	6
	mv	2	mv	6	mv	6
	M1M2	p<0.01	M2M3	p<0.01	M1M3	p<0.01
L̄&W̄1:	M1	30	M2	67	M3	21
	mv	1.03	mv	2.31	mv	2.33
	M1M2	p<0.01	M2M3	p<0.05	M1M3	p<0.05
L̄&W̄2:	M1	11	M2	16	M3	0
	mv	1.83	mv	2.66	mv	0
	M1M2	p>0.05	M2M3	p -	M1M3	p -
L̄&W̄3:	M1	3	M2	3	M3	0
	mv	1	mv	1	mv	0
	M1M2	p<0.01	M2M3	p -	M1M3	p -

[1]mv = medium value for subject

we noted a tendency in the group considered towards reduction of
response capacity (foreplay, 1.2; coitus, 1.0) a quantitatively
small, but statistically significant figure, with an incomplete
spontaneous correction on remission of depression for the first
and no correction at all for the second of the two situations
considered. Also in this case the correlation of the handicap
to the intensity of the depressed state is clear (foreplay: H3,
1.75, H2, 1.7, H1, 0.6; coitus: H3 - H2, 1.45, H1, 0.35).

In three other groups we can see a greater reduction of the
erectile response capacity: in group defined R1, that is, with
a good sexual repertoire before the onset of depression[4] in $\overline{L\&W1}$,
that is with minimal concomitant damage in the marital relationship; and in L&W3, that is with a better quality of marital relationship preexisting the depression.

This seem to be due to the exceptionally low value (that is,
minimal difficulty in the erectile response) of the measurement
of baseline before depression, but indicates that this shift in
value does not go beyond a certain point even under less privileged
departure conditions.

CONCLUSIONS

We would like now to sum up the more important observations
which have emerged from evaluation of new points we have been able
to deal with in the time allotted.

First let us point out the, more than evident, relationship
between the "double standard," which in terminology more familiar
to us can be described as the differential historical conditioning
of the sexes, and the direction of the changes in the sexual repertoire in depression. Linked to this is the discovery of more
stable patterns (see "activity") and of more unstable behavioral
patterns in depression, connected always to the duration and
strength of the conditioning of a certain learned behavior.

Another point to remember is the clear correlation which has
emerged between the extent of the diminution and the intensity of

----

[4]Three categories of sexual repertoire were considered: good,
average, poor, arrived at through the evalution of 7 fundamental
behavioral items.

the depression (first hypothesis confirmed) evident in all the behavioral components considered.

The clinician must take heed of this and it is hoped that there will be maintained a dynamic and open mind towards the other important factor which is, the correlation between the level of concomitant damage to the marital relationship and the degree of limitation in the sexual repertoire found in all the behavioral units examined, and in both sexes, with a regularity and parallelism forming a real deep impression. When the onset of the depression is accompanied by damage to the marital relationship we can then see the fullest expression of damage to one of the behavioral instruments of relationship: the sexual one.

It is satisfying to discover, apropos to this point, that research methodologies, which foresee the examination of groups rather than single units, show, with unhoped for sensitivity, data coherent to certain psychodynamic and transitional observations.

That which in our introduction we defined as a "sometimes difficult protagonist" now appears to us confirmed in its "malignant" role in sexuality, but sufficiently redimensioned, if in no other way but quantitatively, with the exclusion of some situations indicated before in which its "malignant" connotation is more suitable, and which, moreover, explain the modest changes of the whole group.

We believe that there has been an artefact, a sexological artefact, which has created a frightening giant, because the point of observation (that of the sexologist) allowed evalutions only on a population already selected through the appearance of the sexual handicap.

Anyway, the hypotheses and the conclusions that have been presented are meant to be very tentative. We think that, in this area, the kind of questions we have been asking are in a state of flux. New possibilities suggest themselves continuosly and undoubtedly the hypotheses will have to be revised and new ones developed.

We do think we are developing methods for studying the relationship between depression and sexual behavior. Perhaps this constitutes progress.

REFERENCES

Bagadia, V.N. et al. (1972). A study of 258 male patients with
    sexual problems. Indian Journal Psyc. 14 (2): 143-151.

Bailey, H.R. (1973). Studies in depression: treatment of the
    depressed frigid woman. Medical Journal of Australia.

Brown, R.G. (1973). Sex ratio in relative of patients with af-
    fective disorders. Genet. Curriculum Bio. Psyc. 6 (3):
    307-309.

Hamilton, M. (1960). A rating scale for depression. Journal
    Neurol Neurosurg Psychiatr. 23 (56): 56-62.

Horn, H.G. (1971). Endougenous depression and sexual behavior.
    Fortschr Neurol Psychiatr. 39 (12): 668-699.

Knoff, W. (1975). Loss of libido in depressed woman. Medical As-
    pect of Human Sexuality Nov.: 83-89.

Renshaw, D.C. et al. (In Press). Somatic manifestation of de-
    pression. Excerpta Medica.

Winokur, G. and Roth, M. (1969). Manic Depressive Illness, C.V.
    Mosby Co., St-Louis.

SEXUAL DYSFUNCTION IN PATIENTS WITH NEUROLOGICAL DISORDERS

Per Olov Lundberg

Sweden

For the last five years at the Department of Neurology in Uppsala we have systematically studied the occurrence and symptomatology of sexual dysfunction in patients with all types of neurological disorders. Sexual problems may exist in many types of central and peripheral nerve lesions. In the following I shall concentrate on four different groups of patients, namely those with 1) hypothalamo-pituitary disorders, 2) temporal lobe lesions usually also resulting in epilepsy, 3) multiple sclerosis in a mild phase of the disease and 4) peripheral nerve disorders involving the sacral cord segments.

I have chosen these four groups because they represent four different types from the anatomical and physiological point of view and because these patients do not have a severe physical handicap as for example the paraplegics and quadriplegics. Besides, patients belonging to the groups mentioned are not uncommon in general practice and, sexual problems may be an early or sometimes even a presenting symptom (Lundberg, 1974).

METHODS

Information on the sexual life of the patients was obtained from careful personal case histories and, when possible, from their partners. Repeated interviews over a long period of time increased the reliability of information. Most of the patients have been under my care for many years.

The clinical examination included a general physical examination where special care was taken to study the body hair distribu-

129

tion, skin pigmentation, absence or presence of galactorrhea and
examination of the genital organs. Testicular volumes were measured. The neurological examination was especially directed to
the lower segments of the spinal cord. Voluntary contractions of
pelvic floor muscles such as the levator ani, the bulbocavernous
muscles, the ischiocavernous muscles and the muscles of the anal
sphincter were tested. Genital sensitivity was tested with a bio-
thesiometer. With the help of this apparatus the threshold for
vibration sense can be determined in different skin and mucocutaneus
areas. A number of reflexes were used to evaluate patients with
suspected lesions of segmental somatic nerves in the genital region
or in parts of the autonomic nervous system related to this region:

1. Scrotal reflex. This is a local, axonal reflex. A
slow vermicellar contraction of the dartos muscle (tunica dartos)
is provoked by application of a cold object to the scrotum, perineum or inner parts of the thigh. This reaction is often seen
spontaneously immediately after the patient has undressed. The
dartos muscle is contracted during full erection.

2. Cremasteric reflex. This reflex is superficial, somatic
and ipsilateral. The reflex arc goes through the genitofemoral
and ilioinguinal nerves. The reflex center lies in the lumbar
segments 1 - 2. This reflex is elicited by stroking the skin
on the upper inner aspect of the thigh with a blunt point. The
response consists of contraction of the cremasteric muscle on the
ipsilateral side, with elevation of the testicle. This muscle is
contracted during full erection. Absence of the cremasteric reflex
may result from a lesion of the central motor neuron and from a
lesion interrupting the peripheral reflex arc.

3. Bulbocavernosus reflex. This reflex is spinal, somatic
and bilateral. The reflex arc goes through the pudendal nerves
and the reflex center lies in the sacral cord segments 2 - 3.
The reflex is elicited by stroking or pinching the dorsum of
the glans penis or clitoris. The response consists of a contraction of the bulbocavernosus muscle and some other striated muscles
in the pelvic floor. Absence of the reflex may result from a lesion interrupting the reflex arc. The reflex may be exaggerated
following damage to the central motor neuron.

4. Superficial anal reflex. This reflex is superficial,
somatic and bilateral. The reflex arc goes through branches of
the pudendal nerves and the reflex center is located in the sacral
cord segments 2 - 4. In response to stroking of the skin in the
perineal region, the external anal sphincter visibly contracts.
Absence of the reflex may result from a lesion interrupting the
reflex arc. However, it may also be absent, or in certain cases
exaggerated, following a central motor neuron lesion.

5. Anal sphincter reflex or the internal anal reflex.
This reflex is supplied by sympathetic, postganglionic nerve fibres
passing through the hypogastric plexus and presacral nerves. The
reflex centre is probably located in the lumbar cord segments 1 -
2. On dilatation of the internal anal sphincter a contraction of
the sphincter is observed. Absence of this reflex may result especially from damage to the hypogastric plexus or presacral nerves.
The reflex is of special interest in investigating disorders of
seminal emission and in patients with retrograde ejaculation.

The routine laboratory investigation included blood tests for
assay of FSH, TSH, testosterone, oestradiol in women and prolactin
(Radioimmunoassay, L. Wide). Recently determination of sex hormone binding globulin in the blood has also been included. A skull
X-ray and visual field examination were performed in most cases.

In certain cases in addition, an intravenous glucose
tolerance test, an intravenous LH-RH test, mitotic and meiotic
chromosome analysis, seminal sample analysis and testicular biopsy
were included, as well as a series of EEGs, pelvic floor muscle
EMG, urodynamic tests, pneumoencephalography, Amipaque myelography
and spinal fluid protein studies. Computerized tomography of the
skull and brain will replace the pneumoencephalography.

SUBJECTS

The subjects were all patients from the Department of Neurology
in Uppsala (Sweden), with known or suspected neurological disorders
belonging to the four different groups. The hypothalamo-pituitary
patients, 140 altogether, constituted almost all cases of that kind
treated at the hospital for the last five years. The other three
groups also contained a large number of patients but these cases
were highly selected and the study is still in progress. I shall
therefore only give figures for the hypothalamo-pituitary patients.

FINDINGS

Patients with hypothalamo-pituitary disorders

It is well known that patients with pituitary tumors may
have sexual problems. It is believed that in many of these cases
this is due to a lack of androgen caused by combined gonadal and
adrenal gland insufficiency. Patients affected with sexual insufficiency caused by pituitary damage often notice a very obvious
decline both in libido and potency. This may come about rather
suddenly, during the course of a few months.

The present investigation included 65 males with tumors of
the sellar region. Forty-eight of the patients reported a decreased
or absent sexual libido and potency. This was the initial symptom
in 20 patients but in itself it did not lead to medical consultation in more than one case. The patients had usually suffered from
their sexual problems for quite a time before diagnosis.

A clear difference in the frequency of sexual insufficiency
was found when the patients were divided into two groups: one with
a small intrasellar tumor and the other with a larger tumor with
suprasellar extension. In the first group 11 out of 21 had decreased or absent libido and potency, while in the latter group
as many as 37 out of 42 patients had these problems. Nineteen of
the tumours were hormone producing; five of 11 acromegaly cases
had sexual problems, but as many as 7 out of 8 patients with prolactin producing tumors, irrespective of size, were affected in
this way.

Clinical hypoandrogenism was found in most cases and correlated
well with the loss of sexual libido and potency. The results of
radioimmunoassay of blood testosterone were below the limit for
healthy blood donors in 35 of the patients and were normal in only
five (Fig. 1). The testosterone values correlated very well with
the occurrence of sexual problems. It should be noted that in the
borderline cases with sexual insufficiency the tumors were either
prolactin producing or craniopharyngiomas involving the hypothalamus.

In 47 of the patients an LH-RH infusion test, with 100 mg, was
performed. The increase in serum LH was compared with that in a
control group of healthy males. There was a very obvious correlation between the results of these tests and the sexual libido and
potency. Eleven of the 14 patients with a normal response to LH-
RH, but only one of 33 with a pathological response, had normal
sexual functions.

For many reasons it was much more difficult to evaluate the
female tumor cases. Women are less concerned about a decrease in
libido but instead react rapidly when their menstrual periods disappear, which is the rule in patients with hypothalamo-pituitary disorders. However, the figures for the 75 females in the present
study were largely the same as those for the males in regard to the
relation between a decrease in libido and the occurrence, size and location of a tumor. Half of the acromegaly cases and all but one of
19 females with prolactin producing tumors noted a decrease or
absence of libido. The females with the so-called empty sella
syndrome usually noticed a decrease in libido. Low serum oestradiol
values correlated well with the sexual insufficiency, as did an absent response to intravenous LH-RH.

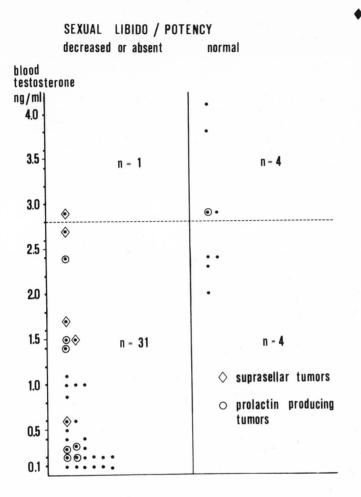

Fig. 1. Sexual libido and potency in 40 male patients with sellar tumors: blood testosterone N: 2.8 - 8.2 ng/ml.

All males were offered androgen substitution in the form of testosterone esters in a depot preparation and all females oestrogens orally and topically. This treatment was started after surgery, radiotherapy and substitution of other hormone deficiencies. However, some of the males, half of the females over 50 years of age and one third of the younger females declined such treatment despite much sound advice. They said that they and their partners had adapted themselves to a life without overt sexual activity and did not want any change. Cortisol and thyroxine substitution alone

did not normalize the sexual dysfunction. For most patients given
gonadal steroids the results were excellent in terms of both libido
and potency, frequency of sexual outlets and physical changes of
the sex organs. In some females injections of testosterone esters
had to be added to the treatment before normalization was achieved.

In 10 cases, however, both male and female, the gonadal steroids
had little or no effect despite normalization of the blood levels
of the steroids. These patients had either prolactin producing
tumors or extensive damage to the basal hypothalamus. The patients
with prolactin producing tumors are now being treated with bromo-
criptin, which has been claimed by other authors (Besser and Thorner, 1976) to restore sexual function in such cases. Unfortunately,
there does not seem to be any effective treatment for patients with
an extensive lesion in the supposed libido centre in the basal
hypthalamus.

Patients with Damage to the Temporal
Lobes Including Epilepsy

It has been reported many times that patients with focal brain
lesions with or without epilepsy may have symptoms of sexual dysfunction. Usually a decrease in libido is present and often there
are also erection or ejaculation problems in the males and anorgasm
in the females. In addition, patients with brain lesions sometimes
have gender identity problems and may show disorder of sexual object. Sexual delusions such as erotomania have also been described
in patients with brain lesion.

Since ancient times there has been considerable speculation
about the relationship between epileptic fits and sex. However,
from the neurophysiological point of view there are no similarities
between the psychic changes in orgasm and the unconsciousness in
the grand mal fit. In very rare cases orgasm can provoke a focal
epileptic fit. Genital sensations as well as genital motor activity
and orgasm can in themselves occur as focal epileptic manifestations.
An increase in sexual arousability may also be a post-paraxysmal
phenomenon after an epileptic fit.

It has been shown by other authors (Gastaut and Collomb, 1954;
Freemon and Nevis, 1969; Taylor, 1969; Bancaud et al., 1970; Blumer,
1970), that sexual problems are more common in patients with temporal lobe lesions, but the mechanisms are not completely understood. The present study was therefore concentrated on patients
with temporal lobe epilepsy. They all had typical EEG changes, but
showed no signs of a gross brain lesion. Patients with further
handicaps such as hemiparesis and mental retardation were not included.

In the present group of patients the most common finding was a decrease in libido and difficulty in becoming sexually aroused. This was found in both males and females. The males claimed that they had difficulty in achieving and maintaining an erection. This probably means that the mechanism of cerebral erection was impaired. Unfortunately, there is no objective method available for testing this mechanism. However, many patients declared that they had no problems in getting a reflex erection by genital stimulation, and if stimulated sufficiently, ejaculation and orgasm were possible.

As a rule, the patients did not perform better sexually during treatment with the anticonvulsive drugs phenobarbital, phenytoin or primidone. On the other hand, when the medication was changed to carbamazepine or benzodiazepines an increase in libido and in sexual arousability were sometimes noted. It is well know that antiepileptic drugs of the phenobarbital-phenytoin type have an effect on both the hypothalamo-pituitary-adrenal gland axis and on steroid metabolism. In a Danish study recently published (Christiansen et al., 1975), a decrease in androgen metabolites was found in the urine of males with epilepsy. This was hypothetically explained by an increase in steroid hormone metabolism due to induction of liver enzymes caused by the anticonvulsants. Another possible explanation of the decrease in androgen metabolites is that it is an effect of certain anticonvulsant drugs on sex hormone binding globulin, resulting in a decrease of active sex steroids in the blood (Victor et al., in press).

In none of the present cases was there any apparent increase in libido. On the other hand, three females presented symptomatology of rather severe erotomania. Four patients had epileptic fits which included disrobing, but this phenomenon may not necessarily be interpreted as a sexual symptom.

Patients with Multiple Sclerosis

In patients with multiple sclerosis, many different types of sexual dysfunction were observed. These sexual problems were often early symptoms appearing before gross disability. Typical of the symptoms was a rather sudden onset with the trouble often disappearing after a while. In more advanced cases the symptoms persisted indefinitely.

Impotence was found to be the most common symptom in the males. It may have been caused both by a lesion of the suprasegmental nerve tracts, or possibly by a lesion interrupting the reflex arc in the spinal cord. Most of the patients in early phases of the disease still had at least some erection capacity. It was often mentioned by a patient that he could no longer get an erection from fantasies or visual stimulation, whereas he could easily get full erection by genital manipulation. In other cases, normal erection occurred but there was ejaculatory failure.

In females, lack of vaginal lubrication and anorgasm were present as often as sexual dysfunction in the males.

Changes in sensitivity were very common in both sexes and the genital region was fairly often involved. There was almost never complete anaesthesia, but paraesthesias in the form of numbness or dysaesthesia were found. The deep sensitivity and vibration sense were more commonly lost than superficial cutaneous sensitivity. These changes had two different effects. Firstly, any kind of touch on the affected body region was disagreeable to the patients. These patients therefore avoided bodily contact, especially coitus. Secondly, when the vibration sense in the genital region was affected, sexual stimulation could no longer be achieved by direct genital contact. Probably the spinal nerve tracts conveying impulses from the specific mucocutaneous end-organs, sometimes called Krause's end-bulbs or genital corpuscles, located in the glans penis and clitoris, were interrupted.

The disturbed sensitivity mechanism sometimes produced another type of sexual disability. The patients complained of intense discomfort or even pain in the clitoris or glans penis just at the moment of orgasm. In addition, a decrease in libido was also reported by many patients with multiple sclerosis. However, this was more often found in advanced cases with considerable disability resulting in substantial social and psychological problems. In a few cases, an increase in libido was noted by the patient. This came about suddenly and disappeared again. In advanced cases, a certain sustained increase in libido was also noticed and in these patients it was interpreted as a part of a personality change in the direction of euphoria.

Sexual symptoms were often correlated with bladder disturbances and impaired perspiration. On the other hand, there was little correlation with ocular or cerebellar symptoms or with extremity paresis, unless the patient was almost totally paraplegic. For evaluation of these patients, it was therefore necessary to use the neurological examination methods mentioned, i.e., vibration sense, voluntary motor activity of pelvic floor muscles and genital reflexes. There were good correlations between positive findings in these examinations and sexual dysfunction. The occurrence of these signs may thus be taken as an indication of a somatic cause of the sexual problems in a particular patient.

There is no specific treatment of sexual problems in multiple sclerosis. The fact that in early and mild cases the symptoms are transitory often makes any treatment apart from counselling unnecessary. In other cases, the patients can be instructed in the use of

specific sexual stimulation or alternative methods of sexual activity. In motor dysfunction of the pelvic floor muscles these
muscles can be trained. In some cases, pain and discomfort caused
by sensitivity disturbances have been treated by local anaesthetics
with good results. Advanced cases of multiple sclerosis need further help of the same type as has been advocated for paraplegics.

Patients with Disorders of the Peripheral
Nerves Involving the Sacral Cord Segments

A lesion of the erection and ejaculation center in the spinal
cord usually results in complete sexual incapacity. However, disorders involving the peripheral nerves going from these centers to
the sex organs, as a rule, only partially interrupt the efferent
and afferent nerve fibres, leading to incomplete failure.

A unilateral rhizopathy of the sacral nerve II or III gives
ipsilateral impairment of the sensitivity of all qualities in parts
of the penis, scrotum, vulva and vagina (Bohm et al., 1956). Usually this does not cause impotence, ejaculatory failure or anorgasm.
Only in those cases where these sacral nerves have been affected
bilaterally is the ability to produce or maintain an erection
seriously affected and ejaculation impossible. Equivalent reactions of the female genital organs are also affected in a similar
way. Sequestrated disc hernias and arachnoiditis may lead to such
results.

However, the pain radiation into the genital organs that usually occurs in sacral rhizopathy is the problem that gives rise to
most of the sexual dysfunction in these patients. This pain may
be very intense at the moment of orgasm or sometimes shortly afterwards. Surgery is usually the best treatment for the rhizopathy
patients.

Polyneuropathy is another type of disorder that sometimes involves both the autonomic nerves and the somatic nerves going to
the genital organs. In the vast majority of cases this polyneuropathy is caused by diabetes mellitus. Alcoholic polyneuropathy
or polyneuropathy caused by intoxications or inborn errors of
metabolism are also common. Partial impotence is seen in about
50 per cent of all males with diabetes, according to most authors
(Neubauer, 1971; Ellenberg, 1971; Kolodny, 1971, 1974). Disturbed
sexual response in females was found in about the same frequency
in the present study. The patients complained, for example, of
diminished vaginal lubrication. Some kind of ejaculatory response
and orgasm was usually present but the patients sometimes declared
their experience of the orgasm to have been changed. Retrograde

ejaculation has been described by other authors (Greene et al.,
1963) in a few per cent of diabetic males. This symptom is caused
by a neuropathy of the sympathetic nerves innervating the internal
bladder sphincter.

Diabetic patients with sexual dysfunction often had a reduced
vibration sense in their genital organs. Genital reflex disturbances were also found. Tests of sensitivity, reflexes and voluntary
pelvic floor muscle activity were therefore of great importance in
evaluating these cases, as well as those with rhizopathy. Electro-
myography of the pelvic floor muscle was also useful. Impotence
was often an early symptom in diabetic males. Unfortunately, the
prognosis in this respect, is unfavorable in most cases.

Sexual counselling and instruction in the use of alternative
methods of sexual activity, including technical devices, seems to
be the only help that can be offered at this time. Causal treatment
of the underlying disease is possible only in a limited number of
the polyneuropathy patients.

CONCLUSION

This paper was presented to give some examples of sexual dysfunction that may exist in patients with neurological disorders.
Neurological disorders are quite common in most age groups. However, it seems to be completely unknown to what an extent neurological disorders are the acutal cause of sexual problems in the
general population.

REFERENCES

Bancaud, J., Favel, P., Bonis, A., Bordas-Ferrer, M., Miravet, J.
        and Talairach, J. (1970). Manifestations sexuelles paro-
        xystiques et épilepsie temporale. Rev. neurol. 123: 217-
        230.

Besser, G.M. and Thorner, M.O. (1976). Bromocriptine in the treat-
        ment of the hyperprolactinaemia-hypogonadism syndromes.
        Postgrad. Med. J. 52. Suppl. 1: 64-70.

Blumer, D. (1970). Hypersexual episodes in temporal lobe epilepsy.
        Amer. J. Psychiat. 126: 1099-1106.

Bohm, E., Franksson, C. and Petersén, I. (1956). Sacral rhizo-
    pathies and sacral root syndromes (SII-S V). Acta Chirurg.
    Scand. Suppl. 216: 5-49.

Christiansen, P., Deigaard, J. and Lund, M. (1975). Potens, fer-
    tilitet og kønshormonudskillelse hos yngre mandlige epilep-
    silidende. Ugeskr. Laeg. 137: 2402-2405.

Ellenberg, M. (1971). Impotence in diabetes: the neurologic fac-
    tor. Ann. Int. Med. 75: 213-219.

Freemon, F.R. and Nevis, A.H. (1969). Temporal lobe sexual seizures.
    Neurology. 19: 87-90.

Gastaut, H. and Collomb, H. (1954). Etude du comportement sexuel
    chez les épileptiques psychomoteurs. Ann. Méd.-Psych. 112:
    657-696.

Greene, L.F., Kelalis, P.P. and Weeks, R.E. (1963). Retrograde
    ejaculation of semen due to diabetic neuropathy. Fertil.
    Steril. 14: 617-625.

Kolodny, R.C. (1971). Sexual dysfunction in diabetic females.
    Diabetes. 20: 557-559.

Kolodny, R.C., Kahn, C.B., Goldstein, H.H. and Barnett, D.M. (1974).
    Sexual dysfunction in diabetic men. Diabetes. 23: 306-309.

Lundberg, P.O. (1974). Sexual function in men with neurological
    disorders. In Hafez, E.S.E. (ed.), Human Semen and Fer-
    tility Regulation in Men, C.V. Mosby Co., St-Louis.

Neubauer, M. (1971). Die Behandlung von Potenzstörungen beim
    Diabetiker. Therapiwoche. 21: 614-620.

Taylor, D.C. (1969). Sexual behavior and temporal lobe epilepsy.
    Arch. Neurol. 21: 510-516.

Victor, A., Lundberg, P.O. and Johansson, E.D.B. (1977). Induction
    of sex hormone binding globulin by fenytoin. Br. Med. J.,
    In press.

Not very thorough review of outcome studies.

EFFECTIVENESS OF SEX THERAPY

Sallie Schumacher

United States

The purpose of this paper is to review the published data concerned with sex therapy with regard to effectiveness of present treatment methods.

BACKGROUND

Treatment approaches to problems of sexual dysfunction vary considerably and are related directly to the therapist's background, training, and personal philosophy. In this paper, treatment methods have been grouped into six main categories based upon what the author of the study described as the primary treatment method: (1) Psychoanalysis; (2) Psychotherapy; (3) Desensitization; (4) Masters and Johnson; (5) Modified Masters and Johnson; (6) Group Therapy.

1. As a therapy, psychoanalysis has as its goal the resolution of conflicts originating in certain stages of the patient's psychological development, with exploration and reorientation of the total personality rather than limited, direct focus upon a single symptom such as a specific sexual disability. O'Connor and Stern (1972), however, designed a study to evaluate the effectiveness of psychoanalysis and psychotherapy specifically with respect to the isolated symptom of sexual dysfunction. Psychotherapy in this study was defined as psychoanalytically oriented therapy.

2. Psychotherapy in the other studies to be reviewed was described as: exploration of personality traits and their influence on sexual activity, explanation of anatomy and physiology,

and medication when necessary (Lesnenko, 1967); superficial psychotherapy consisting of explanation, education, reassurance and support, combined with sex education and relaxation techniques (Cooper,
1968; 1969; 1970); insight therapy, sometimes combined with physical examination (Faulk, 1971); directive psychotherapy, sex education, and drugs and medication as indicated (Bailey, 1973).

3.   Desensitization is a fundamental technique of behavior
therapy in which anxiety responses are deconditioned by exposing
the patient to graded anxiety producing stimuli, either verbal or
situational, under conditions of relaxation and acceptance.

Desensitization procedures applied to the treatment of sexual
dysfunction are designed to alleviate sexual performance anxiety
and, usually, are combined with other interventions, such as, drug
therapy (Friedman, 1968; Friedman and Lipsedge, 1971), education
in sexual technique (Lobitz and LoPiccolo, 1972), and assertive-
ness training (Obler, 1973).

4.   Masters and Johnson (1976) advocate an authoritative,
educational approach to problems of sexual dysfunction. They
adhere to a rigid psychotherapeutic format which consists of:
treatment of the sexually distressed couple as a unit, treatment
by a male/female therapy team, isolation of the dysfunctional
couple from its everyday family and work setting, participation
in the therapy program on a daily basis for a two week period of
time, and five years of treatment follow-up.

Because this approach is not practical for most patients and,
sometimes, not appropriate (Raboch, 1974), there are no reports in
the literature on the effectiveness of this particular treatment
method other than that presented by Masters and Johnson.

5.   Other therapists have modified the approach of Masters
and Johnson without apparent loss of treatment effectiveness. One
major change introduced by almost all therapists is treatment of
patients within their everyday social setting on a weekly basis.
Other modifications include: more attention given to psychiatric
diagnoses (Meyer, et al., 1975); more extensive biochemical and
physiological diagnoses and treatment (Schumacher & Lloyd, 1976);
treatment by only one therapist (Bianco, 1974; Kaplan, 1974; Mc
Carthy, 1973; Prochaska & Marzilli, 1973); the integration of sex
therapy technique with more traditional psychodynamic therapy
(Kaplan, 1974; Panel Highlights, 1976).

6.   There are three reports in the literature of group therapy
as a specific treatment method for sexual dysfunction. In two
studies (Barbach, 1976; Lesnenko, 1967), patients in the group
shared a common dysfunction and group discussion was structured

by the leader to include sex education and explanation as well as
sharing of experiences by the group members. In a third study
(Obler, 1973), group therapy was "traditional" in orientation with
the focus on open discussion of the participants' sexual and social
problems. The group leaders provided analytical interpretations
of etiology and recommendations for overcoming the dysfunction.
In addition, films and slides of specific sexual content were used.

Laughren and Kass (1975) have carefully reviewed the literature describing desensitization of sexual dysfunction, and Munjack
and Kanno (1976) have reviewed treatment methods and effectiveness
in problems of frigidity. Some of the studies they include are
not reviewed here because of methodological problems. The present
review does not include: single case studies, studies with fewer
than 10 subjects, or studies in which general, over-all results
are presented, rather than definitive results for the specific
sexual dysfunctions (Fabbri, 1976; Schumacher and Lloyd, 1974).
Also omitted from this review are two major reports which emphasize theory and technique, generalize about treatment effectiveness, but do not report specific results (Hartman and Fithian,
1972; Kaplan, 1974). There also may be unintentional omission of
important studies.

PROBLEMS IN CRITICAL ANALYSIS

Any attempt to analyze critically what is presently known
about the effectiveness of sex therapy meets head-on with so many
problems that, at first, the task seems impossible. Some of these
problems are: (a) lack of agreement in the use of diagnostic
labels; (b) imprecision in diagnosis; (c) differences in training
and orientation of therapists; (d) inconsistencies in definitions
of terms and concepts; (e) differences in selection of patients;
(f) variable definitions of success and failure; (g) problems of
adequate follow-up.

Most of these problems are interrelated. For many years,
impotence and frigidity have been general terms used to describe
sexual dysfunction in males and females. However, specific categories of impotence and frigidity have been defined differently
by separate investigators and clinicians according to their training, experience, and theoretical orientation. Correspondingly,
definitions of treatment success and failure are directly related
to problem diagnosis and the defined goals of treatment.

For example, in the 17 studies reviewed for this paper, there
were nine distinct categories of impotence, six separate descriptions of ejaculatory disorders, thirteen different definitions of
orgasmic dysfunction, and twelve varying definitions of treatment
success and failure.

A similar situation existed with regard to methods of patient selection. Four investigators (Cooper, 1968; 1969; 1970; Faulk, 1971; Johnson, 1965; O'Connor and Stern, 1972) reported that their patients presented in a psychiatric outpatient clinic with a primary complaint of sexual dysfunction; four (Bailey, 1973; Barbach, 1976; Bianco, 1974; Lesnenko, 1967) were unclear about their patient referrals. One therapist (Lazarus, 1963) selected only difficult cases with histories of previous psychotherapeutic failure, and in five studies (Friedman and Lipsedge, 1971; Jones and Park, 1972; Lobitz and LoPiccolo, 1972; Masters and Johnson, 1970; Meyer, et al., 1975), only highly selected patients who were well motivated and without neurotic or psychotic disorder of serious consequence were treated. In all studies, some attempt was made to eliminate from treatment patients with obvious physical disease associated with sexual dysfunction.

Although the follow-up data of Masters and Johnson are confused and unclear, they take a firm position about the importance of long-term follow-up in the evaluation of therapeutic effectiveness. They insist that treatment has no significant value if the positive results of improved sexual functioning observed at the end of their two-week acute treatment phase are not maintained for a minimum of five years (Masters and Johnson, 1970).

There are many methodological problems involved in adequate follow-up studies. Some investigators interested in long-term treatment results consider follow-up data from three to twelve months after treatment to be adequate. Other investigators do not consider follow-up to be an essential part of treatment.

While differences in opinion, methods, and interpretation can be expected, it is important to be aware of what these differences are and how they may influence the interpretation of and approach to problems of sexual dysfunction. As existing reports are examined, the significance of the difficulties involved in critical analysis of different studies will be readily apparent. At the same time, however, some consistent information emerges, and certain themes and patterns appear which warrant comparisons of studies even in the face of these difficulties.

TREATMENT EFFECTIVENESS

Table 1 shows five different treatment methods and their effectiveness in the treatment of problems of impotence in terms of percentage of patients who were cured or improved. Whether or not follow-up is part of the study is also shown. While Masters and Johnson report their data using failure rates, for purposes of comparison it is assumed that their non failures are either cured or improved.

TABLE 1

TREATMENT METHODS AND EFFECTIVENESS: IMPOTENCE

Therapy	Authors	Number of Patients	Cured or Improved	Follow-up
Psycho-analysis	O'Connor & Stern, 1972.	unclear	86%	yes
Psycho-therapy	Cooper, 1968, Johnson, 1965, *Lesnenko, 1967, O'Connor & Stern 1972	31 21 300 unclear	42% 52% 85% 57%	no yes yes yes
Desensiti-zation	*Friedman & Lipsedge, 1971	19	74%	yes
Masters & Johnson	Masters & Johnson, 1970	245	72%	yes
Group Therapy	*Lesnenko, 1967	300	90%	yes

* Combined with drugs or medication.

In Table 1, it can be seen that with the five different approaches, treatment results can be comparable. The higher rates
of improvement, 86%, 85% and 90% compared with 74% and 72% may be
explained by the fact that erectile problems and ejaculatory disorders are combined by O'Connor and Stern, and Lesnenko. Masters
and Johnson report a very high rate of reversal for ejaculatory
disorders.

The Cooper (1968) and Johnson (1965) studies, showing only
42% and 52% improvement, are reports of treatment of unselected
patients from a general psychiatric setting. In the report of
O'Connor & Stern (1972), there is an obvious discrepancy between
the improvement rate of 86% in patients treated by psychoanalysis
and 57% in those who had psychotherapy. This, in part, may be

explained by O'Connor and Stern's statement that patients who had psychoanalysis had less mental illness than those who received psychotherapy.

In the Lesnenko (1967), and Friedman & Lipsedge (1971) studies, both patient selection and psychological status of the patient are unclear.

Table 2 shows three treatment methods for ejaculatory disorders. Here, again, higher improvement rates are reported for selected patients. In Cooper's study (1969), three separate types of premature ejaculation were identified. Type 1: premature ejaculation with good erections that has been present constantly since adolescence. Type 2: acute onset premature ejaculation, sometimes with insufficient erection. Men in this category were comparatively inexperienced, inhibited, and had little sexual knowledge. Premature ejaculation had come on acutely in response to a discrete physical or psychological precipitant. Type 3: premature ejaculation with insidious onset combined with poorly formed or absent erections. The most significant feature of this group was a gradual decline in erotic interest and performance over

TABLE 2

TREATMENT METHODS AND EFFECTIVENESS:
EJACULATORY DISORDERS

Therapy	Authors	Number of Patients	Cured or improved	Follow-up
Psycho-therapy	Cooper, 1969 Premature Ejaculation	30	43%	no
Masters & Johnson	Masters & Johnson 1970 Ejaculatory Incompetence	17	82%	yes
	Premature Ejaculation	186	99%	yes
Masters & Johnson Modified	Bianco, 1974	32	100%	no

months or years. The figure of 43% improvement in Table 2 represents the over-all improvement rate for the three types of
premature ejaculation. In Type 2, the acute onset group in which
the men were anxious and needed education and experience, psychotherapy was effective in 86% of the cases.

Table 3 summarizes different treatment methods and their effectiveness in the improvement of orgasmic dysfunction in females.

TABLE 3

TREATMENT METHODS AND EFFECTIVENESS:
FEMALE DYSFUNCTION

Therapy	Authors	Number of Patients	Cured or Improved	Follow-up
Psycho-analysis	O'Connor & Stern, 1972	unclear	73%	yes
Psycho-therapy	*Bailey, 1973	100	85%	no
	Cooper, 1970	50	48%	no
	Faulk, 1971	40	43%	no
	O'Connor & Stern, 1972	unclear	38%	yes
Desensi-tization	*Jones & Park, 1972	69	89%	no
	Lazarus, 1963	16	56%	yes
	Lobitz & Lo-Piccolo, 1972	22	73%	yes
	Obler, 1973	13	85%	yes
Masters & Johnson	Masters & Johnson, 1970	342	81%	yes
Masters & Johnson Modified	Bianco, 1974	16	66%	no
	Meyer et al., 1975	14	79%	yes
Group Therapy	Obler, 1973	11	37%	unclear
	Barbach, 1976	17	88%	yes

*Combined with drugs or medication

Here, it is also noted that higher treatment success rates occur
in patient populations in which criteria for selection include
absence of serious psychological and/or difficult marital problems
(Lobitz and LoPiccolo, 1972; Obler, 1973; Masters and Johnson, 1970;
Meyer et al., 1975). Conversely, with one exception (Obler, 1973,
Group Therapy), lower success rates are associated with unselected
and more disturbed patients (Cooper, 1970; Faulk, 1971; Lazarus,
1963; O'Connor & Stern, 1972, Psychotherapy).

PRESENT STATUS

From this brief review, several generalizations can be made
about therapy methods and results. As has been shown in some outcome studies of psychotherapy in general, much of the variance
associated with therapy outcome can be accounted for by initial
patient variables rather than specific treatment methods. From
present reports, evidence seems to indicate that positive results
in sex therapy are obtained in well-motivated patients who begin
therapy with a minimum of personal and interpersonal difficulty,
and in patients in whom the sexual dysfunction is associated with
anxiety and inexperience.

Two other factors related to successful treatment outcome are:
acute onset of distress, and association of the distress with a
specific, identifiable psychological trauma such as divorce, un-
faithfulness, illness or death of a spouse. In most studies, the
importance of a cooperative, loving, and understanding partner was
emphasized. Even in therapies in which only one person was treated,
partner cooperation was mentioned as an important factor in treatment outcome.

The historical development of medical specialties and psychotherapy is marked by a more or less predictable sequence. In nearly
all instances, various kinds of therapy have been accepted and
promoted by both practitioner and patient before adequate attention
has been given to basic scientific and technical aspects. Advances
in practice tend to precede integrated scientific knowledge. The
announcement of new treatment methods in psychotherapy has usually
been followed by exaggeration and oversimplification of their role
in modifying complex behavioral disorders. Initial enthusiasm then
gives way to systematic interest, and longer, more careful investigation.

If we ask the question, "Where are we now in the field of sex
therapy and research?", we find: (1) Sex is accepted professionally
and publically as a legitimate area of treatment and study. (2)
Present methods of treatment appear to be comparably effective
when used with selected patient populations. (3) High rates of

treatment success are reported when sexual dysfunction is primarily the result of anxiety and fear, or lack of information. (4) In unselected patient populations, there is a hard core of patients with sexual dysfunction with which no present method is successful.

If the goal in sex therapy is to cure people of sexual dysfunction, it should be recognized that methods currently in use are effective only in some cases and of limited value in others. It should also be recognized that there is almost total lack of information about the subtle physiological events involved in normal sexual response, and their variations in patients with sexual disorder. As has been appropriately pointed out, "Masters and Johnson's physiological investigations have focused primarily on the correlates of sexual response at the peripheral organ level." Little is known about systemic effects.

Further emphasis on demonstrations that one particular treatment method is better than another, does not appear to be a productive means of achieving the goal of increased effectiveness in the treatment of sexual dysfunction.

At the American Psychiatric Association meeting in 1976, a panel of experts, led by Levay, agreed that current, short-term, directive treatment approaches to sexual dysfunction need to be combined with psychodynamic concepts for maximum effectiveness (Panel Highlights, 1976). In addition, attention must be redirected toward increasing the small body of knowledge now available concerning basic physiological mechanisms and their relationship to psychological processes and behavior.

REFERENCES

Bailey, H.R. (1973). Studies in depression, II. Treatment of the depressed, frigid woman. Med. J. Aust. 1: 834-837.

Barbach, L.G. (1976). For Yourself: The Fulfillment of Female Sexuality. Anchor Press/Doubleday, New York.

Bianco, F.J. (1974). Marital sexual dysfunction: Presentation of a fundamental therapeutic program. Paper presented at the meeting of the International Congress of Sexology, Paris.

Cooper, A.J. (1968). A factual study of male potency disorders. Br. J. Psychiatry, 114: 719-731.

Cooper, A.J. (1969). Clinical and therapeutic studies in premature ejaculation. Comp. Psychiatry, 10: 285-295.

Cooper, A.J. (1970). Frigidity, treatment and short-term prognosis. J. Psychosom. Res., 14: 133-147.

Fabbri, R., Jr. (1976). Hypnosis and behavior therapy: a coordinated approach to the treatment of sexual disorders. Am. J. Clin. Hypn., 19: 4-8.

Faulk, M. (1971). Factors in the treatment of frigidity. Br. J. Psychiatry, 119: 53-56.

Friedman, D. (1968). The treatment of impotence by Brietal relaxation therapy. Behav. Res. Ther., 6: 257-261.

Friedman, D. E. and Lipsedge, M.S. (1971). Treatment of phobic anxiety and psychogenic impotence by systematic desensitization employing Methohexitone - induced relaxation. Br. J. Psychiatry, 118: 87-90.

Hartman, W.E. and Fithian, M.A. (1972). Treatment of Sexual Dysfunction. Center for Marital & Sexual Studies, Long Beach, Calif.

Johnson, J. (1965). Prognosis of disorders of sexual potency in the male. J. Psychosom. Res., 9: 195-200.

Jones, W.J. and Park, P.M. (1972). Treatment of single-partner sexual dysfunction by systematic desensitization. Obstet. Gynecol., 39: 411-417.

Kaplan, H.S. (1974). The New Sex Therapy. Brunner/Mazel, New York.

Laughren, T.P. and Kass, D. (1975). Desensitization of sexual dysfunction: the present status. In A. Gurman & D. Rice (Eds.), Couples in Conflict, Aronson, New York.

Lazarus, A.A. (1963). The treatment of chronic frigidity by systematic desensitization. J. Nerv. Ment. Dis. 136: 272-278.

Lesnenko, W.N. (1967). Vergleichende Katamnese von Kranken mit funktioneller Impotenz, die mit aufklärender Individual - und Gruppenpsychotherapie behandelt wurden. Psychiatr. Neurol. Med. Psychol., 19: 215-218.

Lobitz, W.C. and LoPiccolo, J. (1972). New methods in the behavioral treatment of sexual dysfunction. J. Behav. Ther. Exp. Psychiatry, 3: 265-271.

Masters, W.H. and Johnson, V.E. (1970). Human Sexual Inadequacy. Little, Brown, Boston.

Masters, W.H. and Johnson, V.E. (1976). Principles of the new sex
    therapy. Am. J. Psychiatry, 133: 548–554.

McCarthy, B.W. (1973). A modification of Masters and Johnson sex
    therapy model in a clinical setting. Psychother. Theory
    Res. Practice, 10: 290–293.

Meyer, J., Schmidt, C.W., Jr., Lucas, M.J. and Smith, E. (1975).
    Short-term treatment of sexual problems: Interim report.
    Am. J. Psychiatry, 132: 172–176.

Munjack, D. and Kanno, P. (1976). An overview of outcome on
    frigidity: treatment effects and effectiveness. Comp.
    Psychiatry, 17: 401–413.

Obler, M. (1973). Systematic desensitization in sexual disorders.
    J. Behav. Ther. Exp. Psychiatry, 4: 93–101.

O'Connor, J.F. and Stern, L.O. (1972). Results of treatment in
    functional sexual disorders. N.Y. State J. Med., 72: 1927–
    1934.

Panel Highlights (1976). Modification of Masters-Johnson sex
    therapy utilize psychodynamics. Roche Rep.: Frontiers of
    Psychiatry, 5, October, pp. 1–2.

Prochaska, J.O. and Marzilli, R. (1973). Modifications of the
    Masters and Johnson approach to sexual problems. Psycho-
    ther. Theory Res. Practice, 10: 294–296.

Raboch, J. (1974). Causes and therapy of male impotency. Paper
    presented at the meeting of the International Congress of
    Medical Sexology, Paris.

Schumacher, S., and Lloyd, C.W. (1974). Interidsciplinary treat-
    ment and study of sexual distress. Paper presented at the
    meeting of the International Congress of Medical Sexology,
    Paris.

Schumacher, S., and Lloyd, C.W. (1976). Assessment of sexual
    dysfunction. In Hersen, M. and Bellack, A.S. (Eds.),
    Behavioral Assessment: A Practical Handbook, Pergamon
    Press, New York.

M + J better > communication training for ♀ complainants. Results ē both not v. good ē ♂ subjects.

COMPARATIVE STUDIES OF SHORT-TERM TREATMENT METHODS FOR SEXUAL INADEQUACIES

Walter Everaerd

The Netherlands

Since 1972 a number of comparative studies of short-term methods for the treatment of sexual inadequacies have been conducted.[1] Three of these studies are now completed. This paper is a brief summarization of some of the main data. My presentation will cover: 1) treatments studied, 2) designs, and 3) a brief report of results.

The following research questions were formulated at the studies inception.

1. Can a difference in effect be established between a number of widely used treatment strategies?

2. Can the treatment procedure in a therapist's manual be so formulated that the treatment can be carried out in a simple and uniform way?

3. Can treatments be carried out by therapists with minimum training?

The questions originated from our cooperation with a number of assistance organizations. The organizations are limited in their financial and personnel resources. Thus for their service they prefer short-term effective and inexpensive treatments.

---

[1] These studies were conducted in cooperation with Dr. Herwig Schacht and several students of our department.

METHODOLOGY

Methods of Treatment

The treatment methods studied included:

1. An adaptation of the treatment of Masters and Johnson
(1970): from their description of treatment methods, an approximate procedure which consisted of six phases was adapted.

2. A variant of systematic desensitization: using relaxation and imagination followed by in vivo training at home, both
partners discussed their wishes for sexual interaction and at the
same time established the items for which both were desensitized.
The main variation from the normally used procedure was in the
construction of the hierarchy.

3. A set of communication exercises: these exercises were
formulated on the analogy of the work of Bach (1968), and the work
on territoriality of Bakker (1973). Eight exercises were specified
for active and passive listening, verbalization and reflection of
feelings, fair fighting and assertive behavior.

The treatments were always carried out according to the same
pattern. After the (first) initial interview, the couples were
given a sex information questionnaire. Then we had anamnestic
interviews separately for both partners, followed by a problem
formulation by the therapists and a discussion about that formulation. This was followed by treatment sessions as specified in a
therapist's manual. Six months after treatment, we had a follow-
up interview by an external judge.

Subjects

For the first and second study couples were selected with
female partner complaints of inadequate sexual interaction, and
conversly, in the third study couples with male partner complaints.
To eliminate incidental fluctuations in the interaction of the
couple, complaints must have been present for more than one year.

Therapists

Postgraduate students of the department of clinical Psychology and Psychotherapy worked as male/female cotherapists. After
completing a short intensive training, they implemented treatment
programs according to stipulated procedures in a manual. During
their work, the therapists were supervised in treatment problems

and adherence to manual procedures, was carefully controlled.

Measurements

From Frenken's Sexual Experience Scale (SES) (1976), **scale** 3
"appetitive versus aversive sexual motivation" was used. This
scale provides a measure for satisfaction with sexual interaction
and experience of orgasm. As an indication of satisfaction with
the relationship in general, a combined score from Schutz's Marital
Attitude Evaluation Scale (MATE) (1967) was used. These two measures
were used in all studies in addition to anxiety ratings, subjects
and "therapists" ratings of change, a rating of self esteem and in
the second and third study, diaries for some weeks after treatment.

DESIGNS AND A BRIEF VIEW OF RESULTS

Study I

Forty-eight couples with sexual dissatisfaction of the female
partner, were randomly assigned to four groups. a) Masters and
Johnson adaptation; b) desensitization variant; c) a combination
of a and b; d) waiting-list control (Table 1).

Design Study I. In this first study we decided to compare
effects after a fixed number of sessions (the intermediate test):
we chose the 12th session as a point for comparison. At this
point, only 5 couples in the Masters and Johnson adaptation group,
had completed treatment successfully. There were dropouts in all
groups for external reasons: one couple in the Masters and Johnson
group, four couples in the desensitization group, one couple in
the combination treatment group and three couples in the waiting-
list group dropped out. One couple from the waiting-group reported
having no further problems.

Outcome per method of treatment. The outcome of treatment
is summarized in Table 2. Different numbers of couples in follow-
up data are due to non-responders to follow-up. Those who did not
respond to the follow-up request differed systematically from those
who did respond. The male partners of the non responding group
were significantly more satisfied with the relationship (MATE).
They were also less sexually motivated (SES-3) than the responding
males. The females of the non responding couples were significantly
less sexually motivated (SES-3) than responding females.

TABLE 1

DESIGN STUDY I: A COMPARISON OF MASTERS AND JOHNSON
AND SYSTEMATIC DESENSITISATION: COUPLES COMPLAINING OF ORGASMIC DYSFUNCTION

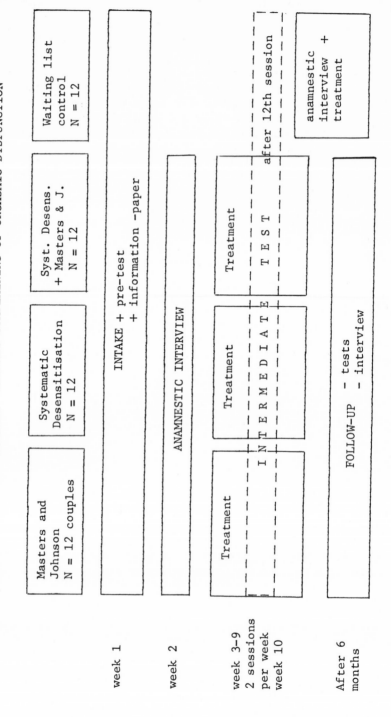

TABLE 2

OUTCOME PER METHOD OF TREATMENT FOR SES-3
AND COMBINED MATE SCORES IN STUDY I (T-TESTS)

a) Pre-Test vs. Intermediate Test (N=42)
After the 12th session

Methods of Treatment	Subject	SES-3		MATE	
		t	p	t	p
Masters & Johnson adaptation	Females	2.43	$<$.025	2.89	$<$.01
	Males	2.33	$<$.025	2.03	$<$.05
Desensitization variant	Females	2.48	$<$.025	2.63	$<$.05
	Males	1.47	ns	0.28	ns
Desensitization + Masters & Johnson	Females	1.29	ns	1.11	ns
	Males	1.25	ns	1.57	ns
Waiting-list control	Females	1.27	ns	1.84	ns
	Males	0.14	ns	0.18	ns

b) Pre-Test vs. Follow-up (N=23)
After six months

Methods of Treatment	Subject	SES-3		MATE	
Masters & Johnson adaptation	Females	1.26	ns	2.44	$<$.025
	Males	1.81	ns	1.94	$<$.025
Desensitization variant	Females	2.47	$<$.025	2.28	$<$.05
	Males	2.90	$<$.025	1.80	ns
Desensitization + Masters & Johnson	Females	1.62	ns	1.32	ns
	Males	2.55	$<$.025	2.36	$<$.05
Waiting-list control	Females	-	-	-	-
	Males	-	-	-	-

In general the results of the Masters and Johnson adaptation and desensitization variant were significant both on SES-3 and MATE after treatment. In follow-up, we saw a slight decrease in SES-3 scores for the Masters and Johnson adaptation and an increase for desensitization. On MATE scores males and females in the Masters and Johnson group were still better. Combined treatments and waiting-list groups did not show significant changes within twelve sessions.

Comparison of methods. Methods were compared on three criteria: 1) difference in SES-3 scores; 2) speed of treatment, that is number of sessions required; 3) effects on other areas than sexual interaction for example MATE scores.

Using quick and successful results as a criterion indicates that the Masters and Johnson approach is superior. Within 12 sessions 5 couples successfully completed treatment whereas in the other groups none of the couples did so. For both SES-3 scores and MATE scores we used F tests to decide whether there were significant differences between treatment groups. F values were nearly significant on a .05 level for females on SES-3. Females treated by the Masters and Johnson adaptation and by desensitization did better than females in the other groups. At follow-up, the differences between treatment groups were not significant. Effects on other than sexual interaction areas, for example MATE scores, were most clear for the Masters and Johnson adaptation and desensitization groups. Here also these differences did not reach a significant value.

Study II

Many therapists assume that there will be a consistent positive correlation between satisfaction about the general relationship and satisfaction about the sexual interaction. In many assistance situations therapists tend to approach problems by treating the relationship in general. They expect as a consequence of this strategy that specific problems will subside. To test this hypothetical relationship between relationship satisfaction and sexual satisfaction we designed a second study (Table 3). Forty-eight couples complaining of sexual dissatisfaction in the female partner were randomly assigned to two treatment conditions. One treatment was the same as in study I; an adaptation of Masters and Johnson. In the case of high anxiety problems, we also used desensitization procedures. This approach was called sex therapy in contrast to the treatment method where communication about feelings

TABLE 3

DESIGN STUDY II: A COMPARISON OF SEX
THERAPY (MASTERS AND JOHNSON - SYSTEMATIC DES.)
AND COMMUNICATION TRAINING: COUPLES
COMPLAINING OF ORGASMIC DYSFUNCTION

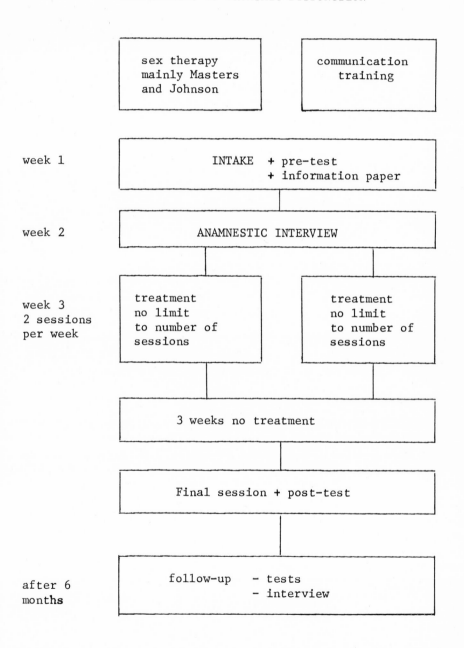

was the focus of treatment; in the communication treatment there was no explicit stress on sexual interaction. In the sex therapy group there were four dropouts, and in the communication training three couples dropped out. Couples dropped out of treatment for external reasons only.

Outcome per method of treatment. The outcome is summarized in Table 4. Sex therapy clearly resulted in more significant changes in the direction of improvement of satisfaction both on SES-3 and MATE scores. It is quite striking that in the communication group sexual satisfaction increases in the females only. In follow-up tests it seems that the male partners showed a decrease in satisfaction about the sexual interaction.

Comparison of methods. Table 5 shows that, with the relationship in general males from the communication group seem to be more satisfied. It appears that sex therapy is the method of choice when the goal of treatment is for an increase in sexual satisfaction. The complicated results in the communication group, will be analyzed in detail elsewhere.

Study III

In study III (Table 6) the treatment of male complaints about satisfaction in sexual interaction was studied. The comparison of an adaptation of Masters and Johnson and a variant of desensitization was repeated. In both methods attention was paid to the specific fear of failure which according to the literature, and our own experience, plays an important role in male sexual disorders. As there was a lack of males requesting treatment, a waiting period for obtaining "own control" data was used. There were two dropouts; one couple in each of the two treatment programs.

Outcome per method of treatment. Table 7 shows that outcome of both methods was weak. Effects on SES-3 and MATE did show some significance. In follow-up interviews most couples reported that they were satisfied with the results of therapy, although they had not solved the initial problems.

Comparisons of methods. There were no significant differences for either methods nor for males or females.

TABLE 4

OUTCOME PER METHOD OF TREATMENT FOR SES-3
AND COMBINED MATE SCORES IN STUDY II (T-TESTS)

a) Pre-Test vs. Post-Test (N=41)

Methods of Treatment	Subject	SES-3		MATE	
		t	p	t	p
Sex therapy	Females	4.56	/.005	1.51	/.08
	Males	3.09	/.003	1.85	/.04
Communication Training	Females	1.96	/.04	1.56	/.07
	Males	0.03	ns	0.61	ns

b) Pre-Test vs. Follow-up Test (N=31)

Sex therapy	Females	2.63	/.009	2.69	/.007
	Males	2.36	/.02	1.89	/.06
Communication Training	Females	2.72	/.006	1.29	ns
	Males	1.89	/.06 D	2.17	/.03

D = decrease in satisfaction

TABLE 5

COMPARISON OF METHODS OF TREATMENT
ON SES AND MATE SCORES IN STUDY II (T-TESTS)

Sex Therapy vs. Communication Training

Tests	Subjects	At Post-Test		At Follow-up	
		t	p	t	p
SES-3	Females	1.44	ns	0.46	ns
	Males	1.83	∠.07 sex	2.86	∠.004 com
MATE	Females	0.79	ns	0.63	ns
	Males	1.36	ns	0.71	ns

sex = sex therapy > communication training

com = communication training > sex therapy

DISCUSSION

An examination of the research questions suggest the following answers:

1. Some differences between methods of treatment were identified. Therapy focused on the sexual problem (Masters and Johnson,
Desensitization) seems to be superior to communication training.
The difference in outcome was more important when comparing female
and male complaints. Our therapists were not very successful with
male complaints.

2. In our opinion, more specific training of therapists is
needed to work on male complaints. Resistance to change, i.e., non-
cooperation in treatment was a difficult problem. Speculatively,

TABLE 6

DESIGN STUDY III: A COMPARISON OF
MASTERS AND JOHNSON AND SYSTEMATIC DESENSITISATION:
COUPLES COMPLAINING OF IMPOTENCE PROBLEMS

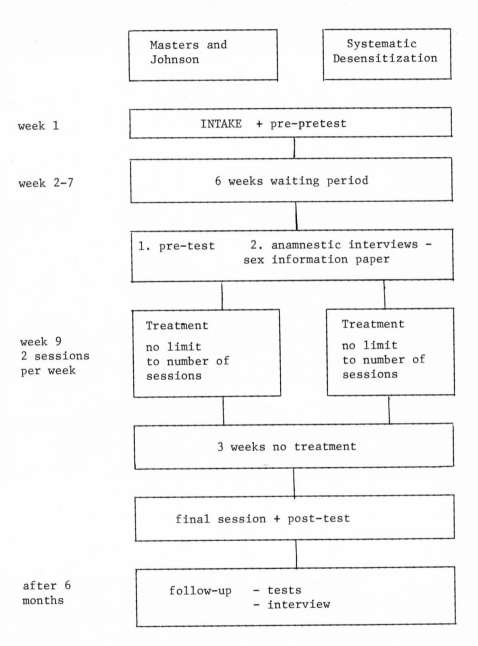

TABLE 7

OUTCOME PER METHOD OF TREATMENT
FOR SES-3 AND COMBINED MATE
SCORES IN STUDY III (T-TESTS)

a) Pre-test vs. Post-test (N=22)

Methods of Treatment	Subjects	SES-3		MATE	
		t	p	t	p
Masters and Johnson	Females	1.60	ns	0.53	ns
	Males	2.44	∠.02	0.20	ns
Desensitisation variant	Females	2.19	∠.03	0.40	ns
	Males	1.93	∠.06	0.75	ns

b) Pre-test vs. Follow-up (N=17)

Methods of Treatment	Subjects	SES-3		MATE	
Masters and Johnson	Females	1.86	∠.07	0.51	ns
	Males	2.38	∠.02	0.49	ns
Desensitisation variant	Females	2.25	∠.03	0.12	ns
	Males	1.95	∠.06	0.63	ns

there seems to be bias in sex therapy as evidenced by the over-whelming results with females.

The results of communication training might give an important indication. In this method no concept of sexual interaction was introduced which is in contrast with sex therapy approaches. In this communication approach females did gain sexual satisfaction, while at the same time males lost some satisfaction. In this situation, where females become more assertive, there may also be a need for discussion about the concept of sexual interaction. This could be an added advantage of the treatment, but to date there is no verification.

3. It appears that therapy for sexual inadequacies can be done, by therapists with minimum training. They needed about 16 one-hour sessions in study II and 23 sessions in study III. However, to improve results of therapy a better understanding of male sexual complaints seems necessary.

REFERENCES

Bach, G. (1968). The Intimate Enemy, William Morrow and Company, Inc., New York.

Bakker, C.B. and Bakker-Rabdau, M.K. (1973). No Trespassing! Chandler and Sharp, San Francisco.

Frenken, J. (1976). Afkeer van de Sexualiteit (sexual aversion), Van Loghum Slaterus, Deventer.

Masters, W.H. and Johnson, V.E. (1970). Human Sexual Inadequacy, Little, Brown & Co, Boston.

Schutz (1967). The FIRO-scales, Manual, Palo Alto.

Modest results. (? in some cases a useful addition to R+I)

STIMULATION THERAPY FOR SEXUAL DYSFUNCTION

Patricia W. Gillan

England

Most traditional sex therapy emphasize anxiety reduction but neglect sex drive. My general approach in an experimental study in 1973 was to stimulate the appetites of sexually dysfunctional patients by any method that was socially acceptable. Pictures of heterosexual sexual activity, as are commonly circulated in London were shown. Stories taken from books as <u>Memoirs of the Life of Fanny Hill</u> by John Cleland or <u>Lady Chatterley's Lover</u> by D.H. Lawrence and current literature magazines were read by the patients. A tape recording called "Japanese Sounds of Sex," in which women vocalize the ecstasy of orgasms, was played to the patients. In addition erotic films were recommended, e.g. "Belle de Jour," "Danish Blue," "Quiet Days in Clichy." Stimulating music as Indians evening ragas, Reggae, Ravel's Bolero was recommended to accompany sexual play. Patients were encouraged to discuss and explore their erotic fantasies and masturbatory techniques, and also encouraged to practice oral sex at home. Patients were seen conjointly once a week and treated individually using a battery of methods to increase sexual stimulation. In addition to those techniques previously mentioned Systematic Desensitization and a modified Masters and Johnson treatment program were used (Gillan, 1973).

THE PRESENT STUDY

In the present study an attempt was made to control some of the variables of the previous study. Erotic stimuli treatment with relaxation was used as the only treatment for this trial. Two groups plus a control group were treated in the following way:

Group 1:   Visual Stimuli

Erotic pictures and slides of nude couples in overt sexual activities were presented. Photographs of paintings as ancient Japanese prints and Allen Jones' work were included.

Group 2:   Auditory Stimuli

Patients were asked to silently read old and new erotic literature. Stories from <u>Vibrations</u> and <u>New Dimensions</u> and <u>Forum</u> letters, articles were included. Patients listened to Japanese "sex tapes" and wrote their own erotic fantasies.

Group 3:   Control Group

The minimal stimuli patients (NS) were asked to talk about their sex problems and an effort was made to divert their attention in discussion of other nonsexual topics.

All the patients in the above engaged in deep relaxation for 15 minutes at the beginning of each session. After an initial case history taking session, each patient attended 6 sessions (approximately once a week) without a partner.

THE PATIENTS

As impotent men responded so well in the previous study, I decided to include women in this study. Twenty-four patients were included: 14 men with erectile problems, and 10 women (5 reporting no pleasure during sex and 5 anorgasmic).

All the patients were shown an erotic or pornographic picture of sexual intercourse and were asked to read an excerpt from <u>Fanny Hill</u>. Their interest and pleasure to such stimuli was measured pre, post and 1 month after treatment. All patients were treated on their own without partners.

RESULTS

Evaluation of therapy usually consists of rather vague "improvement" measures. Few studies include rating scales done by patients and a "blind assessor." An effort has been made in Europe to standardize assessment criteria by using the International Sex

Scales. These rating scales include conventional measures like
frequency of sexual intercourse, but emphasis is also placed on
sexual feelings and pleasure, and on a satisfactory sexual relationship with the partner.

Results based on rating scales in the present study show no
significant difference between the different modes of stimulation,
i.e., visual or auditory, and both these stimulation groups show
a significantly greater improvement than did the control group after
treatment over measures used as pleasure and frequency of intercourse
(Figure 1 and 2) and a better sexual relationship with the partner
(Figure 3). All these measures were usually accurate at the one
month follow-up. Although men were inclined to prefer visual
stimulation, there were no sex differences.

In the stimulation therapy groups, one third of the men were
evaluated as needing further treatment, although 66% reported good
erections. The women fared less well. Fifty-seven percent of the
women showed an improvement. This only included the low sex drive
women, as none of the anorgasmic women were able to reach orgasm

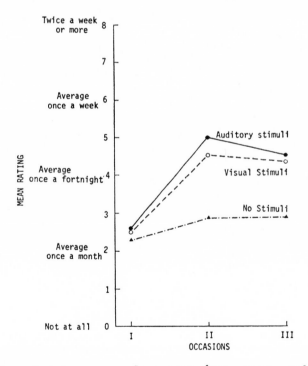

Fig. 1. Sexual intercourse frequency (pre, post, and one month
after treatment).

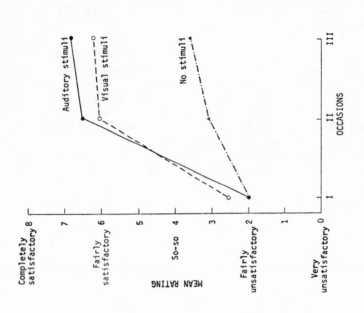

Fig. 3. Sexual relationship with partner (pre, post, and one month after treatment).

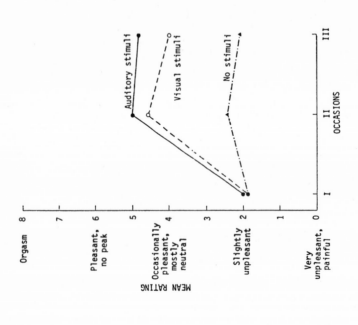

Fig. 2. Sexual feeling (pre, post, and one month after treatment).

after 6 sessions of therapy, although most found they enjoyed sex more and had a better partner relationship.

There was no significant lowering of anxiety for any group, so relaxation and anxiety reduction were not the important variables in this study. The significant variable was increasing sexual arousal.

Those who had not achieved success after the 6 sessions received further treatment. Treatment for those in the control group who were able and willing (7 men and 5 women), did continue. They were treated with a combined audio-visual stimulation programme, supplemented with masturbation instructions similar to those of Lobitz and LoPiccolo (1972), plus a modified Masters and Johnson therapy with additional oral sex instruction. Patients were invited to bring their partners along at this stage and most of them did so. After an average of 10 sessions all the women reported enjoying sex more and 4 out of 5 were orgasmic and 5 out of 7 men became potent. Seventy-five percent of all patients improved.

This mixed method has been applied effectively in groups for women with low sex drive and their partners. So far 3 groups have been treated and 11 of 13 women have improved with stimulation therapy combined with graded Masters and Johnson tasks for one group or reversing the Masters and Johnson, i.e., starting off with the FSP (Female Superior Position) and ending with Sensate Focussing. After 6 sessions there appears to be no significant difference between these two methods of treatment.

REFERENCES

Gillan, P. (1973). Behavioral reeducation in impotence. Paper
    presented at the European Association of Behavioral Psy-
    chotherapy Conference, Amsterdam.

Lobitz, W.C. and LoPiccolo, J. (1972). New methods in the behavioral
    treatment of sexual dysfunction. J. Beh. Ther. and Exp.
    Psychiat. 3: 265-271.

Poor study - confined. Sexual fantasy ff positively correlated c̄ outcome of therapy.

THE EFFECT OF SEXUAL FANTASY FREQUENCIES ON THE OUTCOME OF SHORT-TERM TREATMENT PROGRAM FOR SEXUAL INADEQUACY IN HETEROSEXUAL COUPLES

Edouard Beltrami, André Dupras and Réjean Tremblay

Canada

Although psychoanalysis has conducted in depth studies on the content of sexual fantasies, there has been little research as yet on the frequency of such fantasies in relation to the intensity of sexual response.

Investigations on 193 variables have surprisingly revealed that, independent of their content, the frequency of sexual fantasy was the best indication of a person's sexual health or, of a favorable outcome in the course of sex therapy, and of a positive motivation that prevented treatment dropouts.

METHODOLOGY

Subjects

The sexual fantasies of fifty-eight people, that is, twenty-nine couples, have been studied and treated during their first session of sex therapy. The majority (44) of the patients were between twenty-one and thirty-five years of age, drawing salaries ranging from $9,000 to $15,000, and 30 held positions in the liberal professions and 35 in the civil service. Thirty were college or university graduates, 50 were married, 54 had been raised in the Catholic faith and 50 were born in Quebec and were French-speaking.

We identified thirty-seven cases of masculine sexual dysfunction and forty-seven cases of feminine inadequacy in diagnosing

these patients. Over one half (56 per cent) of these disorders
had been life-long occurrences as opposed to 34.8 per cent of the
problems which had originated one to six years previously. Six
medical pathologies were discovered in the course of medical examination; psychiatric disorders were observed in 26.2 per cent of
the population examined: ten cases of neurosis, three of psychosis,
two borderline cases and six incidences of serious conjugal maladjustment. Six patients received psychotherapy, two for sexual
problems and four for psychological disorders.

Therapeutic Technique

We use the Masters and Johnson technique with two important
modifications: we employ only one male therapist and the sessions
between patient and therapist are held once weekly during a period
of fifteen weeks. One of the required conditions is that the patients have three periods (of one hour) in the intimacy of their
home to practice the exercises recommended during the therapeutic
interviews. To this, we have added one obligatory "free evening
out" each week for the couple, alone, without children, with the
female partner being free from domestic duties. The couple habitually made this outing coincide with a meal in a restaurant during
the week.

Each partner in the couple is seen alone for two distinct
evaluations; there is a brief psychosocial case history taken,
followed by a special questionnaire of our own diagnostic grid of
sexual inadequacies. Then the couple is referred to a medical
doctor for a complete physical checkup. At the fourth session,
evaluations are completed and the patients given a series of cor-
poral sensitization exercises. Most couples are asked to refrain
from intercourse, a condition which could be enforced beyond the
seventh session. Of course, certain cases require variations in
this rule, but all are required to abstain from active sex relations prior to the session in which they could stimulate their
genital organs.

In the second part, which extends from the seventh to the
fifteenth session, we make use of specific procedures, such as
the squeeze technique for premature ejaculators. Vaginismus patients are treated with Hegar or Young dilators.

Measuring Instruments

At the Department of Sexology, (UQAM), we have computerized one
hundred and ninety-three data files for storage on each patient.

A multiple part questionnaire allows us to locate and identify data easily.

Psychosocial anamnesis. Information, such as sex (gender), age, profession, ethnic origin, annual salary, education, religion, history of psychological or sexual problems is recorded.

Sexual evaluation diagnostic grid. The patients are asked a number of questions on many aspects of their sexuality (Table 1). We have found that if we would obtain complete evaluation of sexual functioning, we must not depend on the degree of satisfaction which may sometimes be overemphasized by the patient who would allow himself the minimum of sexual activity, or on the level of performance which often does not indicate the level of satisfaction; yet we deem it extremely important to correlate the agreeable and disagreeable sensations accompanying these activities. Thus, we have recorded: the monthly frequency of activity that the patient estimates was truly performed; the number of times these true activities entailed a sense of pleasure or any other positive reaction; the patient's desired frequency of such monthly activities; and the number of times such activities produce negative reactions, such as shame, guilt, regret, disgust, marked indifference, or pain.

When we have obtained the frequency of activity, a notion of congruence, as to whether the activity in question was desired or not, we then obtain an almost complete picture of the patient's sexual profile. In evaluating frequency, the therapist at first asks the patient a very general question and then according to the patient's answer, attempts to establish a more precise frequency.

The first step toward improvement is to lower the frequency recorded in the negative reaction column. The next step is to increase the number of activities procuring a sense of enjoyment.

FINDINGS

Following the therapy administered to each couple, the data on failure, success, improvement, or withdrawal, relative to each category diagnosed, are recorded and stored. Precoded criteria are used to determine failure, improvement, or success, according to the category under diagnosis. For instance, in the case of primary anorgasm, a lack of orgasm was considered as a failure, one orgasm during the final month an improvement, and three orgasms or more during the final month a success.

TABLE 1

DIAGNOSTIC GRID OF SEXUAL FUNCTION: MONTHLY FREQUENCY

	Carried out	Desired	Carried out with pleasure	Carried out with displeasure
FANTASIES				
EXCITATION WITHOUT PARTNER				
ORGASM				
ATTRACTION TO A PARTNER				
EXHIBITING ONE'S BODY UNCLOTHED				
OBSERVING A PARTNER UNCLOTHED				
NONGENITAL FONDLING OF PARTNER'S BODY (ACTIVE PARTICIPANT)				
EXPERIENCING NONGENITAL FONDLING FROM A PARTNER (PASSIVE PARTICIPANT)				
TOUCHING A PARTNER'S GENITALS				
BEING TOUCHED GENITALLY BY A PARTNER				
EXCITATION PHASE WITH A PARTNER				
NONCOITAL ORGASM EXPERIENCED WITH A PARTNER				
PENILE PENETRATION				
ORGASM BY PENILE PENETRATION				
RESOLUTION AND RELAXATION				

Results by Diagnostic Category in Men

As seen in Table 2, our diagnoses of male patients have revealed 21 percent cases of premature ejaculation, 3 percent absence
of ejaculation, 8 percent ejaculations without enjoyment, 11 percent
male dyspareunia, 11 percent secondary impotence and finally, 46
percent lack of masculine interest. The last disturbance is responsible for 56 percent of withdrawals, not only on the part of
the men involved, but also of the women, because withdrawal affects
the couple. Male dropout averaged 43 percent, which had an important effect on the outcome of the treatment. Indeed, if we eliminate
the number of dropouts, we would average 84 percent success in the
results of male therapy, but if our statistics retain the dropout
cases, our rate of success is only 43 percent. This is an important factor because in most studies the dropout cases are not mentioned and such cases are indicative of improvement needed in the
technique.

Results by Diagnostic Category in Women

In our women patients, we observed 23 percent of cases of
primary or secondary excitation inability, 10 percent with an absence of feminine interest, 15 percent primary and 4 percent secondary orgasmic incapacity, 34 percent coital orgasmic incapacity,
8 percent female dyspareunia, and 4 percent vaginismus.

Total results (Table 2) show that the withdrawal rate is the
same for the men as for the women, as droping out is done by the
couple; however, men lacking interest are responsible for 60 percent of dropout cases whereas not one woman lacked enough interest
to abandon therapy. There is a very close correlation between the
lack of sexual fantasy and the incidence of dropout; in fact, when
monthly frequency declines to less than four per month, this category would include most of the cases exhibiting a lack of masculine
interest, withdrawal, and failure.

Subject's Sex and Age in Relation
To Monthly Sexual Fantasy Frequency

Sex and age have an important determination on fantasy frequency and on the subject's desire to have such fantasies as well
as on the positive or negative reactions experienced while fantasying.

Table 3 shows that a man has more erotic fantasies than does
a woman (89 percent have over four per month, as opposed to 50 percent in women). Women also wish to avoid sexual fantasies (67
percent of women as compared to 33 percent of the men). A man

TABLE 2

RESULTS OF THERAPY (58 PATIENTS) (1972–1974)

Diagnosis	Cases (N)	Cases (N)	Success (N)	Improvement (N)	Failure (N)	Withdrawals (N)	% Success – Improvement Total	% Success – Improvement Total (–withdrawals)
Premature Ejaculation	6	21	4	1	1	2	62%	83%
Absence of Ejaculation	1	2.7	0	0	0	1	0%	0%
Ejaculation without Enjoyment	3	8	2	0	0	1	66%	100%
Secondary Impotence	4	11	2	0	0	2	50%	100%
Lack of Interest	17	46	3	2	1	9	29%	83%
Masculine Dyspareunia	4	11	2	0	1	1	50%	66%
Total of Cumulative Diagnoses (Male)	37*	100	13	3	3	16	43%	84%

*One patient could have received more than one diagnosis.

TABLE 2 (CONTINUED)

WOMEN

Excitation Inability I	4	8.5	1	0	2	0	25%	33%
Excitation Inability II	7	15	3	0	1	3	42%	75%
Orgasmic Inability I	7	15	0	0	5	2	0%	0%
Orgasmic Inability II	2	4	1	0	1	0	50%	100%
Coital Inability	16	34	6	1	2	7	43%	77%
Lack of Feminine Interest	5	10	4	0	1	0	80%	80%
Feminine Dys-pareunia	4	8.5	2	0	0	2	50%	100%
Vaginismus	2	4	1	0	0	1	50%	100%
Total of Cumulative Diagnoses (Female)	47*	100	18	1	12	16	40%	61%

*One patient could have received more than one diagnosis.

E. BELTRAMI, A. DUPRAS, AND R. TREMBLAY

TABLE 3

DISTRIBUTION OF SEXUAL FANTASIES ACCORDING TO THE SEX OF THE SUBJECTS (58 PATIENTS)

Characteristics	Men		Women		Total	
	N	%	N	%	N	%
TRUE FREQUENCY						
Four times or more per month	16	80	8	40	24	71
Less than four times per month	2	20	8	80	10	29
DESIRED FREQUENCY						
Four times or more per month	15	63	9	37	24	73
Less than four times per month	3	33	6	67	9	27
FANTASIES WITH NEGATIVE FEELINGS						
49% and less	9	50	9	50	18	75
50% and more	2	33	4	67	6	25
FANTASIES WITH POSITIVE (PLEASURABLE) FEELINGS						
49% and less	0	0	5	100	5	15
50% and more	17	61	11	39	28	85

χ^2, p<.01

more willingly accepts and enjoys erotic imagery than a woman does
(61 percent as compared to 39 percent) and women experience more
negative feelings (shame, regret) than do men (67 percent to 33
percent). In brief, men have, and desire, more fantasies; they
take more pleasure in such imagery and feel less remorse than
women feel.

Age seems a significant factor in imaginative activity. Older
subjects have less sexual fantasies (45 percent) than their younger
counterparts (80 percent) and have less desire to sexually fantasy
(23 percent as compared to 72 percent). They also feel more ashamed
(72 percent to 23 percent) and experience less enjoyment (13 percent
to 25 percent) (Table 4).

Monthly Frequency of Sexual Fantasies
(MFSF) Indicative of the Outcome of Therapy

The patients successfully treated exhibited MFSF more than
four times per month (67 percent) whereas, failures and withdrawals
averaged 20 percent (Table 5). Of the potentially successful cases,
90 percent experienced pleasure during erotic fantasies, whereas
only 60 percent of the other cases showed equal enjoyment.

Data in the other two categories gave paradoxical results
which only clinical experience can determine: the desire to have
and retain present fantasies is about the same in the successful
and the unsuccessful cases (50 percent to 46 percent); moreover,
failures exhibited less negative reaction (11 percent related to
their fantasies) than the successful cases (33 percent).

CONCLUSION

1. We now have at our disposal a diagnostic grid of sexual
functioning, sufficiently accurate for prognostic value.

2. Sexual fantasy is one of the most sensitive indications
of a person's sexual potential: young men capable of maintaining
high levels of excitation under adverse conditions and who can attain orgasm during every active sexual encounter have the highest
sexual fantasy frequency; statistics show that those who had less
sexual fantasies are women, elderly persons and those suffering
from sexual inadequacy, groups that are usely known as having more
trouble maintaining excitation and experiencing orgasm at every
coital occurrence.

3. An individual who desires having fantasies and enjoys
having them will experience increased frequencies of sexual activity.

TABLE 4

DISTRIBUTION OF SEXUAL FANTASIES ACCORDING TO THE AGE OF THE SUBJECTS (58 PATIENTS)

Characteristics	21 to 35 Years		36 to 55 Years		Total	
	N	%	N	%	N	%
TRUE FREQUENCY						
Four times or more per month	20	83	4	17	24	71
Less than four times per month	5	50	5	50	10	29
DESIRED FREQUENCY						
Four times or more per month	19	79	5	21	24	71
Less than four times per month	6	60	4	40	10	29
FANTASIES WITH NEGATIVE FEELINGS						
49% and less	13	72	5	28	18	75
50% and more	5	83	1	17	6	25
FANTASIES WITH POSITIVE (PLEASURABLE) FEELINGS						
49% and less	3	60	2	40	5	16
50% and more	21	78	6	22	27	84

χ^2, p<.01

TABLE 5

DISTRIBUTION OF SEXUAL FANTASIES ACCORDING TO THE THERAPEUTIC RESULTS OBTAINED (58 PATIENTS)

Characteristics	No Diagnosis		Success		Failure		Total	
	N	%	N	%	N	%	N	%
TRUE FREQUENCY								
Four times or more per month	7	100	12	86	2	14	14	50
Less than four times per month	0	0	6	37	8	63	14	40
DESIRED FREQUENCY								
Four times or more per month	7	100	6	60	4	40	10	48
Less ghan four times per month	0	0	7	64	4	36	11	52
FANTASIES WITH NEGATIVE FEELINGS								
49% and less	5	100	6	43	8	57	14	78
50% and more	0	0	3	75	1	25	4	22
FANTASIES WITH POSITIVE (PLEASURABLE) FEELINGS								
49% and less	0	0	2	33	4	67	6	21
50% and more	7	100	17	74	6	26	23	79

χ^2, p<.01

4. The sense of guilt or uneasiness relative to fantasies does not seem to inhibit sexual activity. Fantasying may place one in either an illicit or licit situation and one's personal transgression, even in fantasy, may prove to be an essential element of human sexuality.

VAGINISMUS

John A. Lamont

Canada

Vaginismus is defined as the involuntary spasm of the pelvic
muscles surrounding the outer third of the vagina, specifically
the perineal muscles and the levator ani muscles (Masters and
Johnson, 1970; Kaplan, 1974; Ellison, 1972). In severe cases of
vaginismus the adductors of the thighs, the rectus abdominis and
the gluteus muscles may be involved. This reflex contraction is
triggered by imagined or anticipated attempts at penetration of
the vagina, or during the act of intromission or coitus.

In the past some authors have attempted to dichotomize organic
and psychogenic causes (Novak, 1948; Harlow and McCluskey, 1972).
British literature uses dyspareunia to describe coital pain with
organic cause while vaginismus encompasses all painful coitus without organic cause. More recently, the emphasis in the literature
has focussed on the need for integrating psychogenic and organic
investigation (Kaplan, 1974). From Figure 1 we can see that the
terms vaginismus and dyspareunia are undeniably linked in the
symptom of perineal muscle spasm (Lamont, 1974). Repeated dyspareunia is likely to result in vaginismus, but vaginismus may be
the causative factor in dyspareunia.

Most authors agree that an essential step in diagnosing the
problem is the physical demonstration of this involuntary spasm
(Masters and Johnson, 1970; Kaplan, 1974; Ellison, 1972). The
general consensus of professional opinion states that this disorder
is relatively rare (Kaplan, 1974); and vaginismus can occur among
sexually responsive or unresponsive women.

The objectives of this descriptive study are as follows:

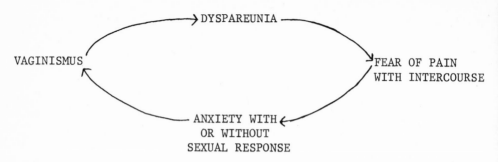

Fig. 1. Dyspareunia and vaginismus cycle.

1) to support or deny the contention that vaginismus occurs more
frequently than is suggested in the professional literature; 2)
to carefully describe the types of patients by history and physical assessment and relate those findings to types of therapeutic
interventions and outcomes; 3) to evaluate therapeutic interventions working with women individually in short-term therapy where
ongoing supportive partners were not available or involved; 4) to
assess the sexual responsiveness of this group of patients. It is
our impression that many patients with vaginismus are being mis-
diagnosed.

MATERIALS AND METHODS

This descriptive study includes 80 consecutive patients seen
in our Human Sexuality Clinic who were diagnosed as having vaginismus between 1972 and 1976. The patients presented chief complaints of difficult, painful or impossible vaginal penetration or
unconsummated coital relationships. Data were collected from the
referring source, the patients and the physical examination. Historical data were obtained to evaluate the specific details of the
complaint of difficult penetration as well as to evaluate sexual
attitudes, the woman's attitude to her genitals, the present sexual relationship, and the non-sexual relationship. During the
pelvic or conjoint physical examination the presence and degree
of levator and/or perineal spasm was documented. Pressure on the
perineal muscles had to reproduce the patient's discomfort or difficulty in order to make the diagnosis. The author arbitrarily
classified the degree of vaginismus into four categories (Table 1).

Of the 80 patients described, four patients refused physical
and pelvic examination. These four patients, although not documented by vaginal examination, were included because of their

TABLE 1

DEGREE OF VAGINISMUS (80 PATIENTS)

1. PERINEAL AND LEVATOR SPASM - RELIEVED WITH REASSURANCE   27

2. PERINEAL SPASM - MAINTAINED THROUGHOUT PELVIC   21

3. LEVATOR SPASM AND ELEVATION OF BUTTOCKS   18

4. LEVATOR AND PERINEAL SPASM, ELEVATION, ADDUCTION AND
    RETREAT   10

REFUSED EXAMINATION   4

classical description of introital spasm at attempts of penetration
of the vagina. Each couple stated "the penis hits a 'brick wall'
about one inch inside the vagina."

Of the 80 patients presented, 40 were assessed on pelvic examination alone, 36 underwent conjoint physical examination with
their partners and the four who refused examination underwent
attitudinal assessment only.

Looking at the total 80 patients with vaginismus, all were
assessed, but 14 were not included in the treatment sample. Sixty-
six patients were treated. The shortest duration of complaint was
one month, the longest complaint was 216 months (18 years). The
average duration of symptoms in both the sample assessed and the
sample treated was approximately 36 months, (Table 2).

SUBJECTS

Age

The average age of our patients was approximately 27-28 years,
the youngest patient being 18 years of age, the oldest being 58
years of age. The majority of patients in this sample were in
their 20's.

Marital Status

The majority of patients were married with six patients being
single, one patient separated, one divorced and three living common-
law.

TABLE 2

DURATION OF SYMPTOMS (80 PATIENTS)

TREATMENT SAMPLE   -   35.6 MONTHS   (66 CASES)

ASSESSMENT ONLY   -   37.4 MONTHS   (14 CASES)

SHORTEST CASE   -   1 MONTH

LONGEST CASE   -   216 MONTHS

Presenting Symptoms

The patients were classified in five categories, including the apareunias, or patients who were unable to accomplish coital contact (primary and secondary), primary apareunia meaning an unconsummated relationship and secondary apareunia meaning successful comfortable coitus prior to the onset of presenting symptoms but no coitus since; the dyspareunias, patients who are capable of coital contact but had pain from vaginismus (primary, meaning pain with each attempt since first coitus; secondary, meaning comfortable coitus initially, followed by onset of pain with each subsequent attempt); and patients labelled as having primary vaginismus. There were 2 patients with primary vaginismus, both patients referred because of vaginismus specifically experienced during pelvic and self-examination. Both patients had not, at this point, attempted coitus (Table 3).

TABLE 3

PRESENTING SYMPTOMS

SYMPTOMS	NUMBER OF PATIENTS	
Primary Apareunia	27	
Secondary Apareunia	11	
Primary Dyspareunia	22	80
Secondary Dyspareunia	18	
Primary Vaginismus (Pelvic)	2	
Complete Vaginismus	62	
Situational Vaginismus	18	80

The study group was further divided into those who experienced complete vaginismus (62 patients), meaning those who had perineal spasm at attempts to insert anything in the vagina including tampons, finger, speculum or penis. The other patients labelled as situational vaginismus (18 patients) were those who had specific vaginismus related to a specific situation, such as coitus, but no problem with a tampon, or those who had severe vaginismus except under the influence of alcohol, or in the doctor's office, etc.

Physical Factors

Vaginismus may be present as a primary problem, best seen in the unconsummated relationship, or it may develop in response to dyspareunia from some other cause (Figure 1).

In reviewing our 76 pelvic assessments we found 22 patients had evidence of physical factors other than perineal spasm that may have been related to the onset of vaginismus. The remaining 54 patients had no physical factors noted on pelvic assessment other than their vaginismus (Table 4).

TABLE 4

PHYSICAL FACTORS RELATED TO VAGINISMUS

Previous Surgery	2	(Vaginal hysterectomies)
Episiotomy	6	(2 infected, 1 granuloma)
Atrophic Vaginitis	4	
Monilia Vaginitis	3	
Trichomonas Vaginitis	1	
Constipation	2	
Retroversion	2	
Pelvic Congestion	2	
None Noted	54	

N.B. 12 Patients had E.U.A. and/or hymenotomy and only one found results helpful with symptoms.

The patients were assessed by the author regarding sexual knowledge and attitudes as well as self-image and the ability to accept responsibility for their own sexual pleasure. Forty-one were judged by the author to have moderate to severe intrapersonal problems, a further 36 having intrapersonal problems related specifically to their coital dysfunction.

Similar attempts were made to assess the interpersonal relationship. Forty-nine couples were felt to have moderate to severe interpersonal discord, such as lack of communication skills and lack of ability to negotiate, etc. A further 25 couples were felt to have interpersonal discord specifically related to their coital difficulties.

MANAGEMENT

All 80 patients were assessed historically and attitudinally regarding their presenting complaints of difficult, painful or impossible vaginal penetration. Each patient and her partner, if involved, were provided with detailed education regarding the nature of the problem along with reassurance that the problem could be solved. Intrapersonal or interpersonal problems were identified at this point and strategies for management were discussed. Of the 80 patients initially assessed, 14 were not accepted into the treatment group because a contract could not be negotiated. Of the 80 patients assessed, 43 had an involved male partner, 37 women requested individual therapy.

The treatment involved weekly, one hour sessions where possible, aimed at systematic desensitization to vaginal penetration. A range of interventions were employed including deep muscle relaxation, progressive sexual fantasies, physical and verbal communication and pleasuring exercises, Kegel and modified Kegel vaginal exercises and the use of some form of vaginal dilator (including organic or inorganic dildo, the patient's finger, partner's finger, vibrator, speculum or penis).

Any identifiable physical factor related to the vaginismus was corrected including such things as revision of episiotomy, treatment of vaginitis, treatment of inadequate conception control, etc. (Table 5).

Exclusion of coital attempts was negotiated with the patient and partner until the patient(s) and therapist agreed this was appropriate, in the course of therapy. At each session the previous week's assignment was assessed as well as some evaluation made of the interpersonal and intrapersonal problems in the relationship during the previous week. A new assignment was negotiated at each visit. After successful completion of therapy, a follow-up visit

TABLE 5

PHYSICAL THERAPY

1 LAPAROSCOPY AND TUBAL DIATHERMY

2 REVISION OF EPISIOTOMY

1 EPISIOTOMY INJECTED WITH KENELOG

7 VAGINITIS TREATED   -   4   ESTROGEN
                                 2   MYCOSTATIN
                                 1   FLAGYL

2 TREATED CONSTIPATION

1 DESENSITIZATION TO HOSPITALS AND DOCTORS OFFICES

was negotiated for six weeks to three months time. Although three
months is the minimum follow-up available at this time with this
group of patients, many of them have been followed for over two
years duration.

RESULTS

Four outcome groups will be discussed: Assessment Only, No
Success, Technical Success, Success with Coital Pleasure (Table 6).

TABLE 6

OUTCOME BY PRESENTING SYMPTOMS

PRESENTING SYMPTOM	N	ASSESSMENT ONLY	NO SUCCESS	TECHNICAL SUCCESS	SUCCESS WITH COITAL PLEASURE
Primary Apareunia	27	4	3	2	18
Secondary Apareunia	11	1	1	3	6
Primary Dyspareunia	22	6	0	3	13
Secondary Dyspareunia	18	3	0	0	15
Primary Vaginismus	2	0	0	1	1
	80	14	4	9	53

Fourteen patients were assessed only. These patients were seen for one session only, usually one and a half hours with four patients refusing physical examination and 10 having a pelvic assessment. Sixty-six patients were treated. Sixty-two patients had success in overcoming their presenting complaint and 53 had success in engaging in coitus with pleasure and comfort. Four patients had no success.

Assessment Only. Of the patients who were seen for assessment only, four patients complained of primary apareunia, one patient of secondary apareunia, six patients of primary dyspareunia and three patients of secondary dyspareunia. Included in this group were the four patients who refused examination. Contracts could not be negotiated with these 14 patients so they were not offered therapy. Seven women were the reluctant partner, five men were identified as the reluctant partner and in two cases both partners agreed with terminating after assessment only.

No Success. Of the patients accepted into treatment, there were four patients with no success. Three presented with primary apareunia and one with secondary apareunia. All were described as complete vaginismus. They were seen for an average of 7.5 sessions. Of the three unconsummated relationships, two could not break the struggle for control in the relationship. One woman sabotaged therapy and one man sabotaged therapy. The third couple separated during therapy. The fourth couple presented with problems following vaginal hysterectomy and repair because of an extra tight vaginal repair. She had one surgical attempt to enlarge her vagina before seeing us. On examination vaginismus was identified but organic causes of her pain could not be ruled out. Many family and relationship problems were identified and during the course of family therapy the couple dropped out of treatment. They sought further gynecologic opinion and the patient underwent a third perineal repair which seems to have corrected the problem.

Technical Success. This group includes those patients who had qualified success in that they were able to learn to relax the perineal and levator muscles and control involuntary spasm. Some of these patients were able to accomplish penetration but did not find coitus a pleasurable experience. Nine patients were classified as technical success, two presenting with primary apareunia, three with secondary apareunia, three with primary dyspareunia, none with secondary dyspareunia and one with primary vaginismus. One couple was interested only in sex for reproduction and was successful with two subsequent pregnancies. One woman insisted on coital orgasms and was unsuccessful in achieving this goal. Five women did not have an interested male partner so at termination and follow-up had not experienced pleasurable coitus. This included one patient with primary vaginismus. One woman was not interested in pleasurable coitus but only in being able to function as a "normal female" during coitus. One woman has no further coital difficulty but continues to have some difficulty with vaginismus during gynecologic examination in the supine position.

The remaining 53 patients had success in conquering their vaginismus and experienced pleasurable coitus. Five treatment sessions were required on the average for the 66 successful patients.

In comparing the different degrees of vaginismus, as evaluated at pelvic examination, the patients with a more severe degree of vaginismus required on the average more treatment sessions. Patients with fourth degree vaginismus required an average of 7.3 visits in treatment whereas patients with first degree vaginismus averaged 3.4 sessions in treatment (Table 7).

Of the 80 patients presented 43 included an ongoing, involved partner. Thirty-seven women were seen in individual therapy (Table 8). Of the sample in individual treatment 8 were seen for assessment only and 29 were treated. Of this sample 22 had successful therapy with coital pleasure and the remaining 7 had a technical success as described above. As one would expect 16 of the 29 treated patients had associated physical factors initiating the vaginismus and these factors were managed during treatment.

TABLE 7

COMPARING SEVERITY OF MUSCLE
SPASM TO TIME IN THERAPY

Degree of Vaginismus	Duration of Symptoms	Treatment Sessions	Successes/ # Patients Treated
1°	28.4 months	3.4 (1 - 12)	21/23
2°	41.5 months	4.8 (1 - 10)	17/18
3°	38.7 months	6.0 (2 - 11)	15/16
4°	29.2 months	7.3 (3 - 17)	9/9

TABLE 8

OUTCOME FOR WOMEN SEEN IN INDIVIDUAL THERAPY

Presenting Complaint (Women seen Individually)	# Patients	Success	Technical Success	Assessment only
Primary Apareunia	3	1	1	1
Secondary Apareunia	7	3	3	1
Primary Dyspareunia	10	5	2	3
Secondary Dyspareunia	15	12	0	3
Primary Vaginismus	2	1	1	0
	37	22	7	8

In the literature there is often association made between the complaint of vaginismus and lack of sexual responsiveness. Table 9 shows the number of women in each outcome group responsive to orgasm. Fifty-five of the 80 patients had experienced or were experiencing orgasm when first seen. Eleven patients stated that they developed secondary orgasmic dysfunction as a result of their difficulties with coitus. Three patients reported experiencing their first orgasm during successful therapy.

TABLE 9

FEMALE RESPONSIVENESS - TO ORGASM   (69%)

ASSESSMENT ONLY	4/14
NO SUCCESS	3/4
TECHNICAL SUCCESS	6/9
SUCCESS	42/53

* 11 patients developed secondary orgasmic dysfunction which they related to the onset of their vaginismus.

* 3 patients became orgastic with resolution of their vaginismus.

During therapy certain male problems were identified. Fifteen men experienced situational impotence during treatment. Nine of these cases occurred during consummation of relationships. All of these cases were associated with successful treatment of vaginismus and were resolved before termination of therapy. Six men complained of premature ejaculation. These complaints were resolved with education and therapy before termination.

CONCLUSION

We feel vaginismus is a more common female sexual problem than previously reported. Without a careful pelvic assessment and re-production of the pain with levator muscle pressure, it is most often overlooked as a complaint of "psychological dyspareunia," and the patient goes home feeling it's all in her head. Careful examination of the introitus will diagnose these patients and provide satisfying results with short-term office or conjoint therapy. Individual therapy can be offered to many women who do not have an ongoing, interested, supportive partner with the ex-pectation of a success rate comparable to conjoint therapy as long as the problem does not stem from a conflicted relationship. On physical evaluation the degree of vaginismus may aid in predicting the duration of therapy needed to resolve the problem. Many pa-tients with the complaint of vaginismus have no difficulty with sexual responsiveness or sexual appetite and their problem is confined solely to involuntary perineal muscle spasms and the resulting coital difficulties. At present this material is being used to develop a protocol to educate health care workers and to further clarify the subtleties of vaginismus and dyspareunia.

REFERENCES

Ellison, C. (1972). Vaginismus. Medical Aspects of Human Sex-
    uality, August, p. 34.

Harlow, R.A. and McCluskey, C.J. (1972). Introital Dyspareunia.
    Clinical Med. 27.

Kaplan, H.S. (1974). The New Sex Therapy, Brunner/Mazel, New York.

Lamont, J.A. (1974). Female Dyspareunia. Canadian Family Phys-
    ician, 20 (8): 53-56.

Masters, W.H. and Johnson, V.E. (1970). Human Sexual Inadequacy,
    Little, Brown and Co., Boston.

Novak, J. (1948). Nature and Treatment of Vaginismus. The Ur. &
    Cut. Review 52: 128.

Interesting. Have noticed that in masturbation — men c̄ situational ejac incomp — often used unusual methods v. dissimilar from coital stimulation. Interesting case history

RETARDED EJACULATION AND TREATMENT

Jay Mann

United States

Retarded ejaculation is a disorder in which the ejaculatory component of the sexual response cycle is totally or partially impaired without impairment of the erectile component. It may be regarded as one end of a continuum of ejaculatory control, with premature ejaculation as the other end.

INCIDENCE

The sparse clinical literature describing retarded ejaculation encompasses only a handful of cases; therefore, it is difficult to estimate the incidence of this condition. Masters & Johnson (1970) reported 17 cases in their original sample of 510 couples treated. Only a few men with the complaint of retarded ejaculation have been treated at the Human Sexuality Program at the University of California School of Medicine. During a three-year period 10 men (of a total of 297 treated for sexual dysfunction) received treatment for retarded ejaculation. Of these, eight have been evaluated one year after treatment. Seven were treated conjointly; three were treated in a men's group augmented by individual counseling but without partner involvement. Four of the above cases were functioning adequately one year after treatment; three did not succeed in reversing the complaint; two are able to ejaculate intravaginally in about 50% of coital episodes, and one ejaculates intravaginally in almost all instances, but requires varying degrees of masturbatory preparation. Nine of these men were able to ejaculate extravaginally before entering treatment; one was not. The Program is currently evaluating an additional five cases now in treatment or less than one year post completion of treatment. I have personally treated an additional four cases conjointly in private practice. Of these, the two most recent cases were able to reverse the complaint within the course of treatment; the two earlier ones were not.

197

I shall first discuss the etiology of retarded ejaculation and describe the condition.   I shall outline some principles of treatment and illustrate them with examples from a case report.

ETIOLOGY

In the psychiatric literature only a few authors have described retarded ejaculation.   In fact, as late as 1968, Ovesey and Meyers (1968) were unable to find a single paper devoted entirely to the subject.   Most authors prior to that time viewed the condition from a psychoanalytic perspective and attributed it to a variety of unconscious factors.   Fenichel (1945) emphasized fears of death and castration, and anal, oral, sadistic and masochistic strivings. Alexander (1950) cited comparable factors, ascribing the condition to regeneration of retaining anal-sadistic tendencies which he regarded as a response to anxiety connected with loss of semen.   Ferenczi (1950) viewed retarded ejaculation as a defense against fear of destruction by the female genitals.   In contrast, Bergler (1935) saw the condition as symptomatic of the man's fear that his ejaculation would destroy the woman.   Although each of these formulations is consistent with psychoanalytic theory, they all lacked adequate clinical data to support their validity.

On the basis of the patients treated privately or at the Columbia University Psychoanalytic Clinic, Ovesey and Meyers (1968) conceptualized retarded ejaculation as "... an attempt to ward off retaliation through the control of symbolic aggression... a withdrawal from competition in anticipation of ultimate defeat."   Masters and Johnson (1970), reporting on the treatment of 17 men with the complaint of "ejaculatory incompetence" over an 11-year period stated that "a multiplicity of factors" may contribute to the development of the condition, a position consistent with social learning theory.   Contributing factors found in subsamples of their treatment group included religious orthodoxy, male fear of pregnancy, negative feelings toward of lack of interest in the partner, and, in a few cases, evidence of homosexual orientation or maternal dominance.   In those instances in which men had lost a preexisting capacity to ejaculate, psychological trauma related to a specific event was most common.

Kaplan (1974) identified both physical and psychogenic factors as potential causes of retarded ejaculation.   Physical factors include anti-adrenergic drugs and diseases that destroy portions of the neurological apparatus that subserve ejaculation.   Kaplan's view of the psychogenic factors influencing retarded ejaculation is eclectic, as is consonant with her view that intrapsychic, interpersonal, and immediate or situational factors all may influence sexual response.   Among intrapsychic factors identified in her patients, are a fear of being abandoned, problems with hostility and

aggression and the use of "holding back" as a defense. She identifies ambivalence or conflict in the dyadic relationship, anxiety
associated with traumatic events, and severe religious upbringing
as additional contributing causes. As do Masters and Johnson,
Kaplan acknowledges that her formulations are derived from relatively limited experience with the disorder.

In our own program at the University of California, the initiating and maintaining factors that we have identified in the few
cases treated have coincided to a large extent with those identified
in the original Masters and Johnson sample. Certainly, rigorous
religious upbringing is one of the more common themes often expressed in a scrupulous or moralistic attitude toward sex. Fear of impregnating the partner has also been noted in some instances. Several of the men seen at the University of California tend to be
super-rational, emotionally controlled individuals, who observe
rather than experience the events of their lives. They have difficulty expressing any strong emotions, particularly anger. They
withdraw from emotional closeness, yet feel an obligation to please
their partners.

Individuals who have lost the capacity to ejaculate after a
period of normal functioning usually report a stressful event that
proceeded the onset of the problem. One man in our sample became
dysfunctional with a new partner after repeatedly practicing coitus
interruptus with a previous one as a means of avoiding pregnancy.
Another man developed partial ejaculatory incompetence after learning of his wife's recent infidelities. A third man lost the capacity to ejaculate when his wife's mother and sister came to live with
them. One man reported that he developed the problem after repeated
episodes of voluntarily delaying ejaculation for long periods to
satisfy his wife.

One additional factor is noteworthy. In interviewing men with
retarded ejaculation our therapists noted that in masturbating, several of them used techniques which provided stimulation varying
greatly from that experienced in coitus. For example, one man would
masturbate by striking the shaft of the penis forcefully with the
heel of his hand; another lightly stroked the urethral meatus with
a throat swab; a third stimulated only one spot on the shaft with
rotary movements of the index finger. Thus, these individuals had
succeeded in conditioning the ejaculatory response to forms of
stimulation not provided by coitus. The framework within which
our group conceptualized retarded ejaculation and its causes is
best described as a social learning formulation. In other words
we view retarded ejaculation as a psychosocially conditioned avoidance response, initiated by avoidance of an aversive stimulus. In
the case of ejaculation, the response acquires aversive connotations
which vary from individual to individual. The avoidance response,
withholding ejaculation, is reinforced and maintained by successful

avoidance of the presumed aversive consequences although the aversive situation that formerly maintained the response may no longer
pertain, the inability to ejaculate often remains firmly entrenched.

We are in agreement with Masters and Johnson that a multiplicity of factors may initiate or maintain the disorder. Given that
the aggregate reported treatment experience is still very limited,
it seems important to consider a range of etiological factors as
potential contributors rather than focusing only on a few presumed
root causes.

DESCRIPTION

Retarded ejaculation may be absolute or partial. I have personally treated a 37-year old client who had experienced nocturnal
emissions but had never been able to ejaculate either through masturbation, coitus, or any other form of direct stimulation. Such
absolute inability to ejaculate is rarely reported. More common
is the inability to ejaculate intravaginally either with a specific
partner or with all partners. In some men, this inability is in-
variant; others are able to ejaculate sporadically, Kaplan (1974)
uses the term "partial retarded ejaculation" to describe a condition
in which little pleasurable sensation is experienced with ejaculation. She attributes this dysfunction to impairment of the urethral and muscular contraction ejaculation phase without impairment
of the emission phase of orgasm.

Cases of retarded ejaculation can also be classified as either
primary or secondary. Primary complaints date from the earliest
onset of sexual activity; secondary complaints are those that develop in individuals who previously had functioned satisfactorily.
Thus the disorder of the 37-year old patient who had never ejaculated would be classified as both primary and absolute.

TREATMENT

The objectives and basic procedures of treatment are as follows:

1. A primary goal is to identify and neutralize any negative
attitudes or emotions, such as guilt or anxiety, that the patient
has come to associate with sexual activity, and, specifically, the
act of ejaculation. The neutralization process may involve exploration of traumatic events or the influence of repressive rearing
patterns. In addition to the more common psychotherapeutic interventions, we have found it useful to have some clients participate
in a weekend sexual attitude reassessment program, in which they
view a variety of explicit erotic films over a period of several
hours, interspersed with large and small group discussion.

2. A second goal is to develop a behavioral context relatively free of anxiety in which the client can learn to experience enhanced levels of stimulation, to focus on them, and to detach his focus from the act of ejaculation itself. If a client enters treatment without a partner, these goals are achieved through assigning self-exploration exercises, the goal of which is to enable the patient to discover for himself what areas of the body are responsive to what kinds of stimulation. The client is taught to stimulate his entire body, not just his genitals, with both the dry and lubricated hand, as well as swatches of chamois, velvet, sateen, and other textured materials, feathers, and in some cases a vibrator. He is taught masturbation techniques approximating coital stimulation and is told to focus only on pleasurable sensation. He is instructed to switch his attention to sexual fantasy in the event that he finds himself focusing on ejaculation as a goal. The patient is also instructed to discontinue stimulation when he has reached a high level of arousal to allow his arousal partially to subside, then to resume stimulation. If the client is tense, he is assigned deep muscle relaxation exercises. The client being treated without a partner is asked to fantasize that the stimulation is being provided by a partner. As he progresses through the stages of treatment, he would fantasize that the imaginary partner is engaged in the same activity that an actual partner would be performing if he were in couples treatment.

If the man enters treatment with a partner, he also begins with self-exploration exercises. The couple is then assigned a graded series of exercises, involving mutual caressing of the entire body. These exercises are diffuse and sensual at first. Later, they become more focused on teasing and titillating touches designed to produce erotic arousal. The couple is instructed to focus merely on sensation and to avoid any activity that implies a demand for ejaculation. Couples may be asked to discontinue coitus temporarily or to relegate it to times other than those devoted to caressing exercises. These procedures are designed on the one hand to raise the input and perception of pleasurable stimulation and on the other to reduce performance anxiety and the obsessive focus on the act of ejaculation-stimuli that presumably interfere with the spontaneous occurrence of ejaculation.

If the man is able to masturbate to ejaculation or becomes able to do so in the course of treatment, he is encouraged in later stages of treatment to masturbate to the point of ejaculatory inevitability before effecting intromission. Once having experienced intravaginal ejaculation by this method, he can insert at a slightly earlier point in time. By continuing to use masturbation as a mode of arousal but by inserting at longer and longer intervals preceding ejaculation, the client becomes able to ejaculate with coital thrusting and can fade out the masturbatory stimulation.

   3. A third objective of treatment is to identify factors in
the client's current life situation that may be maintaining the
dysfunction. If there are difficulties in the client's relationship, often it is necessary to turn attention to the couple's interaction. The couple may need to be taught communication skills
to help them to exchange needed information and to facilitate the
expression of both positive and negative emotions. It is also
important to deal with the patient's expectations. On occasion the
patient may see reversal of his dysfunction as a panacea for all
personal problems, anomie, low self-esteem, depressed affect, or
as an antidote for difficulties in forming or maintaining relationships. If he persists in viewing his emotional well-being as con-
tingent on successful treatment of the ejaculatory problem, treatment becomes a desperation measure and the process of treatment a
new source of tension. Conversely, we have found that a number of
men treated for retarded ejaculation believed at some level of awareness that their dysfunction guarded them against intimacy or commitment to a partner. Before treatment can proceed the client must
learn to recognize that the issue of intimacy or commitment can be
dealt with directly whether or not he is sexually functional. Failure by the therapist to identify the variables in the individual's
life that maintain the dysfunction often becomes apparent when the
man is approaching the culmination of treatment. After making consistent progress, he slows down or relapses. At this point the
therapist can suspect that a crucial variable has been overlooked.

   In order to illustrate some principles of treatment and to
emphasize the importance of identifying elements of the patient's
history that may be maintaining the dysfunction, I will summarize
the case of the 37-year old male referred to previously.

   The client, I shall call him Williams, was the product of a
rigorous religious upbringing by a widowed mother and two unmarried
aunts. He recalled two incidents of mutual genital exploration with
a male classmate at age 9. After each incident he had gone to con-
fession where he had been severely reprimanded by the priest. Thereafter he recalls no sexual activity before marriage except for sporadic attempts at masturbation, accompanied by pangs of guilt and
never culminating in orgasm. By mid-adolescence he had even stopped
masturbating. He and his wife entered therapy at her insistence
seven years into their marriage. They had adopted two children.
Both Williams and his wife were pleasant, self-effacing, religious
people. They described their relationship as compatible and placid
and there was every evidence of mutual affection and respect. Closer
scrutiny of the relationship revealed, however, that both were reluctant to express minor resentments or negative feelings toward
one another for fear of damaging the relationship. Consequently,
each had accumulated a residue of unexpressed resentments toward
the other. Sex was not particularly pleasurable for him although
he could obtain an erection with little stimulation and hold it

indefinitely. His wife enjoyed sex thoroughly and was capable of
multiple orgasms in response to oral, manual, or coital stimulation.
He had never in his life ejaculated except for nocturnal emissions;
however, he was able to maintain penile thrusting until his wife indicated that she was thoroughly gratified. She wanted him to overcome the dysfunction so that he would enjoy sex as much as she did.
Both were asked whether desire to have a biological child was also
a motive. They replied that they might want to do that at some
future time but that procreation was not a priority because they
already had "two adorable adopted children." They reiterated that
their main goal was for him to enjoy sex.

Therapy concentrated on three elements: first, neutralizing his
guilt and anxiety about early sexual experiences and his years of
failure to ejaculate; second, teaching him and his wife to be more
open in expressing their feelings, both positive and negative, to
one another; and third, allowing him to learn new forms of stimulation and ways to sharpen his focus on pleasure in a relaxed setting.
It was hoped that therapy would enable him to masturbate to ejaculation and that he could then generalize the ejaculation to coitus.

Williams and his wife seemed highly motivated and were very
faithful in carrying out assignments and keeping appointments. They
learned to express emotions to one another and found that doing so
improved their relationship. They enjoyed the stroking exercises,
and his pleasure in sexual contact increased steadily.. Viewing
explicit films in the sexual attitude reassessment course repelled
them and outraged their values, according to their report. However,
interestingly enough they reported an exceptionally high level of
erotic pleasure in doing the stroking exercises on the evening after
viewing the films, although they made no causal connection. Williams
was also taught relaxation exercises as a means of reducing his anxiety level. To provide impetus, we had agreed to contract for a
maximum of twelve one-hour sessions. By session eleven, Williams
was still unable to masturbate to ejaculation. Both he and his wife
professed to be very pleased with the effects of therapy on their
relationship, and with his enhanced pleasure in sexual activity.
When asked if there were unrealized goals, other than ejaculation
he said regretfully, almost as an afterthought, that now they would
not be able to realize their dream of having a biological child.
The tone of his voice was revealing. I realized that we had erred
in accepting the couple's original statement that procreation was
a low-priority goal. Perhaps, their loving and loyal feelings for
their adopted children had prevented their admitting even to themselves how much they wanted a biological child. Thus an issue that
both the therapists and clients had passed over lightly proved to be
crucial. Immediately after the session I telephoned a colleague
who had done male fertility research with rhesus monkeys and asked
her advice. She assured me that viable sperm could be drawn from
Williams' epididymis with a hypodermic syringe and could be used

to inseminate his wife. Without double-checking the validity of
the method, I telephoned the good tidings to Williams. He sounded
pleased, but I also noted a moment of silence after I mentioned the
hypodermic.

Between the time of my call to him and the final session, he
succeeded in masturbating to ejaculation three times in three trials.
He said that it felt as though a weight had rolled off his shoulders
when he learned that he would be able to father a child. He also
confessed to some apprehension about the syringe. The couple was
given instructions for generalizing the masturbatory ejaculation to
coitus and told to request further therapy sessions if any difficulties were encountered. He ejaculated on the first coital attempt,
impregnated his wife within the month, and has been functioning very
well for the past three years, except for a few widely spaced incidents of retarded ejaculation which he attributes to transitory
situational factors, such as fatigue.

Although it is difficult to be certain what role the syringe
intervention played in the patient's reversal of the dysfunction,
one might conjecture that detaching procreation from ejaculation
may have drained some of the desperation from his efforts. What
this case clearly illustrates is the importance of identifying and
continuing to track all the historical or current factors in the
patient's life that may be maintaining the problem and working them
through. Although standard techniques for treatment exist, each
patient must be regarded as unique and the strategy selected must
be geared to the specific factors maintaining his problem.

REFERENCES

Alexander, F. (1950). Psychosomatic Medicine, Norton, New York.

Bergler, E. (1935). Some special varieties of ejaculatory dis-
       turbance not hitherto described. Int. J. Psychoanal., 16: 84

Fenichel, O. (1945). The Psychoanalytic Theory of Neurosis, Norton,
       New York.

Ferenczi, S. (1950). The Symbolism of the Bridge, In Selected
       Papers, Vol. 2, Basic Books, New York.

Kaplan, H.S. (1974). The New Sex Therapy, Brunner/Mazel, New York.

Masters, W.H. and Johnson, V.E. (1970). Human Sexual Inadequacy,
       Little, Brown and Co., Boston.

Ovesey, L. and Meyers, H. (1968). Retarded ejaculation: psycho-
       dynamics and psychotherapy. Amer. J. Psychother., 22: 185-201.

MEDROXYPROGESTERONE ACETATE AS AN ANTIANDROGEN FOR THE REHABILITA-

TION OF SEX OFFENDERS

Paul A. Walker

United States

Most sex offenders are male and are properly diagnosed as paraphiliacs. The paraphiliac is totally reliant on a particular
behavior or erotic image for sexual expression. This inappropriate
behavior or image is an imperative, not an option, for arousal.
Although the offender may engage in what appears to be conventional
socially-approved sexual activity with a consenting partner concur-
rent with the paraphiliac behavior, in most cases the approved behavior depends on paraphiliac imagery for adequate arousal and for
erection and orgasm.

Studies of the efficacy of various psychologic intervention
methods demonstrate that the paraphilias are not readily responsive to conventional psychotherapeutic techniques. Should suppression of inappropriate erotic behavior be obtained as a result of
psychotherapy, it may be at the expense of a parallel suppression
of all erotic desire or libido. Alternatively, the inappropriate
erotic behavior may be suppressed but the imagery of that behavior
may persist in erotic fantasy.

The treatment program used since 1966 in the Psychohormonal
Research Clinic at Johns Hopkins Hospital in Baltimore combines
psychologic counseling with the medication medroxyprogesterone-
acetate (Depo-Provera[R], Upjohn) -- an antiandrogen which lowers
the levels of plasma testosterone produced by the testes. It may
also have a direct and beneficial effect on pathways in the central
nervous system which mediate sexual imagery and practice. The goal
of this therapy is to reduce erotic desire (measured by self-reports
of imagery, erections, and orgasm frequencies) so that the patient
is given a "vacation" from his previous sex life. The thresholds

205

or barriers that block the release of erotic arousal and behavior
respectively are temporarily and beneficially raised, so long as
the medication continues. During this period of lessened sexual
tension, psychologic counseling is offered and the patient achieves
a new ability of self regulation which is maintained as the medication schedule is reduced.

The usual dosage regimen is 400 mg, intramuscularly, per week,
for 8 weeks. Thereafter the dosage is gradually lowered in 50 mg
increments so long as maximal testosterone depletion is maintained
and sexual arousal and behavior are still within tolerable and self-
controllable intensities. The combined endocrine therapy and psychologic counseling are then continued long-term (6 months to 2
years or longer) until such time as a gradual final weaning from
the medication seems warranted. In case of a relapse or suspected
imminent relapse, endocrine therapy may be re-started at any time.
Dependent on the patient's body mass and on the severity of his
paraphiliac behavior (as in extreme sadism) the beginning dosage
may be set at 500 mg/week, or higher.

RESULTS

In our most recently published follow-up study (Money, Wiedeking, Walker, Migeon, Meyer and Borgaonkar, 1975) data were reported
on the treatment of 15 sex offending paraphiliacs, including pedo-
philiacs (heterosexual and homosexual), exhibitionists, a masochist,
and an incestuous pedophiliac transvestite. Five of these have completed the therapy program and have evidenced long-term omission of
the sex offending behavior. All of those treated evidenced a decrease, self labeled as significant, of sexual desire and behavior.

DILEMMAS

Therapeutic intervention, even when requested by the patient,
carries with it the supposition that the therapeutic goal is ethically correct. The difficulty with this supposition is that there
are no universally accepted criteria for what is ethically correct.
In our clinics we use a working rule that a paraphilia form of
sexual expression warrants an attempt at treatment when that expression requires that the partner be a nonconsenting adult or
child or, even with consent, when the outcome of the sexual activity brings grievous bodily harm to one or both partners.

In cases where grievous body harm is essential for erotic
arousal (as in rape, sadism, lust murder, and masochism), the use
of an antiandrogen with relatively rapid cessation of erotic arousal is preferred over other forms of therapies whose beneficial
results, if any, are dangerously too long delayed.

The current concern over informed consent for prisoners who are sex offenders is another dilemma. In the present ill-defined situation prisoners are caught in a paradox. Zealots who claim to be protecting prisoners' rights have, in effect, stripped the prisoner of any rights whatsoever in obtaining the therapy of their choice. The sex-offender prisoner usually cannot obtain parole without demonstrating a realistic and prognostically favorable treatment program and the most prognostically favorable form of treatment is denied to them, because it is still considered investigational, until after they are paroled. Likewise, the arrested sex offender, awaiting trial, is denied access to therapy even though it is precisely at that time that they are most likely to ask for help. People seek help when they hurt, and the sex offender rarely hurts until arrest occurs or is imminent.

The pendulum of prisoner's rights has swung dangerously too far toward the conservative. The solution will be complex and will require a close cooperation between law, ethics, and medicine.

In my own recently established clinic at The University of Texas Medical Branch at Galveston, three potentially dangerous sex offenders were voluntarily begun on combined antiandrogen therapy and psychologic counseling literally hours before arrest -- at which time they would have been disqualified for therapy, in the supposed protection of their free-will.

REFERENCES

Money, J., Wiedeking, C., Walker, P., Migeon, C., Meyer, W., and Borgaonkar, D. (1975). 47,XYY and 46,XY males with antisocial and/or sex-offending behavior: antiandrogen therapy plus counseling, Psychoneuroendocrinology, 1: 165-178.

THE USE OF AUDIO-VISUAL MATERIALS IN THERAPY

Wardell B. Pomeroy

United States

In dealing with the sexual problems of patients, whether these patients are presenting a sexual dysfunction, a marital problem involving sex, or some form of sexual inhibition, it appears to me that one of the first and foremost functions of a therapist is to undo the negative conditioning of the past, and to supplant it with a receptivity and an exuberance toward sexual variety and sexual abandonment that will enable patients to move toward a more functional and healthy sexual life. One of the ways this can be done is through audio and visual materials. There is a body of data on the effect of sexually explicit materials on the average person; but, to my knowledge, there is little or no research of this kind on sexually dysfunctional people. Because there are little, if any, data to support the value of such stimuli, I will report on my own clinical practice, my own observations, and my own patient feedback which have helped me develop the procedures I have used with my own clientele.

When one reviews the history of our sexual mores one is struck by the overwhelming weight of the sexual repressions that continues to burden all but the most fortunate. "Don't talk about sex," "treat sex as a joke," "don't think about sex," "don't fantasy sex," "sex is dirty," "sex is bad," "God and Christ are sexless," "don't flaunt sex," "keep your dress down and your fly zippered." The list of prohibitions and restraints imposed on us by our culture is endless. Anthropologists tell us there is scarcely a culture in the world, be it primitive or advanced, with more sexual repression than our own; and don't forget that culture is really all of us in the aggregate.

Some of the restraints mentioned earlier that must be overcome
if one is to be able to get more out of his or her sexual life are
inhibitions against nudity, places where sex can take place, times
when it can occur, variations in positions and techniques, oral and
anal sex, verbalizations and vocalizations, fantasy, to mention
only a few. How a therapist tackles these various behavior changes
depends on the training, background, and personality of the therapist. I use a variety of means including role modeling, exhorta-
tion, specific homework, behavior modification and audio and visual
materials.

DIFFERENT APPROACHES FOR USE OF AUDIO-VISUAL MATERIALS

There are at least three different types of approaches for
use of audio-visual materials which are part of the armamentarium
of therapists.

Information

The first approach is simply informational: How does one masturbate? What are various positions in intercourse? How does
sensate focus work? What do female genitalia look like? Where is
the clitoris? What is one's body imagery? How is a sexological
examination taken? The old dictum "a picture is worth a thousand
words" is certainly true in this situation. However, don't be
fooled by the idea that only information is being given. A much
more important aspect to this process is attitudinal. When showing a "how to masturbate" film for example, the message is not only
"this is one way to masturbate," but more importantly the message
is: "it is all right to masturbate," and "it is all right to observe someone else masturbate," and "see I, the therapist, am watching this with you and I feel this is a worthwhile film or I wouldn't
be showing it to you." Patient feedback after viewing such films
is almost universally favorable as evidenced by such statements as
"now I can picture it better" or "I feel less anxious or fearful
about my own sexuality."

Seeing pictures or watching films with the patient should be
done in a nonerotic atmosphere. This does not mean that patients
do not get aroused while viewing this material, for they often do.
However, if the therapist brings to the attention of the patient
the erotic nature of the film or is perceived by the patient as
being aroused, this will in many cases become threatening to the
patient. I find that at some later time, either in masturbation
or socio-sexual activity, prior viewing of the audio-visuals will
serve as fantasy material for the patient.

There is a great need for both an increased number and better
quality films of an educational nature. A proliferation of such

audio-visuals in the near future is inevitable. I believe that many
therapists dealing with sexual problems will develop libraries of
these films and further, because of the expense involved, will become associated with lending libraries and joint libraries owned by
groups of therapists. Because audio-visuals of a sexual nature are
often difficult to acquire and because many patients are embarrassed
to purchase them publically, it would be helpful if therapists who
possess them could lend or rent them to selected patients. More
films showing "ordinary" people, by this I mean not the young and
the beautiful, but the old, the fat, and the unbeautiful, will help
patients relate to the subjects in the films in a more meaningful
way than is presently allowed by the Hollywood type films that represent the beginning of this genre. An additional need is for
shorter films of 7 to 10 minutes in length; these films can be more
useful in many cases than the more prevalent 20 to 30 minute films.

     Bibliotherapy can be a very useful device in sex therapy. The
therapist's knowledge of relevant books in this area is imperative.
Permission-giving books such as The Joy of Sex, The Yes Book of
Masturbation, For Yourself, Liberating Masturbation, and The Sen-
suous Woman can be particularly helpful. Books dealing with fantasy
such as My Secret Garden, Forbidden Flowers, and To Turn You On can
give patients subject matter and situations that they can incorporate
into their own fantasies.

     Resistance, however, is a common reaction to bibliotherapy.
This takes the form of forgetting to do homework, not being able
to get the recommended books, not finding time to read them, forgetting what they said, and a hundred other ways of negating the
message that the therapist and the authors are trying to get across.
The job of the therapist, as I see it, is to confront the patient
with his resistance and attempt to break through it. In fact, I
believe that the primary job in sex therapy is to deal with the
myriad resistances that are constantly encountered.

                         Erotic Enjoyment

     The second approach for use of audio-visual material is that
which deliberately appeals to the erotic enjoyment of the recipient.
This is given as homework to the patient, although I prefer to call
it "home play." Erotic movies such as "Deep Throat," "The Devil in
Miss Jones," "The Naughty Victorians," etc. are sometimes recommended. Films that have a believable plot, are well acted, and well
produced usually are preferable to the so-called fuck films. A
sensitive and delicate skill is needed by the therapist to determine
when a particular patient or couple are ready for this kind of "home
play" and to determine then which films are best for them. For example, soft core films such as "The Story of O" (although the sado-
masochistic theme in it is usually contraindicated) are better as

a first exposure than hard core films such as "Deep Throat." The
very act of going into a theater where such a film is being shown
may be an important breakthrough for the patient.

In addition to films, there are records available which have
nothing but the recorded sounds people make when they are building
up to and having orgasm. I have been surprised to learn how many
people engage in sex in deadly silence. These records have proven
useful in allowing people to express their mounting sexual excitement
verbally, vocally, and hence, releasing another inhibition which prevents their abandonment.

Sex Attitude Restructuring Program

The third approach for use of audio-visual materials is through
a Sex Attitude Restructuring program (referred to as a SAR). This
program was developed at the National Sex Forum in San Francisco and
is now being used, expanded, and modified in many parts of the country. Heavy use is made of audio-visual materials as a means of first,
desensitizing people to viewing sexually explicit behaviors and second, as a consequence, allowing them to more willingly accept their
own sexual behavior.

Research on the effects of pornography for the average person
almost universally shows that erotic arousal is transitory (2 days
to 2 weeks), and that overt behavior is effected only in a limited
way. A quarter of the people in a SAR program will engage in some
different type of sexual behavior but will rarely engage in behavior they had not already thought of doing. In other words, the
SAR gave them the permission they needed to do what they already
wanted to do. Females report that the most important thing they
got out of their SAR program was the freedom and ability to talk
more openly about sex. Males reported that the actual scenes of
sexual activity were an endorsement of their own feelings and behavior. If this is the case, then the question may legitimately
be asked why it is of value in sex therapy. The answer, as I see
it, is twofold. First, people who have sexual dysfunctions are
not average; in particular, they have a higher degree of fear,
anxiety, and inhibition in the sexual area. And second, they need
a push, a mechanism, a way of releasing their sexuality, which can
be helped by audio-visual stimuli. Because of the transitory nature of such materials it is seldom indeed that patients get "hooked"
on them and continue to use them regularly as part of their sexual
life.

CONCLUSION

Finally, the point must be made that various techniques or gimmicks if you will, do not strike at the heart of good sex therapy. Sex therapy is first and foremost <u>therapy</u> of a specialized nature. To think of a stockpile of good audio-visual materials as the quintessence of good sex therapy is analogous to thinking of a surgeon with the sharpest or newest scalpel as the best. Unpublished research indicates that if the therapist is uncomfortable with films showing explicit sexual activity or if the therapist has low expectations of their efficacy, the target patient will get little or no help from them and further might even be harmed by them. The same can be said for the use of sensate focus, the squeeze technique, conjoint therapists or any other tool or device that has been developed in sex therapy. The focus on training sex therapists has, in my estimation, been too much in the direction of teaching devices or interventions and too little in the direction of sound, basic psychotherapy. Thus it is my hope that these remarks about the use of audio-visual materials will be taken in their proper perspective.

THE EROTIC-BODILY CONTACT APPROACH IN SEXOLOGY

Jean-Yves Desjardins, Willy Pasini & Claudette Isabelle

Canada - Switzerland

The historical evolution of sex therapy in recent years has
gone through the two major streams illustrated by the psychoanalysis and by the therapy practiced by Masters and Johnson. The first
of these has given us an interesting theoretical model and basic
concepts which have resisted much repeated criticism. We owe to
psychoanalysis an outlook on sexuality which is partly autonomous,
because Freud was the first to rediscover and valorize infantile
sexuality wherein the natural biology is nonreproductive. We must
also give credit to psychoanalysis for other fundamental concepts,
from sexual problems - conflicts related to personal development
beyond the negative and repressive restraints imposed externally or
socially on sexual impulses. Finally, we must thank psychoanalysis
for those principles which today are widely applied in sex therapy,
such as the importance of quality in sexual responsivity as opposed
to quantity, and the value of the imaginary and of fantasy considered to be an infinite reserve of eroticism. Traditional criticism
of psychoanalysis includes the theory which does not consider childhood to be the source of numerous sexual problems but rather relates
these problems to a reflex phenomenon or else to pathologic dysfunctions affecting the involved couple.

Personally, our overall criticism of psychoanalysis is for having ignored the body, at least in its perceptive dimension. Of course,
the body is represented in the imaginary, but direct perception is
minimized and the body itself is not sufficiently present in therapy
because both words and verbalization of the affect constitute the
basic tools used in psychoanalysis.

The historic work of Masters and Johnson, with codification
of brief therapy for the couple, allows for an improved reinstatement of the body inasmuch as the couple's sensorial dialogue is the
prelude to satisfactory sexual responsivity. Exploratory exercises,
intelligently measured between the permissible or otherwise, performed on one's own body as well as on the partner's, become an
effective solution in many cases of sexual dysfunctioning. In a
social context where both the verbal and written languages are frequently alienated, the possibility of a couple's rediscovery of a
privileged form of communication through reciprocal sensory exchange
is one of the great scientific acquisitions we have from William
Masters and Virginia Johnson.

In regard to the objective of this exposé, i.e., the body, Masters' approach is still limited, because there is a lack of physical contact between therapist and subject (apart from the initial
somatic examination) and therapy consists in exercises to be performed by the couple behind closed doors.

Even though the psychoanalytic approach as well as that of
Masters have been applied by the Geneva Clinic for Sexual Dysfunction
during the past seven years, the therapists are now sounding out the
idea of a more frequent use of the body itself in the course of sex
treatment. The immediate reaction blocking this attitude was the
negative medical outlook; the philosophy was either to asepticize
the body through gynecological or urological exploration and consider it as a functioning or organic entity, or else the body would
be referred to specialists in eroticism (Thai masseurs, for example),
where it became evident that medical massage or kinesitherapy prescribed to relieve pelvic or spinal discomfort allowed the body to
discover a new dimension of sensation and eventual erotic prospects.
On the other hand, the dialectic understanding of psychoanalysis
and the Masterian concept have provided an effective integrated
form of therapy of which an excellent example would be vaginismus
and unconsummated marriages, wherein over 30 per cent of the 140
cases under treatment during two years have been cured by means of
psychodynamic understanding combined with the appropriate form of
exercise, as opposed to gynecological intervention or various types
of psychotherapy, considered separately.

Bodily contact - between the couple and eventually in larger
groups - may be applied through various forms of massage, relaxation, body expression and individual gestures. This should also
include the valuable organization of psychosexual life-rhythm and
the possibility of vocal expression.

PRINCIPLES PERTAINING TO BODILY CONTACT

These principles have been applied during the past two years

in cases studied at the Geneva Clinic for Sexual Dysfunction and
at the Montreal Professional Centre of Sexology:

1. The reinstatement of bodily integrity and of the
    image of the body as an entity.

Certain patients have divided feeling concerning their body,
denying some of its parts in favor of others. While exercises
upon mutual communication may be palliative, other pathological
situations may require the active assistance of a therapist.

2. Revival of sensations and their explicitation.

People often say they feel nothing, or else, they are so intent upon the expectation of erotic sensations and of the orgasm
which does not take place that they should be made aware of the
situation. Others experience sensations which seem disagreeable
to them but which may be the only means of rediscovering coenes-
thesis. This recalls to mind an anorgasmic woman whose reactions
were negative during her first therapeutic sessions and who later
complained of an aggravating feeling of cold feet and of perspiration; yet, this very chilliness allowed her to remember a childhood experience which had traumatized her entire sexual outlook.

3. The energizing revival in the bioenergetic perspective.

The fundamental principle in bioenergetics holds that there
are certain blocks, at the muscular and characterial levels of certain individuals whose vital energy may be liberated by active techniques and more effectively utilized. In opposition to some forms
of Gestaltism, unfortunately, bioenergetics is too long a therapy
(often lasting over several years) to satisfy anxious patients who
require therapy giving efficacious and reasonably swift results.

4. Authorized modulated regression.

Take the case of a "self made" businessman, long accustomed
to forging ahead and saving face, ever active, even during the
weekend, who is no longer able to keep up the pace. His sexuality
may undergo the same reaction because of the increasing demands of
the woman in his life. This situation may be alleviated through
massage and by adopting certain types of posture which allow him to
retire within himself, (such as curling up in the fetal position);
this constitutes a fundamental modulated regression in order to attain an energizing recuperation on both the physical and psychic

levels. This regression may occasionally be brought about in situations related to everyday living (going to the barber, taking
a shower, etc.), but it may, at times, require expert therapeutic
assistance.

5. Privileged communication when there is alienation or
nonemotional investment in language.

This topic has already been discussed in our introduction.

6. Awareness of one's role.

When sexological requirements conceal more important psychological problems (relationship between a couple or a problem affecting an individual member) postural exercises may fill an urgent
need. In certain instances, verbal counselling may correct faulty
communication on the pathologic level, an approach advocated by
Masters, and especially applied by Philip and Lorna Sarrel of Yale
who insist on communication at the outset of sex therapy. But in
other situations, whether in sex therapy or in para-hospital psychiatry, there seems to be a sort of psychic blindness toward one's
own attitudes and behavior. Therefore, it is necessary to introduce
both experiment and verification so that individuals and couples
may really understand themselves.

This is where audio-visual aids render great services. Alternating the use of the body, of gestures and their meaning, appears
in our eyes a novel course of action in sexual pathology wherein
perception and representation are harmoniously combined as they
naturally exist in everyone.

Finally, a political reference is necessary here, as the bodily contact program tends to democratize sex therapy. Indeed,
many of those who seek consultation (especially those in less-
favored ranks of society) find their "modus vivendi" and their
means of communication in everyday life. It is therefore a delu-
sion - not to say, a form of cruelty - to oblige such patients to
submit to verbal therapy when words mean little to them. Under
these circumstances, bodily contact, instead of replacing psychotherapy, becomes an excellent propaedeutic practice.

The bodily approach may assume various forms. Among other applications, it has been used in cases of erectile insufficiency in
the male and coital anorgasm in the female. Let us now examine the
erotic bodily contact approach in sex therapy.

EROTIC BODILY CONTACT: A THERAPY FOR
MEN SUFFERING FROM SEXUAL PROBLEMS

This procedure is applied by a female therapist at the Professional Centre of Sexology of Montreal; the patients are men without sexual partners, either because they have never attempted sexual relationship with women or because of precarious erotic bonds between their present partners, or else the female correspondent has constantly refused to submit to therapeutic measures. This procedure has been developed during the past two years of our own therapeutic work.

The therapeutic goals sought in this procedure are: 1) to discover the elements in the patient's erotic dynamics; 2) to detect the manifestation related to the patient's sex disturbances; 3) to induce genital focussing in sex experience through verbal and bodily approach methods.

The principal psychological and bodily elements of disturbed behavior as well as the necessary therapeutic steps to be taken will be illustrated from the approach used for men suffering from erectile insufficiency because the findings in the final analysis show that erectile insufficiency rests on faulty genital focussing in sex experience. We know how complicated it is to elaborate the clinical aspect of erectile insufficiency; therefore, we shall limit our observation to the therapeutic bodily approach, i.e., the lack of genital focussing in sexual activity, which may or may not be evident.

The conscious demand

Most men who consult us admit to erectile impotency and seem obsessed by the desire to function normally. Not only does this obsession influence all their sexual behavior but it also affects their entire range of intimate activities. Thus, we see a conscious preoccupation focussed on the possibility of "having an erection."

The erotic imaginary

What can be learned from the conscious images present in those obsessed by this dysfunction? To put it simply, whatever the type of imaginary investment, it is rare - or even impossible - to find the penis as the basis of sexual fantasy. The proprioceptive dynamism of the penis may be lurking in the shadows, but its exterioceptive dynamism is completely forgotten. Creative imaginary eroticism may not even exist, or if it does, it adheres to sentimental or affective norms in which genital desire plays little part. It is not

rare to observe the erotic imaginary wherein fantasy denies the
importance of phallic activity.

Psychosomatic reactions

There are two behavioral choices in men who suffer from erectile insufficiency. The first may be described as complete renunciation with regard to any erotic attempt whatsoever, whereas the
second consists in a frantic search for sensations capable of pro-
voking erection:

1. It is not difficult to observe that patients who seem to
have renounced all hope of erection are among those who deny their
physical ability to accomplish this function. Such men present a
visible form of relaxation based on voluntary muscular slackness as
a cover for their inability to function, but they also exhibit muscular tension in the buttocks or in the thigh adductors or even
involuntary spasms, all of which are body barriers to penile sensory
investment.

2. However, most of the men seen in therapy will cover the
field of sexual activity, indulging in gestures, caresses, movements,
rhythmic contractions of the pelvis and excessive penile agitation,
in a conscious attempt to activate erotization...but all of which
counteracts the possibility of conversion into true sexual tension.
The outward signs displayed momentarily sidetrack and obscure the
importance of genital functioning.

Therapeutic objectives

The first of these is to attempt to focus the subject's attention and concentration (however unpleasant) on the erotic interest
of genitality. In our opinion, one of the most efficacious and
rapid methods of discerning vital genitality is through the postural
approach and therapeutic bodily attitude which reinforce perception
and assume that genitality truly exists (even if it be inadequate).

The bodily approach should be capable of eliciting full erectile responsivity, which is the only aim of this procedure. Responsivity should lead to the re-establishment of erectile functioning
in the patient's erotic make-up, that is, his ability to perform,
which is the visible sign of his virility and the basis of his sexual activity as well as the guarantee of the fulfillment of his
desire.

This first step includes verbal exchange, because this aspect
is also part of erectile recovery and has its role in the ensemble

of the subject's sexual life. Modification in the orientation of
the subject's imaginative creativity is almost always apparent and
the existence of erection with its erotic interrelative potential
becomes increasingly significant.

The second step in the erotic bodily approach should encourage
the subject's ability:

1. to organize his somatic motility from the pelvic axis, so
that motility may become an extension of erectile consistency;

2. to have access to the body of another person (partner) at
the moment when erection allows for erotic interaction.

The subtlety of this therapy lies in the sequence of action
which promotes an approach toward another person without, however,
jeopardizing erectile consistency. And this approach is possible
only when the male subject has imaginatively, emotively, and physically integrated his erection with its dynamic potential.

EROTIC-BODILY CONTACT: A THERAPY FOR
WOMEN SUFFERING FROM COITAL ANORGASM

The erotic bodily approach, as applied by a male therapist to
female sexual dysfunctions, will be confined to incidences of coital
anorgasm.

As previously mentioned, somatic therapy applied to the male
subject stresses the phallic dimension, which is the indispensable
starting point of his sexual tension regarding interaction with a
female partner. However, this concept is not the same when the
subject is a woman. We are now referring to one of the many dysfunctions observed in the women treated during the past twelve
years: coital anorgasm. Coital anorgasm is the impossibility for
a woman to reach orgasm during coitus even if orgasm may be attained
during other allo or auto-sexual activities.

Without elaborating upon the entire range of therapy applied
here, we shall examine the erotic bodily approach and the reasons
underlying this method. Experience has led us to set down seven
postulates which can be found more detailed in "La complémentarité
érotique" (Crépault and Desjardins, 1976):

1. Apart from its initiating circumstances, such as lack of
rehearsal, repeated vaginal infection, competitive ideology, the
partner's incapacity, etc., coital anorgasm is more a dysfunction
of a woman's erotic identity in regard to the man than the result
of inadequate sexual behavior.

2.   Although it cannot be physiologically separated from vulvar orgasm, coital orgasm substantially differs according to the
subjective outlook of each woman.

3.   Coital orgasm should be viewed by the subject as a source
of personal bodily pleasure, but the subject should also consider
her body and vagina in direct relation to man and his phallus.

4.   Orgasm provoked by stimulation of the vulva and the clitoris affects a woman's sensoriality and excites very localized
regions of her body, whereas coital orgasm is a more global mechanism of excitation and has more interiorized repercussions.

5.   In a coital anorgastic woman, the threshold of excitability is sufficiently developed to bring on orgastic spasms to the
critical point.   Excitability is centered principally at the vulvar region or at, or near, the clitoris.   Such women are accessible and easily aroused by caressing, especially with a gentle touch.

6.   These women, however, are generally cold to an approach
which does not include epidermic fondling.

7.   The low level of bodily motility is due to the fact that
the focus of excitability is confined to a specific physical zone.

The aim of our erotic bodily approach is to make the subject
aware of a different erotic dimension than that which has given her
extra-coital satisfaction - a dimension which is global, diffuse,
and interiorized.   The treatment should take into consideration
the following general postulate: some types of erotic bodily approach are capable of promoting either female sensoriality or vaginality (i.e., interiority) and the approach should be adapted
to the subject's needs (sensoriality or else, vaginality).

To treat coital anorgasm, the erotic bodily approach must
endeavor:

1.   to use a touch-type which will not arouse the subject's
sensoriality;

2.   to avoid tactile methods in the erogenous zones capable
of launching extra-coital orgasm;

3.   to employ a slow, practically static tactile method, muscular rather than epidermal, directed mainly toward the medial or
dorsal parts of the body the flanks, belly and abdomen.   When performed slowly, with undulating strokes, a powerful emotional reaction ensues, accompanied by violent abdominal spasms.   In the course
of the following interviews, the emotional reactions are recorded on

a determined rating scale as to their erotic and vaginal progress.

The subject is thus made aware of a kind of excitation which is more general, convergent, and in accordance with her vaginal universe. It is this erotic interiority (studied here for some years now) that has been left out of contemporary sex research, although it is the connerstone of harmonious male-female sexual relationship. As this dimension has not been quantified in the current methods of sex therapy, it would seem that it simply had never been heard of.

It is not surprising, therefore, that the North American male, and we dare say, North American sexology itself, has unconsciously exercised a kind of reductivism in human eroticism, and we are even tempted to add that in America, sexology limps painfully along, deprived of the diversified enrichment of feminine sexual tension.

In conclusion, we are reminded of an Oriental saying: "sexuality is not only sensation: it is also emotion." Erotic interaction is not only coitus, fellatorism, cunnilingus, or even orgasm, it is also a ritual, an emotion, even tenderness; it is warmth, ecstasy, in fact, a symphony.

When a society which proclaims through its most qualified experts in the field of sexuality that such fundamentals of human eroticism should be denied, or else, belittled, the time has come for self inspection.

REFERENCES

Crepault, C., Desjardins, J.-Y., (1976). "La complémentarité
        érotique." Educom, Montréal.

MICROPHALLUS: THE SUCCESSFUL USE OF A PROSTHETIC PHALLUS IN A

NINE-YEAR-OLD BOY

Tom Mazur

United States

Microphallus, also known as micropenis and partial agenesis
of the penis, is a condition in which the corpora of the penis are
agenetic or vestigial to a variable degree.   There is no other defect of embryogenesis of the external genitalia.

In microphallus, the corpora of the penis are primarily affected.   The penile skin, glans, urethra, and urethral meatus are
intact.   The testes may be of normal size, and descended, though
they may also be small with one or both undescended.   The entire
organ is extremely small.   At the age of nine, the patient I am
reporting on had a penis the stretched length of which was 3 cm.
The internal genitalia are differentiated as male and the chromosomes are 46, XY.

There is no way, surgically or hormonally to enlarge a microphallus so that it can function completely as a penis of normal
size in adulthood.   Consequently, the preferred treatment for an
infant with partial agenesis of the penis is sex assignment at
birth as a female with appropriate surgical, hormonal and psychologic habilitation.   In the past, many microphallic infants have
been assigned at birth as males.   Typically they have differentiated a masculine gender identity.   For one of them in boyhood, we
were able to obtain a prosthetic phallus of juvenile size.

This phallic prosthesis (Figure 1) is made of nontoxic flexible plastic.   It is hollow and has a hole for urinary use.   It
fits into a specially prepared athletic support (jock strap) that
acts as a belt to hold it in place, so that it can be used for urination in the standing position.   Without the prosthesis, the boy's

own penis itself is too small to manipulate for standing to urinate
while fully clothed. When not used for urinating, the prosthesis
is soft enough not to appear conspicuous within the pants, but to
create a natural-looking genital bulge.

The patient has been wearing the prosthetic phallus for over
a year now. He wears it on the average five days a week, and has
had no chaffing, rash, or other type of skin irritation. His initially high level of excitement about wearing the prosthesis has
gradually given way to a matter-of-fact acceptance. He says, "it
feels good" and he "feels happy" about being able to urinate through
it. Hypothetically, he would advise another microphallic boy to
wear a prosthetic phallus, " 'cause it would help him to stand up
to urinate."

Manufacturing improvements of phallic prostheses, including
graduated sizes and skin-color matching, are presently being negotiated. Even though not perfect, there is no doubt in the minds
of all concerned that the present model has proved therapeutically
beneficial. It has enhanced the boy's self-esteem and self-confi-
dence as a male. Hypothetically, it will be incorporated into his
body image so that he will be able to put it to erotic use when
the time comes for him to begin having sexual intercourse.

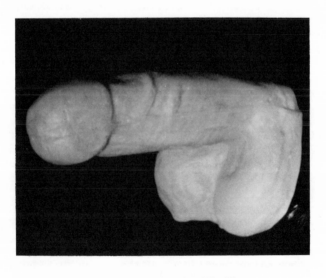

Fig. 1.   Prosthetic Phallus.

a) Hymeneal strand .

b) Cassette records — EEG, ECG, vaginal
photoplethysmography during stim. ⇒ org.

BIOLOGICAL ASPECTS OF SEXUAL FUNCTION

Philip M. Sarrel

United States

The importance of biological factors in human sexual functioning is clearly delineated in the work of William Masters and Virginia Johnson (1966). The same investigators also demonstrated
highly successful results in the treatment of sexual dysfunction
when using a therapeutic approach influenced by the observations
established in the laboratory (Masters and Johnson, 1970). Since
their initial reports, there has been an ever-increasing interest
on the part of other biologically oriented scientific investigators
in applying their own particular disciplines to the study and understanding of sexual function.

The two subjects selected for discussion in this presentation
fall under the general topic of "Biological Aspects of Sexual Function." Our work at Yale involves sex therapy and sex education,
as well as sex research. We cannot and do not separate the psychological and the biological. Instead, we are always aware of the
interaction of the mind and the body when considering the meaning
of a finding that relates to sexuality. Thus, the first subject -
the presence of an epithelial strand subdividing the hymeneal
aperture - is an old anatomic finding reported herein because of
its significance in the development of fear of vaginal penetration.
The second part of the paper - a description of a system for simultaneous recording of brain, cardiac and pelvic physiology during
sex response in an at-home environment is one way of shedding some
light on the interaction of mind and body.

THE HYMENEAL STRAND

In an adult woman who has not experienced vaginal penetration

227

of any kind (no intercourse, no masturbatory penetration, no use of
tampons), the hymeneal membrane has a central opening allowing the
out-flow of normal vaginal secretions and of the menstrual flow.
The tissue about the opening is pliable and can normally be stretched
to permit a 15 mm tampon to be inserted without discomfort arising
from the hymen itself. It is also usually possible to insert a
30 mm diameter vaginal speculum and open it to expose the cervix
without causing pain. The position of the membrane at the junction
of the urogenital sinus and the lower vagina is invariable, the
membrane having been formed as a by-product of the embryological
process involved in the formation of the vagina. Interestingly,
in a survey of 300 college women, Lorna Sarrel and I have found
that 54% believed the hymen was situated directly in front of the
cervix, just beyond the point a tampon reaches. Many of these
women believed it was a closed membrane but semi-permeable allowing
the menstrual flow to pass.

     Figure 1 summarizes the processes involved in the formation
of the vagina. There is a stage when the vagina is a solid core
of tissue which becomes hollowed-out due to recanalization by invading epithelial cells. These invading columns can be split by
one or more mesodermal septa resulting in many different types of
hymeneal and vaginal anatomy. (See Bulmer (1957) for a fuller
discussion). Figure 2 illustrates some of the variants which have
already been described including the hymeneal strand variety to
which I would now like to direct your attention.

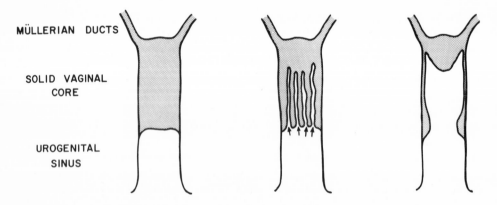

Fig. 1. Processes involved in the formation of the vagina.

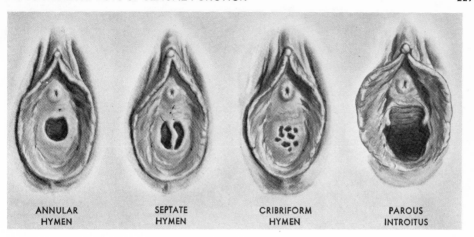

| ANNULAR | SEPTATE | CRIBRIFORM | PAROUS |
| HYMEN | HYMEN | HYMEN | INTROITUS |

Fig. 2.   Hymeneal strand variety.

In our work with adolescent and young adult women we have seen 15 patients who chose to come to our sex counseling program and who were found to have a hymeneal strand on pelvic examination. Figure 3 illustrates the "typical appearance" in women who have not had intercourse. The intact strand is approximately 5 mm in diameter. It extends from the anterior to the posterior rim of the hymeneal ring usually intersecting the rim at a 90° angle but this may vary. In women who have experienced vaginal penetration, including 4 women in our series, who had had sexual intercourse, the strand can be intact. In such cases, it is usually elongated and dis- placed, laterally (Figure 4). Four of the 15 women were found to have broken strands. The separated stumps could be easily iden- tified and approximated (Figure 5). All of the women showed a vaginismus reaction.

Incidence

The incidence of the strand is not established. In this re- gard, Bulmer (1957) wrote:

"In many instances it appears, the root of the sinus upgrowth is split at its origin from the dorsal wall of the sinus by the inclusion of a small mesodermal septum . . . The persis- tence of such a septum, as in the 112 mm. foetus, and its development into a hymeneal septum, as in the 140 mm. foetus, must be fairly common, and occurred in many of the specimens examined by Meyer (1934-38). The persistence of a more ex- tensive septum in the utero-vaginal canal would account, in a similar manner, for a congenital duplication of the vagina."

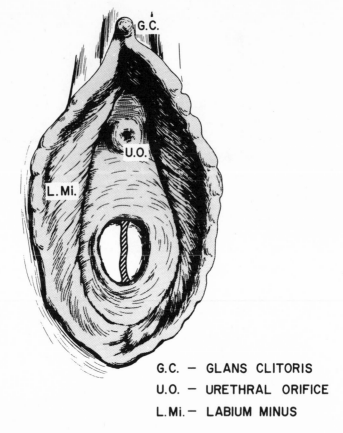

G.C. — GLANS CLITORIS
U.O. — URETHRAL ORIFICE
L.Mi. — LABIUM MINUS

Fig. 3.   Typical appearance of hymeneal strand in women who have not had intercourse.

We are presently examining infant females to determine the incidence of the hymeneal strand at birth.   According to the work of Kravitz (1973) over 90% of female infants finger-penetrate their vaginal orifices before the end of their first year.   This may break the strand and make diagnosis of its presence extremely difficult, the only true incidence therefore would be found by examining newborns.   Unfortunately, the newborn study has not progressed adequately to report the findings at this time.

In the young adult population, I have found nine women with strands among 200 consecutive young women seen in the Yale Sex Counselling Program.   This pre-selection factor, however, makes the 4.5% incidence only an approximation of the true incidence in the general population.   Described elsewhere (Sarrel and Sarrel, 1971), the Yale Counselling Program, started in 1969, is a function

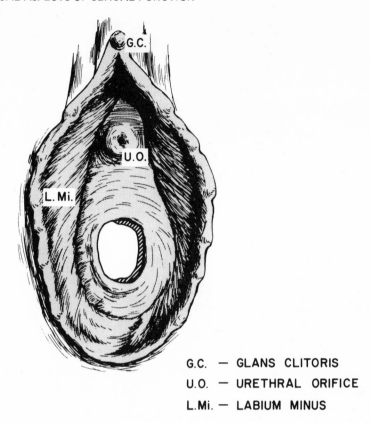

G.C. — GLANS CLITORIS

U.O. — URETHRAL ORIFICE

L.Mi. — LABIUM MINUS

Fig. 4.   Intact but displaced hymeneal strand in women who had had sexual intercourse.

of the Dept. of Obstetrics and Gynecology and the Dept. of Mental Hygiene. The primary focus of the program is the delivery of sexual health services to Yale students. Since 1969 over 2,000 women and more than 500 men have been seen. It is from this experience that most of our thinking about sexuality development has generated.

Clinical Considerations

Among the fifteen women:

1. All were aged seventeen to twenty-three. This age group constitutes 90% of our clinical practice;

2. Eight women had had sexual intercourse. Four of the remaining seven had made unsuccessful attempts at vaginal containment of the penis;

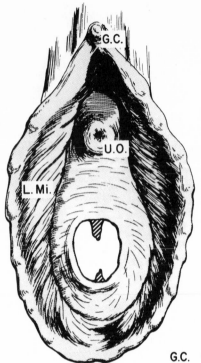

G.C. — GLANS CLITORIS
U.O. — URETHRAL ORIFICE
L.Mi.— LABIUM MINUS

Fig. 5.   Broken hymeneal strand in women.

3. All of the women expressed the feeling of fear of penetration. Four of the fifteen were afraid to insert a tampon.

Eleven of the fifteen women had previous pelvic examinations.
The presence of the hymeneal strand had not been mentioned to any
woman. This group included one woman who I had previously examined.
At her first visit I was not yet aware of the hymeneal strand as a
factor in causing dyspareunia. Her strand was flattened against
the side wall of the vagina. When she first had intercourse she
had had no pain. However, on a number of subsequent occasions,
particularly at times when she felt relaxed and sexually turned
on, attempts at penetration by her fiancee, were accompanied by a
sharp, "knife-like" (her words) pain at which time he would rapidly
ejaculate externally. Gradually, penetration became associated with
pain at all times and eventually became impossible as mild and then
severe vaginismus developed. The second time we saw the couple the
presenting complaint actually was premature ejaculation. The detail

which helped in finally making the diagnosis was the description
of the intermittent nature of the initial pain. The 4th figure
illustrates the condition found. Apparently, at some times, perhaps with the expansion of the introitus due to sex response, the
strand separated from the side wall and penetration was inadvertently attempted in the smaller side channel. Fortunately, the
couple responded quickly to removal of the strand and the rapid
therapy approach to vaginismus treatment.

One of the women apparently tore the strand when a tampon
became trapped behind it. After that experience she had been unable to insert tampons. Later, when she attempted intercourse she
found penetration impossible. She had developed severe vaginismus
which was easily demonstrable upon pelvic inspection. The three
women who had broken strands had all experienced dyspareunia
secondary to mild vaginismus. A straightforward demonstration
of the condition and an explanation of the importance of having
vaginal penetration experiences not associated with discomfort
led to a satisfactory resolution of the problem in all three.

To summarize. Eight of the women had had intercourse. In
three the strand was broken. The three women experienced pain with
penetration but it was not severe and they responded to sex counselling. Five of the women had intact strands. All five expressed a fear of penetration. One 17 year old woman had had intercourse a total of less than 8 times and had had no discomfort
despite her fear. The other four had all experienced sharp pain
with intercourse and had developed vaginismus.

The seven women who had not had intercourse also feared vaginal penetration. All showed a vaginismus response to even
gentle touching of the vulva during the physical examination.

Discussion

As indicated by Greer (1975), in a recent article, the hymen
has been a somewhat forgotten organ in medicine. While citing
many potential hymeneal sources of sexual problems, neither his
nor Hamelin's more exhaustive discussion of the hymen literature
stress the sexual significance of the hymeneal strand (Hamelin,
1974). Hamelin does cite a case of Vesalius in which a women had
a bifurcated hymen. As reported, she was "Vierge d'un coté, femme
accomplie de l'autre." No mention is made of any sexual difficulties.

It may be that women who have an epithelial strand dividing
their hymeneal opening do not have problems. A gynecologist recently told me he had seen such a case and offered to remove the

strand but the woman felt she was having no difficulties and decided to not have anything done.

Our experience however, suggests that in thinking about this
anatomic variant several points should be considered:

1. Fear of vaginal penetration is a widespread phenomenon
especially in a population of young women who have not had an opportunity to associate pleasurable experiences with vaginal penetration.

2. Most young women have vaginal penetration experiences before initiating sexual relations with others. The very first experiences are probably in the first year of life. Pre-pubertal and
pubertal penetration experiences with masturbation and/or menstruation now include most young women.

3. Early experiences, particularly at puberty, bear great
significance to subsequent experiences. For example, Kinsey (1948)
pointed out that the first ejaculation was the most important experience in the development of male adolescent sexuality. If early
experiences of vaginal penetration are associated with pain then
they are bound to influence subsequent sexuality development.

4. Random pain is particularly powerful in behavioral conditioning. Unfortunately, the anatomy of the hymeneal strand can
create just such an experience.

5. Although it is easy enough to recognize and remove a hymeneal strand (the office procedure is painless and takes less than
5 minutes to do) it is also easy to miss it especially if the examiner is not meticulously looking for its presence. Eleven of the
fifteen women herein reported had been examined and in all the strand
had been undetected.

6. All but one of the women demonstrated a vaginismus response.

Based upon these observations, the following suggestions are
made:

1. That all women having a pelvic examination be carefully
evaluated to ascertain whether or not a hymeneal strand is present.
If either an intact or broken strand is found, discussion should be
initiated to explore the possibility that it may have influenced
sex attitude, behavior and response.

2. In all cases of dyspareunia, sexual aversion, and even nonorgasmic response one should not rule out the hymeneal strand and
the possibility of concommitant vaginismus as a contributing factor.

3. When a strand is detected, removal is probably indicated. However, it is important to also look for vaginismus and to treat that condition as well.

4. Perhaps my last thought about the hymeneal strand is a little premature but this is a condition I have been thinking about for the last four years, a time in which our professional energies have shifted from the treatment of sexual dysfunctions to the development of a primary prevention program. In this regard, it seems to me that it may prove beneficial to examine the hymen of all newborn infant females and if a strand is present to remove it while the infant is still in the hospital. This is a time period when the infant vagina is still protected by the effects of maternal hormones so that the procedure should be simple and uncomplicated.

A CASSETTE RECORDER FOR MONITORING
PHYSIOLOGICAL CHANGE DURING SEX RESPONSE

Figure 6 is a picture of a cassette recorder designed to record four channels of physiological data. The recorder has been used at the Neurology Institute in Montreal, for ambulatory studies of EEG activity (Ives and Woods, 1975). It has been used

Fig. 6. Cassette recorder adapted for sexological investigations.

elsewhere for prolonged, up to 24 hours, recording of ECG (Goldberg et al. 1975). As reported, it has been shown to be useful in detecting abnormal physiological events, tachycardias and heart block as well as epileptic foci, not diagnosed using the usual laboratory approaches. The recorder has proved practical and reliable when used by patients during their usual daily activities.

The channels have been adapted for sexological investigations, to record EEG, ECG, and vaginal photoplethysmography, (VP) (Sarrel et al., In press). An event marker has been wired into the ECG channel. The VP used is based on the design described by Geer (1975). Basically, photoplethysmography involves emission of a red light wave which is reflected by red blood cells. The reflected light is then recorded by the photoreceptor cell and the signal is recorded. When more red blood cells are present there is a greater deflection of light and less is returned to the photoreceptor. In this way, the VP can indicate the changes of vascular congestion, if the distance of the photoreceptor from the vessels remains constant. With vaginal expansion and contraction, however, this basic relationship is altered and the recorded results must be assessed accordingly. The tampon-like device can be worn during daily activities except those which involve vaginal penetration.

Six recordings have been done during female sexual response. All recordings have been done by the women at home and in private and during masturbation. The following figures, all taken from one woman's recording, show some of the changes that have been recorded.

Figure 7 shows three channels; EEG, ECG and V.P. Recorded while ambulatory, the EEG pattern is of low amplitude, at a rate of 12-13 alpha discharges per second. The ECG and V.P. correspond, each recording a rate of 60 beats/minute. There is no sexual stimulation at this time.

Figure 8 illustrates the sensitivity of the EEG recording channel. The increased amplitude generated when eyes are closed can be clearly differentiated from the pattern seen with eyes open.

Figures 9 and 10 show changes recorded with sexual stimulation. In the first, after 3 minutes of looking at pornography but experiencing no sense of sexual arousal, the EEG, ECG, and V.P. remain as in the non-aroused state. After 7 minutes, and with eyes open, to look at the pornography, there is a subjective feeling of "slight arousal." There is no change in ECG or V.P. but there is an increase in amplitude of the alpha waves.

This alpha wave increase continues with the onset of manual

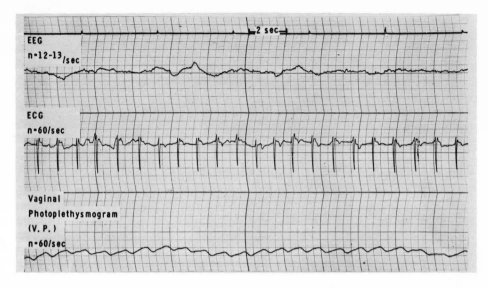

Fig. 7. One woman's recording of EEG, ECG and V.P. At rest, eyes open. (EEG electrodes Left post-ear, Mid-occipital; 3-channel recording - At rest, eyes open).

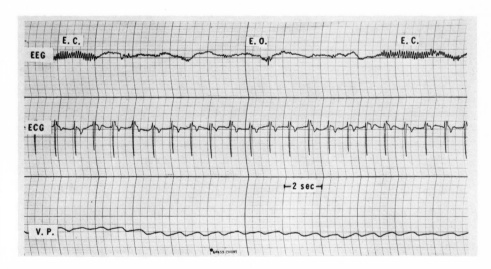

Fig. 8. One woman's recording of EEG, eyes closed (E.C.) eyes open (E.O.) (3-Channel record illustrates EEG change to Open and close eyes).

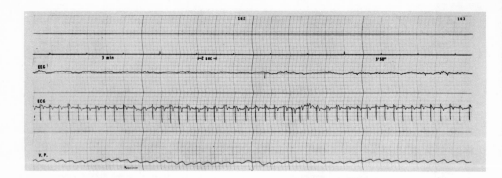

Fig. 9. One woman's recording of EEG, ECG and VP after 3 minutes
exposure to pornography. (3 minutes of visual stimulation. No
change in EEG, ECG. Regular vaginal pulse. Subjective feeling.
No arousal).

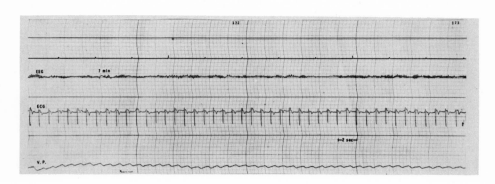

Fig. 10. One woman's recording of EEG, ECG and VP after 7 minutes
exposure to pornography. (7 minutes visual stimulation (eyes open).
No change in ECG or VP. EEG shows increase in size of alpha wave.
Subjective feeling – slight sexual arousal).

stimulation, (Figure 11). Interestingly, during this particular
recording, the woman was inadvertently interrupted at a moment when
she felt she was about to have an orgasm. Her subjective feeling
was one of anger (Figure 12). However, she did indicate the moment
by pressing the event recorder and did resume manual stimulation.
The EEG recording at the moment of interruption shows the beginning
of slow-wave activity superimposed upon the increased alpha discharge which suddenly reverts back to the non-aroused pattern.

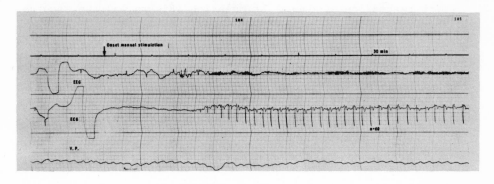

Fig. 11. One woman's recording of EEG, ECG and VP in manual stimulation. (Onset manual stimulation).

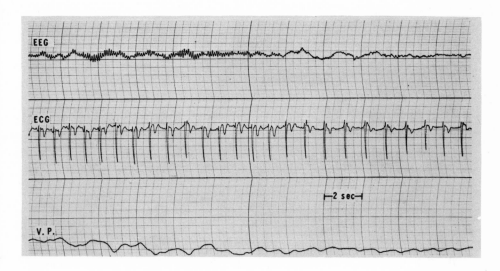

Fig. 12. One woman's recording of EEG, ECG and VP when interrupted at pre-orgasmic moment. (At pre-orgasmic moment (subjective feeling) subject startled and interrupted; EEG and ECG changes immediate. V.P. pattern also changes).

Increased heart rate and V.P. changes suggestive of vaginal expansion also rapidly revert to the patterns associated with a lesser degree of sexual arousal.

With resumption of manual stimulation (Figure 13) the recordings show return to the aroused pattern within 14 to 16 seconds.
The next recording (Figure 14) which includes the events of orgasm,
shows the slow wave discharge reported by Kinsey (1953) many years
ago, the vaginal contractions as reported earlier this year by
Gillan (1976) and the peak heart rate which follows the vaginal

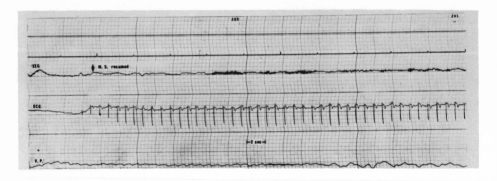

Fig. 13. One woman's recording of EEG, ECG and VP after interruption and resumption of manual stimulation. (Manual stimulation -
post interruption; EEG pattern re-established. V.P. change within
30 seconds).

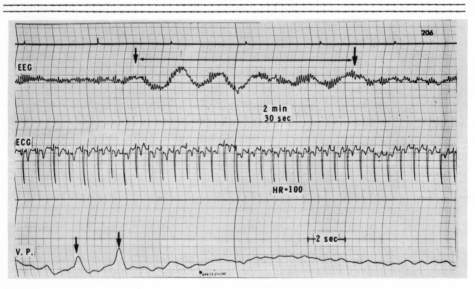

Fig. 14. One woman's recording of EEG, ECG and VP during and after
orgasm. (Orgasm. Arrows indicate slow-wave EEG change reported by
Kinsey and vaginal contraction noted on V.P. by Gillan. Time scale
indicates time from re-onset of M.S.).

and central nervous system events. At 60 seconds post-orgasm (Figure 15) the heart rate, vaginal pulse and brain activity have returned to patterns seen in the early aroused state.

The last figure (Figure 16) shows the entire recording with paper speed run at 30 times the rate shown in the previous figures. By looking at the entire response cycle one can follow the shift in baseline of the V.P., a shift which probably indicates increasing vascular congestion.

There are a number of potential values for recording data in this way:

1. The problems of establishing a laboratory are by-passed. The recorders cost about $2500 each and a playback equipment about $7500. Therefore, for a relatively small amount of capital investment the investigatory system can be purchased.

2. It may be that values for physiologic parameters established in the laboratory will be different when a person records at home. New information about the sex response cycle might become available.

3. The ability to simultaneously record several different body systems may enhance our understanding of the interactions of these systems during sexual response. For example, work to be reported soon from the Radcliffe Infirmary at Oxford will demonstrate the relationship between EEG recorded events and subsequent cardiac events (Pickering, 1976).

4. Clinically, the recorder may find application for the study of sex response change in patients in whom there is some question about biological ability to respond or physical capacity to withstand the stress of sex response. Post-coronary patients, for example, could do home recordings for the cardiologist to analyze before advising resumption of pre-coronary activities including sex.

                              CONCLUSION

I have not tried to present the fullest of discussions for either of my topics. Rather, I have tried to indicate that the study of biological factors which influence sexuality has been and can continue to be an important pathway for the sexological investigator. On this point, Dr. Masters said just a few years ago, - "We don't know what we don't know." I believe the original Masters and Johnson work has already proved to be a most important beginning in orienting sex researchers to establishing biological sex facts in human beings and to using those facts in sex therapy.

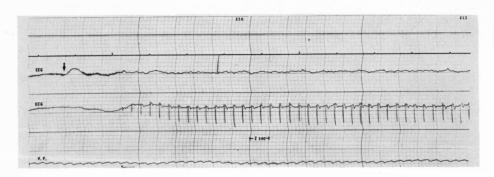

Fig. 15. One woman's recording of EEG, ECG and VP at 60 seconds
post-orgasm. (Post-orgasm indicates 60 seconds from maximal heart
rate).

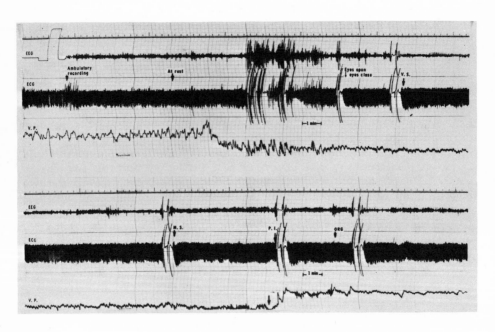

Fig. 16. Entire recording of EEG, ECG and VP for one woman.
Entire recording (Paper speed 12 min/page compared to 24 sec/page
of other figures). Drift in baseline of vaginal plethysmograph is
thought to reflect pooling of blood in vaginal wall.
U.S. - Visual stimulation.
M.S. - Manual stimulation.
P.I. Pre-orgasmic interruption.
ORG. - Orgasm.

I think we can look forward to the coming decade as a time in which we will learn more about the biology of sex and its psychological significance.

REFERENCES

Bulmer, D. (1957). The development of the human vagina. J. Anat. 91: 490-509.

Geer, J.H. (1975). Direct measurement of genital responding. Am. Psychol., 30 (3): 415-418.

Gillan, P. (1976). Objective Measures of Female Sexual Arousal. Proceedings of the Physiological Society.

Goldberg, A.D., Raftery, E.B. and Cashman, P.M.M. (1975). Ambulatory electrocardiographic records in patients with transient cerebral attacks or palpitation. British Medical Journal, 4: 569.

Greer, B.E. (1975). Painful coitus due to hymeneal problems. Medical Aspects of Human Sexuality, 9 (2): 160-169.

Hamelin, J.P. (1974). The hymen. La Nouvelle Presse Médicale, 3 (Feb).

Ives, J.R. and Woods, J.F. (1975). 4-Channel 24 hour cassette recorder for long term EEG monitoring of ambulatory patients. Electroencephalography and Clinical Neurophysiology, 39: 88-92.

Kinsey, A.C., Pomeroy, W.B. and Martin, C.E. (1948). Sexual Behavior in the Human Male, Saunders, Philadelphia.

Kinsey, A.C., Pomeroy, W.B., Martin, C.E. and Gebhard, P.H. (1953). Sexual Behavior in the Human Female, Saunders, Philadelphia.

Kravitz, H. (1973). Hand to Body Part Discovery in Normal Infants. Am. Acad. Ped. Annual Meeting, Oct.

Masters, W.H. and Johnson, V.E. (1966). Human Sexual Response, Little, Brown & Co., Boston.

Masters, W.H. and Johnson, V.E. (1970). Human Sexual Inadequacy, Little, Brown & Co., Boston.

Pickering, T. (1976). (Private Communication)

Sarrel, P.M. and Sarrel, L.J. (1971). A sex counselling program
     for College students. <u>Amer. J. Pub. Health,</u> 61 (July):
     1341-1347.

Sarrel, P.M., Foddy, J. and McKinnon, J.B. (In Press). Investiga-
     tion of Human Sexual Response Using a Cassette Recorder.

PLIABLE PENILE PROSTHESES IN TREATMENT OF ORGANIC IMPOTENCE

Louis Subrini

France

Classically, organic impotencies are less frequent than functional impotencies. After a thorough study of problems, we found
that this proportion can be considerably modified. In particular,
a clinical triade seems to us characteristic of an organic origin:

1) Rare or weak morning erections often being totally absent
is considered a pathonomonical sign. 2) Ejaculation with flaccid
penis notably during masturbation is always found. 3) Intravenous
injection of dextro moramid associated with manual stimulation shows
no erection response in contrast to the normal male.

ORGANIC IMPOTENCIES CLASSIFICATION

Hoping to clarify the problem, we have classified the organic
impotencies into 3 groups:

Hormonal Impotences

They are and can benefit from medical treatment.

Neurological Impotences

They represent about a third of organic impotencies. They
may appear during a number of central nervous system diseases,
among which we point out traumatic paralysis and multiple sclerosis,

often touching the young adult.

They may be of peripheral origin either by neuropathy (as
seen in diabetes mellitus) or by lesion of the hypogastric plexus.
This plexus is a kind of sub center which commands erection and is
located beside the pelvic viscera. Rectal amputation, total cys-
tectomie with urethral rupture, severe fractures of the pelvis,
frequently cause lesions to this plexus.

Vascular Impotency

Vascular impotency has been misunderstood for a long time.
It is responsible for more than 50% of organic impotencies. We
differentiate two groups according to their origin: arterial or
cavernosum.

An erection is an active arterial phenomena and any obintera-
tion of the arterial tree leading to the penis will be a factor of
impotency. Thrombosis as in Leriche's syndrome is a characteristic
example but distal thrombosis iliac or pudendal are the most frequent and their revascularisation by surgical procedure is uncertain, if not impossible.

An erection demands a supple and normally extensible corpus
cavernosum. Any fibrosis of the corpus compromises this possibility as in Peyronnie's desease, where fibrous plaques infiltrate
the tunica albuginea of the corpus cavernosum and the diffuse fibrosis, seen following priapism or direct trauma to the corpus
cavernosum. These vascular lesions could be discovered by
arteriography and cavernosography.

Arteriography will sometimes confirm the diagnosis that the
clinical examination has already posed: the arterio sclerotic
lesions are sometimes multiple and disseminated, or the internal
pudendal artery is completely obliterated at its origin. In these
cases, erection was reduced to a simple swelling insufficent to
permit penetration. On the other hand, the same lesions are not
always seen in severe arterio sclerosis. The lesions are frequently
isolated and overlooked without arteriography. Occasionally, the
lesions are distal. Here interpretation of the rays should be
prudent and carefully combined with the clinical picture.

The Cavernosography is useful to demonstrate the characteristic lesions of intra cavernosum fibrosis.

PRINCIPLE OF THE INTERVENTION

The principle of this intervention is to reproduce the func-

tion of the penis as close as possible to a physiological erection.
To do this, we must not only restore its rigidity but also increase
its length and diameter. These conditions are essential for achieving good sexual intercourse. However, given this size we must assure that every day life will not be troubled; normal mobility must
be preserved. For this, we have developed since 1970 a penile prosthesis which corresponds to these different obligations.

These prostheses are an elastomer of pure silicone, manufac-
tured for medical use. Each prosthesis is a rod 20cm long with 2
segments: the first segment which is rigid is the distal portion.
The second segment more pliable is the proximal portion. With the
prostheses is given a trial prosthesis of a different color and
easily recognized and with no difference in rigidity. This will
be inserted first and shortened to the desired length. Using this
as a model, the definitive prostheses will be cut. This avoids
unnecessary handling of the definitively placed silicone. Each
rod of the pair will occupy the entire space of a corpus cavernosum.

Why did we chose the corpus cavernosum? Because of two distinct characteristics: first, the wall or tunica albuginea is
thick and extremely solid and provides an excellent covering. The
two cul-de-sac distal and proximal are extremely resistant and
firmly block the prostheses in place. Thus protrusion or recoil
are prevented. The second characteristic is the solt alveolar
tissue inside the corpus cavernosum. It can be easily dilated for
the insertion of the two rods. Once in place they should occupy
the entire length of the corpus cavernosum (Figure 1).

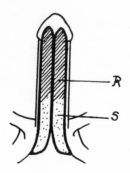

Fig. 1. Two silicone rods composed of a rigid (R) and supple (S)
segments.

The rigid segment is distale in the penal portion of the corpus. The more pliable segment is proximal in the perineal portion and permits an excellent mobility (Figures 2 and 2a).

SURGICAL TECHNIQUE

To reach the corpus cavernosum, three approaches are possible: 1) a direct perineal incision, 2) a longitudinal penile incision and 3) our preference, a circular incision and approach of the corpus cavernosum by pealing back the skin. This permits a sufficiently large operating field far away from the skin incision. The skin is dissected entirely down to the base of the penis. The corpus cavernosum is incised laterally. Two suture wires are used to open the tunica albuginea. This incision will be opened large enough to permit the dilation with beniqués or Hegar's dilators (Figure 3).

We calibrate first the distal portion being sure that the beniqué reaches the distal cul-de-sac. We increase the caliber up to a number 30 (French). In the same way, calibration of the posterior corpus cavernosum is done. A rough measurement of the corpus cavernosum is take in order to cut the trial prosthesis inserted first in front then in back. The silicone is never touched by the gloves for aseptic reasons and for avoiding any fixation of talcum powder on the silicone.

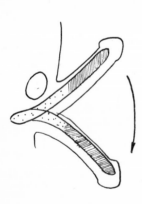

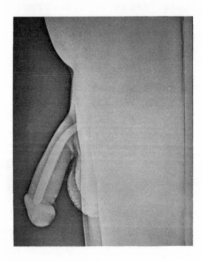

Fig. 2. Illustration of the mobility of the pliable prostheses.

Fig. 2a. Illustration of the flexibility of the silicone prostheses.

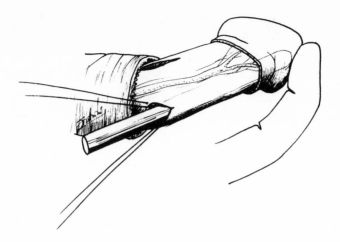

Fig. 3.   Insertion of dilators.

Using the trial prothesis as a model it is then possible to cut the definitive prostheses.   These are inserted and perfect position in the corpus cavernosum is verified (Figure 4).

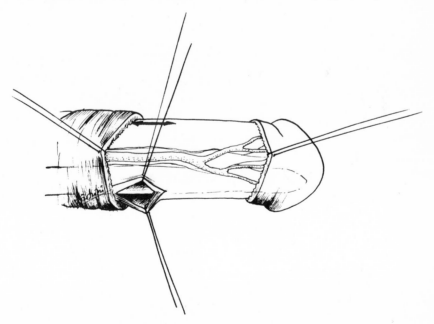

Fig. 4.   Prostheses in place.

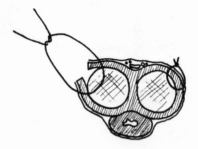

Fig. 5.   Transfixing sutures.

When the second prosthesis is inserted with the first one
already in place, it is often slightly difficult to insert the
second one. To avoid any secondary movement the prosthesis is
fixed in place by a transfixing suture (Figure 5).

The tunica is closed with a continuous suture. Colles fascia
is closed in the same way. The skin is replaced and circumcision
is performed. Finally the skin is closed with interrupted sutures.
After characterization, a circular dressing is applied if desired.

                                RESULTS

We performed this operation since 1970 on 53 patients.

From a surgical point of view, this operation gives immediate
good results in 95% of the cases. In the remaining 5% we had to
remove one of the two prostheses. Its replacement will give the
same good results. We feel that after 3 months post-operative the
tolerance is definitive.

This operation permits sexual intercourse as soon as 2 months
after surgery. The excellent mobility permits typical wearing of
clothes and does not prove to be awkward in every day life. Most
important, these prostheses provide the couple with the possibility
of intercourse on a regular basis and the elimination of a dysfunction which has hindered typical sexual enjoyment.

CERTIFICATION FOR SEX THERAPISTS

Albert Ellis

United States

It is often erroneously assumed that sex therapy began with the famous researches of Masters and Johnson, during the 1960's, and culminated in the publishing of their notable book, Human Sexual Inadequacy, in 1970. Hardly so. Richard von Krafft-Ebing (1922) and Havelock Ellis (1936) laid many of the foundations for modern sex therapy before the close of the nineteenth century; many pioneer sexologists, such as August Forel (1922) and Iwan Bloch (1908) made significant contributions to the field in the early 1900's; and long before Masters and Johnson began their original researches in the 1950's, many European and American sexologists outlined virtually all the elements of the sensate focus, the squeeze technique, the use of sexual imagery, and practically all the other treatment techniques that modern sex therapists have made so popular. Early innovators in the field, from whom Hartman and Fithian (1972), Joseph LoPiccolo (1971), Helen Kaplan (1974), and other recent authorities have taken a great deal of their methods include LeMon Clark (1937, 1949), Robert L. Dickinson (1933), Albert Ellis (1953, 1954, 1960, 1976), G. Lombard Kelly (1948), Alfred C. Kinsey and his associates (1948, 1953), W.F. Robie (1925, 1927), William J. Robinson (1929, 1937), J.H. Semans (1956), Hannah and Abraham Stone (1952), T.H. Van de Velde (1926), and Joseph Wolpe and Arnold Lazarus (1966).

Almost all the pioneering sex therapists had high professional standing, usually in the field of medicine or psychology; and nobody questioned the fact that they treated sexual problems themselves or widely promulgated their methods among members of the public. The same high professional standards, alas, often seem lacking among the new "sex therapists." Many of the recent converts to the field

do, of course, have a fine professional background and years of
experience in related clinical fields - particularly the fields
of psychotherapy, marriage and family counseling, and gynecology.
But many - and perhaps most - of them have training, and that with
little supervision, only in the specific area of sexual dysfunctioning. They seem to have attended a few workshops, often by
Masters and Johnson, Hartman and Fithian, or myself, read fairly
widely in the field of sex, and then set themselves up as self-
styled "sex therapists." Others take a much dimmer view of their
preempted titles; and Masters and Johnson, in some of their press
interviews, have claimed that as many as 90 per cent of those who
operate "sex clinics" or who otherwise call themselves "sex therapists" in the United States and Canada would much more justifiably
merit the label of "quacks."

Such a situation has its obvious dangers - first, to members
of the public who patronize so-called "sex therapists" with little
professional training; and, second, to legitimate therapists, who
tend to get blamed and restricted for some of the not too ethical
practices of the poorly trained people. In view of this deplor-
able condition, many outstanding sex therapists have called for
the setting up of standards that would help keep things, at the
very least, from becoming more alarming; and several legislative
committees in various parts of the world have also begun to consider the possibility of legalizing the profession of sex therapist and, in the process, forcing all legitimate members of this
profession to abide by rules of training, practice, and ethics.

Not everyone, naturally, agrees that standards for sex therapists should exist in a precise form; and those that do agree have
distinct differences over what form of such standards would better
get established. Naturally, I have my own views in this connection,
and since I feel somewhat wary of official organizations and of
legislatures, I cannot wax enthusiastic about such bodies taking
over the entire field of sex therapy and instituting either too
rigorous or too lax standards. Over-rigorousness can well lead
to undue infringement on human liberties; and over-laxness can
lead to standards that remain so loose that members of the public,
and particularly those that have sex problems and come for treatment, have virtually no protection whatever. All of which poses
a real dilemma.

Fortunately for my peace of mind, I was asked to chair, a few
years ago, the Sex Therapy Certification Committee of the American
Association of Sex Educators, Counselors, and Therapists (AASECT);
and Dr. Patricia Schiller, Executor Director of AASECT, filled out
the Committee with some of the best minds and outstanding authorities on sex practice in the United States, including Leroy Graham,
James Leslie McCary, Armando and Dorothy de Moya, Warren J. Gad-

paille, Ulysses Grant Turner III, William R. Stayton, Leon and
Shirley Zussman, and David Mace. I found these people, together
with Dr. Schiller herself, quite devoted to the cause of trying
to hammer out a suitable code of standards and ethics for AASECT
members who wanted to get acknowledged by the organization as
Certified Sex Therapists, and I found that they had an unusual
degree of open-mindedness, fairness and wideranging experience
in the field that enabled them to do a fine job in this respect.

As something of a sex revolutionist and enfant terrible for
the last thirty years, I cannot honestly say that I entirely go
along with all the sex standards and codes of ethics which my
AASECT committee on sex therapy certification has instituted since
1973. I take a more liberal view of many things than several members of the committee and a more rigorous view of certain other
things than some committee members hold. In matters of this sort,
however, a good degree of compromise seems inevitable for any fi-
nalization of important issues. And the compromises that have
come out of the many deliberations that we have held appear to me
quite good. So I can willingly go along with all of them, albeit
my personal reservations in some respects.

AASECT CODE OF STANDARDS

To begin with, the sex therapy certification committee of
AASECT saw fit to adopt the two notable body of rules previously
laid down by its Committee on Training and Standards, chaired by
Dr. David Mace since 1972. AASECT has published these rules under
the titles of The Professional Training and Preparation of Sex
Educators (1972) and The Professional Training and Preparation of
Sex Counselors (1973). I would strongly advise all those interested
in the area of sex therapy to read these two fine documents. I can
briefly summarize them by noting that according to their statements,
both sex educators and sex counselors and therapists, in order to
receive recognition as well-trained individuals, get enjoined to
acquire a considerable body of knowledge of human sexuality in
eight major areas: (1) the process of reproduction, (2) sexual
development, (3) sexual functioning, (4) sexual behavior, (5) sex
and gender, (6) marriage, family, and interpersonal relationships,
(7) sex and health, (8) the study of sex. The reports suggest that
at least a year of intensive study would seem advisable in these
areas.

Along with these study requirements, the AASECT training manual strongly recommends that sex counselors and therapists receive
basic training in the area of counseling or psychotherapy itself,
including intensive courses in counseling theory, counseling methodologies, patterns of counseling, technique of the interview, consultation, collaboration and referral, and counseling management.

The manual assumes, in other words, that a reputable sex therapist
will receive academic and practicum training as a counselor or
psychotherapist first, and that then he or she will receive specialized training in human sexuality. Finally, to complete his
or her training, a full year of supervised clinical internship
goes along with the academic requirements.

Considering this kind of training fair, adequate, and requi-
site to good counseling preparation, the AASECT Sex Therapy Certification Committee took off from there and added several other
requirements before any AASECT member could receive a sex therapy
certificate. Let me briefly summarize these as follows:

Academic Diplomas

A minimum of a Masters Degree, equivalent, or doctorate in
a clinical field as, M.D., D.D., or Ph.D. in psychology is needed.

Experience

One thousand hours paid experience as a sex therapist or
equivalent experience spread over a longer time frame is required.
This includes the one year (or 200 hours) of internship mentioned
above.

Examination

AASECT requires that all applicants, other than those under a
temporary Grandperson Clause, have to take a written examination
embodying the essential knowledge listed under content in the training manual.

Attitudes and Professional Behavior

All applicants have to participate in a two-day weekend workshop where the applicant will have an opportunity to sift through
and sort out his or her attitudes and values concerning human sexuality. The applicant will also set forth, in a letter of application, his or her personal impressions and views of sexual "normality."

As you can see, these basic requirements for anyone who wants
to obtain a certificate from AASECT as a Certified Sex Therapist
seem pretty rigorous; and, again, I feel sure that many people in
the field will tend to argue with them. Certainly, some of the
outstanding leaders in the field today could not have fulfilled
these requirements when they first started out as sex therapists;

and many who have already received the AASECT certification under the Grandperson Clause never will fully qualify under the post-Grandperson rules (which finally go into effect when the Grandperson Clause expires in June, 1978).

Why, then, this rigor? For several good reasons that I can see: (1) Although some people may well have the ability to do fine sex therapy without basic professional training and experience, most probably do not. In this connection, I do not think we can safely make the exception amount to the rule; (2) while highly trained and professionally reputable sex therapists may sometimes act unethically and do harm to their clients as several recent legal cases have shown, much less chance of this occurring among poorly than well-trained therapists seems to exist. Proper professional status hardly assures ethical behavior; but it certainly seems to help; (3) policing bodies, such as professional organizations and courts of law, had better have some kind of standards to go by, in order to judge whether the behavior of certain sex therapists actually falls into ethical or unethical categories. If groups like AASECT do not do something to establish such standards, who will? (4) Rigorous professional and ethical standards rarely prevent capable people from working in their field, since the great majority of them can, even though at some sacrifice to themselves, do something to achieve these standards; and they will usually benefit both themselves and their clients if they do this something; (5) although incompetents and unethical people in any field can often, if sufficiently motivated, pass strict training requirements, a great many of them get discouraged from doing so, and tend to leave the field rather than achieve goals that they can only with great difficulty accomplish.

I contend, in other words, that for all the problems raised by requiring sex therapists to meet a reasonably high level of professional training and ethical conduct, more problems lessen or vanish if we insist on their meeting such standards. No set of rules has only advantages and zero disadvantages, and that undoubtedly includes the certification standards that AASECT has so far established. Time will tell whether these training requisites will have the benefits that the AASECT Committee on Certification of Sex Therapists predicts that they will have. And if the committee proves wrong, it or its successors will certainly give careful thought to changing these standards in the future.

AASECT CODE OF ETHICS

The same thing goes, and perhaps even more importantly, for the code of ethics which AASECT has tentatively set up for its members in general and for certified sex therapists in particular.

The Committee on Certification recommended this code only as a temporary stopgap, to serve as potential guidelines in the cases of
practicing sex therapists who have managed to run afoul of the law
or to get into other legal or professional difficulties. The Committee, along with the Board of Directors of AASECT, sees this
ethical code, at the present time, mainly as a proposed set of
rules that will engender a great deal of discussion and criticism,
and that will get adopted in any final form only after several years
of this kind of discussion have taken place. For sex therapy as a
formal profession has only a short history, and for any group to
adopt conclusive ethical standards for all sex counselors and therapists under all conditions of practice would seem exceptionally
presumptuous.

        The preliminary and temporary AASECT code of ethics contains,
in summary, the following kinds of provisions: (1) that AASECT
certified sex educators and/or therapists "not be judgmental in
promoting or propagandizing a sexual point of view;" (2) that
"patient and/or therapist nudity in an alleged therapeutic modality
is prohibited in a one-to-one therapy situation;" (3) that "the
therapist shall refrain from examining male or female patients for
the purpose of stimulating the patient in order to elicit a sexual
response;" (4) that "the therapist shall refrain from any body contact with a patient for the purpose of either giving or receiving
erotic stimulation;" (5) that "all personal information records,
and communication received about the clients are considered confidential unless clients waive their right in written permission;"
(6) that "sex therapists are encouraged to use traditional professional forums for announcing their practice;" (7) that "an individual or group of individuals who misrepresent by a trade name the
specific professional function performed, or misrepresent explicitly
or by inference the number of professional persons involved in the
performance of sex therapy shall be censored, or other appropriate
action taken;" (8) "it shall be unethical for any sex therapist to
pass judgment on the practice of other sex therapists without having
substantial research and data concerning the value of any other therapist's work."

        In addition to these rules, the AASECT board of directors has
indicated that unethical or substandard behavior on the part of an
AASECT certified sex therapist arises when that individual has had
his or her training mainly under the supervision of a co-therapist,
husband, wife, professional, or social partner; and also when the
sex therapist participates, in the course of treatment, in any conduct that his or her state or country clearly designates as illegal.

                              CONCLUSION
    Let me say again: I can hardly give my total endorsement to

or enthusiastically go along with all the foregoing AASECT rules of ethics. Some of them seem a little too proscriptive for my own personal tastes. But I can definitely see, at the present time, the distinct value of tentatively setting up these kinds of rules, offering them to the whole field of sex educators, counselors, and therapists and to the related fields of marriage and family counseling and of psychotherapy, as issues for serious consideration and discussion, and after prolonged investigation and experience finally adopting some of them and radically revising or abandoning others. If this kind of an open-ended approach to establishing standards for sex therapists continues, a set of sensible rules that will benefit them, their clients, and the public in general will most likely emerge.

REFERENCES

Bloch, I. (1908). The Sexual Life of our Time, Rebman, New York.

Clark, L. (1937). Emotional Adjustment in Marriage, Mosby, St. Louis.

Clark, L. (1949). Sex and You, Bobbs-Merrill, Indianapolis.

Dickinson, R.L. (1933). Human Sex Anatomy, Williams and Wilkins, Baltimore.

Ellis, A. (1953). Is the Vaginal Orgasm a Myth? In Pillay, A.P., and Ellis, A. (Eds.), Sex, Society and the Individual, Bombay: International Journal of Sexology Press, Bombay.

Ellis, A. (1954). The American Sexual Tragedy, Twayne Publishers, New York.

Ellis, A. (1960). The Art and Science of Love, Lyle Stuart, New York.

Ellis, A. (1976). Sex and the Liberated Man, Lyle Stuart, New York.

Ellis, H. (1936). Studies in the Psychology of Sex, Random House, New York.

Forel, A. (1922). The Sexual Question, Physician's and Surgeon's Book Company, New York.

Hartman, W.E., and Fithian, M. (1972). The Treatment of the Sexual Dysfunctions, California: Center for Martial and Sexual Studies, Long Beach.

Kaplan, H.S. (1974). The New Sex Therapy, Brunner/Mazel, New York.

Kelly, G.L. (1948). Sex Manual for Those Married or About to Be,
    Southern Medical Supply Company, Augusta.

Kinsey, A.C., Pomeroy, W.B., and Martin, C.E. (1948). Sexual
    Behavior in the Human Male, Saunders, Philadelphia.

Kinsey, A.C., Pomeroy, W.B., Martin, C.E., and Gebhard, P.H. (1953).
    Sexual Behavior in the Human Female, Saunders, Philadelphia.

LoPiccolo, J. (1971). Case study: systematic desensitization of
    homosexuality. Behavior Therapy, 2: 394-399.

LoPiccolo, J., and Lobitz, W.C. (1972). The role of masturbation
    in the treatment of primary orgasmic dysfunction. Archives
    of Sexual Behavior, 3: 265-271.

Masters, W.H., and Johnson, V.E. (1970). Human Sexual Inadequacy,
    Little Brown and Company, Boston.

Robie, W.F. (1925). The Art of Love, Rational Life Press, Ithaca.

Robie, W.F. (1927). Rational Sex Ethics, Rational Life Press,
    Ithaca.

Robinson, W.J. (1929). Woman: Her Sex and Love Life. Eugenics
    Publishing Company, New York.

Robinson, W.J. (1937). Sexual Truths, Eugenics Publishing Company,
    New York.

Semans, J.H. (1956). Premature ejaculation: a new approach.
    Southern Medical Journal, 49: 353-357.

Stone, H.M., and Stone, A. (1952). A Marriage Manual, Rev. ed.,
    Simon and Schuster, New York.

Van de Velde, T.H. (1926). Ideal Marriage, Covici-Friede, New York.

von Krafft-Ebing, R. (1922). Psychopathia Sexualis. Physicians
    and Surgeon's Book Company, Brooklyn.

Wolpe, J., and Lazarus, A.A. (1966). Behavior Therapy Techniques,
    Pergamon Press, New York.

Somewhat confused argument & apparently little scientific basis. ✓ Quite interesting on differences in fantasy of behaviour ♂ + ♀. Claim that sexual dysf. very often due to deviant fantasies & wishes to & unacceptable. Not borne out by clinical experience.

ROLE OF FANTASY IN PAIR-BONDING AND EROTIC PERFORMANCE

John Money

United States

EROTIC FANTASY IN HISTORY AND DIAGNOSIS[1]

Erotic fantasy is dangerous. Less than three centuries ago, rendered guilty by accusation and tortured into falsely confessing an erotic fantasy of adultery with the devil, you could have been burned at the stake. The aftermath of the Inquisition is still with us. It is manifest in today's residual ecclesiastical taboo on masturbation with its accompanying erotic fantasy as either morally degenerate or morally harmful. It shapes today's legal policy by which creators and merchants of erotic fantasy in print or on film are classified, not exactly as devil-possessed, but as moral degenerates or pornographers, for which they are prosecuted and persecuted.

From the era of the Inquisition until today, erotic imagery has been attributed successively to demonic possession, moral degeneracy, or perversion. In each instance there has been a hidden assumption of moral decision in which the individual chose to go wrong. Small wonder, then, that even today patients for sex therapy formulate their chief complaint in terms not of erotic imagery but of sexual behavior, and bodily malfunction.

There are three chief categories of behavioral erotic complaint – too much (hyperphilia), too little or inadequate (hypophilia), and unacceptable in content (paraphilia, for which the stigmatizing term

---

[1]Supported by USPHS Grant HD00325 and by funds from the Grant Foundation, New York.

is perversion). The criteria of what is too much, too little, or
unacceptable may be either personal or social. They are not absolute criteria, but are subject to fluctuation over time and space.

Each of the three categories of behavioral erotic complaint
has its counterpart in imagery. Erotic imagery is especially prominent in the first of the three phases of eroticism. These three
phases are proception, acception, and conception.

Proceptive Phase

Erotic Signals. Proception is the phase of mutual solicitation and courtship, of being attractive while being attracted. It
may be extended in duration, as when two adolescents fall in love
for the first time; or telescoped into minutes or hours, as when
two established lovers signal their erotic anticipation, to one
another.

In many, if not most of the sub-human mammalian species, proception is more a function of the nose than the eyes. The female
and the male are attracted to one another by reason of the odori-
ferous signal, or pheromone, that is emitted from her vagina at the
time of her ovulation, or heat. Having established pheromonal contact, they proceed to engage in an elaborate and phyletically stereotyped courtship ritual, consummated in coitus.

Among human beings, present evidence neither rules out nor
strongly endorses a pheromonal erotic attractant. It does appear,
however, that in the human species the eyes supplant the nose as
the primary organs of erotic attraction between two people before
they establish body contact. The ears, of course, may play a part,
but it is the visual image par excellence that initiates erotic
arousal. The image of arousal may be an actual perception, or it
may be a memory image, with or without additional fantasy elaboration.

When the image or images signaled from one of a pair of people
evoke responses of erotic arousal in the other, those responses
become, in turn, new erotic signals to the partner. It is possible
that a couple will simultaneously evoke the onset of mutual erotic
arousal and response. Then a kind of reverberating circuit or reciprocal feedback occurs, of which the ultimate culmination is reciprocal orgasm and postorgasmic rest. This kind of reciprocality
often happens when two already pair-bonded lovers reunite, say at
the end of the day. Even before the actual reunion, the proceptive
phase may have begun in the imagery of rehearsal.

The interval between the onset of proception and its transition to acception and orgasm ranges from minutes or hours, at one

extreme, to days or months, at the other. The extended interval
is characterized by a ritual of courtship prescribed by cultural
convention.

Pair-bonding. When two people simultaneously reciprocate proceptive signals, they become potential lovers. More prosaically,
they embark on what could become the first stage of a long lasting
pair-bond. Durable pair-bonding is not unique to the human species,
nor is selective partner preference.

Regardless of species, the determinants of preference and long-
term bonding are poorly understood. For human beings, one likely
hypothesis, stated aphoristically, is that we fall in love not with
a partner but with a fantasy of what that partner could become. If
the first proceptive signals from the partner fit the fantasy well
enough, rightly or wrongly it is taken for granted that the fantasy
will materialize in its entirety.

To illustrate: the transvestite man for whom erection and ejaculation are dependent on the imagery (perceptual or in fantasy) of
his wearing women's garments while copulating cannot prophecy in
the early, proceptive stages of a partnership that his partner will
be able to mutualize his transvestite imagery and/or practice. In-
choately, perhaps, he recognizes in her certain of the attributes
that his transvestite fantasy requires in a partner, and he projects
onto her the others. If they do not materialize, then illusion becomes disillusion and the pair-bond becomes unbonded. If they do
materialize, then the couple become strongly pair-bonded, even to
the extent of being reciprocally irreplaceable.

Statistically speaking, it is difficult for the transvestite
to become strongly pair-bonded, for it is difficult to find a person whose own fantasy is to have a transvestite for a partner. The
same applies to anyone with an unorthodox erotic imagery. Even for
those whose erotic imagery is orthodox, highly compatible matching
is difficult, witness the current U.S. divorce rate of approximately
40%.

Idiosyncratic Variability and Paraphilia. Proceptive matching
in some animal species is phyletically programed in such a way as
to be maximally stereotypic and minimally idiosyncratic. Among human beings, the reverse holds true. Idiosyncratic variability with
respect to the imagery of erotic arousal is as widespread as idiosyncratic variability in the use of language and speech.

Idiosyncracy in both cases may, to a certain extent, be programed into the brain before birth, but to a far greater, if not
exclusive, extent such programing takes place after birth; it is
extremely sensitive to social determinants. The full range and
nature of these social determinants has not yet been traced. It

is likely that perhaps a majority of them are products of our society's sexual taboo on early sexual rehearsal play which, judging
from other primate species, is statistically normal and natural in
infancy and childhood. Prohibited and penalized, sexual rehearsal
play and the imagery associated with it becomes covert. In content,
it becomes inaccessible to adult guidance and direction. Consequently, it may develop not only in a covertly idiosyncratic way,
but also in an unorthodox, pathological or paraphiliac way. Then
difficulty in proceptive matching is the ultimate outcome.

The varieties of paraphilia, each with its own specific imagery
or fantasy, are listed in Table I. According to present evidence,
both the range and incidence of the paraphilias found in men is far
more extensive than in women. Women's paraphilias could prove to
be virtually restricted to tactual fetishes and bondage masochism.

Male/Female Difference in Imagery. One hypothesis to explain
this sex difference in paraphiliac imagery is that the male is designed to be more dependent on the visual image for erotic arousal,
than is the female, she being relatively more dependent on tactual
arousal. A corollary of this hypothesis is that boys, during the
critical years of gender-identity differentiation, can more easily
than girls be "misprinted" with respect to erotic imagery. The
misprint will then manifest itself in full bloom after the onset
of hormonal puberty which lowers the threshold for the manifestation of erotic imagery. With great ease, a boy's erotic imagery

TABLE I

LIST OF PARAPHILIAS

Apotemnophilia	Necrophilia
Coprophilia	Pedophilia
Exhibitionism	Pictophilia
Erotic Strangulation Suicide	Rape
Fetishism	Sadism
Frotteurism	Scoptophilia
Gerontophilia	Telephone Scatologia (lewdness)
Kleptomania	Transsexualism*
Klismaphilia	Transvestism *
Lust Murder	Troilism
Masochism	Urophilia or Undinism
Mysophilia	Voyeurism or Peeping Tomism
Narratophilia	Zoophilia

*These two manifestations of gender transposition are classified as
paraphilias whereas homosexualism and bisexualism are classified
only as transpositions.

expresses itself after puberty in masturbation fantasy and/or copulation fantasy, as well as during sleep in wet dreams.

There is in the adolescent girl no counterpart of the boy's
wet dreams, with their eidetic imagery, culminating in an orgasm
during sleep. Most adolescent boys are insistently confronted in
dreams with the imagery of their erotic arousal, whether it be or-
thodoxly heterosexual or unorthodoxly paraphiliac.

Though nature is very clear in the imagistic message of proceptive sexuality she thrusts upon the typical adolescent boy, there
are a few males who manifest a syndrome of proceptive apathy and
inertia -- proceptive hypophilia. They have no masturbation imagery; they do not masturbate. They have no wet dreams and no erotic
dream imagery. With a partner, they do not get erotically aroused.
Girls also may manifest the syndrome of proceptive hypophilia (apathy and inertia).

Hyperphilia of the proceptive phase, and sex difference related thereto, are still not very well documented in medicine and
science, possibly because affected individuals do not necessarily
define themselves as suffering. Phenomenologically, proceptive
hyperphilia is manifested as seduction without follow-through.

Acceptive Phase

Reciprocality. In animal sexology, the phase that follows
proception is commonly designated as receptive, on the basis of
the female's posture in receiving the male. In actual fact, it
is equally correct to say that the penis receives the vagina, as
that the vagina receives the penis. Preferably, one may say that
the penis and the vagina mutually accept one another, and so avoid
any covert confusion of sexology with sexism. As a mnemonic device, and without doing too much injustice to the facts, one may
equate proception with eroticism above the belt, and acception
with eroticism below the belt.

The transition from proception to acception in an erotically
successful partnership is one in which imagery fades from its proceptive prominence and yields to total engrossment in body awareness
experienced in the here and now. A reverberating circuit or feedback becomes established between each partner as, oblivious to all
else, body motion and sensation reach their culmination in ecstatic
orgasm.

Sex and Aging. There are no statistical data on differences
between men and women concerning the duration of the proceptive
relative to the acceptive phase. In all probability, individual

difference outweighs sex difference, in this respect. The reciprocal fit, or match of tempo and content of proceptive imagery
and sensory interchange between two partners is probably much more
important than their being male and female, with respect to the
proceptive/acceptive ratio.

There are also no statistical data on the effects of aging on
the duration of the proceptive relative to the acceptive phase.
Individual differences notwithstanding, the common sense of clinical inference suggests that the younger the partners and the newer
the partnership, the greater the likelihood of speedy performance,
both proceptively and acceptively; and also the shorter the refractory interval between successive performances. With increasing age,
it is also possible that a man or woman becomes more dependent on
what happens during the proceptive phase in order to make the transition to the acceptive phase.

With youth there may be more versatility. Thus, the young man
may be able to get an erection and ejaculation despite a proceptive
phase which is impaired by being too short and not conforming to the
imagery of his personalized, maximally stimulative erotic fantasy.
Later in life, it may be imperative for this same man to have concordance between what is acutally happening, proceptively, and what
should happen according to the idealized erotic fantasy which has
always promoted his maximum "turn-on" since puberty. Women and men
are, so far as is known, not different in this respect. Each individual has a maximal "turn-on" fantasy, and it is remarkably stable
and persistent throughout life.

Reversion to Forbidden Imagery. There is some clinical evidence to suggest that, under the pressure of a severe life crisis,
an individual may revert to, and re-enact the imagery of a pubertal
erotic fantasy that, despite its maximal "turn-on" value, has been
forbidden in adulthood, and suppressed. Thus, at a time of voca-
tional or domestic crisis, a respectable business executive may in
middle age revert to long-suppressed exhibitionism and be picked up
by the police. Under the threat of debilitating and progressively
deteriorative disease, a professional man may relive and re-enact
the imagery of his homosexual life as a teenager at an all-boy's
boarding school. Under similar circumstances, a monogamous house-
wife may revert to flirtatious teenage and new affairs. And so on.

Covert Paraphilia. One of two partners may have an idealized
proceptive fantasy the enactment of which is anerotic for the other
partner. The transvestite's fantasy (see previous illustration) is
an example. In such a case, the discordance in the erotic imagistic
expectancies of the two partners creates what best may be called a
psychic distance between them. From this isolation issues the la-
ment: "You don't love me. You want me only for my body."

This type of proceptive mismatching impedes, and may block
the fulfillment of acceptive function. For example, the complaint
of a candidate for sex therapy may be impotence. Behind this hypophiliac symptom, however, may hide a covert and forbidden ephebo-
philiac fantasy of having as a partner a pubescent boy (or girl).
If this fantasy can be allowed to enter the mind, either during
masturbation or copulation with an older woman, then the penis is
no longer impotent. The situation is still not ideal for the woman
partner, however, for she senses that somehow she is excluded from
what is going on in her man's mind, as indeed she is.

This type of case justifies the aphorism that behind every
hypophilia lurks a fantasy as for example a paraphilia. There is
a touch of hyperbole here, but it does draw attention to the fact
that covert paraphilia should always be listed in the differential
diagnosis when the presenting complaint is hypophilia or inadequacy
of the functioning of the sex organs in the acceptive phase (Table
2). The other diagnoses are uncomplicated inhibition of genital
function without imagistic involvement; and impairment of genital
function secondary to vascular or neurological disease.

It is quite possible that a covert paraphilia may lurk also
behind a hyperphilia. There are few facts to go by, since hyperphilia is more often regarded as a joke or a crime, rather than a
legitimate subject of sexological inquiry. This is particularly
so when a hyperphilia expresses itself directly as a high incidence
of coitus and orgasm, whether with many partners or one, and even
if the solo partner finds the frequency excessive.

In sex therapy, when a covert paraphilia is masked by either
hypophiliac or hyperphiliac symptoms, the chance of therapeutic
success is proportional to the insistence and demanding quality of
the paraphiliac imagery. In the present state of knowledge, ame-

---

TABLE II

HYPOPHILIAS, MALE & FEMALE
(Partial or Complete)

Male	Female
Erotic apathy	Erotic apathy
Penile anesthesia	Vulval anesthesia
Anorgasmia	Anorgasmia
Erectile impotence	Vaginal dryness
Premature ejaculation	Vaginismus
Coital pain	Dyspareunia

lioration and rehabilitation, rather than cure, may be the most that can be achieved.

Conceptive Phase

Imagery of the possibility of procreation may have either a positive or negative effect on both the proceptive and the acceptive phases to which conception may be the sequel. Imagery also may influence the course of pregnancy and delivery and, subsequently, the course of parenthood. Pregnancy and childrearing, however, are essentially another topic for another occasion, not for today.

SUMMARY

Sexual syndromes can be classified as hyperphiliac, hypophiliac, or paraphiliac, and as belonging predominantly to the proceptive, acceptive, or conceptive phase of eroticism. Proception is the phase of attracting and being attracted, of solicitation and courtship, and of dependence on fantasy and imagery, especially visual. Acception is the phase of erotic conjunction, in which an oblivious state of erotic body awareness replaces fantasy and culminates in orgasm. Conception and parenthood may or may not follow.

People tend to fall in love not with a person, as is, but with that person as the idealized recipient of a projected image or fantasy of what he or she should become. If the projection is the reciprocal of the fantasy of the partner, a strong pair-bonding ensues. Otherwise, illusion eventually becomes disillusion, and the pairbond weakens. The omnipresent sexual taboo in our society allows - in fact encourages - many children to develop with an idiosyncratic or paraphiliac fantasy. This impairs the chances of durable pairbonding. Boys are probably more vulnerable than girls. Aging may favor reduced imagistic versatility of eroticism. Life crises may induce reversion to the imagery of erotic experience at puberty which subsequently had become replaced or forbidden in young adulthood. Behind every hypophilia, or hyperphilia, there may lurk a paraphilia, so that disclosure of erotic imagery is indispensible to effective sex therapy.

EROTIC IMAGERY IN WOMEN

Claude Crépault, Georges Abraham, Robert Porto and

Marcel Couture

Canada - Switzerland - France

Sexuality may appear to be an entity among those most deeply rooted in the notion of the REAL. Sexuality refers to the physical forms which precisely characterize the differences between the sexes; it is based on elaborate physiological mechanisms and it must feed upon a relational reality outlining its own sociological dimension. Yet, it is the world of sexuality that the imaginary finds one of its most consistent sources and wherein it plays an indispensable supporting role.

Although it may be one of several original and excentric factors in relation to a fixed physiological process, erotic fantasy tends to become repetitive and consequently a fixed state in itself. Once the erotic imaginary has proven capable of adhering closely to erotic excitation, or even if it appears to be the cause of this excitation, the individual seems to refer back to the fantasy with exact attention in repeating the smallest detail. The situation seems paradoxical: on the one hand, erotic fantasy is perceived as a factor aiming at a totally different aspect of the actual sexual activity in progress, an alternative, or else an elaboration of reality on the other hand, erotic fantasy becomes an element whose presence is needed at all costs to maintain certain intrapsychic stimuli, to break the persistant monotony which limits them. Whatever the case may be, fantasy may possibly occupy a true intrapsychic erogenic zone and in some ways be considered an authentic metaphysical mechanism of erogeneity.

Let us now examine the problem of fantasmic function. Psychoanalysis describes it as a defensive mechanism against conflicts;

267

but erotic fantasy is capable of adapting itself to compensate for
the insufficiency of external or personal reality. It plays a
feedback part by correcting sexual activity as the latter unfurls.
Thus, an inclination toward fantasmic activity is noted especially
when sexual relations with a partner are of long duration or frequency. It seems that fantasies replace the decreasing stimulation
offered by the partner.

However, erotic fantasies may also be considered not only as a
compensatory phenomenon but also as a sort of erotic enrichment,
more all-embracing than the erogenous possibilities of the subject.
This would lead to the notion that, even though it occasionally
betrays symptoms of neurosis or pervert pathological tendencies,
erotic fantasy is usually described as a normal occurrence and the
possibility of using the imaginary in the process of excitation,
without allowing it to become an indispensable element of sexual
health, would confirm a sexual and psychoaffective state of well-
being. The psychopathologic problem lies not in the existence of
such fantasies, but more in their avoidance, or else in one's inability to produce and use the imaginary during sexual activity.

The appearance of erotic fantasy independent of sexual performance may also be regarded as compensatory for an actual deficiency of sexual activity, but it could also represent a preparation for future performance. Indeed, any such fantasy is in itself a kind of erotic function and may be considered as such.
Certain periodic or recurrent fantasies, unrelated to precise sexual
performance would seem to automatically maintain a psychophysiological sexual impulse. We should add that the relation between female
hormonal periodicity and her eventual fantasmic periodicity has not
as yet been fully explained.

Is there a difference between the erotic fantasies surrounding
the excitation stage and those accompanying the act which leads to
orgasm? This interesting question has not yet been fully answered,
prepartory fantasies (pre-excitation stage) would seem unstable,
changeable and more dependent on external conditions whereas those
preceding orgasm are more stereotyped and less subject to circumstantial influences.

The possibility of creating such a fantasy and of embodying
it within an actual sexual context does not in any way lessen its
inherent stimulating force. In truth, the fantasy often dwells
upon memories elaborated and arranged in a most personal setting
by the subject herself. Various experiences encountered in real
life which more or less relate to the subject's fantasmic desires
may serve as a kind of "launching pad" for successive reinforced
sexual fantasies. Nor does fantasy seem to weaken physical erotic
sensations although excessive imaginative activity may distract

the subject from the physical sensations involved in sexual activities; but this would seem to be the result of neurotic evasion into fantasy which betrays an intensification of mental eroticism at the expense of the sum total of the actual function and of the adequate concept of the subject's own body and the enjoyment it is capable of giving.

This introduction to erotic fantasy leads us to two more questions: 1) is there a fundamental difference between the erotic fantasies of the male and the female subjects? All our observations demonstrate that such a difference is based more on the needs resulting from their cultural context than on their diametrically opposed functional bases. 2) would erotic fantasy persist in the course of an ideal sexual existence wherein every erotic desire is fully satisfied? To this, we would give a convincing, yet hypothetical answer: eroticism does not require full perfection but a lack of such which ensures its eternal striving to attain such perfection, and fantasy is part and parcel of this striving toward a goal which is always one step removed from reality.

AN EMPIRICAL CONTRIBUTION TOWARD
THE STUDY OF EROTIC FANTASIES IN WOMEN

Our main objective here was to determine the incidence, frequency, and nature of erotic fantasies in women in the course of their sexual activities. We were also interested in learning of the existence of intercultural constants relative to fantasmic content. We have limited our inquiries to female subjects as they are more readily inclined than men to describe their erotic fantasy.

Subjects

We were not content with a probabilistic sampling but chose a more limited group which included sixty-six women, forty from Quebec, thirteen from Marseille, France, and thirteen of varied cultural origins living in Geneva (Switzerland) for at least a few years. All the subjects were 20 to 40 years old and were living with a male companion during the past twelve months. None of these subjects were subjected to previous sex therapy.

Procedure

The required information was obtained by means of semi-structured interview, a self-administered questionnaire and of a monthly diary. The aforementioned interview lasted approximately one hour (the longest, about two hours).

Following the interview, the subject was asked to fill out a questionnaire on fantasmic content. The questionnaire was in two parts: in the first part, the subject was asked to indicate which of the thirty-one proposed erotic fantasies she had experienced during her sexual activities with her habitual partner. The answers were to range from "often," "occasionally," or "never." The second part was concerned with these same fantasies accompanying masturbatory activity. The content of the proposed fantasies had been drawn chiefly from a pilot-project conducted among some thirty Quebec women and selection was done according to clinical reports and research.

To obtain more detailed information on the nature of these erotic fantasies, each subject was asked to keep a diary spanning her entire menstrual cycle. She was asked to write down daily, the precise moment of her sexual activities and the content of the fantasies accompanying such activities as well as those occurring under other circumstances.

Besides keeping a monthly diary, the subject was required to fill out another questionnaire bearing chiefly upon her orgasmic experiences. She was asked, among other things, whether there was a difference between her coital and extra-coital orgasms, and if so, to describe the difference. It should be noted that a state-trait anxiety inventory was given to the women from Quebec.

Findings

EROTIC FANTASIES OCCURRING
DURING HETEROSEXUAL ACTIVITY

Incidence

What is the proportion of erotic fantasy in women during heterosexual activity? On this point, there is a lack of consensus in the various reports obtained through research. As illustrated in Table 1, estimations range from 8% to 75%. Almost all the women we have questioned report having had occasional recourse to such fantasies during heterosexual performances. An affirmative answer was given by 93.9% to the question: "Do you have recourse to erotic mental imagery during sexual activity with your usual partner?" The high percentage obtained is due to the fact that the question was not limited to a certain type of erotic fantasy (as was the case in previous soundings) but embraced all possible types of image. The breakdown reveals that 13.6% out of sixty-six women indicated that they always resorted to sexual mental images during such activity; 39.4% declared they often did so, whereas 40.9% rarely did so. As seen in Table 2, there is no significant difference ($X^2 = 6.13$, df = 6, n.s.) in women from Quebec, France,

TABLE 1

INCIDENCE OF EROTIC FANTASY DURING HETEROSEXUAL ACTIVITY:
(RESULTS OBTAINED FROM PREVIOUS STUDIES)

	%	N
Hamilton (1929)	25	100
De Martino (1963)	23	30
" " (1969)	44	102
" " (1969)	39	73
" " (1974)	39	329
Hollender (1963, 1970)	75	8
Fisher (1973)	75	40
Hariton and Singer (1974)	65	141
Wilson (1975)	11	1370
Hessellund (1976)	8	38

TABLE 2

FREQUENCY OF EROTIC FANTASY
DURING HETEROSEXUAL ACTIVITY (%)

	Women from Quebec (N = 40)	Women from France (N = 13)	Women in Geneva (N = 13)	Total (N = 66)
Always	17.5	7.7	7.7	13.6
Often	47.5	23.1	30.8	39.4
Rarely	30.0	61.5	53.8	40.9
Never	5.0	7.7	7.7	6.1

$$X^2 = 6.13, \text{ df} = 6, \text{ n.s.}$$

and Geneva as to the frequency of recourse to erotic fantasy during heterosexual activity.

Onset and Duration

One half (50.9%) of the women interrogated admitted that erotic mental images appeared immediately prior to the pre-orgasmic phase of their heterosexual activities, and became, so to speak, the launching pad toward orgasm. In about one fourth (24.5%) of the subjects, such fantasies appeared spontaneously, or were evoked, only during the pre-excitation or excitation stages, and in these cases, such fantasies aroused or enhanced sexual desire. Finally, almost one fourth (24.5%) of the subjects stated that fantasy occurred at the excitatory phase and lasted until the first orgasmic sensations. It is noteworthy that not one woman reported having erotic fantasies during the orgasmic period, which may indicate an antithesis existing between imagination and the orgasmic explosion. As seen in Table 3, there is no significant difference (X^2 = 1.66, df = 4, n.s.) between the women from Quebec, France, or Geneva as to the onset and duration of their erotic fantasies during heterosexual activity.

TABLE 3

ONSET AND DURATION OF EROTIC
FANTASY DURING HETEROSEXUAL ACTIVITY (%)

	Women from Quebec (N = 34	Women from France (N = 9)	Women from Geneva (N = 10)	Total (N = 53)
Excitatory phase only	20.6	22.2	40.0	24.5
Pre-orgasmic phase only	52.9	55.6	40.0	50.9
Excitatory and pre-orgasmic phases	26.5	22.2	20.0	24.5

$$X^2 = 1.66, df = 4, n.s.$$

Fantasy Content

In the course of their studies on female erotic fantasy,
Hariton and Singer (1974) emphasized two predominant themes: being
with another male partner and feeling irresistably attracted to an
ardent lover, vaguely outlined, but faceless. The prevalence of
the first is confirmed by the results of this work; the second
theme, however important, does not seem equally predominant. If
we analyze the incidence, we see that two fantasies occupy first
place: reviving a former sexual activity and being with a different partner. To narrow things down, 78.8% of the subjects
interrogated stated having resorted to these two fantasies, often
or occasionally. When we consider to the rank obtained from frequency (often - 3; occasionally - 2; never - 1), the fantasy reviving a former sexual encounter takes first place. Table 4 contains more information on the incidence and frequency of each one
of the thirty-one fantasies studied as well as the rank obtained
from the averages. It is interesting to note that in thirty of
the thirty-one fantasies set down, there is no marked difference
in the answers from the women of Quebec and those from other
countries. The one exception concerns the fantasy: "to be the
object of sexual desire in several men" which is more frequently
noted in Quebec women than in the others. In fact, 60% of the
former admit to having entertained this fantasy often or occasionally as compared to 39.5% of the women from France and 30.8% of
those from Geneva. (X^2 = 10, 11, p< .05).

Fantasy Associations

Factor analysis has permitted us to regroup fantasmic content
according to its degree of association and to identify six principal factors. The first factor includes the following fantasies:
being the victim of aggression; being the aggressor; being a prostitute; having sex against one's will with a known partner; being
overpowered and compelled to have sex with one or more strangers;
pretending to struggle and resist before submitting to a man's
sexual advances (see Table 5). As we can see, all these fantasies
to some extent deny responsibility for sexual pleasure and this
is most evident in cases of masochistic fantasies. The same phenomenon appears, more subtly, perhaps, in the prostitute fantasy
because a woman who indulges in this image enjoys the situation
while absolving herself of guilt; she is no longer herself -
catharsis lays the blame on "the other person." It may be true
that the aggressor fantasy occupies an identical place because
aggression exculpates and denies responsibility for sexual enjoyment.

Four fantasies are closely related (.50 +) in the second factor: the romantic scene, embracing a man's genitals, having a man
embrace one's own genitals, being tied up and sexually stimulated

TABLE 4

NATURE INCIDENCE AND FREQUENCY OF EROTIC FANTASIES
OCCURRING IN THE COURSE OF HETEROSEXUAL ACTIVITIES

	Incidence (%) N = 66	Frequency (%) Often	Frequency (%) Ocasionally	Rank in Average Score
1. Scene reviving a former sexual encounter.	78.8	25.8	53.0	1
2. Scene with a different sexual partner.	78.8	19.7	59.1	2
3. Scene from a sexually-exciting movie seen.	71.2	16.7	54.5	4
4. Scene in which you embrace male genitals.	63.6	33.3	30.3	3
5. Scene in which a man embraces your genitals.	63.6	24.2	39.4	4
6. A romantic scene.	60.6	24.2	36.4	6
7. Scene in which a seducer excites you sexually.	54.5	15.1	39.4	9
8. Scene where you are the sex object of several man.	50.0	21.2	28.8	7
9. Scene where you witness the sexual performance of other persons.	50.0	13.6	36.4	10
10. Scene where you are tied up while being sexually stimulated by a man.	48.5	22.7	25.8	7
11. Scene where an enormous penis penetrates you.	42.4	15.1	27.3	11
12. Scene where you witness group sex activities.	42.4	13.6	28.8	12
13. Scene in which you are a victim of aggression.	42.4	9.1	33.3	13
14. Scene where you pretend to struggle and resist before submitting to a man's sexual advances.	39.4	12.1	27.3	13
15. Scene where you find yourself with an imaginary lover.	39.4	7.6	31.8	15
16. Scene in which you are observed during your sexual performance.	37.9	3.1	34.8	19
17. Scene where you have sex relations with another woman.	34.9	7.6	27.3	18

TABLE 4 (CONTINUED)

	Incidence (%) N = 66	Frequency (%) Often	Ocasionally	Rank in Average Score
18. Scene where you receive male ejaculation in your mouth.	33.3	13.6	19.7	15
19. Scene in which you receive anal penetration.	31.8	12.1	19.7	17
20. Scene where you see yourself with another body.	30.3	7.6	22.7	20
21. Scene where you see yourself as a prostitute.	30.3	7.6	22.7	20
22. Scene where you are being fondled by a faceless lover.	28.7	4.5	24.2	22
23. Scene where your sexual activities are performed in public.	27.2	4.5	22.7	23
24. Scene in which you yourself are the aggressor.	27.2	4.5	22.7	23
25. Scene in which you are overpowered and forced to have sex with one or more strangers.	22.7	4.5	18.2	25
26. Scene in which you are obliged to have sexual relations against your will with someone you know.	19.7	3.0	16.7	27
27. Scene where you initiate a boy in sexual functions.	18.2	6.1	12.1	26
28. Scene where you perform actions considered dirty or forbidden.	18.2	1.5	16.7	28
29. Scene where you are the object of humiliation.	15.1	1.5	13.6	29
30. Scene where you receive a beating.	13.6	1.5	12.1	30
31. Scene where you are the sexual partner of an animal.	10.6	1.5	9.1	31

TABLE 5

FACTOR ANALYSIS (VARIMAX) OF EROTIC FANTASIES
OCCURRING DURING HETEROSEXUAL ACTIVITY

Factor I   (S*)

FACTOR I	(S*)
To undergo aggression	.76
To be the aggressor	.54
To be a prostitute	.58
To be compelled to have sexual relations against one's will with a familiar person	.80
To be overpowered and compelled to have sexual relations with one or more strangers	.77
To pretend to struggle and resist before submittint to a man's sexual advances	.59
Percentage of variance	42.7%

FACTOR II	(S)
A romantic scene	.69
To embrace a man's genitals	.53
To have one's own genitals embraced by a man	.58
To be tied up and be sexually stimulated by a man	.54
Percentage of variance	13.3%

FACTOR III	(S)
Group sex Activities	.66
Sexual relations with another man	.62
To be the sex object of several men	.52
To see oneself with another body	-.56
Percentage of variance	9.5%

FACTOR IV	(S)
To initiate a boy	.72
To be penetrated by an enormous penis	.58
To be excited by a seducer	.52
Percentage of variance	7.6%

FACTOR V	(S)
To receive a beating	.71
To receive male ejaculation in one's mouth	.68
To be humiliated	.58
Percentage of variance	5.9%

FACTOR VI	(S)
To witness the sexual performance of other persons	.55
To perform sexually in public	.69
Percentage of variance	5.1%

(S*) = factor loading

by a man. In the romantic fantasy, the object is global and personalized, but in the scenes depicting fellation and cunnilingus,
there is a sense of depersonalization: a person is reduced to a
thing or a part thereof. Being tied up and sexually stimulated
indicates denial of the responsibility for sexual enjoyment as
well as a certain desire to become a sex object. Therefore, it
would seem that the fantasies correlated to the second factor are
essentially of the dialectic type wherein personalization confronts
the depersonalization of the object.

The third factor includes the following fantasies: group sex
activities, sex relations with another woman, being the object of
the sexual desire of several men, and imagining oneself with another
body. This last fantasy is negatively correlated to factor 3 and
therefore in opposition to the other three fantasies in which we
observe a narcissistic element. The inclination toward narcissism
is also apparent in the fantasy portraying a desire to be the sex
object of several men. However, if we accept the fact that group
sex activities are often associated with latent homosexuality and
that homosexual inclinations include a narcissistic element, it is
possible to relate factor 3 to fantasies of the narcissistic type.
The need to be loved is also probably woven into the content of
narcissistic fantasies.

The fourth factor is imbued with the content of three fantasies:
initiating a boy in sexual activity, being penetrated by an enormous
penis, and being sexually excited by a seducer. There is a common
denominator in the three: the child-adult relationship and the inherent generation conflict, both of which imply a need for confirmed
adult status.

Factor 5 reveals the strong correlation of three fantasies
(.50 -): being beaten, humiliated, and receiving male ejaculation
in one's mouth. Although the last fantasy seems less apparent, we
are inclined to associate these fantasies with a kind of moral masochism.

Factor 6 is seeped in two such contents: witnessing the sexual performance of other persons and having sex oneself in public.
The first case retains a "voyeur" element, whereas the second points
to exhibitionism. Both fantasies have a common trait: they imply
a need to confirm one's physical image.

Those familiar with factor analysis know that it is not always
simple to qualify a factor; interpretations are often unsubstantial
and open to criticism. We are aware of our limitations and of the
condensed character of the interpretations suggested and we know
they are provisional analyses which should be further amplified.

Intervening Variables

An accurate score for each subject was set up by means of the answers obtained from the ensemble of the fantasies suggested in the questionnaire. The score was evaluated as follows: each subject was marked 1, 2, or 3, corresponding to the answers: "never" "occasionally" or "often." There were thirty-one fantasies therefore, the score ranged from 31 to 93. Seven of the independent variables are significatively related to the complete score of fantasies: schooling, the onset of masturbation, infantile and pubertal sex plays, frequency of masturbation, the nature of orgasmic experience, the time of stimulation required to arrive at an extra-coital orgasmic state, and finally, the frequency of erotic fantasies outside the active sexual context.

Schooling. Women with higher education are more inclined to use erotic fantasy during their heterosexual activities than those with less schooling. To be more precise, women with twelve years or less of schooling averaged 44.4 compared to those with thirteen to fifteen years (45.3) and sixteen or more years of schooling averaged 55.3 (the significant difference statistically is F = 6.08, df = 2.58, p< .01).

Onset of masturbation. The women who started masturbating during childhood are more inclined toward erotic fantasies during heterosexual activity than those who began doing so during the pubertal or postpubertal periods. Moreover, those who totally abstained from masturbation had the lowest fantasy average (38.9) (the significant difference is p< .05, F = 3.65, df = 3.62).

Infantile and pubertal sex games. The women interviewed were asked if they had indulged in sexual activities (sex play) during childhood and puberty and to describe the nature of these activities. In order to simplify classification, we have distinguished between those who never resorted to such play during these periods, those whose games were exclusively heterosexual or homosexual, and those indulging in both hetero and homosexual play. The women who totally abstained from such play had fewer erotic fantasies during their present heterosexual activities; on the other hand, those who played hetero and homosexual games during their childhood and pubertal periods of life were the most inclined toward such fantasies (F = 4.73, df = 3.53, p< .01).

Frequency of present masturbatory practice. The women who masturbate frequently, or irregularly, have greater propensity for fantasy during heterosexual activity than the non-masturbating subjects. Those who indulged in one or more masturbatory activities per week recorded an average of fantasy of 50.0 compared to an average of 47.2 for women indulging in similar activity less than once a week and of 41.2 for those who do not masturbate (the significant difference is p< .05, F = 4.08, df = 2.64).

The nature of orgasmic experience. Several questions asked during the interview dealt with the nature of orgasm in the subject; additional information was obtained by means of a self-administered questionnaire. We have established a difference between predominantly vulvar orgasmic experience and those predominantly vaginal or vulvovaginal. In the first, vulvar and especially clitoral stimulation is essential for a woman to attain orgasm. Predominantly vaginal orgasm results from vaginal instead of vulvar reaction, whereas in vulvovaginal orgasm, there is no special erogenous zone; orgasm may be achieved by various stimulative means ; the vulva and the vagina are two distinct erogenous and synergistic sources. Women who arrive easily at coital or extra-coital orgasm are of the vulvovaginal type; those who require coitus to do so are classified as vaginal subjects. Finally, those who experience extra-coital orgasm without difficulty but who have some trouble reaching coital orgasm (without direct vulvar stimulation) are considered belonging to the vulvar type.

When the nature of orgasmic experience is related to the total score of erotic fantasies surrounding heterosexual activities, it is evident that women with predominantly a vaginal-type orgasm have the lowest average (42.3), women with predominantly vulvar orgasmic experience occupy second place (average: 44.5) and those with vulvovaginal experience have the highest average (50.3). A significant statistical difference was observed in these groups (F = 3.70, df = 2.63, p< .05).

The time required to arrive at an extra-coital orgasmic state. Women whose extra-coital orgasmic arousal periods are longest tend to fantasy less during heterosexual activity than those who experience extra-coital orgasm more rapidly or, to be more explicit, the women taking ten minutes or less to reach orgasm have a fantasy average score of 50.9, which is higher than those who take eleven minutes or more (average: 43.4) (significant difference is p< .01, F = 806, df = 1.49).

The frequency of erotic fantasies outside the sexual activities context. The frequency of erotic orgasm during heterosexual activity is in direct proportion to that experienced independently of such activity; in other words, women enjoying erotic imagery when not engaged in active sex are liable to have more fantasies during sexual performance than women who do not, or do infrequently, fantasy in nonsexual activity. We observed a significant difference (p < .01, F = 6.19, df = 2.63) in the three categories of frequency (more than once a week, once a week or less, never).

Women enjoying the greatest number of erotic fantasies in the course of heterosexual activity have several common traits: they have the highest degree of schooling (sixteen or more years), they began masturbating at an early age and continue to do so regularly, they experienced hetero and homosexual activity during childhood and puberty, they are of the vulvovaginal orgasmic type, they attain extra-coital orgasm rapidly, and they frequently resort to the erotic imaginary outside sex activity. In opposition, the women who have the fewest erotic fantasies during heterosexual activity are less schooled (twelve years maximum), have never masturbated, have abstained from sexual activity during childhood and adolescence, belong to the predominantly vaginal-orgasmic group, and are slower to reach extra-coital orgasm (ten minutes or longer). Moreover, they never use erotic imagery independently of sexual functions.

In the course of their studies, Hariton and Singer (1974) observed that the women enjoying multiple fantasies during heterosexual activity were more anxiety-prone than others. A situational and a general anxiety test was given to Quebec women and a weak negative correlation was noted between the levels of anxiety and the sum total of erotic fantasies arising in the course of heterosexual activity. To be exact, the Spearman test indicated a correlation of $-.14$ (p = .21) in the situational anxiety test, and $-.11$ (p = .28) in the general anxiety test.

FANTASIES ACCOMPANYING MASTURBATORY ACTIVITY

In the course of their extensive studies on female sexuality, Kinsey and his collaborators (1953) established that 64% of the women who masturbated (n = 2475) almost always (in 50% of the cases) or occasionally (14%) used erotic imagery in the course of self-manipulation. We questioned sixty-six women, fifty (75.8%) who occasionally masturbated, and all these women said they had always, frequently, or occasionally, had erotic fantasies during such activity.

Referring to his own clinical experience, Hollender (1963, 1970) affirmed that a woman's erotic fantasies during heterosexual activities are identical with those perceived during masturbation and the results obtained in this study generally confirm this notion. For instance, out of the ten fantasies most frequently present in heterosexual activity, nine appear most often during masturbation. Those most frequently noted in masturbatory action are as follows: reviving a former sexual relation (shared by 91.9% of self-manipulators); being with a different sexual partner (79.6%); imagining a scene from a movie (77.1%).

On the other hand, women having the greatest number of erotic fantasies during masturbation share these characteristics: they started masturbatory activity during childhood, they rapidly attain a state of coital orgasm, they are more inclined to erotically fantasy during heterosexual performance. These were the only variables significantly related (p< .05) to the frequency of erotic fantasy during self-manipulation.

CONCLUSION

Not too long ago, men were said to have much stronger sexual impulses than women. Being phallic, they identified themselves with Eros. Women on the other hand were compared to Anteros and this concept was deeply rooted in traditional sexological literature. For instance, in 1882, Krafft-Ebing did not hesitate to qualify as abnormal a man who avoided a woman and a woman who sought sexual pleasure. Freud adhered to the same theory when he said that "libido is constantly and regularly masculine in its essence" (Freud, 1905: 129). His faithful disciple, Helen Deutsch (1945) stated that a woman's sexuality is more inhibited and spiritualized than a man's. As for the erotic imaginary, it was usually considered essentially masculine in nature and the outward manifestation of a man's impulsive needs.

It is possible that a woman's erotic imagery is less developed than a man's but this remains to be seen. One thing is certain: the erotic imaginary is not the prerogative of the male but rather that of all humanity. The results obtained from our investigations have shown it to be very active in women. Indeed, the majority of the women we interviewed admitted having entertained erotic fantasies regularly, both during and independently of auto and allosexual activities. The use of such imagery during sexual performance seems in no way a marginal phenomenon.

However, we have observed that fantasmic content gravitates around three main types: fantasies denying the responsibility for pleasure perceived; dialectic fantasies wherein personalization and depersonalization of the object oppose each other; fantasies oriented toward narcissism. The content of such fantasies remains substantially the same, regardless of their increased frequency during masturbatory activity than during heterosexual functions.

We have also noted that the use of erotic imagery during sexual performance was related to several factors. In general, women with full and diversified sexual lives tend to more frequently fantasy when they engage in sex, which could mean that the imaginary has developed in proportion to the degree of their awareness of sexuality and its pleasures. For instance, women who easily achieve coital or extra-coital orgasm are those who usually entertain the

most fantasies of erotic nature during their heterosexual functions
and these fantasies not only ventilate their unfulfilled or impo-
sible desires but also make up for a less-than-exciting situation...
Many women consider these fantasies as indispensable accessories in
the scenario of their sexual encounters and a guarantee of orgasmic
achievement.

In our opinion, the erotic imaginary of woman still lies in
the twilight zone and further systematic studies are required to
better discern it. Future investigation should be undertaken on
larger samples. It would also be useful to analyze in detail
fantasmic dynamics and their therapeutic implications.

REFERENCES

De Martino, M.F. (1963). Dominance-feeling, security-insecurity,
        and sexuality in women, in M.F. De Martino (Ed.): Sexual
        Behavior and Personality Characteristics (pp. 113-143).
        Citadel Press: New York.

De Martino, M.F. (1969). The New Female Sexuality. Julian Press:
        New York.

De Martino, M.F. (1974). Sex and the Intelligent Woman. Springer:
        New York.

Deutsch, H. (1945). La psychologie des femmes. Presses Univer-
        sitaires de France, 1969: Paris.

Fisher, S. (1973). The Female Orgasm. Basic Books: New York.

Freud, S. (1905). Trois essais sur la théorie de la sexualité.
        Gallimard, 1962: Paris.

Hamilton, G.V. (1929). A Research in Marriage. Medical Research
        Press: New York.

Hariton, E.B., Singer, J.L. (1974). Women's fantasied during sexual
        intercourse: normative and theoretical implications. Jour-
        nal of Consulting and Clinical Psychology, 42: 313-322.

Hessellund, H. (1976). Masturbation and sexual fantasies in mar-
        ried couples. Archives of Sexual Behavior, 5: 133-147.

Hollender, M.H. (1963). Women's fantasies during sexual inter-
        course. Archives of General Psychiatry, 8: 86-90.

Hollender, M.H. (1970). Women's coital fantasies. Medical Aspects
        of Human Sexuality, 4, no. 2: 63-70.

Hollender, M.H. (1975). Women's use of fantasy during sexual inter-
     course, in I.M. Marcus et J.J. Francis (Eds): Masturbation
     From Infancy to Senescence (pp. 315-328). International
     Universities Press: New York.

Kinsey, A.C., Pomeroy, W.B., Martin, C.E., Gebhard, P.H. (1953).
     Sexual Behavior in the Human Female. Saunders: Philadelphia.

Krafft-Ebing, R. (1882). Psychopathia sexualis. Payot, 1963:
     Paris.

Spielberger, C.D., Gorsuck, R.L., Lushene, R.E. (1970). Manual of
     the state-trait anxiety inventory (self-evaluation question-
     naire). Palo Alto: Consulting Psychologists.

Wilson, W.C. (1975). The distribution of selected sexual attitudes
     and behaviors among the adult population of the United States.
     Journal of Sex Research, II: 46-64.

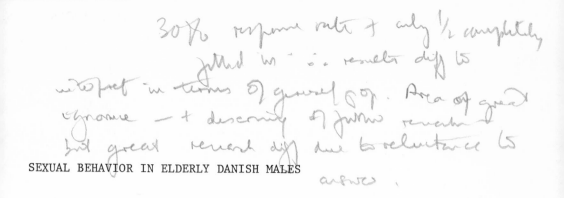

SEXUAL BEHAVIOR IN ELDERLY DANISH MALES

Sten Hegeler and Mei-Mei Mortensen

Denmark

We shall never be able to know what our sexuality will be when we get older before we are old ourselves. Nor are we able to describe the situation among the elderly Danish males as a whole group. We are therefore, presenting some preliminary findings from the subjects who answered our questionnaire during October 1975.

SAMPLE SELECTION AND PROCEDURE

There are about five million people in Denmark. Seven hundred thousands (700,000) elderly men are more than 50 years old. We have been questioning men that were between 51 and 95 years old by sending a questionnaire to 6214 elderly Danish men, asking them about their sexual activities and experiences. From our four previous pilot studies we knew, that only 15-20% would send back the questionnaire. In fact 30% were returned, with half of them filled out satisfactorily.

As shown in Table 1, the subjects were divided in nine subgroups from 50-55 years old to 91-95 years old. As we knew that only a limited number were going to answer out questions, we aimed at having about 100 respondents inside each of these nine five year groups. We also knew that it was more difficult to get the oldest men to answer us. So although we asked at random, we sent out twice as many questionnaires to the oldest groups. We received 936 questionnaires, properly answered. Since 227 men had answered the questionnaire in our four pilot studies, we will present the data for 1163 elderly Danish males instead of personal interviews

TABLE 1

DISTRIBUTION OF QUESTIONNAIRE SENT AND ANSWERED BY AGE SUB-GROUPS

Age-Group	1	2	3	4	5	6	7	8	9	Total
Aged	51-55	56-60	61-65	66-70	71-75	76-80	81-85	86-90	91-95	51-95
Numb. of men alive	146,000	134,000	128,000	100,500	73,500	48,000	25,000	10,000	2,400	670,000
Quest. sent to	493	493	551	581	622	758	762	978	976	6,214
Answer back from	108	117	105	89	102	106	91	124	94	936
Resp. in %	22%	24%	19%	15%	16%	14%	12%	13%	10%	15%

we sent by mail primarily for economic reasons. Since people were
answering anonymously, we hope more sincere data about intimate
sexual activities was supplied.

FINDINGS

Table 2 shows that more than 90% of the men in their fifties,
75% of those in their sixties, 45% of those in their seventies,
whereas only 3% of those in their nineties have experienced coitus
and other sexual activities with a woman in the year prior to our
research.

Figure 1 shows that most of these men seem to enjoy a certain
degree of privacy, with more and more becoming widowers and living
alone, especially after the age of seventy. It can also be seen
that even when living with a woman, many men did not have coital
or other sexual activities. The explanation might be, that the
woman were less interested and/or less able to participate.

When asked if they were still masturbating, up to 31% did not
answer the question and from comments made, we interpret a lot of
guilt about masturbation. Table 3 shows that 23% of the men in
the oldest group answering the question"confessed" masturbating
from time to time, whereas 50% did in the age group under seventy.

Table 4 shows that every second man at least claims to wake
up with an erection from time to time, until the age of 85. Every
third man does so over 85.

We also evaluated our subject's interest in sex, regardless
of potency and of presence of a partner (Table 5). We made this
evaluation based on all the answers to the questionnaire as well
as additional comments. To our best judgement we found that up
to age 75, most of the men seem to be somewhat interested in sex,
whereas every second to every third man over 75 expresses some
short of positive interest in sex.

Finally if we compare the above mentioned findings· (the sex
interest, the morning erection, the masturbation and the coital
activities) we find that: 1) the interest in sex and the morning
erection are much related to one another; 2) the percentage of those
who masturbate is almost at the same level over the age of 80; 3)
the percentage of those indulging in coital activities decreases
the most over the years (Figure 2).

TABLE 2

COITUS OR OTHER SEXUAL ACTIVITIES WITH A WOMAN DURING THE
LAST YEAR PRIOR TO THE RESEARCH (IN PERCENTAGE)

Aged	51–55	56–60	61–65	66–70	71–75	76–80	81–85	86–90	91–95
No answer in %	1%	2%	5%	6%	2%	9%	8%	19%	5%
Coit. or other activities	94%	91%	78%	75%	56%	36%	18%	12%	3%
No coit. nor other activities	6%	9%	22%	25%	44%	64%	82%	88%	97%

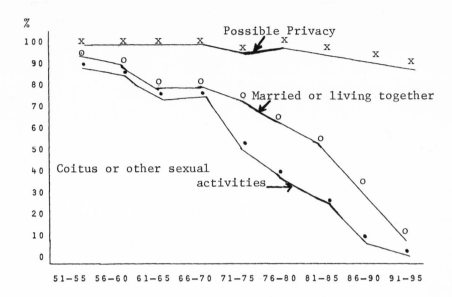

Fig. 1. Privacy, life-style and sexual activities (N = 936).

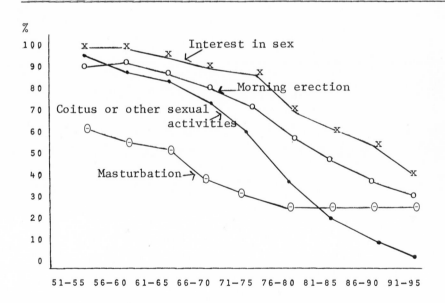

Fig. 2. Interest in sex, morning erection, masturbation, coitus
or other sexual activities (N = 936).

TABLE 3

MASTURBATION (IN PERCENTAGE)

Aged	51–55	56–60	61–65	66–70	71–75	76–80	81–85	86–90	91–95
No answer in %	5%	9%	9%	12%	14%	21%	24%	26%	31%
Never been masturb.	4%	13%	17%	12%	22%	30%	30%	32%	26%
Not any more	37%	36%	28%	44%	35%	46%	43%	47%	52%
Still mast.	60%	51%	55%	45%	43%	24%	26%	21%	23%

TABLE 4

MORNING ERECTION (IN PERCENTAGE)

Aged	51-55	56-60	61-65	66-70	71-75	76-80	81-85	86-90	91-95
No answer in %	1%	3%	3%	5%	7%	9%	13%	21%	20%
Not any more	11%	10%	19%	14%	25%	39%	51%	63%	69%
Still morning erection	89%	90%	81%	86%	75%	61%	49%	37%	31%

TABLE 5

INTEREST IN SEX, REGARDLESS OF POTENCY AND POSSIBILITIES (IN PERCENTAGE)

Aged	51–55	56–60	61–65	66–70	71–75	76–80	81–85	86–90	91–95
No answer in %	1%	0%	4%	6%	4%	13%	25%	24%	25%
Int. in Sex*	98%	100%	95%	92%	86%	61%	46%	51%	35%

* Evaluation, based on total answers as well as additional comments.

REPRODUCTIVE HORMONE LEVELS AND SEXUAL BEHAVIORS OF YOUNG COUPLES

DURING THE MENSTRUAL CYCLE[1]

Harold Persky, Harold I. Lief, Charles P. O'Brien,
Dorothy Strauss and William Miller

United States

The classic studies of Kinsey and his coworkers (1948, 1953) and of Masters and Johnson (1966) provided a major stimulus for the scientific investigation of human sexual behavior. Since those pioneering efforts, a number of reports have appeared concerned with physiological (Masters and Johnson, 1970), behavioral (Fisher, 1973) and social (Chesser, 1957) determinants of human sexuality.

Although endocrine factors, and particularly gonadal hormones, have been examined for their role in the sexual behavior of several mammalian species, similar studies for humans are almost nonexistent. The very few human studies which have been reported have used techniques for the assessment of endocrine status which are not deemed acceptable today. For example, one of the most cited studies used a technique for assessment of estrogen secretion which is presently known to be unreliable. Benedek & Rubinstein (1942) determined the number of exfoliative cells in vaginal smears obtained from women at various times during their menstrual cycles. These women's moods and feelings were gauged simultaneously while they were in psychoanalytic treatment. Maximum vaginal cell count was found by these investigators to be associated with peak sexual desire. On the assumption that maximum cell count reflected maximum estrogen secretion, an event known to be associated with ovulation, they concluded that sexual desire was most intense during the menstrual cycle around the time of ovulation.

---

[1]This study was supported by grants from the National Institute of Mental Health, number MH21044 and MH 18374.

Although this inference would appear to be a reasonable one, Waxenberg and his coworkers (1960) have denied its validity. These investigators studied a group of women using the same technique for assessment of estrogen secretion as did Benedek & Rubinstein. They were unable to demonstrate a significant relationship between vaginal cell count and either sexual desire, sexual activity or sexual responsiveness. They consequently inferred that human sexual behavior for the female was not seriously estrogen-dependent. This group, like that of Benedek & Rubinstein, was not a normative one.

Although Waxenberg and his associates did not obtain a significant relationship between any of the sexual behaviors assessed and vaginal smear count, they did note that these women with metastatic breast cancer, who had been bilaterally oophorectomized and adrenalectomized, experienced major reduction in all 3 types of sexual behavior following surgery (Waxenberg et al., 1959). In a follow-up approximately one year after surgery 14 of 17 of their patients reported some loss of sexual desire with the majority reporting loss of all desire. About half of all their patients also reported stopping all sexual activity. Almost all of the 12 patients who had experienced sexual responsiveness presurgically, experienced a reduction to near unresponsive levels postsurgically. These investigators further noted that adrenalectomy had a far greater effect on sexual behavior than either breast cancer itself or any other previous surgery including oophorectomy. From this study, they inferred that sexual desire, activity and/or responsiveness was probably related to androgens secreted by the adrenal gland.

In one of the only known studies in which gonadal hormones were determined directly, Persky, O'Brien & Khan (1976) measured plasma estradiol, progesterone and testosterone levels of a group of healthy, young women at 3 times during their menstrual cycle: early follicular, ovulatory peak and late luteal stages. They assessed only one aspect of sexual behavior, namely the subjects' average frequency of sexual intercourse in the two months prior to hormone assessment. Subjects who were rated as either High or Medium with respect to intercourse frequency exhibited significantly higher testosterone levels at the ovulatory peak (Figure 1) and significantly higher progesterone levels (Figure 2) in the late luteal stage of their cycles than did the subjects who were rated as Low. No significant differences were obtained among subjects with respect to plasma estradiol level.

While the preceding study tended to bear out some of the conclusions drawn by Waxenberg, assessment of sexual behavior was very limited. We therefore decided to reexamine the problem of the relationship of gonadal hormones to human sexual behaviors in

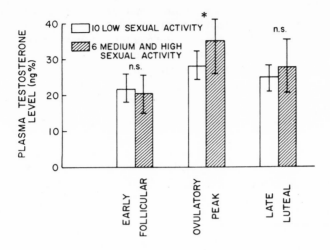

Fig. 1. Plasma testosterone levels (Mean ± S.E.) of Low vs. Medium - High Sexual Activity subjects on 3 occasions during a single menstrual cycle. The asterisk indicates a difference significant beyond the 5% level.

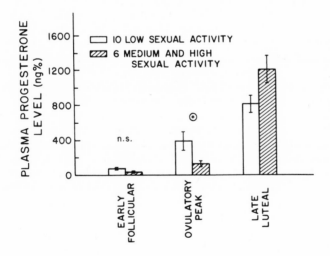

Fig. 2. Plasma progesterone levels (Mean ± S.E.) of Low vs. Medium - High Sexual Activity subjects on 3 occasions during a single menstrual cycle. The circled asterisk indicates a difference significant beyond the 10% level, the uncircled asterisk, a difference beyond the 5% level.

a normative population using modern analytical methods for hormone
determinations. Both hormone levels and behaviors were determined
for both sexual partners in order to ascertain whether dyadic interactions affect psychoendocrine relationships. The present paper is
a preliminary report of such a study of 11 married couples, ages
21-31 years and followed for a period of 3 consecutive menstrual
cycles.

SUBJECTS, EXPERIMENTAL DESIGN AND METHODS

Eleven couples married for at least one year were the subjects
of the study. Five of the couples had children, 4 having one a
piece and one having two children. All of the wives had not used
a contraceptive steroid preparation for at least 6 months prior to
the start of the study and were not using one during the course of
the study. At least one partner of each couple was a student in
the same college.

After being accepted as a candidate for the study, each subject filled out the Minnesota Multiphasic Personality Inventory
(MMPI), was examined by a physician and was interviewed by a psychiatrist (HIL). The MMPI was intended to assist the psychiatrist
in rejecting unacceptable candidates and to provide some additional
background information for the study. No couple was accepted if
one partner scored more than two standard deviations above the mean
on more than one of the 10 MMPI diagnostic scales. Furthermore,
anyone who scored more than 5 on the MMPI-Lie Scale was automatically rejected as an unreliable reporter. The physical examination
was intended to rule out any individual with a serious illness and
particularly an endocrinopathy. The combination of psychiatric
interview and MMPI helped to eliminate from the study psychotics,
severe neurotics and individuals with serious psychosomatic ill-
nesses.

Following the selection phase, each wife was instructed how
to keep a basal temperature record, menstrual period record and
sexual intercourse frequency record using a single chart suitable
for 3 consecutive menstrual cycles. Wives also were required to
fill out a brief sexual gratification form daily.

All couples were seen in the laboratory twice weekly, on
Mondays and Thursdays, at the same time of day, for a period of
3 consecutive menstrual cycles of the wife. No couple missed more
than two testing occasions during the entire study. A heparinized
blood sample was drawn from each partner on arrival in the laboratory and then each one was interviewed individually by the clinical
psychologist who had been trained as a marriage counselor (DS).

Testosterone was determined for both husbands and wives while estradiol and progesterone were determined only for the wives. All determinations were done on plasma by radioimmunoassay (Wu and Lundy, 1971; Furuyama and Nugent, 1971; Furuyama et al., 1970) and in duplicate; all results were corrected for recovery.

The brief interview with the clinical psychologist was open-ended and intended to provide information about the subjects' current sexual behavior. A typescript of each interview, from which all reference to phase of menstrual cycle was deleted, was given to the two psychiatrist-raters (HIL, CPO'B). Every interview was rated independently by each psychiatrist; the final ratings were an average of the two estimates. Five different sexual behaviors were rated including initiatory sexual behavior, sexual responsivity, sexual avoidance, couple interaction relative to sexual feelings and mood as related to sexual feelings. Table 1 gives word definitions for each scale unit of every scale. Reliability estimates were obtained between raters and between ratings made at different times by the same rater. The two ratings invariably agreed closely, the correlation being at least at the 1% level of significance and frequently much better.

RESULTS

Some Characteristics of the
Wives' Menstrual Cycles

Table 2 summarizes some features of the 3 consecutive menstrual cycles obtained for the 11 wives. The mean cycle lengths were 30.9, 28.5 and 29.0 days for the first, second and third cycles respectively. Bleeding persisted for 5.6, 5.9 and 5.6 days respectively. Nine of the 11 women had 3 consecutive ovulatory cycles as judged by a temperature rise at midcycle of at least $0.8^{\circ}F$. One subject had two anovulatory cycles as judged by this criterion and another subject became pregnant during her second cycle. Consequently, 30 out of 32 possible cycles were deemed to be ovulatory. The length of the luteal phase, the time from ovulation to onset of the next menses, averaged 12.0, 13.8 and 13.2 days respectively with an individual range from 7 to 17 days. The combination of normal cycle lengths, normal bleeding periods, normal luteal phase lengths and ovulation strongly support the contention that these women had normal menstrual cycles and confirm the impression gained during the screening period that these 11 women were physically and mentally healthy.

Gonadal Hormone Levels during the Cycle

1. Wives' Testosterone Levels. The mean testosterone levels

TABLE 1

THE INTERVIEW RATING SCALES
AND THEIR QUANTIFICATION

A. Sexual Initiation

   1. Absence of sexual overtures or cues
   2. Ambiguous cues and/or actions
   3. Low-keyed signalling
   4. Moderately aggressive overtures or strong signalling
   5. Highly aggressive sexual actions directed toward partner

B. Sexual Receptivity

   1. Indifferent
   2. Acquiescent
   3. Slightly responsive
   4. Moderately responsive
   5. Highly responsive

C. Sexual Avoidance

   1. No avoidance
   2. Emphasis on "busyness," tension, preoccupation, etc.
   3. Moderately provocative behavior
   4. Highly provocative behavior
   5. Outright refusal

D. Couple Interaction

   1. Strongly hostile
   2. Moderately rejecting
   3. Tolerant
   4. Moderately affectionate
   5. Very affectionate

E. Mood Level

   1. Depressed
   2. More sad than happy
   3. Neither happy nor sad
   4. Contented
   5. Elated

TABLE 2

SOME CHARACTERISTICS OF THE MENSTRUAL CYCLES OF THE SUBJECTS

Ss	Age (Years)		Length of Cycle (Days)			Duration of Menses (Days)			Ovulation			Length of Luteal Phase (Days)		
	H	W	I	II	III	I	II	III	I	II	III	I	II	III
1	25	22	29	29	29	7	7	7	+	+	+	12	13	14
2	21	21	26	?		5	4		+	+		14	?	
3	23	25	30	31	34	6	5	6	+	+	+	15	14	17
4	25	22	30	31	27	6	5	6	+	+	+	12	10	7
5	24	23	33	34	30	5	5	5	+	+	+	15	16	11
6	31	31	24	25	27	5	8	5	+	+	+	11	14	14
7	22	22	39	21	30	5	6	4	+	-	-	11	-	-
8	24	25	32	27	29	5	6	6	+	+	+	7	15	14
9	26	26	29	28	26	6	7	6	+	+	+	11	14	15
10	24	24	31	30	30	8	7	6	+	+	+	10	12	16
11	25	25	25	37	29	4	5	5	+	+	+	14	16	11
X̄	24	24	30.9	28.5	29.0	5.6	5.9	5.6				12.0	13.8	13.2
S.D.	2.6	2.8	4.3	3.6	2.3	1.1	1.2	0.8				2.4	1.9	3.1

for all female subjects expressed as a function of their individual days of ovulation are shown in Figure 3. Inspection shows a maximum value in each cycle of approximately 20-25 ng/100 ml and occurring about the day of ovulation, Day 0 on the chart. Such a peak testosterone value at ovulation has been reported previously (Lobotsky et al., 1964; Judd and Yen, 1973; Persky et al., 1973). A second testosterone elevation also occurs at approximately 7 days following ovulation in each cycle. To determine whether this second peak was merely an artifact of computation, each wife's testosterone chart was inspected. Two peaks were found in cycles #1 and 2 for 8 of the 11 women and in cycle #3 for 6 of the 10 women. Furthermore, the same 3 women, subjects #1, 10 and 11, failed to show a biphasic peak on any of their 3 cycles. To our knowledge, no report of such a biphasic pattern for testosterone secretion has ever been reported previously for women.

2. Wives' Progesterone Levels. Figure 4 gives the average progesterone levels for all 11 women across the 3 cycles. Three distinct peaks occur at +7, +7 and +10 days after ovulation in each of the 3 cycles respectively and amounting to 1705, 1397 and 994 ng/100 ml respectively. These values closely resemble values reported previously from this and other laboratories (Abraham et al., 1972; Persky et al., 1974; Sherman and Korenman, 1974).

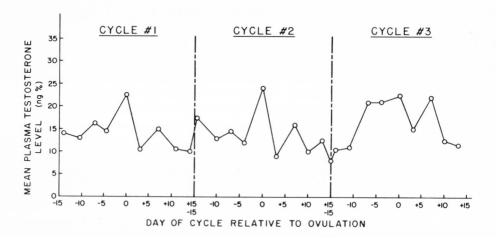

Fig. 3. Mean plasma testosterone levels of 11 young wives during 3 menstrual cycles. Each point is the average for the 11 subjects on the respective day relative to each individual subject's day of ovulation.

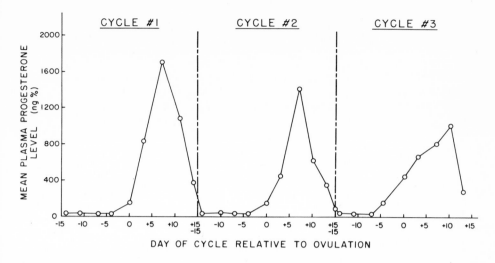

Fig. 4. Mean plasma progesterone levels of 11 young wives during
3 menstrual cycles. Occasions are represented as in Figure 3.

3. <u>Wives' Estradiol Levels</u>. Figure 5 gives the mean estradiol
levels for all wives across the 3 menstrual cycles. A peak value
occurs in each cycle on the day of ovulation and amounted to 48,
62 and 57 ng/100 ml respectively. This value closely resembles
the values reported in the literature (Abraham <u>et al</u>., 1972; Persky
<u>et al</u>., 1974; Sherman and Korenman, 1974). A second peak occurs
in each cycle at +7, +7 and + 10 days after ovulation and tended
to be slightly lower in value than the first peak of each cycle.
This second peak coincided with the second testosterone peak and
the progesterone peak in each cycle. This second peak was not an
artifact of calculation; it occurred in 26 of 32 cycles.

4. <u>Husbands' Testosterone Levels</u>. Testosterone average values for all husbands are plotted against day of their wives' cycles
in Figure 6. The overall grand average amounted to 589 ng/100 ml
with subjects range from 445 to 753 ng/100 ml. A maximum value
occurred for each husband at about +7 days after his wife's ovulation in at least one of her cycles. The +7 day peak occurred in
a total of 25 of 32 cycles. It should be recalled that the wives
showed a progesterone peak and second estradiol and testosterone
peaks on this day in each cycle. How the husbands' testosterone
level peaked at a specific phase of their wives' menstrual cycles
is not known.

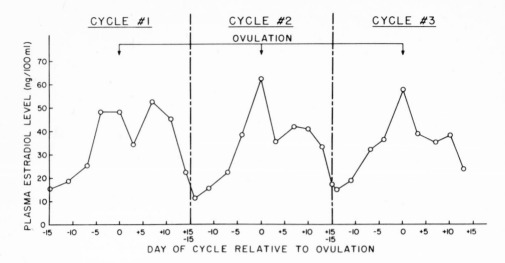

Fig. 5. Mean plasma estradiol levels of 11 young wives during 3 menstrual cycles. Occasions are represented as in Figure 3.

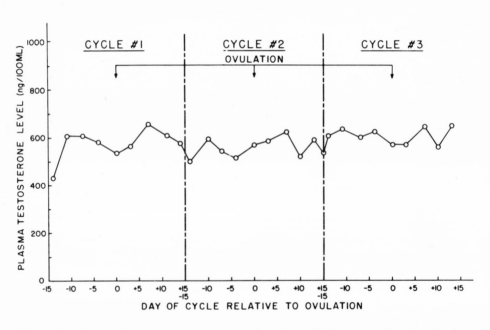

Fig. 6. Mean plasma testosterone levels of 11 young husbands during 3 of their wives' menstrual cycles. Occasions are represented as in Figure 3; i.e., relative to each subject's wife.

Sexual Behavior During the Menstrual Cycle

1. Sexual Intercourse Frequency and Gratification. Turning
away momentarily from the hormone data to the sexual behavior data,
Table 3 gives the number of sexual intercourse experiences for each
couple in each menstrual cycle. Average intercourse frequency for
the group amounted to 11 occasions per cycle with a low for one
couple of 3 occasions and a high for another couple of 18 occasions.
Couples tended to maintain their intercourse frequency relative to
the group as a whole across the 3 menstrual cycles as shown by the
significant coefficient of concordance, W.

TABLE 3

INTERCOURSE FREQUENCY
DURING THREE MENSTRUAL CYCLES

Couple	Cycle 1	Cycle 2	Cycle 3
1	10	7	9
2	10	9	
3	4	3	3
4	11	16	11
5	11	17	10
6	8	7	9
7	18	7	14
8	16	12	11
9	12	16	15
10	14	13	13
11	13	13	13
$\bar{X}$	11.5	10.9	10.8

$W = 0.70$ $X^2 = 21.0$ d.f. $= 10$ $p < .05$

In Table 4, the sexual gratification scores of the wives are given as average values per subject per cycle. Scores range from a possible 0 to a possible 5.5. The higher the score, the higher is the self-report of sexual gratification of the wife. An overall value of 2.03 was obtained for all wives with individual subjects ranging from 0.39 to 4.00 per cycle. Wives tended to hold their positions relative to the group with respect to sexual gratification self-ratings as shown by the highly significant coefficient of concordance.

The question logically arises whether sexual gratification of

TABLE 4

WIVES' SEXUAL GRATIFICATION FORM SCORES

Ss	Cycle 1	Cycle 2	Cycle 3
1	4.00	2.59	2.28
2	2.67	2.63	
3	0.56	0.39	0.42
4	1.45	1.92	1.75
5	2.12	2.16	1.87
6	1.20	0.83	0.84
7	2.39	2.62	3.00
8	2.54	1.94	1.52
9	2.94	3.09	3.06
10	2.11	1.96	1.83
11	2.22	2.17	2.04
$\overline{X}$	2.20	2.03	1.86

W = 0.91	$X^2 = 27.3$	d.f. = 10	$\underline{p} < .01$

the wife was related to the frequency with which she engaged in
sexual intercourse. Correlations were obtained between the self-
rated sexual gratification scores and intercourse frequency amounting to 0.45, 0.48 and 0.75 for the first, second and third cycles
respectively. Although all of these correlations are statistically
significant, it should be recognized that their magnitudes indicate
that factors other than intercourse frequency play a more important
role in the gratification feelings of the wives. We have not yet
established which factors are the more important ones. We have
also not yet performed a similar analysis for the husbands.

     2.   The Interviews and Sexual Behavior Ratings. A total of
513 interviews were obtained by the clinical psychologist from the
11 couples. These semiweekly interviews were converted to type-
scripts and given to the psychiatrists who rated each interview
independently for the 5 different sexual behaviors. The average
behavior scores across the 3 menstrual cycles are given separately
for wives and husbands in Figure 7. Although initiatory behavior
and responsivity of the partners tended to parallel one another,
these relationships did not achieve statistical significance.
However, significant correlation coefficients were obtained between
the husbands' sexual initiation scores and the wives' responsivity
scores; the converse was also true in that wives' initiation scores
correlated significantly with husbands' responsivity scores. An
implication from this finding is that couple interaction scores of
wives and husbands should also be related and this was found to be
true. Neither sexual avoidance scores nor mood scores related significantly between sexual partners.

     While the wives' sexual initiation scores did not show a reg-
ular pattern related to their menstrual cycles, they appeared to
have a greater degree of responsivity around the ovulatory peak.
The wives also appeared to display a greater need for affection
at about the same point. No systematic patterns of mood were noted
for either partner. These sexual behavior ratings are presently
being examined at greater length by a variety of statistical techniques.

Reproductive Hormone Relationship

     Figure 8 shows the average testosterone levels of the husbands
and the average testosterone, estradiol and progesterone levels of
the wives on one composite chart. The important point in connection with this graph is the presence of elevations in the female
subjects' testosterone and estradiol levels around the ovulatory
peak and of another elevation of female testosterone, estradiol
and progesterone levels and of male testosterone levels at approximately +7 days after ovulation. This unique set of male and
female hormone peaks will be discussed more fully at the end of
this paper.

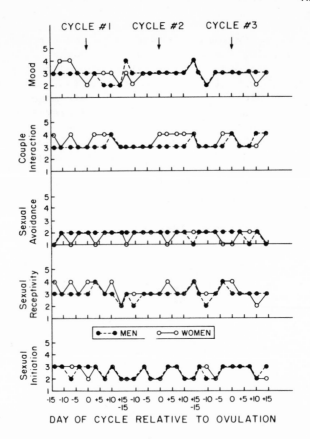

Fig. 7. Mean sexual behavior scores of 11 young husbands and 11 young wives during 3 menstrual cycles. Occasions are represented as in Figure 3.

Hormone-Sexual Behavior Relationships

The statistical analysis of the psychoendocrine relationships have just started and consequently we must severely limit the remarks to be made at this point. The relationship between the male testosterone level and the 5 male sexual behavior ratings has been determined for each husband across the individual testing occasions. Multiple correlation coefficients (R's) ranging from 0.21 to 0.67 were obtained for individual subjects; when the 5 sexual behavior ratings for their wives plus their wives' self-ratings and intercourse frequency are included, these multiple correlation coefficients increased significantly. The coefficients rose in value to 0.67 to 0.97, significant beyond the 0.1% level. The increment

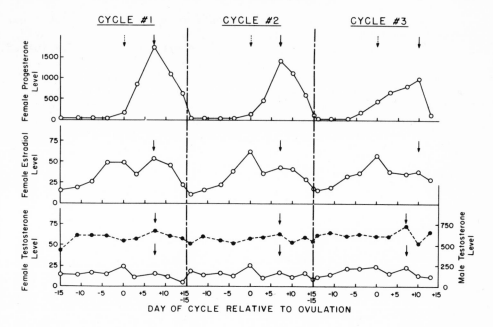

Fig. 8. Mean plasma estradiol, progesterone and testosterone levels of 11 wives and mean plasma testosterone levels of 11 husbands during 3 menstrual cycles. Occasions are represented as in Figure 3.

in correlation indicates that female sexual behaviors, sexual gratification of the wives and frequency of sexual intercourse contribute significantly to the variance in male testosterone.

The opposite relationship, female testosterone level to female sexual behaviors, yielded multiple correlations also ranging from 0.27 to 0.67. Adding the male sexual behaviors, female sexual gratification scores and intercourse frequency raised the correlation coefficients but not to the same degree as in the previous instance. In this connection, the role of the adult female monkeys on individual, young adult male monkeys as reported by Rose and his coworkers (1972) should be recalled.

Plasma estradiol levels of the wives were significantly related to the 5 female sexual behaviors for each wife; adding the husbands' sexual behavior scores did not markedly affect the correlations. Plasma progesterone levels of the wives were also moderately related to the 5 female sexual behavior scores; adding the male scores here markedly elevated the multiple correlation coefficients.

Similar analyses using testosterone/progesterone, testosterone/
estradiol and progesterone/estradiol ratios as the dependent variable have been performed. The results are presently being evaluated.
Correlation of endocrine-behavioral measures in the preceding comparisons were made over the entire period of the 3 menstrual cycles.
Specific comparisons are now under way for more limited aspects of
the cycle; such correlations for the early follicular, ovulatory
peak and late luteal stages will permit comparison with the initial
study of Persky, O'Brien & Khan (1974).

DISCUSSION

Obviously this study remains to be completed. Most immediately, it is necessary to decide whether specific hormonal correlates of sex drive, sexual activity and sexual responsivity
really do occur and for which partner. All efforts are presently
being made in our laboratory to provide answers to these questions.

Two important findings have emerged from this study and have
been mentioned in this talk. The first concerns the patterning of
the male and female gonadal hormone levels. A peak at ovulation
or Day 0 was demonstrated for estradiol and testosterone in the
women while another group of peaks were demonstrated on the +7 day
following ovulation for the female testosterone and progesterone
levels and the male testosterone level. It should be recalled
that sampling in this study occurred twice a week and not daily.
Consequently, the patterning of these peaks may be even closer than
the current measurements indicate. While the meaning of changes
in these hormone levels is not yet elucidated, the specific cluster
of hormones suggests the possibility that all of these substances
may play an important role in ensuring fertilization of the egg at
ovulation.

A second important finding concerns the specific patterning
of the male testosterone levels. Doehring and his coworkers (1975)
have suggested that male testosterone level is cyclical in nature
and that at least for some sizeable proportion of men is related
to the female menstrual cycle. The present study of the reproductive dyad, i.e., the partners in the marriage relationship, has
shown that the husband's testosterone level peaks in an ordered
fashion with respect to the female partner's menstrual cycle and
particularly to her day of ovulation. How the information necessary for this dyadic interaction is transmitted is not yet known.

Finally, although the information was not presented here, data
are available which will shortly demonstrate whether specific sexual behaviors are associated with individual gonadal hormone levels. This information is not intended to prove a priority of
biological processes over psychological or social factors or vice

versa. Rather, it is the intent of this study to demonstrate the complex interrelationships between systems of organization best termed servoregulatory for the reproductive and sexual acts.

REFERENCES

Abraham, G.E., Odell, W.D., Swerdloff, R.S. and Hopper, K. (1972). Simultaneous radioimmunoassay of plasma FSH, LH, progesterone, 17-hydroxyprogesterone, and estradiol-17β during the menstrual cycle. J. Clin. Endocrinol. & Metab. 34: 312.

Benedek, T. and Rubinstein, B. (1942). The Sexual Cycle in Women: The Relation Between Ovarian Function and Psychodynamic Processes, National Research Council, Washington, D.C.

Chesser, E. (1957). The Sexual, Marital and Family Relationships of the English Woman, Roy, New York.

Doehring, C.H., Kraemer, H.C., Brodie, H.K.H. and Hamburg, D.A. (1975). A cycle of plasma testosterone in the human male. J. Clin. Endocrinol. & Metab. 40: 492.

Fisher, S. (1973). Female Orgasm: Psychology, Physiology, Fantasy, Basic Books, New York.

Furuyama, S., Mayes, D. and Nugent, C.A. (1970). Radioimmunoassay for plasma testosterone. Steroids 16: 415.

Furuyama, S. and Nugent, C.A. (1971). A radioimmunoassay for plasma progesterone. Steroids 18: 91.

Judd, H.L. and Yen, S.S.C. (1973). Serum androstenedione and testosterone levels during the menstrual cycle. J. Clin. Endocrinol. and Metab. 36: 475.

Kinsey, A.C., Pomeroy, W. and Martin, C. (1948). Sexual Behavior in the Human Male, Saunders, Philadelphia.

Kinsey, A.C., Pomeroy, W., Martin, C. and Gebhard, P. (1953). Sexual Behavior in the Human Female, Saunders, Philadelphia.

Lobotsky, J., Wyss, H.I., Segre, E.J. and Lloyd, C.W. (1964). Plasma testosterone in the normal woman. J. Clin. Endocrinol. and Metab. 24: 1261.

Masters, W.H. and Johnson, V.E. (1966). Human Sexual Response, Little Brown, Boston.

Masters, W.H. and Johnson, V.E. (1970). Human Sexual Inadequacy,
    Little Brown, Boston.

Persky, H., O'Brien, C.P., Schneider, P. and Basu, G.K. (1973).
    Plasma testosterone level (T) and aggression scores during
    the menstrual cycle. Endocrinology 92: A-252.

Persky, H., Khan, M.A. and O'Brien, C.P. (1974). Plasma proges-
    terone level (P) and sexual activity in normal, anovulatory
    and steroid-blocked menstrual cycles. Endocrinology 94:
    A-287.

Persky, H., O'Brien, C.P. and Khan, M.A. (1976). Reproductive
    hormone levels, sexual activity and moods during the mens-
    trual cycle. Psychosom. Med. 38: 62.

Rose, R.M., Gordon, T.P. and Bernstein, I.S. (1972). Plasma
    testosterone levels in the male Rhesus: Influence of
    sexual and social stimuli. Science 178: 643.

Sherman, B.M. and Korenman, S.G. (1974). Measurement of plasma
    LH, FSH, estradiol and progesterone in disorders of the
    human menstrual cycle: the short luteal phase. J. Clin.
    Endocrinol. and Metab. 38: 89.

Waxenberg, S.E., Drellich, M.G. and Sutherland, A.M. (1959). The
    role of hormones in human behavior. I. Changes in female
    sexuality after adrenalectomy. J. Clin. Endocrinol. and
    Metab. 19: 193.

Waxenberg, S.E., Finkbeiner, J.A., Drellich, M.G. and Sutherland,
    A.M. (1960). The role of hormones in human behavior.
    Psychosom. Med. 22: 435.

Wu, C. and Lundy, L. (1971). Radioimmunoassay of plasma estrogens.
    Steroids 18: 91.

↓ in finger temp while visual erotic film

FINGER TEMPERATURE AS A MEASURE OF SEXUAL AROUSAL IN MALES AND FEMALES

Linda Kabbash, William Brender and Tom Bowman

Canada

In recent studies of human sexual arousal (Heiman, 1975; Kutchinsky, 1970), investigators have exposed men and women to erotic visual, narrative or auditory stimuli and recorded their immediate and delayed responses to the stimuli by means of verbal self-report and/or physiological measures. In comparison to self-report measures, physiological indicators of sexual arousal offer the advantages of objectivity and continuous response tracking and therefore have received increasing research attention in recent years. Mann (1971) and Zuckerman (1971) reviewed studies employing physiological measures to assess magnitude or direction of erotic interest in men and women. They reported that indirect physiological measures of sexual arousal such as galvanic skin response, pupillary dilation, blood volume and pressure, heart rate, respiratory rate, biochemical response and evoked cortical response have tended to be either unresponsive or unreliable indices. In contrast, direct physiological measures such as penile erection (e.g. Bancroft et al., 1966; Freund, 1963; Freund, Sedlacek and Knob, 1965; McConaghy, 1967) and vaginal blood flow (Geer et al., 1974; Heiman, 1975; Hoon et al., 1976, in press; Shapiro et al., 1968) have proven to be more reliable indicators of sexual arousal in males and females, respectively. Recording from the genitals, however, can create certain kinds of problems, e.g. sexual excitement or anxiety resulting simply from attaching the device. Penile plethysmography is subject to distortion through movement artifacts (Lader, 1967), adaptation effects (Cairns, 1968) and voluntary control (Cairns, 1968; Laws and Rubin, 1969). Because of the intrusiveness of the penile and vaginal devices it is posssble that (a) subjects who would agree to use the apparatus are atypical in some respect (e.g. very liberal), thereby creating biases in the subject sample; (b) insertion or attachment of such devices

might contribute to making the experimental situation somewhat artificial and contrived (Amoroso and Brown, 1973); and (c) the direct
genital measures might cause undue discomfort in a clinical population already experiencing anxiety concerning their sexual response.
For these reasons it would appear desirable to develop a less ob-
trusive measure of sexual arousal in men and women.

Surface temperature of the finger has recently received attention as an index of sexual arousal (Corman, 1968; Romano, 1969;
Wenger et al., 1968). Unlike direct genital measures, finger temperature is fairly unobtrusive to record and can be monitored continuously and identically in both males and females. Finger temperature has been found to decrease in response to reading erotic
material (Wenger et al., 1968) and viewing an erotic film (Corman,
1968). All subjects in these experiments were males. There are no
studies on finger temperature changes in women in response to psychosexual stimulation.

One critical aspect of experimental studies of sexual arousal
is the selection of sexually arousing stimuli. It is clearly essential to assess the degree to which stimuli used in these experiments are, in fact, sexually arousing. But researchers have
often neglected the specification of their independent variables
and have usually selected stimuli on the basis of intuitive jud-
gements about their erotic value (Mann, 1971; Zuckerman, 1971).
Recent evidence suggests that erotic movies produce considerably
more sexual arousal in male subjects than Playboy nudes (Corman,
1968) or slides depicting sexual activities (Sanford, 1974). Comparable studies using female subjects are not available. The
erotic stimuli in the present experiment were selected on an empirical basis. Videotapes of erotic scenes were pretested on males
and females in order to obtain independent ratings of the erotic
value of these stimuli. The episodes judged equally arousing by
both sexes were chosen as the erotic stimuli in this experiment.
By constructing stimuli judged equally arousing by males and females any difference between the sexes in finger temperature change
in response to these stimuli could be attributed to characteristics
of the subjects rather than the stimuli.

The present experiment was designed to answer two basic questions. First, is sexual arousal produced by exposure to visually
presented erotic material accompanied by a decrease in finger temperature in females as well as males? Second, do changes in finger
temperature in response to viewing stimuli judged highly and moderately sexually arousing bear any relation to the level of erotic
content in the stimulus material. To answer this question subjects
viewed videotapes constructed to be either highly or moderately
erotic while subjects in a control condition viewed neutral films.

METHOD

Subjects

Thirty male and 30 female students at Concordia University in Montreal, whose mean age was 22 years, were used as subjects. Initially, subjects were told that the experimenters were interested in their emotional reactions to several videotapes. Ten male and 10 female volunteers were randomly assigned to each of three groups. Two female subjects in the high arousal group declined to participate in the experiment when given the option to do so. Therefore, two new female subjects were recruited for the high arousal group.

Apparatus

A one hour-long videotape, a Sony videotape recorder and a monitor were used to present the stimuli. Finger temperature was recorded from a thermistor attached to the most distal section of the subject's right index finger and was monitored continuously by means of a two-channel pen recorder (Yellow Springs Instrument Company) located in the adjoining room.

Stimuli

Forty-five segments of film, varying in duration from 10 to 20 seconds, were videotaped. The segments depicted nude or partly clad men and women involved in various forms of explicit sexual behavior. Each film segment was rated by 106 male and 46 female university students on a five-point ascending scale of sexual arousal. Eleven segments, found to be most sexually arousing by both males and females were transposed to another videotape in random order. The mean rating by both males and females of these selected segments was 2.6. A two-second interval was placed between each segment and the total running time of the videotape was $3\frac{1}{2}$ minutes. The film segments on this tape served as the highly erotic stimulus materials.

Two film segments, each approximately 15 seconds in length, judged least sexually arousing by the raters were transposed as well to a second videotape. The mean sexual arousal rating of these segments by males was 1.5 and by females, 1.4. These segments, separated by a two-second blank interval, were presented in alternating order for a total time of $3\frac{1}{2}$ minutes. This videotape served as the moderately erotic stimulus material.

Two videotape segments, each running $3\frac{1}{2}$ minutes, consisting of a small black square moving at random on a blank screen, were also placed on a videotape and served as neutral stimulus material.

Self-Report Measures

Immediately after viewing the videotaped material subjects rated their responses on two 15 centimeter lines. One line indicated a continuum of not sexually arousing to highly sexually arousing, and the other line, unpleasant to pleasant feelings.

Design

Subjects were assigned at random to one of three groups: a) high arousal, b) moderate arousal, and c) erotic suggestion. Within each group each subject viewed two, $3\frac{1}{2}$ minutes videotape segments. The first segment consisted of the neutral stimulus material (black square moving at random on a blank screen). The content of the second segment of stimulus material corresponded to the group (high arousal, moderate arousal, erotic suggestion) to which the subject was assigned. Two levels of erotic stimulus were included in the study (highly erotic and moderately erotic) to determine not only if finger temperature changed as a function of viewing erotic material but also if the magnitude of finger temperature change would be related to the degree of eroticism of the stimulus materials.

The erotic suggestion condition consisted of informing subjects, prior to the second videotape segment, that the black square moving on a blank screen would simulate men and women engaged in various forms of explicit sexual behavior - to black square in fact moved at random on the screen. This condition was included to control for the effects of attending to a video monitor as well as instructions which generated expectations of viewing erotic subject matter.

Procedure

All subjects were treated identically for the first 20 minutes of the experiment. Each subject was brought to the experimental room and seated in a confortable reclining chair six feet in front of a television monitor. Males were seen by a male experimenter and females by a female experimenter. Subjects were told that certain of their subjective and physical reactions to viewing two videotape segments were under study. A thermistor coated with electrode paste was then attached to the tip of the subject's right index finger and the temperature was recorded continuously for the remainder of the session. Room temperature was measured for one minute at three time intervals during each session, using the same recording equipment and a thermistor suspended two feet from the ceiling. Following the instructions, each subject rested in the chair for 10 to 15 minutes to allow finger temperature to stabilize.

All subjects then viewed a $3\frac{1}{2}$ minute neutral tape. At the conclusion of this first tape subjects in the high arousal group were informed that they were to view a second tape which depicted men and
women engaged in various forms of explicit sexual behavior.   Subjects were also given the option to refuse further participation
in the experiment.   Subjects remaining in the experiment were then
shown the highly erotic tape.   Subjects in the moderate arousal
group were given the same instructions as subjects in the high
arousal group but were shown the moderately erotic tape.   Subjects
in the erotic suggestion group as previously described were instructed that the black square which they would be seeing on the
monitor would simulate men and women engaging in various forms of
sexual behavior.   Subjects in this group then viewed a second
neutral stimulus tape.

Following each tape segment subjects rated the segment for
sexual arousal and pleasantness on 15 centimeter scales.

FINDINGS

The temperature of the experimental room was found to be
relatively stable (± 0.1 C).

Finger Temperature

Finger temperature was sampled from the continuous record
every three seconds and a mean temperature was calculated for
each subject during a) the last $3\frac{1}{2}$ minutes of the resting period,
b) the $3\frac{1}{2}$ minutes of the neutral tape, and c) the $3\frac{1}{2}$ minutes of
the treatment tape. These data were evaluated in the initial
analyses. Sex-of-subject did not prove to be a statistically
significant variable in any of the data analyses. Thus, sex-of-
subject is not included as an independent variable in the analysis
presented below.

Figure 1 presents mean finger temperature for high arousal,
moderate arousal and erotic suggestion groups during the rest
period, neutral and treatment tapes. An analysis of covariance
with temperature during the rest period as the covariate indicated
that the three groups did not differ significantly in finger temperature during the neutral stimulus tape. A similar analysis of
finger temperature during the treatment tapes indicated a significant group effect, F (2,53) = 4.50, $p<.02$. Pairwise comparisons
(Newman-Keuls two-tailed test procedure) indicated that both the
moderate arousal and high arousal groups exhibited significantly
lower finger temperatures during the treatment conditions than
did the erotic suggestion group (both p's<.05). The moderate and

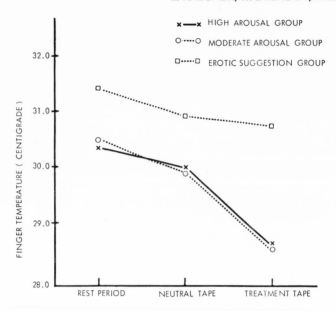

Fig. 1. A comparison of the high arousal group, the moderate arousal group and the erotic suggestion group with respect to mean finger temperature response during rest period, neutral tape and treatment tape.

high arousal groups did not differ significantly in finger temperature during the treatment conditions.

Finger temperature response during the viewing of erotic material can be examined more closely by following its temporal pattern during the neutral and treatment tapes. Each stimulus tape was therefore divided into five time blocks. A mean finger temperature response was calculated for each block within the tape. Each block comprised 14 consecutive samples of finger temperature taken at 3-second intervals. The mean finger temperature for each block during the neutral and treatment tapes for all three groups is presented in Figure 2. A two-way (group x time block), 3 x 5 mixed design analysis of variance, with repeated measures on one factor was performed on the five blocks of the neutral videotape. Neither the group x block interaction nor the main effect due to groups was significant. The block effect approached significance however, indicating a tendency for the finger temperature of subjects in all groups to decrease as the neutral tape progressed. A similar analysis carried out on the treatment tapes revealed no significant main effects due to groups or time blocks. A significant group x block interaction ($\underline{F}$ (8,228) = 11.89, $\underline{p}$<.001) suggested that subjects reacted differently to the neutral and erotic tapes during the treatment condition. Comparisons of subjects' finger temper-

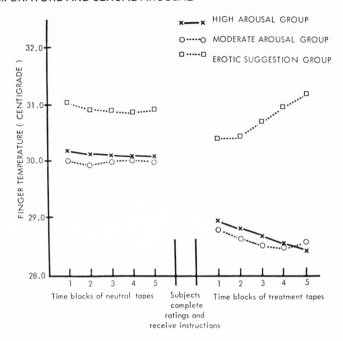

Fig. 2. Mean finger temperature of experimental groups for five consecutive time blocks of the neutral and treatment tapes.

ature during the first time block with temperature during the last time block of each tape revealed the following. The mean finger temperature for the high arousal group was significantly lower during the last time block than during the first time block, $p<.05$. There was no significant difference in finger temperature at these particular time segments within the moderate arousal group. Subjects in the erotic suggestion group showed a significantly higher finger temperature in the last time segment than in the first segment of the tape, $p<.05$. In addition, the high arousal and moderate arousal groups were compared with respect to the mean finger temperature during the first time segment of the treatment tape. There was no significant difference between the two groups for this time segment. The analysis of temperature change under the treatment film condition presents the following pattern. Beginning at equivalent levels, the finger temperature of subjects viewing a highly erotic tape decreased significantly over $3\frac{1}{2}$ minutes, while the temperature of subjects viewing a moderately erotic tape did not. By contrast, finger temperature of subjects viewing the erotic suggestion tape increased significantly from the beginning to the end of the tape.

Pleasantness and Sexual Arousal Ratings

As in the case of finger temperature, sex-of-subject did not prove to be a statistically significant independent variable. Therefore sex-of-subject was not treated as an independent variable in the following analysis.

Table 1 presents mean pleasantness ratings for each of the groups in response to both neutral and treatment videotapes. A two-way, 3 x 2 mixed analysis of variance was computed to assess the effects of group and tape shown (neutral tape vs. treatment tape) on the subjective ratings. The analysis of the pleasantness ratings revealed a significant tape effect, indicating that the subjects rated the treatment tapes significantly more pleasant than the neutral tape, F (1,54) = 8.26, p<.01. Pairwise comparisons indicated that the highly erotic tape was perceived significantly more pleasant than either the moderately erotic or erotic suggestion tapes. However, subjects in the erotic suggestion group rated the erotic suggestion tape equally as pleasant as the neutral stimulus tape.

TABLE 1

MEAN PLEASANTNESS RATINGS FOR NEUTRAL
AND TREATMENT TAPES

Group	Neutral Tape	Treatment Tape
High arousal group	5.92*	8.75
Moderate arousal group	5.91	7.16
Erotic suggestion group	5.89	6.33

*Tape ratings may range from 0 (unpleasant) to 15 (pleasant).

TABLE 2

MEAN RATINGS OF SEXUAL AROUSAL FOR
NEUTRAL AND TREATMENT TAPES

Group	Neutral Tape	Treatment Tape
High arousal group	0.69*	8.96
Moderate arousal group	1.13	5.90
Erotic suggestion group	1.28	2.40

*Tape ratings may range from 0 (not sexually arousing) to 15 (highly sexually arousing).

Table 2 presents the mean ratings of sexual arousal for each group in response to the neutral and treatment tapes. A similar analysis of the ratings of sexual arousal indicated significant group (F (2,54) = 7.75, p< .01) and tape (F (1,54) = 141.72, p< .001) effects. Several pairwise comparisons were computed to further examine a significant group x tape interaction, F (2,54) = 27.12, p< .001. These showed that the highly erotic tape was perceived as significantly more erotic than either the moderately erotic or erotic suggestion tapes (p<.05), and the moderately erotic tape was perceived as more erotic than the erotic suggestion tape, p<.05. Within the erotic suggestion group there were no differences between the ratings of sexual arousal for the erotic suggestion tape and the neutral tape.

DISCUSSION

The result of this study provide evidence for a relationship between finger temperature changes and sexual arousal induced by erotic videotapes. The finger temperature of male and female subjects was significantly lower in response to viewing two video-tapes varying in degree of eroticism than in response to a neutral tape. Examination of subjects' finger temperature during exposure to erotic videotape conditions as compared to an erotic suggestion control condition revealed that the observed temperature decreases were due to the effects of the erotic tapes rather than expectations and attentional factors only. In addition, the analysis of the course of finger temperature changes during the treatment tapes provided evidence that finger temperature could discriminate between the highly and moderately erotic tapes in a manner consistent with their erotic value as rated by a group of subjects prior to the study as well as by subjects in the present experiment. The ability of finger temperature to reflect differences in the level of erotic value of the two videotapes is particularly interesting because the subjective ratings of the two stimulus tapes were not markedly dissimilar. Finger temperature of subjects in the erotic suggestion group who viewed a film devoid of any sexual content was also noteworthy. Their pattern of temperature change was quite different from the groups who viewed the two erotic tapes. Finger temperature of subjects in this control condition actually increased significantly from the beginning to the end of the tape. It appears that, after scrutinizing the movements of the black square presented in the film, subjects soon became aware that, contrary to the information they were given, there appeared to be no hidden sexual images. After an initial decrease, relative to finger temperature during the neutral tape, suggesting an anticipatory effect, finger temperature increased to baseline level.

Some discussion is warranted on the finger temperature decreases which appeared to have occurred between tape presentations. It will be recalled that during this interval subjects filled out rating forms and were told that they would be viewing explicit sexual material. Although it was not possible to analyze the finger temperature decreases occurring in this period in a systematic manner, it is possible that these decreases reflect subjects' anticipatory responses. Exposing the subjects to one or more additional sessions of viewing visual material (as in Heiman, 1975), would have the advantage of familiarizing subjects with the experimental routine and possibly stabilizing their anticipatory responses.

This experiment also marks the first attempt to use finger temperature as a measure of sexual arousal in women. It will be recalled that the erotic stimuli used in this experiment were pretested and selected to be equally sexually arousing to both males and females. In the cross validation of the erotic stimuli inherent in the design of this study the material was again judged equally sexually arousing by males and females in the present experiment and generated equivalent decreases in finger temperature in both sexes.

The pleasantness ratings, which subjects were also required to provide, were used to check for the presence of strong emotional reactions in addition to sexual arousal to the erotic stimuli. The highly erotic, moderately erotic and erotic suggestion tapes were rated by subjects as significantly more pleasant than the neutral tape. Unlike the results of Schmidt and Sigusch (1970), who found that subjects rated very sexually stimulating material as unpleasant, the tape rated as most erotic in this experiment was also rated as the most pleasant. The pleasantness ratings suggest that on the whole the response of sexual arousal to the videotapes was not confounded with any negative emotional responses.

Although the results of this study provide support for the use of finger temperature as a measure of sexual arousal in males and females, further validation studies are in order. Finger temperature might be recorded in conjunction with penile plethysmograph and vaginal photoplethysmograph measures in experimental situations designed to produce sexual arousal. There is some evidence that finger temperature decreases in response to stress (Boudewyns, 1976) and to other strong emotions (Malmo, 1975). Thus, the capacity of finger temperature to differentiate sexual arousal from other intense affective states must be investigated as well. Unlike penis and vagina based measures, finger temperature is quite unobtrusive. The fact that it appears to reflect different levels of sexual arousal as well, suggests that it may be a valuable physiological measure in investigations of human sexual arousal.

REFERENCES

Amoroso, D.M. and Brown, M. (1973). Problems in studying the effects of erotic material. Journal of Sex Research, 9: 187-195.

Bancroft, J.H., Jones, H.G. and Pullan, B.P. (1966). A simple transducer for measuring penile erection with comments on its use in the treatment of sexual disorders. Behavior Research and Therapy, 4: 239-241.

Boudewyns, P.A. (1976). A comparison of the effects of stress vs relaxation instruction of the finger temperature response. Behavior Therapy, 7: 54-67.

Cairns, R.B. (1968). Psychological Assumptions in Sex Censorship: An Evaluative Review of Recent Research (1961-1968). An expanded version of a talk given at Indiana University to the Commission on Obscenity and Pornography, July, 13.

Corman, C. (1968). Physiological Response to a Sexual Stimulus. Unpublished B.Sc. Thesis, University of Manitoba.

Freund, K. (1963). A laboratory method for diagnosing predominance of homo- and hetero-erotic interest in the male. Behavior Research and Therapy, 1: 85-93.

Freund, K., Sedlacek, F., and Knob, K. (1965). Simple transducer for mechanical plethysmography of the male genital. Journal of the Experimental Analysis of Behavior, 8: 169-170.

Geer, J.H., Morokoff, P., and Greenwood, P. (1974). Sexual arousal in women: The development of a measurement device for vaginal blood volume. Archives of Sexual Behavior, 3: 559-564.

Heiman, J. (1975). Responses to erotica: An Exploration of Physiological and Psychological Correlates of Human Sexual Response. Unpublished doctoral dissertation, State University of New York at Stony Brook.

Hoon, P. W., Wincze, J.P., and Hoon, E.F. (1976). Physiological assessment of sexual arousal in women. Psychophysiology, 13: 196-204.

Kutchinsky, B. (1970). The effect of pornography: An experiment on perception, attitudes and behavior. Technical Reports of the Commission on Obscenity and Pornography, Volume 8, U.S. Government Printing Office, Washington, D.C.

Lader, N.H. (1967). Pneumatic plethysmography. In Venables, P.H. and Martin, I. (Eds.), A Manual of Psychophysiological Methods, North Holland Publishing Company, Amsterdam.

Laws, D.R. and Rubin, H.B. (1969). Instructional control of an autonomic sexual response. Journal of Applied Behavior Analysis, 2: 93-99.

Malmo, R.B. (1975). Our Emotions, Needs, and our Archaic Brain, Holt, Rinehart and Winston, Inc., New York.

Mann, J. (1971). Experimental induction of human sexual arousal. Technical Reports of the Commission on Obscenity and Pornography, Volume, 8, U.S. Government Printing Office, Washington, D.C.

McConaghy, N. (1967). Penile volume change to moving pictures of male and female nudes in heterosexual and homosexual males. Behavior Research and Therapy, 5: 43-48.

Romano, K. (1969). Psychophysiological Response to a Sexual and Unpleasant Motion Picture. Unpublished B.Sc. Thesis, University of Manitoba.

Sanford, D.A. (1974). Patterns of sexual arousal in heterosexual males. Journal of Sex Research, 10: 150-155.

Schmidt, G. and Sigusch, V. (1970). Sex differences in response to psychosexual stimulation by films and slides. Journal of Sex Research, 6: 268-283.

Shapiro, A., Cohen, H., DiBanco, P. and Rosen, G. (1968). Vaginal blood flow changes during sleep and sexual arousal. Psychophysiology, 4: 394.

Wenger, M.A., Averill, J.R. and Smith, D.B. (1968). Autonomic activity during sexual arousal. Psychophysiology, 4: 468-478.

Zuckerman, M. (1971). Physiological measures of sexual arousal in the human. Psychological Bulletin, 75: 297-329.

13 ♂'s reporting ability to have repeated orgasms without ejaculation. Confirmed in one case by physiological recording

MULTIPLE ORGASM IN MALES

Mina B. Robbins and Gordon D. Jensen

United States

This is a preliminary report of a variation in the usual pattern of orgasm in men. It consists of repeated orgasm without ejaculation, except for the final orgasm which is simultaneous with ejaculation. We have called this pattern multiple orgasm in men.

It had been traditionally believed and stated by investigators that orgasm and ejaculation are always one continuous physiological process and that ejaculation inevitably accompanies orgasm in the normal male. However, it has been recognized that under abnormal conditions, the two can occur separately: impotent men can ejaculate without the sensations or orgasm, and some men with spinal cord injury or other nerve lesions report a sensation of orgasm without ejaculation.

The complete process has been described by Masters and Johnson (1966) as occurring in two stages: (1) the expulsion of seminal fluid substrate from the accessory organs of reproduction into the prostatic urethra; and (2) the progression of seminal fluid content from the prostatic portion of the urethra through both the membranous and penile segments of the urethra to the urethral meatus. As seminal fluid collects in the prostatic urethra, there is simultaneously, a two-to-three fold involuntary expansion of the urethral bulb. This expansion develops in anticipation of the expulsive urethral contractions of the second stage. The second stage is initiated by the relaxation of the external sphincter of the bladder, which allows the seminal fluid to flow into the distended bulb and penile urethra. The seminal fluid is propelled from the prostatic urethra along the penile urethra by the perineal

musculature, the bulbospongiosus and the ischiocavernosus muscles
and the sphincter urethrae. These contractions together with the
accompanying total body response (muscular, vascular, respiratory,
psychological, etc.) have been labeled orgasm. Masters and Johnson
noted that a few males below the age of 30 experienced repeated
ejaculation and orgasm within minutes, without a more lengthly
refractory period. However, in these cases such repeated orgasms
were each accompanied by ejaculation. These men were termed multi-
ejaculatory.

While we do not disagree with this description of the basic
process for men who always ejaculate with orgasm, our study indicates that the orgasmic response does not always proceed in this
unitary way. This report describes the experiences of normal men
for whom orgasms occurred either with or without ejaculation.

The subjects were men who were either attending university
or were engaged in professional work. Men were asked to volunteer
for interview if they felt they had, or presently were experiencing multiple orgasmic response.

At the initial interviews, each subject was asked to describe
in detail his experience of multiple orgasm. In order to avoid
biasing their responses, the subjects were not informed of our
definition in advance. Their personal accounts enabled us to
reliably identify and eliminate from the study group men who spoke
of repeated orgasm each with ejaculation, who experienced penile
urethral contractions with urination following ejaculation and
called these orgasms, and who described other variations which
did not fit our definition.

The thirteen men whose descriptions of multiple orgasmic response fulfilled the criteria of our definition were interviewed in
detail. They ranged in age between 22 and 56 years, the average
age was late 30's, and the majority of subjects (8) were between
33 and 36 years of age. Seven men were married, all were white,
and all had had sexual experiences with more than one partner.
None had any sexual dysfunction problems. All of the men in
this study were heterosexual, although some had had homosexual
experiences in the past. (Two male homosexuals were interviewed
after the study who also reported multiple orgasms with their partners). None of the subjects used drugs for sexual "highs," nor
were on prescribed medications. Most first began having multiple
orgasmic response after having had considerable sexual experience.
One man described his becoming sharply aware of his multiple response pattern shortly after his marriage, when his wife asked him
if he had always had trouble "coming."

The subjects described their repeated orgasms as including
most of all of the following aspects of the orgasmic response:

increased respiratory rate, increased heart rate, myotonia, hyper-
ventilation, increased penile tumescence, urethra contractions,
and an altered state of consciousness, all without ejaculation.
Immediately after orgasm the increment of the penile tumescence
subsided but the penis retained full erection. These men apparently inhibit or control ejaculation and thereby withhold it until
the final orgasm of a series, which they describe subjectively as
being the most intense. After this final orgasm with ejaculation,
they all experienced complete detumescence and a usual refractory
period. All subjects reported differences between lovemaking sessions: there were times when they experienced one orgasm with
ejaculation and felt fulfilled; and there were other times when
they experienced many orgasms, all without ejaculation, and at
these times they also reported a feeling of physical and emotional
satisfaction.

The men reported from 3 to 10 orgasms per lovemaking session
(prior to ejaculation) and while their responsiveness appeared to
have something to do with the mood and circumstances of the sexual
encounter, they found their multiple orgasmic response to be fairly
reliable, experiencing it in approximately 4 out of 5 intercourse
experiences. Under optimal conditions when his partner was cooperative one male experienced as many as thirty orgasms in one
session of sexual intercourse lasting approximately one hour.

All of the men reported having the multiple orgastic response
by masturbation as well as by coitus.

The multiple orgasmic response was not partner specific for
these men, although some of their partners greatly enhanced the
orgasmic response by their awareness and accommodation to allow
for the man's need to stop thrusting, or to deep breathe in order
to control ejaculation, yet all the while continuing to experience
orgasms. These men related that as they experienced multiple orgasms reliably over a period of months, they generally needed less
or no conscious effort to control ejaculation compared with their
earlier experiences.

The physiological responses of one subject were monitored during a coital episode in which three orgasms occurred (Figure I).
This was carried out in the research laboratory of the Center for
Marital and Sexual studies by W. Hartman and M. Fithian with collaboration by B. Campbell, University of California, Irvine. The
tracings show three orgasms of a series in which ejaculation accompanied the last recorded orgasm. The top graph shows cumulative
heart rate, rising to 143 beats/min. peak during orgasms. The
second graph shows anal contractions of which there are three sets,
and the bottom graph shows frequency and amplitude of respiration.
The peaks of activity in each of the measures coincide and were
simultaneous with the subject's subjective report of orgasm.

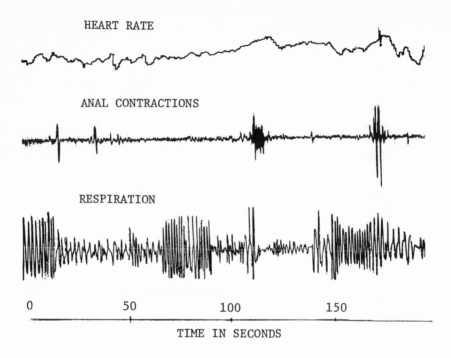

HEART RATE

ANAL CONTRACTIONS

RESPIRATION

| 0 | 50 | 100 | 150 |

TIME IN SECONDS

Fig. I. Polygraph tracing from one patient during one intercourse
episode: three orgasms are indicated by simultaneous increases in
heart rate, anal contractions and respiration.

These data indicate that the essential physiological responses and most of the clinical criteria for orgasm in the traditional
sense are present with multiple orgasm in men. We hypothesize the
orgasmic response and the ejaculatory response can be separate
physiological reactions in a normal state.

At present, explanation of the mechanism in speculative. Multiple orgasmic response should not be confused with a controlled
prolonged plateau phase with rising and falling levels of excitement before reaching orgasm with ejaculation. Possibly the multiple orgasmic response is achieved by conscious or unconscious
control or inhibition of movement of the ejaculate which is usually

caused by contractions of the accessory organs of reproduction (the
vasa efferentia of the testes, the epididymis, the vas deferens,
the seminal vesicles, and the prostatic gland) thereby allowing
for an orgasmic response without the inevitability of ejaculation.
Although it has been said that the relaxation of the external
sphincter of the bladder is involuntary (Masters & Johnson, 1966),
perhaps this can be brought under voluntary control. Without relaxation of the sphincter, the seminal fluid would not flow into
the urethral bulb and penile urethra. With continued orgasmic
response, a higher level of pelvic vasocongestion may occur over
a wider area, and thereby reinforce the ability to continue at
high levels of response with orgasm. A similar mechanism has been
postulated for multiple orgasm in females (Sherfey, 1972). In
comparing men and women, Masters and Johnson have emphasized the
similarities rather than the differences in sexual response. This
basic principle supports the probability that a similar physiological mechanism underlies male and female multiple orgasmic response.

It is well to bear in mind some differences between men and
women with respect to total body arousal. Women, by virtue of
socialization and learning, seem to be able to respond to a wider
variety of simuli integrating a larger portion of their bodies.
Further, their sensitivity during orgasm goes beyond that of the
genitals and they report floating, disconnected, letting-go sensations. Some of the multi-orgasmic men also reported such sensations. Perhaps they are representative of a small group of men
whose psychological and emotional responsivity is more closely
aligned with that of orgasmic women.

We acknowledge that this is a preliminary report of a phenomena which needs thorough study. However, there is heroistic value
in a definition and description. A general belief that men are
capable only of single orgasm and that it inevitably includes
ejaculation would decrease the chances of men experiencing or
achieving multiple orgasm. Just opening up the possibility should
enable some men to possibly acquire the response if they want to
and after some experimentation and learning.

The percentage of orgasmic women who are multi-orgasmic has
been reported to be 12% by Masters and Johnson (1966) and 32% by
Kaplan (1974). Possibly many more are potentially multi-orgasmic
Experience treating pre-orgasmic women (M. B. Robbins) shows that
as they learn to become orgasmic many also become multi-orgasmic
Our clinical experience teaching women to be multi-orgasmic indicates that this response, like single orgasm, can be learned.
The histories of our men subjects in this study and our experience
in teaching other men to become multi-orgasmic suggest that men
too can learn the response.

REFERENCES

Kaplan, H.S. (1974). The New Sex Therapy, Brunner/Mazel, New York.

Masters and Johnson (1966). Human Sexual Response, Little, Brown
     and Co., Boston.

Sherfey, M.J. (1972). The Nature and Evolution of Female Sexuality,
     Random House, New York.

PATTERNS OF SEXUAL RESPONSIVENESS DURING THE MENSTRUAL CYCLE

Heidi Markowitz and William Brender

Canada

One interesting facet of human sexual research is the study of female sexual responsiveness during the menstrual cycle. This topic has engaged the efforts of a growing number of investigators whose findings have, by no means, been consistent. Summarizing the research of the last few years, some workers have found the peak of erotic desire to occur just after menstruation (James, 1971; McCance et al., 1937), others have reported it to be just before menstruation (Davis, 1929; Kinsey et al., 1965), some have found the peak of heightened sexuality around the time of ovulation (Udry and Morris, 1968, 1970), others have found two peaks (Hamilton, 1929; Hart, 1960), or three peaks (Moos et al., 1969) during the course of the menstrual cycle while finally, a few studies report no periodicity in female sexual interest (Diamond et al., 1972; Wineman, 1967). Clearly, there is a certain amount of contradiction as to when the periods of greatest erotic desire occur. Many of the discrepancies in findings may be due to differences in both study design and the statistical procedures used. The most common method of data collection has been some sort of retrospective questionnaire in spite of evidence that retrospective reports bear little correspondence to day-to-day records (McCance et al., 1937). The typical data collected has largely been restricted to questions concerning coitus, orgasm and sexual feeling although it has been demonstrated that there are other very important indicators of female sexual interest such as masturbation (Kinsey et al., 1965; Masters and Johnson, 1970).

The present study was undertaken to obviate many of the previous problems described by including a number of measures that have not been used before, and by using daily reports rather than

retrospective data. It may also be noted that minimal attempts
have been made to date to establish ovulation for the individual
subject. Separation of ovulatory from anovulatory women during
any cycle might be important in testing the hypothesis that changes
in sexual arousability and sexual activity are hormonally based.
Therefore, this project undertook to specify the point of ovulation within a cycle and to identify ovulatory from anovulatory
women by having a panel of two gynecologists independently evaluate temperature graphs of all cycles contributed. Volunteer
subjects, who were unpaid, were selected from the practices of
several Montreal gynecologists. The sample consisted of 25 white,
educated, middle-class women, between the ages of twenty and forty,
who were either married or maintaining a stable sexual relationship for a minimum duration of six months. None were using contraceptive agents. All reported regular menstrual periods. Each
contributed daily reports for an interval of two to five consecutive menstrual cycles. Subjects were asked to supply information for the preceding 24 hours on a specially designed questionnaire. This information concerned basal body temperature, sexual
thoughts and feelings, sexual activity with partner, masturbation
and orgasm. Since the menstrual cycles varied considerably in
length, all cycles were normalized to 24 time categories in order
to facilitate statistical comparison. Twenty-four time categories
were employed so that all menstrual cycles of 24 to 33 days would
be included since it is these cycle lengths which previous research
has demonstrated to be most representative of regularly menstruat-
ing women (Haman, 1942). All reported data were also converted to
standard Z scores so as to readily permit comparison to each other.

Initial statistical analysis revealed that consistent significant effects were observed in Cycle 1 only, with no evidence
of cyclic fluctuations in sexual behavior being apparent in Cycles
2, 3, 4 or 5. Therefore, the discussion thus far will be confined
to the patterning found in Cycle 1. Of the six measures of sexual
interest, three showed a significant days effect. The main result
of Cycle 1 seems to provide evidence for a biphasic distribution
of sexual activity. Peak periods appear to occur immediately after
menstruation and around mid-cycle. Figure 1 shows changes in sexual thoughts and fantasies produced by the 25 subjects. Peaks after
menstruation and in the middle of the cycle are clear. These observations are supported by a significance level of .003 in a one-
way analysis of variance, repeated measures design. Figure 2 plots
changes in frequency of heterosexual activity and in the number of
orgasms. Again, there seems to be a sharp peak at the beginning
of the cycle with a second peak around the time when ovulation
might be expected to occur. As for the measures which did not
attain statistical significance, our impression is that the tendencies are in a similar direction. For example, Figure 3 illustrates changes in level of sexual desire. Much the same effects
are evident here - a peak after menstruation and a peak around mid-
cycle.

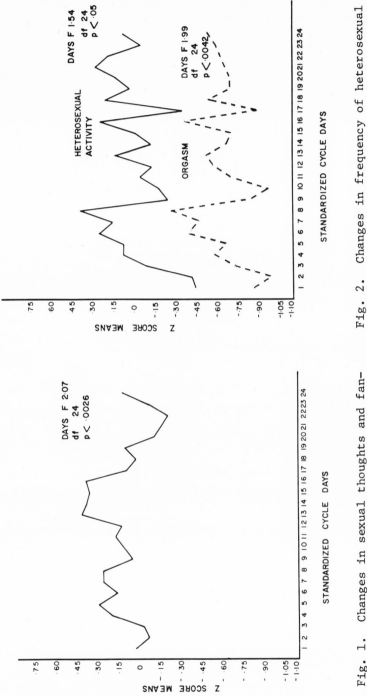

Fig. 2. Changes in frequency of heterosexual activity and orgasm as a function of standardized days.

Fig. 1. Changes in sexual thoughts and fantasies as a function of standardized days.

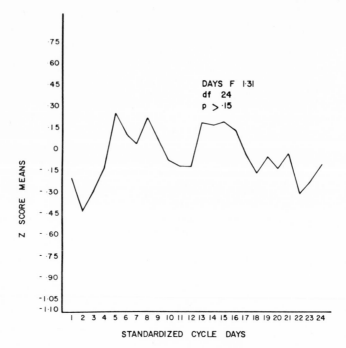

Fig. 3.   Changes of level of sexual desire as a function of
standardized days.

Inspection of these three graphs strongly suggests that there
is considerable variance in our measures of sexuality in Cycle 1.
This may possibly reflect the fact that some subjects ovulated during this cycle while others did not. When the gynecologists assessed the temperature graphs we submitted, they made use of the
classical, operational definition for ovulation (Cohen, 1966;
Haller, 1972; Van de Velde, 1947). This is a drop in basal body
temperature followed by a sustained thermal rise which is, at
least, 0.5 degrees higher than the temperatures recorded in the
earlier part of the cycle. Subjects who met this criterion were
regarded as ovulatory and subjects who did not meet this criterion
were defined as anovulatory. We reanalyzed our data by separating
ovulatory women (those subjects who ovulated according to the judgment of both physicians) from anovulatory women (those subjects
who did not ovulate according to both raters). We carried out a
two-way analysis of variance, repeated measures design. Our sample
size was reduced at this point because several subjects employed
in the one-way analysis had to be deleted from the two-way since
the judges could not agree upon their ovulatory status. We were
left with 8 subjects in the ovulatory group and 10 subjects in the

anovulatory group. These subjects were subsequently reduced in the succeeding Cycles 2 and 3. Yet, interestingly enough, significant findings were obtained throughout these three cycles. Group effects were noted in Cycle 2 for heterosexual activity and in Cycle 3 for heterosexual orgasm, masturbation, and orgasm achieved through masturbation. The most pronounced group effect was in the measure of masturbatory activity where the anovulatory subjects seem to masturbate with greater frequency than the ovulatory group. Day effects were found in only one cycle and thus, may appear to be unreliable. Until we have done further testing, our only impression at the present time is that the anovulatory group displays a higher frequency of masturbation at mid-cycle. Finally, significant group by days effects were found on a number of measures in the three cycles. Further statistical tests remain to be carried out before more precise statements can be made about this interraction. It is our impression, however, that there are no consistent differences in the timing of sexual activity in the two groups.

In summary, this study indicates a bimodal pattern of female sexual interest with one peak just after menstruation and another peak around mid-cycle. There are some suggestions that the cyclical activity might be timed differently in ovulatory and anovulatory women but we cannot conclude that there are consistantly different patterns of sexual behavior for the two groups. One implication of this study is that further research in this area should consider separating ovulatory from anovulatory subjects in examining patterns of sexual responsiveness during the menstrual cycle.

REFERENCES

Benedek, T. and Rubinstein, B. (1939). The correlation between ovarian activity and psychodynamic processes. Psychosom. Med. 1: 245-270.

Cohen, M. R. (1966). Detection of ovulation by means of cervical mucus and basal body temperature. In Greenblatt, R.B. (ed.), Ovulation: Stimulation, Suppression, and Detection, J.B. Lippincott Co., Philadelphia.

Davis, K. B. (1929). Factors in the Sex Life of 2200 Women. Harper Brothers, New York.

Diamond, M., Diamond, L.A. and Mast, M. (1972). Visual Sensitivity and Sexual arousal levels. J. of Nerv. Ment. Dis. 155 (3): 170-176.

Haller, J. (1972). Hormonal Contraception. Geron - X, Inc. Los Altos, California.

Haman, J. (1942). The length of the menstrual cycle. Am. J. of Obs. and Gynec. 43: 870-873.

Hamilton, G.V. (1929). A Research in Marriage. Medical Research Press, New York.

Hart, R.D. (1960). Rhythm of libido in married women. Brit. Med. J. 1: 1023-1024.

James, W. (1971). The distribution of coitus within the human intermenstruum. J. of Biosoc. Science. 3: 159-171.

Kinsey, A. C., Pomeroy, W. B., Martin, C. E. and Gebhard, P. (1965). Sexual Behavior in the Human Female. Pocket Books, New York.

Masters, W. H. and Johnson, V. E. (1970). Human Sexual Inadequacy. Little, Brown & Co. Boston.

Moos, R. H., Kopell, B. S., Melges, F. T., Yalom, I. D., Lunde, D., Clayton, R. B. and Hamburg, D. A. (1969). Fluctuations in symptoms & moods during the menstrual cycle. J. of Psychosom. Res. 13: 37-44.

McCance, R. A., Luff, M. C., and Widdowson, E. E. (1937). Physical and emotional periodicity in women. J. of Hygiene, 37 (4): 571-611.

Udry, J. R. and Morris, N. M. (1968). Distribution of coitus in the menstrual cycle. Nature, 220: 593-596.

Udry, J. R. and Morris, N. M. (1970). Effect of contraceptive pills on the distribution of sexual activity in the menstrual cycle. Nature, 227: 502-603.

Van de Velde, T. H. (1947). Ideal Marriage, Heenemas, London.

Wineman, E. W. (1967). Some of the Psychological Correlates of the Human Menstrual Cycle. Unpubl. Diss., U. of Calif.

Esoteric studies

HUMAN VAGINAL FLUID, PH, UREA, POTASSIUM AND POTENTIAL DIFFERENCE DURING SEXUAL EXCITEMENT[1]

Gorm Wagner and Roy J. Levin
Denmark - England

The vaginal epithelium in women is a stratified epithelium with no glands (Figure 1). It is constantly renewed from the mitosis in the basal layer, with cellular exfoliation from the surface.

When women become sexually excited a fluid is produced on the surface of the vagina that acts as a lubrication for penile penetration and is the medium that semen is first ejaculated into. It has been suggested that the fluid is a transudate of plasma but no studies on its composition have yet been undertaken.

We have investigated, by a number of techniques, vaginal fluid produced in healthy young women.

After packing off the cervix, we inserted into the vaginas of the women a plastic bar whose dimensions are shown on Figure 2. Preweighed filter papers were strapped to the bar with two elastic bands. The bar and papers were left in the vaginas of the women for approximately 8 minutes. On removal, the papers were rapidly placed into a capped, preweighed bottle and reweighed. The increase in weight represented the vaginal secretion collected. This sample was obtained in women who were in an asexual or basal state. A second bar and papers were then inserted vaginally and the woman was allowed to stimulate herself sexually until she attained an

---

[1]Acknowledgements to the British Council for financial support of RJL.

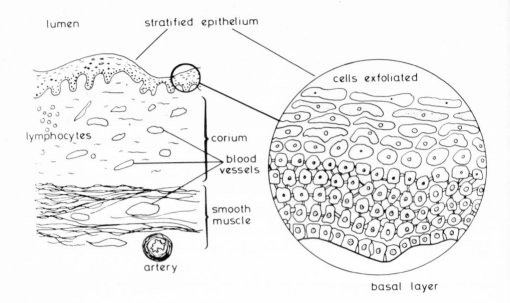

Fig. 1.   Vaginal epithelum in women.

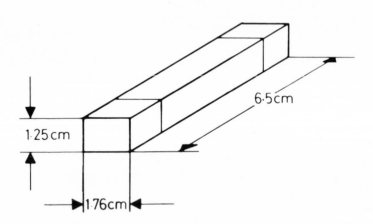

Fig. 2.   Plastic bar used in investigation of the composition of
vaginal fluid.

orgasm. The time for this varied between 8 and 28 minutes. Immediately after orgasm the bar was removed, the papers placed in the bottle and reweighed.

Table 1 lists the six subjects in the study. Three of the subjects came back to the laboratory for a repeated visit. The first and second visits are shown as 1 and 2 in brackets. The types of contraception used varied: NW, had a copper T intrauterine device; KC & BP, were on a steroid contraceptive pill; MS & SG, used a diaphragm and AJ, did not employ contraception.

None of the women had had intercourse earlier than 3 days previous to the experiments. The amount of vaginal fluid collected in mg. during the basal, sexually unstimulated state is shown in the last column, that marked "basal." The amount collected during the sexual stimulation is shown in next column, headed "vaginal fluid." Generally, the amount collected during the sexually excited state is greater than that obtained in the basal state but of course, the collection times of the two conditions are sometimes very unequal. The basal values represent the fluid production in approximately 8 minutes. We do not believe that the weight of fluid we collected by the filter papers necessarily represents a true measure of total fluid production, as the rugose structure of

TABLE 1

AMOUNT OF VAGINAL FLUID (MG) COLLECTED IN SIX
SUBJECTS, THE SEXUALLY UNSTIMULATED STATE (BASAL)
AND DURING SEXUAL STIMULATION (VAGINAL FLUID)

Subject	Contraception	Time to orgasm (min)	Vaginal fluid (mg)	Basal (mg)
NW	CU-T	8	155	195
KC(1)	PILL	13	283	178
KC(2)	PILL	24	248	196
MS(1)	DIAPHRAGM	28	71	43
MS(2)	DIAPHRAGM	26	369	48
AJ(1)	NONE	8	48	47
AJ(2)	NONE	15	85	45
BP	PILL	20	172	142
SG	DIAPHRAGM	21	216	69

the vagina makes it difficult to obtain a quantitative collection
of all the fluid formed.

The vaginal fluid samples and plasma samples taken by vene-
puncture, were analysed for urea and K^+. We hypothesized that if
the fluid was a transudate of plasma then the fluid obtained after
successful sexual excitement to orgasm should have values close to
those of plasma.

The urea concentration (in mg. %) of the plasma and in the
sexually unstimulated (basal) and sexually stimulated vaginal fluid
are shown in table 2. In 2 subjects (KCL, BP and KC2) urea concentration in basal fluid was 2-3 times the plasma value. This
could be due to urine entering the vagina in these women or to
the vagina absorbing fluid and leaving the urea in the lumen in
high concentration. In the case of KC this fell to very near plasma
levels in both visits (1 and 2) but in the case of BP there was
hardly any change (59 to 51). BP however, produced very little
fluid during her sexual stimulation. MS and SG had urea concentrations in basal and stimulated fluid very similar to plasma. AJ
is asterisked because she had a kidney complaint leading to high
plasma urea values. Her basal urea was lower than plasma but it
elevated after sexual excitement.

TABLE 2

UREA CONCENTRATION (IN MG. %) OF THE PLASMA AND
IN THE SEXUALLY UNSTIMULATED (BASAL) AND SEXUALLY
STIMULATED (AFTER ORGASM) VAGINAL FLUID, IN SIX SUBJECTS

		Vaginal Fluid	
Subject	Plasma	Basal	After Orgasm
KC(1)	21	54	21
MS	29	32	32
AJ*	37*	18	29
BP	25	59	51
SG	29	32	21
KC(2)	22	70	32

Thus in general, it can be said that the vaginal urea tends to plasma levels after sexual excitement.

Table 3 tabulates the values for K^+ concentration of the plasma and the basal and "sexual" vaginal fluids. One fact is dramatically obvious, both the basal vaginal fluid and that obtained after sexual stimulation have a potassium concentration very much greater than that in the plasma (a range between 2.2 → 11.9). Sexual excitement did not appear to have a consistent increasing or decreasing effect on the K^+ concentration. In some women, the vaginal K^+ fell while in others it rose - but in all cases the concentration was always very much higher than plasma.

This high concentration of K^+ is interesting in the fact that the spermatozoa are ejaculated in a K^+ rich fluid - semen.   In humans this has a K^+ concentration of 20-30 Meq/l. Thus the high K^+ in vaginal fluid may be an important feature of the vagina for spermatozoal viability.

What mechanisms could create the high K^+. Cell shedding (desquamation) and their consequent disruption in the lumen could cause the release of high K^+ concentrations into the vaginal fluid or the vagina could actually secrete K^+ into its lumen. Another possibility

TABLE 3

K^+ CONCENTRATION (IN MEQUIV/LITRE) OF THE PLASMA
AND OF THE "BASAL" AND SEXUALLY STIMULATED
VAGINAL FLUIDS IN SIX SUBJECTS

Subject	Plasma	Vaginal Fluid	
		Basal	After Orgasm
KC(1)	3.7	21	12
MS	4.1	9	17
AJ	4.0	18	24
BP	3.7	23	44
SG	3.7	22	17
KC(2)	4.0	28	19

was that a high potential difference occurred across the organ's wall - if this was orientated correctly this could drive the K$^+$ from the plasma into the luminal fluid.

We set about examining this possibility by measuring the transvaginal potential difference.

Figure 3 shows in diagrammatic form the technique employed.

The cervix was packed off with a gauze tampon (cervical pack). Electrical contact was made with the wall of the vagina by means of a luminal electrode which consisted of a plastic tube plugged at the end with a gauze wick saturated with 0.9% NaCl. The other electrode was a small plastic cannula inserted subcutaneously in the skin of the forearm. The cannula was also filled with 0.9% saline.

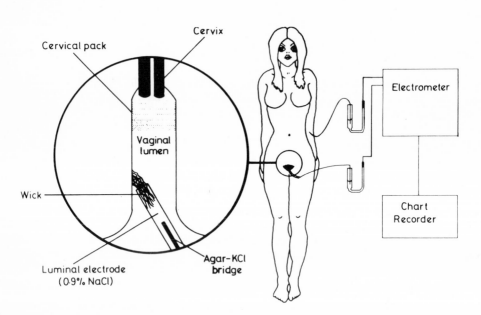

Fig. 3. Technique for measuring the transvaginal potential difference.

The vaginal and the subcutaneous electrode were connected by Agar - KCl bridges to two calomel cells arranged back-to-back across the input terminals of a battery powered Keithley electrometer. The output of the electrometer was displayed on a chart recorder to give a permanent record.

The polarity of all the transvaginal potential differences measured was always lumen negative to the subcutaneous tissue reference site.

Table 4 represents the transvaginal potential difference in mV during the basal, unstimulated condition and immediately after the orgasm. In all cases the post-orgasmic potential was less than the basal condition. In one or two subjects the decrease in potential was very marked, in others this was not so.

What is obvious in this series is that the transvaginal potential is large (28 - 59mV) and the polarity is so oriented that it would drive K^+ ions into the lumen to a concentration much higher than that in the plasma. Thus one possible reason for the high K^+ in the vaginal fluid could be the high transvaginal potential difference.

Figure 4 shows the continuous recording of the transvaginal potential in one subject before, during and after sexual excitement to orgasm by digital autostimulation of the clitoris.

TABLE 4

VAGINAL POTENTIAL DIFFERENCE (IN mV)
DURING THE BASAL CONDITION AND AFTER
ORGASM IN FIVE SUBJECTS

Subject	Basal	After Orgasm
MS	37	13
AJ	42	36
KC	28	22
BP	56	35
SG	59	54

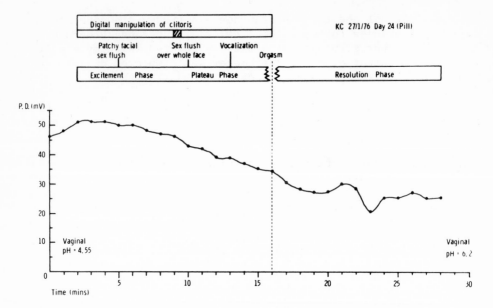

Fig. 4. Continuous recording of the transvaginal potential in one subject.

During the excitement phase, the potential slowly decreased. This decrease was maintained in the plateau phase. At orgasm no specific change in the potential occurred. During the resolution phase the potential continued to decrease reaching a plateau some 8 minutes after orgasm. The fall in vaginal potential during sexual excitement is probably due to the vaginal fluid making the wall oedematous and thus reducing its resistance.

We also made measurements of the pH of the vaginal wall before and immediately after the orgasm using a glass pH electrode. The basal values were on the acid side (Table 5). Often different pH's existed in different regions of the vagina. We tried to get values for the right and left walls; the extreme range of values is shown by the arrows. In nearly all cases a considerable increase in pH was shown after successful sexual stimulation to orgasm.

CONCLUSION

1. Vaginal fluid displays a variable urea concentration; in two subjects the basal level was 2-3 times that of plasma, in 2

TABLE 5

VAGINAL WALL pH DURING THE BASAL CONDITION
AND AFTER ORGASM IN SEVEN SUBJECTS

Subject	Basal	After Orgasm
KC(1)	4.15	5.2 → 5.8
MS(1)	5.5 → 6.2	5.9 → 6.1
AJ	5.2 → 6.1	6.2
BP	4.2 → 4.6	4.5 → 4.8
SG	4.2 → 5.2	5.6 → 6.2
KC(2)	4.4 → 4.6	5.2 → 5.7
MS(2)	5.3 → 5.7	5.9 → 6.3

subjects it was similar to plasma. After orgasm high values usually fell and lower ones were unchanged.

2. Vaginal fluid displays K^+ concentration basal level 2-7 times that of the plasma, and which is the same after orgasm.

3. Vaginal fluid displays a basal pH (wall) acid (4.15-6.2). After orgasm it increased sometimes by 1.3 pH units.

4. The transvaginal potential difference fell after orgasm. A continuous record in one subject showed steady decrease from excitement through plateau to resolution phase. No specific change occurred at orgasm. Its maintained high value, lumen negative to interstitial fluid, may be an important factor in creating the high K^+ concentration of vaginal fluid.

5. The decreases in transvaginal potential difference may be index of oedema of vaginal wall.

Thus high K^+ and the changes in pH of vaginal fluid would both be beneficial to sperm survival in the vagina.

Since the work was reported further experimental observations have been undertaken. The results are to be found in Levin & Wagner (1977) and Wagner & Levin (1977).

REFERENCES

Levin, R.J. and Wagner, G. (1977). Human vaginal fluid - ionic composition and modification by sexual arousal. J. Physiol. 266: 66-67P.

Wagner, G. and Levin, R.J. (1977). Vaginal fluid. In Hafez, E.S.E. and Evans, N. (eds.), The Human Vagina, Elsevier-North Holland, Amsterdam.

SEXUAL CHEMISTRY IN MONKEYS: THE EFFECT OF VAGINAL SECRETIONS ON MALE SEXUALITY

Gordon D. Jensen and Ethel Sassenrath

United States

The reports that vaginal secretions, and particularly certain chemical compounds in them, motivate sexual behavior of male rhesus monkeys (Michael and Keverne 1968, Curtis et al. 1971) attracted a great deal of interest by professionals and the laity. These studies inspired an investigation of the chemical composition of vaginal secretions in women (Sokolov et al. 1976) and have lent support to the long held notion that body odors have an effect on human sexuality.

More recently, a group of investigators at the Wisconsin Regional Primate Research Center (Goldfoot et al. 1976) reported on similar studies which indicated little or no effect of vaginal secretions on the sexual behavior of male monkeys. However, they did find indication that traces of semen on the female had a sexually stimulating effect on the male, presumably mediated through olfaction. They concluded that if the odor of vaginal secretions does have an effect, it probably works primarily by way of a learning mechanism, for example, by providing a cue for copulation. At present, it is fair to say that the matter of odors and sex in monkeys is controversial. More work needs to be done to answer many questions about vaginal secretions. Do monkeys smell them or not? If they do smell them, do they effect sexual arousal or not? What chemicals are they smelling? During what phase of the cycle are the odors produced? If a male is so stimulated, what behaviors are evoked?

This paper presents the results of a pilot study of olfactory mediated evocatants of social and sexual behavior, particularly vaginal secretions, utilizing a different approach compared with the previous studies. Instead of using spayed females and treating them with estrogen in order to bring them into a simulated estrous condition as was done in previously reported studies, we used intact females as our subjects. Thus, we were dealing with the entire hormonal system with its potential for producing several different olfactory stimuli. The intact female is subject not only to the effects of estrogen on the monthly cycle, but also by complex effects brought about by progesterone and testosterone in various phases of the monthly cycle. Our studies included measurements of plasma testosterone in the male in addition to the traditional behavioral measures. However, we are not ready to report results of the hormonal measures at this time.

The subjects of the study were two mature, sexually adequate and experienced rhesus males and two mature female rhesus monkeys who had been part of a breeding colony but had not conceived. The males' home cages, approximately 12 feet by 12 feet by 7 feet, were located outdoors, equipped with perches and separated by an intervening 10 foot cage with visual obstruction. The testing procedures were carried out in each male's home cage. The females lived in smaller individual cages in a separate building.

Each male was paired with each female under four different conditions: 1) non-estrus, 2) non-estrus with vaginal secretions applied to her rear (perineum), 3) non-estrus with vaginal secretions applied to the top of her head, and 4) estrus. In addition, we presented each male with two test conditions of vaginal secretions applied to inanimate objects: 1) applied to a plain six-inch block of wood, and 2) applied to one end of a surrogate monkey, a hobby horse with a vinyl rug covering.

The vaginal secretions were obtained by swab from separate donor estrous females who were part of a breeding program. These females lived in individual cages and were swabbed before any mating during their current menstrual cycle. Fifteen water-moist swabs were used for each application of vaginal secretions.

Objective behavioral observations were taken during the first 50 minutes of each test condition using a standard check list method; operationally defined behaviors included proximity, sniffing, aggression, grooming, and an array of sexual behaviors such as mounting, thrusts, and masturbation.

Prior to each test condition the female was placed in a cage in the corridor within view of the male for two hours. After the female was introduced the pair remained together for the next four hours. Each female was tested twice a week at 2 or 3 day intervals.

Figure 1 shows the results for male J and C, tested with each female, X and Y, with regard to number of mature complete mounts.

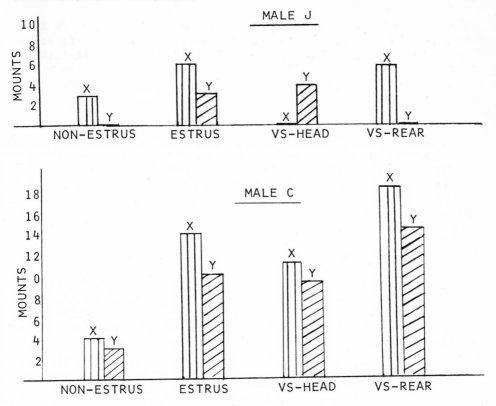

Fig. 1. Number of complete mounts of each male (J and C) with each female (X and Y) under test conditions of non-estrus, estrus, vaginal secretions applied to female's head, and vaginal secretions applied to female's rear (perineum).

C mounted the estrous females more frequently than he did when they were in the non-estrous condition. He also mounted the "painted" non-estrous female (vaginal secretions applied to either head or rear) more frequently compared with the "plain" non-estrous female. As for J he showed a greater number of mounts during the estrous condition contrasted with non-estrus. He also mounted the "painted" non-estrous female (vaginal secretions applied to either head or rear) more then the "plain" non-estrous female although he was not consistent with each female.

It appeared to the observers that J preferred female X. This was supported by data from several measures: mounting, proximity, closeness, and a lesser amount of aggression directed towards X, compared with Y. Male C also appeared to prefer X in the first three weeks of the testing and then switched to Y. The initial preference for X was supported by greater amounts of proximity and grooming. However, his later preference for Y was corroborated by the mounting data.

Table 1 summarizes masturbation data regarding the conditions of vaginal secretion applied to the inanimate objects; the wooden block and the surrogate. Both males showed definite olfactory interest in the objects which had vaginal secretions applied to them as indicated by sniffing and masturbation. The increase in masturbation is striking for the condition of vaginal secretions applied to the wooden block.

In summary, acknowledging that this study was pilot in nature, the data suggest several effects of vaginal secretions: 1) that vaginal secretions applied to an inanimate object, even a wooden block, can effect the sexual response of the male. This supports the hypothesis that vaginal secretions are evocatants of sexual behavior. 2) Vaginal secretions applied to a non-estrous female are generally effective in evoking an increased number of mounts by the male, sometimes even more than does an estrous female. These findings also support a vaginal secretions evocatant hypothesis. 3) Vaginal secretions placed on the rear of the non-estrous female generally evoked more mounts than vaginal secretions placed on the female's head. This suggests that the appropriateness of location of the odor plays a role in its effect.

TABLE 1

FREQUENCY OF MASTURBATION REGARDING THE CONDITIONS OF
VAGINAL SECRETION APPLIED TO INANIMATE OBJECTS

♂ J	0	7	3	4
♂ C	0	17	0	2
	Block Control	Block Vaginal Secretion	Surrogate Control	Surrogate Vaginal Secretion

Because of the difference in the hormonal system of the primates used in our tests, compared with those used in other studies, our data are not interpreted as either supportive or contradictory of the previous studies of vaginal secretions on male response. They do suggest the existence of some type of a pheromone-like mechanism, i.e., olfactory mediated chemical evocatants of social and sexual behavior. There is the possibility of different pheromones (chemical substances) operating at the different phases of the normal menstrual cycle. It is evident that more studies need to be done to clarify the role of odors in the sexual functioning of monkeys.

REFERENCES

Curtis, R.F., Ballantine, J.A., Keverne, E.B., Bonsall, R.W. and Michael, R.P. (1971). Identification of primate sexual pheromones and the properties of synthetic attractants. Nature 232:396.

Goldfoot, D.A., Kravetz, M.A., Goy, R.W., and Freeman, S.K. (1976). Lack of effect of vaginal lavages and aliphatic acids on ejaculatory responses in rhesus monkeys: Behavior and chemical analysis. Hormone and Behavior, 7:1.

Michael, R.P. and Keverne, E.B. (1968). Pheromones in the communication of sexual status in primates. Nature 218:746.

Sokolov, J.J., Harris, R.T., and Hecker, M.R. (1976). Isolation of substances from human vaginal secretions previously shown to be sex attractant pheromones in higher primates. Archives of Sexual Behavior 5:269.

Have demonstrated rise in extra uterine p during orgasm followed by development of neg p. ? — increases 'intake' of semen. Buffering of semen reduces 'motile', pH of vagina (≈ 4) pH semen ≈ 7. ? also very stimulation may cause ovulation (evidence that conception in rape occurred more often > expected during 1st part of cycle)

ORGASM AND FERTILITY

Cyril A. Fox

England

Recently an industrial psychologist, surveying an area of high population in the United Kingdom, interviewed a mother of ten children; "You must enjoy intercourse," he said, to which she replied in all honesty, "No, I just lie there like a fish on a slab." This is shattering news for all sexologists who have realized the full strength and profundity of the female orgasm in the past decade, and would feel that here is a source of great pleasure and release of tension, beyond which lies a deep biological significance.

We have to accept, not merely from the example that I have quoted, that fertilization and conception can and does occur in the absence of any external evidence of orgasm. This leaves several possibilities; firstly, that the spermatozoa make the journey unaided through the cervix and into the fallopian tubes - and after all, they do most of this in artificial insemination. Secondly, that there are internal secretions in the female which are released reflexively by the male or by his secretions, as well as the more obvious oxytocic substances such as the seminal prostaglandins, which may work independently of orgasm. Another suggestion is that the act of intercourse may induce ovulation in some women, whether they experience orgasm or not, and hence enhance fertility.

In this paper I shall briefly consider the evidence for and against coital-induced ovulation, and then concentrate on the physiological facts of the female orgasm as we know them. As we progress, the evidence should show that there are several mechanisms which facilitate sperm transport and conception, preferably, but not necessarily aided by female orgasm.

COITAL-INDUCED OVULATION

Cogent arguments for the existence of this phenomenon in the human have been advanced by Jöchle (1973, 1975); but there are many critics of his thesis. Jöchle reminds us that animals such as the ferret, rabbit and cat are reflex ovulators following coitus, and that other mammals, while ovulating spontaneously may have this process accelerated by intercourse. He even argues that for a short time, the "period of standing heat," the same conditions as in the ferret, rabbit and cat exists in species such as the rat, sheep, pig and cattle. We have considered the comparative aspect of coital physiology (Fox and Fox, 1971) in terms of vaginal ma-nipulation and enhancement of ovulation or sperm transport in some mammals, and have suggested four criteria for orgasm: (1) changes in blood pressure, respiratory pattern and heart rate; (2) changes in muscular tension (including vaginal and uterine contraction); (3) hormonal changes; (4) emission of sound. These criteria may be seen in other mammals to a varying extent as well as in the human, and suggest a biological connection between orgasm and re-production.

Further evidence of coital-induced ovulation in the human is adduced from the distribution of conceptions through the menstrual cycle. An analysis of data from conceptions reported as a result of rape or limited exposure is illustrated in Table I. As we can see the fertility is higher in the early days of the cycle than would be expected if ovulation had occurred at the usual time.

TABLE I

DISTRIBUTION OF CONCEPTIONS REPORTED
AS RESULTS OF RAPE OR LIMITED EXPOSURE*

		Days of cycle		
		1-11	12-16	17-30
	N	Distribution (%)		
Conceptions from rape	651	44	27	29
Conceptions from limited exposure	100	49	26	25

*Adapted from Jöchle, 1975.

Despite criticisms of the method of obtaining data of this nature, since pregnancies were much more likely to be reported than non-pregnancies, we do have the paradox that conception has apparently occurred after a single coition outside the usual time for ovulation. It has been suggested that the fear and anger of rape may in a humoral manner mimic sexual excitement and facilitate conception. One other explanation could be that ovarian contraction occurs during intercourse and leads to ovulation, but this would be more likely in an orgasmic situation.

Quality of Orgasm

If we are to accept that the female orgasm has some facilitatory effect on conception, how does this come about? Studies have shown that the uterus contracts during orgasm (Fox, Wolff and Baker, 1970) and the type of orgasm may have some quantitative effect on these contractions. To clarify what I mean by type of orgasm I shall employ the classification of Singer (1973): a) vulval orgasm, which as measured by Masters and Johnson (1966) can be induced by coital or non-coital stimulation and is not physiologically terminative; b) uterine orgasm, which is deeply satisfying, involves apnea (Fox and Fox, 1969) and uterine contractions and is physiologically terminative; c) and finally blended orgasm, which is a mixture of the above two.

I should explain how we measured intra-uterine pressure. This was made possible by the development of the radio-telemetry pressure capsule, which could be inserted into the uterus and by a change in the frequency of its signal show when any pressure changes took place. We were able to conduct these experiments in the subject's own bedroom without the presence of observers, and it was found that female orgasm increased the intra-uterine pressure to + 40 cm H_2O to be followed by a post-orgasmic drop in pressure to a negative value of -26 cm H_2O. Further experiments showed that in the more satisfying or uterine orgasm the pressure changes were enhanced (Fox, 1976). These findings lead us to postulate that as a negative intra-uterine pressure has been shown to occur one may still think in terms of "uterine insuck" of spermatozoa, or at least of an active role for the female genital tract in sperm transport. As previously mentioned, ovulation may be induced or enhanced by active contraction of the ovary or surrounding structures, but this is speculation.

Other Relevant Aspects of Coital Physiology

Vaginal pH. It has often been stated that the vagina is a hostile environment for human semen since the former is at pH4 compared with the latter at pH7 (approximate figures). As spermatozoa are immobilized at pH6 or less, it follows that the quicker the semen enters the relatively alkaline uterus the better. We have, however, shown that human semen has remarkable powers of buffering and in a normally fertile subject the vaginal pH changes from pH4 to pH7 within 8 seconds of the arrival of semen in the vagina during coitus. These observations were made during unobserved coitus by the use of the radio-telemetry pH capsule (Fox, Meldrum and Watson, 1973). We also found that the semen of sub-fertile and infertile men did not buffer at all well, so that in their case the vagina was indeed a hostile environment.

Moreover we observed that orgasm per se did not change the vaginal pH, but vaginal lubrication occurs mainly in the outer 2/3 of the vagina whereas our capsule was placed high up in the fornix where we expected the device (25mm x 9mm) would not interfere with the penis. Important work by Levin and Wagner (1976) may be of significance in infertility due to poor ejaculation as well as insufficient sexual arousal in the female. These researchers have shown a rise in vaginal pH during sexual stimulation if measurements are made at varying levels in the vagina, with values as high as pH6.3 being recorded.

Taking these results together, it would appear that sexual stimulation alone is of benefit to the survival of spermatozoa within the female genital tract, and presumably orgasm enhances this effect. However, due to the powerful buffering effect of semen there is a built-in mechanism for sperm survival even in the "fish on the slab" woman.

Humoral release. The presence of oxytocin in female peripheral blood after orgasm has been reported (Fox and Knaggs, 1969). This finding would bias one to the thought that orgasm is beneficial to conception since one could postulate a direct effect on the female genital tract. Although the nonpregnant human uterus is said to be unaffected by oxytocin, one must consider the uterus to be in a more active state during orgasm than in the usual in vitro or even in vivo studies. At the same time a local release of prostaglandins by the uterus might enhance the activity of plasma oxytocin.

CONCLUSION

The evidence presented suggests that active participation in the sexual act by the female, culminating in orgasm is likely to enhance fertility by assisting sperm transport. It has, however, been shown that factors exist which make it possible for the nonorgasmic woman to conceive. The balance, in terms of fertility, would appear to shift in favor of the orgasmic woman and the quality of the orgasm may be of significance. Where sperm quality is

poor in regard to buffering power, fertility may be enhanced by
the raising of vaginal pH levels during sexual excitement and orgasm. There is conjectural but not firm evidence for the possibility of coital-induced or coital-accelerated ovulation.

REFERENCES

Fox, C.A. (1976). Some aspects & implications of coital physiology.
J. Sex & Marital Therapy, In Press.

Fox, C.A. and Fox, B. (1969). Blood pressure & respiratory patterns
during human coitus. J. Reprod. Fert. 19: 405-415.

Fox, C.A. and Fox, B. (1971). A comparative study of coital physiology, with special reference to the sexual climax. J. Reprod.
Fert. 24: 319-336.

Fox, C.A. and Knaggs, G.S. (1969). Milk ejection activity (oxytocin)
in peripheral blood in man in association with coitus. J.
Endocr. 45: 145-146.

Fox, C.A., Meldrum, S.J. and Watson, B.W. (1973). Continuous measurement by radio-telemetry of vaginal pH during human coitus.
J. Reprod. Fert. 33: 69-75.

Fox, C.A., Wolff, H.S. and Baker, J.A. (1970). Measurement of intravaginal and intra-uterine pressures during human coitus by
radio-telemetry. J. Reprod. Fert. 22: 243-251.

Jöchle, W. (1973). Coitus-induced ovulation. Contraception, 7:
527-564.

Jöchle, W. (1975). Current research in coitus-induced ovulation:
a review. J. Reprod. Fert. Suppl. 22: 165-207.

Levin, R.J. and Wagner, G. (1976). Human vaginal potential difference, pH, fluid & potassium concentration during sexual
excitement. Abstract at Annual meeting Society for Study
of Fertility, Sheffield, England, and personal communication.

Masters, W.H. and Johnson, V.E. (1966). Human Sexual Response,
Churchill, London.

Singer, I. (1973). The Goals of Human Sexuality, Norton, New York.

OVULATION INDUCTION

S. Muazzam Husain, R. Husain and P. Brazeau, Jr.

Canada

Ovulation, or the release of the egg from the mature Graafian follicle, occurs as a consequence of a complex series of timely co-ordinated events. Much of our understanding with regard to the mechanism of ovulation was obtained through successful induction of ovulation in various laboratory animals and in women.

Ovulation involves the participation of the central nervous system, the pituitary gland and the ovary. Under natural circumstances the mammals can be classified either as spontaneous or as non-spontaneous (reflex or induced) ovulators. In the former category the females have a reproductive cycle and ovulation occurs cyclically during a particular phase of this cycle: examples of spontaneous ovulators are the rat, mouse, hamster, guinea pig, horse, cow, monkey and man. In the second category no such reproductive cycle is discernible and ovulation in the female animal occurs following copulation: examples of this category are the rabbit, mink, cat, ferret, etc. It is interesting, however, that ovulation can be experimentally induced in both the spontaneous ovulators and the reflex ovulators in about the same manner.

The purpose of this paper is to discuss the ways ovulation can be induced with some chemical agents in certain female animals and in women.

Ovulation occurs due to the influence of the pituitary gona-dotrophic hormones on the ovarian follicle. The gonadotrophins are FSH or follicle stimulating hormone and LH or luteinizing hormone. The secretion of the gonadotrophic hormones are in turn regulated by the RFs, the releasing factors (or releasing hormones),

secreted by the hypothalamus. The secretion of the RFs are in
turn influenced by the ovarian hormones, particularly estrogen,
via a feedback mechanism. Secretion of RFs is said to be also
influenced by other endogenous factors like prolactin (another
pituitary gonadotrophic hormone) and certain brain catecholamines,
as well as by some external factors like light, odors, etc.

The gonadotrophic hormones are glycoproteins. The releasing
factors are much smaller decapeptides. It has not yet been resolved to everybody's satisfaction whether it is the same RF that
causes the release of both FSH and LH or whether separate RFs exist,
one for FSH release and one for LH release. In any event RF stimulation brings about prompt release of pituitary gonadotrophins.

Also, cyclical variations in FSH and LH release occur during
the reproductive cycle of the spontaneous ovulators. Fluctuations
occurring in FSH secretions appear to be more gradual where as a
sudden increase in LH release takes place several hours prior to
ovulation time. LH (in presence of FSH) is, therefore, regarded
as the ovulating hormone.

The exact mechanism by which the egg is released from the
Graafian follicle under the influence of LH surge is still a matter of debate. Apparantly the buildup of intrafollicular pressure,
local effects of LH and other hormones including prostaglandins are
somehow involved in it.

Ovulation can be easily detected in the laboratory animals by
laparotomy. In rats, for example, all the ovulated eggs remain
together within the fallopian tube causing the characteristic bulging of the tube. The eggs can be squeezed out in a gelatinous mass
by simply puncturing this bulging with a sharp needle and can be
easily detected under the microscope and counted (Husain and Saucier,
1970). Detection of ovulation in women, on the other hand, is based
upon indirect evidences like increased plasma progesterone level,
progestational endometrium, rise in basal body temperature, etc.
Needless to add that such methods are open to severe criticisms.
The only unquestionable evidence of ovulation in women is the establishment of pregnancy.

With the isolation of gonadotrophin releasing factor and the
synthesis of gonadotrophin releasing factor analogs by various laboratories (Matsuo et al., 1971; Schally et al., 1971a; Guillermin
R., 1972; Banik and Givner, 1975) a rather large number of investigations are now being done with regard to the potency of these
compounds as ovulation inducing agents. These agents have been
found to be potent stimulants of both FSH and LH secretion (Schally
et al., 1971-b).

The gonadotrophin releasing factor has been found to be an excellent diagnostic tool for the evaluation of the anovulatory patient with particular reference to testing the hypothalamo-pituitary axis. Several laboratories have reported induction of ovulation and pregnancy following gonadotrophin releasing factor therapy.

The synthesis of these agents open up many possibilities which should be further investigated, e.g., possible contraceptive action, repeated use without causing ovarian refractoriness, etc.

The two main reasons for using ovulation inducing agents in women are the regulation of the menstrual cycle and induction of pregnancy, anovulation being already diagnosed in both cases.

The mechanisms which govern the menstrual cycle and ovulation are complex and delicate and can be easily disturbed by internal and external factors. The possible causes of anovulation are varied and many. Consequently, prompt diagnosis of anovulation at times is difficult.

It is now accepted that failure of ovulation during one or more cycles is not uncommon and would result in temporary infertility and often menstrual disturbances. It is also agreed that a significant percentage of the adult female population suffers from sterility. The cause of sterility in some of these women is long-term ovulatory failure. Recent development of ovulation inducing agents has made induction of ovulation possible in cases of anovulatory infertility.

Apart from gonadal defects, anovulatory patients (with accompanying infertility and menstrual dysfunction) usually also manifest other endocrine problems, e.g., hirsutism, galactorrhea, vasomotor instability, adrenal and thyroid disorders, etc. Factors like emotional trauma, stress, environmental changes, etc. may also cause ovulatory failure and menstrual dysfunction.

A thorough examination of the patient before the onset of treatment is regarded essential. This is to ascertain whether the problem is indeed anovulation, and if so, what is the cause. That is, whether the defect is at the hypothalamic, pituitary or ovarian level. A high plasma gonadotrophin level is generally regarded as indicative of problem at the ovarian level. On the contrary, low gonadotrophin level is regarded as indicative of disturbance at the hypothalamo-pituitary level. Simple functional hypogonadotrophism may be attributed to psychogenic factors. Lesions in the hypothalamic-pituitary area, enlargement of sella turcica, Cushing's syndrome, Stein-Levinthal syndrome, etc. are serious circumstances accompanied by anovulation.

Anovulatory patients in most cases present themselves for treatment due to menstrual dysfunction or infertility. The decision concerning the need for treatment is influenced by many factors such as desire for fertility, presence of a distrubing menstrual disorder, etc. Some patients simply insist that they would feel better when they menstruate regularly. For a physician it is important to rule out any underlying organic lesions or systemic disease before the treatment is initiated. A physician's decision not to treat also should imply that long-term anovulation would not produce any untoward effect in the future. Prompt therapy to cause anovulation is usually initiated when the patient expresses strong desire for pregnancy.

The first principle in the treatment of anovulation is evidently the correction of the underlying cause. The second principle relates to the choice of therapy. The physician of course selects those agents which are most appropriate to initiate ovulation and with the least untoward effect. However, a serious and complete work up has been emphasized by many workers before any attempt to induce ovulation. Such a work up, according to Rioux (1974), must ultimately reach the following conclusions, e.g., willingness to cooperate fully and has strong desire for progeny, the male is fertile, the female is anovulatory and her genital tract is normal or corrected, and the ovaries contain follicles which retain the capacity to respond to stimulation.

The hypothalamo-pituitary-ovarian axis not only gets easily disturbed, it may also get easily self-corrected. At times the very contact between the patient and the physician may exert a favorable effect and some workers report pregnancy in 10% of women seeking treatment for anovulation even before the actual treatment with therapeutic agents is initiated.

Besides the above placebo effect anovulation has been treated by the following pharmacological agents, e.g., estrogens and estrogen derivatives (like epimestriol), progesterone, retroprogesterone, cyclofenil or Sexovid, clomiphene citrate, gonadotrophins, gonadotrophin releasing factor, etc. as well as diverse methods like irradiation of pituitary and ovary, and surgical procedure like wedge resection in certain cases. During the past years the two methods that stood out are the gonadotrophin therapy and the clomiphene therapy. More recently a surge of interest has been shown by many investigators to induce ovulation with gonadotrophin releasing hormone. It should be pointed out at the outset that ovulation has been induced with all these methods with variable degree of success. Not only has it been possible to induce ovulation using one or the other methods in otherwise healthy women, but such induced ovulation was followed by successful pregnancies in women suffering from different pathological conditions as well as in women previously hypophysectomized (Corral et al., 1972).

Attempts to induce ovulation with gonadotrophins from animal sources met with little success. Gonadotrophin preparations like PMSG (pregnant mare serum gonadotrophin), sheep pituitary extract etc. are no longer acceptable for such therapy. The real break-through in anovulation therapy came when Gemzell and his coworkers described in 1958 the successful induction of ovulation and preg-nancy in the human utilizing gonadotrophin derived from human pi-tuitary glands. The works of Genzell and his coworkers and others showed that gonadotrophins isolated from human pituitaries and human menopausal urine could be used in combination with HCG (hu-man chorionic gonadotrophin) to induce ovulation in women. Since then tens of thousands of ovulations have been induced with these drugs, and thousands of pregnancies have been reported.

The gonadotrophin therapy is based on providing FSH and LH stimulation which is thought to mimic the endogenous hormone se-cretion during the normal menstrual cycle. All gonadotrophin therapies use both FSH and LH preparations since both are required for follicle maturation and ovulation. Two different gonadotrophic preparations are, therefore, required – one providing the required amount of FSH and another providing sufficient LH activity to pro-voke ovulation. The FSH-rich material may be obtained from the human pituitary or from the postmenopausal urine called HMG, Huma-gon (Organon) or Pergonal (Searle). To provide the LH surge either pituitary LH or HCG can be used.

The treatment schedule adopted in treating anovulation is probably the most important single factor influencing results obtained. This appears to be particularly true in gonadotrophin therapy.

Treatment with gonadotrophins is extremely effective in induc-ing ovulation and pregnancy. With proper treatment it may be pos-sible to obtain an ovulation rate of as high as 90% and pregnancy rate 60% or more (Taymor, 1973). The chances of a woman taking home a living child, according to some workers, is between 65-70% (Katz et al, 1973).

The complications from gonadotrophin therapy are high rate of multiple pregnancies, fetal wastage and the occurrence of hyper-stimulation syndrome.

Clomiphene citrate is commonly referred to as the fertility pill and is presently the most successful single agent for the induction of ovulation. It is orally active and is related to the nonsteroidal estrogen diethyl-stilbestrol. It is available under the trade name of clomid. The preparation consists of a mixture of the <u>cis</u> and <u>trans</u> isomers with most of the biological activities attributable to the <u>cis</u> form.

When it comes to the choice of therapy many physicians argue about the selection of the clomid therapy over the gonadotrophin therapy or <u>vice versa</u>. According to some investigators such argument may be put to rest by using the following guidelines in the choice of therapy: the anovulatory patient who displays gonadotrophin and estrogen production but does not cycle should be subjected to clomiphene therapy, where as the anovulatory patient who is deficient in gonadotrophin and estrogen, and as a result can not cycle, should be treated by gonadotrophins.

Clomiphene does not have estrogenic or progestational properties in the human. It is believed that clomiphene induces ovulation by acting at two levels. It stimulates pituitary gonadotrophin release and also increases the ovarian sensitivity to gonadotrophins by acting locally on the ovaries. To be responsive to clomiphene the patient must have potentially normal pituitary and ovaries.

There are many variations of clomiphene therapy. One such method is to initiate treatment with one 50 mg tablet daily for 5 days, beginning on the 5th day of a spontaneous or induced flow. If ovulation and menstruation has not occurred, a flow is induced and the treatment is repeated.

According to some investigators an ovulation rate of as high as 80% and pregnancy rate of as high as 50% can be expected following clomiphene therapy (Kase, 1973).

The complications from clomiphene therapy are multiple pregnancies, fetal wastage, hyperstimulation syndrome, and several minor side effects like vasomotor flush, abdominal distention or pain, visual simptoms, irritability, depression, headache, loss of head hair, etc. Clomiphene therapy is contraindicated in the patient with ovarian cysts.

It may be mentioned here that sometimes combined clomiphene and gonadotrophin therapies are also used with some success.

Ovulation has been successfully induced in large number of mammalian and non-mammalian species using various pharmacological agents. Ovulation has been induced in mature, immature and pregnant animals. Ovulated eggs recovered from the immature animals have been found to be qualitatively as potent as eggs from mature animals, such eggs were made to undergo successful implantation and gestation.

Experimentally ovulation has been induced in many mammalian species some of which are rats, mice, hamsters, guinea pigs, rabbits, cattle, sheeps, chinchillas, monkeys, pigs, etc. The ovulation inducing agents used are gonadotrophins, steroids, clomiphene, prostaglandins, gonadotrophin releasing factors and synthetic analogs, prostaglandin, cyclofenil (Sexovid), etc. and many new chemicals like tamoxifen, epimestrol, centachroman, etc. The mode of adminstration of these agents varied, e.g., subcutaneous injection, intraperitoneal injection, intravenous adminstration, oral adminstration, cerebral implants, etc.

Attempts to induce ovulation in laboratory animals result in overstimulation of the ovaries (like in women) causing the release of more than the "normal" number of eggs. The phenomenon is called superovulation. Also, in some laboratory species the immature animals are better suited for such studies due to the fact that it is easier to induce ovulation in these young animals. Studies using mature laboratory animals are relatively few (Husain and Saucier, 1970).

We wish to take this opportunity to present some data that we obtained using mature rats when we tried to regulate the degree of ovarian stimulation and observed the effects of contraceptive and other steroid pretreatment on the gonadotrophin induced ovulation. We were able to induce ovulation consistently in mature Sprague Dawley rats with PMSG and HCG. PMSG was injected in the morning of Day 1 and HCG was given 52-54 hours later. Autopsy was done in the morning of Day 4. The eggs were recovered from the fallopian tubes and were counted under the microscope.

Our first observation was that irrespective of which particular phase of the reproductive cycle we initiated the PMSG treatment (i.e., estrous, metestrous, diestrous or proestrous), we were always able to induce ovulation.

We used different combinations of doses of PMSG and HCG. The doses of PMSG varied from 10 IU to 500 IU, whereas the doses of HCG varied from 10 IU to 5,000 IU. It was observed that injections of 50 IU of PMSG and 50 IU or more of HCG are necessary to obtain maximal ovulatory response. We also noted that it is possible to change both the number of eggs ovulating as well as % of rats in a given population ovulating by varying the doses of PMSG below or above 50 IU.

When we studied the effect of steroid pretreatment on the maximal ovulatory response obtained in the way described above, we observed the following: androgens do not have any effect on gonadotrophin induced ovulation, progestagens in lower doses have no effect but in higher doses somewhat depress gonadotrophin induced ovulation, estrogens alone or in combination with progestagens (as in some oral contraceptive pills) significantly facilitate gonadotrophin induced ovulation.

Similar studies were then conducted in hypophysectomized animals (in order to eliminate the endogenous source of gonado- trophins) and the results basically strengthen the observations made with intact animals.

These studies demonstrate that it is possible to regulate the degree of ovarian response while attempting to induce ovula- tion in animals. These studies also show that the effect of gonadotrophins in inducing ovulation can be amplified by estrogen pretreatment. Implications of such observations in animals, we trust, are important in relation to ovulation induction in women.

REFERENCES

Banik, U.K. and Givner, M.L. (1975). Ovulation induction and antifertility effects of an LH-RH analogue (AY-25, 205) in cyclic rats. J. Reprod. Fertil., 44: 87-92.

Corral, J., Calderon, J. and Goldzieher, J.W. (1972). Induction of ovulation and term pregnancy in a hypophysectomizid woman. Obst. & Gynecol., 39: 397-400.

Gemzell, C.A., Diczfalusy, E. and Tillinger, K.G. (1958). Clinical effects of human pituitary follicle stimulating hormone (FSH). J. Clin. Endocr., 18: 333.

Guillemin, R. (1972). Physiology and chemistoy of the hypothalamic releasing factors for gonadotrophin: a new approach to fertility control. Contraception, 5: 1-20.

Husain, S.M. and Saucier, R. (1970). Induction of superovulation in mature rats with gonadotrophins. Can. J. Physiol. Pharmacol., 48: 196-199.

Kase, N. (1973). Induction of ovulation with clomiphene citrate. Clin. Obstet. Gynecol., 16: 192-200.

Katz, M. Lunenfeld, B. and Insler, V. (July 28, 1973). Induction of ovulation with gonadotrophins. S.A. Med. Journal Suppl. S.A. Journal of Obstet. Gynecol., p. 1272-1280.

Matsuo, H., Arimura, A., Nair, RMG, Schally, A.V. (1971). Synthesis of porcine LH and FSH releasing hormone by the solid phase method. Biochem. Biophys. Res. Commun., 45: 822-827.

Rioux, J.E. (1974). Ovarian stimulation and laparoscopy in women.
        In Husain, S.M. and Guttmacher, A.F. (ed.), Progress in
        Reproduction Research and Population Control, Publications
        Internationales, Montreal: 185-199.

Schally, A.V., Kostin, A.J., Arimura, A. (1971a). Hypotholamic
        stimulating hormone (FSH) and luteinizing hormone (LH)
        regulating hormone: structure, physiology and clinical
        studies. Fertil., Steril., 22: 703-718.

Schally, A.V., Arimura, A., Kastin, A.J., Matsuo, H., Baba, Y.,
        Redding, T.W., Nain, RMG, Debeljuk, L., White, W.F. (1971).
        Gonadotrophin releasing hormone: one polypeptide regulates
        secretion of luteinizing and follicle stimulating hormones.
        Science, 173: 1036-1039.

Taymor, M.L. (1973). Induction of ovulation with gonadotrophins.
        Clin. Obstet. Gynecol., 16: 201-220.

Art. n. interesting

INFERTILITY IN THE UNWED

Herbert H. Keyser

United States

The fact that social and sexual mores have changed dramatically over the past decade is well known in the medical and non-medical communities. In some areas, the medical profession has been slow to adjust to these changes.

The material collected deals with the availability, or lack of availability, of care for infertility in the unmarried female or couple. An attempt has been made to determine, when such facilities are not available to the unwed, what social, religious, legal, economic and sexual forces are at work.

MATERIALS

On the three thousand questionnaires sent out to members of the American Society of Sterility, and hospitals in the United States having infertility clinic services, there were 603[1] recordable responses received. All the questionnaires were to remain anonymous, in the hope that it would help to yield accurate information in a highly sensitive subject.

The questions dealt with the incidence of patients requesting such care. Among the patients apparently unable to conceive are included:

---

[1]In the 603 responses, some gave data for both private practices and a functioning clinic facility so that data was available for 588 private and 393 clinic facilities.

1. Unmarried couples in permanent cohabitation.

2. Couples contemplating marriage.

3. Single women participating in unprotected intercourse who are concerned about why they have never been "caught."

4. Single women desirous of pregnancy.

Statistical information concerning the frequency of such requests, reasons why the services were or were not available, external pressures affecting the decision and demographic information concerning those physicians involved was accumulated.

Of the data collected from 588 private practitioners, there were 348 who had received such requests for help. Of those physicians, there were 153, or 44% who felt that there had been a significant increase of such patients in the preceding year.

In responses from 393 clinics, 181 were being requested to provide such services. Seventy-four, or 41%, felt the incidence was increasing.

The frequency of the requests in both categories is shown in Table 1.

TABLE 1

FREQUENCY OF REQUESTS FOR INFERTILITY
CARE BY UNMARRIED WOMEN

Frequency of Requests	Private Practice	Clinic
More than once a week	30	13
Once a week	49	29
Once a month	76	52
Less than once a month	143	59
Frequency not indicated	50	28
Total	348	181

As can be easily noted, the largest category of practitioners and clinics see these patients with the low frequency of less than once a month.

There were twenty-eight clinics that stated their hospital policy disallowed such treatment. In eleven other cases, both private and clinic, the respondents felt there was a law forbidding such care.

The questionnaire offered five possible reasons why patients requesting care might be rejected. The results are shown in Table 2.

In the private practices, there were sixteen who are not presently treating such patients but are considering reversing their decision. Of all those responses from private physicians, there were only two who were concerned about pressure from women's rights organizations.

In fifty-six cases, hospital clinics felt that eventually they would be forced by the courts to treat these patients.

In 338 questionnaires reporting giving the treatment, 296 began with the initial request, and 42 began subsequently; but of that group, twenty were considering reversing their decision, and another twenty felt they were in legal jeopardy because they were offering the services.

TABLE 2

REASON FOR REJECTION OF PATIENTS (N = 191)*

	Morality	Legality	Effect on Community	Interpretation of Newborn Rights	Religion
Yes	81	34	73	65	32
No	36	66	31	45	70

*There were 191 rejections of which some had more than one reason for the rejection.

Table 3 identifies, when there was some reluctance to treat even though the care was being offered, the frequency and causes of that reluctance.

In fifteen cases where treatment was given, the physician stated that women's rights organizations had affected their decisions.

In a rather sensitive question, physicians were asked if, under their care, the patient had successfully become pregnant and subsequently decided she wanted it aborted, would they be willing to perform the procedure. The question applied only where abortion was legal. One hundred and forty-eight answered affirmatively, and one hundred and seventeen in the negative.

Among those offering treatment, in response to whether they would accept minors, 237 answered "yes," 87 answered "no" and 14 had no response.

The demographics of the responding group appear in Table 4. Certain interesting observations could be made from that information.

TABLE 3

BASIS OF RELUCTANCE WHERE
CARE IS BEING OFFERED (N = 338)*

	Yes	No
Legality	31	272
Morality	56	249
Effect on Community	74	231
Interpretation of Newborn Rights	66	235
Religion	20	283

*Of the 338 offering care some had no reluctance and others had more then one basis for their reluctance.

TABLE 4

DEMOGRAPHY OF RESPONDENTS

Type Of Practice Community

Urban	Suburban	Rural	Combinations of all three	No Response
393	108	33	58	11

Size of City

Under 25,000	25-100,000	100-500,000	500-1,000,000	Over 1,000,000	No Response
45	140	139	100	169	10

Base of Practice

Med. School	Private	Vol. Hosp.	Priv. Hosp.	Gov. Hosp.	Other	No Response
125	82	68	49	29	75	175

Year of Graduation

Before 1935	1935 1940	1941 1945	1946 1950	1951 1955	1956 1960	1961 1965	After 1965	No Response
50	49	80	87	97	140	55	9	36

Patients' Economic Classification

Upper	Middle	Lower	Combinations of the three	No Response
39	414	52	86	12

Those physicians and clinics whose patient load was restricted to the lower-income group were willing to treat minors over 70% more frequently than those physicians caring for the middle and upper-income patients.

In the question dealing with the reason for the reluctance to treat, all three economic groups were rejected equivalently on the basis of "Legality," "Morality," "Religion" and the "Rights of the Newborn Child." But, on the question of its "Effect on the Community," the lower-income group was rejected four times as frequently as either of the other two.

DISCUSSION

An understanding of what circumstances initiated this project may help in the appreciation of the accumulated data. In the author's affiliated institutions, as well as in the private practice of infertility, an increasing number of such patients were appearing. In the involved institutions, there was an attitude of non-acceptance of such patients. In the private sector there was, at best, an awkwardness in the handling of such cases and some indecision concerning their acceptance. This situation offered no comfort to the patients. Certainly, the physicians' general lack of preparation in handling such matters placed them in a difficult psychological situation.

It was hoped that by collecting data on how and why such matters were being handled presently, other physicians might be enabled to make well-considered decisions in advance. This might eliminate hasty subjective decision-making, whether positive or negative.

Information was elicited from two sources in the medico-legal field. A concern about legal consents was expressed, specifically in the treatment of minors. One legal problem deals with aspects of artificial insemination. Legal opinion also holds that third-party payers, such as insurance companies, may not agree to participate. It was felt that changing mores would lead the courts and legislatures to set up guidelines upon which a physician could place more reliance. It may be noted that both the acceptance of liberalized forms of treatment, such as abortion, as well as the rejection, such as restrictions on sterilization, have led physicians into legal confrontations.

It was quite interesting to note that, in a response from a women's equality organization, though it was totally in support of the availability of such care, it was specifically noted that it should be offered only after counseling was coupled with it. There is little doubt that counseling is an urgent matter in these situations.

In questioning sources of governmental welfare organizations, it was found that subsequent economic, social and psychological responsibility were the main concerns. This must be weighed in relation to how these same responsibilities are, or are not, being handled by the parents of children born in wedlock. Would attempts at evaluating such attributes, in either the married or unmarried, fall within the realm of the duties or the rights of a physician?

In considering the previous opinions, how does the physician make such a decision? It may be worthwhile for the doctor to consider whose problem it is, and why.

For the patient it is a medical and, probably, psychological problem. The physician may have both of these, plus a moral, religious and/or legal problem. The hospital is most likely concerned legally, but may well have a religious affiliation. Finally, the community will think mostly in terms of an economic concern, though all of the other problems may be present as well.

The obvious consideration involves the physician's acceptance or rejection of childbirth out of formal wedlock. This is occurring with much greater frequency throughout our society. If this phenomenon is accepted, then is there a difference between a married or a single infertile patient?

A noted obstetrician-gynecologist explained that the laws in her state are unclear on such matters. However, she felt that if it is not illegal to treat unmarried women for contraception, she assumed it would not be illegal to treat them for infertility; though she had not, as yet, treated such a patient.

The physician of today will be faced not only with questions of a medical and scientific nature, but with massive changes in life-styles. The word is out now, clear and sharp, that gynecologists have spent the past decades treating women the same way the rest of society does. But women will no longer be willing to accept the status of second-class citizen, and will certainly not be patronized by male chauvinist gynecologists. The physician will have the right to decide, on some basis, whether or not it is proper for him or her to treat unmarried individuals for infertility. But they must be prepared, regardless of the position they take, to supply responsible answers as to how they view sexuality in the unmarried and associated problems, such as infertility.

Interesting review & quite useful recommendation of how to approach ♀ who have diff expell.

THE EFFECTS OF ORAL CONTRACEPTIVES ON SEXUAL BEHAVIOR

Jean Cohen

France

Just as the different types of sexual behavior tend to influence the decision to use contraception as well as the choice of method, all contraceptives affect sexual behavior. Many contradictory conclusions have been made about the subject and particularly about the influence of oral contraceptives. Although there are many scientific papers about the effects of estroprogestins on different metabolisms or on blood circulation, very few serious studies have been done on this problem.

All types of contraception imply that woman must consider the possibility of two basic components of her sex life: the desire for intercourse and the desire to have children. Estroprogestins are 100% effective and can be taken orally. There is probably a relationship between this method of contraception and personality types, as oral contraception has a different effect on sexual behavior than do other methods. It is not our intention to claim, that the pill only has negative effects on libido. Undoubtedly, it has just as many positive effects as negative ones, but the latter are more controversial and less well-known.

MODIFICATION OF SEXUAL BEHAVIOR

An overview of extremely different effects on sexual behavior and highly varying frequencies have been reported as follows:

Frequency of Intercourse

Rice-Wray's research (1963) indicates that there is an increase

of sexual intercourse frequency in 54% of the cases with a decrease
in 3%, and no change at all for 43% of the users. According to
Wibaut (1972), the frequency of daytime intercourse increases in
30% of the cases in his research. In a double-blind statistical
survey Udry (1970) shows that the frequency of intercourse is not
modified by oral contraception. Glick (1967) finds that the frequency of sexual intercourse increases in 50% of the cases. Pasini
(1974) interviews 300 women in Geneva and notes an increase of sexual intercourse in 23% of the cases.

Orgasm

From a study based on 143 women Wibaut (1972) concludes, that
for 50% of the users orgasm had greater intensity, 33% of the women
said they had orgasm more frequently and that it coincided with
their partner's more often than before, and that only 5% of the
users in this study experienced a decrease in their capacity to
have orgasm. Cullberg et al. (1969) interviewed 99 Swedish women
and found no change at all in their sexual satisfaction. Having
studied 300 women, Pasini (1974) reports an improvement in 32.2%
of the cases.

Frigidity and Loss of Libido

Eicher (1972) interviewed 586 users and found that 35 of them
(6%) complained of a decrease in their sexual desire and had difficulty in reaching orgasm. However, the survey of a control group
shows the existence of related factors: social and psychological
problems, marital conflicts, etc.

Fucs and Coutinho (1975) also report 113 women who complained
about a decrease in sexual desire, while Cullberg (1969) records the
same problem in 5% of the cases. Pasini (1974) notes an improvement
of the libido in 12% of the cases with estroprogestins as compared to
21% with mechanical means of contraception. The cases of primary
frigidity prior to contraception are not modified. Aznar-Ramos
completed a prospective experiment with 147 women who just had a
miscarriage and ardently desired to be pregnant again. They were
given a placebo and told that it was a pill designed to block ovulation in view of an ultimate improvement in fertility. At the end
of one year period, more than 50% were pregnant, 33% did not have
any side effects, 30% complained of decreased libido, 15% of ce-
phalagia, 13% of pelvic pain, 6% of dysmenorrhea and 8% of pain
in the lumbar region, due to the pill. In Ebranti's opinion (1973)
libidinal decrease is more frequent with ethinyl estradiol than
with mestranol. Other researchers as Marcotte (1970) and Ground
et al. (1970) believe that negative effects are mainly connected
with the use of progestatives.

Satisfaction/Dissatisfaction with Sexual Intercourse

Our research on 100 users of an estroprogestative mini pill, in coded questionnaire form, which identified symptoms the women thought they had, indicated the following: 10% consider that they now have more satisfying sexual intercourse; 14% find that their relations are less satisfying , (9% attribute this to lack of response during intercourse, 5% blame it on lack of desire; 9% experience pain at penetration, 3% feel pain deeper inside, 9% have pain after intercourse). In our opinion, the latter cases seem to prove an indirect, organic effect on the sexual compatibility between partners, as well as on mycosis, vaginal dryness, etc. that we encounter frequently.

Disappearance of Pelvic Pain Related to the Cycle and Regularity of Menstrual Bleeding

Haspels (1974) reports the disappearance of dysmenorrhea, premenstrual syndromes and pain connected with ovulation that interferes with sex. The same is true of menorrhagia. These can be considered positive effects.

Male Partner's Reactions

Musaph (1969) described the aggressive attitudes of the pill users' husbands as feelings of rejection in being deprived of the decision-making role surroundings contraceptive use or non use for sexual intercourse and procreation and their feelings of doubt and jealousy. The disappearance of the pretext connected with the fear of pregnancy makes some men behave in a way that has repercussions on the couple's sex life.

In summary, the results are highly dissimilar and depend greatly on the sample, the researcher's specialty and commitment.

NEGATIVE PHARMACOLOGICAL EFFECTS

The existence of negative effects is further confirmed by the fact that after the beginning of oral contraceptive use certain changes in sexual behavior occur only after a certain period of time. Once the patient stops taking the pill, these problems disappear and the patient is in the same state as before.

Vitamin B6 Deficiency and Disorders of Tryptophane Metabolism

A relative or total deficiency in vitamin B6 causes psychic disorders, such as pessimism, unhappiness, weeping, irritability and loss of libido.

The syndrome which is discernible to a greater or lesser
degree in the case of many women taking estroprogestin seems to
result from the action of estrogens rather than that of progesterones. Adams et al. (1973) carried out a survey on 22 depressed
users: 11 of them had total vitamin B6 deficiency, confirmed by
a considerable drop in the elimination of its metabolites, as well
as by disorders in tryptophane metabolism. This amino acid is
instrumental in the synthesis of nicotinic acid and 5- hydroxytrip-
tamine, also known as serotonin. This synthesis requires the
presence of pyridoxal phosphate, an active form of vitamin B6.
Estrogens seem to favor the synthesis of the sequence leading to
nicotinic acid at the expense of the synthesis resulting in serotonin. A deficiency of serotonin was found in the cephalo-spinal
fluid of people suffering from depression and suicidal tendencies
and it was suggested that the precursors of serotonin be given as
treatment for these disorders.

Haspels (1974) studied a group of 11 women using estroprogestins a delayed-action progestin, along with a control group of
women who had an IUD. He came to the same conclusion: the urinary
elimination of the metabolites of tryptophane increases under a
treatment of estroprogestins. However, he also remarked that certain
progestins, such as medroxy-progesterone acetate had the same effects. This might be attributed to the estrogenic properties
of certain synthetic progestins. Haspels concludes that the tryptophane metabolism of women taking estroprogestin is disturbed, but
for 20% of these women there is a compensatory mechanism that comes
into play.

The administration of 100 mg of pyridoxal hydrochloride cor-
rects the biological effects and produces clinical improvement.
However, an overdose of vitamin B6 would have two unwelcomed consequences: it would orient the synthesis of tryptophane toward
serotonin to the expense of protein production, and it would facilitate the transfer of tryptophane through the cerebro-meningeal
barrier. The synthesis of serotonin would thus be hindered.

However, there is a type of pill (Ciclosequer) composed of 0.05
mg of ethinyl-estragiol + 1 mg ethynodiol diacetate and 25 mg of
pyridoxine hydrochloride which is reputed to have very few side
effects on the psychic level.

EFFECTS ON SEXUAL COMPATIBILITY

A number of direct effects, although varying with the products
and the dosage employed, can be identified: the mucus of the vagina
has a luteal, slightly congestive, sometimes atrophic appearance,
occasionally accompanied by a decrease in the amount of secretion;

cervical mucus is poor, coagulated and not very ropy, except when
sequential pills are used; there is bleeding and spotting between
periods; finally, the appearance of recurrent vaginal mycose was
mentioned by a great many authors.

EFFECTS OF OLFACTORY COMMUNICATION
AND THE CENTRAL NERVEOUS SYSTEM

Keverne (1974) showed the importance of olfactory communication by "queen substances" in monkeys. When males are in the
presence of females that have undergone ovariectomy, there is no
attraction. If, however, these females are treated with estradiol,
the males do respond, unless they have been made anosmic. Once
the anosmia is cured, sexual attraction is reestablished. If some
vaginal secretion is taken from the females that have been treated
and it is introduced into non-treated females, the male monkeys
will become sexually excited. Another experiment shows that the
male's sexual performance can be improved by giving progesterone
to the female.

In man, many studies have shown how hormones and the particular phase of the menstrual cycle can influence the perception of
odors. These differences reflect the equilibrium between the positive effects of the adrenergic central processes and the inhibiting effects of the cholinergic processes. It is well known that
the latter are influenced by sexual steroids.

The odor of vaginal secretions plays an important role in
human sexuality. To quote Zwang (1976), "This cocktail combines
the tangy bitterness of the vagina and the musky sebum of the vulva,
sugar and salt, glycogen and lactic acid, yoghurt and milk. There
is no end of comparisons, from the warm seas to seashells, none
of which quite manage to render this inimitable uniqueness." Huggins and Preti (1976) studied the volatile constituents of human
vaginal secretions by means of gas chromatography and spectrophoto-
metry throughout the cycle. Lactic acid, acetic acid and urea
undergo cyclic variations of concentration. Aliphatic volatile
C_2-C_5 acids that bring on the sexual response in male rhesus monkeys
were found during the period of ovulation and in the luteal phase.

The role of sexual steroids in generating sexual behavior was
thoroughly explored in the animal world. In rats, the positive
action of estrogens is sufficient to trigger a lordosis for females
that have had their ovaries removed. Progesterone has a two-stage
action: instigating then inhibiting. Hormones act at successive
sections of the spinal cord and the brain stem and of the hypothalamus
and the rhinencephalon and also at the level peripheral sensory
receptors.

Although no such surveys have been carried out with humans, various authors mentioned by Klotz (1974) call attention to the fact that estrogens cause the libido to increase, while progesterones cause it to decrease.

Ferin (1974) postulates the following hypothesis: testosterone and DHT acting on unspecified central nervous structures constitute the hormonal basis of the sex drive. By increasing the vagina's receptivity for the phallus, estrogens could, secondarily modify sexual desire through actual sexual fulfillment. Owing to their anti-androgenic property and as a consequence of their negative feedback on LH secretion, progesterone and progestin would reduce the libido. Unfortunately, surveys on the proportion of testosterone and DHT contained in the plasma under oral contraception are as yet too few and far too contradictory.

EFFECTS CONNECTED WITH THE
SYMBOLIC SIGNIFICANCE OF THE PILL

Many authors have reported the effects of oral contraceptives on sexuality and have discussed the symbolic meaning of the pill. The pill destroys the equilibrium between motherhood and sex by inhibiting at least temporarily the procreative aspect of sexual relations. Some women have a more satisfying sex life under oral contraception, while others have ambiguous attitudes to the pill.

According to Maruani (1974), women have the same attitude to the pill as babies to their mother's breast: they value it as a source of pleasure, but wish to devour it at the same time, hence a feeling of guilt and the danger of being devoured. Half the women who had tried the pill before consulting Maruani (1974) were frigid. In the author's opinion, the fact that frigid women prefer the pill is a proof of these reassessments. Other psychological symptoms the pill is accused of being responsible for seem to provide other evidence as the user would end up resembling a bad mother; she would be fat, bald, have varicose veins and even cancer.

It is known that the pill is more often preferred by women who understand little about their genitalia; they have misconceptions about genital anatomy and refuse local and mechanical contraceptives. Thanks to use of the pill, they can go on ignoring their sexual organs (provided there are no side effects) and thus maintain the ambiguous awareness. Consequently, the choice of the pill as a method of contraception seems to reflect a predisposition to disorders of sexual behavior.

The desire to have a child is another aspect that interferes with sexual intercourse. Oral contraception is 100% effective, so women are conscious of being <u>totally</u> deprived of their status as

potential mothers (this is not the case with other means of contraception). According to Melon (1972) "for women, whose phallic
needs happen to be satisfied through procreation, even the temporary
suppression of the possibility to have children would result in a
loss of self-esteem and ultimately, depression... The women for
whom pregnancy is a state of happy fulfillment are the least apt
to tolerate the pill that blocks ovulation, precisely because this
pill symbolically (and in reality) prevents them from becoming
pregnant."

CONCLUSIONS

The information reported tends to show that for the time
being there are no satisfactory studies from which the effects of
oral contraception on sexual behavior could be objectively evaluated.
The presently available works are quite dissimilar and they still
show the influence of the authors' own philosophical frame of reference. It is significant, that psychiatrists and psychologists
report more on psychological effects, while gynecologists report
primarily the physiological occurences. The practician's own
behavior at the moment of giving a prescription and later at the
time of subsequent check-ups, has an effect on the percentage of
women incurring ill-effects. One way to avoid this risk of an
intervening variable would be in the future to have the women fill
out a questionnaire. This must be done systematically and on a
large scale. However, experience indicates that many women refuse
to answer questions concerning sex.

There is not a single survey exploring the influence of different steroids and their doses, however, judging from my practical
experience, some disorders can be eliminated simply by changing the
progestin's dosage or composition.

RECOMMENDATIONS

When a patient using oral contraception expresses negative
sex behavioral effects, an understanding of the exact nature of
her problems is indicated. If the disorders are recent and have
never been noticed before, and if from the point of view of general
health the pill is well tolerated then the following approaches
are evaluated: a) if there is an element of depression, we suggest
a one-month test treatment of vitamin B6; b) if there is a notion
of sexual incompatibility, we systematically search for mycosis
and prescribe a local test treatment which consists of estrogen
capsules and antifungal medicine; c) if the patient complains of
general malaise, we advise her to switch from a traditional pill
to a minidosed one with a different progestin, or else to a sequential pill that has the advantage of providing only estrogens

in the first part of the cycle, thereby increasing cervical secretions that have a positive influence on sexual harmony.

However, if the patient expresses her reluctance to take the
pill, we suggest that she try an IUD, if possible. In each case
we must try to make the patient aware of the various considerations implied by her choice. She should be directed to a counsel-
lor or a psychologist if she thinks she might benefit from their
advice.

Unfortunately, these disorders often occur in women who have
never been pregnant or given birth and we must change the pill's
composition or dosage. Oral contraception must not be interrupted
unless a substitute is found.

Present information does not allow definite conclusions about
the frequency of positive or negative effects oral contraception
might have on sexual behavior.

The existence of ill-effects is beyond doubt, although the
predominance of the biochemical or the psychological mechanism
is not understood.

REFERENCES

Adams, P.W., Wynn, W. and Rose, B. P. (1973). Lancet, 1: 897-904.

Cullberg, J. et al. (1969). Acta Psychiat. Scand. 45: 259.

Ebranti, E. (1973). Psicopatologia e contraccettivi orali. Ses-
    suologia 14 (2): 16.

Eicher, W. (1972). Munch. Med. Wschr. 114: 1286-1289.

Ferin, J. and Veldekens, P. (1974). Determinisme hormonal du désir
    sexuel chez la femme. Congrès International de Sexologie
    Médicale, Paris.

Fucs, G.B. and Coutinho, E.M. (1975). Estudo sobre o tratamento
    das alteracoes da resposta sexual causadas pelo uso de
    anticonceptionais. Reproduction 2 (2): 97-104.

Grounds, D. et al. (1970). The contraceptive pill side effects
    and personality. Brit. J. Psychiat. 116: 169.

Haspels, A.A. (1974). Oral contraceptives and sexuality. Inter-
    national Congress of Medical Sexology, Paris.

Huggins, G.R. and Preti, G. (1976). Volatile constituents of human vaginal secretions. Amer. J. Obstetr. Gyn. 1: 129-136.

Keverne, E.B. (1974). 8th International Congress of Fertility and Sterility.

Klotz, M. (1974). Le rôle des hormones sexuelles dans la sexualité. Contraception-Fertilité-Sexualité, 2 (5): 315.

Marcotte, D.B. (1970). Psychophysiologic changes accompanying oral contraceptive use. Brit. J. Psych. 116: 165.

Maruani, G., Lagroua Weill Halle, M.A., Atlan, P. (1974). Cent premières consultations de contraception en centre spécialisé. Rev. Franc. Gynec 69 (12): 731-735.

Melon, J. (1972). Incidences psychopathologiques de la contraception orale. Revue médicale de Liège, XXVII (11): 362-365.

Musaph, H. (1969). Psychopathologische aspecten van oral contraceptie. Ned. T. Geneeskunde 113: 1988-1994.

Pasini, W. (1974). Contraception et plaisir. In Abraham, G. and Pasini, W. (eds.), Introduction à la Sexologie Médicale, Plon, Paris.

Rice-Wray, E., Goldzieher, J., Aranda-Rosell, A. (1963). Oral progestatives in fertility control, a comparative study. Fertil. Steril. 14: 402.

Szwang, G. (1976). L'odorat dans la sexualité humaine. Contraception, Fertilité, Sexualité 4 (4): 275-281.

Udry, R.J. and Morris, N. (1970). Effects of contraceptive pills on the distribution of sexual activity in the menstrual cycle. Nature, 227: 502.

Wibaut, F.P. (1972). Hormonale anticonceptie, Stafler Leiden.

Subtracting Evidence of ∧ ⌐ in testosterone levels in rats following vasectomy. ∨ Human studies contradicting — many neg.

POSSIBLE EFFECTS OF VASECTOMY ON SEXUAL FUNCTION[1]

Gordon A. Kinson

Canada

Reference to the effects of occlusion of the vas deferens was made more than 200 years ago by the English surgeon, John Hunter (1775). Some years later, Cooper (1830) experimented with dogs and compared the effects of unilateral vasoligation to occlusion of the vascular supply to the contralateral testis. He subsequently noted that, whereas the testis deprived of its blood supply became gangrenous and necrotic, the gonad subjected to blockade of its ductal outflow retained a healthy appearance. Guyon (1883), a French physician, was then soon to claim that blockade of the vas deferens led to atrophy of the prostate. This encouraged surgeons of the day to use such procedures in an effort to treat conditions involving enlarged prostate glands and diseased epididymides. The practice has continued into modern times even though it was never conclusively demonstrated that vasectomy altered prostate size in man. Only quite recently has evidence emerged to suggest that prostate function is affected after vasectomy. Renewed interest in the possible effects of vasectomy was generated by Steinach (1920) who claimed that vasoligation produced rejuvenating effects in aging men and led to hypertrophy of the interstitium and germinal atrophy of the rat testis. This implication that blockade of the vas deferens leads to enhanced testicular endocrine function was then to be refuted by Moore (1932) and Young (1933) and vasectomy was somewhat ignored until the 1950s when rams were vasectomized to act as "teasers" for the detection of estrus in ewes (Webster, 1954).

---

[1] The financial support of this work by the Medical Research Council (Canada) and the Bickell Foundation (Toronto) is gratefully acknowledged.

It was in the 1950s that some of the eastern nations, faced with severe overpopulation and nutritional problems, began to adopt vasectomy as part of their family planning programs. The acceptance of vasectomy as a safe and convenient means of male fertility control is illustrated by the fact that 6 million were performed in India alone between 1968 and 1972. In addition, the application of vasectomy has exceeded numbers of female sterilizations and intrauterine device insertions for several years now in countries such as Pakistan, Bangladesh and Nepal. In Europe and North America, vasectomy began to take hold in the late 1960s and appears to have reached a maximum level in 1971 in the USA and Canada when 750,000 and 100,000 were performed respectively. By 1974, the numbers had dropped considerably to 500,000 and 50,000 respectively in these countries.

The criteria for an ideal contraceptive method for men are generally considered to be: (1) reliability, (2) ease of application, (3) reversibility, (4) maintenance of accessory sex characteristics with special reference to libido and (5) the absence of significant, untoward side effects. There can be little doubt that vasectomy meets the first two of these requirements and, indeed, current statistics for failure rates of available methods of contraception and fertility control clearly show that vasectomy is the most effective method in current usage. Vasectomy is essentially a reversible procedure, as surgical resection of the vas deferens has met with considerable success, particularly in recent years. From a re-fertility standpoint, however, it would be inaccurate at this point in time to regard the method as reversible on account of the antisperm antibody response to vasectomy and the significant incidence of infertility in men following resection of the vasii.

A certain degree of concern over possible side effects to vasectomy involving the maintenance of accessory sex characteristics and gonadal function has attracted the interest of investigators during the 1970s, both from the basic sciences and clinical environments. By 1972, the entire literature concerning vasectomy and vasoligation consisted of approximately 400 published reports of which most were devoted to the psychosocial and minor surgical aspects of the operation. A workshop conference was convened in December 1971 under the sponsorship of the Agency for International Development (Johnson, 1972) to consider the current status and future directions for research, in relation to reversible male sterilization. It was concluded that several areas merited further research and, while recognizing the limitations in terms of clinical relevance, the importance of pursuing controlled animal experimentation was pointed out. Research was encouraged into granuloma formation and ductal dilation and the possible involvement of hydrostatic pressure development or denervation of the vas deferens.

Further study of the fate of spermatozoa, functions of the epididymis and the immunological consequences of vasectomy was considered desirable. The possibility of alteration in testicular hormonogenesis and systemic metabolic consequences after vasectomy were additional areas which have since been investigated in this laboratory over the last 3 years.

While controversy continues as to whether or not vasectomy leads to deranged testicular function in the mammalian organism, the emergence in the literature of clinical studies of hormone levels in vasectomized men would seem to indicate that such a possibility is being seriously considered. The available clinical data is largely negative in nature but, studies to date have been exclusively of short-term duration. The appearance of this information is, however, highly encouraging for several reasons and one is tempted to suggest that clinical interest has been provoked, to some degree at least, by the somewhat controversial reports of animal invesigations. In keeping with the clinical theme of this Congress, a description of the human aspects would seem appropriate before presenting the animal work that has been carried out in my laboratory and those of other investigators.

ENDOCRINE CONSEQUENCES OF VASECTOMY IN MEN

Follow-up of the endocrine consequences of vasectomy in men has, in most instances, entailed the measurement of follicle-stimulating hormone (FSH), luteinizing hormone (LH) and testosterone in the blood. In a few studies, plasma estradiol and prolactin levels have been determined after vasectomy. Blood titers of these hormones are reported to be unchanged or within the normal ranges by Weiland et al., (1972), Varma et al. (1975), Johnsonbaugh et al. (1975) and Skegg et al. (1976) when determined at various intervals to 5 years post-vasectomy. Interestingly, Hagedoorn and co-workers (1974) have examined spermatogenesis within 7 years of vasectomy to find no lack of germinal elements on histological specimens from testes of vasectomized men, but a significant tendency for spermatozoa to be associated with the Sertoli cells near the basement membrane rather than in their usual luminal location was apparent. This may reflect subtle changes in the spermatogenic cycle of man leading to more drastic effects on spermatogenesis which will only be revealed through more longer-term investigation. Spermatogenesis has been studied in greater detail in several animal species for considerably longer periods of the reproductive lifespan of the organism, post-vasectomy. Species differences are clearly evident here and, while spermatogenesis appears not to suffer after vasectomy in some animals, it is seriously impaired in guinea pigs and transiently inhibited in dogs and rabbits.

Several groups of workers have reported a tendency for LH
levels to be enhanced in the short-term after vasectomy (Rosemberg
et al., 1974; Whitby et al., 1976) and Smith and coworkers (1976)
have also recorded elevations in blood testosterone within 2 years
of surgery. While these changes were statistically significant,
the levels of hormones in vasectomized subjects were invariably
still within the normal ranges. Several tentative interpretations
can be applied to these findings such as, short-term stimulatory
effects of vasectomy on pituitary-testicular endocrine activity or
the beginnings of end-organ (testis) failure giving rise to higher
levels of gonadotrophin due to lack of feedback action. Kobrinsky
and associates (1976) have reported acute suppression of FSH levels
in vasectomized men without concomitant elevations in circulating
testosterone. They suggest that their data are compatible with
either diminished production of a positive feedback factor or
enhanced production of a negative feedback factor following vasectomy. They favored the latter hypothesis and the increased resorption after vasectomy of the products of the germinal epithelium
containing the FSH-specific negative feedback factor, the all-
illusive "Inhibin." The results of a detailed study carried out
in Diczfalusy's laboratory have just been published, where the
levels of several hormones in the plasma of 20 Mexican men were
determined, both before and at regular intervals to 12 months after
vasectomy (Purvis et al., 1976). No consistent changes in plasma
FSH, LH and testosterone were found, but significant decreases in
plasma levels of pregnenolone, dehydroepiandrosterone and androstenedione were recorded. In addition, vasectomy was associated
with decrease in the seminal plasma concentrations of dihydro-
testosterone, androstenedione and dehydroepiandrosterone, with
increase in estradiol. These changes in hormone titers were of a
gradual nature and it was suggested that vasectomy might be associated with long-term alterations in adrenocortical activity, as
well as with effects upon the epididymal-gonadal elaboration of
hormones. This group emphasized the need for the immediate initiation of large scale, multi-center studies of long-term duration
and the importance of employing carefully-matched control groups
of non-vasectomized males.

ENDOCRINE CONSEQUENCES OF VASECTOMY IN ANIMALS

In 1972 evidence appeared to indicate that vasectomy in adult
dogs and rats gave rise to stimulation of testicular endocrine activity. At 2 months after vasectomy, Kothari and Mishra (1972) found
increased Leydig cell volumes in dog testis and Thakur and coworkers
(1972) observed increases in maltase activity and fructose concentrations in the accessory sex organs of the rat. Leydig hyperplasia of
the rat testis was later reported by Easterday et al. (1973), with some
elevation in circulating testosterone. Concurrently, two independent studies of longer-term duration in the rat did much to draw
attention to the possibility of severe detrimental consequences of

vasectomy on the function of the testis. Lacy's group in London examined hormonogenesis in vitro with testis preparations from vasectomized and sham-operated rats after 1, 3 and 12 months to find progressive alterations in steroid metabolism (Collins, Bell and Tsang, 1972; Lacy and Collins, 1973). It was concluded that vasectomy in adult rats gave rise to premature aging of the testis with changes in steroid metabolism which constituted an acceleration of the changes that normally take place with advancing age. Sackler and coworkers (1973) then applied vasectomy and vasoligation to immature rats and after 7 months found decline in urinary 17-oxosteroids with marked discoloration and atrophy of the testes. However, Neaves (1975) and Mock et al. (1975) have since refuted claims that vasectomy leads to impairment of testis function in the rat, based upon their observations of lack of significant alteration in circulating testosterone within 7 months of surgery. Significant atrophy of the prostate gland following vasectomy (Mock et al., 1975) was explained in terms of the interference with the ductal supply, rather than systemic concentrations of androgen hormones to the accessory sex structures. Nickell and associates (1974) had previously provided, however, further evidence of degenerative effects on both testicular endocrine and gametogenic function, together with alterations in lipid metabolism and impaired hepatic enzyme activity, 12 months after vasectomy in adult rats.

Our initial investigation into the long-term actions of vasectomy in adult rats provided more direct evidence of serious decline in endocrine activity through the measurement of androgen levels in testicular venous blood. Eighteen months after vasectomy, marked reductions of testosterone and androstenedione in testicular vein blood were observed and these changes were accompanied by significant atrophy of the testis, ventral prostate and kidneys (Kinson and Layberry, 1975). There occured some degree of pituitary enlargement and vasectomized rats displayed obvious obesity, possessing excessive quantities of abdominal "fatty" tissue. The general appearance of these vasectomized rats amounted to what might be described as premature aging of the animal organism. Further investigation at regular intervals after vasectomy, for a period of one year, was then pursued in an effort to clarify the course of events leading to the eventual demise of the testis.

All studies to date in this laboratory have involved vasectomy and sham-operations by the abdominal approach. It can be legitimately argued that this does not provide the best model for clinical extrapolation but this approach was preferred in order to avoid risk of traumatization of the testes, the primary focus of the investigations. Blood samples have been collected for hormone analysis from the testicular vein, tail vein or the right ventricle. Plasma androgen concentrations have been determined by radioimmunoassay and spermatogenesis was assessed by conventional histological pro-

cedures.   Adrenocortical status has been monitored by spectrofluo-
rometric measurement of circulating corticosterone, the major glu-
cocorticoid of the rat.

   Monthly examination after vasectomy of young adult rats (Kinson
and Narbaitz, 1976a) has revealed acute enhancement of androgen
status, with significant elevation in circulating testosterone at
2 months following surgery.   The effect was transient in nature
since, one month later, blood levels of hormone in vasectomized
rats were virtually identical to those of control animals.   After
6 and 7 months there occurred some tendency for testosterone levels
to be lower than control values but differences were not significant.
Plasma testosterone was significantly reduced at the 11 month interval following vasectomy.   A comparison of the temporal changes
in androgen levels in control and vasectomized rats might suggest
that vasectomy did give rise to some interference or instability
of the peak in testosterone rhythm which appeared at 6 to 8 months
following the surgery.   Furthermore, these events coincided with
an elevation in circulating corticosterone which was evident at 6
months after vasectomy.   This was the only significant alteration
in plasma corticoid level over the entire 12 month period of investigation and may reflect some change in adrenocortical activity,
perhaps in response to subtle alterations in testicular endocrine
activity.   In order to ascertain whether or not this actually involved increase in the adrenal secretion of androgens merits the
further study of hormone levels in adrenal venous blood in order
to circumvent possible steroid metabolic influences.   This is particularly important since Nickell and coworkers (1974) have demonstrated that vasectomy causes alterations in hepatic enzyme activities, the liver being the primary site of metabolism of steroid
hormones.

   Functions of the testis were directly evaluated at 4, 8 and
12 months following vasectomy.   Endocrine activity was stimulated
in the short-term, at 4 months, as witnessed by significantly
higher levels of testosterone and androstenedione in vasectomized
rats (Kinson, Narbaitz and Bruce, 1976).   Subsequently, androgen
levels did not differ significantly from control values at 8 and
12 months.   At the latter time interval, however, significant
atrophy of the testis had occurred and spermatogenesis had been
seriously influenced in one-third of the vasectomized rats.   Inhibitory actions upon gametogenesis were characterized by atrophy
of the seminiferous tubules with a marked thickening of the basement membrane and extensive destruction of the germinal epithelium.
Such morphological changes are considered to be a feature of the
natural aging process of the mammalian testis (Bishop, 1970).

   To summarize the implications of these investigations with
the adult rat; vasectomy is followed by short-term increases in

testicular endocrine function and systemic androgen status. If
similar clinical findings are eventually confirmed, this may provide some explanation for the claims, by many individuals, of increased sexual activity after vasectomy which was originally con-
tended by Steinach around 1920. Subsequently, there follows long-
term decline in testis function which starts to become manifest at
around 12 months after vasectomy, progressing towards serious demise of the testis as a functional organ. Several independent
reports have appeared in the literature over the last few years
which provide support for this hypothesis. It would appear that
the long-term consequences of vasectomy, in rats, amounts to a
premature aging of the testis involving impairment of spermatogenesis and the creation of hormonal imbalances which are conducive
to accelerated aging of the organism. The loss of androgens with
age and its relation to muscle wastage and osteoporosis is well
recognized and the involvement of several other hormones in lipid
metabolism together with the increasing incidence of cardiovascular
sclerotic conditions in man prompts further thought for research
into several areas related to the consequences of vasectomy in
animals and man. Since the mammalian testis undergoes a natural
and progressive decline in function with advancing age, it is quite
conceivable that the sensitivity of the gonadal and reproductive
system to vasectomy might be related to the age of the organism
at the time of surgery. This raises the clinical question as to
whether or not there might be a critical age range during adulthood after which vasectomy, in its present form, might lead to
accelerated effects on gonadal activities and the subsequent health
of the individual. There is currently no suggestion in the literature that the question of age at surgery has been considered in the
study of vasectomized men. Experiments are now in progress with
rats in my laboratory to ascertain if age is a major factor in determining the nature and course of events after vasectomy. Some
results of the short-term aspects of the investigation are available
(Table 1) and, indeed, provide support for this contention (Kinson
and Narbaitz, 1976b). Adult rats have been vasectomized at 10, 20,
30 and 50 weeks of age for subsequent study at several time intervals following the surgery. Investigation of possible effects on
lipid composition in the blood and tissues, the histology of the
heart and aorta and muscle metabolism is envisaged, in addition to
further investigation of changes in hormonal status and testicular
functions. Observations from the initial 2 months study have provided confirmation of our earlier findings of enhanced androgen
status after vasectomy in young adult rats. Vasectomy in 10 week
old animals led to significant increase in mixed venous testosterone and was accompanied by hypertrophy of the ventral prostate
gland. Vasectomy was without effect upon the weight of the kidneys,
testis weight, spermatogenesis and circulating corticosterone. Essentially similar results were noted in rats vasectomized at 20
weeks of age, although the elevations in circulating testosterone

TABLE 1

INFLUENCE OF AGE AT SURGERY ON RESPONSES TO VASECTOMY AFTER TWO MONTHS

Experimental groups	Body weight (g) at		Organ weights (mg/100 g body)				Circulating hormone (µg/100 ml plasma)	
	Surgery	Study	Testis	Kidneys	V. Prostate	Pituitary	Testosterone	Corticosterone
10 weeks old at surgery								
Sham controls (10)	320±4	503±18	354±12	647±13	100±7.5**	2.85±0.22	0.610±0.153	39.1±2.9
Vasectomized (10)	313±3	462±9	363±10	655±16	128±6.5	3.25±0.14	0.769±0.071*	35.2±3.3
20 weeks old at surgery								
Sham controls (9)	429±12	574±13	321±13	611±11	108±7.8	2.80±0.08	0.205±0.028	34.1±3.0
Vasectomized (10)	425±14	561±21	316±13	597±17	138±7.8**	2.82±0.11	0.301±0.044	38.5±2.6
30 weeks old at surgery								
Sham controls (7)	569±19	633±26	292±14	626±30	97±10.4	2.93±0.17	0.211±0.056	32.2±4.8
Vasectomized (10)	527±14	604±15	290±18	627±20	81±6.9	2.91±0.17	0.172±0.022	29.7±2.3
50 weeks old at surgery								
Sham controls (8)	608±12	657±13	277±18	613±17	110±10.1	2.90±0.32	0.233±0.034	30.6±3.2
Vasectomized (9)	576±9	628±7	261±19	659±17	83±10.3	2.84±0.15	0.252±0.054	29.3±1.2

All values are the mean ± standard error. Numbers in parentheses () are the numbers of rats in the group.
* indicates significantly different from control value with P less than 0.05
** indicates significantly different from control value with P less than 0.02

did not quite achieve statistical significance. Quite different
responses, however, were obtained with animals which received the
surgery at 30 and 50 weeks of age. There were no significant elevations in blood testosterone and, in fact, some degree of prostatic atrophy, although not significant, could be indicative of
suppression of testicular endocrine activity. There were definite
signs of deleterious consequences to gametogenesis at this comparatively early period after vasectomy in older rats. Two vasectomized rats from both age groups presented histological evidence
of extensive destruction of the germinal epithelium in many seminiferous tubules. Once again there was atrophy of the tubules and
thickening of the basement membrane perhaps denoting a marked acceleration of aging of the testis. These rats also possessed huge
unilateral cysts of the epididymis which were 2 to 4 times the
weight of the testis and were filled with green pus. Histology
revealed that these structures were full of spermatozoa, debris
and blood cells. Erosion of the epididymis may have been initiated
by the swift intraductal development of hydrostatic pressure (Howards
and Johnson, 1974) following blockade of the outflow of the vas deferens. These findings conceivably bear witness to an increased
susceptibility with age of the gonadal-epididymal complex of the
rat to the detrimental effects of vasectomy. Damage to the epididymis did not occur with young adult animals in our earlier investigations, even at 12 and 18 months after vasectomy. The completion
of these investigations will hopefully further clarify the possible
importance of age in the consequences of vasectomy, at least in the
experimental rat. Investigation along similar lines with vasectomized men is also envisaged.

REFERENCES

Bishop, M.W.H. (1970). Ageing and reproduction in the male. J.
Reprod. Fert., Suppl. 12: 65-87.

Collins, P.M., Bell, J.B.G. and Tsang, W.N. (1972). J. Endocrinol.
55 (2): XVIII-XIX.

Cooper, A.C. (1830). In Observations on the structure and diseases of the testis. In Cooper B.B. (ed.), A Collection of
the lectures of A.C. Cooper, Churchill, London, 1941.

Easterday, J.L., Nickell, M.D., Fahim, Z., Fahim, M.S. (1973).
Effects of vasectomy on endocrine and hepatic function. Res.
Commun. Chem. Pathol. Pharmacol. 6 (1): 301-312.

Guyon, F. (1883). In The History of experimental and clinical
work on vasectomy. Jhaver, P.S. and Ohri, B.B., 1960. J.
Intern. Coll. Surgeons. 33 (4): 482-485.

Hagedoorn, J. and Davis, J.E. (1974). Fine structure of the semini-
    ferous tubules after vasectomy in man. The Physiologist, 17
    (3): 236.

Howards, S.S. and Davis, J.E. (1974). Micropuncture studies of the
    hydrostatic intratubular pressure in the seminiferous tubu-
    les and the tubules of the epididymis of the hamster before
    and after vasectomy. Program of 7th Annual Meeting of the
    Soc. Study Reprod. Ottawa, Canada, Aug. 19-22.

Hunter, J. (1775). In, Vasectomy-reviewed. Hackett, R.E. and Water-
    house, K. (1973). Amer. J. Obstet. Gynecol. 116 (3): 438-
    455).

Johnson, D.S. (1972). Reversible male sterilization: Current sta-
    tus and future directions. Contraception 5: 327-338.

Johnsonbaugh, R.E., O'Connell, K., Engel, S.B., Edson, M. and Sode,
    J. (1975). Plasma testosterone, luteinizing hormone, and
    follicle-stimulating hormone after vasectomy. Fertil.
    Steril. 26 (4): 329-330.

Kinson, G.A. and Layberry, R.A. (1975). Long-term endocrine res-
    ponses to vasectomy in the adult rat. Contraception 11 (2):
    143-150.

Kinson, G.A. and Narbaitz, R. (1976a). Effects of vasectomy on
    testicular function in rats. J. Endocrinol. 71 (2): 100 –
    101.

Kinson, G.A. and Narbaitz, R. (1976b). Short-term gonadal respon-
    ses in rats vasectomized at different ages. Proc. Can. Fed.
    Biol. Soc. 19, abs. 322.

Kinson, G.A., Narbaitz, R. and Bruce, N. (1976). Gonadal function
    following vasectomy in the rat. Intern. J. Fertil. (In
    press).

Kobrinsky, N.L., Winter, J.S.D., Reyes, F.I. and Faiman, C. (1976).
    Endocrine effects of vasectomy in man. Fertil. Steril. 27 (2):
    152-156.

Kothari, L.K. and Mishra, P. (1972). Vasectomy and the endocrine
    function of the testis. Lancet I: 438.

Lacy, D. and Collins, P.M. (1973). Hormones and contraception in
    the male and the relative merits of hormonal control and
    vasectomy. J. Reprod. Fert., Suppl. 18: 185-198.

Mock, E.J., Kamel, F., Wright, W.W. and Frankel, A.I. (1975). Plasma testosterone levels in vasectomized rats. J. Reprod. Fert. 44: 575-578.

Moore, C.R. (1932). In, Sex and Internal Secretions, 1st Edition, ed. by Allen, E: 281-371. Williams and Wilkins, Baltimore.

Neaves, W.B. (1975). The androgen status of vasectomized rats. Endocrinology 96 (2): 529-534.

Nickell, M.D., Russell, R.L., Fahim, Z. and Fahim, M.S. (1974). Long-term effect of vasectomy on reproduction and liver function. Fed. Proc. 33: 531.

Purvis, K., Saksena, S.K., Cekan, Z., Diczfalusy, E. and Giner, J. (1976). Endocrine effects of vasectomy. Clin. Endocrinol. 5: 263-272.

Rosemberg, E., Marks, S.C., Howard, P.J. and James, L.P. (1974). Serum levels of follicle stimulating and luteinizing hormones before and after vasectomy in men. J. Urol. 111: 626-629.

Sackler, A.M., Weltman, A.S., Pandhi, V. and Schwartz, R. (1973). Gonadal effects of vasectomy and vasoligation. Science 179: 293-295.

Skegg, D.C.G., Mathews, J.D., Gillebaud, J., Vessey, M.P., Biswas, S., Ferguson, K.M., Kitchin, Y., Mansfield, M.D., and Sommerville, I.F. (1976). Hormonal assessment before and after vasectomy. Brit. Med. J. 1: 621-622.

Smith, K.D., Tcholakian, R.K., Chowdhury, M. and Steinberger, E. (1976). An investigation of plasma hormone levels before and after vasectomy. Fertil. Steril. 27 (2): 145-151.

Steinach, E. (1920). Rejuvenation by means of experimental animation of the ageing sex gland. Arch. Entrw. Mech. Org. 46: 553-618.

Thakur, A.N., Sheth, A.R., and Rao, S.S. (1972). Biochemical studies on rat testes and sex accessory organs after vasoligation operation. Fertil. Steril. 23 (11): 834-837.

Varma, M.M., Varma, R.R., Johanson, A.J., Kowarski, A. and Migeon, C.J. (1975). Long-Term effects of vasectomy on pituitary-gonadal function in man. J. Clin. Endocrinol. Metab. 40: 868-871.

Webster, W.M. (1954). Vasectomy-how and why. N.Z. vet. J. 2: 10-
       13.

Weiland, R.G., Hallberg, M.C., Zorn, E.M., Klein, D.E., and Luria,
       S.S. (1972). Pituitary-gonadal function before and after
       vasectomy. Fertil. Steril. 23 (10): 779-781.

Whitby, M., Gordon, R.D., Seeney, N. and Thomas, M.J. (1976).
       Vasectomy: a long-term study of its effects on testicular
       endocrine function in man. Andrologia 8 (1): 55-59.

Young, W.C. (1933). Resorption of the efferent ducts of the mouse
       and its bearing on the ligation of the testicular-epididymal
       system. Z. Zellforsch. mikrosk. anat. 17: 729-757.

FACTORS AFFECTING THE USE OF CONTRACEPTION IN THE NONMARITAL CONTEXT

Constance Lindemann

United States

This paper, part of a larger social-psychological study of the birth control behavior of young, unmarried women (Lindemann, 1974), is based on interviews with 2500 young women between the ages of 13 and 26 in the Free Clinics and Public Health Youth Clinics in the Los Angeles, California metropolitan area. Its purpose was to 1) isolate the relevant variables in the birth control behavior of young, unmarried women, 2) generate categories of behavior and hypotheses that would help to explain this behavior, and 3) integrate these categories and hypotheses in a theoretical model of the social-psychological processes of birth control behavior in the nonmarital context.

The model that was derived from this data states that young, unmarried, sexually active women go through three stages of birth control behavior: the natural stage when no contraceptives are used; the peer stage when methods learned from peers are used; and the expert stage when experts and professionals are consulted. Each of these stages is characterized by typical birth control behavior along with conditions that influence this behavior at given stages.

This is a social process consisting of a complex of patterns of behavior that has evolved and is continuing to evolve in the course of finding a solution to the problem of avoiding pregnancy. It has evolved in response to perceptions and interpretations of the social environment in the absence of an institutionalized norm for birth control behavior. This gap in the social structure has been filled by the actors on the scene in the course of their day-to-day behavior.

METHOD

The method that was used to generate this model and its numerous hypotheses was Grounded Theory. This a systematic method for data collection, coding and analysis of qualitative data. The strategies of the method are described at greater length in <u>Discovery of Grounded Theory</u> by Barney Glaser and Anselm Strauss (1967) and, together with its application for the present research, in <u>Birth Control and Unmarried Young Women</u> by the author of this paper (Lindemann, 1974).

The major three strategies of the method are 1) theoretical sampling; 2) constant comparative analysis; and 3) simultaneous collection, coding and analysis of data.

In theoretical sampling the comparison groups are not chosen by preplanned design as in research studies that are designed for the verification of hypotheses. Groups are chosen in the course of the research in order to answer research questions that arise in the process of the research. The choice of the first group is based on the investigator's interest in the problem area to be studied. Thereafter, the choice of groups is based on the emerging theory in order to help generate emerging categories, develop to the fullest extent as many properties of the categories as possible, and help relate categories to each other and to their properties. This differs from research for verification of hypotheses where the selection of groups and categories to be studied takes place prior to data collection.

Constant comparative analysis is the continuous comparison of data from these groups. The comparison takes place throughout the course of the research. Again, this differs from research for the verification of hypotheses in which data comparison takes place only after all the data has been collected.

The comparison takes place by the simultaneous collection, coding and analysis of data. These three tasks are intertwined and constitute a process which is continuous throughout the course of the research. This means that the data is collected and immediately coded and compared with data already collected.

In this way the theoretical model is systematically worked out in relation to the data. This insures that the theoretical model with its categories and hypotheses is relevant to and has explanatory power for the study problem.

FINDINGS

This paper will present some of the factors that inhibit the

use of contraception in the first stage of birth control behavior
when no contraception is used.

Some of the factors that inhibit contraception in the first
stage, the natural stage are: patterns of sexual behavior, level
of awareness, indecision about sex and contraception, aspects of
the boy-girl relationship and parental attitudes and behavior.

Patterns of Sexual Behavior

Patterns of sexual behavior are in a state of constant flux
in the nonmarital context. These changes in sexual behavior in
turn, exert a powerful influence on birth control behavior. Birth
control needs change in accord with changes in sexual patterns.
There are several dimensions of sexual activity that influence
birth control behavior. These dimensions are predictability of
coitus, belief in the spontaneity and naturalness of sex, frequency
of coitus, type of sexual activity, and duration of sexual activity.
In the natural stage the very nature of sexual activity is not
conducive to the use of contraceptives.

Predictability. Coitus is unpredictable in the early phases
of sexual activity. Contraceptives are not used at the first
coital experience because intercourse is unplanned and unantici-
pated. The range of circumstances surrounding first coitus is
enormous (Lowry, 1969; Eastman, 1972). Where there are no immediate and concrete prospects of sexual intercourse, there is
reluctance to prepare with a contraceptive. This lack of predictability (of knowing if, when, and with whom sexual intercourse
will take place) inhibits the use of birth control.

There are three components to predictability: time, place
and partner. One or all three of them may be unpredictable. There
is no way of knowing when a meeting will take place that will develop into a sexual encounter. There may be no suitable place (a
place with no parents) available. If a place is available the
time may still be unpredictable. If there is no present involvement with a partner, there is no way to predict with whom a sexual
involvement will develop. All of these aspects of unpredictability
inhibit the use of contraceptives.

Spontaneity and Naturalness. The second dimension of sexual
activity that influences behavior in the natural stage is the
belief in spontaneous, natural sex. The belief is that sex is
better if it's "natural"; birth control is artificial. This belief
in spontaneity and naturalness has a direct effect in inhibiting the
use of contraceptives. It also has an indirect effect by reinforcing unpredictability and by giving it a rationale.

Frequency. The third dimension of sexual activity that inhibits use of contraception is frequency of coitus. Coitus is
apt to be an infrequent event during the natural stage. One effect of infrequent coitus is that if there are thoughts about birth
control, they occur briefly around the time of a specific sexual
experience. The time span allows for concern with birth control
to dissipate between experiences. Another effect is that since
chances of pregnancy seem minimal with infrequent sexual intercourse, contraceptives are considered unnecessary. The infrequency
of coitus at this stage means that it is not part of regular patterns of behavior. This also contributes to the difficulty of
anticipating and predicting. Frequency of coitus has a major influence on contraceptive use. The most frequently stated reason
for seeking birth control services by the women in this study was
that they were having intercourse more frequently.

Type. A fourth dimension of sexual activity that inhibits
the use of contraceptives is type of sexual activity. In changing
from homosexual to heterosexual relationships, a girl who said she
was "messing around with women" was not prepared with a birth control method when she subsequently had sexual intercourse with a
man.

Duration. A fifth dimension of sexual activity that affects
birth control use is the length of time of sexual activity without
contraception. Although time usually increases the likelihood that
a birth control method will be used, it may well have the opposite
effect. When a young woman has intercourse over a period of time
and does not get pregnant, she becomes increasingly convinced that
pregnancy will not occur. It may be because she herself does not
get pregnant or that someone she knows has had intercourse without
getting pregnant.

The Problem of Awareness

Adoption of new sex behavior does not automatically bring with
it the recognition of the need for birth control. Changes have to
take place in awareness of sex behavior itself, awareness of the
possibility of pregnancy, and awareness of the need for birth control. A new self-concept has to be acquired that includes these
new behaviors and possibilities. The girl has to define herself
as sexually active, capable of reproduction, and in need of contraception.

Awareness of Sexual Behavior. There are varying levels of
awareness of sexual behavior. In extreme cases, it is possible
to be completely unaware of having sexual intercourse. This occurs
when there has been trauma connected with it or when the stakes
are very high. In one such case, there was no awareness of sexual

intercourse and the possibility of pregnancy was denied up until the time that the baby was born. The pregnancy meant forever losing the chance to continue in school which provided the only means of escaping the poverty cycle in the girl's particular country. There was no possibility of abortion.

At the other extreme is full awareness. In this case, sexual behavior, its implications and consequences, and the need for a birth control method are fully realized. This makes it possible to prepare with a birth control method either before sexual intercourse takes place for the first time or immediately afterwards. In cases like this the natural stage is skipped completely.

But these extremes are atypical and the level of awareness usually falls somewhere in between. For instance, there may be a high level of awareness around the time of intercourse, but no self conception as a sexually active person between experiences. Or there may be a drift into sexual activity on a low level of awareness and continuation in this manner for some time. In either case, intercourse is still an accident, a fluke. The new sexual behavior is not yet integrated into the standard repertoire of behaviors. Under these circumstances a new self concept is hard to maintain.

Awareness of Possible Pregnancy. There is generally a low level of awareness of the possibility of pregnancy at the natural stage. Pregnancy, like sexual behavior, is not part of the self concept; there is no identification with the possibility of pregnancy.

Growing Awareness. The natural stage is a time of growing awareness. Awareness may grow either slowly and gradually or rapidly and suddenly. Gradual growth of awareness has quantitative and qualitative components. Quantitatively, growth of awareness is the result of more sexual experience in terms of the number and frequency of incidences of coitus and longer duration of sexual activity. The more sexually active a girl is, the greater her chances of becoming aware of her behavior and the need for birth control. Thus, frequency and duration of sexual activity have a marked effect on awareness. Qualitatively, awareness is manifested as a greater degree of comfort and familiarity with sexual behavior.

Rapid and sudden growth of awareness usually stems from an encounter with pregnancy, such as a late menstrual period, or a friend's pregnancy, or when the girl herself gets pregnant.

As awareness grows there is greater recognition of the implications of sexual behavior. Growing awareness exerts constant pressure toward the next stages in which different behaviors are chosen to resolve problems. Although, the same factors may be present,

behavior differences are a consequence of changing interpretations
of sexual experiences. The ill-defined concept of self becomes
replaced with a clearer definition of self as a sexually active
person capable of reproduction and in need of birth control. The
problems of awareness and ill-defined concepts are present in other
aspects of the natural stage. These will be discussed in the section on the boy/girl relationship.

Indecision about Sex and Contraception

There is a great deal of indecision on the part of the girl
about pacing the acquisition of birth control during the natural
stage. Should it be acquired in anticipation of the first sexual
experience when there are no immediate prospects of sex? After a
relationship with a boy has begun, but before first coitus? After
one or more sexual experiences have taken place? Indecision about
when to get birth control really reflects ambivalence about sex.

Commitment to Sex. Indecision does not necessarily end after
sexual intercourse has occurred. Having sexual intercourse once
or even many times does not mean commitment to sex. Ambivalent
feelings about sex do not deter sexual activity; they do deter
getting a birth control method. One girl who was pregnant and
seeking abortion information explained that she had not been using
a contraceptive because:

"I couldn't get the pill without telling my parents. I would
feel guilty about taking the pill behind their back."

Indecision and guilt about sex get focused on birth control.
It is not coitus itself that means commitment to sex--it is the
acquisition of a birth control method. Sexual activity is background, in a sense, to commitment, but does not mean commitment,
just the possibility of commitment. It is the decision to get a
birth control method that means commitment to sex. This was expressed clearly by a girl who had not yet had intercourse:

"I've been thinking about it, the pill, that is. I've been
persuaded by my boyfriend that I ought to get it. Haven't
made up my mind yet. I won't get the pill tonight. I'll
discuss it with my boyfriend again. If I get the pill I'm
open. Then I can screw around when I want. I like the idea
of having drawbacks."

The fact that commitment to sex gets focused on birth control
rather than on sex itself, that it is birth control that means
commitment to sex and not sexual intercourse causes delay in getting a birth control method until after sexual intercourse has
taken place.

The Boy - Girl Relationship

There are many aspects of the relationship between the girl and the boy that influence the use of contraceptives. Three of these are: the definition of the relationship; changing standards of sexual behavior; and the boy's level of awareness.

Definition of the Relationship. Ability to define the relationship is a contributing factor to birth control behavior. A prevalent hypothesis about why girls don't use contraceptives is that they want to promote marriage (Pohlman, 1967). They define the relationship as one that will lead to marriage. This is true in some cases. But there is evidence that birth control is also used or not used to accomplish other ends with regard to relationships with the opposite sex. A girl who previously had not used contraceptives said:

"I'm going with somebody now and I don't want anything to interfere with the relationship. I think a pregnancy would interfere with the relationship so I need a contraceptive."

A twenty-six year old woman who had been casual about the use of condoms and was adamant about having an abortion said that she had no intention of ever marrying and did not want children. One girl who knew what she wanted said the boy didn't "do anything" about sex. She wanted sexual intercourse and since she defined herself as the "aggressor" she prepared with foam for her first sexual experience. Such motives with regard to relationships are not confined to young women. Young men have them too. One young man said that he would not mind getting involved in a pregnancy situation with someone he cared something about, but if it were someone he didn't care about he would not want to get involved and would be more careful about using something. In another case a young man deliberately refrained from using a birth control method because "that was the girl I wanted to marry." The point is that not using birth control in order to promote marriage is only one instance in a class of behaviors that is characterized by a definition of what is wanted in the way of a relationship with the opposite sex. Where there is a clear definition a decision will be made about birth control and it will be used or not used according to the needs of the situation. When the conditions of the relationship are not well defined and there is a choice between use and nonuse, the tendency is toward nonuse. This is similar to the awareness problem and ill-defined self concept that was discussed earlier. In the natural stage these definitions are not clear and given the other inhibiting factors the tendency is to be lax about birth control.

Changing Standards. Another factor in the relationship between the girl and the boy that influences birth control behavior is the

change in standards of sexual behavior. The old double standard
(Reiss, 1967) meant that boys could be sexually active before
marriage, but girls were obliged to remain virginal until their
wedding night. Now girls are sexually active as well. New twists
on the double standard come out around questions like: Who is
supposed to start the talk about birth control? Who decides
whether to use it? Who initiates the action to get birth control?
Who should provide it?

When old social relations are breaking down and new ones are
evolving, new forms of communication and behavior need to evolve
(Daniels, 1971). At this time, there are no customs, rules of
thumb, or norms about what to expect in terms of birth control
in the relation between a girl and boy, and no standardized way
to communicate about it. There is no etiquette to provide a
framework for discussing birth control. There is no customary
way for the girl to ask the boy if he has a condom, or for her to
raise the question if she is not prepared with a method. Each may
arrive at the scene with different expectations and not be able
to communicate or check out the situation because of the lack of
an etiquette. Communication on the physical level does not guarantee communication on the level that is necessary for checking
about birth control even when there is a high level of knowledge.
An example of this is a twenty-two year old graduate student in
health education who had previously attended medical school for a
year and a half who said that he did not always broach the subject
because it was a "clumsy question."

Communication is effected by the nature of the involvement
between the boy and girl. When asked why, in such an intimate
situation, it was so difficult to ask about birth control, someone
in a rap session replied, "That's the trouble, it's not intimate."

Like expectations about communication, confusion surrounds
the actual provision of birth control methods. When they arrive
at the coital moment, the boy may expect that the girl is taking
oral contraceptives. The girl, on the other hand, may expect
something else: "The guy is expected to have something. After
all, if he takes you out.... ."

A marked twist on the double standard is evident around initiating the action to acquire a birth control method. At the same
time that sexual intercourse may be anticipated or is already taking place, there is a fear of what the boy may think if the girl
is prepared with a method or initiates action to acquire one. The
fear is that being prepared, using, showing knowledge, or experience
about birth control means loose sexual morals. It is preferable
in these situations, for the idea to come from the boy. It is the
display of knowledge or experience about birth control that means
looseness, not sex itself. Here, again, as in the ambivalence about

sexual activity and birth control, the question of looseness gets
focused, not on sexual intercourse itself, but on birth control.

The Boy's Level of Awareness. Just as the question of ambivalence recurs in the boy-girl relationship, the problem of awareness
also recurs. The boy's awareness of the problem is a contributing
factor in much the same way as the girl's. Growth of awareness
takes place in the boy in much the same way as in the girl.

The problems of definition, ambivalence, awareness, and expectations that are found in the girl are similarly found in the
boy as well as in the nexus between them.

Parental Attitudes and Behavior

The family is not a place where one can readily make inquiries
about birth control. The same lack of awareness and ambivalence,
if not downright opposition, to premarital sex is present in the
family and is manifested in the interaction between the girl and
her family around the issue of birth control. Even in families
where there is a permissive attitude toward premarital sex they
are not able to help their daughters plan for birth control in
concrete terms. When it comes to what to do, where to go and which
method to use because of immediately contemplated or already ongoing sexual activity, they don't tell and the girls don't ask.
The following incident, which occurred at a community meeting on
overpopulation, illustrates this:

"A woman kept asking why on earth these girls don't use anything. After the meeting she told me that she had been involved with three young girls in their efforts to obtain
abortions and had gone with them to Tijuana (a popular place
in Mexico for illegal abortions). She just couldn't understand why they hadn't used contraception. Immediately she
went on to say that she had not been able to discuss the subject with her own daughter despite the urging of her husband
(who was obviously also reluctant). The outcome was that her
daughter was given oral contraceptives by a physician to correct menstrual irregularity. The woman said she was greatly
relieved by this. (Field Notes, 1968).

She was absolved of responsibility for her daughter's birth
control planning, and although she herself considered it a "cop
out" she welcomed the intervention of a third party.

The reluctance to discuss birth control in concrete, here
and now terms is evident on the part of girls as well as parents
in the permissive family. Girls find it is not possible for them

to actually ask or let their parents know when sexual intercourse is imminent. In an extreme case, a very young girl did not use foam, although it had been given to her by her mother. She was afraid to let her mother know that she was actually using it. Another girl had already been having sexual intercourse for a month. Her mother found out and sent her to the Free Clinic for a birth control method. In this case, it was the direct impetus of the parent that moved the girl into another stage of birth control behavior. Although this is about the most permissive type of attitude that exists on the part of parents, the girl still had been having intercourse for one month without using contraception. In most cases, even in permissive families, this type of direct intervention is not forthcoming. However, the permissive attitude does provide a setting and background for more readily using contraception.

In other permissive families premarital sex is recognized as a probable event, but parents do not want to appear to sanction it by offering information on birth control. They fear that this will be pushing the girl into premarital sex, that it will be a go-ahead sign for sex. These parents will consider giving birth control information and advice at an early age, but concrete help only when sex is in the offing. But even in a case like this the girl has to initiate the procedure. Since there is reluctance to disclose sexual activity the girl may not initiate the discussion until she has been having sexual intercourse for some time. She may not raise it with her parents at all. She is more likely to solve the problem in some other manner, but not until she has been having sexual intercourse for a period of time.

In some permissive families premarital sex is acceptable, but there is some question about the safety of oral contraceptives. In this case opposition to birth control is usually overcome in recognition of the necessity of preventing pregnancy.

The posture of parents in permissive families toward premarital sex and birth control indicates that ambivalence is not characteristic of the girl only, but is also manifested by parents.

In most families premarital sex is completely unacceptable. The girl is expected to abstain from sex until she is married. Under these conditions, there is no discussion, information, or advice on birth control methods. In one such family, the girl constantly approached her parents for discussion and help, but was rebuffed each time. The benefits and need for such a discussion were not perceived by them. In many families like this, if the girl gets pregnant she is forgiven for one mistake, but she is expected to abstain after the pregnancy until she is married. At the other extreme, she may be thrown out of the house or she may elect to leave so that her parents do not discover her plight.

In most cases, the family is reconciled to the situation and the girl acquires a method of birth control after an abortion or the birth of a baby.

In a few families the emphasis is on the unacceptability of birth control. This is usually for religious reasons. As in the non-permissive family, the girl is expected to abstain and if she does get pregnant she is expected to abstain afterwards. The result is often more than one pregnancy.

In addition to not being able to use parents as a resource, the parent-daughter relationship has another profound effect. It is necessary for the formation of a new self-concept to have it recognized and accepted by others, especially key persons like parents (Goodenough, 1963). If the parents have difficulty or cannot accept a new concept for their daughter it will retard her in her achievement of a new self-concept and this, as has already been discussed, inhibits the use of contraception.

CONCLUSION

Factors affecting the use of contraception by young, unmarried women in the earliest stage of sexual activity include patterns of sexual behavior; level of awareness about the sexual activity, the possibility of pregnancy and the need for contraception; decision making about sex and contraception; aspects of the boy-girl relationship; and parental attitudes and behavior.

These factors are part of the social environment and influence behavioral responses to the environment. The behavioral responses are part of a social process that has evolved in the absence of institutionalized norms for conduct of sexual activity in the nonmarital context.

REFERENCES

Daniels, A.K. (1971). Sexual social types and the etiquette of sex relations. Paper read at Pacific Social Meeting, April 1971, Hawaii.

Eastman, W.R. (1972). First intercourse. Sexual Behavior, 2:22-27.

Glaser, B.G., and Strauss, A.L. (1967). Discovery of Grounded Theory, Aldine Publishing Co., Chicago.

Goodenough, W.H. (1963). Cooperation in Change, John Wiley and Sons, New York.

Lindemann, C. (1974). Birth Control and Unmarried Young Women,
     Springer Publishing Co., Inc., New York.

Lowry, R.P. (1969). First Coitus. Medical Aspects of Human Sex-
     uality, 3:91-97.

Pohlman, E. (1967). The Psychology of Birth Planning, Schenkman
     Publishing Co., Cambridge.

Reiss, I.L. (1967). Contraceptive Information and Sexual Morality.
     Journal of Sex Research, 2:51-57.

ATTITUDES OF NURSES TO PREMARITAL SEX AND THEIR CONTRACEPTIVE

ROLE ORIENTATION[1]

Edward S. Herold

Canada

In recent years professional health organizations have increasingly recognized the need to provide contraceptive educational
services to youth. A survey of students and faculty in nursing
schools in the United States found 75% agreeing that family planning education should be given to anyone who deserves it (Shea et
al., 1973). Although there has been a considerable increase in
the number of nursing schools instructing students in the methods
of contraception, there has been a lag in preparing nurses to deal
with attitudinal aspects (Garret, 1972). In particular, nurses
have not been trained to examine their own attitudes which might
inhibit them against disseminating contraceptive knowledge (Garret,
1972: 27).

Forty percent of the nurses surveyed in one study agreed or
were uncertain whether a nurse's personal beliefs should prevent
her from discussing family planning with her patient (Howard et
al., 1972). To deal with this issue, nursing and medical schools
have instituted programs of attitudinal reassessment for their
students in order to provide them with insight into their own
attitudes and the manner in which these attitudes can prevent the
provision of needed services to patients.

[1]Sponsored by Family Planning Grant #4460-5-2 made by the Department of National Health and Welfare

HYPOTHESES

Although there has been speculation concerning the relationship between personal attitudes and the provision of professional
contraceptive services, there has been, to the author's knowledge,
no research of this relationship.[2] The major objective of this
study was to test for this relationship.

Hypothesis 1: nurses with permissive attitudes to premarital
sex are more willing to provide contraceptive education.

It was also anticipated that nurses having more permissive
attitudes to premarital sex would place less emphasis on abstinence
for youth.

Hypothesis 2: nurses with permissive attitudes to premarital
sex will place less emphasis on abstinence as a means of decreasing pregnancy rates among adolescents.

A related question is whether nurses' attitudes are related
to their perception of the extent of sexual activity among youth.
Sorensen (1973) in research with adolescents found a relationship
between adolescent attitudes to premarital sex and their perception of the extent of premarital sexual behavior among youth in
general.

Hypothesis 3: nurses with permissive attitudes to premarital
sex will estimate higher rates of sexual activity among adolescents.

DATA COLLECTION

The sample consisted of 209 female nursing students and nurses.
Included were 114 nursing students registered in a two year community college program in a small city in Southern Ontario and 95
registered nurses enrolled in an evening course in human sexuality
at a university in Toronto. Questionnaires were distributed during
regular class periods. Questions relating to this study were included as part of a larger project evaluating the effectiveness
of films about contraception.

---

[2]In a somewhat related area, Knapp (1975) found a significant relationship between the personal attitudes of marriage counsellors
with respect to non-monogamous marriage and the type of counselling
they provided to clients who were involved in non-monogamous relationships.

MEASUREMENT OF VARIABLES

Premarital Sexual Attitudes

To measure attitudes to premarital sex, a modified form of the Reiss scale (1967) was constructed on the basis of pretest results in 1974 with a sample of 200 undergraduate students. The scale consisted of three items:

1. I believe premarital intercourse is acceptable when one feels strong affection for one's partner.

2. I believe premarital intercourse is acceptable when one is engaged to be married.

3. Premarital intercourse is not acceptable to me under any condition.

Factor analysis (varimax) showed that these items did form a scale. The factor loading for each of the items was .88, .94 and .92 respectively.

Contraceptive Role Orientation

To measure the willingness of respondents to provide contraceptive education to youth a contraceptive role orientation scale was constructed consisting of these items:

1. I feel somewhat uncomfortable at the thought of my teaching high school students about contraception.

2. In my professional role I am willing to provide contraceptive information to high school students.

3. A professional in my field should be willing to provide contraceptive information to high school students, when the professional thinks it is needed, even if the students do not request it.

4. In my professional role, if I had my choice, I would like to spend more time working in the area of contraceptive education.

5. I am willing to attend workshops on contraceptive education.

Factor analysis provided verification for this scale as the respective factor loadings were .52, .78, .52, .65 and .70.

Abstinence for Adolescents

Respondents were asked to indicate their attitudes towards abstinence as a solution for unwanted pregnancy by responding to the item, "In order to decrease adolescent pregnancy rates, there should be an increased emphasis on abstinence before marriage."

Perception of Sexual Activity

To measure perception of sexual activity among youth respondents were asked, "What percentage of high school students do you think will experience sexual intercourse before leaving high school?" They were asked to give separate estimates for males and females. To facilitate analysis estimates for both sexes were combined to form a single index.

RESULTS

Pearsonian correlation coefficients (with significance being taken as .01 or better) were obtained to test the hypotheses. As shown in Table 1 all three hypotheses were confirmed. Separate correlations were obtained for individual items of the contraceptive orientation scale. Each of the individual items was also found to be significantly correlated with PMS, with the highest correlation (.34) being obtained for the item "In my professional role, if I had my choice, I would like to spend more time working in the area of contraceptive education."

TABLE 1

CORRELATION AND PARTIAL CORRELATION COEFFICIENTS FOR PREMARITAL SEXUAL ATTITUDES AND DEPENDENT VARIABLES

Dependent variables	Correlation Coefficient	Partial Correlation Coefficient Controlling for Age and Religiosity
Contraceptive role orientation	.35*	.24*
Emphasis on abstinence	.57*	.49*
Perception of sexual activity	.38*	.31*

* Significant at .01 level

The strongest relationship was found between the attitudes to premarital sex of the nurses, and emphasis on abstinence (Hypothesis 3).

It was anticipated that the variables of age and religiosity might influence the relationships, and these variables were controlled by partial correlation. Age and religiosity were chosen as controls as previous research has found them to be related to attitudes to premarital sex (Reiss, 1967). Religiosity was measured by the question "About how often do you attend church or synagogue services?" In this study age and religiosity had correlations of $-.23$ and $-.41$ respectively with premarital sexual attitudes. After the effects of age and religiosity were controlled by using partial correlation, the three hypotheses were still confirmed.

Those having less permissive attitudes to premarital sex were less interested in working in the area of contraceptive education, less willing to provide contraceptive education to high school students and more uncomfortable at the thought of teaching contraception to high school students. They also placed a greater emphasis on abstinence than did those having more permissive attitudes to premarital sex, and gave lower estimates of the extent of sexual activity among youth.

DISCUSSION

The results indicate that personal sexual attitudes of nursing students and nurses influence their professional attitudes toward providing contraceptive education to adolescents. This finding supports the emphasis being placed today on health professionals recognizing and dealing with their own sexual feelings (Carrera and Calderone, 1976). This affective component needs to be included in the training of health professionals especially when they are being asked to provide services to clients whose values are different from their own.

REFERENCES

Carrera, M.A. and Calderone, M. (1976). Training of health professionals in education for sexual health. Siecus Report, 4 (4): 1-2.

Garret, N. (1972). Population, family planning and related health care: a working paper. Canadian Nurses Association, Ottawa.

Howard, J., Lawrence, J. and Rasile, K. (1972). A survey of public
     health nurses' knowledge and attitudes about family planning.
     American Journal of Public Health, 62: 962-968.

Knapp, J. (1975). Some non-monogamous marriage styles and related
     attitudes of marriage counsellors. The Family Coordinator,
     24 (4): 505-514.

Reiss, I. (1967). The Social Context of Premarital Sexual Per-
     messiveness, Holt, Rinehart and Winston, New York.

Shea, F., Werley, H. and Rosen, R.A. (1973). Survey of health
     professionals regarding family planning. Nursing Research,
     22 (1): 17-24.

Sorensen, R.C. (1973). Adolescent Sexuality in Contemporary America.
     The World Publishing Company, New York.

UNMARRIED YOUTH AND ACTUAL ACCESSIBILITY TO ORAL CONTRACEPTIVES

AND CONDOMS

Robert Gemme

Canada

At first sight, oral contraceptives and condoms seem to be easily available, in North America, at least. Almost every drug store sells condoms without considering the marital status of the client and the majority of medical practitioners will prescribe oral contraceptives to healthy unmarried young patients. In theory, therefore, these two types of contraceptive methods are easy to obtain, but in practice, we may suppose such contraceptives quite hard to get when we consider the sexual and contraceptive experience of young people. There is indeed a disparity between theory and fact regarding the facility of procuring oral contraceptives and condoms for the young unmarried.

SEXUAL AND CONTRACEPTIVE EXPERIENCE
AMONG THE YOUNG UNMARRIED

It is interesting to analyze the true availibility of contraceptive methods because we are aware of the widespread sexual activity among young people who, however, do not always have recourse to adequate and uninterrupted means of protection. The studies undertaken in this field show that increased sexual activity in youth, became noticeable some ten years ago in Canada. Surveys done by Mann (1967, 1970) stated that between 1965 and 1969 the percentage of young persons indulging in such activities has risen from 35 per cent to 50 per cent in young males and from 15 per cent to 37 per cent in young females. Our own survey (Crépault and Gemme, 1975) reveals that 42.8 per cent of the girls and 52 per cent of the boys in our probabilistic sampling had experienced coital relations during six months prior to the survey. It is

logical to assume that at least one out of two young unmarried
people has had sexual intercourse in 1976. Several factors allow
us to assume that such an increase will continue and Quebec will,
in the near future, match the statistics set down by Denmark where
according to Christensen and Gregg (1970), about 95 per cent of
young men and women indulged in sexual intercourse in 1968.

However, regardless of an increasingly active sex life, many
young people do not resort to adequate and sustained preventive
behavior. Evaluations made by the Center for Disease Control
(1976) show that 32.7 per cent of the 763,479 legal abortions
practised in the United States in 1974 were performed on women
under twenty years of age. If we consider births out of wedlock,
or those legitimized by marriage in the course of pregnancy, as well
as the induced and spontaneous abortions in unmarried women, the number would total approximately 20,000 pregnancies out of wedlock in
Quebec (Gemme, 1974). In the United States, Settlage et al., (1973)
report that 96 per cent of young female consultants seeking contraceptive assistance for the first time at a Family Planning Center
were already sexually active and that 58 per cent had been so for
ever a year. Finally, in their probabilistic national sampling,
Zelnick and Kantner (1974) reported that only 50.9 per cent of
the sexually-active girls had availed themselves of contraceptive
methods during their recent sexual activities, and worse still,
only 25 per cent of the latter had used ovulation-suppressive
means, 21.8 per cent had resorted to condoms whereas 33 per cent
had used interrupted coitus (48.2 per cent in the fifteen-year-
old group).

As already stated, oral contraceptives and condoms are theoretically easy to obtain; therefore, there must be psychological
and/or social obstacles responsible for such disparity between
theory and fact.

PSYCHOLOGICAL AND SOCIAL OBSTACLES
IN ORAL CONTRACEPTIVE USE

There seem to be two particularly important factors which
explain why oral contraceptives are actually not so accessible
to a certain category of young women as is generally believed.

Emotional Adherence to Virginity

It is not an overstatement to say that the majority of girls
in Quebec begin active sex lives in a context where both adults
and the young women themselves still adhere to the importance of
premarital virginity. In an unpublished work of this writer, it

is reported that 65 per cent of the adults between the ages of thirty-five and fifty-five disapproved of young girls having sexual relations even when the girl is in love. Other studies undertaken in the United States and Canada reveal that teenagers of fifteen and sixteen believe in the importance of virginity. Ménard (1973) has reported that 71 per cent of young girls in Grade Eleven believed that men preferred to marry a virgin.

In such a context where only a small number of adults patronize sex for the unwed, it is not surprising that some young women undertake sex activities without also resorting to adequate and sustained contraceptive methods nor is it strange that oral contraceptives are not more widely used. Indeed, such use presupposes a decision taken some weeks prior to intercourse, due to the time required for an appointment with a gynecologist. Therefore, some young women refuse to prepare for behavior which they consider unacceptable, immature, or immoral, or behavior which they think, betrays a lack of self-control. To anticipate contraceptive measures would indicate complicity before the act itself. So, our opinion is that only those who have wholly integrated the notion of sexual activity into their personalities are capable of arranging for active sex outside the marital context, and at the same time, willing to prepare themselves for the preliminary means of protection.

For those who have not yet arrived at this psychosexual stage in their lives, the emotional adherence to virginity is a lingering psychological block as regards the use of contraceptives in oral form, and they are liable to forego "the pill" in favor of interrupted coitus and douches. This situation will continue until they finally convince themselves to accept a definite or anticipated active sex life and estimate premarital or out-of-wedlock sex as an acceptable alternative to virginity.

A Must: The Doctor's Prescription

The request for a contraceptive prescription on the part of a young girl is tantamount to the admission that she will eventually indulge in non-marital sex and the length of time required to obtain this prescription implies that this decision has already been taken, an acknowledgment which some young women find psychologically impossible to take, even to themselves, and especially to an adult physician. Even those who have integrated active sex into their way of living may cringe before the anticipated moral judgment of the doctor prescribing the pill, especially as the prescription is usually accompanied by a check-up, including a pelvic examination, which some girls find most embarrassing when performed by a male gynecologist. And finally, certain young women are loath to reveal their sexual intentions to a third party, just as some married men find it awkward to buy condoms at a drug store.

However integrated non-marital sex may be in their lives, the necessity of obtaining medical authorization is a very real obstacle which decreases the theoretical accessibility of oral contraceptives.

PSYCHOLOGICAL AND SOCIAL OBSTACLES
IN THE USE OF THE CONDOM

In recent years, society has increasingly insisted that young men assume their responsibilities in the use of contraceptive methods, and the only effective masculine means to date is the condom. Theoretically, condoms are totally accessible and all drug stores stock and sell them; actually, however, they are not all that easy to obtain. Indeed, the purchase of condoms is an embarrassing moment, even for adult married men who often order them by mail or over the telephone, or else have them bought by their wives. A woman druggist whose business concern had no delivery service, reports that a certain male customer requested that his condoms be put in a bag marked with his name which he would pick up at the store simply by asking for "Mr. So-and-so's bag." We may infer that such embarrassment is also shared by young people for whom sexual intercourse are not yet part of the self-concept. Certain indications lead us to presume that the fact that condoms are not displayed in drug store open show cases and are not readily accessible to customers has constituted an obstacle to their use by some young men; this explains why we undertook a widespread survey in 1974 to discover how available these articles were in Quebec pharmacies and the percentage of stores which obliged customers to ask for them (the types "available on demand") as well as the percentage of stores which allowed customers to have direct access to this merchandise (the types "self-service").

Methodology

In the courses dealing with the social dimension of sexuality given in the Department of sexology at the Université du Québec à Montréal, some of the students were asked to visit ten drug stores near their homes, in Montreal, or elsewhere. The students were to verify the true accessibility of condoms and the reasons justifying the type of access. A research assistant then selected and verified the findings of each student.

The research project, which covered a period from November 1974 to December 1975, allowed us to compile the findings obtained from 601 pharmacies concentrated especially in the Montreal area

(440) but otherwise extending from Val d'Or to Sherbrooke and from
Valleyfield to Chicoutimi (161). In consideration of the information supplied by the Order of Pharmacists of Quebec and by consulting the Yellow Pages in the Montreal telephone directory, we may
say that we have approached 51 per cent of the drug stores in the
Province of Quebec (601/1175), 79 per cent of those located on the
Island of Montreal (346/435), and 85 per cent of the pharmacies in
Montreal itself (261/305). The results obtained are evidently more
representative of the Montreal area than of the whole of the Province of Quebec.

Results Obtained

Type of accessibility. The following results concern 598
drug stores (three others did not stock condoms). Tables 1 to 4
illustrate the distribution of drug stores according to whether
condoms were available on self-service or else available on demand
only. Table 1 represents the ensemble of drug stores; Table 2,
those located in the Montreal area; Table 3 and Figure 1, the
pharmacies on the Island of Montreal, Table 4, those in the City
itself.

A more detailed study shows that availability differs according to the regions. For instance, in the city of Sherbrooke, eight
out of ten drug stores offer condoms at their self-service counters,
whereas in St. Jerome, only three out of eight stores do the same.

TABLE 1

TYPE OF ACCESSIBILITY IN THE PHARMACIES
IN THE PROVINCE OF QUEBEC (N=598)

Type of accessibility	N	%
On demand	327	54.69
Self-service	271	45.31
Total	598	100.00

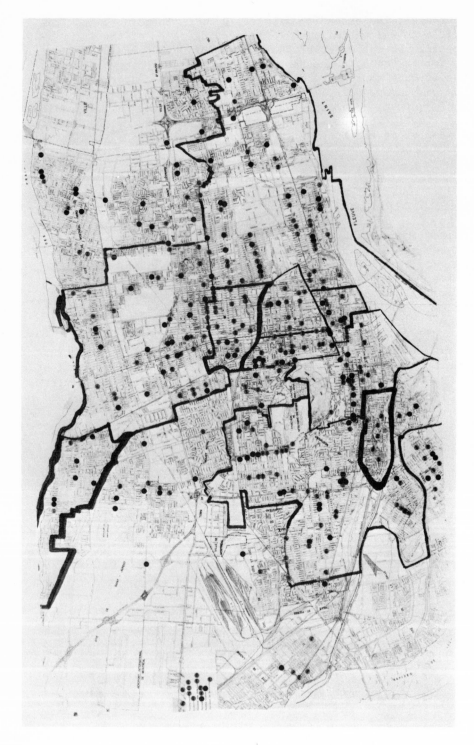

Fig. 1. Type of accessibility of condoms in pharmacies of the Island of Montréal (N = 343).
Pale dot = on demand (N = 203 or 59.18%) — Dark dot = self-service (N = 140 or 40.08%).

TABLE 2

TYPE OF ACCESSIBILITY IN
THE PHARMACIES IN THE MONTREAL AREA (N=437)

Type of accessibility	N	%
On demand	247	56.52
Self-service	190	43.48
Total	437	100.00

TABLE 3

TYPE OF ACCESSIBILITY IN THE PHARMACIES
ON THE ISLAND OF MONTREAL (N=343)

Type of accessibility	N	%
On demand	203	59.18
Self-service	140	40.82
Total	343	100.00

TABLE 4

TYPE OF ACCESSIBILITY IN THE PHARMACIES
IN THE CITY OF MONTREAL (N=261)

Type of accessibility	N	%
On demand	161	61.69
Self-service	100	38.31
Total	261	100.00

This difference is also apparent in the various districts of Montreal, as is illustrated in Table 5.

When we examine the St. Edouard district (Figure 2), which extends from Park Avenue on the west to Jean-Talon on the north and from Iberville Street on the east to the CPR tracks near St. Grégoire Street on the south, it is not hard to understand how difficult it is for a young man to buy condoms without the embarrassment of having to ask the druggist for them. If this young person lives in the center of the aforementioned district ▭, he would have to cover several streets before finding a store that sells condoms at its self-service counter. A breakdown shows he would have to cover 24 streets to the east, 10 to the west, 8 to the south and 6 to the north; moreover, he would be obliged to leave this district in three out of four possible directions.

Justification for the type of accessibility on demand. As previously stated, the druggists were required to justify the reasons for a particular type of accessibility. Table 6 illustrates the reasons put forward by 296 pharmacists to justify their decision to sell condoms on demand only.

TABLE 5

TYPE OF ACCESSIBILITY IN THREE DISTRICTS
IN THE CITY OF MONTREAL

Accessibility	Districts					
	St. Henri (N=6)		St. Edouard (N=22)		Cartierville (N=8)	
	N	%	N	%	N	%
On demand	6	100	19	86.4	2	25
Self-service	0	0	3	13.6	6	75
Total	6	100	22	100.0	8	100

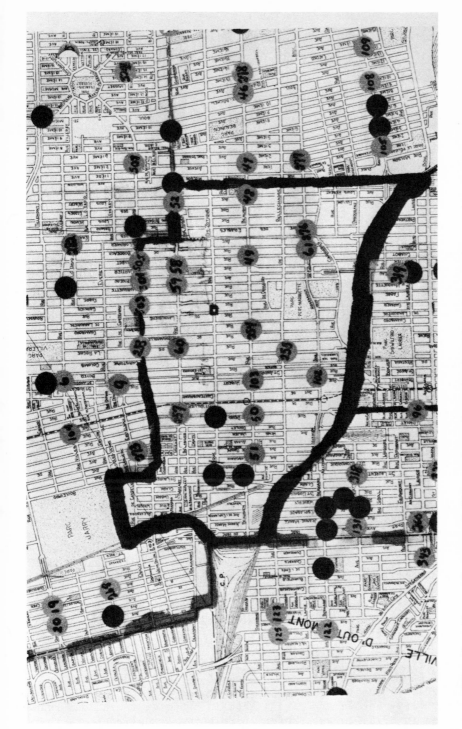

Fig. 2. Type of accessibility of condoms in St.Edward district.
Pale dot = on demand   -   Dark dot = self-service   -   □ = youth living at this place.

TABLE 6

REASONS JUSTIFYING THE TYPE OF
ACCESSIBILITY ON DEMAND (N=296)*

Reasons	%**
Lack of space	32.09
Moral reasons	28.38
Fear of theft (shoplifting)	26.01
No reason given	15.54
Other reasons:	
Out of habit	8.11
Little demand	3.04
Shielding the customer	2.70
Forbidden by law	1.01
Refusal to answer	2.70

* This question was not asked in 31 cases and the result obtained concerns 296 pharmacists out of a possible 327.

** The total exceeds 100 per cent because a single pharmacist may have given several reasons.

As we can see, the three main reasons given are lack of space, fear of shoplifting, and moral reasons. However, we may question the veracity of such excuses as "lack of space" or "theft." Indeed, spermicide foam is easily obtainable and generally displayed on most drug counters, although this merchandise is not greatly in demand and it takes up the same space as a box of condoms. We may even ask ourselves why condoms should be more likely to be stolen than spermicide foam, shaving cream, and after-shave lotion. Perhaps these reasons are given to disguise moral reasons, at least on the part of some druggists.

Table 7 presents certain allegations regarding moral attitudes. Of course, this does not represent the attitude of the ensemble of conservative pharmacists regarding their policy of condom accessibility, but we are citing them in order to remind our readers that even in 1976, in our present permissive sexual context, there

TABLE 7

ALLEGATIONS INDICATING MORAL RESTRICTIONS

"I know of no drug store that puts <u>that</u> at the customer's disposal."

"We do not display condoms because we have no space for <u>those</u> <u>things</u>."

"There must be some kind of control over young people and they should not be allowed to <u>go too far</u>."

"I'm not in favor of <u>bad habits</u> and <u>dirty customs</u>."

"We will not sell condoms to customers who are too young."

"It is against professional ethics to display forbidden articles."

"Our drug store is near a church and priests sometimes drop in."

---

are still some adults who retain and enforce a restrictive and negative attitude towards sexuality.

All in all, the theoretical availability of condoms is considerably lowered because this merchandise is hidden away in the drawers beneath or behind drug store counters. This obliges the young customer to openly ask for the product and subjects him to an anticipated embarrassment which, in turn, might force him to delay such a purchase and resort to interrupted coitus or else, to rely heavily on his sexual partner.

SOLUTIONS

We believe that effective and continuous contraception methods must be made available to young people by overcoming the barriers, e.g., psychological (the emotional adherence to virginity, embarrassment, etc.,) and social (obligatory medical prescription, concealed condoms and difficult access to them).

Breaking Down the Psychological Barriers

To do this, it will be necessary to generalize sexual education in school curricula and in extracurriculum activities, in view of emphasizing contraceptive methods for young people and giving premarital relations and virginity equal value. In the absence of such educational means, sexual intercourse will continue

to outdistance proper contraceptive behavior and such behavior
will continue to precede sexual intercourse until young, sexually-active individuals ascribe importance to the alternative
premarital sexuality. To reach this attitude, the young person
planning on becoming sexually active must feel supported by the
community in which he lives. Only a positive and permissive sexual education is capable of breaking down the psychological ram-
parts resulting from the emotional attachment to virginity and
the embarrassment of exhibiting one's intentions to indulge in
sex.

Breaking Down Social Barriers

The oral contraceptive. As regards oral contraception the
results of the studies undertaken in numerous countries and the
recent research on the innocuity of the pill as well as on the necessity of a physical examination indicate that there should be
reevaluation of the formality of a medical prescription before
purchasing oral contraceptives. Black (1974) reports that contraceptive medication without prescription has always been available in 30 of 45 countries affiliated with the International Planned
Parenthood Federation (IPPF) and that at least seven other countries have since adopted an identical policy. Furthermore, reports
from Antigua and Columbia confirm that no major complications have
as yet been observed (Bailey and Correa, 1975; Gemme, 1977).

The harmlessness of oral contraceptives, as recorded in the
literature, (Gemme, 1976), has allowed us to highlight the following facts which weigh in favor of a new evaluation regarding the
obligation of a medical prescription:

1. A prospective survey undertaken by the Royal College of
   General Practitioners in England (RCGP, 1974) involving
   23,611 contraceptive users as opposed to a control-group
   of 23,611 non-users has shown that, within five years,
   more users (2866 per 100,000) have benefited from the
   use of contraceptive medication than those who were in-
   convenienced by its use (1147 per 100,000);

2. Serious, irreversible adverse effects rarely occur; the
   cerebrovascular accidents reported between users and non-
   users totalled 3/1000 of 1 per cent (RCGP, 1974) and
   moreoever, this difference was noted before the widespread
   use of minimal doses of estrogen in contraceptive medication;

3. The mortality rate in the 15 - 19 age group due to the
   use of oral contraceptives was 1.3 per cent per 100,000

users, or 1.3/1000 of 1 per cent, as compared to that of
10.8 per 100,000 pregnancies and deliveries (Tietze, 1976),
showing that the risk in pregnancy and childbirth is eight
times higher than when using oral contraceptives;

4. Most adverse effects are reversible upon withdrawal of
   contraceptive medication;

5. Users experiencing discomforting adverse effects would
   discontinue medication or consult a physician if recommended to do so on the container's indications for use.

An analysis of the practical medical examination itself leaves
a doubt in the mind as to its utility. The pilot-survey wherein
general practitioners, physicians, and gynecologists were interviewed (Gemme, 1977) brought the following facts to light:

1. Twenty-seven out of the twenty-nine physicians refused a
   prescription to only 3.5 per cent of their patients, a
   figure approaching the 4.9 per cent (Huber and Huber, 1975)
   reported after a survey on 1021 clients in a Family Planning
   Clinic with extremely high standards;

2. Among the physicians questioned, 72.4 per cent stated that
   the first visit gave no indication of the resulting adverse
   effects which later required withdrawal of medication;

3. Most doctors disregard the various dosages available; 78.8
   per cent habitually prescribe the same type of oral contraceptive and may subsequently modify the original prescription.

Our own results are confirmed by Cartwright (1970) whose studies
show that 34 per cent of the doctors prescribing the pill had not
previously inquired whether the patient had a history of phlebitis,
81 per cent had not taken the patient's blood pressure, and 85 per
cent had not proceeded with breast inspection.

We feel that reevaluation of the obligatory medical prescription in purchasing oral contraceptives is justified, especially
when it entails a delay in time between effective use and the first
incidence of sexual activity. Its abolition would eliminate a young
girl's embarrassment in veiling her future intention to a doctor
and when faced with a gynecological examination.

The condom. There are two potential solutions to the accessibility of the condom: the first is that druggists should display this merchandise in full view and thereby allows the customer
self-service. The only embarrassing moment would occur when the
client presents his purchase to the cashier. This leads to a second

solution wherein condoms could be dispensed in vending machines in the washrooms of high schools, CEGEPs,[1] universities, discotheques, and cinemas, etc.

We must not forget that most young people do indulge in sexual intercourse and that the difficulty in obtaining contraceptives is in part responsible for the lack of use and consequently a recourse to ineffective methods of protection.

---

[1]Colleges in Quebec are called CEGEP (Collège d'Enseignement Général et Professionel).

REFERENCES

Black, T.R. (1974). Oral contraceptives prescription requirement and commercial availability in 45 developing countries. Studies in Family Planning, 5 (8): 250-254.

Cartwright, A. (1970). Parents and Family Services, Atherthon Press, New York.

Center for Disease Control (1976). Abortion Surveillance: Annual Summary 1974, U.S. Department of Health, Education and Welfare, Atlanta.

Christensen, H.T. and Gregg, C.F. (1970). Changing sex norms in America and Scandinavia. Journal of Marriage and the Family, 32: 616-627.

Crépault, C. and Gemme, R. (1975). La Sexualité Prémaritale, Presses de l'Université du Québec à Montréal, Montréal.

Gemme, R. (1974). Education sexuelle et contraception. In Samson, J.M. (éd), Education Sexuelle à l'Ecole? Guérin, Montréal.

Gemme, R. (1976). La distribution extra-médicale du contraceptif oral: revue de la littérature. Contraception, Fertilité et Sexualité, Vol. 4, No. 8: 637-651.

Gemme, R. (1977). La distribution extra-médicale du contraceptif oral: analyse critique de l'opinion de 29 médecins québécois. Contraception, Fertilité et Sexualité, in press.

Huber, D.H., and Huber, S.G. (1975). Screening Oral Contraceptives Candidates and Inconsequential Pelvic Examinations. Studies in Family Planning, 6 (2): 49-51.

Mann, W.E. (1967). Canadians trends in premarital sexual behavior. Bulletin, 198: 1-64.

Mann, W.E. (1970). Sex at York University. In Mann, W.E. (ed),
     The Underside of Toronto, Mc Clelland and Stewart, Toronto.

Ménard, R. (1972). Hétérosexualité des Etudiants de Onzième Année,
     unpublished thesis, University of Montréal, Montréal.

Royal College of General Practicionners (1974). Oral Contracep-
     tives and Health: An Interim Report from the Oral Contra-
     ception Study, Pitman Publishing Corp., New York.

Settlage, D., Baroff, S., and Cooper, D. (1973). Sexual experience
     of young teenage girls seeking contraceptive assistance for
     the first time. Family Planning Perspectives, 5 (4): 223-226.

Tietze, C., Bongaarts, J., and Schearer, B. (1976). Mortality
     Associated with the Control of Fertility. Family Planning
     Perspectives, 8 (1): 6-13.

Zelnick, M., and Kantner, J. (1972). Sexuality, Contraception and
     Pregnancy among Unwed Females in the United States. In
     Commission on Population Growth and the American Future,
     Vol. 1, U.S. Government Printing Office, Washington.

PHYLOGENETIC AND ONTOGENETIC ASPECTS OF HUMAN AFFECTIONAL

DEVELOPMENT

James W. Prescott

United States

The failure to develop peaceful behaviors represents the single greatest threat to the quality of human life and to the survival of human civilization. It is unnecessary to catalogue the history of human violence nor to note that the human mammal is unique in its ability to engage in collective action to destroy its own species. Some would point to the evolution of language and complex cognitive functioning as indispensable in accounting for the uniqueness of human violence. Others would argue that it is our evolutionary heritage where the most aggressive individuals survived hostile and violent environments which thereby perpetrated their own aggressive genotype. No such genotype has, of course, been found and it is highly unlikely that such a genotype exists. The enormous extent and diversity of human violence throughout the world defies any simple genetic explanation.

It is the purpose of this paper to outline a different theory of the origins of human violence which is primarily an ontogenetic theory but which has unique phylogenetic characteristics. In brief, the theory states that the failure to develop affectional bonds in human relationships is the primary cause of human violence. The beginning of this failure is in the parent/offspring relationship where sensory deprivation of the emotional/affective senses (tactile and vestibular sensory modalities) are permitted to occur. It is these sensory modalities that mediate somatosensory pleasure experiences in the parent/offspring relationship which are held to be necessary for the development of primary affectional bonds between parent and offspring. Failure to develop this primary affectional bond is proposed to result in an impaired ability to develop secondary affectional bonds, i.e., the expression

431

of physical affection through human sexual relationships. This
failure to establish adult affectional bonds prevents adults, as
parents, to provide the essential physical affectional experiences
to their children who are then emotionally and affectionately impaired and will with high probability, as adults, pass on their
impairments to succeeding generations. Central to this theory
is the role of physical pleasure in inhibiting physical violence
and the primacy of the cutaneous and vestibular sensory modalities
in ontogenetic development.

The unique evolutionary characteristic of this theory is proposed to reside in the human emotional/affective capacity to experience and integrate pleasure with other human capacities and
functions in a manner that is not possible with infra-human mammals. This evolutionary advantage to experience and integrate
pleasure is considered to be sexually dimorphic, i.e., it is
uniquely developed in the human female and thus confers upon the
human female a biological advantage to experience and integrate
pleasure when compared to the human male. The ability to integrate
somatosensory pleasure with higher cortical functions is considered
to be less well developed in the human male than in the human female. It is this difference which is proposed to underlie sex
differences in aggression although these sex differences can be
abolished and reversed by specific ontogenetic experiences. A
corollary of this theory is that the human female is also more
vulnerable to somatosensory pleasure deprivation experiences and
consequently will manifest greater impairments than the human male
when subjected to somatosensory pleasure deprivation. Before pro-
ceeding with the identification of this unique evolutionary characteristic that is considered to be sexually dimorphic and the biological and behavioral evidence that supports it, it would first be
helpful to review the evidence in support of the ontogenetic theory
of human affection and violence which has been summarized elsewhere
(Prescott, 1971, 1975, 1976a, 1976b).

ANIMAL STUDIES

This ontogenetic theory of human affection and violence has
its origins in the primate isolation rearing studies of The Harlows
and their many students and colleagues (Harlow, 1958, 1964, 1971;
Harlow, et al., 1963; Harlow and Harlow, 1965; Harlow, et al., 1966;
Harlow and Seay, 1966; Mason and Berkson, 1975; Mason and Kenney,
1974; Mason, 1968, 1971; Mitchell, 1968, 1970, 1975; Mitchell and
Clark, 1968; Kaufman, 1973a, 1973b; Kaufman and Rosenblum, 1967,
1969; Lichstein and Sackett, 1971; Sackett, 1970a, 1970b; Suomi,
1973; Suomi and Harlow, 1972; Gluck, et al. 1973; Seay, et al.,
1962, 1964; Berkson and Mason, 1964; Jensen et al., 1968, 1973;
Hinde, 1974; Eastman and Mason, 1975; Arling and Harlow, 1967).

In these studies it was found that rearing infant monkeys from birth in single cages but in a colony room where they could see, hear, and smell other monkeys but could not touch or be touched by other monkeys resulted in severe emotional and social pathologies. Symptoms included depressed, withdrawn and autistic-like behaviors; movement sterotypies; self-stimulation; and as juveniles and adults: self-mutilation, pathological violence and abnormal sexual behaviors. Mitchell (1968, 1970, 1975) has, in particular, documented their pathological violence. In addition to these abnormalities it should be noted that these isolation reared animals develop an aversion to touching as well as impaired pain perception. Lichstein and Sackett (1971) have experimentally documented this paradoxical relationship between aversion to touching (a form of hyperreactivity) and impaired pain perception. It should also be recognized that the chronic self-stimulation of these animals (toe and penis sucking early in life and self-mutilation later in life) reflect a high need for tactile stimulation as does the sterotypical rocking behaviors reflect a need for vestibular-cerebellar stimulation. There is sufficient experimental data that documents compensatory chronic stimulus-seeking behaviors consequent to sensory deprivation during the formative periods of development. In other words, there is a greater need for sensory stimulation in the specific sensory modality that has been deprived (Lindsley, et al., 1964; Prescott, 1968, 1971, 1975, 1976). These behaviors in isolation reared monkeys also appear in humans who have been deprived of physical affectional experiences during the formative periods of development and it will be illustrated how parental affectional deprivation is also linked to disturbances in human sexual functioning.

One of the most dramatic findings reported by Mason (1968) and his colleague Berkson (1974) was that artificial movement (vestibular) stimulation provided by a "swinging-mother" surrogate could prevent most of the abnormal emotional-social behaviors from developing in the isolation reared infant monkey. Figure 1 illustrates how the infant monkey reared on its "swinging-mother" surrogate freely interacts with a human attendant showing no fear, no avoidance of touching and no social withdrawal. In contrast, Figure 2 illustrates how the infant monkey reared on the "stationary-mother" surrogate crouches in fear, avoids touching and is socially withdrawn. These behaviors are more dramatically illustrated in the film "Rock-a-Bye Baby" (Dokecki, 1973).[1] It is emphasized

---

[1]The film "Rock-a-Bye Baby" which illustrates many of the abnormal social-emotional behaviors in animals and children subjected to parental-social deprivation can be obtained from Time-Life, Inc., Time-Life Bldg., New York, N.Y.

that vestibular stimulation (movement) is the critical variable
in accounting for the differences in these animals. Figure 3
illustrates two 8 month isolate reared monkeys that were paired
together by the author for a film study of social behaviors and
movement stereotypies. Note the catatonic posturing of the hind
limb of one animal while the other looks on and that they have
physically separated themselves from each other to avoid physical
touching which is highly traumatic to these animals. These behaviors are also vividly portrayed in the film "Rock-a-Bye Baby."
Figure 4 illustrates how two infant monkeys touch and cuddle one
another when they have not been reared in social isolation (deprivation of touch and body movement). It should be noted that physical
touching - grooming and play-movement - are two of the most dominant
social activities in developing mammals and in primates, in particular. Figure 5 illustrates the self-biting and self-mutilation
of the adult isolation reared rhesus. The pathologic violence of
the juvenile and adult rhesus monkey in their attacks against other
monkeys has been extensively documented by Mitchell (1968, 1970,
1975). The pathological attacks of young juvenile isolate monkeys
against large adult monkeys and against helpless infants were particularly noted by Mitchell. Normally reared rhesus are rarely,
if ever, observed to engage in such pathologic violent behaviors.
Figure 6 illustrates a "motherless" mother monkey attacking its
infant and crushing its head to the cage floor. Seay, et al.
(1962, 1964) have documented extensively this "infant abuse" in
"motherless" reared mother monkeys. Harlow and Harlow provide
a vivid description of "motherless" monkey mothering:

> "Female monkeys that fail to develop affection for members
> of their species in their first year of life are ineffective,
> inadequate, and brutal mothers toward their first-born off-
> spring . . . . All seven infants would have died had we not
> intervened and fed them by hand. Five of the mothers were
> brutal to their babies, violently rejected them when the
> babies attempted maternal contact, and frequently struck
> their babies, kicked them, or crushed the babies against the
> cage floor. The other two "motherless mothers" were primarily
> indifferent and one of these mothers behaved as if her infant
> did not exist." (Harlow and Harlow, 1965: 309.)

In addition to the above behavioral pathologies of isolation
reared rhesus monkeys, there is also sexual dysfunctioning in
these animals (Figure 7). As can be seen neither the male nor
the female engage in correct sexual posturing. This issue will
be returned to later.

HUMAN STUDIES

The findings from Harlow's laboratory and his many students

Fig. 1. "Swinging" surrogate reared monkey freely interacts with human attendant.

Fig. 2. "Stationary" surrogate reared monkey avoids interacting with human attendant.

Fig. 3. Two 8 month old isolate reared monkeys who avoid touching and social interaction.

Fig. 4. Two normally reared monkeys touch and cuddle one another.

and colleagues have direct relevance to human behavior in several
respects.   The issue of child abuse and human violence in general
is one such example; impaired sexual functioning is another.   There
are intrinsically interrelated and the nature of their interrela-
tionship will be illustrated later.

Child Abuse Studies

The literature on child abuse has grown extensively and appears
to parallel the increase (actual or reporting patterns) of child
abuse.   Lash and Sigal (1976), for example, have reported a 1,026%
increase in child abuse between 1964 and 1974 for New York City.
Needless to say, it is not possible to ascertain what portion of
this increase is real and what portion reflects better reporting.
The observation that for the United States (1970-1971) accidents
ranked fifth and homicide ranked thirteenth for infant deaths; and
accidents ranked first and homicide ranked fifth for child deaths
(Simopoules, 1976) suggests the degree of societal neglect and
abuse of children that exists in the United States.   It is not
possible to even begin to review the child abuse literature for
this paper; rather the intent is to illustrate the relevance of
primate isolation rearing studies to human child abuse.

Figure 8 illustrates a case of child abuse where this 3 month
old infant had scalded milk thrown on its face.   There are worse
examples of child abuse than what is illustrated here.   The relevance of child abuse to this paper are the findings that parents
who abuse their children were invariably deprived of parental
physical affection, i.e., were subjected to somatosensory pleasure
deprivation during their infancy and childhood.   Steel and Pollack
(1968) have reported in their studies of child abuse that abusing
parents rarely experience pleasure in day-to-day living and that
their sexual lives are especially impoverished.   In personal discussions between Dr. Steele and the senior author he mentioned
that of the hundreds of women he interviewed only a few had ever
reported experiencing orgasm.   Thus, the deprivation of physical
affection and sexual pleasure in adulthood has been linked with
deprivation of parental physical affection and these deprivations
of physical pleasure during two stages of development (pre-pubertal
and post-pubertal) have been linked with adult human violence.
Unfortunately, Dr. Steel did not assess the degree of sexual pleasure experienced by fathers who abuse their children and it should
be noted that ejaculation should not be equated with orgasm.   Ejaculation is a basic reflex which may be associated with very high
or very low degrees of pleasure.   We will return to these issues
later.

Fig. 5. Self-biting and self-mutilation of an adult isolation reared rhesus.

Fig. 6. Motherless mother crushing 20 day old infant to the floor.

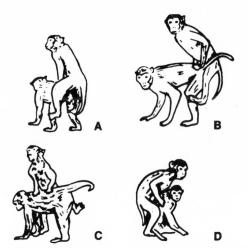

Fig. 7. Normal sexual posturing in the normal male & female rhesus (A, B). Abnormal sexual posturing in the isolation reared male & female rhesus (C, D).

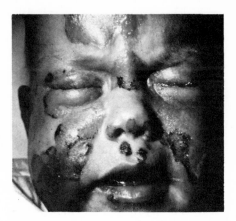

Fig. 8. Physical pain in child abuse: 3 month old child with scaled milk thrown on its face.

Cross-Cultural Studies

In an attempt to provide more substantive data that would
link deprivation of parental physical affection to adult physical
violence and impaired sexuality cross-cultural studies were conducted on pre-industrial cultures.[2] The author is indebted to
Professor John Whiting for bringing his attention to the resources
of the Human Relations Area Files and to R.B. Textor's (1967) A
Cross-Cultural Summary which was the principal source for the
cross-cultural studies. From Textor, the relationships among the
following coded scales were examined: a) infant physical affection provided by Barry et al. (1967); b) repressive sexuality
provided by John T. Wesbrooke (1963) and Ford and Beach (1951) and
c) adult physical violence provided by Philip E. Slater (1967).

For the following Tables the code column is the Textor code
number with the initials of the cultural anthropologist who coded
the variables (s) under Descriptor. This is followed by the value
of the chi square statistic, its level of significance, the number
of cultures in the sample, the phi coefficient and the percent
"correct" classification of cultures in the comparison.

Table 1 presents some of the social and behavioral characteristics of cultures which inflict pain on the infant by the
nurturant agent. Such cultures are characterized by:

a) practice of slavery (P = .03);

b) polygyny has high incidence (P = .001);

c) women status is inferior (P = .03);

d) desire for children is high (P = .003);

e) low infant physical affection (P = .03);

f) low overall infant indulgence (P = .0000);

g) developing nuturant behaviors in children is low (P = .05);

h) supernaturals are aggressive (P = .10);

i) high god is present (P = .08);

j) fears of supernatural forces greater than fears of natural
    forces (P = .03).

----

[2]Some of these findings have been previously reported (Prescott,
1975).

TABLE 1

SOCIAL AND BEHAVIORAL CHARACTERISTICS OF CULTURES
WHICH INFLICT PAIN ON THE INFANT BY NURTURANT AGENT (324-BBC)

CODE	DESCRIPTOR	CHI SQ	P	N	PHI	%
110-EA	Slavery is Present	4.74	.03	66	.27	64
175-EA	Community Not "Kin-Heterogeneous"	5.47	.02	66	.29	64
243-WCS	Polygyny has High Incidence	9.84	.001	34	.54	79
277-LWS	Women Status is Inferior	3.43	.03	14	.50	78
282-BCA	Desire for Children is High	7.22	.003	28	.51	79
299-EA	Post-Partum Sex Taboo Lasts One Year or Less	6.89	.007	36	.44	78
314-WCS	Incidence of Mother-Child Households is High	3.99	.05	45	.30	64
317-BBC	Low Infant Physical Affection	4.71	.03	63	.27	65
318-BBC	Low Overall Infant Indulgence	18.05	.0000	66	.52	77
321-BBC	Immediate Reduction of Infant Drives is Low	3.48	.06	58	.25	64
322-BBC	Consistency of Reducing Infant's Drives is Low	5.08	.02	57	.30	67
340-BBC	Developing Nurturant Behavior in Child is Low	3.87	.05	45	.29	67
425-LTW	Supernaturals are Aggressive	2.17	.10	36	.25	64
426-GES,EA	High God is Present	3.05	.08	57	.23	64
438-WC,JFG	Fears of Supernatural Greater than Fears of Natural Forces	3.88	.03	28	.37	71

The above cluster of interrelationships illustrates a pattern of exploitation and deprivation of women and children being associated with inflicting pain upon the infant by the nurturant agent. It is emphasized that these data document an inverse relationship between infant physical affection and infant physical pain. In this context a "high desire for children" reflects a measure of exploitation and deprivation rather than high nurturance. In many primitive cultures large families are desired to demonstrate "potency" in the male and "fertility" in the female, to provide a labor source, and to provide protection and security in old age.

Table 2 presents some of the social and behavioral characteristics of cultures which provide "high infant physical affection." Selected characteristics of these cultures are highlighted below:

a)   low incidence of theft (P = .02);

b)   low infant physical pain (P = .03);

c)   weaning age is 2.5 years or longer (P = .05);

d)   low demands for child responsibility (P = .004);

e)   killing, torturing or mutilation of enemy is negligible (P = .004);

f)   low religious activity (P = .003).

The variable of particular significance in the above cluster of characteristics is "killing, torturing or mutilation of the enemy" which provides direct support for the main hypothesis that deprivation of infant physical affection is associated with adult physical violence and thereby supports at a high level of statistical significance the extrapolation of effects of infra-human primate isolation rearing (somatosensory deprivation) to consequences of human primate child rearing practices which are also characterized by somatosensory deprivation.

Table 3 presents the distribution of the 49 cultures which relate infant physical affection to adult physical violence. The first two columns include 36 cultures whose physical violence was correctly classified according to the somatosensory pleasure deprivation theory. 13 cultures in the last two columns were not correctly classified according to this theory. It is recognized that a theoretical system must deal with the exceptions and it will be illustrated how these exceptions can be accounted for within the somatosensory pleasure deprivation theory.

TABLE 2

SOCIAL AND BEHAVIORAL CHARACTERISTICS OF CULTURES
WHICH PROVIDE HIGH INFANT PHYSICAL AFFECTION (317–BBC)

CODE	DESCRIPTOR	CHI SQ	P	N	PHI	%
137–PES	Invidious Display of Wealth is Low	3.54	.06	50	.27	66
138–BBW	Super Ordinate Justice is Absent	2.55	.07	22	.34	68
149–BBC	Incidence of Theft is Low	5.51	.02	36	.39	72
318–BBC	Overall Infant Indulgence is High	21.00	.0000	66	.56	80
320–BBC	Degree of Reducing Infant Needs is High	11.95	.0005	65	.43	74
321–BBC	Immediacy of Reducing Infant Needs is High	5.66	.02	59	.31	68
324–BBC	Infant Physical Pain is Low	4.77	.03	63	.27	65
330–BBC	Weaning Age is 2.5 Years or Longer	3.72	.05	63	.24	63
338–BBC	Child's Anxiety Over Performance of Responsible Behavior is Low	8.49	.004	65	.36	68
354–BBC	Child's Anxiety Over Performances of Obedient Behavior is Low	4.61	.03	63	.27	65
368–JKH	Dissociation of Sexes at Adolescence is High	4.43	.03	18	.50	78
421–PES	Killing, Torturing or Mutilation of Enemy is Negligible	8.38	.004	49	.41	73
424–JMH	Low Religious Activity	7.73	.003	27	.54	81
433–GES	Belief in Reincarnation Absent	2.91	.05	17	.41	76
434–JFG	Low Asceticism in Mourning	3.58	.06	41	.30	66
441–WC	Fear of Human Beings is High	6.58	.007	38	.42	71
446–GES	Witchcraft Low or Absent	2.91	.05	17	.41	76

TABLE 3

DISTRIBUTION OF 49 CULTURES WHICH RELATE INFANT
PHYSICAL AFFECTION TO ADULT PHYSICAL VIOLENCE

High Infant Physical Affection - Low Adult Physical Violence	Low Infant Physical Affection - High Adult Physical Violence	High Infant Physical Affection - High Adult Physical Violence	Low Infant Physical Affection - Low Adult Physical Violence
ANDAMANESE SIRIONO	ALORESE	CHEYENNE	AINU
ARAPESH TALLENSI	ARANDA	CHIR-APACHE	GANDA
BALINESE TIKOPIA	ARAUCANIANS	CROW	KWAKIUTL
CHAGGA TIMBIRA	ASHANTI	JIVARO**	LEPCHA
CHENCHU THROBRIAND	AYMARA	KURTATCHI	PUKAPUKA
CHUCKCHEE WOGEO	AZANDE	ZUNI	SAMOANS*
CUNA WOLEAIANS	COMANCHE		TANALA
HANO YAHGAN	FON		
LAU	KASKA		
LESU	MARQUESANS		
MAORI	MASAI		
MURNGIN	NAVAHO		
NUER	OJIBWA		
PAPAGO	THONGA		

—————— Premarital sex punished
- - - - - Premarital sex permitted

N = 49
XSQ = 8.38   PHI = .41
P = .004   % = 73

* According to Derek Freeman, Professor of Anthropology, Australian National University the Samoan culture is misclassified and belongs to column 2. (Personal communication).

** According to Harner (1972) the Jivaro also belongs in column 2 (Personal communication).

For the cultures in the third column, their violence should have been low since they had high infant physical affection. It should be noted that four of the six cultures are punitive toward premarital sex and from other sources the Zuni are also considered to be punitive toward premarital sex (Raoul Naroll, personal communication). Consequently, five of the six cultures are characterized by punitive premarital sexuality. The interpretation of this relationship is that the advantages of early infant physical affection can be negated later in life through repressive sexual pleasure and it is this which accounts for their adult physical violence. The Jivaro is the only exception and this may be due to their religious belief that "killing leads to acquisition of souls which provide a supernatural power conferring immunity from death" (Harner, 1972). A more parsimonious explanation would involve the extension of the somatosensory pleasure deprivation (SPD) theory to the next developmental stage - marital sexuality. The Jivaro strongly punish extramarital sex and wife stealing is punished by death. Given this additional criteria this theory accurately classifies the physical violence in the cultures. It is also of interest to note that Jivaro males appear to prefer hunting to engaging in sexual relations and are "reluctant to engage in sexual intercourse more often than about once every six to eight days." It is also reasoned "that a second wife permits a man to spend more time hunting and thus reduces the frequency of his acts of sexual intercourse" (Harner, 1972). Clearly, the Jivaro do not appear to be a highly sexual active and expressive culture even though premarital sex is accepted. Additionally, Harner (1972) considers the Jivaro as providing low infant affection which places the Jivaro in Colunm 2.

Needless to say it is a subject of future research that should attempt to relate frequency of sexual relations to incidence of physical violence. A necessary consideration for such an inquiry is whether the sexual relation reflects an act of dominance/exploitation or a mutual sharing of physical pleasure. The central issue is the degree of sexual pleasure experienced and not just the frequency of sexual activity, although the two are often assumed to co-vary.

For the cultures in the fourth column their violence should have been high since they had low infant physical affection. All seven of these cultures were characterized by expressive premarital sexuality. The interpretation of this relationship is that the disadvantages of early infant physical affection can be compensated for later in life by enriched physical affection and pleasure experienced through expressive premarital sexuality.

Derek Freeman, professor of Anthropology, Australian National University in a personal communication indicated that the Samoan

culture belongs in column 2 not column 4. Given these revisions
by anthropologists Harner and Freeman there are now 38/49 cultures
whose physical violence is accurately classified from the infant
physical affectional variable with X^2 = 14.69; P = .0002; PHI = 55;
78% correct classification.

In brief, the single variable of physical affection or physical
pleasure experienced in two stages of development (infancy and
adolescence) can correctly classify the physical violence in 48
of 49 pre-industrial cultures which are distributed throughout the
world. An extension of this theory to three stages of development
to include issues of marital sexuality results in a 100% correct
classification of physical violence in these 49 cultures. A re-
classification of the Jivaro in column 2 also results in a 100%
correct classification. Needless to say these data offer no support for a genetic-evolutionary theory of human violence but does
provide substantial support for an ontogenetic-developmental theory
of human violence.

Table 4 provides a summary of social and behavioral characteristics of cultures which are punitive toward premarital sexuality.
It can be seen that these cultures can be characterized as violent,
criminal, sexually dysfunctional and dehumanizing.

Table 5 provides a summary of social and behavioral characteristics of cultures which are punitive toward extramarital sexuality. The statistical relationships are much stronger than for
repression of premarital sexuality and reflect even stronger as-
sociations of violence, criminality, militarism, exploitation of
women and children and dehumanization with repressive extramarital
sexuality. It should also be noted that belief in a "high god in
human morality who is punitive and aggressive" is also a characteristic of these cultures.

Cross-Cultural Studies in Perspective

A systematic review of cross-cultural studies on aggression
is beyond the scope of this paper, however, it would be remiss not
to mention selected studies by cultural anthropologists who have
previously linked certain parent-child relationships and other
cultural factors to the development of social and asocial behaviors (Whiting and Child, 1953; Bacon, Child and Barry, 1963; Whiting et al., 1958; Whiting, 1969, 1971; Ainsworth, 1967; Barry et
al., 1967; Russell, 1972; Rohner, 1975; Otterbein, 1970; Naroll,
1970; Slater and Slater, 1965; Freeman, 1971; Alcock, 1976).

The longitudinal study of the development of aggression by
Lefkowitz, et al. (1977) is an additional essential reference which

TABLE 4

SOCIAL AND BEHAVIORAL CHARACTERISTICS OF CULTURES
WHICH ARE PUNITIVE TOWARD PREMARITAL SEXUALITY (389-392-JTW,EA)

CODE	DESCRIPTOR	XSQ	P	N	PHI	%
81-EA	Community Size is Larger	13.11	.0003	80	.41	73
91-FW	Societal Complexity is High	5.13	.01	15	.56	87
102-EA	Class Stratification Present	6.25	.01	111	.24	60
110-EA	Slavery is Present	7.87	.005	176	.21	59
127-JKB	Low Female Income	2.84	.09	24	.34	71
148-BBC	Personal Crime is High (392)	3.45	.05	28	.35	71
149-BBC	Incidence of Theft is High (392)	2.70	.07	31	.30	68
186-EA	Kin Group Exclusively Patrilineal	4.39	.04	114	.20	62
190-EA	Kin Groups Patrilineal or Double Descent Rather than Matrilineal	10.10	.002	62	.40	64
240-EA	Small Extended Family	7.13	.008	63	.34	70
262-EA	Wives are "Purchased"	5.58	.02	114	.22	54
278-LWS	Women have Property Rights	5.41	.008	9	.78	100
301-EA	Longer Post-Partum Sex Taboo	4.86	.03	50	.31	62
393-FB	Extramarital Sex is Punished	7.96	.005	58	.37	71
397-JKH	Sex Disability is Present	6.94	.004	23	.55	83
399-WNS	Castration Anxiety is High	5.23	.009	37	.38	65
420-PES	Bellicosity is Extreme	3.50	.04	37	.31	68
421-PES	Killing, Torturing, Mutilating is High	3.26	.07	35	.31	69
428-GES	High God in Human Morality	5.44	.01	27	.45	81
472-PES	Narcissism is High	3.31	.04	38	.30	66
475-PES	Exhibitionistic Dancing Emphasized (392)	4.16	.04	66	.25	65

TABLE 5

SOCIAL AND BEHAVIORAL CHARACTERISTICS OF CULTURES
WHICH ARE PUNITIVE TOWARD EXTRAMARITAL SEXUALITY (393-FB)

CODE	DESCRIPTOR	XSQ	P	N	PHI	%
110-EA	Slavery is Present	10.12	.002	83	.35	67
133-GES	Contracted Debts Highly Present	3.43	.03	14	.50	79
137-PES	Display of Wealth Emphasized	3.05	.08	44	.26	63
148-BBC	Personal Crime is High	4.38	.02	20	.47	80
149-BBC	Incidence of Theft is High	5.86	.008	21	.53	81
175-EA	Community Not "Kin-Heterogeneous"	3.12	.08	84	.19	60
190-EA	Kin Group Patrilineal or Double Decent Rather than Matrilineal	2.76	.10	52	.23	63
258-WNS	High Avoidance of Son's Wife	4.13	.02	17	.49	76
282-BCA	Desire for Children is High	3.41	.05	27	.36	70
295-BCA	Abortion is Highly Punished	3.14	.05	17	.43	76
301-EA	Greater Post-Partum Sex Taboo	3.01	.08	43	.26	65
320-BBC	Low Degree of Reducing Infant's Needs	3.34	.05	37	.30	68
321-BBC	Infant Needs Not Immediately Met	3.01	.07	31	.31	68
337-BBC	Child Responsibility: High Child Anxiety	3.26	.05	37	.30	68
345-BBC	Child Autonomy: High Child Anxiety	9.24	.001	39	.49	77
353-BBC	Child Obedience: High Child Anxiety	5.24	.02	38	.37	71
392-JTW,EA	Premarital Sex Strongly Punished	7.26	.005	58	.37	71
399-WNS	Castration Anxiety is High	13.33	.0001	30	.67	87
419-PES	Military Glory Strongly Emphasized	9.52	.002	53	.47	62
420-PES	Bellicosity is Extreme	10.10	.002	43	.49	77
421-PES	Killing, Torturing, Mutilating is High	9.33	.002	42	.47	76
425-LTW	Supernaturals are Aggressive	4.54	.02	19	.49	79

has contributed significantly to the literature on childhood experience and later violence. Their findings that parental rejection and lack of parental nurturence of the child is significantly
linked to the expression of aggression is consistent with the findings of Mantell (1974), Rohner (1975) and the point-of-view developed herein and elsewhere (Prescott, 1975).

Limitations of space, unfortunately, preclude the reporting
of extensive psychometric studies on the consequences of parental
affectional deprivation upon sexual functioning, social/moral
values and alcohol/drug usage. These studies fully support the
conclusion that females are more vulnerable to deprivation of
parental affection than are males. These findings will be reported
in full elsewhere which are related to the conceptualization of
physical pleasure as a sexually-dimorphic characteristic.

EVOLUTION OF PHYSICAL PLEASURE:
A SEXUALLY DIMORPHIC CHARACTERISTIC?

It has been previously argued that the sensory neurobiological
mechanisms of physical pleasure are the somesthetic (touch) and
vestibular (movement) sensory systems. These emotional senses and
associated brain mechanisms should be expected to show sexually
dimorphic characteristics associated with pleasure and pain experiences. Thus, these primary sensory processes and the central
neural integrative mechanisms of these afferent processes become
subjects for systematic study with respect to the hypothesis being
proposed.

The specific evolutionary process that is being proposed which
confers upon the human female an evolutionary biological advantage
of experiencing and integrating physical pleasure to an extent
that is not shared by the human male involves the relationship
between ovarian cyclic processes and sexual behavior. A major
evolutionary change in mammalian sexual behavior is the emergence
of human female sexuality that is relatively autonomous from ovarian
cyclic processes and reproductive intent. This dramatic evolutionary
change of sexual function observed in the human female is not shared
by the human male since mammalian males, except for seasonal breed-
ers, have always had the potential for sexual activity when presented with an estrous female. What then is the primary function
intended by this evolutionary change in sexual receptivity and
activity of the human female? Clearly, it is no longer primarily
"reproductive intent" which is characteristic of infra-human mammals except for certain primates under conditions of captivity,
e.g., stumptail macaques (M. arctoides) (Slob et al., 1975; Bielert,
1976; Goy, 1977).

There can be only one alternative: physical pleasure. It is clear that the primary function of human sexuality is for the experiencing of physical pleasure; and "reproductive intent" is clearly secondary. This is so obvious that it hardly needs stating except that there are strong religious viewpoints to the contrary. It is only necessary to compare the number of children in a family to the total incidence of intercourse in a lifetime of a couple to be convinced that the primary function of human sexuality is physical pleasure.

With respect to the unique role of physical pleasure in human female sexuality other phenomena can be cited, e.g., multiple orgasms which are common experiences for many women but are rare, if non-existent, in men. The distinction between multiple (absence of refractory phases) and sequential (presence of refractory phases) orgasm becomes an important consideration in this context and it is recognized that these differences are a subject of considerable discussion and research. It is not necessary to take an extreme sexually dimorphic view of multiple orgasms to support the hypothesis, i.e., to posit non-overlapping distributions between the sexes with respect to the phenomena of multiple orgasms. It is probable that an extremely small percentage of men may experience multiple orgasms which would not invalidate the criteria of multiple orgasms as being primarily a human female sexual characteristic that denotes an unusual capacity to experience and integrate physical pleasure (Masters and Johnson, 1966). It is recognized that there is a difference of opinion on the interpretation of multiple orgasms in women, particularly those that are induced by clitoral stimulation with vibrators. Frankl (1974) has argued that such phenomena represent orgasmic spasms and not orgasmic discharge and that women who terminate many such orgasms from physical exhaustion are not necessarily gratified in the Reichian orgasmic sense. The commentary on these issues by Frankl is worth reading in full. (Frankl, 1974: 153-154.)

This does not, however, exclude the existence of genuine (Reichian) multiple orgasms in women which are not characteristic of the male sexual response, although it may be experienced in some males (Robbins, 1976). Needless to say, these issues require systematic research to clarify more specifically the pleasure dimensions of the male and female orgasm. Consistent with the theoretical point-of-view being developed herein it is suggested that the male human orgasm is more "reflexive" and less "integrative" which reduces states of physiological tension rather than producing positive states of "integrative-pleasure." The increased capacity of the human female to experience and integrate sexual pleasure with her somatic and psychological life is proposed to account for sex differences in aggression. Such integrative capacity appears to be more developed in women than men. The descriptive reports of physical pleasure and orgasm by women presented in The Hite Report are supportive of this interpretation. A common report is that the whole body is involved in the orgasmic pleasure experience – from head to toe; suspension of time – no past and no future; emergence and integration of one's body with her partner – "as we two become one." In addition, it is of interest to note that descriptions involving vestibular-cerebellar mediated sensations are reported, e.g., "floating," "drifting," "flowing" and identification with the universe or cosmos, etc. Similar reports were given by Seymour Fisher in The Female Orgasm (1973). Unfortunately, no comparable data appears to exist for men. Space does not permit even a brief outline of how these differences in experiencing and integrating physical pleasure between men and women may be represented in brain mechanisms. Consistent with previous theoretical speculations it would seem that cerebellar-frontal/cortical-limbic system interrelationships are to be emphasized.

It is heuristic to relate the issue of integrating physical pleasure with higher levels of consciousness to Bakan's (1966) concept of agency (male) and communion (female) in human sexuality where "agency" manifests itself in the formation of separation, isolation, alienation and aloneness; and "communion" manifests itself in contact, openness and union. Similarly, within this context, Koestenbaum's (1974) concept of existential sexuality as pre-sexual, pre-erotic, pre-biological and pre-somatic, as a manifestation of "pure consciousness," deserves systematic attention that is not possible to develop herein. Bakan (1966), Koestenbaum (1974), Marcuse (1962, 1964, 1969), and Frankl (1974) provide rare resources to explore more fully the philosophical, social and psychological dimensions of human sexuality that have been illuminated by the pioneering studies of Reich (1942, 1945, 1971).

EPILOGUE

It is the conclusion of this writer that deprivation of physical affection in human relationships, particularly, the repression of female sexuality constitutes the single greatest source of physical violence in human societies. It is also held that as somatosensory pleasure inhibits physical violence, its coexistent of mutual sharing in the male/female relationship also neutralizes power and authority in that relationship. Thus, physical pleasure mutually shared constitutes a psychobiological substrate for egalitarian democratic relationships which is antithetical to authoritarian, fascist relationships. It is for these reasons that religious systems that place a high moral value on pain, suffering and deprivation and place immoral values on physical pleasure, which emphasize the virtues of virginity and celibacy contribute substantially to authoritarian, fascist societies and the prevalence of physical violence (Prescott, 1975, 1976).

A moral revolution is necessary if human societies are to become humanized. The morality of physical pleasure mutually shared must be affirmed and the immorality of pain, suffering and deprivation must be acknowledged.

REFERENCES

Adorno, T.W., Frenkel-Brunswik, E., Levinson, D.J. and Sanford, R.N. (1950). The Authoritarian Personality, The American Jewish Committee, Norton, New York.

Ainsworth, M.D.S. (1967). Infancy in Uganda: Infant Care and the Growth of Love, Johns Hopkins Press, Baltimore.

Alcock, N. (1976). The Logic of Love, Canadian Peace Research Institute, Oakville, Ontario.

Arling, G.L. and Harlow, H.F. (1967). Effects of social deprivation on maternal behavior of rhesus monkeys. Journal of Comparative and Physiological Psychology, 64: 371-377.

Bacon, M.K., Child, I.L. and Barry, III, H. (1963). A cross-cultural study of correlates of crime. Journal of Abnormal and Social Psychology, 66: 291-300.

Bakan, D. (1966). The Duality of Human Existence. Beacon Press, Boston.

Barry, III, H., Bacon, M.K. and Child, I.L. (1967). Definitions, ratings and bibliographic sources for child-training practices of 100 cultures. In Ford, C.S. (ed.), Cross-Cultural Approaches: Readings in Cooperative Research, HRAF Press, New Haven, Connecticut.

Barry, III, H. and Paxon, L.M. (1971). Infancy and early childhood: cross-cultural codes 2. Ethnology, 10 (4): 466-508.

Berkson, G. and Mason, W.A. (1964). Stereotyped behaviors of chimpanzees: relation to general arousal and alternative activities. Perceptional and Motor Skills, 19: 635-652.

Berkson, G. (1974). Social responses of animals to infants with defects. In Lewis, M. and Rosenblum, L.W. (eds.), The Origins of Behavior, Academic Press, New York.

Bielert, C., Czaja, J.A., Eisele, S., Scheffler, G., Robinson, J.A. and Goy, R.W. (1976). Mating in the rhesus monkey (Macada Mulatta) after conception and its relationship to oestradial and progesterone levels throughout pregnancy. Journal of Reproductive Fertility, 46: 179-187.

Dokecki, P.R. (1973). When the bough breaks . . . what will happen
    to baby? Film review of "Rock-a-Bye Baby". Contemporary
    Psychology, 18: 64.

Eastman, R.F. and Mason, W.A. (1975). Looking behavior in monkeys
    raised with mobile and stationary artificial mothers. De-
    velopmental Psychobiology, 8: 213-221.

Fisher, S. (1973). The Female Orgasm, Basic Books, New York.

Ford, C.S. and Beach, F.A. (1951). Patterns of Sexual Behavior,
    Harper, New York.

Ford, C.S. (1967). Cross-Cultural Approaches: Readings in Com-
    parative Research, HRAF, New Haven, Connecticut.

Frankl, G. (1974). The Failure of the Sexual Revolution, New
    English Library Ltd. Mentor Editor, Great Britain.

Freeman, D. (1971). Aggression: instinct or symptom. Australian
    New Zealand Journal of Psychiatry, 5: 66-73.

Gluck, J.P., Harlow, H.F. and Schiltz, K.A. (1973). Differential
    effect of early enrichment and deprivation on learning in
    rhesus monkey (macaca mulatta). Journal of Comparative and
    Physiological Psychology, 84: 598-604.

Goy, R.W. (1977). Personal Communication.

Harlow, H.F. (1958). The nature of love. American Psychologist,
    13: 673-685.

Harlow, H.F., Harlow, M.K. and Hansen, E.W. (1963). The maternal
    affectional system of rhesus monekys. In Rheingold, H.L.,
    (ed.), Maternal Behaviors in Mammals, John Wiley, New York.

Harlow, H.F. (1964). Early social deprivation and later behavior
    in the monkey. Unfinished Tasks in the Behavioral Sciences,
    In Williams and Wilkins, Baltimore, Maryland.

Harlow, H.F. and Harlow, M.K. (1965). The affectional systems. In
    Schrier, A.M., Harlow, H.F. and Stollnitz, F., (eds.), Be-
    havior of Nonhuman Primates, Vol. II, Academic Press, New
    York.

Harlow, H.F., Harlow, M.K., Dodsworth, R.O., and Arling, G.L. (1966).
    Maternal behavior of rhesus monkeys deprived of mothering and
    peer association in infancy. Proceedings of the American
    Philosophical Society, 110: 58-66.

Harlow, H.F. and Seay, B. (1966). Mothering in motherless mother monekys. The British Journal of Social Psychiatry, 1: 63-69.

Harlow, H.F. (1971). Learning to Love, Albion Publishing Company, San Francisco, California.

Harner, M.J. (1972). The Jivaro, National History Press, New York.

Hinde, R.A. (1974). Mother/infant relations in rhesus monkeys. In White, N.F. (ed.), Ethology and Psychiatry, University of Toronto Press, Toronto.

Hite, S. (1976). The Hite Report: A Nationwide Study of Female Sexuality, MacMillan Publishing Company, New York.

Jensen, G.D., Bobbitt, R.A. and Gordon, B.N. (1968). Effects of environment on the relationship between mother and infant pigtailed monkeys. Journal of Comparative Physiology and Psychology, 66: 259-263.

Jensen, G.D., Bobbitt, R.A. and Gordon, B.N. (1973). Mother and infant roles in the development of independence of Macaca Nemestrina. In Carpenter, C.R. (ed.), Behavioral Regulators of Behavior in Primates, Bucknell University Press, Lewisburg, Pennsylvania.

Kaufman, I.C. and Rosenblum, L.A. (1967). The reaction to separation in infant monekys: anaclitic depression and conservation - withdrawal. Psychosomatic Medicine, 29: 648-675.

Kaufman, I.C. and Rosenblum, L.A. (1969). Effects of separation from mother on the emotional behavior of infant monkeys. Annals of the New York Academy of Sciences, 159: 681-695.

Kaufman, I.C. (1973). Mother-infant separation in monekys. In Separation and Depression, AAAS.

Kaufman, I.C. (1973). The role of ontogeny in the establishment of species-specific patterns. Early Development, A.R.N.M.D., 51: 381-397.

Kennell, J.H., Jerauld, R., Wolfe, H., Chesler, D., Kreger, N.C., McAlpine, W., Steffa, M. and Klaus, M.H., (1974). Maternal behavior one year after early and extended post-partum contact. Developmental Medicine and Child Neurology, 16: 172-179.

Koestenbaum, P. (1974). Existential Sexuality: Choosing to Love, Prentice Hall Spectrum Book, New Jersey.

Lash, T.W. and Sigal, H. (1976). State of the Child: New York City, Foundation for Child Development, New York.

Lefkowitz, M.M., Eron, L.D., Walder, L.O. and Huesmann, L.R. (1977). Growing up to be violent, Pergamon Press, New York.

Lichstein, L. and Sackett, G.P. (1971). Reactions by differentially raised rhesus monkeys to noxious stimulation. Developmental Psychobiology, 4: 339-352.

Lindsley, D.B., Wendt, R.H., Lindsley, D.F., Fox, S.S., Howell, Jr., and Adey, W.R. (1964). Diurnal activity behavior and EEG responses in visually deprived monekys. Annals of the New York Academy of Sciences, 117: 564-587.

Lynch, J.J. (1970). Psychophysiology and development of social attachment. Psychophysiology, 151: 231-244.

Mantell, D.M. (1974). True Americanism: Green Berets and War Resistors, Teacher's College Press, Columbia University, New York.

Marcuse, H. (1962). Eros and Civilization. Alfred A. Knopf, New York, Vintage Books Edition.

Marcuse, H. (1964). One-Dimensional Man. Beacon Press, Boston.

Marcuse, H. (1969). An Essay on Liberation. Beacon Press, Boston.

Mason, W.A. (1968). Early social deprivation in the non-human primates: implications for human behavior. In Glass, D.E. (ed.), Environmental Influences, The Rockefeller University Press and Russell Sage Foundation, New York.

Mason, W.A. (1971). Motivational factors in psychosocial development. In Arnold, W.J. and Page, M.M. (eds.), Nebraska Symposium on Motivation, University of Nebraska Press,

Mason, W.A. and Kenney, M.D. (1974). Redirection of filial attachments in rhesus monkeys dogs as mother surrogates. Science, 183: 1209-1211.

Mason, W.A. and Berkson, G. (1975). Effects of maternal mobility on the development of rocking and other behaviors in rhesus monkeys: a study with artificial mothers. Developmental Psychobiology, 8: 197-211.

Masters, W.H. and Johnson, V.E. (1966). Human Sexual Response, Little, Brown, Boston.

Meadows, R. (1934). A Private Anthrological Cabinet of 500 Authentic
    Racial-Esoteric Photographs and Illustrations, Privately Is-
    sued. Copy #965 Falstaff Press, New York.

Melzack, R. and Scott, T.H. (1957). The effects of early experience
    on the response to pain. Journal of Comparative Physiology
    and Psychology, 50: 155-161.

Mitchell, G.D. (1968). Persistent behavior pathology in rhesus
    monkeys following early social isolation. Folia Primatol-
    ogy, 8: 132-147.

Mitchell, G.D., and Clark, D.L. (1968). Long-term effects of social
    isolation in nonsocially adapted rhesus monkeys. The Jour-
    nal of Genetic Psychology, 113: 117-128.

Mitchell, G.D. (1970). Abnormal behavior in primates. In Rosen-
    blum, L.A. (ed.) Primate Behavior: Developments in Field
    and Laboratory Studies, Academic Press, New York, 195-249.

Mitchell, G. (1975). What monkeys can tell us about human violence.
    The Futurist, April: 75-80.

Otterbein, K.F. (1970). The Evolution of War, HRAF Press, New
    Haven, Connecticut.

Prescott, J.W. (1967). Invited commentray: central nervous system
    functioning in altered sensory environments (Cohen, S.I.).
    In Appley, M.H. and Trumbull, R. (eds.) Psychological Stress,
    Appleton-Century-Crofts, New York.

Prescott, J.W. (1971). Early somatosensory deprivation as an on-
    togenetic process in the abnormal development of the brain
    and behavior. In Goldsmith, I.E. and Moor-Jankowski (eds.),
    Medical Primatology 1970, Karger, Basel.

Prescott, J.W. (1972). Before ethics and morality. The Humanist,
    Nov/Dec: 19-21.

Prescott, J.W. (1973). Commentary: sexual behavior in the blind.
    In Gillman, A.E. and Gordon, A.R. (eds.), Medical Aspects
    of Human Sexuality, June: 59-60.

Prescott, J.W. (1975). Body pleasure and the origins of violence.
    The Futurist, April: 64-74.

Prescott, J.W. (1976a). Somatosensory deprivation and its relation-
    ship to the blind. In Jastrzembska Z.S. (ed.), The Effects
    óf Blindness and Other Impairments on Early Development,
    American Foundation for the Blind, New York.

Prescott, J.W. (1976b). Violence, pleasure and religion. In The Bulletin of the Atomic Scientists, March 1976 (b).

Reich, W. (1942). The Function of the Orgasm, Farror, Straus and Giroux, New York.

Reich, W. (1945). The Sexual Revolution, Farror, Straus and Giroux, New York.

Reich, W. (1971). The Invasion of Compulsory Sex - Morality, Farror, Straus and Giroux, New York.

Rheingold, H.L. (Ed.) (1963). Maternal Behavior in Mammals, John Wiley and Sons, Inc., New York.

Riesen, A.H. (1961). Stimulation as a requirement for growth and function. In Fiske and Maddi (eds.), Functions of Varied Experiences, Dorsey Press, Homewood.

Riesen, A.H. (1975). The Developmental Neuropsychology of Sensory Deprivation, Academic Press, New York.

Robbins, M.B. (1976). Multiple orgasm in male. International Congress of Sexology, Montreal, Canada, October 1976.

Rohner, R.P. (1975). They Love Me, They Love Me Not: A World Wide Study of the Effects of Parental Acceptance and Rejection, HRAF Press, New Haven.

Russell, E.W. (1972). Factors of human aggression: a cross-cultural factor analysis of characteristics related to warfare and crime. Behavior Science Notes, HRAF Quarterly Bulletin, 1: 275-312.

Sackett, G.P. (1970). Innate mechanisms, rearing conditions, and a theory of early experience effects in primates. In Jones, M.R. (ed.) Miami Symposium on Prediction of Behavior: Early Experience, University of Miami Press, Miami.

Sackett, G.P. (1970). Unlearned responses, differential rearing experiences, and the development of social attachments by rhesus monkeys. In Rosenblum, L.A. (ed.), Primate Behavior: Developments in Field and Laboratory Research, Vol. 1, Academic Press, New York.

Seay, B., Hansen, E. and Harlow, H.F. (1962). Mother-infant separation in monkeys. Journal of Child Psychology and Psychiatry, 3: 123.

Seay, B., Alaexander, B.K. and Harlow, H.F. (1964). Maternal be-
    havior of socially deprived rhesus monkeys. Journal of Ab-
    normal and Social Psychology, 69: 345-354.

Simopoules, A.P. (1976). Maternal and child health research com-
    mittee on maternal and child health research. Division of
    Medical Sciences, Assembly of Life Sciences, National Re-
    search Council, National Academy of Sciences, Washington,
    D.C.

Slater, P.E. and Slater, D.A. (1965). Maternal ambivalence and
    narcissism: a cross-cultural study. Merrill-Palmer Quar-
    terly of Behavior and Development, 11: 241-259.

Slater, P.E. (1967). Unpublished coding guide for the cross-cul-
    tural study of narcissism. Walthom, Massachusetts, 1964.
    Source for code on "Killing, Torturing or Mutilating the
    Enemy", R.B. Textor.

Slob, A.K., Wiegand, S., and Goy, R.W.   Unpublished manuscript.

Steel, B.F. and Pollack, D.B. (1968). A psychiatric study of
    parents who abuse infants and small children. In Helfer,
    R.E. and Kempe, C.H. (eds.), The Battered Child, University
    of Chicago Press, Chicago.

Suomi, S.J. and Harlow, H.F. (1972). Social rehabilitation of
    isolate-reared monkeys. Developmental Psychology, 6: 487-
    496.

Suomi, S.J. (1973). Surrogate rehabilitation of monkeys reared in
    total social isolation. Journal of Child Psychology and
    Psychiatry, 14: 71-77.

Textor, R.B. (1967). A Cross-Cultural Summary, HRAF Press, New
    Haven.

Westbrooke, J.T. (1963). Unpublished coding modified by the
    Ethnographic Atlas, Column 78: 116.

Whiting, B. (1963). Six Cultures. Wiley, New York.

Whiting, B.B. (1965). Sex identity conflict and physical violences:
    a comparative study. American Anthropologist, 67: 123-140.

Whiting, B.B. and Whiting, J.W.M. (1975). Children of Six Cultures:
    A Psycho-Cultural Analysis, Harvard University Press, Cam-
    bridge, Massachusetts.

Whiting, J.W.M. and Child, I.L. (1953). Child Training and Personality. Yale University Press, New Haven.

Whiting, J.W.M., Dluckhorn, R. and Anthony, A. (1958). The function of male initiation ceremonies at puberty. In Maccoby, EE., Newbomb, T.M. and Hartley, E.L. (eds.) Readings in Social Psychology, Henry Holt and Company, Inc., New York.

Whiting, J.W.M. (1969). The place of aggression in social interaction. American Anthropological Association, Annual Conference, New Orleans.

Whiting, J.W.M. (1971). Causes and consequences of the amount of body contact between mother and infant. American Anthropological Association Annual Meeting, New York.

SEX ATTITUDES AND PRACTICES IN TWO LANGUAGE GROUPS IN SOUTH AFRICA

Colin M. Shapiro and Eric D. Stillerman

South Africa

To the best of our knowledge no study has ever been accomplished comparing sexual attitudes of Afrikaans-speaking (AS) and English-speaking (ES) groups. We examined this question as part of a larger study on sex attitudes in South Africa.

South African society comprises a mosaic of different socio-cultural groups with a variety of normative patterns of attitudes and behavior in many spheres. The Caucasian community contains two major groups, the Afrikaans-speaking community and the English-speaking community. Afrikaans as a language is derived mainly from Dutch and German and is only spoken in South Africa.

Historically, English-speaking and Afrikaans-speaking communities have encountered long periods of social, cultural, political and economic separation within South Africa. The Afrikaner, with a rural and pioneering background, maintains a strong community identity, expressed not only in politics, but in almost exclusive allegiance to Afrikaans' language, churches, schools, universities and cultural institutions. Integral to the strong community identity and pioneering background is a certain degree of isolationism from the mainstream of Western European cultural evolution as compared to the English-speaking group.

METHODS AND SUBJECTS

Questionnaire

There are definite research advantages in using personal interviews to study sex attitudes and practices. It was felt, however,

that in the South African context an anonymous questionnaire would
be more likely to produce honest replies and hence a more valid
survey. A questionnaire was designed adapted from validated and
reliable questionnaires in print. Over one thousand questions
were considered, the major sources of which were: The Reiss scale
of premarital sexual permissiveness, the Bentler and Zucherman
scales of Heterosexual Behavior, the Sex Inventory devised by J.C.
Thorne, the Kinsey reports, and the recent Sorensen report on
adolescent sexuality.

After evaluation by a team of judges of the Medical Faculty
and at the National Institute for Personnel Research, a final form
of seventy-six questions was designed. Questions were judged and
selected for their validity and reliability and for their comparison
value with previous research. The entire questionnaire covered a
wide range of attitudes, knowledge and behavior while not being too
demanding on the respondents in terms of questionnaire "test-fatigue.
Each question was presented in both English and Afrikaans.

The first seventeen questions covered demographic variables
known or expected to relate to sex attitudes and behavior. Among
these variables were age, sex, religion, religious commitment,
income, language, education and birth order. The next thirty
questions contained interspersed questions relating to knowledge
of sexual medical facts, and of sexual activities, attitudes and
practices concerning topics as sex education, abortion and contraception.

The final group of questions consisted of modified versions
of two published and validated Guttman scales, one dealing with
attitudes and the other with sexual behavior. The twelve item
version of the Reiss scale of premarital sexual permissiveness
(i.e., attitudes) form a Guttman scale implying an ordinal sequence
of behaviorally-anchored attitudes, such that agreement with the
most "difficult" item implies endorsement of all the less "difficult"
items. For example, agreement with "sexual intercourse between
unmarried couples who have no particular affection" implied agreement with "sexual intercourse between unmarried couples who are in
love." In this manner, the Reiss scale measures the acceptability
of three levels of premarital sexual behavior (i.e., kissing,
petting and sexual intercourse) interacting with four levels of
emotional commitment between unmarried couples (i.e. no affection,
strong affection, love and being engaged to be married). The terms
kissing, petting, sexual intercourse, strong affection and love
were defined in the questionnaire in the same way as they appear
in the original form of the shortened Bentler scale of Heterosexual
Behavior, comprising eleven items in parallel form for males and
females. The Bentler scale and the closely related Zuckerman scale
both yield reproducible Guttman scales with activities ranging from
"one minute's continuous mouth-kissing" to "mutual oral-genital

manipulation to mutual orgasm."

The advantage of using the above two scales is that they are based on far larger numbers of questions from which ordinal sequences were empirically derived. From the longer lists a smaller number of questions were extracted by the original authors, correlating almost perfectly ($r \simeq 0.97$) with the full lists of items.

Sample

To compare the ES population to the AS population, two matched samples were drawn from the predominantly English-speaking nurses at the Johannesburgh General Hospital and the predominantly Afrikaans-speaking nurses at the J.G. Strydom Hospital. Both hospitals are in Johannesburg which has a population of one million.

The two samples were matched for age, education, income and, of course, for occupation. The main significant difference between the two groups, besides language, was their religious affiliations and levels of religious commitment, with the AS nurses belonging to typically Afrikaans denominations and being more religiously committed, and the ES belonging to predominantly English community denominations and being less committed. This difference is one of the central distinctions between English and Afrikaans-speaking communities. The scope of the language comparison is limited by the female bias in both groups of nurses, but the matching design of the two samples makes the comparison valid within this limitation.

The questionnaire administration was completely confidential and it was clearly indicated that if the respondents objected to any particular question they were free to leave it blank, and further that if respondents objected to the questionnaire in principle, they were free to return it unanswered. It was attempted in such cases, however, to obtain responses to the demographic questions, to enable an analysis of possible biases in the sample.

RESULTS

The two nursing samples have been pooled and subdivided into two homogeneous language groups i.e., English and Afrikaans-speaking. Demographic characteristics, such as age, education, income, birth order, travel experience and marital status were similar in the two groups. Exceptions to this similarity were significantly different, urban-rural ($\alpha < 0.04$ using the X^2 test) with Afrikaans speakers more likely to have been brought up in a "large city" and

English speakers in a "large town," and both religious affiliations
and levels of religious commitment were significantly different with
most of the Afrikaans-speaking group belonging to the traditional
Afrikaans denominations (such as the Dutch Reformed Church) and
being more religiously committed, and the English group belonging
to other denominations and being mainly "not very" or "not at all"
religious. The urban-rural difference is in the opposite direction
expected, and thus provides and ad hoc control of a possible nuisance
variable, i.e., that the English/Afrikaans difference may, in fact,
be associated with urban-rural differences in the more commonly
expected direction.

The ES group and the AS group shared similar responses to
many of the attitude, knowledge and behavior questions, but numerous
differences emerged.

Sex education questions revealed no significant differences
between the groups. In both groups, 35% felt that contraception
should be the woman's responsibility. "Abortion on demand" is
favored by only 21% of the AS group as opposed to 40% in the ES
group. Knowledge of medical terms was similar in both groups in
the cases of "sterility" and "frigidity," but the meaning of "impotence" was significantly less often identified in the AS group
than in the ES group ($\alpha < 0.03$: ESG 95% correct, ASG 60% correct).
"Cunnilingus" and"fellatio" were also less often correctly defined
by the AS group, but it is suspected that the problems of translation underscore this finding. Only 25% of both groups stated that
sterilization of the male always or usually leads to impotence,
and 66% of both groups correctly responded that it usually takes
the female longer than the male from time of arousal until orgasm.
Of the AS group, 25% would approach their doctors for advice on a
sex problem, as opposed to none of the ES group.

The first experience of sexual intercourse among the ES group
tended to be with a "boyfriend or girlfriend," but the AS group
often had had their first experience with their spouses or fiances
($\alpha < 0,01$). A majority (71%) of the AS group disapproved of premarital sexual intercourse for their children of both sexes as
opposed to 29% of the ES group ($\alpha < 0.02$). The AS group would be
more concerned about marrying a non-virgin ($\alpha < 0.03$) and would be
more likely to divorce or react strongly to their spouses in the
event of extramarital sex ($\alpha < 0,05$). In both groups 75% found the
idea of any orgy unacceptable or disgusting, and 84% had never been
attracted to a member of their own sex. Less than 20% of both
groups had ever been physically attracted to a person of their own
sex. A comparison of responses of the ES and AS group to the Reiss
and Bentler scales is shown in Tables 1 and 2. One important point
to note is the time lapse since Reiss (1960) and Bentler (1968)
published their scales.

TABLE 1

BENTLER SCALE OF HETEROSEXUAL BEHAVIOR: FEMALES

BENTLER SCALE ITEMS	BENTLER ORDER	ENGLISH NURSES		AFRIKAANS NURSES	
Have you experienced:	No.	No.	%	No.	%
One minute continuous mouth kissing	1	1	(89)	1	(100)
Manipulation of nude female breasts	2	2	(89)	2	(93)
Kissing female nipples	3	3	(83)	3	(67)
Mutual manipulation of covered genitals	4	6	(67)	5	(60)
Manipulation of nude male genitals	5	5	(78)	4	(67)
Sexual intercourse ventral-ventral	6	4	(83)	6	(53)
Oral manipulation of male genitals	7	7	(61)	8	(27)
Mutual oral-genital manipulation	8	9	(56)	9	(27)
Sexual intercourse ventral-dorsal	9	8	(61)	7	(47)
Mutual oral-genital manip. to orgasm	10	10	(44)	10	(20)
Coefficient of Reproducibility	0.98	0.92		0.98	
Coefficient of Scalability	–	0.69		0.92	
Sample size	175	28		23	
Sample mean	5.23	3.50		2.36	
Standard deviation	3.17	2.64		2.41	

Bentler-English Spearman Correlation (rho) $p = 0.97$

Bentler-Afrikaans Spearman Correlation (rho) $p = 0.95$

English-Afrikaans Spearman Correlation (rho) $p = 0.95$

TABLE 2

REISS SCALE OF PREMARITAL SEXUAL PERMISSIVENESS

REISS SCALE – ORDER OF PRESENTATION	REISS SCALE No. %		ENGLISH No. %		AFRIKAANS No. %	
Sexual Intercourse is acceptable:						
1. when there is no affection	1	(11)	1	(15)	1	(22)
2. when there is strong affection	2	(16)	4	(65)	5	(67)
3. when there is love	3	(18)	5	(75)	6	(67)
4. when engaged to be married	4	(20)	6	(75)	3	(63)
Petting is acceptable:						
5. when there is no affection	5	(29)	2	(25)	2	(28)
6. when there is strong affection	6	(54)	7	(75)	7	(78)
7. when there is love	9	(59)	8	(80)	8	(78)
8. engaged to be married	7	(61)	9	(80)	11	(100)
Kissing is acceptable:						
9. when there is no affection	8	(58)	3	(60)	4	(61)
10. when there is strong affection	10	(90)	10	(85)	9	(83)
11. when there is love	11	(94)	11	(90)	10	(89)
12. when engaged to be married	12	(95)	12	(95)	12	(100)

Sample size			28	23
Coefficient of Reproducibility	> 0.90		> 0.92	> 0.84
Coefficient of Scalability	> 0.65		> 0.62	> 0.32
Spearman Correlations:				
Reiss – English (rho)	p = 0.82			
Reiss – Afrikaans (rho)	p = 0.77			
English – Afrikaans (rho)	p = 0.94			

DISCUSSION

The differences between the English and Afrikaans-speaking nurses showed the Afrikaans group to be almost as knowledgeable about sexual terminology, but more conservative in their sexual experience as shown by the Bentler scale. While attitudes as shown by the Reiss scale were similar in the two groups, other questions, for example the attitude on abortion and premarital sex of their own children (as opposed to youth in general), showed the AS group to be more conservative in this regard as well.

The comparison of matched samples of English and Afrikaans-speaking nurses has served to illustrate expected areas of both similarity and difference. The language division paralleled a religious affiliation and commitment division as expected, while the higher urbanization of the AS group served as a control of this variable from intervening in the comparison. The causal status of religion in determining language differences in sex is debatable, particularly since separate analyses of each variable, with the other controlled statistically, reveal parallel differences; that is, English versus Afrikaans-language groups differ in a similar way to English versus Afrikaans denominations. Religious denomination is unrelated to any of the variables measured within the English-language group, even with respect to contraception and abortion, and yet the presence of a religious difference between Dutch Reformed and all other denominations, even within the Afrikaans-speaking group, suggest the possibility of causal priority in the religious factor. A further confounding variable is the level of religious commitment, wherein the most highly committed are more sexually conservative, but also predominantly Afrikaans-speaking members of the DRC. Descriptively, a clear picture emerges in terms of the profile of this conservative group, but causal priority among these variables is difficult to infer. Some of the recent literature accords little priority to religious differences (Sorensen 1973), while Reiss (1960) has stated that "political, economic, religious and sexual life have been repeatedly shown to be highly interrelated." Our data support Reiss' statement, but do not enable any further explanatory refinement among this set of variables.

Although some authors, for example Morgenthau and Sokoloff (1972), consider the recent descriptions of a sexual revolution to be more myth than reality, most authors observe a fundamental change to have occurred, at least in the last 15 years, particularly in female sexual attitudes and behavior, with a marked increase in premarital sex among females approximating the male level which has remained static since the turn of the century. Sigush and Schmidt (1971) report that by 20 years, 67% of females had experienced sexual intercourse, while in our samples 57% of the two nursing groups had experienced sexual intercourse by that age. This is, however, largely due to the more liberal practices of the ES group.

It would appear that the ES and AS groups are clearly distinct in sexual behavior, even though they are part of the same society with much daily interaction. The overall impression is that the much spoken of sexual revolution has occurred for the ES group but not completely for the AS group.

REFERENCES

Bentler, P.M. (1968a). Heterosexual behavior assessment: I. Males". Behavior Research and Therapy, 6 (1): 21-25.

Bentler, P.M. (1969b). Heterosexual behavior assessment: II. Females. Behavior Research and Therapy, 6 (1): 27-30.

Morgenthau, J.E. and Sokoloff, N.J. (1972). The sexual revolution: myth or fact? The Pediatric Clinics of North America, 19 (3): 779-791.

Reiss, I.L. (1960). Premarital Sexual Standards in America, Free Press, New York.

Sigush, V. and Schmidt, G. (1971). Lower Class Sexuality: Some emotional and social aspects in West German males and females. Arch. Sexual Behavior, 1: 29-66.

Sorensen, R.C. (1973). The Sorensen Report on Adolescent Sexuality in Contemporary America, The World Publishing Co., New York.

RESULTS OF THE SEX KNOWLEDGE AND ATTITUDE TEST OF MEDICAL STUDENTS

IN ISRAEL[1]

Zwi Hoch, Hadassa Kubat (Seidenros) and J. M. Brandes

Israel

At the Paris Congress of Medical Sexology (1974) and at a later
W.H.O. meeting on "Education and Treatment in Human Sexuality"(1975),
the conclusion reached was that there is an urgent need for human
sexuality courses to be included in medical schools' curricula. Paul
H. Gebhard (1974) stated at the W.H.O. meeting: "The medical profession should be reminded that sex research, sex education and
sex therapy are all its clearly-evident responsibilities ... ."
This was already recognized by a large number of medical schools
in the United States and Europe, and Harold I. Lief (1974), who
was one of the first scientists to call for formal sex education
for the medical student, summarizes, at the same W.H.O. meeting,
the situation in the United States today, "The human sexuality
course is offered for academic credit in 88% of medical schools."

Human sexuality courses for medical students were nonexistent
in Israel until 1974, at which date the students at the Aba Khoushy
School of Medicine in Haifa were offered such an elective during
their clerkship in Obstetrics and Gynecology (Hoch, 1975; Hoch and
Peretz, 1975).

In order to construct a human sexuality course most suitable
for the specific needs of the local student, a previous evaluation
of basic knowledge and attitudes concerning this subject appeared self-evident. A pilot study on 45 fifth-year Haifa medical
students using the S.K.A.T. (Sex Knowledge and Attitude Test - an

---

[1]The research was made possible by funds granted by the Brunner
Foundation, New York, and by the Israel Family Planning Association.

instrument successfully used for this purpose in many medical schools
in the USA and other countries) showed serious lack of knowledge on
basic sexual items as well as quite conservative attitudes regarding the subject. As a result, we decided to embark on a nation-wide
study of medical students, using the same instrument, in order to
have a statistically significant sample before any final conclusions
were reached on the matter. Permission was sought and obtained to
use a Hebrew translation of the S.K.A.T., somewhat changing some
of the questions in order to adapt it to Israeli needs. The questionnaire was administered to medical students of all four schools
of medicine in Israel, in groups of 9 - 12 each, mostly during their
clerkship in obstetrics and gynecology. Statistical evaluation was
done, mainly by using the SPSS statistical package for the social
sciences. Interrelations between items were analyzed by standard
nonparametric techniques, contingency tables and nonparametric
correlations. When appropriate and justified, we used parametric
techniques such as the T-test.

RESEARCH INSTRUMENT

The S.K.A.T. (Sex Knowledge and Attitude Test) has been developed by Harold I. Lief and David M. Reed, from the University
of Pennsylvania, School of Medicine, Philadelphia, as a means for
tabulating, scoring and reporting data on sexual attitudes, knowledge, degree of experience in sexual encounters and a diversity
of biographical information. Accordingly, the S.K.A.T. has four
parts: 1. Attitude section; 2. Knowledge section; 3. Demographic
data; 4. Personal sexual behavior data. The Attitude section is
divided into four scales: 1) Heterosexual Relations (H - R); 2)
Sexual Myths (S - M); 3) Abortion (A); 4) Autoeroticism (M).

The Knowledge section contains 71 questions, fifty of them
being test items. The average performance for the American medical student on the Knowledge section (true - false answer possibility) is 50 with a standard deviation of 10. Scores less
than 50 indicate a lesser degree of knowledge while 50 or more
indicate superior performance. The same is true for the Attitude
section (50 ± 10). High scores (above 60) imply liberal attitudes,
low scores (below 40) imply conservative ones.

FINDINGS AND COMMENTS

Background Information

The research sample consisted of 189 medical students from
the four medical schools in Israel, 81.2% males and 18.8% females.
The age distribution was 21 - 36, with the mean age of 24.5. The

large majority (94.1%) were Jewish, 3.9% Moslem, 0.7% Christian
and 1.3% belonged to "other religions;" from the Jewish sample,
89% were Ashkenasi Jews and only 11.3% were of Sephardic origin.
Almost thirty-nine percent (38.6%) of the students were married.

To the question on the origin of their sex education, the
large majority of the students indicated "professional literature"
(40%), peers (16%) and "other sources (movies, novels, etc.) (35%)
as main origins for their sex education. Only 8% indicated their
home as the main source of sex education, and "school" rated <u>lowest</u>
(2.2%).

The medical students were asked to rate themselves in comparison with their peer group's knowledge about sex, sexual adjustment
and sexual experience. The majority (57.2%, 64.3% and 62% respectively) did see themselves as knowledgeable, as adjusted and as
experienced sexually as most of their peers, but males felt themselves relatively more adjusted as compared to females. 50.3% of
students rated their homes as "neutral," 28.0% as permissive and
very permissive, and 21.7% as repressive and very repressive during
their adolescent period.

Sixty-seven percent (66.7%) of students felt that their sexual value system is liberal and only 11.5% conservative (41 students did not answer this question). Sixty percent felt in conflict on different levels with their parents. Seventy-six percent
stated that their value system is not at all influenced by religion,
with 13.9% somewhat, and 10.2% definitely so.

Sexual Behavior

Eighteen percent (18.5%) stated not having ever masturbated;
the majority started masturbating between age 13 - 15 (Tables 1,
2). Three percent never dated; 3.8% never went steady; 5.56%
never had sexual intercourse, all of them male students; 1.8% had
intercourse with prostitutes more than five times (5.6% once);
3.2% reported on homosexually derived orgasms more than five times;
84.7% had intercourse more than five times; seventy-four percent
(73.8%) dated with more than five partners and 80.7% had intercourse with two partners or more (Table 3). A number of conclusions could be reached from these findings:

1. During their adolescent years, most of our students use
to date a lot and also with a large number of partners; those
who dated very often did so probably with different partners.

2. The same appears true for their "going steady" experiences—
only 6.7% had one stable partner; the majority had more than
two.

TABLE 1

AGE AT FIRST MASTURBATION
IN ISRAELI MEDICAL STUDENTS (NATIONAL NORMS - 1976)

Age	Percent
Never	18.5
< 10	10.2
10 - 12	16.6
13 - 15	39.5
16 - 18	10.2
19 +	5.1

TABLE 2

MASTURBATION PRACTICE AT DIFFERENT AGES
AND IN DIFFERENT SAMPLES

AGE	PERCENT SAMPLES			
	Israeli Medical Students (%) (Cumulative)	Klausner Sample (%) - (1954)	Lancet Sample (%) - (1974)	
			Boys	Girls
< 10	10.2	5.3		
10 - 12	26.7	60.0	60.0	12.0
13 - 15	66.2	66.7	80.0	21.0
16 - 18	76.4	66.7		
19 +	81.5			

TABLE 3

SEXUAL BEHAVIOR OF ISRAELI
MEDICAL STUDENTS (NATIONAL NORMS - 1976)

EXPERIENCE	NUMBER OF TIMES (%)				NUMBER OF PEOPLE (%)			
	Never	Once	2.5	5 +	Never	Once	2.5	5 +
DATING	3.0	1.8	7.3	87.8	8.3	4.8	13.1	73.8
GOING STEADY	3.8	5.8	42.9	47.4	7.4	6.7	40.9	45.0
SEXUAL INTERCOURSE	7.4	1.8	6.1	84.7	4.8	14.5	33.1	47.6
PROSTITUTES	90.0	5.6	2.5	1.9				
HOMOSEXUAL ORGASM	92.2	3.2	1.3	3.2	88.7	2.6	2.6	5.9

3.   At least 5% never experienced sexual intercourse despite their mean age of 24.5.

4.   More students (84.7%) reported on more than five experiences of intercourse, but only 47.6% on intercourse with more than five partners. In this context we have to remember that 39% of our students were married and therefore had a large number of coital experiences with the same partner.

Frequency of Use and Preferrence for Contraceptive Methods

The large majority (82.3%) had experience with the birth control pill (seventy-two percent (71.7%) clearly preferred the pill to other contraceptives); 19.1% had experience with the I.U.D. and as many as 21.8% (23 males and 8 females) with abortion as a birth control method. 11.2% preferred the I.U.D., 5.9% the condom, 2% the rhythm method and 2.6% withdrawal. It was however interesting to discover that quite a large number (11.2%) preferred the diaphragm (this could be following the late publicity given to side effects of the pill).

Attitudes

The Israeli student's mean standard score is 50.44 with S.D. of 10.1 on the heterosexual scale, but reaches only 41.31 (S.D. - 11.7) on the sexual myths scale, 46.62 (S.D. - 7.9) on the abortion scale and 44.88 (S.D. - 10.0) on the autoeroticism scale, (Table 4). The T-test for comparison between the Israeli medical student and the American medical student shows that on the heterosexual scale there was no difference, but on the other scales our student is significantly more conservative (p<0.05). Statistically significant difference was also found between the four attitudinal scales themselves. The mere fact that the student appears liberal on one scale does not necessarily imply that he has the same liberal stand on other issues.

When further analyzing our results, while looking into the relations between the different variables, we decided not to predetermine what "conservative" or "liberal" means. Instead we classified individuals according to their relative degree of conservativeness in regard to the whole population studied. On the basis of the 35 Attitude statements we constructed our own score with a theoretical range from 35 - 175. The Likert-type scale of the Attitude section of the S.K.A.T. was recoded so that strong agreement with a conservative attitude scored 5 points, while strong disagreement scored 1 point. The scores attained by our students ranged from 54 up to 137. An overall liberal attitude was found (mean 83.4), (Tables 5, 6).

TABLE 4

COMPARED RESULTS OF S.K.A.T. ON SEXUAL ATTITUDES AND SEXUAL KNOWLEDGE OF MALE AND FEMALE ISRAELI MEDICAL STUDENTS (NATIONAL NORMS) AND OF MALE AND FEMALE AMERICAN MEDICAL STUDENTS (NATIONAL NORMS)

| | SEXUAL ATTITUDES | | | | | | | | SEXUAL KNOWLEDGE | |
| | Heterosexual Relations | | Sexual Myths | | Abortion | | Autoeroticism | | | |
	Mean*	S.D.	Mean	S.D.	Mean	S.D.	Mean	S.D.	Mean	S.D.
Israeli Male N = 92	50.64	11.40	43.45	11.20	46.39	8.30	45.72	10.80	N = 90 36.99	10.80
American Male N = 3014	49.26	10.80	49.13	10.10	48.33	10.50	49.59	9.50	N = 3014 49.85	9.70
T. Test	No difference		P = 0.000 Israeli more Conservative		T=2.19 P=0.029 Israeli more Conservative		T=3.59 P=0.000 Israeli more Conservative		Israeli less Knowledgeable	
Israeli Female N = 27	48.44	10.60	42.31	9.90	47.88	7.90	45.56	10.60	N = 2.7 37.62	11.40
American Female N = 460	48.77	10.10	52.97	9.40	48.42	11.20	49.60	10.00	N = 460 50.89	10.60
T. Test	Not significant Difference P = 0.87		P = 0.000 Israeli more Conservative		P=0.69 Israeli		T=1.93 P=0.054 Israeli more Conservative		P = 0.000 Israeli less Knowledgeable	

* Attitude scores below 40 = conservative attitudes. — Knowledge scores less than 50 = lesser degree of knowledge.

TABLE 5

THE FREQUENCY DISTRIBUTION OF ATTITUDE
SCORE FOR INDIVIDUALS ISRAELI MEDICAL STUDENTS

No. of points scored by individual	Percentage of such individuals	Cumulative Percentage
- 60	4.5	4.5
61 - 70	9.1	13.6
71 - 80	23.9	37.5
81 - 90	29.0	66.5
91 - 100	20.4	86.9
101 - 110	8.6	95.5
111 - 120	2.2	97.7
121 - 130	1.2	98.9
131 - 140	1.1	100.0

Number of Valid Cases = 176
Mean 85.295 Stand. dev. 14.685
Median 83.389 Minimum 35.000
Maximum 155.000
Point of indifferent attitude 105.000

TABLE 6

THE FREQUENCY DISTRIBUTION OF ATTITUDE
SCORE FOR INDIVIDUALS ISRAELI MEDICAL STUDENTS
NUMBER OF VALID CASES = 176

Attitude Categories*	Range of points Scored in Category	Percentage of such individuals
Very liberal	54 - 75	25.6
Liberal	76 - 83	25.0
Somewhat conservative	84 - 95	27.8
Conservative	96 - 137	21.6

*Categories in Table express only the relative degree of conservativeness of an individual as compared with the entire sample.

In light of the heated public discussion on abortion policy going on now in Israel, we further analyzed the Abortion scale of the S.K.A.T. We measured the student's attitude to abortion according to the number of points scored on the total of the nine Attitude statements from S.K.A.T. dealing with this subject. The results were: 85% liberal; 14.2% conservative. An interesting finding was that the longer the students were married, the more conservative they became toward abortion. Following are some examples of the items from the four attitudinal scales which did gather the largest number of conservative answers:

Item 1. The spread of sex education is causing a rise in pre-marital intercourse. 62% of Israeli medical students as compared to 24.7% American male medical students (A-M) and 16.5% American female medical students (A-F), agreed to this statement.

Item 13. All abortion laws should be repealed. 40.7% of Israeli medical students as compared to 39.82% A-M and 33.48% A-F disagreed. This statement might not be very relevant to the actual Israeli scene because there are indeed quite severe abortion laws, but everybody quite disregards them, provided that no medical complications occur as a result of the intervention.

Item 15. Laws requiring a committee of physicians to approve an abortion should be abolished. 48.6% of Israeli medical students as compared to 34.97% American males and 35.32% A-F disagreed to this statement. The actual trend in Israel is to liberalize abortion, under the control of such committees, a trend which was also supported by the National Association of Obstetricians & Gynecologists. This Association officially opposes abortion on demand. It is therefore interesting to note that 51% of our students "voted" in favor of liberalization, but 49% "voted" in keeping with the official organisation's view.

Item 24. Boys should be encouraged to masturbate. 71.4% Israeli medical students as compared to 63.57% A-M and 62.17% A-F disagreed to this statement. The student's view appears very conservative on this issue, and heavily influences the Attitude scale. But this conclusion could be rather misleading, as they might have thought that it is unnecessary to purposefully encourage masturbation, but at the same time sanctioning it by simply "looking away" in a rather positive manner.

Item 34. Extramarital sexual relations may result in a strengthening of the marriage relationship of the persons involved. 45.5% Israeli medical students as compared to 38.75% A-M and 43.04% A-F voted against this statement with 19.1% in favor of it. But the most interesting percentage were the "uncertain" answers scoring 30%, results very similar to the American student.

Knowledge

The average performance of the Israeli medical student on the Knowledge section of the S.K.A.T. is 36.26 with a standard deviation of 10.50 compared with a score of 50 with a standard deviation of 10 for the American student, (Table 4). The T-test shows a highly significant difference (p<0.0001) between the two groups of students with the Israeli student much less knowledgeable.

To evaluate knowledge, we contructed a simple score, summing over the 50 best items. Incorrect answers scored 1 point and correct answers scored 2 points. Thus, the theoretical range was 50 to 100. The actual range of our students was 63 - 93 with a mean of 80.742 and S.D. of 5.829.

In order to make a more detailed evaluation of our student's knowledge, we divided the knowledge section of the S.K.A.T. (test items) into four categories of questions or four knowledge scales: medical questions (Med.), medical-psychological questions (Med. - Psych.), psychological questions (Psych.) and sociological questions (Soc.), (Table 7). The student answering incorrectly received a score of 1 on the particular question, and those who did answer correctly received a score of 2. The mean score on the Med. scale was 1.723 with a S.D. of 0.144; Psych. 1.645 with S.D. 0.178; Soc. 1.545 with S.D. 0.167 and Med.-Psych. 1.497 with S.D. 0.173 (Table 8). Significant difference was found between these scores. The Israeli student reaches significantly higher performance on the medical and psychological scores, with pronounced lesser performance on medical-psychological and sociological items.

A selection of some of the items in the Knowledge section with at least 50% incorrect and missing answers will help us to better understand the results:

1. "Masturbation by a married person is a sign of poor marital sex adjustment." Fifty-seven percent of Israeli medical students as compared to 26.14% American male medical students (A-M) and 22.61% American female medical students (A-F) still agree to this statement.

2. "A high percentage of those who commit sexual offenses against children is made up of the children's friends or relatives." Almost sixty percent of Israeli medical students as compared to 28.93% A-M and 27.39% A-F were not aware of this fact.

3. "Impotence in men over 70 is nearly universal." One of the most striking facts was that 52.4% of our students as compared to 20.31% A-M and 14.78% A-F still agree to this statement.

TABLE 7

CATEGORIES OF KNOWLEDGE QUESTIONS
(S.K.A.T. - 1972)

Categories	Item number
Medical questions	1, 4, 5, 7, 17, 21, 22, 25, 27, 28, 33, 34, 37, 38, 47, 53, 70.
Medical psychological questions	11, 12, 18, 23, 36, 40, 42, 43, 48, 52, 57.
Psychological questions	14, 16, 24, 45, 56, 60, 61, 64, 65, 66.
Sociological questions	2, 20, 26, 29, 39, 50, 51, 58, 59, 63, 69, 71.

TABLE 8

RESULTS OF ISRAELI MEDICAL STUDENT
(NATIONAL NORMS, 1976) ON KNOWLEDGE SCALES (S.K.A.T. - 1972)

Medical questions		Medical Psychological questions		Psychological questions		Sociological questions	
MEAN	S.D.	MEAN	S.D.	MEAN	S.D.	MEAN	S.D.
1.723	0.144	1.497	0.173	1.645	0.178	1.545	0.167

INCORRECT ANSWER = 1

CORRECT = 2

4. "Certain conditions of mental and emotional instability are demonstrably caused by masturbation." 45.5% of Israelis as compared to 15.33% A-M and 14.78% A-F agree to this statement; this was difficult to understand, in view of the students' rather liberal attitude on this item.

Following are some additional items which scored less incorrect answers, but are of interest regarding their content:

1. "There are two kinds of physiological orgastic responses in women, one clitoral and the other vaginal." 55.56% of Israeli medical students believe this is true as compared to 42.67% A-M and 38.26% A-F.

2. "One of the immediate results of castration in the adult male is impotence." 33.33% of Israeli medical students believe this as compared to 35.17% A-M and 51.30% A-F.

3. "Menopause in women is accompanied by a sharp and lasting reduction in sexual drive and interest." 21.69% of Israeli medical students as compared to 20.64% A-M and 12.61% A-F believe this statement to be true.

Correlations between S.K.A.T. Variables

The research methodology of survey analysis in our study is not definitely recommended as a means to conclude clear-cut causal links between the different variables studied. Therefore, we scored "why" type questions but did not give definite causal answers.

When constructing our research model based on the information obtained from the S.K.A.T., a number of similar variables could be grouped together under different headings: background information; past-early sexual knowledge and experience; self-rating of sexual knowledge and experience; sexual behavior (actual experience); experience with contraceptive methods; preference of contraceptive methods; military service; actual sexual knowledge and attitudes. By this means a model (Table 9) was constructed, and cross tabulation done between the individual variables from the different groups testing logical hypothesis of possible links. A number of interesting statistically significant correlations were found:

Less conflict on sexual matters was found in homes with higher educated fathers, but no correlation existed between father's education and the degree of permissiveness at home.

On the other hand, a direct negative correlation was found between permissiveness at home and mother's educational status:

TABLE 9

RESEARCH MODEL: TABLE OF VARIABLES
ISRAELI MEDICAL STUDENTS – NATIONAL SAMPLE

Background

| AGE |
| SEX |
| ORIGIN |
| RELIGION |
| NUMBER OF SIBLINGS |
| FATHER'S EDUCATION |
| MOTHER'S EDUCATION |
| FATHER'S OCCUPATION |
| YEARS OF MARRIAGE |

| EXPERIENCE WITH CONTRACEPTIVE METHODS |
| PREFERRENCE FOR SPECIFIC CONTRACEPTIVE METHOD |

Past early sexual knowledge and experience

| ORIGIN OF SEXUAL KNOWLEDGE (SEX EDUCATION) |
| HOME SEXUAL PERMISSIVENESS (PERMISSIVE VERSUS REPRESSIVE) |
| CONFLICT WITH PARENTS ON SEXUAL MATTERS |
| MASTURBATION – AGE OF BEGINNING – FREQUENCY |

| SEXUAL KNOWLEDGE |
| SEXUAL ATTITUDES |
| MILITARY SERVICE |

Self Ratings

| SELF RATING OF SEXUAL KNOWLEDGE |
| SELF RATING OF VALUE SYSTEM WITH REGARD TO SEX (CONSERVATIVE OR LIBERAL ATTITUDES) |
| SELF RATING OF SEXUAL ADJUSTMENT |
| SELF RATING OF SEXUAL EXPERIENCE |
| SELF RATING ON RELIGIOSITY INFLUENCE |

SEXUAL BEHAVIOR (EXPERIENCE)

| DATING |
| GOING STEADY |
| SEXUAL INTERCOURSE |
| INTERCOURSE WITH PROSTITUTES |
| HOMOSEXUAL ORGASM |
| (HOW MANY TIMES; WITH HOW MANY PEOPLE) |

NOTE: THE S.K.A.T. IS NOT MEASURING THE ACTUAL SEXUAL ADJUSTMENT OF THE INDIVIDUAL.

less educated mothers were correlated with more repressive homes and there also was more conflict on sexual matters (especially with daughters).

Students from more permissive homes indicated better sexual adjustment.

Direct significant correlation was found between students' self-rating of knowledge about sex and the self-rating regarding attitudes on sex.

And even more important, the self-rating on attitudes is directly correlated with his actual attitudes about sex, whether conservative or liberal. This acutally proves that our students did indeed answer sincerely to the questionnaire.

It was interesting to note that greater conflict at home on sexual matters did not necessarily negate students' liberal attitudes. But more religious students rated more conservative.

We next wished to know if there are significant factors influencing the student's sexual experience: no significant correlation exists between sexual adjustment and the age of starting masturbation. Those students who rated themselves sexually adjusted, reported on going steady more frequently and with a larger number of partners, and also on more partners with whom they had coital experience. The more conservative student had less sexual intercourse. The student who never had sexual intercourse rated significantly more conservative than those having had more than five times this experience. And vice-versa, those students who rated themselves more experienced sexually, regard themselves as also better adjusted. All these results were statistically significant for both female and male students, $p < 0.005$. (Similar links were found by the Institute for Sex Research, Bloomington, Indiana, in their American College Youth Study).

Fifty-four percent of our students did start medical school after serving in the Israeli army. This is a situation rather specific to our country and we wanted to know if army service caused any change in the student's sexual attitudes or experience. Interesting results emerged: the army probably did not influence the sexual attitudes or experience of Ashkenasi students, but made a definite change in his male Sephardic colleague who gathered significantly more sexual experience (this conclusion based on our rather small number of students of Sephardic origin). We did not find, however, any changes concerning the nine female students who served in the army before their medical school studies.

When analyzing our "research model" for variables which did participate in significant correlation only, it became clear that relatively few items were pertinent, the others being eliminated as lacking significance, (Table 10). As a whole, the student's background has direct influence on the student's past-early sexual knowledge and experience, which by his turn will influence his self-rating of sexual knowledge, sexual adjustment, experience and self-rating of his value system (conservative versus liberal). There is a direct correlation between the student's self-rating on sexual matters, and his sexual behavior, but from all the sexual behavior variables, only "going steady" and "sexual intercourse" were significantly correlated. Each of the last three groups of variables (past-early sexual knowledge and experience, students' self-ratings and students' sexual behavior) is significantly correlated with the students' sexual knowledge and sexual attitudes, and vice versa. It was interesting to note however, that background variables (sex, origin, father's and mother's education), had no direct influence on sexual knowledge and attitudes, but may probably have an indirect influence only. Surprisingly, no direct significant correlations were found between past-early sexual knowledge and experience and the students' later sexual behavior (experience). Self-rating on sexual matters, however, did make the "link" between the two. One sexual behavior variable (going steady), showed some direct correlation with the students' background.

These different factors correlated with, and influencing on knowledge and attitudes, constitute, we think, one of the most interesting findings of this work.

CONCLUSION

The Israeli medical student is significantly less knowledgeable on sexual matters and much more conservative than his American colleague in most of his attitudes regarding sex, except on the "heterosexual scale" items.

In judging the attitudes and sexual values system of Israeli medical students, we must remember that the definition of "liberal" or "conservative" is not necessarily identical in the USA and in Israel, explaining perhaps the stronger "conservativeness" of our students.

The division of the Knowledge section of the S.K.A.T. in four groups of questions: medical, medical-psychological, psychological and sociological, was very helpful in directing our future teaching efforts. We are proposing to add this division as a standard procedure evaluating the knowledge of the population studied.

TABLE 10

CROSS TABULATION OF VARIABLES ISRAELI MEDICAL STUDENTS
NATIONAL SAMPLE (SIGNIFICANT LINKS ONLY)

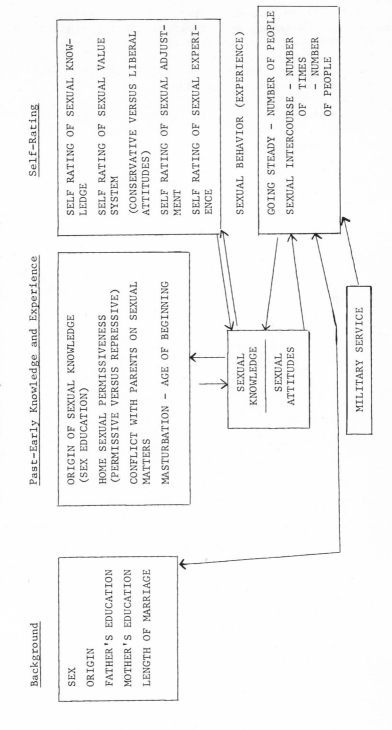

Background

SEX
ORIGIN
FATHER'S EDUCATION
MOTHER'S EDUCATION
LENGTH OF MARRIAGE

Past-Early Knowledge and Experience

ORIGIN OF SEXUAL KNOWLEDGE
(SEX EDUCATION)

HOME SEXUAL PERMISSIVENESS
(PERMISSIVE VERSUS REPRESSIVE)

CONFLICT WITH PARENTS ON SEXUAL
MATTERS

MASTURBATION – AGE OF BEGINNING

Self-Rating

SELF RATING OF SEXUAL KNOW-
LEDGE

SELF RATING OF SEXUAL VALUE
SYSTEM
(CONSERVATIVE VERSUS LIBERAL
ATTITUDES)

SELF RATING OF SEXUAL ADJUST-
MENT

SELF RATING OF SEXUAL EXPERI-
ENCE

SEXUAL BEHAVIOR (EXPERIENCE)

GOING STEADY – NUMBER OF PEOPLE
SEXUAL INTERCOURSE – NUMBER
OF TIMES
– NUMBER
OF PEOPLE

SEXUAL
KNOWLEDGE

SEXUAL
ATTITUDES

MILITARY SERVICE

Correlation analysis between S.K.A.T. groups of variables showed an interesting and rather surprising finding: no significant correlation was found between the students' background and past-early sexual experience from one side, and their actual sexual behavior (experience) from the other. Only self-rating on sexual matters was directly significantly correlated with behavior. Sexual knowledge and attitudes were however strongly correlated with all the groups of variables, except background. S.K.A.T. findings clearly show the urgent need for human sexuality courses as an integral part of Israeli Medical Schools' curricula.

REFERENCES

Congrès International de Sexologie Médicale (1974). Book of Proceedings, Paris.

Gebhard, P.H. (1974). Coping with barriers to sex education and sex research: In W.H.O. meeting on Education and Treatment in Human Sexuality: the Training of Health Professionals, Geneva, 6-12 February.

Hoch, Z. (1975). An educational program on human sexuality at the Aba Khoushy School of Medicine in Haifa, J. Med. Educ. 50: 691 - 193.

Hoch Z. and Peretz, A. (1975). Human sexuality for medical students, Harefuah, 89: 262 - 263.

Klausner, S.Z. (1967). Sex life in Israel. In Ellis, A. and Barbanel, A. (eds), The Encyclopedia of Sexual Behavior, Hawthorn Books Inc., New York.

Lancet M., Modav, B., Kav-Venaki, S., Antonovsky, H. and Shohana, I. (1974). Sexual Knowledge and Behavior of Israeli Adolescents, presented at the 2nd international symposium on sex education, Tel-Aviv, June 26.

Lief, H.I. and Ebert, R.K. (1974). A survey of sex education in United States Medical Schools. In W.H.O. meeting on Education and Treatment in Human Sexuality: The Training of Health Professionals, Geneva, 6-12 February.

Lief, H.I. and Reed, D.M. (1972). Sex Knowledge and Attitudes Test (S.K.A.T.), (2nd edition), Center for the study of sex education in medicine, University of Pensylvania School of Medicine, Philadelphia.

W.H.O. (1975). Education and Treatment in Human Sexuality: The Training of Health Professionals, Report of a W.H.O. meeting, Technical report series 572, Geneva.

YOUTH, SEXUALITY, AND POLITICS

André Dupras and Réjean Tremblay

Canada

The principal objective of this study was to examine the many complex ties between sexuality and politics. Theoretical discussions on this subject have stimulated many interesting arguments, unfortunately, without pertinent empirical data; thus, the reason for this survey among young people.

Initially an accumulation of findings on the sexual and political activities on campus was made. From reviewed research three potential schemas seemed to explain the relationship between sexuality and politics. With reference to Freudian theory, the first approach considered the sexo-political trend as a process tributary to distinctive features of personality. The second approach examined student life, not in the light of emotional reactions, in its interaction with the various institutions and social groups. The third approach recognized the adoption of permissiveness and sexo-political contestation as an unmistakable sign of student adhesion to a counter-culture.

In the first approach, subconscious elements are responsible for political attitudes and activities and psycho-sexual conflicts, (which are the foundations upon which they rest), reveal very specific sexual tendencies and well defined political trends, including sexual options. Farnsworth (1969), Flugel (1945) and Hart (1952) have linked student protest movements to express compensatory personality traits characterized by sexual frustration. However, the numerous investigations in psychology undertaken by Abramowitz (1973) and Kerpelman (1969) have not succeeded in locating particular personality traits among the student activists. The results

obtained show that such psychological features could not explain
adequately a sexo-political orientation. Nevertheless, the manifestations of the personality approach have prompted an investigation
of the sexual and political tendencies of the student body by as-
sociating their behaviors and corresponding attitudes.

The second approach waived intrapsychic conflicts in favor
of relational conflicts. Indeed, sexual and political trends
would seem to rely more heavily on patterns of thought and conduct
transmitted by parents, friends, and clergy. Political and sexual
activism appears to stem from the refusal to adhere to values set
up by a conservative society, represented by the family and the
Church, and to be directed toward the more liberated outlook of
one's peer group. In the course of this differential process of
political and sexual socialization by family, church, school, and
peer group, the protesting student may concurrently develop liberalized sexual and political attitudes which could lead the student's
involvement in controversial sexual and political action (Berns et
al., 1972; Block et al., 1969). This explanation is not satisfactory
however, because it refers to a restricted time or situation indicating the modes wherein attitudes and behaviors are acquired. In such
cases, sexo-political orientation would result from specific socialization whose contents and consequences differ with the various
individuals involved.

As already mentioned, the third approach refers to counter-
culture. In opposition to the concept of campus activities characterized by the sporadic conflicts of opinion and behavior of a
particular group of students, this approach is a more global concept of counter-culture in which the political action challenges
the numerous aspects of social culture and the standards of sexual
activity in particular. Counter-culture youth may be described
as young individuals with controversial sexo-political trends
(Geller and Howard, 1972; Kirby, 1971; Langman et al., 1973).

The three analytical and explicative approaches to the sexo-
political tendencies of our youth are based upon conceptual and
classificatory dividions of somewhat questionable validity. The
inherent logic of these tendencies is constantly creating new
categories which makes the outcome difficult to assess. In this
study, participation in a novel way in discussions of the relation
between sexuality and politics was accomplished by recording and
regrouping the findings by using a technique which is not based
on preconceived theories. A questionnaire dealing with attitudes
and behaviors was distributed among 915 university students in the
Montreal area. Bergonier's typological program (1967) enabled
grouping of our candidates into various sexual and political
profiles without previously defining the possible categories.

The following is a brief description of the algorithm used to form such groups. An individual profile was based on the sum total of questionnaire answers and was compared to a second profile obtained from another individual. If the differences in the two profiles outweighed the similarities, the individuals in question became the first two types; otherwise, they formed a single type. Each new subject was subsequently compared to the original type - or types - and so forth until the maximum number of types determined at the outset had been reached. In this way, an accurate pattern conforming to the intitial data was discovered. The optimal profile (the number of subjects included in our analysis) was arrived at by calculating the proportion of true typological variance relative to change distribution; we now are inclined to agree with Handley (1974) that this approach eases the disparity between theory and practice, as is indicated in the following quotation: "The ideal situation is where both approaches interact in a dynamic research process. Theoretical typologies point the way for empirical verifications. The numerical solutions in turn modify prior theoretical positions, and so forth" (Handley, 1974: 2).

Eight sexual types emerged from the typological regrouping of the sexual findings and a detailed description of each type is one of the highlights of the specific and innovative aspect of this method. Instead of identifying students a priori whose practices classified them as sexually experienced or not, or whose sexual attitudes stereotyped them as radicals or conformists, eight different sexual profiles which represented the mainstream of sexual trends on campus in a most satisfactory manner were identified. Information on political attitudes and behaviors underwent identical treatment and resulted in the identification of nine political types with significant differences among them. This typological methodology allowed us to avoid a predetermined classification of our subjects, such as identifying them as political activists, passivists, or sideline spectators. This would have over simplified a student's political trends and reduced the study to generalities. The many sexual and political formations in the students provided us the opportunity to cross-check the two typologies and to examine the relationship between sexuality and politics.

The purpose of cross-checking these two typological structures was to discover the influence of politics on sexuality and its corrolary, i.e., influence of sexuality on politics; and the results of this cross-checking served to enlighten the three explicative approaches previously described.

In the first place, the results of the relationship between sexuality and politics may be compared with theories on personality. Harold Lasswell (1930) staunchly upholds this approach in his test

wherein the psychanalytical schema is applied to interpret political behavior. Lasswell maintains that political traits stem from
a displacement of personal affects on the public scene. Hart (1952)
goes along with this theory and discerns a passive sexual orientation in student protesters which he claims is the result of an unresolved Oedipal complex. Our findings do not confirm the passive
sexual character of the agitators; on the contrary, it appears that
students engaged in political protest movements adhere to sexual
profiles displaying noticeable erotic and hedonic practices which
may even border on atypical hedonism. Sexual continence, moreover,
tends to correspond to political apathy.

     Our results also contradict the categories propounded by the
Quebec sociologist, Jacques Lazure (1970) in his first work on the
Revolution of Young Québecois. He suggests that these political
reactionists manifest aggressive identification with their fathers;
in certain instances, their unresolved complex becomes an incentive
to violence and especially to an austere sexual life. Our data indicate that young people known for sexual continence are also attracted toward passive political forms.

     Some of our findings reveal that political violence is recip-
rocally associated with hedonic or atypical sexual behavior and
also with homosexuality, which parallels the ideas set down by
Whilhelm Reich (1936) who affirms that sexual repression predisposes
an individual toward servility and political conformism. Our study
indicates that such tendencies (toward political apathy) appear in
sexual abstainers; however, this was the only influence of sexuality
over politics. Indeed, resorting to more challenging sexual attitudes or behavior has very little impact on political activist orientation. It is easy to understand why Reich stresses the integration
of sexual revolution into the political and economic upheaval. All
in all, the results currently obtained encourage an investigation
of the various theories affecting personality to facilitate an exploration of the psychic foundations of sexo-political orientation.

     Another source of information on the relationship linking sex-
uality to politics can be traced in the studies on the transmission
of political trends. The definition of political socialization is
the acquisition of a complex set of values, of emotive reactions
and of information allowing the individual to understand, evaluate,
and relate with the political culture. This complex orientation is
achieved in the process of political socialization and shapes
the individual's political identity. A student is apt to develop
certain sexual or political ideology according to the various
forms of interaction experienced with regard to other persons
or institutions. The family is one of these socializing agents
and is responsible for sexual or political agitation inasmuch as
it allows the free expression of opinions and political or sexual
options. Unfortunately, there is no data available on parental

attitudes; our only source of information is the student's place
of residence, but here again, as already mentioned, students living
with their parents do engage in sexual activities while others in
the same circumstances do not. This has also been observed in
political typologies: left-wing students may or may not choose
to live in a non marital context. A sense of acumen is also needed
to estimate the part played by religion in an individual's orientation. Consequently, socialization involves several variables which
may account for the different sexual or political trends observed
on campus.

Studies on the new youth culture also identify a correspondence between sexuality and politics and changes seen in the psychological and social characteristics of the new generation of
students also suggest the inception and amplification of a collective consciousness in young people. Thus, students have a sense
of revolt when the symbols and values of the dominating culture
are seen as inadequate in the light of radical social change; this
movement extends from the minority and pervades the counter-culture
on campus where values, attitudes and behaviors are shared by many.
The findings of our research make it impossible to verify the effective presence of this culture because to detect a coherent association of such trends implies a study of attitudinal and behavioral structures in various fields, such as one's professional
future, family expectations, cultural options, etc. Only certain
characteristics attributed to this counter-culture will be highlighted.

The counter-cultural approach interprets sexual and political
unrest as the outward signs of a semi-organized culture entrenched
in all sectors of university life and which has given rise to an
overall renewal of attitudes and behaviors. The first stages of
typological analysis disclosed that the impression of sociocultural
isolation had been replaced by an awareness of numerous differential
structures. It was obvious that the general patterns of political
and sexual tendencies were not shared by all types of students, and
it was also clear that religion and independent lifestyles reflected sexual and political orientations. A distribution of sexual
types within the various departments of the university was identifiable. Segmentation of these different trends has not only allowed
observation of some common traits which give the impression of a
general movement but also, and especially, the many sexual and
political facets of this youth culture.

Are common cultural elements, characterized by the rejection
of socially accepted values (both political and sexual) to be
found? Janine Mossuz (1974) declares that this joint rupture indicates an outspoken desire for change. Cross-checking has not
fully confirmed this hypothesis; for instance, even if certain

students assume political traditional attitudes, they also adhere
to sexual profiles which encourage sexual activity in amorous or
even hedonic contexts. The reciprocity between political radicalism
and sexual permissiveness maintained by Mossuz was verified by means
of the following criteria of permissiveness: premarital sex and
homosexuality. The latter also appears in the reciprocal reports
of our study. But if homosexuality is referred to in terms of
sexual behavior one finds that even though homosexual behavior
is an accelerating factor in political activism, such reciprocity
does not have the same meaning as Mossuz gives it: for some students in our sampling, homosexuality is part of organized activism,
whereas others use it as a shield or a means of political withdrawal.

Our cross-checking has been confined to reciprocity between
political and sexual contestation and Mossuz's results on the
tendency of permissive sexual protesters to embrace similar political trends has not been confirmed; in fact, political agitators
whose line of conduct was not overly affected by sexuality and
other sexual types who vehemently denounced amorous and hedonic
abstinence but who associated with apathetic types who were totally
opposed to all political violence were encountered. The results
reflect the conclusions arrived at by Jacques Lazure (1975) in
his latest book which treats the new sexual lifestyles of a group
of young Québecois. Cohabitation prompts these individuals to
adopt new values and behaviors in their personal and sociocultural
environment, yet certain vestiges of the dominating culture also
persist. Such examples of resistance to change may be explained
by referring to the essential findings in the fields of psychology
or of socialization.

In conclusion, this empirical research provides a glimpse
of the complexities linking sexuality and politics. An examination
of other research results recognizing the relationship between
these two dimensions, identify sexuality and politics, as two
relatively-independent realities in most people's lives; nevertheless, our studies indicate that this apparent dichotomy conceals
a very real relationship between the two. The results of typological analysis have, in fact, revealed the many subtleties which
give relative value to this opinion. The empirical data and considerations set forth in this study cannot, of course, give hard-
and-fast answers to the questions which may have come to mind;
they have attempted to portray certain corresponding factors
which cannot easily be explained by a different methodological
approach.

We have not sought to give the final answer to the discussion
on sexuality and politics; instead, we have attempted to revive

this discussion. Our empirical survey of certain sexual and political variables has far from exhausted the possibilities of research in political sexology; new avenues are always open, but
new means of investigating sexual and political trends should be
employed if research is to reveal new findings on an individual's
feelings concerning sexuality and politics. The question should be
asked if this correlation takes into account the opinions and choices
of one particular group of young Québecois or if a comparative study
or survey taken among a larger group of young people would give a
more accurate picture of sexo-political ideologies and conduct,
and allow an evaluation of greater depth on the revolutionary
possibilities of sexuality...

      Jacques Lazure (1975) has this to say: "In the renewed effort
of Quebec to build her own future, it seems that the new sexuality
of our youth will be in the limelight." (p. 469)

REFERENCES

Abramowitz, S.I. (1973). The comparative competence-adjustment of
      student left social political activists. Journal of Per-
      sonality, 41 (2): 244-260.

Bergonier, H., Boucharnec, L. and Irrmann, P. (1967). Une nouvelle
      méthode d'analyse globale des résultats d'une enquête: éta-
      blissement de typologie. Revue Française de Marketing, 25
      (4): 31-41.

Berns, R.S., Bugental, D.G. and Berns, G.P. (1972). Research on
      student activism. American Journal of Psychiatry, 128 (12):
      1499-1504.

Block, J.H., Haan, N. and Smith, M.B. (1969). Socialization cor-
      relates of student activism. Journal of Social Issues, 25
      (4): 143-177.

Farnsworth, D.A. (1969). A university psychiatrist looks at campus
      protest. Psychiatric Opinion, 6: 6-11.

Flugel, J.C. (1945). Man, Morals and Society, Duckworth, London.

Geller, J.D. and Howard, G. (1972). Some sociopsychological char-
      acterics of student political activists. Journal of Applied
      Social Psychology, 2 (2): 114-137.

Handley, D. (1974). Regional variations and supportive attitudes
      toward european integration. Etudes et Recherches, 4: 52.

Hart, H.H. (1952). Masochism, passivity and radicalism. The Psychoanalytic Review, 39: 509-511.

Kerpelman, L.C. (1969). Student political activism and ideology: comparative characteristics of activists and non-activists. Journal of Counselling and Psychology, 16 (1): 8-13.

Kirby, D. (1971). A counter-culture explanation of student activism. Social Problems, 19 (2): 203-216.

Langman, L., Block, R.L., and Cunningham, I. (1973). Counter-cultural values at a catholic university. Social Problems, 20 (4): 521-532.

Lasswell, H. (1930). Psychopathology and Politics, University of Chicago Press, Chicago.

Lazure, J. (1970). La jeunesse du Québec en révolution. Essai d'Interprétation, Les Presses de l'Université du Québec, Montréal.

Lazure, J. (1975). Le Jeune Couple Non Marié, Les Presses de l'Université du Québec, Montréal.

Mossuz, J. (1974). Radicalisme politique et permissivité sexuelle. Revue Française de Science Politique, 24 (1): 52-78.

Reich, W. (1936). La Révolution Sexuelle, Plon, Paris.

PSYCHOSEXUAL MATERIAL IN THE STORIES TOLD BY CHILDREN: THE FUCKER

Brian Sutton-Smith and David M. Abrams

United States

We should make it clear at the outset that the findings in this paper on sexuality were incidental to a larger study on narrative, which we have conducted over the past three years (Sutton-Smith et al. 1975; Sutton-Smith, Botvin and Mahony, 1976; Abrams and Sutton-Smith, 1976; Botvin and Sutton-Smith, in press).   In our collection of the fantasy narratives of children between the ages of five and eleven years, we did not seek to elicit any particular kind of story, psychosexual or otherwise.   We know from several of our studies, however, that there can be both experimenter and stimulus instruction effects in the elicitation of stories.   For example, our male story takers tended to receive stories of higher fantasy content than our female story takers (Peterson, 1976). Furthermore, stories told freely, as compared with stories told to a TAT stimulus or a Rorchach stimulus, were of a more developmentally complex level (Peterson, 1976).   This finding, incidentally, is consistent with recent anthropological studies of narrative in which it has been shown that children tell stories of greater complexity in natural settings than in laboratory settings, and that children tell stories of higher complexity when reporting fantasy rather than personal or vicarious experience (Watson, 1972).   For these reasons, we may suppose that the stories with psychosexual content which we did receive tended to be elicited only by certain story takers.   While the character of such story takers has yet to be analyzed systematically, it is our anecdotal impression at least, that they were those who responded with the most joy at hearing these stories, thus providing a reinforcing response of considerable magnitude to the tellers.

The type of tales reported here were not directly sought.   This may account for the fact that from 150 children between the ages of

five and ten years, each telling two or more tales over a year of
collecting, only 24 children told any tales with any reference to
either romantic, sexual, tabooed behavior of any sort. A further
limitation of the present study is that it deals with sex only
through the medium of fantasy with all the complexities that that
implies about the relationships between fantasy and ordinary behavior.

The two major prior studies of children's psychosexuality as
revealed in fantasy are those of Wolfenstein (1954) and Legman
(1968). In Children's Humor, Wolfenstein gives examples of the
changing nature with age of children's references to sex. Younger
children's jokes tend to focus on dependency, anality, and self
exposure, while older children's jokes more often involve sexual
acts and aggression. By and large, earlier expressions are more
direct and later expressions more indirect. The younger child
thinks it funny to use words directly for sexual organs or bodily
orifices (pee pee, pooh pooh, etc.), but by eleven years he laughs
rather at more indirect expressions as in the childish joke about
the man who felt there was something wrong with his beer. He gave
it back to the waiter, who took it to the scientists (sic), and in
due course the message came back that his horse had diabetes. The
developmental law proposed by Wolfenstein is as follows:

"Children go through a two-sided development in relation
to joking. They progressively incorporate inhibitions
against the simple expression of impulses, and they progressively master technical devices by means of which
these inhibitions can be circumscribed." (1954, p. 214)

This is in effect an application of Freud's dictum (1963) that
the higher a joke rises in polite society the more indirect must be
its form of expression.

The most remarkable collection of fantasies about childish sex,
however, is to be found in Legman's Rationale of the Dirty Joke,
where in a section entitled "Children," he includes jokes about the
primal scene, mock ignorance, penis envy, embarrassments, masturbation, castration, group sex, incest, pedophilia, etc. On closer
examination and in contrast with Wolfenstein's mainly puerile examples, it is clear that the Legman corpus is not comprised of
jokes by children, but rather includes jokes about childishness
often expressed in antagonism to adult authority. These jokes
necessitate an understanding of abstract reasoning and symbolic
reference. They have an adolescent character to them.

"A father is bending over arranging presents under the
Christmas tree in his nightshirt. Little boy's voice,
'Hey pop, who gets the bagpipes?'"

or

> "An old man meets a little girl who is crying. 'I
> want one of those things like my brother's got, that
> sticks out and lays down and sticks out again.' Then
> the old man begins to cry, too."

In order to find these jokes amusing, the perceiver has to be
old enough to understand the relationship between the images presented and images not presented, and to discover the correspondence
asserted, or the effects of the parallel. Such a set of abstract
relationships is usually not appreciated cognitively until at least
early adolescence. Legman interprets these phenomena partly as a
subcultural protest by the young against the sexual hypocrisies of
the old, and partly as an indulgence by adults in the pain of having been children. His developmental hypothesis is that these
jokes are part of that prudential sexual enlightenment, whereby
the young discover that "sex can cause one to be unfairly rejected
or severely punished by those whose love one very much needs. This
is the real sexual enlightenment of the child, and of just as serious nature as that concerning the birds and the bees" (1968, p. 50).

If we wish to contrast Legman with Wolfenstein, it would seem
that he is demonstrating that children's jokes become more complicated with age, but he does not seem to be showing that they become
more inhibited which is Wolfenstein's thesis as well as that of
Freud. While it is not easy to distinguish between complexities
that are due to cognition and those that are due to inhibition, it
seems doubtful that most of the complicated jokes in Legman's book
could rise very far in polite society. These jokes are considerably
more popular with exclusive groups of males and with the lower socioeconomic classes than they are with the more prudish middle classes.
So there may well be a social class limitation to the Wolfenstein
thesis. Most current data on humor seems to suggest that we laugh
at that which matches our understanding (Goldenstein and McGhee,
1972). Probably it must also match our inhibitions, but there is
a great deal of cultural relativity in these inhibitions, so they
are perhaps less susceptible to developmental laws than are simple
cognitive changes.

In the present study, we may ask (although with the same difficulty of measuring) whether the older children become more inhibited in their expression of sex in fantasy stories, or whether
they merely become more complex. It must be added that there may
be a difference between the fantasy of the humor above and the
fantasy of the present stories. Typically in humor the comic hero
cannot control events, whereas in fairy tale stories he gains control over the world. Humor is a rite of reversal, whereas hero
tales are a ritual of identification with some of the major modes
of the society.

RESULTS

In the present sample the psychosexual stories as compared with romance stories were contributed only by the boys. Nine boys told psychosexual stories four boys told romance stories; whereas, no girls told psychosexual stories and eleven girls told romance stories (9:4 - 0:11). This is a significant difference in statistical terms except that it is almost impossible to know in what way the universe of boys and girls is being sampled in this study, so the results are better regarded as a potentially instructive case study. In the obscenity stories there is possibly an age shift with the exploration of impropriety and taboo violations increasing with age. In the present examples seven-year-old and under stories seem to be a trifle less extreme, including spitting, shitting, pants down, naked girls, pee fights, biting weeners, long weeners, sucking buggars, pinching asses and fucking. From eight onwards there are references to having a boner, farting, tits, being horney, a dickey, animalism, having babies, throwing up, massages, cunts, eating shit, leaping on girls, sexual assaults, being pregnant, whores, vaginas and incest. There is also an increasing number of references to direct sexual contact at these later age levels. When all the stories of particular children who gave strings of psychosexual stories are viewed, a progression of rapport with the investigator is also present. In one case, the first story is about pee fights, the second about pulling down pants, the third about seeing naked girls, and the last about fucking. In another case, there is a progression from jumping on girls, to having a boner, to giving massages, to impregnating all the alluring girls in the class. These examples suggest that with encouragement the sample of more extreme stories from all children would be much larger than that collected in the present largely incidental manner.

The age progression in the romance tales is even less pronounced than in these psychosexual ones, though there is perhaps a shift from having friends, staying overnight and playing together at the younger levels to more fairy tale marriages at the older age level, together with some discussion of having babies. Some of these stories show a very close resemblance to classic fairy tales.

In the Appendix I we have included some of the 35 psychosexual tales collected in the present inquiry. For space reasons and because of their more conventional nature, the romance tales are not included.

DISCUSSION

These results for the psychosexual stories, which demonstrate increasing taboo violation with age, do not seem to support Wolfenstei

thesis of increasing inhibition with age. There is both increasingly serious tabooed subjects taken into account, and also increasing complexity of expression. But that complexity seems to
be more of an appeal to more mature insight, than a cover and device for indirection of expression, although admittedly these are
not too easily separated. The present sample was taken from a
public school and an open school where the parents tend to be more
liberal and professional than they are in many other public schools.
There has also been a clear change in public attitudes over the
past twenty years with increasing acceptance of obscenity and pornography in joke circles which may account for the more direct expressions in this sample than in Wolfenstein's earlier work twenty
years ago (Sutton-Smith, 1960).

This conclusion, however is largely sustained by reference
to the stories of the boys in this sample. The romance tales contain relatively more oblique and symbolic references (although the
psychosexual tales are not without these also). Romance tales have
the ring of an earlier historical age compared with the psychosexual
tales, although even within them there is occasionally a marked mod-
ernism (see "Harold Hoot" and "The King's Daughter and the Three
Lovers").

A more important distinction between the psychosexual tales
and the romances, however, is that the latter are very much like
the hero genre of tales with which we have dealt elsewhere (Sutton-
Smith et al., 1975). They are serious and they do model after
cultural realities that are fairly obvious. They can be interpreted
in the way fairy tales are often interpreted, as a wish fulfillment
and an ego bolstering model suited to the childhood years (Bettelheim, 1975). The psychosexual tales, however, do not easily fit
this model. Here the children are not following any genre which is
presented to them in conventional literature or television. Although
the presence of several psychosexual rhymes in our collection, suggests that there may be an underground source of oral psychosexual
lore which is providing the model.

The psychosexual tales perhaps are more like humor in which
the comic hero cannot control events. On the other hand, they do
have elements of hero status in them. ABC Wee-Oh (Story 1) swings
through the air like superman after various obscene adventures and
ends up back in his own bed. In other stories, (Story 2, 5) after
various exposures of organs, pee fights, and millions of babies,
the parties get married. Some of the tales clearly have a developmental plot, although others are more like a series of improper
episodes. In an earlier paper (Abrams and Sutton-Smith, 1976), we
have dealt with the "trickster" figure in children's stories. It
seems probable that the interpretations we used in that case are
those that are most appropriate for the present collection of data.

The trickster figure which is widespread in the folklore of the
world is usually a low order evolutionary figure such as a spider,
frog, raven, rabbit or fox who counters the physical aggression of
more powerful figures with cunning and wit. The most well-known
modern form is Bugs Bunny of television fame. Classically, the
trickster is characterized both by infantile behavior and cunning.
In some literatures his infantile conduct has led to his being
labelled as a symbol of regressive behavior. For example, in
Radin's (1956) collection of the Winnebago Indian tale cycle of
Wakdjunkago, his exploits include his right arm fighting with his
left; telling his anus to watch over roasting ducks as he sleeps;
awakening with an erection holding up his blanket and mistaking
it for the chief's banner; scattering the villagers by breaking
wind; and wading through his own excrement. There are other interpretations of this tale genre however, which emphasize the
trickster's sophisticated cleverness and which may arise from
cultural differences. The Afro-American trickster, for example,
is generally a much more clever and successful figure than the
self-defeating promiscuous trickster of the American Indians. In
our own study of trickster tales from 56 children, we found that
these tales could be arranged in a developmental order. The tales
of the younger children tended to emphasize the more regressive
aspects of the trickster. Their tricksters were noticeable for
their physical clumsiness and their moronic self-defeat, as in
"Numskull" tales. By about the age of 7 or 8 however, the trickster begins to display trickery, though as yet is not successful
with it. But by 9 or 11 years, the stories are characterized by
trickster success. In sum, the trickster as a folktale phenomenon
has its own particular developmental career from Numskull, silly
trickster, to trickster-hero, at least as it appears in children's
spontaneous stories.

     Unfortunately, the present sample of psychosexual tales is not
large enough to positively identify them with all aspects of the
trickster genre, but it is clear that it is their most likely pa-
radigm. This linkage is a most important one, because it suggests
that in these tales we are not dealing simply with obscenity or
regression as such, but are dealing with a spontaneous folk phenomenon or phantasm within which children express for themselves a
growth style or a growth model (as the hero is a growth model),
which does not involve the renunciation of many of their basic
psychosexual concerns. This is not a model that is often approved
by adults, but it may be one that is more important in the lives of
some creative youngsters than we have yet realized.

     What we are saying here is that the trickster is both a reality
on the cultural level, and a reality on the level of individual symbolism. When children tell these psychosexual tales, they are not
simply or episodically being obscene, they are representing a model

of cultural behavior, which may no more be "true" than are fairy
tales, but like fairy tales has a firm cultural significance.   If
fairy tales bolster the belief in good fortune and the feeling that
we shall overcome, trickster tales bolster the belief that there is
scope in this world also for the promiscuous and the wily.   Fairy
tales bring a message of optimism to our character, about ultimate
success (or at least, that is the way in which I read Bettelheim's
cogent interpretation of them, (1976)).   Psychosexual tales similarly bring a message of optimism about the ultimate goodness of
our erogenous life.   But both fairy tales and trickster tales are
also primitive blueprints of the life to be.   They are not merely
a message to character, they are a message to thought, even though
a caricatural and much oversimplified one (Sutton-Smith, in press).
Each gets the teller and the hearer ready for the potentially good
future.   In cultures where the future is not so encouraging the
people tell more defeated kinds of fairy tales (Dundes, 1964).   In
sum, trickster tales and tales of obscenity are pre-adaptive forms
of behavior.   They are not simply epiphenomenal or erratic side
effects in human development.

What is remarkable on a closer analysis of these tales is the
conflicts which they entail between the various psychosexual orifices.   They can be seen as an unusally clear illustration of the
psychoanalytic accounts of the battle between the erogenous zones.
In the younger children's stories (6 to 7 years) in particular,
there is almost a pitched battle between the oral and anal orifices, and the phallic and genital ones.   One six-year-old eats,
farts, shits, has enemas, and runs back to his mother's frying pan,
but also runs round naked, gets married and fucks all over the
world as in Martha's Vineyard, Vermont and Greece (Story 3, 4).
In his development ultimately, higher zones appear to transcend
the earlier ones.   A seven-year-old has problems with monster Nixon,
but finally Nixon's teeth are broken as he bites the hot dog containing the steel weener, and Nixon is disparaged as the (oral)
Fried Egg President (Story 5).   The older children, (9 to 11), seem
to have partially escaped the battle with orality and anality, and
instead invest themselves more completely in stories of fucking
everyone and having thousands of babies all round (Story 6).

As these tales are in their way well organized and yet can be
differentiated from the Trickster by these largely psychosexual
concerns, we feel there might be virtue in thinking of them as a
special sub-category of the Trickster, namely the Fucker.   The
fucker is a character who is the ultimate hero when the battle between psychosexual zones has been fought out.   In him the conflicts
specific to the psychosexual modal world come to issue.   With normal
development, those who take this pathway for representing their inner feelings finally recount a fucker who has a Don Juanish capacity for lovemaking, and the potency of the mythic bull for producing babies.

In a small scale auxiliary study we asked the school principal to describe the level of adjustment of the nine boys telling these psychosexual tales: high, average, or low. One was described as superbly adjusted, one was maladjusted, and the rest as quite average. However, what they all had in common along with their level of adjustment was a degree of quarrelsomeness in their social relationships. They appeared to be mildly rebellious boys. The hypothesis is generated that aggression against authority figures is an intrinsic aspect of the kind of free reportage on psychosexual modes that is recorded here, a conclusion quite consistent with the "protest" explanations of Legman provided above, and certainly consistent with the anti-authority character of the trickster in folklore.

The Fucker then may be a figure in many of our hearts. Perhaps it is time we gave him his due and recognized his development in childhood years. But such recognition is probably more critical to those of a more rebellious strain whose own psychosexual development is worthy of further investigation.

APPENDIX I

PSYCHOSEXUAL STORIES

Story 1

Boy aged seven.

A baby was walking down the street making trouble and when the baby saw a man passing her, she said, "You suck your buggers, two times, yeh, yeh." Then they went to a music studio and they heard, "Keep coming in ABC, ABC, ABC, 1, 2, 3." And then the baby said, "I can do the whole alphabet. ABCDEFGHIJKLMNOPQRS and TUV, W and XYZ. That's how!" And then the baby said, "I spit at you," and then she spitted in the air. Then the baby said, "ABC my bugger!" Then the baby said, "I think I'm so smart just because I have one tooth out." Then the baby said, "I am superman, you can't hurt superman." Then the man said, "You're messing up the whole music studio. Kick the baby out." Then another baby said, "I never saw a baby with a moustache," while putting his fingers on his nose. Then he said, "Me Chinese, me tell joke, me go peepee in your coke." And then the baby that was getting kicked out said, "You're not Chinese, you're American."

Then they saw 3 ladies kicking their legs up and saying, "Legs, legs, legs are here!" Then the girl said, "I shave my eyelashes everyday." And then the baby said, "I think I'm so great because my teeth don't need to be fixed." Then the baby walked into an A&P Wee-O Store and everyone was saying, "Wee-O!"

Then the baby said, "It passed my bed-time, I better find my way home." Then he accidently walked into a museum while the guard was asleep, and he climbed up a plastic tree and there was a rope hanging on it and he said, "Me Tarzan!" Then the baby swinged out the window and about a mile and landed through the chimney into his house and said, "Me Santa Claus." And then he climbed into bed and went to sleep.

Story 2

Boy aged six.

Once upon a time Alfred went to the bathroom. And he took a wee and after that Balfour (he's referring to Balfour Cutchie who is listening nearby) came over and then Dennis (who is also listen-ing) and then they all went to the bathroom at the same time. Then they had a pee wee fight and they kept on having pee wee fights and they kept on having pee wee fights all day. And then they went to

bed and they had a dream of them having a piss fight when they had
to go to the bathroom again. And then there was morning. Ha, ha,
ha. And they didn't have anything for breakfast except for eggs
and they hated eggs and they had to crack 'em, and throw 'em on
their heads. And then they took a drive to Washington Square Park
and then had to go to the bathroom again. And then they wee weed
near a tree. And the coppers came and they said, "Pull down your
pants and your underpants." And then they said, "Take off your
shirts and then take off your shoes and take off your socks" (and
now here comes the funny part) and everybody came to see and look
at them naked. And then they put back their clothes (here comes
the funny part again) and they said, "Oh Cop, please let me go to
the bathroom." And then Alfred came back again and then they all
went home. And then Alfred went to call up his girlfriend and then
they kissed and then they got married. And at the wedding, they
started to take off their clothes and kiss and then they walked
home in the snowy snow, snow, snow. And they forgot their clothes
and they were walking naked, and then someone shot 'em with a snow-
ball and they called it the Naked Ball. And then they all came
around and they made more naked balls. And then they said, "Hey,
give me more naked balls." And then they said, "I want to take my
clothes off and kiss and stuff." And then they said, "I'm going
to marry you, but I'll kiss you and never get divorced." And then
they woke up and got dressed and had breakfast.

Story 3

Boy aged six.

Once upon a time there was Alfred and then he had a girl. Then
he went over to her house. Then they went into bed. And they took
off their clothes. And they pissed together. Then they went to
get married. Then they were going home and then they stopped at
the store to get a bra (he laughs merrily) and then they stopped
at a different store to get a girdle. And then they went back home
to get an enema. And then they kissed together and then they fell
on the floor and took off all their clothes and then they got home
finally.

Well and then they said, "We ought to kiss together first."
Then they went on all through the night until it was morning. Then
they said "I'll draw a picture for you of your butt!" And then
Alfred said, "I got to go home for my mother's frying pan, 'cause
my mother's frying pan is the boss of the house." Then she kisses
goodbye and says, "Do you have to?" Then they watched TV and hear,
"Take a ball of clay, pinch it with your fingers, then they put it
on the wheel, then they pinch it with their fingers. Then they
shit on it. That's how you make a pot, that's how you make a vase,
and that's how you make a pitcher."

And then they went to get a funnel and then they said, "I got
to get a couple more girls and a couple more bras and I'll buy you
a horse and we'll spit in the air and I'll break your hot and I'll
throw you in the do-do dot. If I was the king of the world, I'd
tell you what I'd do. I'll lay a fart and blow you apart, and
that's the end of you." Then they say, "A fart is a fart and I'll
blow you apart, and that's a dot." Then they sat on the couch and
turned on the TV and say, "I hate Western movies." Then she says,
"I like Colgate better, I like Colgate because they use their pitch-
ers." Then they go home to Alfred's house. And then he goes, "I'll
your petticoat (sic) I'll eat' em all up. You get the Colgate Cakka."
He goes, "There's a mouse, a mouse, a mouse. I'll take a worm out
and stuff some chalk down his throat." Then he goes, "I got a tooth.
I need a toothpick." Then Alfred says, "Fuck me, fuck me, fuck me.
Put the Colgate dinosaur, you eat 'em all up. I dream of Jeannie,
swimming in her bikini, sucking on her wienie, and watching her
bikini."

Story 4

Boy aged six.

This kid -- his name was Alfred -- walks down the street one
day and he sees this girl. And then he goes into a little corner
and they both take off their clothes, and they go home and they
get into bed (snicker). And they take off her bra and their clothes
and their underwear (laughs again). And they're all naked. And
they started cooking naked with a blender (he is playing with an
eggbeater). And they had supper and they started F-U-C-K-I-N-G
(spells it). And they went out in the street naked. And then a
man walks by and laughs and says, "Ha, ha, ha, you can't win them
all." And then Alfred and his girlfriend go get married. They
start to go to the store naked and then Alfred comes along and says,
"I gotta go home." And then the girlfriend goes, "Can't you stay
a little longer?" And then he goes, "I'll stay for dinner. What
are we having?" And she says, "Frankfritters." And Alfred says,
"I hate frankfritters. Let's get a divorce." And then they meet
in the street and they say, "Let's get married again."

And then there's another girl that walks by that's even prettier
than Alfred's girlfriend. And the Alfred falls in love with that
girl and the first girl says, "I'm getting out of here." And then
they go, "Let's get married." They get married and they say, "Let's
go to the drive-in and F-U-C-K there and go home and get married
again and go to bed and take off your clothes -- I'll help ...
okay, let's start F-U-C-K-ing, F-U-C-K again. And let's go to
Martha's Vineyard and we will F-U-C-K alot there and we'll come
back and start F-U-C-K-ing again. And then you know what we'll do
is go to Vermont and start F-U-C-K-ing, F-U-C-K-ing, F-U-C-K-ing

again. And come back and go to Greece and F-U-C-K, F-U-C-K there."

Story 5

Boy aged seven.

Once upon a time there were two babies. They loved, they hated
spinach. So once their mother gave them a big pot of spinach, each
with one fried egg on it. And they hated it so much, they threw it
at their mother. She gave them another pot of spinach with two eggs
on it this time and they were even madder and they threw it at their
father this time. Then their mother gave them two pots of spinach
with six fried eggs on it. They threw it at their sister. Then,
when Nixon heard of this, he called them "The Fried Egg Family."
But the baby was angry at Nixon. So when Nixon came to their house,
they did nothing to him. But as he was walking out the door, the
baby saw him and they they stuck out their weenies and then they
put their weenies to work (sic). And when Nixon saw these things, he
flipped. But then, they pulled in their weener and put 2 buns on
top of them and put some catsup and spinach and then Nixon got
right back up and he started to bite. All of a sudden, the babies
went pissing and shot their X-Y-Z. And Nixon was so upset he almost,
his heart almost cracked. But then, they had more strategy.

So when he was walking over the mountain, they made flying hamburgers and then Nixon screamed, "We're being invaded by flying
hamburgers!" And then the babies made flying hamburgers shoot out
missile hotdogs and then Nixon had a very good idea! And he ate it
-- the hotdogs. But Nixon was so dumb, those hotdogs were solid
metal and when he bit on them, they cracked his teeth and he was
so upset. And then a lady came and said, "Will you help me across
the street?" And Nixon said, "Whaaaaaaaaaaah."

"You are weird, Man," the lady said. And then the babies had
little bit more strategy. They started shooting spinach with fried
eggs on top. And then New York called Nixon "The Fried Egg President."

Story 6

Boy aged ten.

Once upon a time there was a boy named Kelly. Kelly had a sister named Booty. Kelly and Booty were in love. They slept in the
same bed together. They had a lot of babies. But Kelly didn't
like Booty, so he found a new girlfriend. His girlfriend's name
was Willa. Willa was just right. Kelly and Willa were madly in
love with each other. So they finally got married. They had

10,000 babies. Kelly was not satisfied, so they had 10,000 more.
Well Willa wasn't right, so he gave up Willa. Kelly married a new
girl named Prudence. Well Kelly knew Prudence wasn't right, so he
gave her up right away. Then he met a new girl. This girl's name
was Starret. Starret was perfect, even better than Willa. Well,
Kelly and Starret had a couple of thousand babies, but Kelly wasn't
satisfied, so they had a couple thousand more. Kelly and Starret
were madly in love. Kelly didn't like her, so he gave her up and
met a new girl. The new girl was named Roberta. Roberta and Kelly
were so happy together so they got married and had 10 million babies. But that wasn't enough for Kelly, so they had 10 million
more.

... My name is Kelly. Let me explain how you have babies. You
lie in bed with all your clothes off with another person of the opposite sex. You come close to each other and whoops, my mother's
coming, we have to continue the story.

Anyway, to get back to the story, Kelly and Roberta were madly
in love. This reminded Kelly of his school days when he and another
girl were kissing in the bathroom, the boy's bathroom of course,
and while they were kissing their braces got caught together. While
their lips were touching each other, the principal walked in. Kelly
didn't mind but he got out of the braces mess and started kissing
the principal who was female. That girl got so mad at Kelly she
slapped him in the ponderosa (rear end) and walked out. Well back
to the story. Kelly and Roberta were having a good time together,
a real good time and they both lived happily ever after. P.S. Very
happily ever after.

REFERENCES

Abrams, D. and Sutton-Smith, B. (1976). The development of the
     trickster in children's narratives. Journal of American
     Folklore.

Botvin, G. and Sutton-Smith, B. (in press). A syntagmatic analysis
     of children's narrative. Developmental Psychology.

Bettelheim, B. (1975). The Uses of Enchantment: The Meaning and
     Importance of Fairy Tales, Knopf, New York.

Dundes, A. (1964). The Morphology of North American Indian Folk-
     tales, FF Communications, No. 195 (Helsinki).

Freud, S. (1963). Jokes and Their Relation to the Unconscious,
     Norton, New York.

Goldstein, J.H. and McGhee, P.H. (1972). The Psychology of Humor, Academic Press, New York.

Legman, G. (1968). Rationale of the Dirty Joke, Grove Press, New York.

Petersen, L. (1976). The effect of the storytaker's sex on the stories the children tell. Paper #2 in Project Report, National Institute of Education, Grant No. NE-G-00-3-0133. Sutton-Smith, B. Principal Investigator: "The enculturation of the imaginative processes between the ages of five and seven years and their effect upon classroom activity."

Petersen, L. (1976). Constraining the child's story telling situation: does it make a difference?, Ph.D. dissertation, Columbia University, Teachers College.

Radin, P. (1956). The Trickster, Schocken, New York.

Sutton-Smith, B. (1960). The cruel joke series, Midwestern Folklore 10: 11-22.

Sutton-Smith, B., Abrams, D., Botvin, G., Caring, M., Gildesgame, D., and Stevens, T. (1975). The importance of the story-taker: an investigation of the imaginative life. The Urban Review 8: 82-95.

Sutton-Smith, B., Botvin, G., and Mahony, D. (1976). Developmental structures in fantasy narratives. Human Development 19: 1-13.

Sutton-Smith, B. (in press). The Dialectics of Play, University of Texas Press.

Watson, K.A. (1972). The rhetoric of narrative structure: a sociolinguistic analysis of stories told by part-Hawaiian children, Unpublished Ph.D. Dissertation, University of Hawaii.

Wolfenstein, M. (1954). Children's Humor, a Psychological Analysis, Free Press, Glencoe.

Quite interesting but not very practical.

Symbiotic relationship ∈ vice officers and prostitutes.

PROSTITUTION AS AN ECOLOGY OF CONFIDENCE GAMES: THE SCRIPTED
BEHAVIOR OF PROSTITUTES AND VICE OFFICERS

Maxine Atkinson and Jacqueline Boles

United States

Most research on prostitution has considered it either a form
of deviant behavior or one of the more extreme examples of occupational professionalization (Gray, 1973; Winnick and Kinsie, 1973;
Hirschi, 1962).   Little research has included the effects of criminal statutes and law enforcement practices on the behavior of
prostitutes even though the illegality of prostitution and police
strategies to control it strongly relate to the behavior, attitudes
and lifestyles of prostitutes themselves (Roby, 1972; James, 1975).

This paper examines the social organization of impersonal sex
(Weinberg, 1975), specifically the scripted behavior of prostitutes
toward vice officers and vice officers toward prostitutes as the
two groups cooperate to achieve their differing but interrelated
goals (Long, 1961).

RESEARCH METHODS

The data for this paper were gathered as part of an ongoing
research project during an eight month period, April to December,
1975.   While collecting structured life histories of arrested prostitutes in a vice officer, we observed the interactions between
prostitutes and vice officers.   We observed the strategies used by
vice officers to arrest suspected prostitutes, and conversely, the
strategies favored by prostitutes to avoid arrest.   Prostitutes
were observed and interviewed as arrestees in the squadroom and in
hustling bars, massage parlors and strip clubs.[1]

_____

[1]A hustling bar is a cocktail lounge which operates almost exclusively for the purpose of providing a meeting place for bar prostitutes and potential customers.

ACTORS AND SCRIPTS

The purposes of vice officers are three-fold: to make arrests to fulfill their quotas (Peterson, 1971; Rubenstein, 1973); to minimize citizen complaints; and to avoid personal danger. Prostitutes' purposes are to make sufficient money to satisfy themselves or their pimps, avoid hassles, arrest and personal harm. These various purposes are not mutually exclusive; they can be accomplished by the actors (prostitutes and vice officers) adhering to a script, i.e., "... an organization of mutually shared conventions that allows for two or more actors to participate in a complex act involving mutual dependence (Gagnon and Simon 1973:20)."

Vice officers must accommodate themselves to the goals of their superior officers and to the expectations of the general public; in the process they must gain the cooperation of prostitutes. Prostitutes, in order to fulfill their goals (making money and avoiding hassles and arrest) must accommodate both "johns" and vice officers. This paper describes the scripted behavior of prostitutes toward vice officers and vice officers toward prostitutes as they cooperate to achieve their differing but interrelated goals.

The Prostitutes' Game with the Vice Officer

Prostitutes, in order to accommodate vice officers, provide services which are both extrinsically and intrinsically rewarding to them, thus meeting their own goals of avoiding harrassment and arrest. The prostitute must structure her game so as to convince vice officers that she can provide services which in turn, help him satisfy his superiors.

Prostitutes counsel and instruct wayward hookers, i.e., those who misbehave by causing trouble which brings them to the attention of the public. Hookers who solicit too aggresively, become offensively drunk, or otherwise cause a disturbance will be counselled by the usually older, wiser, "good hooker" on proper decorum. Often vice officers will ask their hooker friends to counsel with these troublesome young women who are causing complaints.

The prostitute acts as an informant. She knows about new girls coming to town; their troublesome habits and, more importantly, their troublesome friends (Chambliss, 1972; Jackson, 1972). Prostitutes feel no need to be loyal to others who endanger their precarious positions. As one said, "Some girls deserve to be arrested every night." Another respondent explained that some hookers steal from "johns," keep up pimps, neglect their children, fight with other girls, and are too obvious in the way they dress and act. "They'll (the police) treat you right if you watch yourself."

Prostitutes are invaluable sources of information concerning drug traffic and gambling operations. Many lounges, bars and strip clubs serve as distribution points for drugs. Also prostitutes are part of the night people (Boles and Garbin, 1974), and they meet with their friends at after-hours restaurants and clubs where they hear the latest gossip about the opening of new gambling establishments. Often they will be recruited as sticks (shills) for gambling houses and thus are in position to know the owners of these places. Arson is another crime that prostitutes often have inside information on, as clubs and lounges frequently burn.

Prostitutes also offer police officers certain intrinsic rewards. There are only two possible alternate ways of relating to vice officers. Keeping out of their way is one method, but it is, however, more satisfactory to be their friend.

There are a few hustling bars where prostitutes and officers meet as friends. A typical bar scene includes officers and prostitutes sitting around the bar engaging in friendly conversation on topics ranging from a recent football game to the officer's impending divorce. The officers pay no cover charge and are not charged for their drinks. Occasionally these bars host more elaborate affairs. A group of hookers gave a farewell party for a sergeant on the vice squad who had been transferred to an outlying post.

The friendly prostitute helps the vice officer rationalize his role behavior. Many of the street prostitutes whom the officer arrests attack the officer's motivation, behavior, character and integrity. The legitimacy of the laws he seeks to enforce are questioned. The morality of hiding in men's toilets, pretending to be "johns," or spying on people carrying on their private affairs is discussed in vivid terms. The vice officer must legitimate his behavior to those he arrests as well as to himself, his superiors, and his friends and colleagues. The friendly prostitute supports his rationalizations: "You're just doing your job," or "You don't make these laws, you just enforce them."

This type of conversation leads quite naturally to discussion of the prostitute's role. She will often move the conversation into a discussion of the difficulties of her life which led her into prostitution. Add to that the touching story of her two year old whom she "tries to raise right," and the prostitute who is already friendly with the officer protects herself with an age old con.

Prostitutes provide sexual services for police officers; it is difficult for them to refuse. They are also recruited by vice officers and others to service judges, journalists and politicians.

As one hooker said, "I didn't charge for having sex with a state legislator; that was public relations." Two female broadcasters were fired from a local talk show for quoting a lobbyist to the state legislature as saying, "You can get anything you want out of the state legislature by providing booze, broads or porno." Attractive stripper-prostitutes are most often recruited to service influential politicians and their friends.

In sum, prostitutes are able to attain one of their primary goals by helping vice officers attain theirs. The good prostitute avoids arrest by providing services for officers: information, friendship, emotional support, and sex.

The Vice Officers' Game with the Prostitute

Vice officers, like prostitutes, use costumes: leisure suits, blue jeans, overalls, and mod shirts. Many officers' costumes are highly idiosyncratic; one habitually wore a white fur hat, and another had an earring in one ear. Hair styles and length, beards and mustaches are part of the costume. Like prostitutes, officers try to adopt clothing and hair styles which reflect their personalities. On special assignments officers may be dressed as conventioneers with badges, taxi-cab drivers, or street cleaners. Since officers may dress in whatever fashion will enhance their role performance, they have become more difficult for prostitutes to identify. As one prostitute explained, "You just have to learn to pick them out; its instinct I guess. Its harder now 'cause they're sneaky." Another said, "It definitely is easier to get arrested, like with the black guys (officers), they look like average dudes."

The strategy most often used by vice officers to apprehend prostitutes is called encouragement, i.e., "the activity of the policeman or police agent (a) who acts as a victim; (b) who intends by his action to encourage a suspect to commit a crime; (c) who actually communicates this encouragement to the suspect; and (d) who has thereby some influence upon the commission of the crime (Newman, 1975:161)." The vice officer poses as a potential "john" and invites the prostitute to make him an offer.

Officers act their roles in bars, lounges, on the street, and in rooming houses and hotel rooms. Hotel rooms are rented by officers, and clothing and personal toiletries are planted so as to make the room look lived in. One conversation we recorded involved two vice officers planning to pose as street cleaners complete with uniforms and truck.

Officers also hide and listen. Two officers spent over three

hours hidden under a stoop of a rooming house used by prostitutes.
They were able to overhear a prostitute make an offer and thus effect an arrest.   There are a variety of laws which can be used to
arrest prostitutes other than solicitation.   In the city where
this research was conducted, there are twenty-two municipal or-
dinances alone which may be used to arrest prostitutes.   Often the
officer will arrest one prostitute on as many as three or four
separate charges so that he can make several cases out of one arrest.   Further, the quality of arrests is also important: the
more serious the charge, the better the arrest.   It is preferred
to make an arrest for committing an illicit sex act than for just
solicitation.   In order to make an arrest for such an act, the
officer must take the hooker to a room (often his), get undressed
and go through the preliminaries of a sex act just prior to penetration.   The male must have an erection for it to be considered
a sex act, but if he penetrates, he is participating in the act
himself and a case cannot be made.

Vice officers not only arrest prostitutes, they help them.
Vice officers drop or reduce charges in exchange for information,
help prostitutes' friends in court, provide inside information on
the disposition of charges, and help prostitutes solve their personal problems.   As Rubenstein (1973:207) reports: "His (the
vice officer's) steadiest source of information is what he collects as rent for allowing people to operate without arresting
them."

A vice officer can be a good friend to a prostitute, in and
out of court.   In exchange for their friendship and help, vice
officers expect cooperation in regulating prostitution and other
consensual offenses in the community.

SUMMARY AND CONCLUSIONS

In this paper we have detailed some of the strategies used by
prostitutes and vice officers to accommodate and cooperate with
each other to maintain prostitution while achieving their own ends.
Ideally, an ecological balance is maintained so that each occupational group can achieve its own goals while only minimally inter-
fering with goal attainment of the other.   This system breaks down
occasionally; unsocialized prostitutes come into town; raids are
called for by the police administrators for their own purposes; a
murder occurs which draws the public's attention to prostitution;
a crusading reporter does a story on prostitution.   However, the
ecological balance is soon restored and prostitution flourishes.

The scripted relations between prostitutes and vice officers
are part of the myriad of relations between groups which are involved, either directly or tangentially, to prostitution, itself

just a small segment of what is called vice. Pimps, procurers, club and lounge owners, bartenders, and drug pushers are only a few of the occupational groups, many of whose members are engaged in prostitution-related activities. Gambling, narcotics, and pornography and other consensual crimes (Kaplan, 1973) operate similarly to prostitution with each other to accomplish their goals while maintaining a smoothly operating system.

Consensual crimes, because of the nature of their organizational structure, are particularly sensitive to changes in the external environment, i.e., new laws, police commissioners, or police practices.

These changes in the external environment cause readjustment throughout the system as it seeks to accommodate itself to the new situation. Newman and others have argued that police practices in relation to consensual crimes appear highly unpredictable, erratic, and idiosyncratic because they are sensitive to "... pressures from both within and without the police department (Newman, 1975:160)."

We know very little about the relationship between "external pressures," and police practices and the responses of prostitutes, gamblers, pornographers, or other players whose scripts must be altered to meet these new conditions. As Newman stated:

"It is difficult to identify these pressures and to measure their significance in relation to current police practices. The police seldom explain why they concentrate their detection efforts in one direction rather than another. As a consequence, this aspect of current criminal justice administration is little understood (Newman, 1975:160)."

Research on the linkages between changes in the external environment, police practices, and consensual crimes would further our understandings of a variety of problems including changes in arrest rates for consensual crimes, the social organization of various forms of vice, and the decision-making processes among vice officers.

REFERENCES

Boles, J. and Garbin, A.P. (1974). The strip club and stripper customer patterns of interaction. Sociology and Social Research, 58 (2): 136-144.

Chambliss, B. (1972). Box Man: A Thief's Journey. Harper and Row, New York.

Gagnon, J. and Simon W. (1973). Sexual Conduct: The Social Sources
     of Human Sexuality, Aldine Publishing Company, Chicago.

Gray, D. (1973). Turning out: a study of teenage prostitution.
     Urban Life and Culture, 1 (4): 401-425.

Hirschi, T. (1962). The professional prostitute. Berkeley Journal
     of Sociology, 7 (1): 33-49.

Jackson, B. (1972). Outside the Law: A Thief's Primer, Transac-
     tion Books, New Brunswick.

James, J. (1975). Mobility as an adaptive strategy. Urban Anthro-
     pology, 4 (4): 349-364.

Kaplan, J. (1973). Criminal Justice: Introductory Case and Mate-
     rials, Foundation Press, New York.

Long, N. (1961). "The local community as an ecology of games," in
     Edward Banfield, E. (ed.) Urban Government: A Reader in
     Administration and Politics. The Free Press, Glencoe.

Newman, D. J. (1975). Introduction to Criminal Justice. J.B.
     Lippincott Co., New York.

Peterson, D. (1971). Informal norms and police practice; the traf-
     fic ticket quota system. Sociology and Social Research,
     55 (3): 354-362.

Roby, P. (1972). Politics and prostitution: a case study of the
     revision, enforcement, and administration of the New York
     State penal laws on prostitution, Criminology, 9 (Feb.):
     425-447.

Rubenstein, J. (1973). City Police, Farrah, Struss and Giroux,
     New York.

Weinberg, M. (1975). Gay baths and social organization of imper-
     sonal sex. Social Problems, 23 (2): 124-136.

Winnick, C. and Kinsie, P. M. (1973). The Lively Commerce: Pros-
     titution in the United States, Quadrangle, Chicago.

SEXUAL SCRIPTS

Jay Ann Jemail and James Geer

United States

In their book <u>Sexual Conduct</u>, Gagnon and Simon (1973) suggest that there is little that can be truly called spontaneous in human behavior. They propose a psychosocial learning model to account for the social and cultural elements in the learning of scripted behavior. They use the term "script" or "scripted behavior" to describe the conventional and dramatic elements in human conduct. Their model may be used to describe all human social behavior; however, specifically, we are concerned here with its application to sexual behavior, that is to say, with the description of scripted sexual behavior.

Sexual scripting theory predicts that there are conventional-ized patterns of culturally shared sequences of behaviors facilitat-ing the "doing" of sex. Inherent in the theory is the notion that scripts allow a sexual interaction to take place by providing the participants with a program of action. The script defines the sit-uation, names the actors, and plots the sequence of events in a sexual interaction. Hence, internalization of the script allows the partners to proceed with a sequence of behaviors as if there was no need to question what is to follow.

Kinsey and his co-workers (1948, 1953) suggested that a stan-dard sequence occurs in sexual experience. The sequence commonly begins with general body contact and moves on to breast manipula-tion and genital manipulation, and terminates with oral-genital sex and/or intercourse. Bentler, who developed a Guttman-scale to assess sexual conduct, found that there is a hierarchy of ex-perienced sexual behaviors. The Bentler scales suggest that there is a hierarchical element in psychosexual development. Thus, a

513

person who had experienced "more advanced" sexual behaviors, e.g.,
coitus, had also experienced "less advanced" behaviors, e.g., manipulation of breasts. This is in agreement with Gagnon and Simon's
theory, although they go a step further proposing that there is a
sexual script, a conventionalized sequence in the "doing" of sex.

In the present study we attempted to identify this sequence
for both males and females. Thus, it was necessary to obtain a
sequence free from the biases of the experiments by having the sequence constructed by the subject population. Gagnon and Simon
suggest that the conventional sequence is the sequence construed
as sexually arousing. We tested this by having subjects rearrange
a set of 25 sentences each describing an event in a heterosexual
interaction under two sets of instructions. Subjects were asked
to rearrange the sentences in a sequence that was "the most sexually arousing" (Condition A) and "the most likely to occur" (Condition B).

With this procedure we could answer the following questions:
What do males and females construe as the sequence most likely to
occur? What is construed as the most sexually arousing sequence?
How are these sequences related for males and females?

The procedure needed to be flexible enough as to allow for
individual variability in order to avoid obtaining an artificial
sequence, that is, a sequence including events which were not actually part of the subject's repertoire, or his/her preferred sexual behavior. For this reason, subjects were permitted to discard
as many sentences as they wished, or none at all. We could then
look at the discards and ask which sentences were most frequently
discarded under each condition. This was done for both males and
females. The qualitative characteristics of these discards were
also analyzed. This made the findings even more interesting.

The events described in each sentence were collected from the
Bentler scales and from sexually explicit literature. They were in
a narrative form and included events such as kissing, general body
contact, oral-genital contact, manual manipulation of genitals and
intercourse. Some sentences merely described sensations which are
commonly used to portray arousal in males and females. The procedure used in the construction and selection of sentences was complicated as it attempted to take into account grammatical style,
wording acceptable to both sexes and a balanced description of
males and females as the active partner or as the partner receiving the action described by the verb.

First, we will briefly discuss the procedure and some results.
Subjects were seated as a group in a large auditorium. Each received a set of the same 25 sentences under each condition. They

were then asked to rearrange the sentences in a sequence which would make the "most sexually arousing" passage and then to rearrange the sentences in the sequence they would use to describe their "most likely" sexual interaction. Half of the subjects were given instructions for Condition A, followed by Condition B. The other half received instructions in the reverse order. The Bentler scales and a questionnaire assessing demographic data and sexual experience were also administered.

Sequences were correlated by condition and by sex. We also tested for sex differences in the number of discards for specific sentences under each condition and for differences in the number of discards between conditions.

The subjects were 45 female and 78 male undergraduate subjects who participated in this study to fulfill a requirement in an introductory psychology course. The average age was 18.7 years with a range of 17 to 24 years. The sample was 84% college freshmen and sophomores. Forty-four per cent indicated they dated 3 or more times a week; 46% had been involved in, or had ongoing sexual relationships, and 70% reported orgasms in intercourse. Sixty per cent indicated orgasms in petting and 62% in masturbation. By age 18, 97% had experienced intercourse. This is much higher than other similar samples of undergraduates. Forty-three per cent reported they were fairly often exposed to pornographic drawings, 18% to stag movies; 24% read pornographic literature; and only 20% indicated none or minimal exposure to sexual material. Daily sexual daydreams were reported by 43%. The mean Bentler Score for males was 10.9 and for females 12.3. Sexual preference was 80% exclusively heterosexual, 17% heterosexual with some homosexual preference, and 3% described themselves as bisexual. The religious self concept was 43% "somewhat," 28% "not at all" and 13% "very religious."

The data were summarized in four (25 x 25) matrices showing the position of each sentence in relation to every other sentence for males and females separately under each condition. Each entry in the matrix gave the percentage of time a sentence preceeded another sentence when both were included by Ss. By adding the percentages in each row of the matrix and ranking these sums, we obtained a ranking of the sentences. The row with highest sum indicated that sentence preceeded all others the most. The number of discards were also obtained for each condition.

The results strongly support the prediction that there are conventionalized patterns or culturally shared sequences of behaviors facilitating the "doing" of sex. The sequences are presented in Tables 1 through 4. The most arousing and the most likely sequence correlated .84 for males and .77 for females.

TABLE I

AROUSING SEQUENCE FOR MALES

They shared a slow kiss, moving their tongues in and out of each other's mouths.

Taking his hand, she made him squeeze her firm, excited breast.

Roughly stroking his genitals, she made them bulge with a hard-on.

He slid down and began kissing her full breast, bitting each nipple.

Snuggling together, their bodies created more warmth.

Gently, he guided her hand to caress his balls.

His nipples erected as she sucked them gently.

She massaged his hard penis rhythmically.

He fingered her clitoris, feeling her thick, dark hair as she stroked his pulsating cock.

He pressed his groin against her, feeling the warmth of her genitals.

His hard-on swelled, pulsating with pleasure.

When he gently rubbed her swollen lips, she moaned with delight.

Her vagina felt warm as she rubbed her clitoris against him.

She felt a warm throbbing in her genitals.

As his finger played inside her wet lips, she began to moan.

Using his tongue, he licked her clitoris, moving her lips apart gently yet firmly.

She began to cover his peter with kisses.

While he thrusted his tongue deep in her vagina, she sucked his hardened penis.

As she forced his hard-on deeper in her mouth, she caressed him.

Quickly running his tongue over her wet vagina he felt her subtle quivering.

On top of her, he thrusted deeper into her vagina, enjoying the tightness of her.

By raising her hips, she enjoyed the full length of his tool.

Throbbing, his member exploded into orgasm.

Their surging orgasm triggered a pulsing in their genitals.

Her hot vagina exploded into her own orgasm.

TABLE 2

LIKELY SEQUENCE FOR MALES

They shared a slow kiss, moving their tongues in and out of each other's mouths.

Taking his hand, she made him squeeze her firm, excited breast.

He slid down and began kissing her full breast, bitting each nipple.

Snuggling together, their bodies created more warmth.

His nipples erected as she sucked them gently.

Roughly stroking his genitals, she made them bulge with a hard-on.

Gently, he guided her hand to caress his balls.

He pressed his groin against her, feeling the warmth of her genitals.

She massaged his hard penis rhythmically.

He fingered her clitoris, feeling her thick, dark hair as she stroked his pulsating cock.

As his finger played inside her wet lips, she began to moan.

Her vagina felt warm as she rubbed her clitoris against him.

When he gently rubbed her swollen lips, she moaned with delight.

His hard-on swelled, pulsating with pleasure.

She began to cover his peter with kisses.

Using his tongue, he licked her clitoris, moving her lips apart gently yet firmly.

She felt a warm throbbing in her genitals.

Quickly running his tongue over her wet vagina he felt her subtle quivering.

While he thrusted his tongue deep in her vagina, she sucked his hardened penis.

As she forced his hard-on deeper in her mouth, she caressed him.

On top of her, he thrusted deeper into her vagina, enjoying the tightness of her.

By raising her hips, she enjoyed the full length of his tool.

Their surging orgasm triggered a pulsing in their genitals.

Her hot vagina exploded into her own orgasm.

Throbbing, his member exploded into orgasm.

TABLE 3

AROUSING SEQUENCE FOR FEMALES

They shared a slow kiss, moving their tongues in and out of each other's mouths.

Taking his hand, she made him squeeze her firm, excited breast.

He slid down and began kissing her full breast, bitting each nipple.

Gently, he guided her hand to caress his balls.

His nipples erected as she sucked them gently.

Snuggling together, their bodies created more warmth.

He pressed his groin against her, feeling the warmth of her genitals.

Roughly stroking his genitals, she made them bulge with a hard-on.

He fingered her clitoris, feeling her thick, dark hair as she stroked his pulsating cock.

She felt a warm throbbing in her genitals.

As his finger played inside her wet lips, she began to moan.

She massaged his hard penis rhythmically.

His hard-on swelled, pulsating with pleasure.

Her vagina felt warm as she rubbed her clitoris against him.

Using his tongue, he licked her clitoris, moving her lips apart gently yet firmly.

When he gently rubbed her swollen lips, she moaned with delight.

Quickly running his tongue over her wet vagina he felt her subtle quivering.

She began to cover his peter with kisses.

While he thrusted his tongue deep in her vagina, she sucked his hardened penis.

As she forced his hard-on deeper in her mouth, she caressed him.

On top of her, he thrusted deeper into her vagina, enjoying the tightness of her.

By raising her hips, she enjoyed the full length of his tool.

Her hot vagina exploded into her own orgasm.

Throbbing, his member exploded into orgasm.

Their surging orgasm triggered a pulsing in their genitals.

TABLE 4

LIKELY SEQUENCE FOR FEMALES

They shared a slow kiss, moving their tongues in and out of each other's mouths.

Taking his hand, she made him squeeze her firm, excited breast.

He slid down and began kissing her full breast, bitting each nipple.

Snuggling together, their bodies created more warmth.

Gently, he guided her hand to caress his balls.

He pressed his groin against her, feeling the warmth of her genitals.

His nipples erected as she sucked them gently.

He fingered her clitoris, feeling her thick, dark hair as she stroked his pulsating cock.

She massaged his hard penis rhythmically.

As his finger played inside her wet lips, she began to moan.

Roughly stroking his genitals, she made them bulge with a hard-on.

She felt a warm throbbing in her genitals.

Her vagina felt warm as she rubbed her clitoris against him.

When he gently rubbed her swollen lips, she moaned with delight.

His hard-on swelled, pulsating with pleasure.

Using his tongue, he licked her clitoris, moving her lips apart gently yet firmly.

She began to cover his peter with kisses.

Quickly running his tongue over her wet vagina he felt her subtle quivering.

While he thrusted his tongue deep in her vagina, she sucked his hardened penis.

As she forced his hard-on deeper in her mouth, she caressed him.

On top of her, he thrustèd deeper into her vagina, enjoying the tightness of her.

Her hot vagina exploded into her own orgasm.

By raising her hips, she enjoyed the full length of his tool.

Throbbing, his member exploded into orgasm.

Their surging orgasm triggered a pulsing in their genitals.

Correlation between sexes for the most arousing sequence was .84
and for the most likely .77. All correlations were significant
at the .01 level.

These results suggest that both sexes mutually agree on a
script which outlines the sequence of events in heterosexual interaction. Males and females agree on the sequence described as most
likely and most arousing. The conventionalized sequence parallels
that of the stages of development in a heterosexual relationship.
The progression of events goes from kissing and hugging, to petting
above the waist, to manual and body stimulation of the lower genitals,
to oral-genital contact, and finally intercourse.

Both sexes agree that regardless of whether the sequence is
most likely to occur or the most arousing, the sexual interaction
begins by kissing. This event is followed by the male manipulat-
ing the female breast with his hand and then kissing her breasts.
They agree that first the male kisses her nipples and then the
female has oral contact with his. Although males find it more
arousing to have the female manually stimulating his genitals
before he kisses her breast, both sexes agree that this is more
likely to occur later in the sequence.

Description of physiological events or sensations relevant to
each sex and either manual or general body stimulation of genitals
were ordered by both sexes under the most likely and the most arousing conditions in such a way that the male partner briefly becomes
the center or recipient of all the action regardless of who initiates
the event. The female is then briefly the recipient of manual and
general body stimulation of genitals. Thus, the male is stimulated
by the female who caresses his testicles and strokes his penis and
then the male stimulates her clitoris and labia.

In our culture, the lower genitals have been defined as aversive
in terms of taste, odor, cleanliness and excretions. Given the
socio-cultural influence on the script, one would predict that conventionally oral kissing rarely follows oral-genital contact and
similarly oral contact if it occurs conventionally preceeds intromission. The present results strongly support these predictions.

Analyses of the discards produced some interesting results in
agreement with what is publically defined as errogenous for the
sexes. For example, more than a third of the female and male subjects discarded the sentence describing the female kissing the
male's nipples. This was true under both likely and arousing conditions. These results could be predicted if one considers that
conventionally the male's nipples are not defined as errogenous.

Females discarded more items under the "likely to occur" condition than under the "most arousing." There was no significant

difference for males under the two conditions. In 1948 and 1953, Kinsey and his co-workers reported that males are more likely to fantasize about experiences they would like to have, but have not yet experienced, while females are more likely to fantasize about past experiences which were pleasurable. The present results suggest that females include in their fantasy of what is most sexually arousing events which they have not or are unlikely to engage in. For example, in the likely to occur condition 51% of females discarded the sentence describing fellatio and cunnilingus occurring concurrently, while only 27% discarded this sentence in the most arousing sequence.

Sex differences in the number of discards for specific sentences under each condition was found for only four of the sentences. This is much less than anticipated, given the myth that the sexes differ in what they define as sexually arousing. These results are presented in Table 5. One of these sentences which

TABLE 5

RESULTS OF CHI SQUARES TO TEST FOR SEX
DIFFERENCES IN THE NUMBER OF DISCARDS

Sentences	Condition*	Discarded Most By	$\underline{a}$ level
He slid down and began kissing her full breast, bitting each nipple.	A	Males	.01
She began to cover his peter with kisses.	A-B	Females	.001, .01
Throbbing, his member exploded into orgasm.	A	Males	.01
She felt a warm throbbing in her genitals.	A-B	Males	.01, .05

* A = Most Sexually Arousing;

  B = Most Likely.

describes the male orally stimulating the female's breast was discarded in the most arousing sequence by 35% of male, while only by
8% of female subjects. Only 8% of males and females discarded this
sentence in the likely to occur condition. Therefore, the sexes
agree that males are likely to orally stimulate the female's breast.
One may speculate that males engage in this behavior mainly to fulfill the conventional expectation that this is arousing for females.

The wording of the sentences seems to be the important variable in the other three items showing a sex difference in the
number of discards. One of these items describes fellatio and
the female as the initiator of the event. While females discarded
this item more than males under both conditions, this was not true
for another item in the set also describing the female initiating
fellatio. The item showing a difference between sexes used the
word "peter" for penis, the other item uses the term "hard on."
The other items which show a difference between sexes describe a
"throbbing" sensation in the genitals. Males discarded the items
more often than females. This finding may indicate that this sensation is more commonly associated with female sexual arousal and/or
that it is rarely perceived by the male partner.

In general these results support the notion inherent in sexual scripting theory that the sexes have a mutually shared conventionalized sequence which plots the behaviors in a heterosexual
interaction and agree in what is defined as sexually arousing.
This study provides the first data supporting the notion of stability in the sequence. Additionally, these are the first sequences
objectively defined by an undergraduate subject population. Thus,
our results may be of interest to researchers studying erotic
material.

REFERENCES

Gagnon, J. and Simon, W. (1973). Sexual Conduct: The Social
        Sources of Human Sexuality, Aldine Publishing Co., Chicago.

Kinsey, A.C., Pomeroy, W.B. and Martin, C.E. (1948). Sexual Be-
        havior in the Human Male, Saunders, Philadelphia.

Kinsey, A.C., Pomeroy, W.B., Martin, C.E. and Gebhard, P.H. (1953).
        Sexual Behavior in the Human Female, Saunders, Philadelphia.

SEX EDUCATION AND THE STRUCTURE OF MORAL JUDGMENT: EFFECTIVENESS OF A FORM OF SEX EDUCATION BASED ON THE DEVELOPMENT OF FORMAL STRUCTURES OF VALUE JUDGMENT[1]

Jean-Marc Samson

Canada

CONSIDERATION IN EVALUATING
THE EFFECTIVENESS OF SEX EDUCATION

The researcher or the sex educator is confronted with four considerations when evaluating the quality and effectiveness of individual or group sex education. First, measurement of the pupil's acquisition and comprehension of sexological knowledge, second, verification of changes which have taken place in the pupil's sexual behavior as a result of sex education, or third, determination of change in the pupil's attitude about sexuality may all be made. Finally, the fourth consideration might be to examine the influence this experience in sex education has had on the development and change of the pupil's inherent sexual values. It would seem that, the fourth consideration, centered upon values is one of major importance today. Although a more detailed discussion of this fourth consideration is presented in Samson (1974), the following explanations are necessary.

Information

The evaluation of the effectiveness of sex education based on the acquisition of sexological knowledge as a principal criterion would seem to lead to confusion between the terms "sex information" and "sex education": Education outdistances simple information.

---

[1]This research project has benefited from grants by the Canada Council (numbers S69-1465 and S72-1811).

While sex information is confined to the acquisition and comprehension of sexological facts, sex education takes a different approach:
it is a process which guides the student in examining his/her own
sexuality; consequently there is a world of difference between
the two facts. This, however, does not mean that sex education,
which is intended to facilitate the integration of the pupil's own
sexuality, should dispense with precise sexological information;
on the contrary, such personal sexual integration requires sufficient and precise information, but education goes far beyond dissimination of information.

It also seems that the dissemination of sexological information is not yet capable of implementing a methodology with durable
effects; in fact, the studies of Forlando et al. (1970), Fretz and
Johnson (1971), indicate that the current form of sex information
has barely succeeded in dispensing stable sexological knowledge,
a fact which raises doubts as to the merits of this criterion in
determining the effectiveness of sex education. It should also be
noted that such information does not necessarily lead to changes
in sexual behavior. A striking example of this is contraceptive
use: studies have shown that the knowledge of contraceptive methods has not entailed, ipso facto, the personal use of such methods.

Behavior

The difficulty in evaluating sex education according to changes
in sexual behavior seems self-evident; to begin with, evaluation
necessitates extremely delicate methods of investigation, and
further, there may be a considerable interval between learning
and resulting behavior. For instance, contraceptive education
may be acquired in the early adolescent years but practical application may occur several years later, making it impossible to
evaluate the impact of a given session in sex education.

Attitudes

In order to evaluate the effectiveness of sex education according to changes in attitude, a list of attitudes, both "positive"
and "negative" should be set up; but the criterion underlying the
catalogue needs to be justified - an approach which many researchers
and sex educators seem to avoid. One thing, however, seems clear:
beneath the "positive" attitudes lies a hidden human ideal which
is classified as objective, but which, in reality, mirrors the
personal ideal of the researcher or else that of the researcher's
societal environment.

It sometimes happens that the change in itself is to be of
value; to change one's attitude is considered a sign of true and
strong personality. In such a light, any sexual attitude which
does not conform to avant-gardist ideas is considered "negative"
and this consideration would classify as "positive" such attitudes
described as nontraditional. Such oversimplification leads to the
assumption that human progress and change are synonymous and that
change is a sign of advancement.

Both researchers and sex educators are faced with the same
dilemma. It is easily admitted that the latter should assist the
pupil in attaining "positive" attitudes concerning sexuality, but
it is equally easy to neglect justification of the human ideal
which underlies these "positive" attitudes.

As regards attitudes, sex education is vulnerable to indoctrination, however subtle and disguised, and we are convinced that the
researcher who judges the effectiveness of sex education according
to a range of attitudes contributes to strengthening the sex educator's search for patterns on students' ideas and attitudes.

Values

As previously mentioned (Samson, 1973, 1975), it no longer
suffices to break the sexual bonds of yesteryear nor to limit oneself to denouncing so-called "traditional" values. Today, it is
necessary to have the courage to create new sexual values; therefore, sex education would be off-course if it were content to
condemn former sexual values or if it attempted to impose, by
means of a carefully hidden curriculum, ready made sexual goals.
We believe sex education should help students to develop as individuals capable of sexual autnonmy, capable of making personal
decisions and of judging current sexual mores, or if necessary,
of inventing new values.

EFFECTIVENESS OF SEX EDUCATION

As previously suggested, the determination of the effectiveness of sex education implies a definition of its objectives, and
those objectives in sex education do not consist of sex information or in changes in sexual attitudes. Sex education should go
beyond values clarification; it should include programs and methodologies capable of allowing the individual self-evaluation of
personal sexuality, and personal value assignment to sexual expression; most important of all, sex education should allow students
to situate sexuality in the overall picture of one's personal
problematics. This implies educating one's moral judgment in sexual values which, in turn, means that the individual assumes res-

ponsability for personal sexuality, not influenced by external
criteria, but rather by the quality of his discernment concerning
sexual values. Effective sex education encourages discernment of
sexual values whose quality will lead to autonomy in moral reasoning.

Operationalization

It would be too simple to formulate new objectives in group
sex education without outlining the pedagogical operationalization,
and this task has been elaborated during the past years in the
Department of Sexology at the Université du Québec à Montréal
(UQAM). It was necessary at the outset to find a theoretical
format which would outdistance dissemination of sex information
and bypass, more or less, explicit indoctrination in the change
of sexual attitudes.

The format finally adopted is that outlined by Lawrence
Kohlberg in his theory on the development of moral judgment. A
professor at Harvard University (U.S.A.), Kohlberg (1958, 1969,
1971 , 1971 , 1976) demonstrates that the development of moral
judgment in the child, the adolescent and the adult always follows
a well determined and invariable sequence of six stages.

This means that the quality of value-judgment relative to
general morality as well as to sexual values, does not develop in
a haphazard manner, but follows a certain sequence of stages, extremely important in reference to sex education. With this schema
in mind, it is possible to follow the development of moral judgment in sexuality in the child and adolescent and be of assistance
in their slow attainment of sexual autonomy.

The Six Stages

The six stages in the development of moral judgment, with
schematic examples taken from sexual contexts are briefly outlined:

STAGE I: Here, the child perceives the existence of constraint
           over acts, yet still confuses psychological motivation
           with physical necessity. Punishment or the negative
           aspect of an act renders the act morally good or bad,
           at this stage; for example, a child might consider it
           morally wrong to touch genitals if punishment is an-
           ticipated for doing so. But such an act could also be
           considered morally good if reward is anticipated or if
           it entails positive reinforcement; for instance, praise
           for having cleaned the genitals.

STAGE II: This stage represents instrumental relativism orienta-
                tion: the soundness or moral value of an act is deter-
                mined by the desires of the subject or by the benefit
                obtained from such an act. At this stage, an individual
                may perceive masturbation to be a good thing because of
                the pleasure experienced, or else, may consider it to
                be morally wrong because of the resulting consequences,
                sexual or otherwise, which outweigh the pleasure in-
                volved. The moral argument in Stage I refers to punish-
                ment, whereas in Stage II, the argument refers to per-
                sonal advantage.

STAGE III: In this stage, the structure of an individual's moral
                thinking is centered on the concept of interpersonal
                concordance. Here, an act is good if it meets with
                the approval and pleasing of other persons. This is
                the stage of close conformity to the stereotyped forms
                of behavior of the majority, or else to those forms
                known as "natural." In Stage III, the individual seeks
                approval and moral judgment exists in terms of such
                approval, with personal benefit taking second place.
                For example, an individual may consider masturbation
                to be morally good if met with approval on the part
                of other persons rather than for the pleasure procured
                by this action. Or else, the individual may believe
                masturbation to be bad if persuaded that such an ac-
                tivity is not "natural" or if it be frowned upon by
                peer group in spite of the personal pleasure it entails.

STAGE IV: This stage shows an individual's moral judgment influ-
                enced by the perspective of a social system whose con-
                tinuity and stability is sought to be maintained. With-
                out being a rigorist, one adheres to established rules
                and respects the ways and customs observed in one's
                social setting. One fears that disrespect for law and
                order will entail moral and social chaos: law and order
                are personal goals. For example, such an individual
                may regard pornography to be morally wrong because of
                a belief that pornography upsets social order and
                violates social rules and customs. Or one may regard
                pornography to be morally good if convinced that its
                distribution will counteract sexual assault, abduction,
                rape, etc., and thereby safeguard good social order.
                The Vatican document on sexual ethics, issued at the
                end of the year 1975 is a good example of this stage.

STAGE V: Post conventional morality is attained in Stages V and
                VI. In Stage V, the individual abandons the views of
                the social setting to adopt an outlook on moral values

based on a social contract. This social contract favors
the protection of personal rights for each member of
society. In this Stage, the individual may begin to
question the justifying principles of established moral
order, and here, the adult (because this Stage is rarely
attained before the age of 25) will speak of the rights
of an individual or of a group of individuals. For
example, the Geneva Convention on the human treatment
of prisoners of war belongs to Stage V. In sexuality,
a person might consider masturbation or homosexuality
to be morally good, because an individual is entitled
to pleasure and has an inalienable right to orient
sexual inclination as seen fit. Stage V refers to one's
right or rights, and not to upholding a social system.

STAGE VI: It is almost impossible to summarize this stage. Suf-
fice it to say that an individual's criterion of judgment consists in the complete reciprocity of rights
and duties. It is not sufficient to just invoke one's
rights but necessary to evaluate the duties incumbent
to these rights and to rationalize the relationship
between the rights and duties of all persons (physical
and moral) implicated in a given situation. For example, each partner in a couple has a right to orgasm,
but orgasm is not an isolated occurrence; it is part
of other rights...the right to sleep, the right to be
respected as a human entity, etc. In addition, the
right to orgasm entails a series of obligations, such
as to assist one's partner in attaining orgasm, to
respect the partner as a free person whose quality of
orgasm should be intensified (a right to be mutually
observed) in such a manner as to coordinate each element of the sexual procedure of the individual or the
couple into an improved integration of sexuality.
Such reciprocal rights and duties make any evaluation
of sexual values a complex affair, so to simplify this,
we have limited ourselves to the identification of the
rights and duties of the couple only, and have by-
passed those of the persons surrounding the couple.
The family, if any, also has rights and duties toward
the sexual partners: they for example, should not be
disturbed, but the family may require (as a family
should) the couple's attention. Society too, and its
institutions, has rights and duties relative to the
sexual relations of the couple: education should allow
the partners the sexual functioning leading to orgasm;
the work schedule should allow for sufficient leisure
time for sexual encounters. But society has rights
also: for instance, the work schedule should not be

set up solely for the sexual convenience of the couple.
And justice requires society to protect à couple's
intimacy without, however, exposing their intimacy to
those who do not choose to witness it. As we can see,
Stage VI not only proclaims the right to orgasm but
suggests this right among the rights and duties of
the individual and of society.

Each stage may be characterized by the ethical evaluation of
a given sex therapy. Let us imagine, for example, that the sex
therapist considers a technique used personally to be good; however, the arguments may differ in many respects. The therapist
may consider the technique ethically good because psychologists
have not yet condemned it (Stage I), or because it brings great
satisfaction (personal or monetary), which is characteristic of
Stage II. The technique may give the therapist certain scientific
prestige (Stage III) or it may help clients to improve their
sexual functioning and thereby contribute to the betterment of
society as a whole (Stage IV). The therapist's clients have a
right to a cohesive sexology and the therapist as a researcher,
become a factor in the advancement of science (Stage V). The
therapist may consider it a duty, as a scientist, to place personal learning at the disposal of human development, and if in
need of therapy, would take unconditional advantage of such means;
in this opinion, all persons involved directly or indirectly in
the therapeutic activity will benefit from this work (Stage VI).

Thus, one can see the series of arguments slowly progressing
from autocentric toward sociocentric perspectives in order to attain a personal humanistic ideal. Although a detailed discussion of Lawrence Kohlberg's theory of moral judgment development
appears in Samson (1976b), the following explanation are necessary
for clarity.

First, the developmental stages in value judgment are formal
structures, in other words, forms of the organization of mental
activity of moral reasoning and these stages should not be confused
with attitudes or opinions which refer to value content. For instance, it is possible to have a favorable or permissive attitude
toward group sex activities, which represents the content of a
sexual value, whereas the stages define the formal moral types
which are independent of value content. Each stage represents a
mental structure, which is a means of moral judgment. For instance, to state that group sex is or is not, to be encouraged
because such a statement would seem acceptable, or unacceptable,
to one's peers, corresponds to a moral structure in Stage III.
On the other hand, to maintain that such group activities are, or
are not, desirable because they may lead to progress, or deteriora-

tion, of our social structures represents a moral judgment in Stage IV.

Second, the sequence of stages never varies, i.e., it is not possible to by-pass a given stage. The sequence is always from Stage I to Stage II, from II to III, etc. However, the full sequence itself is not obligatory, meaning that every individual works through every single stage. An individual may linger at a particular stage or else remain there indefinitely. In general, the adolescent is situated in Stages II, III, or IV, and it is exceptional for a person to reach Stage V before the age of 25. Stage VI, when it <u>is</u> attained, rarely occurs in subjects before the age of 35.

Third, the passage from one stage to the next is not an automatic process, but results from an interaction with the environmental setting which allows the individual to restructure one's personal functional axis. But an individual is capable of grasping the arguments of only one single stage above the present stage-level. Within the individual's environment, responses will be made to both the arguments at the person's own moral level and to that immediately following this level, but arguments at levels two or more stages above will not be recognized. An individual in Stage III will not respond to elaborate arguments on the right to sexual pleasure because, in that person's opinion, the good or evil inherent to a sexual gesture is stereotyped, according to the individual's milieu or peer group whose approval the individual seeks by conforming personal moral thinking to their expectations. Consequently, the individual in Stage III will reinterpret the arguments in Stage V after his own fashion: "When you refer to the right to sexual pleasure, you mean that sexual pleasure is 'natural' and everyone agrees with this principle ... that is, everyone I know does ..."

<u>Sex Education</u>. We have observed the importance of sex education centered on the <u>quality</u> of moral judgment. Indeed, sex education seen from Kohlberg's theoretical perspective has less tendency to classify as "good" a definite series of attitudes and sexual values; it thereby sidesteps the trap of indoctrination and really assists the pupil in attaining better judgment of sexual things and acts. The tenets of this theory allow sex education to handle moral values without risking indoctrination and help steer the pupil in the direction of sexual autonomy, without forcing a decision for or against group sex activities, from a knowledgeable framework. The sex educator seeks to develop quality in decision making, not in terms of <u>content</u>, but in terms of mature, moral reasoning and insight on sexual values when analyzing a given situation.

This type of sex education does not aim at altering an individual's sexual "ideas" but encourages the development of a more discerning sense of reasoning in the integration of an individual's own sexuality.

Not only does this theory provide a frame of reference, but is also becomes a valuable aid to the sex educator in supplying precise methodology of application. The educator who is aware of the moral stage of a person or of a group may organize his work so as to truly help such a person or group to advance toward the next stage of development and toward sexual autonomy as well. Discussions must be encouraged that center on sexual topics beyond the formal limits of sex information and must present axiological arguments inherent to the stage immediately above the pupil's present level "Stage x + 1" (which is a major contribution of this method). Instead of role playing as a model to be imitated, the educator becomes a professional, capable of orchestrating actions which will further the development of pupils without imposing one's own image upon them.

These observations do not necessarily imply that Kohlberg's theory of the development of moral judgment summarizes all programs of sex and moral education. As Peters (1974) has pointed out, it is not possible to neglect the importance of transmitting certain contents (as Kohlberg seems to have done) which will assure a minimum of social life. As this writer (Samson, 1976[a]) has already indicated, such a theory does not have the pupil identify the elements of a given situation to be evaluated which John Wilson (1972) describes as "γνῶσῃ." Kohlberg's theory also fails to consider the process of acquiring courage in action (a principle we deem necessary) which consists in strengthening the ego in such a manner as to allow the pupil not only to acquire a clearer sense of moral judgment, but also to be capable of "moral action", i.e., to materialize the results of his moral thinking which Wilson (1972) calls "χρατος." It is evident that although Kohlberg's theory is helpful to sex educators, there is still more to be said on the subject.

Hypothesis and Research Procedure

Hypothesis. In the light of the preceding, we have outlined a vast research project. In our first hypothesis, we have proposed that the application of sexual education according to "Stage x + 1" methods could develop sexual moral judgment in an individual.

Before presenting the second hypothesis, it should be mentioned that moral judgment, in terms of stages, may vary if the situation to be evaluated contains sexual elements or otherwise. In her studies on American adolescents, Carol Gilligan et al. (1971),

observed a décalage from one half to one entire stage between general moral judgment (GMJ) and sexual moral judgment (SMJ) and recent work undertaken by Malo et al. (1976) also indicates that
Quebec socio-affective and unadapted teenagers have a statistically significative difference in their general and sexual moral
forms of judgment, with the latter lagging behind the general form.
It must be noted that studies by Jurich and Jurich (1974) and
Speicher (1973) do not indicate a décalage between the SMJ and the
GMJ. Thus, the formulation of our second hypothesis, which is that
sex education administered according to "Stage x + 1" will allow the
pupil to reduce the possible décalage between his general and sexual forms of moral judgment.

Method. One hundred and seventy-four adolescents, both boys
and girls, between the ages of 12 and 18 years, were chosen for
our study. The average age was 15.8 years. There was no significant difference in age or sex between the groups of 100 experiment
subjects and the 74 control subjects. However, there was a slightly
inferior IQ in the control group (p = .0569).

Interview. Each subject was given a personal interview lasting one hour to sound out their moral stage. Each was presented with
five different situations to be judged, three of which contained
explicit sexual dilemmas (early sex relations, homosexuality, abortion, etc.). Each interview was recorded verbatim and was then
coded paragraph by paragraph (issue scoring). The intercoded
correlation was .78; each subject had been evaluated twice: prior
to this experiment (in October, 1973) and after in May, 1974.

Application. The sex education program covered a period of
eight months, on the basis of one hour per week, totalling thirty
hours. Six groups of students from regular classes in the public
schools in the Montreal area participated in the experiment as well
as a seventh group from a rural area out of the city. The sexual
educators (or interventionists) were in full control of the technique used in "Stage + 1;" six out of seven had received three
years training in sexology at UQAM (B.Sc. sexology-education).
The details obtained during each hour spent with the pupils were
fully recorded and the reports allowed us to state that 80 per
cent of application time had been given to serve arguments at the
level immediately above the average stage of the student group.
The remaining 20 per cent was devoted to the presentation of sex
information. The teaching format was: 38 per cent of applied
time was allowed for verbal exchange between teacher and pupil
as well as among the pupils themselves; 22 per cent, to student
reports and role-playing, 17 per cent to formal teaching, and
the remainder, for audio-visual work the correction of individual
exercises, and for other types of teaching activities.

Findings

There was strong correlation among the five situations to be evaluated; in the test, all the intersituational correlations registered over .60; the second test, subsequent to the sex education experiment, registered over .77, indicating the increase in the internal stability of judgment due to this type of sex education.

The results obtained from the test prior to experimentation signify that, in the evaluation of the 174 Quebec adolescents, the breakdown of stages relative to age is identical to that obtained by Kohlberg in his studies on American subjects in the same age group. It is also clear that our study does not confirm the décalage observed by Gilligan et al. (1971) between the GMJ and the SMJ. No significant difference was noted between both modalities of evaluation; however, we analyzed each stage progressively (which had not been done in other studies) and it was ascertained that although there was no décalage between the GMJ and the SMJ in the subjects classified in Stages I, II, and III, those in Stage IV and in Stage IV-V exhibited a significant décalage with a lower SMJ. Analyses allowed the deduction that such a décalage appeared mainly among the boys with an above average IQ. It should be noted that the girls in Stage III exhibited a significant décalage between the GMJ and the SMJ.

The overall influence of applied sexual education set up according to the "Stage x + 1" method in our studies show that the total (GMJ and SMJ combined) moral development was not more marked in the experiment group than in the control group. Although more progress was evident in the subjects belonging to the former group than in their control counterparts, it would seem that thirty hours of applied sexual education is not sufficient time to produce radical changes. The results we obtained are similar to those reported by Blatt and Kohlberg in 1975.

Nevertheless, measuring the central tendency makes it possible to overlook the significant progress made by each category of subjects. For example, our study shows that 36 per cent of the experiment subjects advanced one or two stages, in their SMJ whereas only 23 per cent of the other group did likewise. On the other hand, both groups showed many regressions from Stage IV to Stage III. Statistics based on the averages of the total number of subjects in both groups indicate very little progress, with advances and regressions canceling each other. It is therefore necessary to proceed stage by stage, if a clear picture of the differential effect produced by applied sex education is to be obtained and we have resorted to the usual percentages for each stage, i.e., because all arguments used by an individual in resolving the five situations do not correspond to a given stage; a percentage of use

in a certain stage may be established for each subject and an average of use in a particular stage may be defined for a group.

As regards the sexual dilemmas there was a 17.20 per cent
increase in the experiment group from its original stage as opposed
to a 10.79 per cent increase in the control group, indicating the
direct influence of applied sexual education ("Stage + 1") whereas,
the non-sexual dilemmas produced no significant differences between
the two groups. In this instance, a stage-by-stage analysis is
most revealing: the experiment subjects advanced from their initial Stage I or II, to higher stages at a rate of 29 per cent and
the control subjects in identical initial stages progressed at a
rate of 7.44 per cent. Experiment subjects in the initial Stage
III progressed at a rate of 17.49 per cent and control subjects,
at a rate of 12.63 per cent (a non significant difference). Experiment subjects in Stage IV as of November 1973 advanced at
the rate of 14.10 per cent when evaluated in May 1974, whereas
the control group progressed at a rate of 5.83 per cent. Progress
was noted especially in the girls; the boys tended to regress toward Stage III, as though to "toe the mark" before the sprint on
to Stage V.

The final objective of our research project was to define
the special effect of each teaching format on the development of
moral judgment and so we correlated the time of application in
class for each format (formal teaching, student reports, discussions and exchange of ideas, role playing, audio-visual techniques,
etc.) and the positive results obtained in the sexual moral judgment. Given similar IQ's, ages, and sexes, we have found that for
experiment subjects, role playing is the only format of applied
sex education showing positive and significant correlation
with progress in sexual moral judgment ($r = .21$, $p < .05$).
Formal teaching, however, revealed negative correlation with an
increase in sexual moral judgment ($r = .17$, $p < .05$) and appear to
be a stumbling block in the march toward sexual autonomy. Stage-by-
stage analysis has thrown another light on the outcome: in Stage
I and II subjects, role playing appears to facilitate the development of SMJ ($r = .75$), whereas discussions and the exchange of ideas
seem to have negative effects on these subjects ($r = -.52$). Progress exhibited in subjects at the Stage III level was without
significant correlation with any of the teaching formats applied.
It should be mentioned, however, that progress was minimal in
Stage III subjects, which may explain the lack of correlation with
any of the methods used. The subjects in Stage IV showed interest
in role playing ($r = .34$) and their growth in SMJ correlated significantly with the use of audio-visual methods (ten silent films
entitled "Points of Departure") as well ($r = .31$); the subjects in
Stage IV, however, reacted negatively to formal teaching ($r = -.49$).
The ten subjects in the experiment group classified in early Stage
V exhibited more developed SMJ from these formal teachings ($r = .82$)

and from discussions and the exchange of ideas (r = .81), but the use of audio-visual material was not a contributing factor in their final SMJ (r = -.68).

There does not seem to be any particular magical formula in sexual education, even in consideration of the effectiveness of role playing, and to a lesser degree, that observed in the discussion and exchange of personal ideas. It is obvious that formal teachings have not contributed to progress in sexual moral judgment except in subjects who have already attained a higher degree of moral development (those in early Stage V, for example).

A more subjective observation is required here: all the subjects of the experiment group who participated showed marked enthusiasm for the type of intervention in "Stage x + 1," to the point where such courses in sexual morals were the most sought after; many pupils missed other classes and managed to swell our ranks in order to participate in sessions where questions of sexual ethics were openly discussed. The personal empathy of the interventionist cannot fully explain this wave of enthusiasm: we are convinced that success was due to the "Stage x + 1" method because it responded to the pupil's level of ethical comprehension and allowed for effective intercommunication between instructor and student without the habitual décalage which engenders a lack of understanding, and the boredom and indifference which had formerly characterized these courses.

CONCLUSION

The results obtained from this research project, which have been presented as succinctly as possible, have indicated several conclusions.

Sex education which emphasizes moral values without falling into the trap of indoctrination is not only possible, but welcomed by the students, and what is even more important, such education may become a true contribution in their development.of sexual moral judgment by providing a greater degree of quality in their concept of sexual values. Of course, these results are not always self-evident when one judges the effectiveness of the method, but our study has succeeded in revealing that the individual reacts to different types of teaching during each stage of his moral development. Gradual development, in theory, may be much more complex in fact, which explains the differential progress observed in each stage and in the members of each sex. One outstanding fact in this study is that the subjects whose initial stage was Stage III seemed indifferent to sex education; there are others in their initial Stage IV who tend to revert to Stage III. Such

a magnetic attraction to Stage III may be explained by the moral
atmosphere surrounding the pupils and the population at large
which, in a general sense, corresponds to the characteristics of
Stage III.   Thirty hours of systematic application may have but a
limited influence on the resistance exerted by a convenient "concordance with a certain milieu" which we believe explains the slow
development of the subjects in Stage III and the regression of
others to Stage III.

However, we are convinced that the thirty hours of intervention time has initiated a certain development which may have a
long-term effect on the subject, as studies undertaken in Ontario
by Sullivan and Beck (1974) have shown in slightly younger individuals.   A follow-up project is currently under way and results should
be forthcoming within the year.

In closing, it should be mentioned that the theory formulated
by Lawrence Kohlberg offers valuable guidelines to the sex educator
who may organize a method of application in terms of the actual
ethical level of the pupils and subsequently improve upon the
quality of this level.   The educator who uses the Kohlberg method
is better equipped to describe and use to best of knowledge the
objectives established in sex education, and further is able to
avoid subtle indoctrination which can impair the pupil's personal
sense of moral judgment and distort his values through manipulation by those whose moral outlook is of another order.

REFERENCES

Blatt, M. and Kohlberg, L. (1975).   The effect of classroom moral
      discussion upon children's level of moral judgment.   Jour-
      nal of Moral Education, 4 (2): 129-161.

Forlano, G., May, W. and Schneider, A.J. (1970).   Family Living,
      Including Sex Education, Year-end report, New York State
      Education Department, Division of Research, New York.

Fretz, R., and Waren, J.R. (1971).   Influence of intensive work-
      shop on teachers' sex information and attitudes toward sex
      education.   Research Quarterly, 42 (May): 156-163.

Gilligan, C., Kohlberg, L., Lerner, J. and Belenky, M. (1971).
      Moral reasoning about sexual dilemmas; the development of
      an interview and scoring system.   In Technical Report of
      the Commission on Obscenity and Pornography, U.S. Govern-
      ment Printing Office, Washington, D.C.

Jurich, A., and Jurich, J. (1974). The effects of cognitive moral development upon the selection of premarital sexual standards. Journal of Marriage and the Family, 36 (2): 736-741.

Kohlberg, L. (1958). The Development of Modes of Moral Thinking and Choice in the Years Ten to Sixteen, Unpublished doctorate dissertation, University of Chicago.

Kohlberg, L. (1969). Stages and sequence: the Cognitive-Developmental Approach to Socialization. In Goslin, D.A. (ed.), Handbook of Socialization Theory and Research, Rand McNally, Chicago.

Kohlberg, L. (1971a). From is to ought: how to commit the naturalistic fallacy and get away with it in the study of moral development. In Mischel T. (ed.), Cognitive Development and Epistemology, Academic Press, New York.

Kohlberg, L. (1971b). Stages of moral development as a basis for moral education. In Beck, C.M., Critenden, B.S. and Sullivan, E.V. (eds.), Moral Education: Interdisciplinary Approaches, University of Toronto Press, Toronto.

Kohlberg, L. (1976). Moral stages and moralization: the Cognitive-Developmental approach. In Lickona, T. (ed.), Moral Development and Behavior, Theory, Research and Social Issues, Holt, Rinehart and Winston, New York.

Malo, F., Poirier, G. and Thériault, R. (1976). Développement du Jugement Moral du Consommateur et du Non-Consommateur Adolescents Mésadaptés Socio-Affectifs et les Drogues Illicites, Unpublished study report, Department of Psychology, Université du Québec à Montréal.

Peters, S. (1974). Moral development and moral learning, The Monist, 58: 541-567.

Samson, J.-M. (1973). The significance of sexuality in the contemporary world. Main Current in Modern Thought, 29 (5): 186-191.

Samson, J.-M. (1974a). The objectives of sex education in the schools. Journal of Moral Education, 3 (3): 207-222.

Samson, J.-M. (1975). La liberté sexuelle de demain, Cahiers de Sexologie Clinique, 1 (3): 281-289.

Samson, J.-M. (1976a). Sexuality, morality and Kohlberg's notion
of moral education. Symposium held during the Annual Assembly of Learned Societies, Quebec, Laval University, June
3, 1976.

Samson, J.-M. (1976b). Le développement du jugement moral selon
Lawrence Kohlberg, Unpublished manuscript, Université du
Québec à Montréal, Department of Sexology.

Speicher, M.-E. (1973). Stimulating Change in Moral Judgment: an
Experimental Validation of an Innovative Education Approach
to Sexual Morality, Unpublished, M.A. dissertation, Purdue
University.

Sullivan, E.V. and Beck, C. (1974). Developmental approach to
assessment of moral education programmes: a short commentary. Journal of Moral Education, 4 (1): 61-66.

Wilson, J. (1972). Practical Methods of Moral Education, London,
Heinemann Educational Books Ltd., London.

X

SEXUAL ATTITUDE REASSESSMENT: THE WORKSHOP PARTICIPANT AND

ATTITUDE CHANGE

Jane Barclay Mandel

United States

Sex education in medical schools is now a reality, with 110 out of the 114 American medical schools reporting courses (Lief and Ebert, 1974). The days of urging the adoption of human sexuality courses by medical schools are behind us, but an equally difficult task is before us: the evaluation of a myriad of courses using different formats, teaching techniques, content, class size, and goals, both attitudinal and cognitive.

Lief and Ebert's survey indicated that 60% of medical schools reported sexuality courses which are part of the core curriculum while 32% offered elective courses. The survey does not report the percentage of students who attend electives or the rates of attendance at required courses. The number of medical students actually attending human sexuality courses is not reported in the survey.

Researchers evaluating the effects of sex education courses have also struggled with the problem of what proportion of students are being reached. Golden and Liston (1972) reported no changes as measured by the Sex Knowledge and Attitude Test (SKAT) (Table 1) in a required course offered to UCLA School of Medicine sophomores, but noted that attendance was irregular. As no attendance records were kept, their data do not compare SKAT scores of regular and sporadic attenders.

Garrard, Vaitkus, and Chilgren (1972) reported significant SKAT attitude and knowledge changes resulting from a two-day seminar at the University of Minnesota. The 215 participants, including medical students and their spouses, medical and university

TABLE 1

SKAT SCALE DESCRIPTIONS*

Heterosexual Relations Scale

The heterosexual relations scale deals with an individual's general
attitude toward pre- and extramarital heterosexual encounters. Individuals with high HR scores (above 60) regard premarital sexual
relations as acceptable or even desirable for both men and women.
These individuals view extramarital relations as potentially bene-
fitting, rather than harming the marital relationships of those
involved. Low scores (below 40) imply conservative attitudes in
this area.

Sexual Myths

The sexual myths scale deals with an individual's acceptance or
rejection of commonly held sexual misconceptions. High scores
(above 60) indicate a rejection of commonly held sexual misconceptions, low scores (below 40) indicate acceptance of popular misconceptions.

Abortion

This scale deals with an individual's general social, medical and
legal feelings toward abortion. High scores (over 60) imply an
orientation which sees abortion as being acceptable. Low scores
(below 40) suggest an orientation which sees abortion an unacceptable

Autoeroticism

This scale deals with general attitudes toward the permissibility
of masturbatory activities. Individuals with high scores (over 60)
view auto-erotic activity as healthy or acceptable. Low scores
(below 40) imply an orientation which sees masturbation as an un-
healthy practice.

Normed Knowledge Score

This score relates raw group scores on fifty true-false items to
average scores obtained by medical students. The average score is
50.00 (SD 10.00), thus normed scores of 50 or better indicate knowledge equal to, or better than, the average medical student.

---

*The above information exerpted from SKAT, second edition, Prelim-
inary Technical Manual.

faculty, and community representatives were volunteers. SKAT pre-
test data were gathered on 186 of the participants. Post-seminar
SKATs were completed by 18% fewer participants (N = 153). The lack
of a control group drawn from the same volunteer population and the
decrease in subjects completing the second SKAT make the results
of this study difficult to interpret.

    Marcotte, Kilpatrick, Geyer, and Smith (1976) measured pre
and post SKAT scores given during a required weekly course for 159
first year students at the Medical University of South Carolina.
Student participation in the post-testing was voluntary, but comparison of mean pre-test scores showed no differences between those
who took the post-test and those who did not. Results showed significant changes in attitude and knowledge on all SKAT subscales,
but no control group was used.

    Lastly, a study by Vines (1974) which compared a 15-hour
weekend seminar and five three-hour weekly seminars with similar
content reports significant differences for both experimental formats ("massed" and "spaced") compared to a control group, on the
knowledge section of the SKAT, but no significant difference on
the attitude subscales. This well-designed study is the only
published research which includes a true control group, and its
careful design may account for the absence of significant attitude
shifts.

    This brief overview of research evaluating human sexuality
courses provides us with conflicting results. When significant
results are reported, either volunteer subjects have been used, or
a control group has not been used which would eliminate the rival
hypothesis of testing effects. When a control group has been used,
results seem to diminish.

    Golden and Liston (1972) indicated that poor attendance at the
UCLA human sexuality course may have been related to student avoidance of uncomfortable situations, or situations which were personally involving, such as the small group discussions in the course.
Human sexuality courses may not attract students who are uncomfortable talking about sex or these students may simply stop attending.

    At Northwestern University Medical School about one-third of
the student body attends a 16-hour, two-day Sexual Attitude Reassessment Workshop (SAR) during the course of each academic year.
The workshop uses a multi-media approach: films, slides, audio
tapes, a panel of people from a variety of lifestyles (homosexual,
lesbian, bisexual, group marriage, monogamous heterosexual, celibate)
interspersed with small group discussions led by male-female teams
of trained co-leaders. The workshop encourages participants to
examine their own attitudes toward aspects of human sexuality and
attempts to increase their comfort when interacting with people

whose values or lifestyles may differ from their own. An informal
comparison of students who have attended the SAR with their class-
mates who did not give staff members the overall impression that
SAR participants were more knowledgeable about sex and more tolerant in their attitudes. If this were true, any pre to post attitude and knowledge changes would lessen in significance.

SAMPLE SELECTION AND PROCEDURE

In order to test the impression that voluntary human sexuality
workshops attract the more informed, more liberal segment of a
student body, a workshop was planned for graduate and undergraduate students at the Evanston Campus of Northwestern University during the first week of Spring Quarter, 1975. Over 500 students completed the SKAT test, during class time, in courses including psychology and sociology, education, engineering, theology and premed-
ical. Participation in the test taking was voluntary, but few
students refused. All students who participated were then invited
by verbal announcement and by letter to attend a human sexuality
workshop to be held about one week later. The workshop was described briefly, noting that Northwestern medical students had found
similar workshops valuable.

FINDINGS

From the group of 501 students who completed the SKAT, 57
attended a one-day workshop. All 57 remained for the entire workshop of eight hours duration. Scores from the SKAT administered
before the workshop were divided into two comparison groups, workshop participants and nonparticipants, and showed significant
differences on the knowledge section and three of the four attitude subscales (Table 2, 2A). Persons who attended the workshop
were significantly more knowledgeable about human sexuality, were
less accepting of sexual myths and folklore, and had more liberal
attitudes toward premarital and extramarital sex and masturbation
than their peers who did not attend the workshop. These differences existed before the workshop was held.

Comparison of biographical data from the SKAT shows no significant differences in age, sex, major, religion, or graduate/
undergraduate standing between workshop participants and nonparticipants, nor were differences found in response to items rating the
influence of religion on one's value system, or the degree of conflict between parents values and one's own.

No significant differences were found for frequencies of masturbation, going steady, sexual intercourse, or orgasm with a partner of the same sex, but participants had a significantly higher

TABLE 2

MEAN SKAT SCORE

AND STANDARD DEVIATIONS ( )

OF WORKSHOP PARTICIPANTS AND NONPARTICIPANTS

	HR	SM	A	M	K
Nonpar- ticipants N = 421	48.28 (10.8)	43.80 (14.0)	43.63 (10.50)	44.66 (11.70)	42.51 (11.50)
Workshop Participants N = 57	51.21 (9.0)	52.93 (10.80)	46.09 (11.80)	50.61 (10.60)	50.16 (5.9)

ANALYSIS OF VARIANCE

HR	SM	A	M	K
$F=3.83$	$F=22.02$		$F=13.22$	$F=29.14$
$p< .05$	$p< .001$		$p< .001$	$p< .001$

Key to Scales

HR = heterosexual relations

SM = sexual myths

 A = abortion

 M = autoeroticism

 K = normed knowledge

TABLE 2A

ANALYSIS OF VARIANCE OF SKAT SCALES

FOR WORKSHOP PARTICIPANTS AND NONPARTICIPANTS

Skat Scales	Degrees of Freedom	Mean Squares	F	
HR	1	429.88	3.83	p< .05
	467	112.37		
SM	1	303.80	22.02	p< .001
	467	113.66		
A	1	1770.05	2.67	
	476	133.92		
M	1	3265.43	13.22	p< .001
	462	112.08		
K	1	2781.63	29.14	p< .001
	403	119.19		

Key to Scales

HR = heterosexual relations

SM = sexual myths

 A = abortion

 M = autoeroticism

 K = normed knowledge

frequency of dating encounters than nonparticipants. (X^2 = 12.20, df = 3, p = .0016). Eight percent of nonparticipants had never dated as compared to only two percent of participants. At the other end of the spectrum, 93% of participants had over five dates while only 74% of nonparticipants fell into this category. A trend existed, in that more nonparticipants had been involved in sex for money (18%) as compared to participants (5%). (X^2 = 7.59, df = 3, p = .0553). Self-ratings of sexual experience did not discriminate the two groups, a fairly accurate appraisal. In summary, workshop participants seem to be more social than the nonparticipants having dated more people more times, but not significantly different in their sexual experiences.

Comparisons of family characteristics show that workshop participants tended to come from larger families and were less often only children (7% compared to 22% on nonparticipants) (X^2 = 12.13, df = 4, p = .0164). The educational level of both fathers and mothers of participants was significantly higher than nonparticipants. Forty-two percent of participants' fathers held advanced degrees, compared to 24% of nonparticipants' fathers. (X^2 = 15.54, df = 5, p = .0083). Among participants' mothers, 23% held advanced degrees while only 11% of nonparticipants' mothers had achieved a similar educational level. (X^2 = 16.39, df = 5, p = .0058). Over twice as many nonparticipants' fathers and mothers had a high school education or less. (Nonparticipants' fathers 37% vs 16%. Mothers of nonparticipants 42% vs 22%).

Self-ratings of knowledge about sex and personal sexual adjustment compared to peer group clearly distinguish between participants and nonparticipants. Participants rate themselves as more knowledgeable (X^2= 15.68, df = 4, p = .0035). Twenty-seven percent of nonparticipants felt they knew "less" or "far less" than their peers about sex, compared to seven percent of participants. Fifteen percent feel "far less" adjusted sexually, compared to two percent of workshop participants. (X^2 = 10.36, df = 4, p = .0347).

Lastly, preferred methods of contraception (Table 3) varied greatly, with more nonparticipants (27%) choosing the less effective methods such as rhythm, douching or other unspecified methods compared to 3% of participants choosing one of these as a preferred method. (X^2 = 25.87, df = 9, p = .0021).

CONCLUSION

In summary, the persons who chose not to attend the human sexuality workshop were less knowledgeable about sex, feel less informed about sex, and more often rate themselves as less adjusted

TABLE 3

PREFERRED CONTRACEPTIVE METHOD

OF WORKSHOP PARTICIPANTS AND NONPARTICIPANTS

	Participants		Nonparticipants	
	N	%	N	%
RHYTHM	1	2.6	16	4.6
DOUCHE	0	0	60	17.3
WITHDRAWAL	1	2.0	0	0.0
CONDOM	4	8.0	25	7.2
FOAM AND/ OR DIAPHRAGM	5	10.0	26	7.5
IUD	2	4.0	11	3.2
PILL	35	70.0	191	55.0
STERIL-IZATION	1	2.0	1	0.3
MORNING AFTER PILL	0	0.0	1	0.3
OTHER	0	0.0	16	4.6

sexually than their peers. Students who might possibly benefit most from human sexuality courses are those who did not attend. As they hold more traditional values, they may feel that such workshops are inappropriate, or they may feel uncomfortable, as Golden and Liston hypothesized, and, therefore, avoid the workshops.

The students who did attend the human sexuality workshops came to the workshop with knowledge, attitudes and values which were more similar to the knowledge, attitude and values the workshop hopes to encourage, than their peers. They knew more about sex, had more liberal attitudes, felt more adjusted sexually than their peers, and preferred the more effective contraceptives.

If pre to post change occurs, it is clearly only a matter of degree, not of kind. Future research will have to account for the students who do not attend, or drop out in the process before we can claim than human sexuality courses are achieving their goals among total student populations.

REFERENCES

Garrard, J., Vaitkus, A., and Chilgren, R.A. (1972). Evaluation of a course in human sexuality. Journal of Medical Education, 47: 772-778.

Golden, J.S., and Liston, E.H. (1972). Medical sex education: the world of illusion and the practical realities. Journal of Medical Education, 47: 761-771

Lief, H.I., and Ebert, R.K. (1974). A survey of sex education in United States medical schools. Paper presented at International Congress of Medical Sexology, Paris.

Lief, H.I., and Reed, D.M. (1972). Sex Knowledge and Attitude Test, (2nd ed.), Center for the Study of Sex Education in Medicine, Department of Psychiatry, University of Pennsylvania, School of Medicine, Philadelphia.

Marcotte, D.B. (1973). Sex education and the medical student. Journal of Medical Education, 48: 285-286.

Marcotte, D.B., and Kilpatrick, D.G. (1974). Preliminary evaluation of a sex education course. Journal of Medical Education, 49: 703-705.

Marcotte, D.B., Kilpatrick, D.G., Geyer, P.R., and Smith, A.D. (1976). The effect of a spaced sex education course on medical students sexual knowledge and attitudes. British Journal of Medical Education, 2: 117-121.

Preliminary Technical Manual, Sex Knowledge and Attitude Test,
        (2nd ed.), Center for the Study of Sex Education in Medicine,
        Department of Psychiatry, University of Pennsylvania School
        of Medicine, Philadelphia.

Vines, N.R. (1974). Responses to Sexual Problems in Medical Coun-
        seling as a Function of Counselor Exposure to Sex Education
        Procedures Incorporating Erotic Film, unpublished doctoral
        dissertation, University of Pennsylvania, Philadelphia.

EVALUATING A SHORT-TERM SEX INFORMATION PROGRAM

Jules-Henri Gourgues

Canada

This presentation is an evaluation of a short-term sex information program, the "Programme d'information préventive en milieu
scolaire en matière de planification des naissances et de sexualité"
(Program Information on Family Planning and Sexuality for Schools).
This preventive program is more commonly known as PIPMS.

The first of its kind in Quebec, PIMPS was developed by the
Department of Social Affairs (MAS) within the framework of its
global policy on family planning.

Initially, I shall emphasize the widespread integration of
this program in its general context. Secondly, I shall attempt
a more detailed analysis of its effectiveness and, in conclusion,
I will add a few personal comments inspired by my own experience
with the program.

THE FRAMEWORK

The program is both an offshoot and an integral part of the
policy of the Department of Social Affairs on family planning and
sex education. As published by the Minister on May 10th, 1972
(MAS, 1973), the policy affirms the Department's intention to intervene in this area of family planning and education throughout
the entire province in an effort to reach all levels of society,
most particularly the underprivileged and the young adults. The
primary approach is not restrictive in its effort, as it also seeks
to promote wanted births and considers that family planning has a
psychosocial as well as a medical function. Lastly, it sanctions

549

the principle of cost-free voluntary sterilization and other medical acts having a contraceptive aim.

The policy defined three priorities for action in order to
organize the necessary departmental programs: 1) to reach young
people through the schools; 2) to provide information and counselling services (clinics) for the entire population; and, 3) to promote further training for the various professionals involved in
this particular sphere.

The PIPMS

The Context. As early as 1972, the Department decided to
develop this Information Program on Family Planning and Sexuality
for Schools in an effort to contact young people. The program's
roots are in the context of a very precise social and political
conjuncture which explains in part its orientation.

Although, family planning in Quebec seemed adequately structured at the time, it was for the most part aimed at the adult segmen
of the population. Quebec's social structure was simultaneously
undergoing extreme rapid and far-reaching change and it seemed
clear that the sexual habits of young people needed to be considered
within the scope of a broader governmental intervention. As a consequence, considerable pressure was placed upon the Department to
extend its program inclusive of this new target group.

Concurrently, the Quebec Department of Education was in the
process of developing a systematic sex education program, but, as
is often the case when developing programs in this area, unend-
ing discussions and constraints perpetuated stumbling blocks to
the program's inception.

At the same time, the Department of Social Affairs was beginning to reform health and social services and one of the main
considerations was to shift the emphasis from curative intervention to the preventive intervention. As part of this new philosophy, the Department was also anxious to see developed an information program for the schools which would deal with the principal
areas of intervention such as nutrition, sexuality, and the abuse
of drugs and alcohol. The name of the program, therefore, intentionally reflects this concern.

Nature of the program. Before deciding upon the nature of
its program, the Department participated in a series of consultations with more than 200 health and social service professionals
in an effort to obtain their professional opinions on the merits
of a governmental intervention program and upon the proper strategies to be employed. The results of this collective consultation

proved conclusively that the social climate with respect to this
program justified a swift intervention.

Conscious that the global responsibility for a complete sex
education program was not within its duties, the Department of
Social Affairs, as early as 1973, decided to take responsibility
for prevention, counselling and information, areas which are in
fact within its jurisdiction. The Department felt that a program,
albeit limited, which could be swiftly implemented would provide
a solution for the young people pending the creation of a comprehensive sex education program. The enthusiasm such a program
could engender would more than make up for its being somewhat less
than ideal.

The program was organized within Quebec's educational system
which at present offers secondary school students the services of
a nurse and social worker, employed by the MAS. In an effort to
ensure both a psychosocial and medical intervention approach, the
program provides for group sessions on family planning and sexuality cooperatively given by these two professionals. Small
classes are limited to secondary school students from 13 to 19
years of age. Since this program is particularly aimed at those
students who will enter the labor market at the end of the term, and
who are thus likely to be part of the low income class within a
few years, the Department will ultimately be able to provide services for the pressing needs of this sector of the population.

The program, supported by grants from the MAS to hire regional
program coordinators, is implemented throughout the province by the
fourteen Social Service Centers.

The specialist in sex education and family planning is responsible for regional development, application and evaluation of
the program as well as for directing and aiding the intervention
in the school milieu. Activities in the classroom using audio-
visual materials provide students with an opportunity to exchange
ideas and interact with the program specialist. The specialists,
in turn, provide available resources and encourage consultations
not only with them, but with outside professionals or parents as
well. To help supplement and achieve the program's objectives,
the Department has provided the animators with an audio-visual
document entitled "Sexe: nom masculin et féminin," (Sex: Masculine and Feminine) which inspired lively debate during the
spring of 1975.

The Department of Social Affairs in collaboration with certain
Quebec universities has also organized and funded three professional
training sessions, each 45 hours in length and directed at the
social workers and nurses who are practicing in the schools; at
present, these sessions have reached more than 500 professionals.

Evaluation

Scope. The Department has always accorded PIMPS top priority
because of its innovative character. In spite of numerous difficulties, the Department obtained evaluative data on the program
for each year it has actually been implemented. At the end of
the 1972-1973 school year, immediately after the program was initially implemented, an evaluative report was drafted on the basis
of the reactions of 1300 young people and adults, to whom the program had been presented on an experimental basis (Gourgues, 1973).
For the second school year (1973-74), a random sampling of 160
students out of a possible 4163 who had experienced the program
was polled (Giner et al., 1974; Tremblay, J., 1975). In 1974-75,
959 students from nine different regions were contacted for evaluation. Each region subsequently presented a report to the Department. For the last school year to be evaluated (1975-76), three
questionnaires were prepared by the Department and submitted respectively to the regional program coordinators, to 150 specialist
of PIPMS and to a hundred and some professionals involved in implementing the program at one level or another. (Unfortunately,
I am able to refer only to the first part of the report as the
rest was delayed by strikes in all public schools of Quebec). Finally each of the three training sessions was subject to a specific
evaluation.

Program's development. Ultimately, the program's evolution
proved rapid and constant, in spite of inevitable fluctuations
resulting from public feedback. The following is a brief outline
of this evolution:

1. In 1973-74, four out of fourteen Social Service Centers
    sought to implement it;

2. In 1974-75, twelve of these centers were active in im-
    plementing the program; however, during this period, the
    stir created by mass media publicity of the quarrel over
    the slides (La Querelle du Diaporama) considerably slowed
    down the program's implementation.

3. Last year, thirteen of the fourteen Social Service Centers
    took part in the program in spite of the many labor rela-
    tions conflicts which paralyzed school activities for a
    large part of the year;

4. At the start of the present school year, the program, in
    theory, achieved maximum regional implementation with all
    fourteen regions involved, and for the moment there are no
    predictable problems.

Evaluation of the program on numbers of students contacted shows an increase from 4,163 students during the 1973-74 school year to approximately 26,500 students contacted two years later in 1975-76.

Current state of the program. Recent data obtained from the 1975-76 evaluation give us a clear idea of the present state of affairs (Gagné et al., 1976).

The fact that the program reached more than 25,000 students over the past school year also means that at least 75 of all the educational institutions in the province were contacted. Their breakdown according to the type of institution is the following: 85.2% were secondary schools, 2.7% elementary schools and 9.3% institutions of another nature (such as reception centers, etc.).

The approximate size of the groups contacted gives an idea of the strategies for applying the program: less than 10 students in 4% of the interventions; from 10 to 20 students in 39% of the cases; from 21 to 30 students in 40% of the cases; and more than 31 students in 3% of the cases (does not apply for 14% of the cases). These groups were mixed for 7 interventions out of 10 and, comprised one sex only, for 3 out of 10.

The time spent in each group was as follows: 28% of the interventions lasted less than 3 hours; 23% from 2 to 5 hours inclusively; 21% from 6 to 8 hours; and 8%, more than 9 hours, with a rate of "no response," "no reply," or "does not apply" of 20%.

Since, for now, it is absolutely impossible to reserve a specific period of time for this program inside the official timetable, the interventions took place during the course on "personal and social formation" in 20% of the cases; for another 41% during the religious sciences class time; for yet another 21%, during classroom periods devoted to other courses (Biology, French, English...); for another 10%, approximately, during the periods devoted to pedagogical activities or physical training; and finally, for 5% of the cases, the interventions took place extramurally.

The nurse and the social worker conducted the program during 4/5 of the interventions. The teachers and religious instructors took part in more than 25% of the activities, whereas the psychologists collaborated for more than 10%.

The following are subjects most often presented during these sessions (by order of importance): anatomy and physiology of the reproductive system (presented during 87% of the interventions); the menstrual cycle (79%); family planning and venereal diseases (76%); sexual intercourse (71%); and changes at puberty (65%). Furthermore, other equally popular subjects were presented during less than 60% of the interventions, namely: pregnancy and childbirth

(56%); masturbation (35%); abortion (31%); sterilization (20%);
and homosexuality (17%).

Overall level of satisfaction. The majority of the questionnaires requested that the persons interviewed stipulate the general
level of satisfaction with respect to the program. For example,
among the students contacted at the end of the 1973-74 school year,
71% felt the content of the program was "good" and "very good"; 13%
qualified it as "satisfactory;" 9% felt that it could be improved;
and 2% deemed it "unsatisfactory."

An initial regional evaluation based on the reactions of 500
students, in June 1975, reported that 80% were satisfied with the
program, 2.5% were satisfied to a certain extent and 17.5% were dissatisfied (MAS, 1976). Another similar regional evaluation, limited
to a systematic sampling of 133 students who had followed the program the same year, reported that 93% of the students were in favor
of having the experiment repeated whereas only 7% were not (MAS,
1976).

Finally, with respect to parental reactions, only 10% of the
students interviewed in 1973-74 stated that their parents had reacted positively (Giner et al., 1974).

Impact of the program. The most important consideration was
to determine how the students understood the program and its importance to them.

In the research conducted by the Department in 1974 (Giner et
al., 1974), 28% of the students affirmed having learned about things
they were ignorant of; 59% admitted that the program had made clear
to them information they already had; and 2% felt that the program
had taught them nothing new.

In tapping attitudes about sexuality, 61% of the students reported that the program had sharpened their sense of responsibility,
whereas 32% reported that it had in no way changed their attitudes.
Further, 39% of the students felt much less personally restricted
sexually as a result of the program, whereas 6% had the opposite
impression. Finally 49% reported that their attitudes had undergone no significant change.

Behaviorally speaking, we now know that the most frequently
stated objection to the program was the fear adults had that it
might encourage young people to have more frequent sexual intercourse. We therefore questioned the students about this and their
reply was as follows: 85.3% stated exposure to the program had not
increased the frequency of their sexual intercourse; 2.8% reported
an increase in intercourse; whereas 5.7% confided having less
sexual intercourse as a result of the program. It should be noted,

however, that the sampling comprised for the most part (87%) young
people 17 or 18 years of age and that, at the time of the survey,
more than 50% of them were not having sexual intercourse as yet.

The program also had a certain behavioral influence regarding
the use of contraceptives; 18.3% of the students stated that the
program encouraged them to use contraceptives more frequently,
2.7%, to use these less often; and for 7.3% of the students there
was no perceptible change.

The same research also provided data about parents' fear at
seeing professionals in the schools replace parental influence in
sex education. In fact, one question the students were asked was
whether or not they felt the need to discuss these subjects with
their parents. The number of them replying in the affirmative was
relatively high 32.4% in light of the fact that 38.2% reported
having personally spoken with a professional at the school or with
an acquaintance.

Within the context of the regional evaluations, it is interesting to note the results of a research made by the Jewish Social
Service Center (Jewish, Family Services) and by Concordia University, both in Montreal (Gross et al., 1976). The aim of this research was to make a full evaluation of the increased acquisition
of knowledge 48 target students had acquired during the eight week
program. The research also sought to evaluate to what extent this
new awareness had lessened the students' anxiety about sexuality.
To make this evaluation the following tests were used: the questionnaire on the "IPAT Anxiety Scale" by Cattell and Scheir: the
"Sex Knowledge and Attitude Test" and the "Sex Knowledge Inventory
Test" by Lief and McHugh, appropriately revised by Donna Snowden.

This research showed that the program had encouraged a significant increase in the level of knowledge, 58%, but it was not
able to equate it in any significant way to a related decrease in
anxiety, which remained stable at 27%. Moreover, pertinent to this
absence of a positive correlation between the two phenomena, it is
interesting to note that the researchers arrived at the following
though not the only hypothesis: the increase in knowledge achieved
at the beginning of a course might well lead to a subsequent increase in anxiety which would diminish later on when the newly
acquired knowledge had been well assimilated.

Finally, another regional study by Francine Corbeil and Georges
Letarte in the Gaspé region used a pre and post test measure (MAS
1976). The aim of this study was to verify the impact of the program on knowledge, contraceptive behavior and persistence of certain
sexual myths held by the students. In spite of certain reservations concerning the regional context and the scope of this study
(sampling of 233 students), a few of its conclusions merit our

attention.

With respect to acquired knowledge, the research used both a
blind awareness test and a test on known or unknown terms. The
principal results are as follows:

1. A 10 to 20% improvement in the knowledge of birth control
    methods;

2. An increase in educated decisions regarding the effective-
    ness of contraceptive methods used;

3. A lessening of the gap between the sexes with respect to
    their knowledge of the subject.

As for the known or unknown terms, the study showed that a
total number of 34 unknown terms were mentioned 233 times by 103
students at the beginning of the program, whereas only 10 of these
terms were mentioned 34 times by 20 students at the end.

With respect to contraceptive behavior patterns, the influence
of the program was as follows:

1. A 10% increase in the rate of contraceptive use from 42.2
    to 46% between the pre and post test measurements;

2. The program seems to help make the students more aware
    both of a broader range of possible contraceptive methods
    and of the necessity of carefully choosing the most suit-
    able one;

3. The lessening of the gap between the boys and the girls
    as a possible result of the program was also confirmed
    with respect to the actual use of contraceptive methods.

The researchers noted that, following the dissimination of
pertinent information, most sexual myths seem to have been dis-
pelled with the exception of the virginity myth in which female
virginity is an important criterion in mate selection for marriage.

CONCLUSION

These are the main data concerning the various points used
for evaluating the program; many others could have been mentioned.
Research is underway and the program now seems sufficiently well
established to allow us to develop a longitudinal study to tap the
program's influence on the students over a period of time.

In conclusion, I would like to make a few personal comments on related points.

First, to comment on the often levelled criticism that this type of intervention program cannot compete with a systematic program aimed at the entire educational system from nursery school through the university: it cannot be denied that, in theory, such a program should constitute a long-term objective, but, at present, it seems to me that a short-term limited program on information of a preventive nature affords definite advantages.

For example, when we consider the fact that it has taken us a scant three years to really get this program off the ground and to see it implemented throughout the province, one has to admit that an identical time lapse is scarcely long enough to set up a systematic sex education program - to obtain the necessary authorization and to establish the initial experimental contacts with a limited number of students selected from certain restricted milieus. If four years ago, this more global and idealistic approach had been sanctioned, we would not have reached the thousands of students who have been exposed to the program since its inception, (26,500 last year alone), but would have had to be content with reaching only a negligible number of students. We also realize that it was the only practical intervention possible because of the socio-political climate which gave it birth.

Four years after the program's inception, there are one or several coordinators in every region of the province. Their presence in the school milieu will very definitely stimulate a wider and more thorough application of the program, which is a primary part of the program's objective.

The flexibility of the program's basic structure and the possibilities of adapting it to the individual region may well constitute the distinction between the "teach us what we want to know" and the "we teach you what we want you to know" orientations. For example, the results of various research probes showed that the subjects most often chosen by the students and which they judged most useful were of a practical nature, such as contraceptive methods and venereal diseases, among others (Giner et al., 1974).

If within 5, 6 or even 10 years, we see that this type of intervention program is adaptive to the same orientations and meets the same objectives as a structured sex education program, in addition to satisfying the student's immediate and particular needs, then I believe that the merits of this intervention cannot easily be questioned. Finally organizing such a program is less complicated at every stage (development, implementation, social-political acceptance) than a structured sex education program.

This program caused a great deal of public debate as witnessed
by the number of newspaper articles (134) or the 12,213 lines printe
on the subject of our audio-visual document alone (MAS, 1976). However, in our opinion, any intervention in sex education is always
likely to cause a stir at one level or another. Such arguments are
not purely negative as they stimulate a necessary evolution in the
collective mentality and modify attitudes on the part of organizations or individuals directly implicated, which in the end, compensate for the delays they initially caused. Moreover, this
public debate resulted in very tangible positive repercussions:
for example, we have evaluated responses of approximately 100,000,
young spectators who saw a televised presentation of the audio-
visual document which was transmitted first regionally then nation-
ally (it was estimated that more than $50,000 was saved in broad-
casting time alone). Nevertheless, the approach taken by the program enabled us to minimize public debate which was centered on
the audio-visual document and not on the whole program, and, in
the end, the program's global approach was not compromised as
other substitute documents became available for use. It appears
necessary for sex educators to remain aware of political and social
impacts on the profession and in my judgment we must seek to engra-
tiate the public to our profession by developing practical services
to meet the real needs of the population. In achieving this goal,
we must develop closer ties with the political structure which is
situated in a middle position between our endeavors and the preoc-
cupations of the population.

REFERENCES

Gagné, M.-H., Giner, M. and Villeneuve, C. (1976). Evaluation
    Quantitative du P.I.P.M.S.: année scolaire 1975-1976, MAS,
    Québec.

Giner, M., Villeneuve, C. and Bouchard, P. (1974). Evaluation du
    Programme d'Information Préventive en Milieu Scolaire: la
    Planification des Naissances dans Lévis, Laval et Duvernay,
    MAS, Québec.

Gourgues, J.-H. (1973). Programme d'Information Préventive en
    Milieu Scolaire: Etat du Dossier au 1er juin 1973, MAS,
    Québec.

Gross, P., Levine, S., Rothstein, J., Schneider, S. and Zuckerman,
    S. (1976). The Effects of a Family Life and Sex Education
    Program on Adolescents: A Research Project. The Jewish
    Family Services and the Applied Social Science Department
    of Concordia University, Montréal.

MAS, (1973). Orientations en matière de planification des naissances. In Burt, J.J., Brower, L.A., Cardyn, L.J. and Gauthier, G., (eds.), Education Sexuelle: Concepts et Plans de Cours, HRW, Montréal.

MAS, (1976). Programme d'Information Préventive en Milieu Scolaire: Rapports Régionaux d'Evaluation, Année Scolaire, 1974-75, Québec.

Tremblay, J. (1975). Programme d'Information Préventive en Milieu Scolaire: Données Fragmentaires d'Evaluation, MAS, Québec.

HISTORY, OBJECTIVES, CONTENT OF THE SEXOLOGY PROGRAM AT UNIVERSITÉ DU QUÉBEC À MONTRÉAL

Joseph Josy Levy

Canada

This International Conference on Sexology has clearly demonstrated the great development achieved in sexology as a field of learning and this, in turn, has been paralleled by the organization of various institutions for research as well as programs concerned with the scientific comprehension of sexuality.

In this context, the experiment made by the Module and the Department of Sexology at the Université du Québec à Montréal (UQAM) represents a unique and original attempt to set up a program of sexological studies which will take into account the specificity of this discipline and the socio-cultural conditions characteristic of Quebec.[1]

The purpose of this presentation is to outline a short history of the program, its objectives and structure as set forth by the Module as well as the characteristics of the student body and its integration into the labor market.

When UQAM was founded in 1969, a Module attached to the Department of Education was set up for the purpose of giving courses to future sex educators. It offered a curriculum consisting of twenty courses in psycho-pedagogy and ten courses in sexology leading to a B.Sc. degree in what was called "sexology-education."

---

[1]The Université du Québec à Montréal has set up a twin structure: a special unit which we have called a "Module" and the Department itself. The Module includes the teachers and the students who make up a Committee in charge of programming and of pedagogy; the Department is composed of the faculty members responsible for teaching research and service to the collectivity.

The purpose of this program was to train in both sexology and in pedagogy, teachers to be capable of providing sex education based on scientific findings.

From 1969 to 1976 many reorganizations of the program were made. First, the number of psycho-pedagogical courses was reduced in favor of those in sexology, such as courses in biosexuality, psychosexuality and sociosexuality; then new changes were made and other courses set up, further emphasizing the sexological dimension of the program. In the meanwhile an autonomous Department of Sexology was created and officially recognized in June 1975. At that time the new faculty was composed of 12 professionals with degrees in biology, psychiatry, psychology, psychoanalysis, sociology, criminology, anthropology, education or philosophy. In 1972, it seemed necessary to reorganize the program in consideration of the development in the academic field of sexology and the diversification of social needs in sexology.

In 1973, the Administration of the Université du Québec à Montréal was presented with a new program of "information-sexology" and official endorsement was obtained from UQAM. But in 1976, the Inter-University Council voted against this new program[2] because it felt that there was no opportunity for a new profession. The proposed new program wanted to enable students to work in social agencies as well as in schools. Meanwhile, the "sexology-education" Module has continued to train sexology teachers in the framework of the former study program still in effect.

OBJECTIVES AND STRUCTURES OF
THE CURRICULUM IN "EDUCATION-SEXOLOGY"

The principal objective is to train educators in sexology to intervene, inform, teach, animate, educate or help through research, the different social or school groups affected by sexual problems. Training in counselling and in therapy will be undertaken in a proposed MA program which has already been submitted by the Department of Sexology and has also receive endorsement from UQAM. We are still waiting for a decision from the Inter-University Council.

The courses included in the B.Sc. program give an overall view and general acquisition of knowledge, whereas more specialized train-

---

[2]The number of experts consulted as well as the vague resolutions and unfounded criticism concerning the new curriculum is typical of the reservations surrounding sexology; its unqualified acceptance in the field of significant studies has yet to be approved.

ing in therapy or counselling requires more advanced studies which
far outdistance the modest ambitions of an undergraduate program.

The experience obtained by the Module in its contacts with
the social milieu points to two separate fields where professional
training in sexology may be put to work: the school and social
agencies.

In the framework of the Quebec school system, it is necessary
to train teachers capable of setting up and implementing a program
of sex education adapted to the various levels and age groups whose
problems and doubts require specific solutions. The social setting,
however, disposes of more outlets for "sexo-educateurs": Social
Service Centers (CSSS), local community service centers (CLSC),
hospital centers and individual agencies, as for Family Planning, Unwed Mothers, etc., which have increased their sexology
services (information and animation on sexual problems, contraceptive methods, etc.). Here, the sex educator is often a welcomed
addition to other existing professionals and paraprofessionals.

The training of this new professional requires the student to
follow a program of thirty courses (90 credits) over a minimal
period of three years; however, it is possible for the students
who so desire to take courses part-time which will prolong the
study program. These courses are described in Annex 1.

The program itself is centered on the following:

1) The theories, concepts and fundamentals of sexology through
an interdisciplinary approach, i.e., an integration of the findings
of bioneuro-physiology, psychology, and socio-anthropology into a
theoretical framework of sexuality. This dynamic outlook is specially developed in courses on ontogenesis, from the prenatal
period to old age and in the following courses:

1. Introduction to sexology: its basic aspects and contemporary problems

2. The physio-medical dimensions of human sexual behavior

3. The socio-cultural and psychological dimensions of human
sexuality (2 courses)

4. Ontogenesis: prenatal, pre-adolescent, adolescent and
adult life (3 courses)

5. The analysis of the human sexual response: its objective
and subjective aspects (2 courses)

6. Sex pathology: classification and etiology (3 courses)

In addition to the compulsory courses (20), the student can select from multiple options to develop a specialized theme of personal particular interest. These courses allow the student to assimilate the varieties of information in sexology.

2) Courses in methods, research and in didactic techniques with insistence on the pedagogical aspects appropriate to effective intervention in both school and social settings. Animation techniques, group work and audio-visual aids are also introduced to complete the training in methodology. Finally the program offers specific courses and practical training periods in exploration, observation and intervention in which students are encouraged under supervision to apply their knowledge and professional skills; this makes it possible to fill in any theoretical or methodological gaps in their professional development.

3) The development of the student's own resources and individual and professional maturation by means of courses dealing specifically with the deontological aspects of the sex-educator's profession, personal development and awareness of subjective aspects inherent in training both in individual and group work. The student is required to reevaluate his personal course of study to facilitate the choice of final courses that would complete professional training specialized to personal needs.

Teaching is given by professors who are all members of the new Department of Sexology; their high qualifications assure the successful outcome of the objectives set forth in the curriculum. Interdisciplinary efficiency is assured by the varied professional backgrounds of the faculty members whose close collaboration in teaching and research help provide cohesion and scientific content of courses.

CHARACTERISTICS OF THE STUDENT BODY

Since the foundation of the Module, 204 students have received B.Sc. in "sexology education." Male and female students are almost evenly divided, with 105 female and 99 male students. Among those holding degrees who were admitted to the Module, two groups stood out: 58.8 percent were college graduates or had a B.A., and 30 percent held a degree in education (B.Ed.) and were returning to the university to specialize in sexology. A small percentage included former nurses, social workers and others.

Today, the profile of the student body has changed. Since 1973, new admission requirements are in effect; the candidates who have already received degrees in the science of Education or in Public Health and have acquired sufficient experience are accepted

Classification as to former training is as follows: 45.5 percent
are specialized in the Health Sciences (nursing, social work, psychology) and 30 percent in Education. Among the other students,
10.5 percent hold various degrees in the Social Sciences and 14
percent are adults who have fulfilled certain conditions, one of
which is having sufficient experience.

Today, the majority of our one hundred and fifty students have
sound basic training, especially in the Health Sciences, which indicates a certain interest in social conditions pertaining to sexology. This trend will continue in the framework of the newly-
established curriculum, and the Module will continue to enroll
candidates with suitable academic backgrounds.

INTEGRATION INTO THE LABOR MARKET

The lack of quantitative data makes it impossible to analyze
the degree of integration of the "sexo-éducateurs" into the labor market; the demand will increase proportionately to recognition of
the profession by the public. In the Quebec school setting, sex
information is part of courses in religion and biology, but apart
from a few pilot attempts, there are no true general programs in
sex education. Indeed, the provincial Department of Education in
Quebec has not as yet adopted a precise policy in this field because
of the complexity of the subject matter and the conflicting ideologies concerning the content and administration of such a program.
This state of affairs somewhat limits the employment of future
"sexo-éducateurs" but difficulties will be solved in the long run
when such programs are finally set up.

On the other hand, in the social setting, there are many
"sexo-éducateurs" working in public agencies and ancillary organizations, especially in family planning centers, where the "sexo-
éducateurs" are considered preferential employees. Institutions
for services to youth, unwed mothers, and engaged couples require
"sexo-éducateurs," especially when interest is aroused by the practical work performed by a sexology-trainee in the course of active
probation. Such interest leads to an awareness of the role sexology
may play in improving the services offered to the public at large,
and as our professionals gradually penetrate the labor market, we
foresee a complete recognition of the importance of sexology in
Quebec.

CONCLUSION

In Quebec, sexology is presently in a period of transition
and is gradually being integrated into the academic and social
circles as a definite and acknowledged means of intervention.
The Module program offered by the Université du Québec à Montréal
is an original contribution to the developing science of sexology.

ANNEX I

COURSES TO BE FOLLOWED BY STUDENTS ENROLLED IN THE B.Sc. PROGRAM OF SEXOLOGY-EDUCATION AT UQAM

Integration and Personal Maturation I

The purpose of this course is to allow the student 1) to integrate the knowledge, 2) to form a subjective idea of what should be a professional sexologist (the intellectual, ethical, and social requirements, 3) to understand the necessary and continuous changes in human existence, as regards the professional in human relations, and specifically, the professional sexologist.

This approach is facilitated by a syllabus, prepared at the outset of the session for each student by the instructor, which includes the following elements: the objectives of the first university cycle in sexology; interdisciplinarity; professional deontology, and the requirements of professional "human relations."

Integration and Personal Maturation II

This course allows the student 1) to sound out personal attitudes and the emotions, sensations and sentiments (physical and mental) relevant to his professional experience 2) to become increasingly aware, as an individual and future professional, of the outcome of subjectivity and the results of the reactions and emotions of others. Various experiments (sensitization, nonverbal interaction, bio-energetics, creativity sessions, transcendental meditation, psycho-therapeutics, and in a broad sense, personal development and group development) are possible according to the student's ability and his academic environment. The student will be required to remit a written report on the effect of these experiments and of the adjustment to the acquired sexological knowledge.

The Physio-Medical Dimensions of Human Sexual Behavior

This course deals with the various interactions between the somatic, sexual dimorphism, and sexual behavior. Studies include physio-medical analysis of the urogenital functions and structures, the integration of the reproductive and the other biological systems, organogenesis and the maturation of the urogenital organs, their histology, biochemistry, natural variations and behavioral implications, ovogenesis and spermatogenesis, the genetic, endocrinologic, immunologic, and sex-behavioral data (identity, interest, behavioral types).

Introduction to Sexology: Fundamental Aspects and Contemporary Problems

Problematic fundamentals in the field of sexology are introduced and discussed: multidimensionals, data, myths ("scientific"); actual sex values; integrated sexuality (masculine/feminine; normal/abnormal); the fundamental aspect of the human condition; sexology and its allied disciplines; the diversified roles of the sexologist, etc.

The Socio-Cultural and Psychological Dimensions of Human Sexuality

The application of the socio-cultural and psychological perspectives to sexuality. Analysis of scientific proofs to the relationship between certain sexological facts and the concept of socialization, a multidisciplinary concept uniting the data obtained from sociology, anthropology, psychology and criminology. Emphasis on the role of society in sexual values, attitudes and behaviors. Study of the influence exerted by adherence to a particular social group (culture, sex, age, social status) on sexual values, attitudes, and behavior. Application of the concept of social control to the Quebec situation. Explanation of certain sexual phenomena as regards socio-cultural variables.

Sexopathology I: Classification and Etiology

The criteria of normal and pathological sexuality. Levels of sexopathological interpretation. Organic sexual dysfunctions: hermaphrodism, pseudohermaphrodism, ovarian and testicular deficiency, virilism, hirsutism, venereal diseases, etc. Endocrinological disorders affecting sexuality (acromegaly, the adrenogenital syndrome). Sexual behavior and organic dysfunctions (mental debility, paraplegia, deafness, blindness, etc.). Functional disorders of sexuality: lack of sexual interest, frigidity, impotence, atypical sexual conduct (homosexuality, pedophilia, voyeurism, exhibitionism, transsexualism, prostitution). Sexual conformity, deviance, and deliquency.

ANNEX I (continued)

Sexual Ontogenesis I: Prenatal Life and Childhood

Integration of the knowledge relative to the sexual development in the fetus and in the child. Studies on sexual differentiation and biological systems: genetic and gonadal sex, hormonal, morphological, neurological sex. The acquisition of sexual identity: biological, psychological and socio-cultural factors. The relative importance of assigned and acquired sex. The development of sexuality in the child. The study of psychological, psychoanalytical and socio-cultural problematics. The plasticity of infantile sexuality: the transcultural and historical approaches.

Ethnosexology

The purpose of this course is to make the student aware of the socio-cultural variability in sexuality. Definition of ethnology: its place relative to the other social sciences, especially to sexology. The principal concepts: culture and society; status and role; notions of patterns and structures. The functions of culture. The study of transcultural methods: comparative methods and tests. Transcultural analysis: its characteristics and problems. The social structures: the economy and sexual divisions in the labor market. Parental systems; the incest taboo. Initiation rituals: the analysis and hypothesis of work. Cultural variability in sexual behaviors. Homosexuality. Birth control and abortion. Ideological aspects: the sexual roles in mythical representation, primitive concepts of sexuality. Major anthropological theories and sexuality: evolutionism, definition and methods and the principal theories (Bachofen, Morgan, McLennan). Ethno-psychology: definitions and methods, principal theories (Freud, Malinowski, Roheim, Mead, Bateson and Kardiner). Functionalism and structuralism: definition and methods, principal theories (Malinowski, Radcliffe-Brown, Parsons, Levi-Strauss).

Methodology of Sexological Research

Student elaboration of an interdisciplinary research project in sexology. The development of theoretical schema and formulation of hypotheses. Theoretical and operational projects. Construction of measuring equipment: problems in accuracy and validity. Selection of analysis subjects. Delimitation in experimental context; analysis of results obtained; intervening and conjugate variables. Causal analysis. Reliability of results. Patterns of interpretation.

Seminar on Sexological Theories II

The purpose of this course is to allow the student to make a comparative and critical analysis of sexological theories. Each participant must progressively work out a critical analysis of several sexological theories or of a sexological phenomenon based on various data. The results of this analysis are submitted to group criticism.

Sexuality and Civilizations

The concept of civilization and its pertinence to sexology. The historical methods. Comparative studies of the role of sexuality in the great civilizations: in gesture, social relations, art (the dance, sculpture, painting); ideology (philosophy and religion) as illustrated in Antiquity (Mesopotamia, Egypt, Greece, Rome), in Islam, the Occident and the Orient (China, Japan, India). Studies of the various aspects of romantic love, erotism, the woman, the human body; insistence on the constants and variables in human sexual behaviors in the course of history.

Seminar on Sexological Theories

The purpose of this seminar is to achieve a pluridimensional outlook on a sexual phenomenon and to highlight a sexological theory by means of individual and group motivation. Moreover, the efforts of a single student or of a team of three or four students must meet with group appreciation and/or criticism. Special attention is given to topical essentials, methods, and theoretical problematics inherent to the given situation.

Neuro-Physiological Aspects of the Human Sexual Response

Pertinent bases of neuro-anatomy and neuro-physiology. Conscious sexual sensations: receptors, motor pathways, cortical representation. The motor function of the skeletal muscles in sexual responsivity. The motor function of the autonomous nervous system. Parasympathetic activity and excitation. Sympathetic nerve system and orgasm. Medullary centers of excitation and orgasm. The limbic lobe as a pleasure-giving center. Sexuality and the electric stimulation of the brain. Electroencephalogram during sexual response. Sexuality and dreams. The influence of drugs on sexuality. Sexual hormones and the brain. Biological retro-action and sexuality. Neurophysiological implications in relaxation techniques (meditation, the imaginary) in sexual response. Acupuncture. The nycthemeral rhythm and sexuality.

ANNEX I (continued)

Sexopathology II: Diagnosis and Treatment

Diagnosis of organic sexual dysfunctions: macroscopic and microscopic diagnoses and use of modern instruments. Endocrinological and biochemical methods. Diagnosis of functional sexual disorders: the use of psycho-sexological tests. Treatment of sexual insufficiencies through hormonal, behavioral, analytical therapy. Atypical sexual behavior and possible therapies.

Sexological Action in the School
Setting II: Participation

Operationalism and establishment of circumstantial project in sexological educative action in the school setting. Individual participation in such action in personal or group form, in close collaboration with school personnel. Periodical evaluation of effectiveness and profitability of such action.

Interview Techniques: A Method
of Sexological Intervention

Student sensitization and training in various approaches to affective and sexual problems. The course is divided into three parts: a) a theoretical overview on the interview situation and on the relation of aid; b) a training period "in the field" in which small groups of students are required to conduct interviews supervised by instructors; c) student group discussions on their experience and the relation between theory and practice.

Family Planning: its Social
and Psychological Dimensions

This course completes the bio-medical dimensions of fertility and of contraception with the following studies: the socio-cultural ans psychological factors of fecundity; the social consequences of uncontrolled fecundity; the sociological and psychological factors affecting illigitimacy; the history of contraception; the socio-cultural and psychological factors in the non-use or misuse of contraceptive means; the socio-cultural and psychological dimensions of abortion; the non-biological methods of birth-control; the institutions and philosophy underlying family planning.

Sexological Intervention in a Social Setting I

This session proposes to train the student in the techniques of observation in the social setting and to sensitize him/her to the real problems facing sexologists in the chosen field of work. The session is centered on the exploration of the social sphere serviced by institutions or community centers which gives sexological services. Evaluation and criticism of the observation techniques used and their results.

Sexological Intervention in a Social Setting II

Continuous participation in a particular sexological sphere in a social context. Follow-up relative to objectives set forth in a Social Setting I, with insistence upon the techniques entailing appropriate evaluation of chosen mode of participation.

History of Contemporary Sexological Concepts

The foundations of contemporary sexological concepts. Different sexological periods and their principal representatives. Descriptive period (Krafft-Ebing, Westermarck); heuristic period (H. Ellis, Hirschfeld, Freud, Reich, Guyon, A. Ellis); empirico-quantative period (Malinowski and the ethno-sexological approach, Kinsey and the socio-sexological approach, Masters and Johnson and the psycho-physio-sexological approach). Sexology considered as an interdisciplinary group of studies.

Sexual Phylogenesis

The phylogenetic approach: problematics and methods. Sexual differentiation in the vegetal and animal kingdoms. Description of sexual behavior in the vertebrata and non-vertebrata, mammalia, primates, etc. Studies of phylogenetic foundations of human sexuality: the functions of sexuality in the various species. Analysis of the sexual invariances in animal and human societies. The part played by instinct in human sexual expression. The teleological aspects of feminine orgasm. Ontogenesis and phylogenesis as complementary patterns of human sexuality.

ANNEX I (continued)

Endocrinology and the Development of Human Sexual Behavior

The endocrine control relative to the different aspects of reproduction. The definition of hormones and the endocrine glands; the modern concept of hormonal action; the releasing factor. The development and functions of the glands: the pituitary gland, the ovary, the testes, the adrenal gland, etc. The effect of the steroid and protein hormones on various phases of reproduction, i.e., differentiation of sexual organs, maturation at puberty, the menstrual cycle, ovulation, pregnancy, the menopause, sperm formation, ejaculation, old age in males, etc. The placenta parturition, lactation, synthetic hormones, the effects of castration, hypophysectomy, etc., the influence of hormones on sexual desire, mating, etc.

Applied Sexological Methods and Techniques II

Critical analysis of certain sexological methods of application; the ethnological method (Marshall, Suggs, Stephens, Mead, Ford and Beach); the neurophysiological method (Heath, Maclean, Lisk); the ethnological method (Lorenz, Tinbergen, Wickler); the possibility of integrating method and techniques of research in sexology.

Fertility and Contraception: the Bio-Medical Dimensions

Study of the problems in fertility and contraception from the bio-medical stand. Fertility: generalities. Sperm: capacitation, migration, fecundation, etc. Implantation: fetal life and the newborn. Spontaneous and induced abortion. Infertility and treatment. Artificial insemination. Contraception: the condom, diaphragm, home methods, etc., Hormonal methods for both men and women. Intra-uterine devices, sterilization. Comparative studies of various contraceptive methods and family planning.

Applied Methods and Research Techniques in Sexology I

Sexological applications of methodology in the human sciences. The scientific methodology in sexology: historics, general laws, and obstacles. The application of research principles and experimental schemas of the sexual phenomenon: setting up possible guidelines, the nature and validity of inference. The physiological method applied in sexology: Masters and Johnson, Freud, Fox, etc. The psychological application in sexology: Fisher, Kirkendall, Eysenck, etc. The sociological method applied in sexology: Kinsey, Chesser, Ehrmann, Simon, Schofield, Reiss, etc.

Analysis of the Human Sexual Response: Objective and Subjective Aspects

Account of biological and medical studies in sexual relations. Masters and Johnson: physiological studies of conditions of experiment and of the population. Resumption of their work in present research. Differences and similarities. Genital and extragenital reactions in the male. Sexuality in the elderly male. Genital and extragenital reactions in the female: the nulliparae, multiparae, elderly women. Comparison in male and female orgasm. Physiological response: primary and secondary impotence. Premature or delayed ejaculation. Orgasmic impotence. Frigidity. Re-establishment of normal physiological response.

Sexual Ontogenesis II: Pre-Adolescence and Adolescence

Integration of the knowledge relative to the sexual development of the pre-adolescent and of the adolescent. Pre-adolescence and sexual manifestations. Biological changes at puberty. Sexual manifestations in the adolescent: epidemiological study. The meaning of sexuality for the adolescent. The function of the sexual rites of initiation. The phenomenological, analytical and socio-cultural hypotheses in mate selection. Adolescence, sexuality and sub-culture. The role of peer-groups.

Sexual Ontogenesis III: Adult Life

Integration of the knowledge relative to adult sexuality. Adult sexual behaviors: epidemiological study. The formation of sexual bound. The foundation of married and family life. The emotional role in the expression of adult sexuality. Self-image and sexual interest. Marital sexual interaction. Marital adjustment and sexuality. Differentiation in masculine and feminine expressions of sexuality. Co-marital and extra-marital sexual relations.

Didactics of Sexology: an Approach to Educative Action

Initiation into the explicit approach to educative sexuality. Critical presentation of contemporary concept of sexuality, its objectives, content and the evaluation of such educative action as regards age, milieu, and environment. Criticism of quality in human sexuality educative action according to a axiological orientation: the presentation of educative action centered on structural development of the human being.

ANNEX I (continued)

Didactics of Sexology: Praxiology
And Criticism of Ancillary Material

Initiation into the praxiology of educative action in sexology; study of the modulation in praxiological approaches according to age, milieu, and environment; Operationalism of educative action applied to human sexuality. Systematic criticism and evaluation of pertinent ancillary material: films, slides, diapositives, 3-dimensional models, plates, documentation, manuals, recordings, etc. Introduction to creative ancillary methods and to computerized educative procedures.

The Sexological Action in the School Setting I:
Field Work, Observation and Planning

Knowledge and analysis of physical and human resources in the schools as regards sexological aids and educative action. Elaboration of circumstantial projects in sexological educative action and individual aid relative to present school conditions and dynamic evolution. Analysis of student needs in this field and pertinent planning.

Sexopathology III: Clinical Seminar

Discussion and demonstration of cases relative to topics studies in sexopathology I and II; attention is focussed on drugs and sexuality, transsexuality, transvestism, and ligature of the uterine tubes on sexuality and affectivity. Reparative surgery of sexual functioning in congenital malformation of the female genital tract, maladjustment in interest and sexual reactions.

Sexual Ontogenesis: Aging

Integration the knowledge relative to the sexuality of elderly persons. The menopause, andropause, and biological transformations. Age and the genital and extragenital reactions. The sexual behavior of the elderly: epidemiological and transcultural aspects. Old age and sexual identity. The attitude of society toward sexuality in the elderly.

The Critical Approaches and
Systematic Observation of Body-Language

The body as a means of communication: principles and hypotheses. Sexology and its bodily transcriptions. Muscular rigidity, sexual disorders and body schema. The usefulness of systematic observation in this approach. The development of observation grids to interpret the emotions seen in body reactions. The elaboration of a special vocabulary and the use of systematic observation of body-language as a means of sexological research.

Epistemology and Sexology

The situation of specific contributions of sexology to learning and the definition of the human concept contained therein. The principal elements of criticism in the human sciences. The study of the methodology characteristic of sexology and the delimitation of sexological knowledge. The present state of scientific findings: basic concepts, laws and theories. The relation between sexology and human values. The impact of sexological knowledge on individuals and groups.

Contemporary Theories of Mate Selection

Analysis of various theories of choice and their implications in mate and sexual partner selection. Phenomenological, analytical, and sociological hypotheses. The relation between mate selection and socio-cultural factors: eligibility, contributive agents and process of selection. The relation between mate selection and personality factors: love, complementary needs, search of parent-image, the process of interaction. Choice and attraction. Analysis of studies on interpersonal attraction factors and criteria: the morphological organization of individuals (beauty/homeliness, attractiveness/repulsion). Description of the various hypotheses relative to decision-taking. This course will enable the student to situate the different theories and hypotheses relating to mate-selection or sexual-partner choice within the framework of sexology and the practical assignments stemming from this master-approach will familiarize the student with the Quebec context.

Feminist Movements and Sexuality

The sexual role of women: biological, psychological, socio-economic, cultural and political. The various feminine protest movements. Changes in feminine sexual attitudes in the course of history.

SEX EDUCATION IN MEXICO

Juan Luis Alvarez-Gayou

Mexico

Sex education has always been a controversial subject in countries which traditionally place taboos on sexual themes. There has been very limited research on the sexual attitudes, knowledge and behavior of Mexican people and what is known is based mainly on empiric observation.

Within this context it was very difficult until recently to even consider an institutionalization of sex education. Nevertheless, an important effort was made in the early thirties during the regime of President Lázaro Cárdenas, one of the most progressive rulers our country has had. At that time, the Education Minister Narciso Bassols, proposed to introduce sex education in the school system; unfortunately, his suggestion met widespread opposition. There are classic photographs of the period showing groups of women demonstrating against such an introduction.

Bassols was pressured into resignation; sex education can not be blamed exclusively for his resignation, but the political change directly contributed to the sex education stalemate.

During the fifties, Mexico entered the stream of modernization and although the country was subject to natural upheavals of a growing society, we have witnessed many positive changes in recent years.

Since the thirties, Mexico has been experiencing a demographic transformation which has changed the face of the country. As it has grown in numbers its age structure has changed. Our population under 15 years of age now number around 50 per cent.

Another important factor is the educational reform underway since 1971 which includes free textbooks. To understand the importance of this reform, it should be mentioned that the Education Ministry provides a free textbook for every child in primary school in four areas: Spanish, Mathemathics, Social Sciences and Natural Sciences. Besides these books, there is a teacher's guide for each of the four areas in each of the 6 levels of primary school. This means that the government prints and distributes an average of 65 million books a year.

With sex education reintroduced to the public, there is discussion about it in the media, courses are taught and the whole atmosphere is changing.

OFFICIAL INSTITUTIONS

Sex education is being introduced and integrated into many activities in the official sphere, sometimes in an overt way and sometimes in a more subtle manner.

First of all, under our new Population Law, the National Population Council has been created as a coordinating and executive body in the population field. The Council is very much aware of the contribution sex education can make toward a better understanding of a population policy and a more rational and responsible way of facing reproduction. It is to be the coordinating agency for all sex education activities which are undertaken by the Ministries of the Interior, Health, Education, Labor, Treasury and Rural Development.

The Health Ministry includes some sex education in its lecture program, Direction of Mother and Child Health, for couples planning marriage.

Another official agency, the Mexican Social Security Institute, includes sex education lectures within their Responsible Parenthood Programs and further have contributed pioneering work in introducing sex education in the Pediatric Residency program.

The most important work in the official sphere is being carried out by the Education Ministry, through new free textbooks. Although textbooks for other grades contain some sex information written for all grades the most explicit information on the biology of reproduction is included in the 4th and 6th grade Natural Science books. In the first grade texts reproduction and development are studied, first in plants and animals and then in human beings. This course of study continues, culminating in its focus (at the 6th grade), on the student's own development. The natural sciences textbooks include sex education in subtle ways too. Whereas other textbooks exploit through visual means the idea that boys experiment and girls passively observe, our textbooks from the first grade onward illustrate that boys as well as girls experiment.

In our most conservative states where some feel that sex education should be the sole responsibility of parents, the introduction of sex education has met with some parental opposition. Fortunately this opposition was very localized and often associated to other problems not related to education. One of the best ways to fight such opposition is to train teachers. A beginning in this direction has been made by Dr. Gutiérrez-Vázquez's group which has traveled through out the country meeting with parent-teacher groups to discuss sex education and book content within the natural sciences' curricula. The social sciences textbooks include aspects of sex education, as the study of sex roles, responsible parenthood, etc.

As part of the educational reform, the whole curriculum of the middle school has been reviewed and changed to include sex education. Even the general objectives of middle school include sex education and there are plans underway for a population and sex education textbook for secondary school teachers. Many schools have even organized their own training courses for teachers and parents.

Concern about sex education has been growing in recent years in all official spheres connectioned with education, but no coordinated efforts have been carried out and as a result the entire program was diluted. In view of this situation, the Mexican Association for Sex Education took the initiative of drafting a project which the National Population Council revised and presented to the authorities.

This project was officially presented by the Mexican Government to the United Nations Population Fund and began January 1st of this year (1976). The main features of the project include research, curriculum design and testing, teacher training, adult education, introduction of sex education in schools of medicine, psychology, social work and nursing, all over the country, and others.

Both long term and specific objective were selected. The long term objectives are: 1) to motivate a change of attitude concerning sex, 2) to promote the transformation of stereotyped sex roles into more flexible sex roles, 3) to promote family integration by means of the adoption of attitudes and values which will make sex a creative force for positive interpersonal relations within the family, 4) to support the acceptance of regulation and rationalization of reproductive behavior and 5) to set the basis for the establishment of a Mexican Institute for Sex Education.

The specific objectives are: 1) to obtain reliable information about knowledge, attitudes and practices on sex in Mexico,
at a national and regional level, and how it is related to marital
status, income groups, occupation, religion, schooling, etc., 2)
to design curricula on sex education to be included in elementary
and middle school programs, 3) to train all teachers in the country
in the knowledge and use of sex information, 4) to contribute to
attitude changes concerning sex in the adult population by means
of sex education extended to great sectors of the population,
specially individuals and groups who act as community leaders, and
5) to create permanent mechanisms to train in sex education, teachers
and university students of the health area (nurses, medical, social
work, psychology).

PRIVATE INSTITUTIONS

Many private institutions are involved in isolated activities
in sex education since the early sixties. Among these are the
Fundación para Estudios de la Población, Asociación Pro-Salud
Maternal, Asociación de Caballeros Aztecas and several others.

But it was not until 1972 when the Mexican Association for
Sex Education was created that sex education activities began to
take a more formal and systematic form.

The Mexican Association for Sex Education is a multidisciplinary
private, nonprofit organization which has as its main objectives:
a) to enable people, through a suitable education, to exercise their
sexuality in a rational, enjoyable and responsible way, b) to encourage a change in relationship patterns between the sexes toward
more equalitarian models, and c) to contribute toward the solution
of the population problem in Mexico through the creation of responsible attitudes toward reproduction. The Association works
through three different groups organized in departments.

The information department arranges periodic open meetings to
inform on philosophy, content and methods of sex education and other
relevant questions, promotes the use of mass media, and coordinates
all press interviews and articles.

The education department designs and administers sex educator
training programs, organizes lecture groups and makes presentation
to all community sectors, promotes the use and application of modern
educational technology to sex education, and acts as consultant to
private and official institutions in the development of sex education programs.

The research department promotes and administers pilot research
in sex education and sexology.

As a part of its training program, the association has organized three seminars for sex educators, with a fourth one programmed to begin in mid-May. The association has also been very successful in establishing cordial relationships with many private and official groups. With many of these, there is close collaboration.

Finally, we must stress that most of the work that the association carries out is done on a volunteer basis, with many highly trained people giving freely of their time.

MASS MEDIA

The media has played a very important role in affecting attitudes toward sex education, at least in most urban areas. There had been very little mention of sex education in the daily press until the 1975 textbook problems were reported. Most newspapers with the exception of one, devoted many of their editorial pages to articles which supported the curricular changes and tried to foster good public opinion. Since that time, newspapers have been supporters of the introduction of sex education in and out of school.

Many journals were pioneers in the promotion of sex education; unfortunately, many of them were concerned with role orientation only. The number of journals and magazines which are doing a good job of reporting about sexuality in general, have grown in recent times to include comics, women's magazines, journals for professional groups and others.

Television and radio have also contributed greatly to opinion and attitude changes. Several programs and series have been devoted to sex education and sexuality in general. Members of the Education Ministry, of the Mexican Association for Sex Education and of the Population Council have participated in them.

At the present time, almost any subject can be discussed on television, although no formal programs deal with the matter.

CONCLUSION

Although Mexico is a newcomer to formal sex education, the conditions provided by its social and economic development make it a fertile ground for the growth of all the programs initiated in the past decade. We have no doubt that within the next five years Mexico will become one of the countries in Latin America and other parts of the world including developed countries with the most important sex education projects in and out of school.

CURRENT STATUS OF SEX RESEARCH AND SEX EDUCATION IN JAPAN

Shin'ichi Asayama

Japan

CURRENT STATUS OF SEX RESEARCH

Quite a few studies in sex research have been done on an international basis by Japanese scholars. Most of them, however, are
confined to the medical or biological sciences. The fact is that
there is scarecely any comprehensive or interdisciplinary research
on human sexuality. The synthesis of achievements in different
fields of science or the exchange of scientific knowledge on sex
has never been attemped among Japanese scholars.

The main reason why such circumstances exist can be attributed
to the prejudiced view of Japanese scholars that sex should not be
an appropriate topic for orthodox study and further, that it should
be eliminated from academia. This prejudice is undoubtedly a hang-
over of traditional Japanese sexual morality that once dominated
the feudalistic society of Japan: sex was considered a matter of
filth and shame, and what is worse, an object of social taboo.

Japanese society today has many serious sex problems needing
examination. To cope with the present situation an interdisciplinary
approach to solutions of sexual problems has become an urgent necessity. The scientific study of human sexuality achieved by such an
approach will play an active role in the emancipation of Japanese
sexual life-styles. To undertake this approach, an organization
named "The Japanese Assembly for the Study of Sex" (JASS) has been
established recently in Tokyo. The object of this organization is
to exchange scientific knowledge of sex beyond the narrow territory
of respective academic worlds, and to promote comprehensive research
in human sexuality. Although membership of this organization is
still small at present, there are researchers of various fields of

both natural and civic science, who are earnestly concerned about
the establishment of sexology in Japan. As the planner and or-
ganizer of this assembly I really look forward to lively future
activities of this organization.

In addition to the research movement, a statistical investigation conducted in 1974 on sex development and sexual behavior in
Japanese students is worthy of mention (Asayama, 1974). This
survey was done on a nation-wide scale by the Japanese Association
for Sex Education, entrusted by the Youth Problem Council of the
Prime Minister's Office. This association is a nonprofit public
foundation established in 1972 in Tokyo. As the planner and representative of the survey committee I was responsible for the
arrangement of samples to be collected.

In comparing the findings of the 1974 survey with available
data of studies which had been carried out previously in the Kansai
area in 1952 and 1960, together with recent data obtained in surveys conducted in the Tokyo Metropolis and Kyoto, Osaka and
Kobe areas (Asayama, 1976), the following findings have been
clarified:

1. Physiosexual and psychosexual development of present-day
Japanese students has been intensely accelerated; particularly,
psychosexual development in females (as sex awareness and desire
for intimacy). As a whole, psychosexual development of females
converges on that of the males.

2. Sexual activities have accelerated in both sexes, especially
in females. Cumulative incidence of dating after 14 years of age in
females exceeds that of males. Kissing in a sexual sense and coital
experience are activated in both sexes, though the cumulative incidence by age is much lower than those of foreign studies: (Kissing
36.7% and 25.7%; coitus: 14.2% and 4.2% in males and females of 18
years of age respectively in 1974 survey).

3. Masturbatory activity in females is much accelerated (24%
and 30% by 18 and 21 years of age respectively in the nationwide
survey. Current incidences are three times those of respective age
in the 1960 survey). The masturbation pattern of sexual behavior
in Japanese adolescent females is coming closer to that of European
and American girls.

4. Homosexual contact in male students has distinctly increased: active incidence is twice as much as has been reported
in previous local studies (7% ca. in total samples of the nation-
wide survey), whereas the female still holds the former incidence
(4% ca.).

5. The most common place reported for first intercourse is "own dwelling and partner's dwelling" in both sexes, and the second common place is "hotel, motel and rental room, etc.". Comparing this finding with data from Denmark, Sweden, Canada, United States, France and England. It has become clear that the latter fact is peculiar to sexual behavior of Japanese students but is hardly practiced by foreign youths.

6. Development of sexual desire and overt sexual acting-out conduct shows a basic difference between two sexes: the male develops the desire earlier in age, and shows higher cumulative incidence of sexual acting-out than the female. The motive correlated with the first physical contact for female is love, whereas the motive for males is sexual urge. These differences were consistently found irrespective of date and areas of the surveys.

The cause of the intensive acceleration described above may be in part due to the disintegration of the preexisting value-attitude system together with the traditional sexual morality, and in part to the commercially brutalized information on sex accompanying the intense economic growth of Japan. These extrinsic factors have positively exerted a very strong influence on the younger generation born after the War, and have changed their ideas on sex and selection of overt sexual behavior. These findings suggest that man is a changing being that can be influenced and whose behavior can be modified by environmental factors during the early stage of development.

CURRENT STATUS AND PROBLEMS OF SEX EDUCATION

According to various surveys carried out recently, 80% of teachers up to high school level and more than 90% of the parents think it is necessary to have sex education in the schools. More than 60% of those teachers and parents advocating sex education in schools think that it should be carried out under a close cooperation between homes and schools. In addition, a majority of education boards of local governments have published The Guide-Book of Sex Education which proposes concrete guidance methodologies and curricula depending upon the students personal growth. More than a hundred publications on sex education are available for children, students, parents and teachers. In addition, audio-visual materials such as slides, films and overhead projections are available. Only less than 5% of schools up to the high school level are known to have systematic sex education programs given on a continuous basis. All other schools either have taken no action, avoided the issue, taken a prohibiting attitude or expected that the matter would be handled voluntarily by teachers of physical education. Some teachers are attemting to give sex education on a personal basis as a part of the life guidance program. The following factors make it difficult to effectively teach sex education in the schools:

Peculiarities of the Educational Administration

Although the Government centered patriarchial ethics were
denied soon after the War, the educational administration of the
country is still to a great extent organized in a pyramidal hierachy
with the Ministry of Education at its head whose principle of guidance is still a patriarchial sexual morality. An authoritative
influence of the Ministry through "Teacher's Guidance for Study"
and the certification system of textbooks are not tolerant of
variations practiced by individual schools and teachers. Moreover,
the Ministry has not yet developed any clearcut position as to sex
education.

Education and Training of Sex Educators

Practically, none of the pedagogical colleges and medical school
have interdisciplinary courses on human sexuality organized by
faculties of physiology, psychology and sociology. Opportunities
for reeducation and training of teachers on sex education are also
deplorably inadequate. An appalling discrepancy exists between
teachers' curricula and pupils' anticipation on sex education.
Most mothers still consider sex education as a means to prevent
their sons and daughters from practicing unlawful sexual behaviors
or to protect them from possible pregnancy, sexually transmitted
diseases, etc. To most mothers and fathers the sex education still
means "chastity education" which is useful for protection of their
daughters' virginity.

Problems of Sex Education for the Future

The terminology "sex education" has been used instead of "chastity education" since about 1970. However, there still are many
problems left unsolved regarding establishment of the concept and
concrete methodology of the implementation. The problems can be
summarized in the following two categories:

Establishment of the concept of human sexuality. Presently,
the need for sex education is advocated from a parents and teachers'
perspectives and there is always a danger of having sex education
isolated from the needs of children. In order to establish the
concept of human sexuality based on objective and scientific facts,
not on feudalistic theory of chastity education, we need promotion
of educational activities which take full advantage of current
sexological findings.

Transformation of public attitude. Man's superiority over woman is still predominant in the Japanese society, which makes breaking through double standard and sexism barriers a difficult task. Efforts to change the general public's position need to be exerted in elevating woman's position in society by promoting social consciousness among women. Toward this aim, sex education (which has as its principle the realization of freedom and equality between the two sexes) should be promoted as an effective means in helping Japanese people achieve transformed attitudes.

Japanese people have undergone many variations of the peculiar life philosophy influenced by Buddhism, Confucianism, Shintoism and Christianity. Industrial culture has also exerted a remarkable influence upon the mode of thinking and daily life-style. More than half of the country's population consists of a younger generation born after the World War II. These people obviously have the kind of values, ethical consciousness and international mind that differs from that of the older generation. We are certain that we have made an appreciable step forward in the solution of problems restricting sex education.

REFERENCES

Asayama, S. (1976). Sexual behavior in Japanese students comparisons for 1974, 1960 and 1952. Archives of Sexual Behavior 5 (5): 371-390.

SOCIO-POLITICAL PROBLEMS OF SEXOLOGY AS A DEVELOPING FIELD IN ITALY

Romano Forleo

Italy

It is indeed difficult to expose all of the problems connected with the development of sexology in Italy in an overview; I will attempt, nonetheless, to cover those problems which I feel are actually the most specific in characterizing the Italian cultural attitudes toward sex.

Sexology is, in fact, a science which deals with people as a whole, in their biological, social and sexual components. It depends in part on biological problems but more importantly, on the culture in which an individual is raised. The political life and the ideologies attached to this culture determine individual behavior to a great extent even in the area of sex.

It is well-known to all that the fundamental characteristic of the actual Italian political situation is represented by a relationship between two mass movements: the Communists of the I.C.P. and the Catholics of the Christian Democrate Party (C.D.P.). For however much these two movements refer to two ideologies initially irreconcilable, (marxist materialism and the Christian concept of life) it is undeniable that, with time, there have been great steps made toward closer ties. The I.C.P. is discovering the value of individual liberty, abandoning the concept of proletariat dictatorship, rejecting atheist materialism, rediscovering the value of the middle class, and is insistently holding out its hand to the Christian Democrate Party in order to effectuate a government in common in what has come to be called the "historical compromise." The Christian Democrate of the C.D.P. have progressively attached themselves too strongly to their ties with the bourgeois class and the bureaucracy of the State; they are now searching for their "popular" soul, giving a more important role to the working classes. Both of

these movements feel the need for a series of reforms which will
favor the poor. What is hoped for is a more mature citizen, that
is, one more able to manage both individual and social reality,
and at the same time more aware of collective problems in order
for maturation to not come about through damage to the community.

Participation in management by the workers and a greater ter-
titorial autonomy in cultural development seem to be the best guarantees of individual and collective growth.

It seems to me that to understand achievement and future
prospects of sexology in various fields in our country, we have
to acknowledge that the development of sexology in Italy is also
characterized by this ideological and political situation; even
if the debate on divorce and abortion have met with approval, an
ecclesiastical hierarchy extremely rigid in its position and the
Communist Party have sided with the adversaries.

The prospective to work for would be for a new sexology as
an instrument for the liberation of total man and mankind. We
need a sexuality that abolishes relationships of dominator-dominated
(master-slave), a sexuality that would aid in a language of frater-
nity among men, a sexuality beyond individualism in favor of a
greater solidarity; a sexuality which would reevaluate genitality
and pleasure and favorize the total growth of the individual and
the community; a sexuality which unites rather than divides, man
and woman, man to man, generation to generation, which goes beyond
the agony and solitude in which today's society tries to imprison
us.

It is in the sense that the rediscovery of the value of sexuality, no longer separated from other problems of human development, can be truly an alternative to the present concept of sexual
liberation.

The law establishing the Family Counseling Centers enacted
in July of 1975 and actually being set up in the various regions
of Italy, has brought the problems of the couple and the family
to a political level, taking them away from the individual sphere.
It will be up to the local community to deal with family culture
and to give support and aid to women, the couple and the family.
In spite of the fact that the Catholic authorities continue to
support private Family Centers directly controlled by the Church
and recognized by the law in respect to pluralism, the Catholics
play an important role within public centers along with other laic
forces. The attempts of some feminist movements, inspired by radical bourgeois ideals, to impose basic structures for a feminine
aggregation, seem to fail under the pressure of a more powerful
group desiring men and women together in the fight for emancipation
of the couple and the family.

In this political situation the problem of sexual education
in the schools has been raised. A law proposed to the house by
the I.C.P. last year was not discussed because of the anticipated
elections, and a project studied by a group of democratic deputies
met with a similar fate. These plans had much in common: the
necessity first of all, of training teachers; absolute loyalty to
scientific principals; the respect of the developmental growth of
children and adolescents. In the Communist project the role of State
control was accentuated; in the Christian Democrat project the role
of the parents elected to the school committee and the family in
general was accentuated. The Communist Party's project is being
represented and probably other parties will follow now. As it was
for the law concerning the Counselling Centers, it will probably
be possible to reach an agreement concerning sex education in
schools with all political groups.

Parallel to this situation of some agreement on themes of
development, both cultural and economic, there are also elements
of disagreement between the major parties. On one hand the radical
party, (heirs of the libertarian tradition of the enlightened
bourgeoisie), is preoccupied with the individual's possible suf-
focation by the collectivity; on the opposite hand, the extrapar-
lementary movements, (heirs of the student riots of 1968). Both
parties support the fight for women's liberation, and both up-
hold absolute sexual liberty leaving every choice to the individual
in moral and behavioral fields and denouncing any censure or any
attempt to socialize the problem. The result is a sexuality dominated by instincts, where all is resolved in a spontaneity which
should, by itself, guarantee the genuineness of human relationships. But the responsibility of each individual towards the
creation of new sexual attitudes creates a culture and it is within
this cultural unity that new relationships are formed and grow.
The attitude of the individual must thus be examined within a
cultural whole and one must realize that attitude creates and
guarantees the future of relationships to be experienced within
a society.

These movements, however minority and often extremist they
may be, contribute on one hand to eliminate taboos and on the
other to maintain the tension of respect of ideological minorities.
Parallel to this political world, there is the pressure of the
"system," immersed in and swept away by the irresistible need for
consuption which converts sex into a product of economic value.
Sexual liberty is written about in order to distract attention
from the fight for a greater justice and freedom from need.

In this complex situation medical sexology in medicine remains
absent. Influenced by psychiatry, the new sex therapies are not
well received, and sexology itself has not found a spot in university teaching, nor private or hospital out-patient clinics offering

services in the field.   The initiative is thus still in the hands
of private companies such as the "Centro Italiano di Sessuologia,"
or of some doctors who insist on the necessity of introducing
medical staffs to the profession through conferences or courses.
In truth, doctors and medical students show a notable interest in
the field and it seems possible that, even in Italy, we may soon
provide systematic instruction of sexology in medicine.

In spite of the profound economic crisis, administrative
disorders, the slow development of our public school system and of
our medical schools there exist elements in initial fermenting
stages which can play instrumental roles in the maturation of
new possible solutions.

HUMAN SEXUALITY - BATTLEGROUND OR PEACEGROUND?

Mary S. Calderone

United States

The evolution of scientific knowledge about a specific area does not usually proceed in linear fashion, but rather in a series of step-like plateaus separated from each other by varying time intervals. Whether these intervals are long or short will depend on several factors, e.g., the importance of the area in the eyes of one or more researchers or in the view of social need; the rapidity with which the knowledge spreads coupled with the degree of interest it arouses in workers in similar or related fields; the recognition of its importance by nonworkers in the field and an increasing public demand for it.

Population growth, family planning and human sexuality are three areas that share many of these factors. They also have a common block in the continued inability of the lay public, the health professions and the supporting socioeconomic structure to recognize that they are crucially important, and why. One should remember that only twenty-two years ago the population problem was being generally denied. Malthusians were looked upon as kooks, and contraception was not taught in medical schools, mentioned in obstetrical or gynecological textbooks or provided in public health services. In fact, it was a quite secretive transaction in the private physician's office. There were no simple vaginal contraceptives, intra-uterine devices or contraceptive pills, and the two pages on contraception in the American Medical Association's Handbook of New and Nonofficial Drugs mentioned condoms, diaphragms, suppositories - and vinegar or lemon juice douches!

Twelve years ago the word sexuality was not used in the public or academic presses except in a pejorative or scandalous context;

three medical schools taught something about human sexuality but
did not announce it; and Kinsey was revered by a few and loathed
by many because he had demonstrated so clearly what ordinary people did unofficially in their private sex lives that they officially felt they should be ashamed of. 1964 was also the year
that Masters and Johnson shook the world with their first book.

And, it was the year that SIECUS was formed, with the intention of placing human sexuality in the domain of public health.
And now in 1976, this International Congress of Sexology, the
World Health Organization Technical Report on Education and Treatment in Human Sexuality: the Training of Health Professionals
(1975) and the broad inclusion of professional and preprofessional
sexological course work in medical, religious, social work, nursing, and general education all tell us clearly that the first phase
now has been accomplished and will undergo its own natural expansion. For instance, in the March 1976 SIECUS Report, post-graduate
summer workshops in human sexuality and sex education were listed
for some 58 U.S. institutions. In the University of Minnesota,
twelve sex-related courses were listed apart from the Medical
School's, seven for the Department of Family Social Science, two
for the Department of Sociology, one each for the Divisions of
School Health Education, of Home Economics Education, and for
adult, higher and teacher education. In fact, almost 100% of U.S.
medical schools now include courses in human sexuality.

What remains to be done? A very great deal, for officially
the general public still fails to acknowledge the centrality of
human sexuality to their own lives and those of their children,
and the aforementioned positive changes in attitudes are only among
certain groups of professionals. In other words, in that phrase
"general public" we have to lump not only the nonprofessional elements, but also many of the professional ones, i.e., those who deal
in the other-than-health sciences, such as physics, chemistry, ar-
chitecture, mathematics, and the various technological sciences; also
the business world, that still white-middle-class-American-male-
dominated section of the U.S. population. Planned Parenthood found
it almost impossible to raise significant funds until the specter
of the population crunch was brought home to the influential, by
respected General William Draper in the mid sixties. He formed the
fund-raising arm for Planned Parenthood as a group of concerned
citizens headed by two former U.S. Presidents as honorary chairmen.
Not until then did Planned Parenthood really begin to receive the
support of the business community that it deserved, nor did governmental officials at the high level begin to accept family planning
as part of governmentally-supported health services.

Human sexuality is in a similar case today, and it is the individual who suffers. At no matter what age, it is still being made

clear that one's sexuality is not one's own property. Instead, a
number of other agencies persist in laying claim to it: first in
life, the parental and family agencies - primarily the parents
themselves. Later, while indulgently pretending to try to "control"
the sexuality of their adolescent sons, parents still tend to resist even faintly acknowledging the equivalent sexuality and sexual
needs of their adolescent daughters. And, institutions caring for
the dependent handicapped, aging and adolescents continue to desex-
ualize and thus dehumanize these people.

Historically, the prime contender for control of the sexuality
of a person by an outside agency is, and continues to be, religion.
Although human sexuality has been a dominant theme in the art and
literature of most cultures, control (meaning repression) of this
alleged "rampant" and "uncontrollable" yet universal factor in
human life has been held by most religions to be necessary in order
to restrict its use to its so-called primary or even sole function,
procreation. Therefore, most religions have proscribed various
kinds of sexual behaviors that would presumably circumvent this
function, by labeling these acts as "unnatural" or as "detestable
crimes against nature," terms which eventually found their way into
the criminal codes of most western countries and of all of the
United States. The gambit was, and still is in many cases, to
denounce sexual pleasure per se as sinful unless leading directly
to the possibility of conception.

The back-up gambit was also to make illegal such sexual activities that might circumvent procreation. So, once legally out
from parental control, the individual may find at his or her cost
that the criminal code has stepped in. Although about 15 states
in the U.S. have now quietly changed their sex laws to conform to
the so-called "consenting adults in private" principle, it is still
possible for a couple to be prosecuted if, for instance, in New York
State or Iowa they were to be detected in oral-genital sex while
they are unmarried. Once they are married the New York State law
will protect them in this, but in California until just this year,
even married people could be and have been subject to criminal action for a similar "offense." Although there are no laws against
solitary masturbation, laws against mutual masturbation clearly do
exist in most states, primarily because they have been found useful
for action against homosexuals. In an effort to demonstrate the
effects of such sex laws, a mock trial was recently staged in Indiana by SIECIND, the Indiana affiliate of SIECUS. Based on an
actual case it demonstrated how the state could legally move a-
gainst the "abominable and detestable crime against nature," a
meaningless label from Indiana's sodomy statute that can be and
has been, variously interpreted as 1) oral-genital sex, 2) anal
intercourse, 3) nonsolitary masturbation, or 4) sexual intercourse
with an animal - all of which, of course, occur in nature and form
part of the sexual repertoires of many people in the United States.

Customs, or social mores, can also play a heavy "controlling" role simply by creating in the individual, from earliest childhood on, the profoundly disturbing conviction that he or she is somehow out of step, bad, abnormal, solitary or degenerate, for no matter what genital sexual behavior.

Finally, health practitioners and services can quite innocently exert a malign influence if they are careless about what they tell parents, as for instance, when they quite properly try to reassure parents that their young child's masturbation will not hurt the child, but then hedge their bets by adding "if it isn't done too much." What is "too much?" Physicians also have all too often informed males over the age of 50 who were concerned about their actually quite normal diminution in sex drive intensity and frequency, that they had to expect this because after all they were already "over the hill" when it came to sex. The same doctor might later tell the same patient's wife that her continued and thus only relatively increased sexual drive was obvious evidence of "nymphomania," and the future of the marriage of that couple might well be sealed.

But there are healthy signs that the great general public is stirring out of its fear and inertia and asserting, in sometimes even inappropriate or sensational ways, the right of each person to "own" his or her endowment of sexuality. A study by Miller and Lief (1976) of the findings of over a thousand Sex Knowledge and Attitude Tests (SKAT) administered to pre-med and medical students and residents from various parts of the country clearly shows, for instance, that neither masturbation nor age at first masturbation is related to religious affiliation (Protestant, Jewish or Catholic). Gemme and Crepault's (1975) study at the Université du Québec à Montréal shows that incidence of masturbation among Catholic young people of Montreal was not a function of religious devoutness as measured by church attendance. The recent study by the National Opinion Research Center, reported in the New York Times on March 24, 1976, shows that independent thinking by Roman Catholics has not only led to increased use of birth control but to declines in religious devotion as measured by lowered participation in and financial support of church programs.

Thus increasing insistence by the individual of his or her right to express sexuality in his or her chosen way, stopping short of violence or of exploitation of minors or incompetents, constitutes a significant sector of the sexual revolution. But, as Georges Causse (1975), Chief of the Venereal Disease Unit at WHO, stresses in an article in World Health Magazine, "The curious fact is that the present revolution in social attitudes to sex has not been matched by the spread of intelligent information on sex."

As long as a "monkey-see, monkey-do" belief persists even in a vocal
minority of the general population, this will result in the idiotic
prevention of adequate spread of information about all aspects of
sexuality, as needed by that same population. The give away here
is the almost paranoid fear that exists, not only of sexual pleasure
itself but also of the recognition of one's body as a valid source
of that pleasure. The World Health Organization Technical Report
(1975) appeared to recognize this by its definition of sexual
health, and specifically by a phrase immediately following that
definition:

> Sexual health is the integration of the somatic, emotional,
> intellectual and social aspects of sexual being, in ways
> that are positively enriching and that enhance human person-
> ality, communication and love.

> Fundamental to this concept are the right to sexual informa-
> tion and the right to pleasure.

Persons who oppose all forms of sex education for all ages
because of such a "monkey-see, monkey-do" mentality should look
around them a bit and confront their fears by recognizing that
all that has been happening that they find distasteful or worrisome (and I'll agree that at least some of it is indeed distasteful or worrisome), is exactly because of the lack of knowledge
and education about, and respect for, every person's sexuality
from earliest childhood on. Education and services to allay sexual ignorance and fears, provided in the same spirit of respect,
dignity and scholarly competence as at this meeting, can lead people who are not in the sexual health field to recognition that
exactly the same moral values that apply to all of one's actions
and relationships can also safeguard the area of sex. In fact,
could expected results be any worse than those we see today in
the absence of broad sex education for all? Hardly! The professional world has made epochal advances in this field, but we
have left way behind us our co-citizens who are not also co-
professionals. We have developed a special language and have
accepted special sets of assumptions and facts that they are still
uncomfortable with or even unaware of; we constitute an "élite"
group where élitism has no business to be.

In the face of the need for a universal approach to realistic
sexual knowledge for all ages and socioeconomic groups, we must
take it as possible for others to learn more of the truths about
human sexuality and sexual behavior as has become possible for us
in the past ten years.

I propose a coalition of strengths in this respect. The
world's leading and most broadly respected specialized organiza-

tions and services in the sexual health field - most of them represented here - should be able to pool their efforts and come up
with an agreed upon set of basically simple assumptions, the gist
of whose message might be:

1. That we are born sexual and remain so until death;
2. That our sexuality is of central importance to each of us
   throughout life;
3. That sexuality itself is morally neutral, but that how we
   learn or are taught to use it throughout life has heavy
   moral implications;
4. That the sex education with the most impact is probably
   that done by parents or their surrogates by the age of
   fourteen, but especially before the age of five;
5. That this undoubtedly determines or profoundly influences
   the child's sexuality for the rest of its life;
6. That this influence extends, for good or ill, into the
   areas of gender identity, gender role behavior, erotic
   response, and sex object choice;
7. That in the interests of prevention, the institutions of
   society (educational, religious and health) should be
   called upon to accept primary responsibility for persuad-
   ing, educating and helping parental figures to carry out
   their unique roles as primary sex educators.

Religion can be especially helpful in such a coalition if it
will stand behind assumption 3, for such moral implications should
- and indeed must - transcend differences in religious dogma.

I wonder how simplistic is such an action, how effective such
assumptions might be if disseminated broadly in the names of organizations of stature?

The sexuality of each person has for centuries been a battleground, with religion, the law, social customs and parents struggl-
ing for control of what should be private to each person alone. It
still is a battleground, and as a result, the bewildered and guilty
child grows into the resentful, over-anxious, hostile or sexually-
acting-out young person, who then brings into adult life a sexual
dysfunction blighting to full adult sexual happiness.

We don't need battlegrounds within us as we move through life,
we need peacegrounds - and sex should always be one such.

Whenever I think about these things I experience a real and
deep anger at how, even with the best of intentions, most parents
constantly meddle and interfere between the child and its own most
private self, justifying this interference by their conviction that
without it the child will grow up to express eroticism in "unspeak-
able" ways. We should rather remember that the dysfunctional ex-

pressions of sex identified today appear to be built into the growing individual quite literally during the days of his or her life
that he or she must spend in the company of adults! The results
we see are a far cry from being private peacegrounds. I suspect
that they are found by many of us personally and in our practices
to be closer to being private hellgrounds.

We need to put our goals for the sexual lives of people in
positive ways - to come to terms with our sexuality, to make our
peace with it. Is this purely for the sake of physical pleasure?
In part it is, of course, but the non-physical factors are what
really provide us with the richness and color we all need: sex
for communication, for ego support and formation, for self-reali-
zation, for play, for celebration of life, for the achievement of
intimacy, for the synergistic release of energy between two people,
for the sensing of principles and values, for harmonization of the
physical with the spiritual, for the development of fantasy, for
the balancing of love against hate, and through these and many more,
for the ultimate integrative role erotic sex can play in helping to
harmonize the many thrusts, drives and possible conflicts within
each individual, and between individual and society. These are all
possible uses of sexuality that need today to be accorded positive
values by our whole society. In various, subtle, individualistic
and vital ways the central role of human sexuality in every life
must become clear, and so must the role of the health professional
in fostering and supporting it.

REFERENCES

Causse, G. (1975). World Health, 12.

Crépault, C. and Gemme, R. (1975), La Sexualité Prémaritale, Uni-
        versité du Québec Press, Montréal.

Miller, W. and Lief, H., (1976). Masturbatory attitudes, knowledge
        and experience: data from the Sex Knowledge and Attitude
        Test (SKAT). Archives of Sexual Behavior, 5 (5): 447-467.

W.H.O. (1975). Education and Therapy in Human Sexuality, the Train-
        ing of Health Professionals, Technical Report no. 572, Geneva.

CONTRIBUTORS[1]

ABRAHAM, Georges, M.D., Department of Psychiatry, Geneva and Turino Universities, Switzerland.

ALVAREZ-GAYOU, Juan Luis, M.D., Technical Coordinator of the Sex Education Project, Consejo Nacional de Poblacion, Mexico.

APFELBAUM, Bernard, Ph.D., Berkeley Sex Therapy Group, Berkeley, California, United States.

ASAYAMA, Shin'ichi, D.Sc., Department of Biology, Faculty of Science, Osaka City University, Japan.

ATKINSON, Maxine, M.A., Oxford College of Emory University, United States.

BELTRAMI, Edouard, M.D., Department of Sexology, Université du Québec à Montréal, Québec, Canada.

BOLES, Jacqueline, Ph.D., Department of Sociology, Georgia State University, United States.

BUREAU, Jules, Ph.D., Department of Sexology, Université du Québec à Montréal, Québec, Canada.

CALDERONE, Mary S., M.D., President of SIECUS (Sex Information and Education Council of the United States), New York, United States.

CLARKE, Florence C., B.S., Department of Psychiatry and Behavioral Sciences, The Johns Hopkins University School of Medicine and Hospital, Baltimore, Maryland, United States.

---

[1]Only those contributors who were speakers at the 1976 International Congress of Sexology are listed here.

CLOPPER, Richard R. Jr., M.Sc., The Psychohormonal Research Unit, The Johns Hopkins University School of Medicine and Hospital, Baltimore, Maryland, United States.

COHEN, Jean, M.D., Sèvres Hospital and Paris-Ouest University, France.

CREPAULT, Claude, Ph.D., Department of Sexology, Université du Québec à Montréal, Québec, Canada.

DESJARDINS, Jean-Yves, Ph.D., Department of Sexology, Université du Québec à Montréal, Québec, Canada.

DÖRNER, Günter, Ph.D., Institute of Experimental Endocrinology, Humboldt-University, German Democratic Republic.

DUPRAS, André, Ph.D., Department of Sexology, Université du Québec à Montréal, Québec, Canada.

EHRHARDT, Anke A., Ph.D., Department of Psychiatry and Pediatrics, State University of New York at Buffalo, New York, United States.

ELLIS, Albert, Ph.D., Institute for Advanced Study in Rational Psychotherapy, New York City, United States.

EVERAERD, Walter, Ph.D., Department of Clinical Psychology and Psychotherapy, State University of Utrecht, Utrecht, The Netherlands.

FELICIOTTI SEPPECHER, Marisa, M.D., Unit of Clinical Sexology, The Skinner Institute, Rome, Italy.

FORLEO, Romano, M.D., Department of Obstetrics and Gynaecology, Fatebenefratelli Hospital, Rome, Italy.

FOX, Cyril A., M.D., Joint Academic Unit of Obstetrics, Gynaecology and Reproductive Physiology, St. Bartholomew's Hospital Medical College, University of London, England.

GAGNON, John H., Ph.D., Department of Sociology, State University of New York at Stony Brook, New York, United States.

GEMME, Robert, Ph.D., Department of Sexology, Université du Québec à Montréal, Chairman of the 1976 International Congress of Sexology, Québec, Canada.

GILLAN, Patricia W., Ph.D., Rochford General Hospital and London University, London, England.

GOURGUES, Jules-Henri, M.A., Quebec Department of Social Affairs, Planned Parenthood Division, Québec, Canada.

GREEN, Richard, M.D., Department of Psychiatry and Behavioral Science, State University of New York at Stony Brook, New York, United States.

HEGELER, Sten, Ph.D., Department of Psychology, University of Copenhagen, Denmark.

HEROLD, Edward S., Ph.D., Department of Family Studies, University of Guelph, Ontario, Canada.

HIGHAM, Eileen, Ph.D., Department of Psychiatry and Behavioral Sciences, The Johns Hopkins University School of Medicine and Hospital, Baltimore, Maryland, United States.

HOCH, Zwi, M.D., Center for Sexual Counseling, Therapy and Education, Department of Obstetrics and Gynaecology, Rambam University Hospital, Israel.

HUSAIN, Muazzam S., Ph.D., Department of Sexology, Université du Québec à Montréal, Québec, Canada.

ISABELLE, Claudette, B.Sc., Montreal Sex Therapy Clinic, Québec, Canada.

JEMAIL, Jay Ann, Ph.D.Can., Department of Psychology, State University of New York at Stony Brook, New York, United States.

JENSEN, Gordon D., M.D., Department of Psychiatry, University of California, Sacramento, California, United States.

KABBASH, Linda, M.Sc., Department of Psychology, Concordia University, Sir Georges Williams Campus, Montréal, Québec, Canada.

KALRA, Meryle Anne, M.Sc., St. Mary's Hospital and Concordia University, Québec, Canada.

KEYSER, Herbert H., M.D., Department of Obstetrics-Gynaecology, Stony Brook Medical School, New York, United States.

KINSON, Gordon A., Ph.D., Faculty of Medicine, University of Ottawa, Ontario, Canada.

LAMONT, John A., M.D., Department of Obstetrics and Gynaecology, McMaster University, Hamilton, Ontario, Canada.

LEVY, Joseph Josy, Ph.D., Department of Sexology, Université du Québec à Montréal, Québec, Canada.

LEWIS, Viola G., B.S., Department of Psychiatry and Behavioral
    Sciences, The Johns Hopkins University School of Medicine
    and Hospital, Baltimore, Maryland, United States.

LIEF, Harold I., M.D., Centre for the Study of Sex Education in
    Medicine, University of Pennsylvania, Philadelphia, United
    States.

LINDEMANN, Constance, Ph.D., Department of Social Work, University
    of Oklahoma, United States.

LUNDBERG, Per Olov, M.D., Department of Neurology, University
    Hospital, Uppsala, Sweden.

MANDEL, Jane Barclay, B.S., Division of Human Biology, Long Island
    Research Institute, Department of Mental Hygiene, Chicago,
    Illinois, United States.

MANN, Jay, Ph.D., Human Sexuality Program, University of California
    School of Medicine at San Francisco, California, United States.

MARKOWITZ, Heidi, M.A., Concordia University, Montréal, Québec,
    Canada.

MAZUR, Tom, Ph.D., Department of Psychiatry and Behavioral Sciences,
    The Johns Hopkins University School of Medicine and Hospital,
    Baltimore, Maryland, United States.

MEYER-BAHLBURG, Heino F.L., Ph.D., Departments of Psychiatry and
    Pediatrics, State University of New York in Buffalo, New York,
    United States.

MONEY, John, Ph.D., Department of Psychiatry and Behavioral Sciences,
    and Department of Pediatrics, The Johns Hopkins University and
    Hospital, Baltimore, Maryland, United States.

MORTENSEN, Mei-Mei, M.Sc., Department of Psychology, University of
    Copenhagen, Denmark.

PASINI, Willy, M.D., Service of Psychosomatic Gynaecology and of
    Sexology, Medical School, Geneva University, Switzerland.

PERSKY, Harold, Ph.D., Department of Psychiatry, University of
    Pennsylvania, United States.

POMEROY, Wardell B., Ph.D., Clinical Psychologist, San Francisco,
    California, United States.

PORTO, Robert, M.D., Marseille Hospital, France.

PRESCOTT, James W., Ph.D., Developmental Behavioral Biology, Growth
    and Development Branch, National Institute of Child Health and
    Human Development, Washington, D.C., United States.

ROBBINS, Mina B., Ph.D., School of Nursing, California State Uni-
    versity, Sacramento, California, United States.

SAMSON, Jean-Marc, Ph.D., Department of Sexology, Université du
    Québec à Montréal, Québec, Canada.

SARREL, Philip M., M.D., Yale University School of Medicine,
    Connecticut, United States.

SCHUMACHER, Sallie, Ph.D., University of Pittsburg School of Med-
    icine, Pittsburgh, Pennsylvania, United States.

SCHWARTZ, Mark F., Ph.D.Can., Psychohormonal Research Unit, The Johns
    Hopkins University School of Medicine and Hospital, Baltimore,
    Maryland, United States.

SHAPIRO, Colin M., Ph.D., Department of Physiology, University of
    the Witwatersrand, Johannesburg, South Africa.

SUBRINI, Louis, M.D., Necker Hospital, Paris, France.

SUTTON-SMITH, Brian, Ph.D., Program in Developmental Psychology,
    Teachers College, Columbia University, New York, United
    States.

TAMBURELLO, Antonino, M.D., Unit of Clinical Sexology, Skinner
    Institute, Rome, Italy.

TORDJMAN, Gilbert, M.D., Clinical Therapist, Paris, France.

TREMBLAY, Réjean, Ph.D., Department of Sexology, Université du
    Québec à Montréal, Québec, Canada.

WAGNER, Gorm, Ph.D., Institute of Medical Physiology, University of
    Copenhagen, Denmark.

WALKER, Paul A., Ph.D., University of Texas Medical Branch, Galveston,
    Texas, United States.